ADOLESCENCE

DEVELOPMENT, DIVERSITY, CONTEXT, AND APPLICATION

RICHARD M. LERNER
TUFTS UNIVERSITY

Prentice Hall

UPPER SADDLE RIVER, NEW JERSEY 07458

Library of Congress Cataloging-in-Publication Data
Lerner, Richard M.
    Adolescence: development, diversity, context, and application / Richard M. Lerner
    p. cm.
    Includes bibliographical references and indexes.
    ISBN 0-13-085761-0
    1. Adolescence.   2. Adolescent psychology.
HQ796.L3815 2001   2001036181
305.235—dc21   CIP

VP/Editorial Director: Laura Pearson
Senior Acquisitions Editor: Jennifer Gilliland
Editorial Assistant: Nicole Girrbach
**VP/Director of Production
    and Manufacturing:** Barbara Kittle
Director of Marketing: Beth Gillett Mejia
Executive Marketing Manager: Sheryl Adams
Editor in Chief of Development: Susanna Lesan
Sr. Managing Editor: Mary Rottino
Project Manager: Alison Gnerre
Production Assistants: Meredith Gnerre and Patricia Sleys
Prepress and Manufacturing Manager: Nick Sklitsis
Development Editor: Barbara Muller

Prepress and Manufacturing Buyer: Tricia Kenny
Creative Design Director: Leslie Osher
Art Directors: Anne Bonanno Nieglos and Nancy Wells
Interior and Cover Designer: Thomas Nery
Cover Images: Digital Visions/Groups, Children and
    Teenagers
Line Art Manager: Guy Ruggiero
Electronic Illustrations: Maria Piper
Director, Image Resource Center: Melinda Reo
Photo Research Supervisor: Beth Boyd
Image Permission Supervisor: Kay Dellosa
Photo Researcher: Julie Tesser

Acknowledgments for copyright material may be found beginning on p. 447, which constitutes an extension of this copyright page.

This book was set in 10/12 Sabon by TSI Graphics and was printed by Von Hoffman Company. The cover was printed by Von Hoffman Company.

Pearson Education

©2002 by Pearson Education, Inc.
Upper Saddle River, New Jersey 07458

Printed in the Unites States of America

10 9 8 7 6 5 4 3 2 1

ISBN 0-13-085761-0

Pearson Education LTD., London
Pearson Education Australia Pty. Limited, Sydney
Pearson Education Singapore, Pte. Ltd
Pearson Education North Asis Ltd., Hong Kong
Pearson Education Canada, Ltd., Toronto
Pearson Education de Mexico, S.A. de C.V.
Pearson Education—Japan, Tokyo
Pearson Education Malaysia, Pte. Ltd
Pearson Education, Upper Saddle River, New Jersey

BRIEF CONTENTS

CONTENTS

CHAPTER 5
MORAL DEVELOPMENT, BEHAVIOR, AND CIVIL SOCIETY   106

CHAPTER 6
IDENTITY: THE SEARCH FOR SELF-DEFINITION DURING ADOLESCENCE   132

CHAPTER 7

ROLE DEVELOPMENT AND WORK IN ADOLESCENCE 160

CHAPTER 8

ADOLESCENTS AND THEIR FAMILIES 178

CHAPTER 14:

POTENTIALS OF ADOLESCENTS: COMMUNITY PROGRAMS AND PUBLIC POLICY 326

CHAPTER 15:

BEYOND ADOLESCENCE: LAUNCHING THE YOUNG ADULT YEARS 358

APPENDIX:

STUDYING ADOLESCENT DEVELOPMENT: METHODS AND DESIGNS 376

MEET THE RESEARCHERS

PREFACE

The word *adolescence* can be traced to the Latin word "adolescere," which means to grow into maturity. Growing into maturity involves change, and today, adolescence is regarded, perhaps with the exception of infancy, as the most change-filled period of life. It is a period of transition in which the biological, psychological, and social characteristics typical of children become the biological, psychological, and social characteristics typical of adults.

Most researchers define the second 10 years of life (from ages 10 to 20) as the adolescent period. All people who study adolescence—or who experience it, as either parents or as young people themselves—agree the period is characterized by numerous major changes and also dramatic ones that often are remembered for all the years of life thereafter.

The hopes, challenges, fears, and successes of adolescence have been romanticized or dramatized in novels, short stories, and news articles. It is commonplace to survey a newsstand and find a magazine article describing the "stormy years" of adolescence, the new crazes or fads of youth, or the "explosion" of problems with teenagers (e.g., involving crime or sexuality).

To what extent are these characterizations of adolescence correct? Just what do we know about adolescents and if some adolescents do experience problems, what can be done about it? In turn, aren't there strengths of adolescents? How may knowledge about adolescent development be applied in ways to promote positive, healthy development among all the diverse young people experiencing this period of life? How, in the span of 10 years, does the individual bridge the gap between coping with the several challenges of early adolescence and the launching of a young adult life?

The Goal of This Book

Answering these questions fascinates and engages the energies of scientists, practitioners, parents, teachers, and young people themselves. Providing the key information pertinent to providing answers to these questions is the goal of *Adolescence: Development, Diversity, Context, and Application*.

This book will help you to understand the bases of the *developmental changes* young people experience during the adolescent period; to appreciate the important instances of *diversity* of individuals, families, communities, and cultures that give texture and richness to adolescent development; to recognize the important role played in adolescent development of the different instances of the *context*, or ecology, of human development—for example, the family, the peer group, schools, communities, the media, and culture; and to understand the ways in which knowledge about adolescent development, diversity, and context may be *applied* to promote positive development among young people. In short, the aim of *Adolescence: Development, Diversity, Context, and Application* is to present the best information currently available about the adolescent period and the ways in which scientists and practitioners both understand the period and, take actions to promote positive development among youth.

How Is Adolescence Discussed in This Book?

Throughout this book I illustrate that, by understanding the relations of diverse adolescents and their contexts, we may formulate *applications* that may help improve these relations. These applications may involve community-based programs, professional practices, education curricula, and public policies. But all applications aim to resolve or ameliorate challenges to healthy adolescent development, to prevent problems of adolescent behavior from developing, or to promote positive development among youth.

Accordingly, this book emphasizes that adolescence is a dynamic developmental period marked by diverse changes for different youth, changes brought about because development involves changing *relations* among biological, psychological, and social/ecological processes. Together, these diverse developmental changes involve the relations adolescents have with their biological, social, and cultural contexts, and provide the basis for innovations, in the types of applications just noted, aimed at increasing societal ability to improve the lives of adolescents. If the basis of the development of young people lies in their particular relationships with their social world—with their specific family, peer group, schools, and neighborhoods—then by taking actions improve these relations we may be enacting the key steps needed to promote positive development.

You will find that the four themes in the title of the book—development, diversity, context, and application—are interwoven. Together these themes will help you understand how scholars and practitioners contribute to identifying knowledge that matters in respect to enhancing the lives of the diverse young people in the United States and around the world.

Foci and Features of the Book

The themes of developmental diversity, adolescent-context relations, and the links among theory, research, and applications to programs aimed at enhancing the life chances of young people are key foci in contemporary scholarship and practice pertinent to adolescence. As such, these themes frame the discussion in all chapters of this book. Across chapters, we emphasize several types of information:

- The stress on adolescent *development* involves both the antecedents in earlier life periods of changes in adolescence and the consequences of these changes for later adult development and aging. The treatment of development in this text includes a discussion of the intertwining of the development of youth with the development of their parents and other relatives, with peers, and with other individuals important their lives (for instance, teachers, mentors, and coaches).

- The focus on *diversity* provides understanding of the variation among adolescents associated with race, ethnicity, gender, sexual orientation, and physical characteristics.

- The emphasis on the *context* of adolescence involves discussing (1) the role of culture and history in shaping the processes and products of adolescent development; (2) the role of the social, interpersonal, familial, and physical context in influencing youth development; (3) institutional contributions to adolescent development, including educational, political, economic, and social policy influences; and (4) community needs and assets, including programs promoting positive youth and family development. In addition, several disciplines and several professions involved in understanding the contexts that influence human development are discussed.

- The fact that the changes of adolescence derive from the relations between youth and their contexts constitutes an optimistic and powerful approach to *applications* (for instance, community-based programs, school curricula innovations, professional practices, and public policies) aimed at promoting positive adolescent development. By changing the character of the relations youth have with their social world we may be able to enhance their chances for healthy development. Accordingly, the stress on application involves indicating current foci of policies and programs pertinent to youth intervention programs, education, retraining, and services.

The several foci of the book are not only interwoven throughout the discussions in each chapter but they appear as well in the feature boxes. The book includes "Implications for Parenting" boxes about **parenting adolescents** and "Applications" boxes about **policies** and **programs** pertinent to promoting positive adolescent development. In addition, "Meet the Researcher" boxes present **personal reflections** by leading scholars of adolescence about their current research or applied efforts.

The information in these boxes and in the text itself is enhanced by several learning tools: **vignettes** about adolescent development that begin the text of each chapter, **chapter overviews, learning objectives, issues to consider, chapter summaries, discussion topics,** and **glossaries.**

Aspirations for This Book

Certainly, it is a daunting task to understand the bases of the healthy and successful development of diverse adolescents and to apply such knowledge to ensure that young people are eventually capable of leading themselves, their families, their communities, and their nations productively, responsibly, and morally across the 21st century. I believe all citizens, worldwide, must rise to this challenge if we all are to not only survive but to prosper.

The young people of today represent 100% of the human capital on which the future health and success of all nations rest. To enhance the lives of adolescents requires that we continuously educate all citizens—young and old—about the best means available to promote enhanced healthy lives among *all* youth and the families, schools, and communities involved in their lives. It is my hope that *Adolescence: Development, Diversity, Context, and Application* will motivate you to contribute to this effort. In so doing, this book may play a role in an educational and community collaborative effort to help ensure, for the new millennium, a socially just

and civil society populated by healthy and productive children and adolescents.

Acknowledgments

I am indebted to numerous colleagues for helping me develop this book. I am grateful to all whose basic and applied scholarship about adolescence have provided the information and expertise reflected in the following pages. I am especially appreciative to all the colleagues who contributed to the "Meet the Researcher" boxes, features that enable readers to understand the scholarship and passion that researchers bring to their work, efforts aimed at both furthering understanding of young people and improving their lives. In addition, I am very grateful to my fellow faculty members in the Eliot-Pearson Department of Child Development at Tufts University for their support, encouragement, and enthusiasm for and support of my work. I would also like to acknowledge my great gratitude to the following reviewers: Gerald Adams, University of Guelph; Lisa Crockett, University of Nebraska; Carolyn H. Johnson, The Pennsylvania State University; Beth Manke, University of Houston; Daniel F. Perkins, The Pennsylvania State University; Peggy Perkins, University of Nevada, Las Vegas; and Marie S. Tisak, Bowling Green State University.

Three of my graduate students—Aida Bilalbegović, Elizabeth Dowling, and Deborah Bobek—have been true collaborators with me. They read and provided always useful and insightful comments about drafts of each chapter and were instrumental in designing and developing the learning tools. They have also been the major authors of the learning aids ancillary to this book, for example, the Companion Website, an online Student Study Guide located at **www.prenhall.com/lerner** and the Instructor Resource Manual with tests. They have proven to be invaluable colleagues, providing knowledge, wisdom, organizational efficiency, and a never-flagging positive attitude.

Several undergraduate students—Jennifer Brown, Catherine Hubbard, Scheherazade Tillet, and Angelica Lundquist—assisted as well in the myriad important tasks involved in finalizing the manuscript, from checking references to critiquing the several features of the text designed to engage the interest and enhance the knowledge of readers.

I am grateful as well to my administrative assistant, Holly Maynard, for helping me find sufficient time to complete this book on schedule. I appreciate as well the excellent efforts of my editorial assistants, Lisa Marie DiFonzo and Karyn Lu. Their professionalism and dedication to the project were extraordinary.

I am also indebted to my editor at Prentice Hall, Jennifer Gilliland. Her expertise, insight, and energy were essential ingredients for the creation of this book and for its completion. I appreciate as well the wonderful contributions of Barbara Mueller, who provided developmental editing for the book. Her guidance was critical in shaping the direction and completion of this project. In addition, I appreciate greatly the superb efforts of Alison Gnerre, the Production Editor of the book. Her mastery of the myriad details of producing a high quality book is truly astonishing, and her combination of precision, creativity, and productivity is nothing short of incredible.

Finally, I want to express my love and gratitude to my family. My wife, Professor Jacqueline V. Lerner, has been my most important colleague in my research and scholarship about adolescent development. She has also been my partner in the development of our three children—Justin, Blair, and Jarrett. I know Jackie would agree that our children have taught us more than perhaps we want to recognize about adolescence. When they were all children, we used to describe ourselves as experts in the field of adolescent development. Now, having seen the completion of Justin's adolescence, its imminent completion by Blair, and, at this writing, being immersed in the middle of Jarrett's adolescence, we currently describe ourselves as "people who study adolescence." For all they have taught us and all that we anticipate they will continue to teach us, I dedicate this book to them.

R. M. L.
Medford, Massachusetts
October 2000

ABOUT THE AUTHOR

 Richard M. Lerner is the Bergstrom Chair in Applied Developmental Science at Tufts University. A developmental psychologist, Lerner received a Ph.D. in 1971 from the City University of New York. He has been a fellow at the Center for Advanced Study in the Behavioral Sciences and is a fellow of the American Association for the Advancement of Science, the American Psychological Association, and the American Psychological Society. Prior to joining Tufts University, he was on the faculty and held administrative posts at Michigan State University, Pennsylvania State University, and Boston College, where he was the Anita L. Brennan Professor of Education and the director of the Center for Child, Family, and Community Partnerships. During the 1994–1995 academic year Lerner held the Tyner Eminent Scholar Chair in the Human Sciences at Florida State University. Lerner is the author or editor of 40 books and more than 275 scholarly articles and chapters, including his 1995 book, *America's Youth in Crisis: Challenges and Options for Programs and Policies*. He edited Volume 1, *Theoretical Models of Human Development*, for the fifth edition of the *Handbook of Child Psychology*. He is known for his theory of, and research about, relations between life-span human development and contextual or ecological change. He is the founding editor of the *Journal of Research on Adolescence* and of the new journal, *Applied Developmental Science*.

ADOLESCENCE

1

ADOLESCENT DEVELOPMENT:
THE LAWS AND THE LORE
OF ADOLESCENCE

Janis Brown sat alone in her room. If it were not for the steady sound of her CDs drifting down the stairs, her parents would not have even known she was home. Such relatively unobtrusive behavior was not typical of Janis, but her mother thought she understood why this was occurring.

It had been just two days ago that Janis and Daniel had broken up and, it seemed, only a few days before then that Mrs. Brown had heard her daughter explain how fulfilled she was by her new relationship with Daniel. No other 15-year-old, Janis assured her mother, had ever loved as deeply, as totally. No one had ever felt such intense compassion, devotion, and overwhelming sense of completion.

But now, less than 2 weeks after it began, it was over. Janis was certain that her pain—her depression and feelings of physical agony—had not been experienced as deeply by anyone else. At least, she pointed out to her mother, she was sure that no one who had been so true had been treated so callously, so rudely and publicly humiliated: told by Daniel, in front of everyone, that he just wanted to be friends!

And so Janis sat in her room hardly evidencing enough energy to place a new disk in her CD player. Friday afternoon turned into Friday evening, and then Saturday morning and afternoon. Another evening was now at hand.

Mrs. Brown could not take it any longer. Dinner was on the table and, by Monday morning, there would be chores to do and homework to complete. She had indulged Janis long enough.

She strode up the stairs to her daughter's room. "Janis! Enough is enough now. Come down, eat your dinner, and then start your homework."

"Mom! Leave me alone!" Janis shrilled back. "You don't understand. What do *you* know about love?!"

3

LEARNING OBJECTIVES

1. To appreciate that adolescent development is influenced by biological, psychological, and social contexts.
2. To recognize the inherent diversity of the possible developmental pathways through adolescence, and to recognize that this diversity involves changes within the person across time and between the individual adolescent and parents and peers.
3. To appreciate the life-span approach to human development and its emphasis on multiple levels of the ecology of human development.
4. To recognize that the changing relations between the developing individual and his or her complex and changing ecology constitute the critical process of human development.
5. To appreciate the relevance of applying intervention studies to better understand how healthy and successful development across the life span can be promoted.

6. To know the major developmental tasks of adolescent development.
7. To recognize that adolescent development is influenced by multiple factors, including hormonal development, family, and culture.
8. To appreciate why policies and programs must be tailored to a specific target population and must address that group's particular developmental and environmental circumstances.
9. To understand the stereotypes about young people that have historically defined adolescence and how these stereotypes have created the lore of adolescence.
10. To appreciate the research that supports the existence of different developmental trajectories and thereby challenges the lore of adolescence.

The hopes, challenges, fears, failures, and successes of **adolescence** have been romanticized or dramatized in novels, short stories, and news articles. It is commonplace to survey a newsstand and find a magazine article describing the "stormy years" of adolescence, the new crazes or fads of youth, or the "explosion" of problems with teenagers involving crime or sexuality. Until the past 35 years, when medical, biological, and social scientists began to study intensively the adolescent period, relatively little sound scientific information was available to verify or refute the literary characterizations of adolescence. Today, however, such information does exist, and it is clear that although adolescence presents many challenges, the evidence is not consistent with the frequently reported belief that adolescence is a protracted period of **storm and stress** for most individuals (Feldman & Elliott, 1990; Lerner, 1993a, 1993b, 1995; Lerner & Galambos, 1998; Offer, 1969; Petersen, 1988). As this chapter discusses, although adolescence has its share of challenges and problems, as do all periods of life, for most young people it is a period when health and positive growth predominate.

Adolescence Period of transition spanning the second decade of life during which a person's biological, psychological, and social characteristics undergo change in an interrelated manner and the person goes from being childlike to adultlike.

Storm and stress Phrase often used to stereotype general and universal turmoil throughout the adolescent years.

Adolescence spans the second decade of life (Lerner, 1991a; Petersen, 1988). Young adolescents elicit both curiosity and frustration in many observers, especially—it seems—parents. By the end of the second decade, however, the person seems to be in a time of constant commitment—to partners, family, and work. The middle portion of this period may be a time of mystery, self-examination, and emerging identity. It is a time to bridge the gap between the awkwardness (for both youth and their caregivers) of early adolescence and the launching of a now young adult life at the end of this period.

Each period of adolescence holds its own promise and fascination. For this reason alone it is useful to study adolescent development. But there are other reasons for interest in this period. Only through such a focus can we understand the diversity of life paths that characterize different people. Only through a focus on the scope of development across this period can we evaluate whether paths on which we embark in early adolescence are the ones on which we continue to walk. This book discusses the diversity and scope of adolescence while attempting to answer the following questions:

- Is there a necessary connection between development at age 10 or 12 and the behaviors of the late adolescent period, as the individual enters college, career, or marriage?

- Are there ways in which adolescents may change—for better or worse—as they move from one point of life to the next?
- Are there particular aspects of adolescents' biology (for instance, genes or hormones) and/or their contexts (for example, families, schools, workplaces, or cultures) that either promote connections across life (continuity) or lead to change (discontinuity)?
- *If* adolescents can change, and *if* the bases of these changes can be identified, can means be found to improve their development?
- Can the study of adolescent development help people live lives of greater health, opportunity, and achievement?

A Definition of Adolescence

Issues to Consider
- How do the biological, psychological, and social contexts of adolescence impact development?
- What accounts for the diversity of the developmental trajectories of adolescents?

Adolescence may be described as a phase of life beginning in biology and ending in society (Petersen, 1988). This characterization of adolescence underscores the idea that, whereas pubertal changes may be the most visible and universal features of this period, the social and cultural context within which youth develop textures this phase of life. Adolescence is a period of transition, one when the biological, psychological, and social characteristics typical of children change in an integrated manner to become the biological, psychological, and social characteristics typical of adults (Lerner & Spanier, 1980). When most of an individual's characteristics are in this state of change, that person is an adolescent.

Adolescence is a period of dramatic challenge, one requiring adjustment to changes in the self, family, and peer group. In contemporary society, adolescents typically experience institutional changes as well. Among young American adolescents, there is a change in school setting, typically involving a transition from elementary school to either junior high school or middle school. In late adolescence there is

Young people test different roles during adolescence, often in the context of part-time jobs.

a transition from high school to either the world of work or college.

Understandably, for both adolescents and their parents, adolescence is a time of excitement and anxiety, happiness and troubles, discovery and bewilderment. Although some childhood behavior continues, the adolescent also begins to break with the past. Adolescence is a confusing time for the adolescent experiencing this phase of life, for the parents who are nurturing the adolescent during his or her progression through this period, and for the other adults charged with enhancing the development of youth during this period, such as teachers, coaches, and so on.

The feelings and events that bring about parents' reactions to their adolescent children are well known to parents, teachers, and many writers who have romanticized or dramatized the adolescent experience in novels, short stories, or news articles. Even when "storm and stress" is not attributed to adolescence, the period is often characterized by conflicting behaviors, for example, both trying to "fit in" and attempting to define oneself as a unique person. Moreover, adolescence is characterized by a unique combination of assets and deficits, for example, a great reservoir of physical health together with a propensity to take risks that compromise one's health, such as binge drinking or unsafe sex (Lerner & Galambos, 1998).

The famous writer George Bernard Shaw once said, "Youth is a wonderful thing. Too bad it is wasted on the young." This view epitomizes the idea that adolescents possess many positive and valued characteristics—health, fitness, and energy, for example—and yet also possess charac-

Conflict with parents is a normal part of adolescence.

teristics that place them at risk for problems of development—poor judgment, a proclivity to make dangerous choices (driving drunk, engaging in unprotected sex), and a "live for today, don't worry about tomorrow" attitude. Writers, poets, and members of the mass media focus on the assets and deficits of people traversing this stage of life. Such a focus often helps sell books and magazines, and it creates high ratings for television shows. This media depiction of adolescence is popular because it builds on this stereotypical view of young people.

Given the multiple transitions an adolescent experiences, this period is clearly a dramatic challenge. Not all young people undergo these transitions in the same way, with the same speed, or with comparable outcomes. There is diversity in their paths through life, which are known as **developmental trajectories**. A major source of this diversity is the **context** within which youth live and develop—the family, peer group, school, workplace, neighborhood, community, society, culture, and niche in history.

Developmental trajectories Individual's path through life as influenced by combinations of biology, psychology, and context unique to each person.

Context Environments in which an individual exists such as family, school, work, and culture.

The Goal of This Book The aim of *Adolescence: Development, Diversity, Context,* *and Application* is to present the best information currently available about the adolescent period and the ways scientists and practitioners successfully promote positive development among youth. The book emphasizes that adolescence is a dynamic, developmental period marked by diverse changes for different youth, changes brought about because development involves changing *relations* among biological, psychological, and social/ecological processes.

Diversity in adolescent development occurs as a consequence of systematic relations between youth and their contexts (Lerner & Castellino, 1999, in press). The importance of understanding this system is underscored by the life-span developmental framework—a perspective particularly useful for discussing adolescence in relation to the periods of life preceding and following it and in respect to the important contexts of one's life.

Features of the Life-Span Perspective

Issues to Consider
• How might an adolescent's ecology influence her or his behavior and development?

- What are the two types of diversity stressed in the life-span perspective?
- According to the life-span perspective, what is the goal of intervention studies?

When the life-span perspective was introduced in the 1970s, its features included certain ideas, specifically:

- Development occurs across the life course. It does not end with physical maturity (puberty).
- Individual development occurs in relation to social, cultural, and historical changes. It does not occur because of internal (biological, genetic) influences acting alone or by the isolated action of environmental stimuli.
- Across life, there are important differences between people and within individuals. Not only do people change across life, but also different people change in ways specific to them.
- Attempts to describe, explain, and optimize development across life involve understanding the connections between individuals and their contexts. If we understand development we should be able to improve it. To improve development we need to alter the connections between people and their social and cultural worlds.

A life-span approach to adolescence employs concepts pertaining to the nature of human development—for instance, diversity, context, and application. It uses a specific set of scientific methods, which address issues about these concepts. For example, do youth from different racial, ethnic, and/or socioeconomic backgrounds experience comparable changes in their personality development? What family, school, or community resources are most effective in attempts to promote the development of positive self-esteem among these different groups of youth?

The life-span perspective emphasizes that human behavior and development arise as a consequence of individuals' relationships with the several aspects, or *levels,* of their social context. These levels constitute the **ecology** of human development (Bronfenbrenner, 1979; Bronfenbrenner & Morris, 1998) and include the family, community, society, and culture. In addition, the research of Glen H. Elder, Jr. (1974, 1998) has demonstrated that the period in history within which people live influences their development as they experience unique combinations of economic, political, and techno-logical conditions. Elder's contributio trated in Meet the Researcher Box 1.1.

As a result, the life-span perspective that variability, or diversity, arises in consequence of their relationships with particular constellations of family, community, society, culture, and historical conditions. Two types of diversity are stressed in the life-span perspective. First, there are important differences *among people,* for example, in their racial, ethnic, religious, gender, physical, age-related, community, and cultural characteristics. These may be associated with differing patterns of life-span development. Second, there are often underappreciated differences *within a person* over the course of his or her life. Here life-span scholars emphasize two principles: (1) Development occurs throughout life; children differ from adolescents and adolescents differ from adults; the way you are in childhood or adolescence does not completely determine the rest of your life. (2) Development always involves a combination of gains and losses.

For example, in infancy, gains in visual acuity are accompanied by a loss of neurons that could have been used in other potential visual pathways. In childhood, growth in fluency in one language decreases the probability of gaining similar proficiency in another language. In adolescence, commitment to one **social role** and to its associated beliefs or ideology is associated with a loss of other life paths as potential routes to self-definition. For example, if an individual is committed to becoming a computer engineer and subscribes to the accompanying belief in the importance of technology for society, that choice influences the individual's self-definition and eliminates other choices. In the adulthood and aging years, physical or cognitive losses may be compensated by gains associated with accumulating experience, expertise, or "wisdom" in a particular domain (Baltes, Lindenberger, & Staudinger, 1998; Baltes, Staudinger, & Lindenberger, 1999).

The life-span perspective emphasizes that variations in the changing links, or relationships, between individuals and contexts create diversity in the course of human development. To life-span scholars, *basic* processes of human development are relational in character. Changing

> **Ecology** Levels of a person's social context that influences individual development.
>
> **Social role** Socially prescribed set of behaviors that society believes is important for its maintenance and perpetuation.

MEET THE RESEARCHER BOX 1.1

GLEN H. ELDER, JR.
HISTORICAL INFLUENCES ON ADOLESCENT DEVELOPMENT

A large number of young people who grow up in disadvantaged circumstances manage to rise above the limitations they face in the transition to adulthood. By contrast, other youth from more privileged families lose even the advantage of their background. What influences account for these different pathways to adulthood?

In the 1920s, a small group of American psychologists launched studies of children's development and began to follow them with periodic data collections into adolescence. Before long the young children of these pioneering studies had entered their 20s and 30s at the Institute of Child Welfare, the University of California, Berkeley. I joined the faculty in the early 1960s with the task of working on one of the studies, the Oakland Growth Study. All members of this study (about 40 years old in 1961) were born in the early 1920s, and most of them experienced hard times during the Great Depression (Elder, 1999). Nearly all of the boys served in the Second World War.

These young people were members of a presumed "lost generation" who would never succeed in rising above hardships of the 30s. But as I put the pieces of their lives together, I began to see that most of the men and women from deprived families had done very well in their lives. The question was not one of persistent disadvantage and its consequences, but rather that of pathways of resilience into the 40s and beyond. How did so many young people

Glen H. Elder, Jr., is the Howard W. Odum Distinguished Professor of Sociology and Research Professor of Psychology, Center for Developmental Science, the University of North Carolina at Chapel Hill. He is director of the Carolina Consortium of Human Development at the university. See Web site: www.unc.edu/~elder.

rise above the limitations of their Depression background?

I discovered many years later that this question had become a recurring one in my research career. To answer it I had to "recast" the original longitudinal data archives to enable them to address the new questions of my research. Recasting the data archive refers to a process of developing a new codebook for the study and using it to recode the data. I was also forced to think differently about the course of human development by placing lives in context (Elder, 1998; Elder, Modell, & Parke, 1993). This involved locating them in historical time and place (in the early 40s, most of the men served in WW II). I also had to depict their "lives as lived," following them into the military and theatres of service, into combat and types of skill training. Timing and significant others proved to be most important in depicting their lives, or what we now call the life course. Some men entered the service out of high school, others did so much later in life. "Lived lives" are typically interwoven with other lives—with immediate family, friends, co-workers. Many of the consequences of a change in life course occurred through these "linked lives"—a spouse or children, for example.

The Oakland men who escaped from family hardship through the Armed Forces were better able to experience more life opportunities through the GI Bill and its educational benefits, and through the

relations between the developing individual and his or her complex and changing ecology constitute the critical process of human development. To understand human development across life, scholars and students must appreciate the diversity of life paths, or "trajectories." These variations arise as a consequence of differences across life in the familial, community, cultural, and historical niches of people. This influence of multiple levels implies another important idea of the life-span perspective: To understand the influences of contextual levels requires knowledge that goes beyond psychology or

any other single discipline. Knowledge about multiple disciplines and from multiple professions must be combined to understand the complex ecology of human development.

Another important goal of the life-span perspective is to understand how healthy and successful development across life can be promoted. If we understand the forces that shape development we should be able to influence those forces, especially when they relate to relatively changeable characteristics, such as behavior, family relations, or social conditions, including housing, street safety, and human

usable skills they acquired in the service, such as managerial expertise and technical know-how. I wondered whether this pathway to greater opportunity among surviving veterans would also apply to other veterans who served in the military? I found that it did among young men in the Berkeley Guidance study—these men were born at the end of the 1920s, grew up in hard times, and nearly 3 out of 4 served in the military. This data archive was also housed at the Institute of Child Welfare (now Human Development). Despite the hard times of their childhood, the Berkeley men who served in the military were better able to rise above the limitations of their family disadvantage, when compared to men who did not serve in the military. The Oakland and Berkeley women did not serve in the Second World War, as a rule, but the war involved them in activities that often improved their lives. These included advanced training, employment, and marriage.

Longitudinal studies that follow people across many decades are needed to answer questions concerning resilience and vulnerability in the lives of young people. Unfortunately, very few longitudinal studies were launched before 1960 in the United States and especially in other countries. However, I have made the most of these early studies to shed greater light on changing lives and development in changing times. One example is the famous Lewis Terman data archive, housed for many decades at Stanford University. From the 1960s to the present, longitudinal study samples have increased at an exponential rate in the United States and abroad, and they have been supplemented by the use of retrospective life calendars that enable us to capture basic facts from a "lost past." The calendars record life events and their dates, and enable cross-checking to ensure accuracy. I have taken full advantage of these new studies and techniques to investigate the impact of World War II on Japanese young people and the effect of China's Cultural Revolution on young people who were born around 1950.

But the best example of this new work involves the Iowa Youth and Families Project, housed at Iowa State University, Ames. In the 1980s, a severe agricultural crisis hit the Midwest and especially the prosperous farm state of Iowa. Land values declined by half, forcing countless farm families into heavy indebtedness and bankruptcy. Given the level of distress among family members in 1989–1990 (Conger & Elder, 1994), we were surprised to find little evidence of it 4 years later, even among youth from farm families, and yet these families were hardest hit by the economic crisis. Why were youth with ties to the land doing so well, both socially and psychologically, when their families were still losing income? To answer this question, we focused on a primary source of resilience among farm families—their strong relationships with relatives, friends, and community institutions (Elder & Conger, 2000). Youth with parents who were engaged in farming were most likely to be involved in leadership, athletic, and volunteer roles, and the greater their involvement, the greater their social competence and academic success. Their social involvement reflected the social ties of their parents. We are continuing to following these young people into their 20s, and the influence of their civic engagement remains a powerful factor in their accomplishments to date. One of the keys to human development and life success involves "making the very best" of what we have. Success amid adversity is an example of this accomplishment.

services. And if we can test our knowledge about development by trying to change it, we have an obligation to change it for the better. Scholars have an ethical responsibility to study human life and to use the knowledge they gain to improve life (see Appendix 1). They must go beyond understanding how both positive and negative trajectories occur in adolescence. They must test this understanding in an effort to promote positive trajectories among youth.

In order to accomplish this goal, life-span scholars conduct **intervention studies** in laboratories and in the actual ecologies of human development. Gaining theoretical understanding of how and why development occurs may lead to research designed to explore how people's lives may be improved through change. For example, an individual's social world could be changed through public **policies**, and an individual's functioning

Intervention studies Research designed to understand how changing aspects of the social world or an individual's behavior can lead to improvements in a person's life.

Policies Actions (e.g., the enactment of laws) taken by social institutions, such as governments, to ensure or increase desired behaviors (e.g., better school performance) or to decrease unwanted behaviors (e.g., drunk driving).

might be changed by modifying problem-solving strategies. Therefore, life-span scholars view application as a way to evaluate their assumptions, descriptions, and explanations of human development.

In short, *diversity, context,* and *application* constitute key components of a **life-span perspective** on human development. Individual differences between and within persons, the role of the context of human development, and the emphasis on applications and interventions are hallmarks of this view. We integrate these theoretical themes throughout this book and apply them specifically to the adolescent period.

Key Features of Adolescent Development

Issues to Consider

- What are the major developmental tasks of adolescence?
- How do developmental tasks converge to influence an adolescent's self-definition?

Over the past 35 years, the results of research on adolescence have demonstrated for biomedical, behavioral, and social scientists the importance of individual differences and contextual sensitivity for understanding the nature of human life and development (Lerner & Galambos, 1998; Petersen, 1988). Research on adolescence is an example of the importance of collaborations among multiple disciplines. We have learned that to understand adolescents we need to combine knowledge from biology, medicine, and nursing, the social and behavioral sciences, social work, law, education, and the humanities. The study of adolescence today is not dominated by a purely biological, psychological, or sociological viewpoint. Instead, there is a **multidisciplinary** literature that allows several generalizations to be made about the life of young people and provides information about how best to intervene when adolescents are experiencing difficulties.

Life-span perspective
Approach that characterizes individual development as occurring across a lifetime through the combination of internal and external influences; the approach stresses differences within and between people and attempts to optimize lifetime development.

Multidisciplinary
Research and knowledge from diverse fields.

Developmental tasks
Behavior that must be achieved at a particular age or stage in order for adaptive development to occur.

Multiple Developmental Challenges of Adolescence: Biology, Psychology, and Society

By the beginning of the second decade of life, numerous types of changes begin to occur. Internal and external bodily changes, cognitive and emotional changes, and social relationship changes all take place. Adolescence involves more than just the internal physiological and external bodily changes associated with puberty, it is a period involving changes in the biological, psychological, and social characteristics of the person. To move adaptively across the period of adolescence, the adolescent needs to deal with these three sets of changes, which constitute the major **developmental tasks** of this period of life (Demos, 1986). Meet the Researcher Box 1.2 describes how one investigator approaches the study of these several facets of adolescent development.

Biological Challenges Adolescence is a matter of biology. The adolescent must cope with changing physical characteristics, such as bodily appearance, and with physiological functions, such as the beginning of the menstrual cycle or the first ejaculation. Adolescents see themselves differently: Hair is growing in places where it has not grown before; their complexion is changing; and their body is taking on a different shape. Moreover, new feelings, new "stirrings," are emanating from the body, and adolescents begin to wonder what this all means and what they will become.

Understanding and accepting these biological changes as part of the self protects the adolescent from fear, confusion, or alienation about what is happening. For an adaptive sense of self to emerge, adolescents must understand and cope with these biological changes. This constitutes a developmental task of this period.

Psychological Challenges Interrelated with the biological changes are psychological changes—as shown by the way adolescents react to biological changes. Psychological changes—of cognition and emotion—arise because adolescence is also a matter of psychology (Demos, 1986). New characteristics of thought and emotions emerge. Cognition becomes abstract and hypothetical, and emotions involve feelings about genital sexuality and changing relationships. The adolescent's developmental task is to

MEET THE RESEARCHER BOX 1.2

NANCY L. GALAMBOS
UNDERSTANDING IMAGES OF MATURITY AMONG ADOLESCENTS

When you think back to junior high or high school, can you remember teens who seemed more "mature" than the other kids in your class? Were you one of the these teens, or did you feel young and inexperienced? Did you ever have the sense that some kids who appeared to be older on the outside were *not* mature on the inside? Over the past several years, I have been fascinated by the issue of what it means to be mature in adolescence. I have been interested in both the outer sort of maturity, which includes physical or behavioral maturity, and an inner sort of maturity, which includes characteristics such as a strong work ethic and knowing and being comfortable with who you are.

Through this research, which has been funded by the Social Sciences and Humanities Research Council of Canada, I have found three groups of adolescents who differ reliably on a number of important characteristics. The first group comprises adolescents who engage in "adultlike" problem behaviors such as drinking and smoking. These adolescents feel older or more mature than their same-age peers, but paradoxically, they score low in terms of inner maturity (e.g., they do not believe in the value of hard work). These adolescents may be labeled as pseudomature (or adultoid), for they demonstrate adultlike behaviors in the face of an inner or psychological immaturity. A second group of adolescents— the immatures—have dabbled in problem behaviors, feel younger than do their same-age peers, and are psychologically immature. The third group of adolescents appears to be genuinely mature; they have experimented with adultlike problem behaviors, they feel slightly older than their chronological ages, and they report a strong sense of themselves and a strong work ethic.

Along with Lauree C. Tilton-Weaver and Erin T. Vitunski, I have looked further into what it means to be pseudomature, immature, or mature. We have found that these groups differ in many ways. For example, pseudomature adolescents are likely to be early maturers. They have a very strong desire to be older and although they are peer oriented, they do not feel that they matter a lot

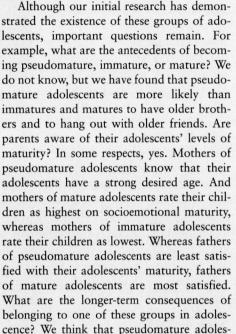

Nancy L. Galambos is a professor in the Department of Psychology at the University of Victoria in British Columbia, Canada. She is director of the Life-Span Developmental Psychology program at the University of Victoria, assistant editor for the *Journal of Adolescence,* and has served on numerous editorial boards in the area of adolescence.

to their friends. Immature adolescents also (perhaps appropriately) feel the desire to be older, but they are less peer oriented, and have some strengths such as being involved in school. Mature adolescents seem to be pretty happy with where they are in the world: They are not heavily involved with peers but they have close friends and are engaged in school.

Although our initial research has demonstrated the existence of these groups of adolescents, important questions remain. For example, what are the antecedents of becoming pseudomature, immature, or mature? We do not know, but we have found that pseudomature adolescents are more likely than immatures and matures to have older brothers and to hang out with older friends. Are parents aware of their adolescents' levels of maturity? In some respects, yes. Mothers of pseudomature adolescents know that their adolescents have a strong desired age. And mothers of mature adolescents rate their children as highest on socioemotional maturity, whereas mothers of immature adolescents rate their children as lowest. Whereas fathers of pseudomature adolescents are least satisfied with their adolescents' maturity, fathers of mature adolescents are most satisfied. What are the longer-term consequences of belonging to one of these groups in adolescence? We think that pseudomature adolescents may be at higher risk of developing difficulties in the future and that mature adolescents are likely to continue to be well adjusted. The direction that will be taken by immature adolescents is unknown. To answer all of these questions requires a longitudinal design following these groups of adolescents and their parents over time.

By learning more about adolescents' maturity, we are gaining an understanding of sets of behavioral and psychological characteristics that together tell us about the relative emotional health of the adolescents. Such knowledge can potentially help us to identify adolescents who may be at risk, to design interventions to increase maturity, and to provide support and guidance to parents who are concerned about their adolescents' levels of maturity.

cope with these new psychological characteristics. To interact adaptively in the world, the adolescent needs to recognize abstractions and hypotheses as different from reality. And to avoid problems of health and adjustment, adolescents need to find ways to deal in socially acceptable ways with their sexuality. Thus psychological tasks clearly involve adolescents in their social world and illustrate the interwoven nature of the tasks of this period.

New cognitive abilities allow adolescents to understand their current physical and physiological characteristics and to project what these characteristics are likely to mean to them as individuals. Given their

Adolescents spend a great deal of time contemplating themselves—their thoughts, feelings, and appearance.

changing characteristics of individuality, it is adolescents' thought capabilities that allow them to know who they are, guess who they might become, and plan what they may do with their new feelings.

The psychological changes of adolescence require the individual to deal with his or her changed biology by forming a revised sense of self—a new **self-definition.** Individuals' self-definition fosters the selection of the niche they pick to occupy in life, that is, the role or roles they plan to play in society.

The Challenges of Society and Culture The psychological nature of adolescence blends inextricably into the third type of challenge of the period. Because adolescents are a part of society and culture, they must learn the range of activities and roles available in the social world and come to understand their value. The developmental task is to find the appropriate role in society by combining who one is physically with who one is psychologically. To fit optimally into a social role, one's sense of self must be well formed.

Self-definition allows the individual to meet the role tasks of the social world. Finding a social role is a crucial developmental task for **adaptive functioning,** that is, functioning that is healthy, positive, and successful. Roles give meaning to life. Responsible and successful performance of roles elicit from society protections, rights, and privileges, which safeguard individuals and allow for continued healthy functioning.

Finding a social role that contributes to society in ways that best suit the individual and is helpful to society will be adaptive for both the individual and the social world. Thus ideally there is a convergence among the three tasks of adolescence, one which allows the person to best integrate his or her changing self with his or her particular social world.

The Influence of Multiple Levels of Context During Adolescence

Issue to Consider

- What other factors, besides hormonal changes, influence adolescent development?

Individual differences are an important part of adolescent development. They involve connections

Self-definition
Understanding of who you are as a person based on how you view yourself physically, psychologically, and socially.

Adaptive functioning
Development that responds to biological, psychological, and social influences in ways that are healthy, positive, and successful.

among biological, psychological, and societal factors. No single influence acts alone or as the "prime mover" of change (Brooks-Gunn & Petersen, 1983; Lerner, 1987, 1993b, 1995; Lerner & Foch, 1987; Lerner & Villarruel, 1994; Petersen, 1988). Thus it is possible to characterize the study of adolescence as a field that focuses on the *relations* between the developing individual and the several levels of his or her changing context (e.g., Lerner & Galambos, 1998; Petersen, 1988).

For example, hormonal changes are part of the development of early adolescence (Susman, 1997), but they are not primarily responsible for the psychological or social developments during this period (Finkelstein, 1993; Petersen & Taylor, 1980; Susman, 1997). The quality and timing of hormonal or other biological changes influence and are influenced by psychological, social, cultural, and historical factors (Elder, 1980; Gottlieb, 1992; Magnusson, 1988; Stattin & Magnusson, 1990; Tanner, 1991).

Other examples of the integrated, multilevel changes in adolescence arise in regard to cognitive development during this period (Graber & Petersen, 1991). Global and pervasive effects of puberty on cognitive development do not seem to exist. When biological effects are found, they interact with contextual and experiential factors, such as the transition to junior high school, to influence academic achievement (Simmons & Blyth, 1987). Perspectives about adolescence that claim behavioral disruptions or disturbances are a universal part of this period of life (e.g., A. Freud, 1969; Hall, 1904) might lead to the assumption that there are general cognitive disruptions over adolescence. However, evidence does not support this assumption. Rather, cognitive abilities are enhanced in early adolescence as individuals become faster and more efficient at processing information—at least in settings where they feel comfortable in performing cognitive tasks (Ceci & Bronfenbrenner, 1985). Moreover, pubertal timing is not predictive of gender differences on such tasks as spatial cognition. Girls' earlier maturation does not result in general sex differences in cognition (Graber & Petersen, 1991).

The relations among biology, problem behaviors associated with personality, and the social context of youth illustrate the multiple levels of human life that are integrated throughout adolescent development. For example, the biological changes of early pubertal maturation have been found to be linked to delinquency in adolescent girls, but only among girls who attended mixed-sex schools (Caspi et al., 1993) or among early maturing girls who socialized with older friends instead of same-age ones (Magnusson & Stattin, 1998; Stattin & Magnusson, 1990). Early maturation among girls in single-sex schools or in same-age peer groups is not linked with higher delinquency.

Changing Relations Among Adolescents and Their Contexts

The period of adolescence is one of continual change and transition between individuals and their contexts (Lerner, 1995). These changing relations constitute the basic process of development in adolescence and underlie both positive and negative outcomes (Lerner, 1995).

Most developmental trajectories across this period involve positive adjustment on the part of the adolescent. For most youth there is a continuation of warm and accepting relations with parents (Grotevant, 1998; Guerney & Arthur, 1984). The most optimal adjustment occurs among adolescents who are encouraged by their parents to engage in age-appropriate autonomy while maintaining strong ties to their family (Galambos & Ehrenberg, 1997).

Most adolescents maintain close and warm relationships with their parents.

The risk of problems occurring in a youth's development is greater when the multiple biological, psychological, cognitive, and social changes of adolescence occur simultaneously, for example when menarche occurs at the same time as a school transition (Simmons & Blyth, 1987). In these circumstances, the adolescent is more often involved than younger individuals in making the behavioral and contextual choices associated with involvement in problem behaviors, such as engaging in drug use with a particular peer group (see J. S. Lerner, 1995). In adolescence, poor decisions, for example those involving school, sex, or drugs, have more negative consequences than in childhood (Dryfoos, 1990), and the adolescent is more responsible for those decisions and their consequences than in childhood (Petersen, 1988).

When necessary, adolescence is an opportune time to intervene into family processes. As discussed in more detail later in this chapter, minor parent-child conflicts are normative in adolescence, for example, regarding chores and privileges. Major conflicts are less frequent, however, and when they occur often in a family, parents should be concerned (Galambos & Almeida, 1992). The continued salience of the family in the adolescent period makes such conflicts an appropriate intervention target.

Individual Differences Among Adolescents

Issues to Consider
- What characterizes the developmental trajectories of adolescence? Why do problems often occur?
- What is a key feature of policy making in the study of adolescent development?

Inter-individual differences Variability between people that leads to different developmental outcomes.

Intra-individual changes Alterations within a person that occur with development.

Programs Standardized procedures followed to enable a person or group to increase desired behaviors (e.g., the enhancement of literacy through instruction in reading) or to decrease unwanted ones (e.g., school dropout).

As discussed in detail later, there are multiple pathways through adolescence (Bandura, 1964; Block, 1971; Douvan & Adelson, 1966; Offer, 1969; Simmons & Blyth, 1987). Normal adolescent development involves both **inter-individual differences** and also **intra-individual changes**, that is, both differences between individuals and differences within in individuals. Good examples of differences among adolescents are temperamental characteristics involving mood and activity level (Lerner & Lerner, 1983, 1987). Inter-individual and intra-individual differences in mood and activity level may influence adolescent behaviors such as substance use and delinquency (Henry et al., 1996). Diversity also exists between and within all ethnic, racial, or cultural groups. Therefore, generalizations that confound class, race, and/or ethnicity are not useful (Lerner, 1995).

Unfortunately, there is a major limitation in the contemporary scientific literature about adolescent development. Despite the value of the extant knowledge base about development in adolescence, the majority of studies in the literature have involved the study of European American, middle-class samples (e.g., Fisher & Brennan, 1992; Graham, 1992; Hagen et al., 1990; Lerner, 1995). There are, of course, some prominent, high-quality investigations that have studied samples other than European American middle-class ones (e.g., Brookins, 1991; Reid, 1991; Spencer 1990, 1991; Spencer & Dornbusch, 1990; Spencer & Markstrom-Adams, 1990) or that have studied adolescents from national or cultural settings other than the United States (e.g., Magnusson, 1988; Mead, 1928, 1930, 1935; Silbereisen, 1995; Stattin & Magnusson, 1990; Whiting & Whiting, 1991). Many of these studies are discussed throughout this book.

In regard to policies and **programs,** any intervention must be tailored to the specific target population and, in particular, to a group's developmental and environmental circumstances (Lerner, 1995; Lerner & Miller, 1993; Lerner & Villarruel, 1994). Because of inter-individual and intra-individual diversity among adolescents, any single policy or intervention cannot reach *all* of a given target population or influence every adolescent in the same way.

The breadth and depth of the high-quality scientific information available about development in adolescence underscores the diversity and dynamics of this period of life. The theoretically interesting and socially important changes of this period constitute one reason why the field of adolescence has attracted an increasing degree of scientific attention. To enhance further both basic knowledge and the quality of the research base used for applications aimed at enhancing youth development, scholarship in adolescence should be directed more increasingly to elucidating the course of development of diverse adolescents.

Adolescence is a period of life marked by diversity, both among different youth and within any given young person. As a result of such diversity, any generalized statement about what is true for "all adolescents" is apt to be inaccurate. Therefore, a stereotyped belief that there is only one type of pathway across the adolescent years—for instance, one characterized by inevitable "storm and stress"—would not be expected to stand up in the face of current knowledge about diversity in adolescence. The life-span perspective provides concepts with which to evaluate this **stereotype,** or cultural lore, that frequently defines the adolescent period.

Adolescence: The Myth of Universal Storm and Stress

Issues to Consider

- What is the lore of adolescence?
- How do historical trends frame the lore of adolescence?

We have defined adolescence as a period of both change and transition. Certainly, other developmental periods also involve changes in both individual and social characteristics, involving biology and psychology as well as relationships with parents and peers. The uniqueness of adolescence is that it is also a period of transition, of development from being childlike to being adult. As already noted, this transition spans almost a decade of life. In fact, with the exception of infancy, adolescence is the major transitional period in the life span (Brooks-Gunn, Petersen, & Eichorn, 1985; Lerner & Foch, 1987).

Because of the dramatic and major ways in which change occurs in this period of life, the developmental tasks of adolescence can be especially problematic. Because it is a period of such pronounced transition and the person undergoing the changes of this period is physically bigger and stronger than a child, adolescent changes can often appear more disruptive and disturbing in their effects on the individual and his or her social world than is the case with changes occurring in other periods of life. It may be that the nature of adolescent change is so great that it can be experienced as

especially stressful and the net effect of the transition may be felt as a time of "storm," or conflict for the developing person and his or her social world.

Does this possibility of adolescence as an especially stormy and stressful period strike you as fitting or as fanciful? It may be that your answer is shaped by the events of adolescence that you, your friends, and/or your siblings experienced. It may also be that your answer is shaped by the influences on you of stereotypes that exist in our culture about what is believed to be the inherent nature of adolescence. These stereotypes, if not held by you, may pervade your own or your parents' generation.

A stereotype is an overgeneralized belief or, in other words, an exceptionless generalization (Allport, 1954). The overgeneralized belief about adolescence is that it is a universal period of storm and stress, of emotional turmoil, and of problem behaviors (e.g., see Anthony, 1969; Lerner, 1986; Lerner & Spanier, 1980; Petersen, 1985). This exceptionless generalization is predicated on the idea that the universal biological changes of puberty inevitably create a developmental disturbance in emotions, thoughts, and social relationships (A. Freud, 1969. Anna Freud's theory is discussed in more detail in Chapter 2). According to the stereotype, stormy and stressful inner and outer conflicts inevitably complicate developmental change in adolescence.

The stereotype about adolescence arises from an interpretation about the meaning for the person of an invariant set of individual changes he or she undergoes, those associated with pubertal maturation. For this reason, it is important to discuss the stereotype, or cultural lore, of adolescence.

Bases of the Lore of Adolescence

All individuals and families have conflicts and negative experiences. Such experiences are a normal part of life. Yet many people believe that the adolescent period is a particularly stormy and stressful one—for youth and their families. Is such conflict actually prototypic of adolescent development? Is there a single nature to, or trajectory for, this period? Is there one universal, inevitable type of adolescent development that exists regardless of historical period or culture?

> **Stereotype** Exceptionless generalization or commonly held belief about a group (e.g., adolescents) or social institution (e.g., fraternities or sororities).

The word *adolescence* itself is not a new invention. It can be traced to the Latin word "adolescere," which means to grow into maturity. However, the word is especially salient for people today (Demos, 1986). One reason for this importance is that in this century there has been both popular and scientific debate over the nature of the developments that occur in this period.

Psychologist G. Stanley Hall (1904), discussed in more detail in Chapter 2, believed that "human development everywhere included a period of *sturm und drang* [German for "storm and stress"] between childhood and adulthood" (i.e., during adolescence) (Demos, 1986, p. 94). As a more or less direct refutation of Hall's theory of universal and inevitable storm and stress in adolescence (Demos, 1986), anthropologist Margaret Mead designed her classic study, *Coming of Age in Samoa* (1928). Mead's view was that storm and stress are **culturally conditioned** and are quite specific to developmental experiences in modern Europe and North America (Demos, 1986).

Anthropologists other than Mead had often "noticed an absence of special concern for adolescence in pre-modern cultures around the world . . . sociologists discovered a similar pattern—i.e., less versus more highlighting of adolescence—in rural as contrasted with urban populations even within the United States" (Demos, 1986, p. 94). Indeed, in his review of the history of the adolescent period, Demos (1986) indicates that the presence and degree of storm and stress in adolescence is related to historical, cultural, and subcultural variations.

For instance, teenage pregnancy—one possible instance of a stressful event for the adolescent—is neither a universal nor an inevitable phenomenon of adolescence (Modell, 1985). Instead, the occurrence and rate of teenage pregnancy is related to two historical trends taking place in particular in the United States. One trend involves "a decline in the capacity of parents and their agents to direct the behaviors of their adolescent children" (Modell, 1985, p. 3). The second trend involves "a temporarily enlarged capacity of adolescents themselves to construct and maintain a coherent path to adulthood for themselves" (Modell, 1985, p. 3).

The characteristics attributed to the adolescent period vary historically and culturally (e.g., Demos, 1986; Keniston, 1970; Modell,

Culturally conditioned Ideas, views, beliefs, attitudes, or values engendered by the social, cultural, and historical environment in which we live.

1985). Given its social character, it should not be surprising that in modern Western societies there is a social stereotype (Anthony, 1969), a lore of adolescence (Lerner, 1986; Lerner & Spanier, 1980; Petersen, 1985; Siegel & Shaughnessy, 1995). As noted, its most general feature is the view that adolescence, universally and inevitably, is a period of storm and stress. There are specific components of this stereotype that are important to note.

Features of the Lore of Adolescence

Issue to Consider

- How does society's view of the developmental tasks of adolescence (e.g., forming a self-definition) contribute to the lore of this period?

At least since the time of G. Stanley Hall (1904), the idea of "storm and stress" captures what many people in Western culture believe is the essence of the adolescent period. Romanticized and envied in fiction, caricatured and condemned in the media, and idealized in song, the stereotype, or lore, about adolescence is that it is a period wherein raging hormones and complicated and contradictory social messages confuse the adolescent about who he or she is and lead erratically from one personally unsatisfying and socially unproductive activity to another (Anthony, 1969; Bandura, 1964; Petersen, 1985). Lacking an enduring sense of self anchored with accurate understandings of one's emotions, values, and ideology, the adolescent is portrayed as unpredictable and often uncontrollable. Such an individual is simultaneously a victim of his or her own inner turbulence and a victimizer of the social institutions and agents charged with guiding the individual successfully into the stability, success, and serenity of the adult years (Anthony, 1969; Lerner & Spanier, 1980; Petersen, 1985).

The emergence of our culture's lore of adolescence has been aided and abetted by the speculations and theorizations of social scientists and psychoanalysts. Undeterred either by contradictory historical and cultural data (Demos, 1986) or by an invariably incomplete and often nonexistent database (Lipsitz, 1977), these pronouncements have pictured adolescence as an inevitable and indeed necessary period of developmental disturbance, as a period of negative and difficult disruptions evoked by universally tumultuous and trying transitions in the young person's biological, emotional, cognitive, and social processes (e.g., Erikson, 1968; A. Freud, 1969; Hall, 1904). Here too the adolescent's false or unstable sense of self, derived from the simultaneity and stress of these several transitions, has been said to lead, in a manner seemingly unpredictable to either the adolescent or his or her caregivers, from one adultlike guise to another (e.g., Erikson, 1959, 1968). As each facade is adopted, the adolescent believes, albeit temporarily, that he or she has coped with the storm and is now mature, directed, and committed.

Not surprisingly, it is little comfort to parents to know that within the mere passage of no more than 10 years the adolescent will look back to these days, understand the individual and interpersonal turmoil produced by this behavior, and, as did the folksinger Bob Dylan (1964), recognize that:

> Yes my guard stood hard
> When abstract threats
> Too noble to neglect
> Deceived me into thinking
> I had something to protect
> My existence led by confusion boats
> Mutinied from stern to bow
> Ah but I was so much older then
> I'm younger than that now . . .

This lore of adolescence is a story fulfilling the purposes of many sectors of society: educators, social and health care providers, novelists, journalists, and poets included (Meyer, 1988). However, the historical and cross-cultural data we have noted (Demos, 1986; Mead, 1928; Modell, 1985) indicate that storm and stress and/or developmental disturbance is neither universal nor inevitable. But does storm, stress, and disturbance characterize today's adolescent in modern Western societies? Did it characterize your own adolescence and those of your friends? Did it characterize the adolescence of your *parents*?

Certainly, many facets of the lore may have the ring of truth to them, especially to those people trying currently to cope with an adolescent son or daughter. Nevertheless, we may question whether the changes stereotyped to follow from pubertal change—conflict and turmoil, **cognitive reorganization,** and emotional upheaval and personal redefinition—in fact occur prototypically among today's adolescents. For today's youth—at least those in modern Western societies—

do the biological transitions of adolescence directly produce a special quality of developmental tasks marked by a psychological disturbance in the young adolescent's cognitive and emotional developments (A. Freud, 1969), and by storm and stress for both the individual and the caregivers? The information available to answer this question consistently and convincingly points to "no."

Research Evidence Regarding Adolescent Storm and Stress

Issue to Consider
- How did Albert Bandura's research contribute to the debunking of the stereotypes related to the period of adolescence?

Every period of life has stresses. There are always challenges imposed by newly emerged or diminishing psychological and behavioral capacities and by changes in our social world, changes to which we must react to be adaptive. Thus across life we must develop the ability to cope with the stressors imposed by our inner and outer changes.

For some youth, the need to cope with the stress of these changes does produce an adolescent period that is stormy. However, research spanning about 35 years—a period that includes the adolescent years of many of the students reading this book and some of their parents—indicates that for most youth this is simply not the case (Laursen, 1995; Lerner & Spanier, 1980; Petersen, 1985).

It is important to evaluate the validity of the lore of adolescence over the course of history. As emphasized by the life-span perspective, development during one period of history may differ from development at other times. Wars, economic depressions, changes in laws, epidemics, and natural disasters may create quite different developmental contexts for youth (Elder, 1974, 1980, 1998). It is possible, therefore, that during a time of considerable social unrest, or of particular quiescence, a pattern of adolescent development may arise that differs from those of other historical eras.

However, we can confidently reject the idea of universal storm and stress for youth if there is no evidence

Cognitive reorganization
Changes in the way a person thinks or reasons.

for it over a historical period when wars have begun and ended (for example, in Vietnam and Iraq), major political systems have eroded (communism), countries have disappeared or emerged (for example, in Africa and in Europe), diseases have reached epidemic proportions (for example, AIDS), and human life has changed fundamentally due to advances in technology (the computer, the Internet). It is important, then, to critically evaluate research pertinent to any feature of adolescent development that has been conducted across such a broad historical period. Given the prominence of the lore of adolescence, such evaluation is critical.

Across adolescence, young people spend more time with peers than with parents.

A study by Albert Bandura (1964) provides a useful point of departure for this historical analysis. Investigating male adolescents in California, Bandura not only found that most youth did not experience a stormy adolescence, but he also found virtually no evidence for the general conflicts thought to exist between adolescents and their parents. Most of the boys Bandura studied adopted parental values and standards and formed friendships with peers who shared these same values and standards. Thus there was no struggle by the adolescents to break unwanted ties with parents and turn instead to peers. Bandura found that parents actually encouraged greater autonomy in their adolescents and began training them for such behavior during their childhood.

Bandura (1964) observed that by adolescence most children had so thoroughly adopted parental values and standards that parental restrictions actually were reduced. In addition, Bandura noted that although the storm and stress idea of adolescence implies a struggle by youth to free themselves of dependence on parents, parents begin in childhood to train their children *to be independent*. In addition, Bandura found that the adolescents' choice of friends was not a major source of friction between adolescents and parents. Adolescents tended to form friendships with those who shared similar values. The peers tended to support those standards of

the parents that already had been adopted by the adolescents themselves.

Bandura pointed out that these observations do not mean that adolescence is a stressless, problemless period of life. As noted, Bandura was also careful to indicate that no period of life is free of crisis or adjustment problems, and any period of life may present particular adjustment problems for some people and not for others. Thus we have to be careful about attributing to all adolescents problems seen in one group of adolescents.

In a portion of his study, Bandura (1964) observed a sample of antisocial boys, whose excessive aggression did lead to an adolescence associated with storm and stress. However, their problem behaviors were present throughout their childhood. When the boys were children, they were physically smaller and the parents were able to control their aggressive behavior better than they could during adolescence. Bandura concluded that one could not appropriately view the problems of these boys as resulting only from adolescence.

Other data are consistent with Bandura's (1964) findings that youth who show problem behaviors during adolescence showed similar problematic behaviors in childhood (Spivack, Marcus, & Swift, 1986). A child who is overly and disruptively involved socially and who fails to modulate his or her behavior to accommodate others is likely to show misconduct and to have conflict with authority figures in adolescence. Similarly, drug use in adolescence was predicted by childhood personality as well as by contemporaneous adolescent personality (Brook et al., 1986). Bandura's (1964) findings, as well as those of others (Brook et al., 1986; Spivack et al., 1986), suggest that some, but not necessarily all, paths through adolescence begin in the childhood years.

Bandura's (1964) study leads to two key conclusions: (1) Even when storm and stress is seen in adolescence, it is not necessarily the result of events in adolescence, but instead may be associated with prior developments. (2) Storm and stress is not necessarily characteristic of the adolescent period; many possible types of adolescent development, many trajectories, can occur. The existence of such different paths through adolescence is supported by the results of other classic studies pertinent to the lore of adolescence.

Offer (1969) also found evidence for multiple paths through early adolescence. Most boys experienced either **"continuous growth"** or **"surgent growth."** Offer described "continuous growth" as involving smooth, nonabrupt change; he described "surgent growth" as involving abrupt spurts or changes in behavior but with no necessarily accompanying crisis, problems, or storm. Only a minority of boys experienced what Offer termed **"tumultuous growth,"** which consistent with Bandura's (1964) findings was the only path deemed "stormy" (Offer, 1969).

In Offer's study (1969), the adolescents in the "continuous-growth" type of development, the category into which most fall, were not in any major conflict with their parents and did not feel that parental rearing practices were inappropriate or that parental values were ones they did not share. Such a pattern is like the one Bandura (1964) describes. In the "surgent growth" trajectory, there was abrupt change but it did not necessarily involve the turmoil associated with storm and stress. Finally, with the "tumultuous growth" type, crisis, stress, and problems are present. The nature of this change is aptly characterized by major emotional and interpersonal distress.

Additional research finds evidence of several different types of developmental trajectories in adolescence. Block (1971) identified at least five different paths through adolescence for males and at least six different paths for females. However, for both males and females only a few of these pathways could be characterized as crisis-ridden or stormy.

In a study of both male and female adolescents, Douvan and Adelson (1966) found very little evidence of either conflict with or rebellion from parents. Adolescents were satisfied with their families and with how they were treated by their parents. Confirming Bandura's findings, Douvan and Adelson (1966) found that both boys and girls shared their parents' basic values and standards. In fact, adolescents were again seen to choose peers who had these same values and standards. Although adolescents spend increasingly more time with peers than with parents (Petersen, 1988; and see Chapter 9), and the influence of peers may actually increase across adolescence (Petersen, 1988), parents remain central in the adolescent's world.

Across the adolescent period youth maintain a high level of discussion with their parents in regard to academic/vocational, social/ethical, family, and peer issues (Petersen, 1998). At the same time, discussions with peers about these issues increase across this age range. Friends may be more influential than parents in some areas such as peer relationships. In other areas parents and peers may have equivalent influences (Chassin et al., 1986). On most major issues, for example life plans, parents have the most influence on adolescents (Kandel, 1974; Kandel & Lesser, 1969, 1972; Petersen, 1987).

The means by which this influence occurs can vary in relation to the structure and/or function of the family. In regard to family functioning, families with good parent-adolescent communication show high cohesion as a unit, high adaptability to change, and high satisfaction with the characteristics of the family (Barnes & Olson, 1985). However, there may be **cross-cultural variation** in the influence of particular types of family functioning. Among Korean adolescents, high parental control is associated with high warmth and

> **"Continuous growth"**
> Developmental path through adolescence characterized by smooth, nonabrupt change.
>
> **"Surgent Growth"**
> Developmental path through adolescence characterized by abrupt spurts or changes in behavior, but not necessarily with turmoil, storm, or stress.
>
> **"Tumultuous growth"**
> Developmental path through adolescence experienced by a minority of adolescents, characterized by turmoil, storm, and stress.
>
> **Cross-cultural variation**
> Differences in values, beliefs, attitudes, and actions that occur between societies.

low neglect in the parent-adolescent relationship. However, among most American youth and their parents, the relationship between control and warmth and neglect is reversed (Rohmer & Pettengill, 1985).

Family structural differences, such as the number of parents in the household, also affect the influence of parents on adolescents. For example, in a study of adolescent-father, adolescent-mother, and adolescent-mother-father interactions in intact two-parent families, the presence of the father enhanced the quality of mother-son relations; but the presence of the mother reduced the quality of father-son interactions (Gjerde, 1986). In addition, mothers treated sons and daughters more differently when the father was present in the group; but fathers treated sons and daughters more differently when the mother was absent from the group. In families with male adolescents, parental role differences increased in the presence of the spouse. In contrast to adolescents in households with two parents, youth in mother-only households are more likely to make decisions without direct parental input and are more likely to show problem behaviors (Dornbusch et al., 1985). However, when another adult joins the household, there is an increase in parental control and influence and a decrease in problem behaviors. This change is especially true for male adolescents.

Although there are structural and functional variations in how influence is expressed, parents do continue to influence their adolescents and share with them key orientations to life. Lerner and Knapp (1975) found substantial attitude and value similarity among male and female adolescents and their mothers and fathers. In the great majority of cases, members of both generations had similar attitudes about such issues as sexuality, drug use, war and peace, and civil and human rights.

The adolescents studied by Lerner and Knapp (1975) believed their attitudes were quite different from those of their parents. Despite the actual high level of similarity that existed, adolescents exaggerated the differences between them and their parents and overesti- mated the extent to which they differed from their parents. Parents, however, underestimated even the small extent to which they differed from their children. The parents saw fewer differences than actually existed. Although the different generational groups present in a family do not actually differ very much in their attitudes, members of one generation (adolescents) overestimate this difference and members of the other (parents) underestimate it.

Recent information indicates that among contemporary adolescents, parents are not the exclusive or even necessarily the major source of social disagreements (Laursen, 1995). Adolescents report that disagreements occur most often with their mothers, but the next most frequent sources of conflict are friends, romantic partners, and siblings (Laursen, 1995). Fathers trail behind these groups as a source of disagreement. In other words, adolescents' disagreements are more likely to involve people of their own generation than their parents. Disagreements with parents are likely to involve responsibilities, school, and autonomy, whereas disagreements with peers tend to arise in respect to friendships and sexuality (Laursen, 1995).

Even in regard to disagreements with peers, there are perhaps more agreements than conflicts. In a study of about 3,500 youth from five countries (the United States, Israel, Costa Rica, the Philippines, and Scotland), there was significant concordance

Parents remain sources of support and guidance for adolescents.

among adolescents and their peers in regard to ideas about major life events involving the nature of and the transition to adulthood (Seltzer & Waterman, 1996). Consistent with past research (Lerner & Knapp, 1975), adolescents also *perceived* that their attitudes were in agreement with those of their peers (Seltzer & Waterman, 1996). Even though adolescents are more likely to have disagreements with age-mates than with both their parents, they believe they have—and in fact do have—marked agreements with their peers.

When the precise nature of conflicts between youth and their parents is examined, there is little evidence for the lore of adolescence (Laursen, Coy, & Collins, 1998). Across the adolescent period there is a decrease in the *rate* of conflict between adolescents and their parents and also a decrease in the *number* of conflictual exchanges youth have with them. Although there is an overall decrease in the frequency of conflict between youth and their parents across adolescence, when they do have conflicts the intensity of emotions increases across adolescence, as well as in relation to pubertal maturation (Laursen et al., 1998).

The findings of recent research, consistent with research from several decades ago, indicate that the patterns of inter- and intra-generational conflict and compatibility are hardly the base on which to build the notion of universal adolescent storm and stress. There may always be stress, conflict, or interpersonal disagreements in the adolescent period, but there are several paths through adolescence, and storm occurs only sometimes. For most youth there is a continuation of generally good and satisfying parent-child relations, relations predicated on the adoption by the adolescent of parental values and standards (Lerner & Spanier, 1980; Petersen, 1985).

As the findings of Laursen (1995) and Laursen et al. (1998) suggest, parents do not always experience their children as perfect and amenable to all their rules and requests. Conflicts can and do occur. As illustrated by Janis Brown and her mother at the beginning of the chapter, these disagreements may even take the form of heated verbal exchanges. However, disagreements, arguments, and even "backtalk" from teenagers are normal parts of parents' experiences with their teenage children. As explained in Implications for Parenting Box 1.1, parents should keep such interactions with their adolescents in perspective.

The lore of adolescence is not fully accurate in depicting the nature of the changes involving the physiological, cognitive, emotional, self-definitional, and role characteristics associated among contemporary youth with the challenges of this period of life. Nevertheless, the way the adolescent meets the developmental challenges of the period will influence the quality of development during this portion of life.

Contemporary scientific literature does not support the belief that adolescence is a period of general disruption of parent-child ties or the belief in the emergence of problematic social behaviors among virtually all youth. The facts of adolescent development allow the study of the social problems that *do* occur during this period to be put in appropriate perspective.

It is also important to highlight the nature of the individual and social problems, which do exist within this period of life. Although only a minority of youth exhibits these problems, on a population basis this frequency translates into millions of people. This book presents information about these problems of adolescent development. However, in order to identify what is problematic or atypical it is crucial to know what is typical and normative (Fisher et al., 1993). This book also elucidates the prototypic characteristics of adolescent development.

Conclusions

Contemporary scholarship about adolescence focuses on the themes of developmental diversity; adolescent-context relations; and the links among theory, research, and application (to youth policies and programs). As such, these themes frame this book in the following manner:

- The emphasis on adolescent development involves both the antecedents of development in earlier life periods and the consequences of changes in adolescence for later, adult development and aging. The treatment of development in this text includes a discussion of the intertwining of the development of a youth with the life-span development of parents and other relatives, with peers, and with other individuals important in the life of an adolescent, such as teachers, mentors, and coaches.

implications for parenting box 1.1

Does Your Preteen Have to Argue About Everything? Yes, But You Can Keep It All in Perspective

Mark Twain once wryly noted, "When I was a boy of 14, my father was so ignorant that I could hardly stand to have the old man around. But when I got to be 21, I was astonished at how much he had learned in seven years."

If you're the parent of a preteen, you know all too well what it's like to be on the receiving end of that attitude. The youngster who once saw you as the source of all wisdom now cuts you off in midconversation with utterances such as "You can't tell me what to do" and "Why do I bother explaining things to you? You can't possibly understand." In addition, he suddenly seems to question every statement that comes out of your mouth. He may even use the occasional obscenity.

It's easy for a parent to lose patience when a child starts mouthing off this way; none of us enjoys being treated disrespectfully or having to justify everything we say. Back talk is also disturbing because it signifies your loss of control over your child's behavior.

But as inappropriate and disrespectful as a preteen's language might be, it's actually a step toward mature behavior. Learning to assert individual opinions is a developmental milestone every bit as significant, and universal, as cutting teeth or walking. As annoying as this stage in your child's life can be at times, there is no way you can absolutely abolish back talk. There are, however, a number of ways for you to recognize and provide outlets for your child's opinions, emotions, and growing skills at debate.

Begin by understanding why your child needs to talk back.

Her "smart mouth" is, in some ways, exactly that—a sign that she's smarter. Her logic is growing more sophisticated, although it's not quite up to adult level yet. She now sees her parents' opinions, once regarded as the absolute truth, as one possible truth—and a version of it that she sometimes finds hard to swallow.

Chalk that up to another aspect of adolescence: your child's need to establish herself as a person separate from you. Just as it is your job to watch over and protect your child, it is your child's job to stake out her own emotional turf, to discover who she is and what she stands for.

An increase in back talk often coincides with a developmental transition, such as starting middle or junior high school. Hanging out with a new group of kids may lead your child to think that a certain level of repartee is expected of her. You may need to tell your adolescent, "I know you talk this way with your friends, but I find it unpleasant to hear that kind of language at home."

Don't belittle your child.

In the heat of the moment, this rule can be tough to follow, but it's crucial. No matter how adult your teen wants to be, he is still a child, with easily hurt feelings and little experience in the art of persuasion.

For example, if you take your child to task for doing his homework in front of the television, he may answer you dismissively with, "This isn't homework. It's just answering questions." You could easily answer him with something like, "That's ridiculous! Do you think I don't know what homework is?"

Although understandable, this response will only serve to embroil you further in an unproductive argument. What you might do instead is say something such as, "Whatever you call it, I want you to try your best at your schoolwork, and I don't think you can do that if you're working in front of the television."

Similarly, if your child is using unpleasant language toward a sibling and you tell him to stop it, he might say, "I'm not being mean; I'm just defending myself!" Your impulse might well be to say, "That's baloney! I heard the way you talked to her." But it's probably more helpful if you respond by saying something like, "Standing up for yourself is a good thing, but you have to try to do it without using words that hurt others' feelings."

- The emphasis on individual *diversity* includes focus on developmental variation between adolescents associated with race, ethnicity, gender, sexual orientation, and physical characteristics. In addition, this emphasis on diversity involves an appraisal of within-person variability, such as that associated with the gains and losses that characterize human development across life.
- The emphasis on *context* involves a discussion of

Fight fair, even when your child doesn't.

Resist the temptation to fight fire with fire, especially if your teen gets so angry during an argument that she curses at you, shoves you, or even spits on you. If something like this happens, as calmly as you can, say, "I want you to let me know how you feel about things, but I can't tolerate this behavior. The conversation is over." Follow up with appropriate discipline.

Stick to your values.

Debates with your child will be more fruitful for both of you if you know what is negotiable and what is not. If you have a habit of arguing and then giving in, you'll get more of an argument from your child because he knows that it pays off. Put forward your deeply held values, and don't retreat from them—but be prepared to justify your position to your child.

Set limits on profanity.

Preadolescents often use foul language to signal their grown-up status. It's hard to deny that cursing is an activity associated with adults. It is as reasonable to set limits on profanity, however, as it is on other adult behaviors, such as staying up late. What those limits are depends on how much foul language upsets you.

If your child says, "How come you get to say any words you want, and I don't?" tell her that using profanity is a habit of yours that you don't especially like and are trying to control, but that it sometimes happens when you're very angry or upset. You can also say to her, "By using those words, you're going to offend someone or create an impression you'll regret later on."

Make sure you give your child credit for what he does right.

Because one of your child's primary motives for talking back is to show that he is capable of holding his own in a grownup conversation, acknowledge him when he succeeds. You won't lose ground by saying, "That's a good point you've made."

Suppose your 12-year-old son wants to sleep over at a friend's house and you say, "No, I don't want you to spend the night there." Blair's parents are lax about supervision."

Your child might respond with "How do you know? *You've* never spent the night there."

Instead of treating this response as insolence, you might reply, "That's absolutely true. I've heard from other parents, however, that Blair's mom and dad sometimes go out and leave the kids alone. Maybe that isn't so, but the possibility worries me because I'm concerned about your safety."

After some discussion, your child might suggest a solution: "I'll call and make sure his parents will be there all night." After you agree to this—with the understanding that you can telephone the parents to confirm the arrangement—praise your child for respecting your concerns and solving the problem creatively.

Don't expect conflicts—or back talk—to be solved overnight.

Arguments often do not have clear-cut resolutions. If you've both had your say and the conversation has become unproductive, you may have to tell your child, "We've been over this too many times. Let's wrap it up. Maybe if we think about it and talk tomorrow, it'll be easier for us to agree on something."

And remember that arguing with a child you love can be a highly emotional and exasperating experience. Don't expect perfection from yourself. Stay as calm and even-handed as you can, and keep reminding yourself how smart you're going to be in just a few years.

Source: Lerner, R. M., & Olson, C. K. (1994, December). "Don't talk back," *Parents* pp. 97–98.

(1) the role of culture and history in shaping the processes and products of adolescent development; (2) the role of the social, interpersonal, familial, and physical context in influencing youth development; (3) institutional contributions to adolescent development, including educational, political, economic, and social policy influences; and (4) community needs and assets, including programs promoting positive youth and family development. In addition, the text discusses several disciplines

and professions involved in understanding the contexts that influence human development.

- Finally, the emphasis on *application* focuses on how the life-span perspective embraces both theoretical and applied research in adolescents' lives. The text also discusses **applied developmental science** (ADS), and how this approach to research about adolescence frames policies and programs pertinent to youth intervention programs, education, retraining, and services.

Applied developmental science Approach that uses research about human development to promote positive changes in individuals, families, and communities.

Many chapters of the book feature an Implications for Parenting box, a key dimension of application. Traditionally, there has been keen interest in understanding how developmental science may be applied to enhance adults' ability to parent their preadolescent offspring. A life-span perspective extends this domain to include issues of parenting youth, such as helping a young person make a successful transition to work. It also includes issues of adolescents' parenting their own children, that is, the issue of teenage parenting.

Summary

- Adolescence spans the second decade of life and is a period of transition wherein a person's biological, psychological and social characteristics go from childlike to adultlike.
- Not all young people undergo the period of transition in the same way. There is variation in the timing, speed, and outcome of the transition.
- Developmental trajectories are the diverse paths through life that an individual experiences based on biology, psychology, and social characteristics.
- The life-span perspective seeks to understand development across the entire course of life, in relation to combinations of biological, psychological and contextual influences. It stresses differences within and among people and attempts to optimize development by understanding these different bases of development.
- The life-span perspective emphasizes two types of diversity: differences among people (inter-individual differences) and changes within a person (intra-individual changes).
- It is important to use knowledge from multiple disciplines and professions to understand human development.
- Life-span scholars use intervention studies to optimize people's development through changes in the social world and changes in individual functioning.
- The major developmental tasks of adolescence are to deal with changes in biology, psychology, and the social world.
- Adolescents must cope with changing physical characteristics and physiological functions.
- Adolescents must deal with new thoughts and emotions and their changed biology to form a revised sense of self.

- The social developmental task of adolescence involves finding an appropriate role in society by combining who one is physically with who one is psychologically.
- Ideally, the three developmental tasks of adolescence converge to allow the adolescent to integrate his or her changing biology and psychology with the social world.
- Adolescents' changing relations with their contexts influence positive and negative outcomes of adolescence.
- When the biological, psychological, and social changes of adolescence occur simultaneously, there is a greater risk of developmental problems.
- The study of adolescence is limited in that the majority of the studies conducted are focused on European American, middle-class adolescents.
- Because of differences among adolescents, policies and programs must be tailored to specific target populations, and any policy or program should not be expected to reach all members of a given target population.
- The lore or stereotype of adolescence is that it is a period of universal storm and stress involving emotional turmoil and problem behaviors.
- Research indicates that the lore of adolescence is not accurate and that storm and stress is neither universal nor inevitable.
- Adolescence is generally a time of continued positive relations with parents, and most adolescents adopt their parents' values and standards as their own.
- How adolescents meet the developmental tasks of coping with changing biology, psychology, and context will influence the quality of their development during adolescence.

Discussion Topics

1. How do *you* define adolescence?
2. How does the life-span approach to adolescence employ concepts pertaining to the nature of human development such as diversity, context, and application?
3. Why is it important to take a multidisciplinary approach to adolescent development?
4. In what way did the onset of puberty affect your development? What other biological, psychological, and/or social/cultural factors influenced your developmental trajectory?
5. What is missing in studies that make broad generalizations about adolescent development?
6. What is your opinion about the lore of adolescence? How do your experiences and/or the experiences of those you know contribute to your opinion on this matter?
7. How do the media contribute to the stereotypes you might hold about the period of adolescence? Is the media portrayal of adolescence harmful? Is the media more or less harmful in their portrayal of males or females?
8. What should parents know about adolescent development to support healthy relationships with their children?

Key Terms

Adaptive functioning (p. 12)

Adolescence (p. 4)

Applied developmental science (p. 23)

Cognitive reorganization (p. 17)

Context (p. 6)

"Continuous growth" (p. 19)

Cross-cultural variation (p. 19)

Culturally conditioned (p. 16)

Developmental tasks (p. 10)

Developmental trajectories (p. 6)

Ecology (p. 7)

Inter-individual differences (p. 14)

Intervention studies (p. 9)

Intra-individual changes (p. 14)

Life-span perspective (p. 10)

Multidisciplinary (p. 10)

Policies (p. 9)

Programs (p. 14)

Self-definition (p. 12)

Social role (p. 7)

Stereotype (p. 15)

Storm and stress (p. 4)

"Surgent growth" (p. 19)

"Tumultuous growth" (p. 19)

2

THEORIES OF ADOLESCENCE

Jason's original plan for making friends in his new high school involved athletics and academics. As he entered his senior year, that strategy seemed to be falling apart. When he and his family first moved to Pathground, Vermont, last fall, he had assumed that moving to a new town in the middle of high school would likely be a social catastrophe. Kids who had probably gone to school together since kindergarten would not necessarily make him a part of their group just because he was new. Although he had never played football back in Ohio, he believed that joining the team would be a way to fit in immediately at his new high school. "If I don't have history going for me," he reasoned, "I can use sports to make friends and be accepted at school." He committed himself to working as hard on football as he could, both to overcome his lack of experience in the sport and to establish himself as a motivated person who could be relied on by others in an activity valued in the school.

Jason was used to working hard in school. However, academic pursuits had been his only "game" in Ohio, and this had earned him the peer status he sought. Fortunately, his new Pathground High fellow students also valued academic achievement. Kids with good standardized test scores and good grades went on to competitive, prestigious colleges. Youth with this course ahead of them were highly esteemed by the students and teachers of Pathground, especially when they were also varsity athletes. "I can overcome this disaster my parents created by moving," Jason convinced himself, "by being as good in football as I know I can be in my classes."

He was right. His junior year grades at Pathground High were terrific, almost straight A's. Although he did not get much playing time during the football season, few juniors did. The coach gave preference to the seniors, and so, like other juniors, Jason worked hard at practice and spent most of the time during games cheering the seniors from the sidelines. The coach promised the juniors that their commitment would pay off next season when they assumed the mantle of Pathground's senior class football team members.

But this expectation was the basis of Jason's dilemma. Now, as a senior, he believed he would be expected by his coach and teammates to contribute to the team's efforts during games, not just during practice. But there were more seniors than the coach could use. Jason would have to work extra hard—his coach recommended a special weight training program—to earn the right to get playing time and to have the strength and skills to succeed when given the chance to play.

Where would this time come from? Jason's scores on the preliminary Scholastic Aptitude Test (SAT), which he had taken at the end of his junior year, were good, but probably not sufficiently high to gain him admission into the most competitive colleges. His guidance counselor and parents urged him to take a special SAT preparation course. But how could he do an extra class and extra weight training, as well as his normal full day of regular classes, football practice, homework, and studying? Even if he decided that he would just skip sleeping for the semester, he could not be in two places at once, both at an after-school weight training session and an after-school SAT preparation course. Something had to give. Greater strength would give him a chance to play. However, about 100 more points on his SAT were required for him to get into the colleges of his choice. The combination of athletics and academics had given him the niche he desired in his junior class. Now, it seemed, this strategy would not be possible. He had to choose, and in so doing, he might have to sacrifice his newly found status in Pathground High School. . . .

* * *

Jason opened the envelope slowly. It contained information that would shape the next four years of his life. He had applied for "early admission" to a highly prestigious college and the letter would tell him whether he had been admitted. Jason let out a whoop of joy. "Mom, Dad," he called to his parents who stood anxiously in the next room awaiting to learn of their son's fate, "I'm in! I'm in! I've been accepted!" The choice to enroll in the SAT preparation course was now vindicated. He had continued to work hard at football practices, but forgoing the weight training program resulted in his inability to compete successfully for playing time during games. When he did get into a game it had been only in its last moments and only when the outcome of the event had been settled much earlier in the match. Clearly the SAT course had done its job. His SAT score had risen substantially over the level he had achieved on the preliminary test, and this outcome had encouraged him to try for the early admission he had now gained.

"I guess my thing is academics after all. It is certainly not football!" he reflected to his parents and a few friends at a dinner celebrating his college acceptance. He laughed and so did his friends. One added, "No one from Pathground is going to the pros anyway. You're lucky that what you are really good at will pay off for you in life." "Yes," Jason intoned with mock seriousness, "and now there's only one small thing holding me back from the good life: getting good grades in college."

LEARNING OBJECTIVES

1. To understand what is meant by the statement "Development occurs as a consequence of relations among multiple levels of organization."

2. To recognize the importance of the diversity of development when designing intervention programs.

3. To understand the theoretical debate of nature versus nurture.

4. To know how developmental contextualism differs from other theories of human development.

5. To recognize that genes can be influenced by characteristics of the context and that, inversely, the context can be influenced by the biological characteristics of those who live within it.

6. To understand the contributions of G. Stanley Hall to the study of developmental psychology and to recognize the problems inherent in Hall's belief that "phylogeny recapitulates ontogeny."

7. To recognize what McCandless meant by *drive states* and how drive states come to influence and determine behavior.

8. To recognize and be able to describe the three different types of interaction theory.

9. To define and describe the five stages of psychosexual development.

10. To recognize Erikson's view on the role of the ego in contributing to development.

11. To understand the special alterations in personality that Anna Freud associates with adolescence.

12. To recognize that Piaget believes that cognitive development occurs in stages and involves the individual's attempt to maintain an equilibration between the processes of assimilation and accommodation.

13. To recognize that Kohlberg's work, like Piaget's, describes a stagewise progression in moral reasoning and to be able to identify the stages of moral reasoning as described by Kohlberg.

14. To define and describe the four levels of human ecology according to Bronfenbrenner. Specifically, to recognize the reciprocal relationship between the individual and his or her contexts within and across levels.

15. To identify and be able to differentiate the components of the SOC model and to recognize that successful development includes the coordinated integration of selection, optimization, and compensation processes.

What Jason experienced during his transition from one school to another illustrates what may be the key challenge for people during adolescence: discovering what they can do—given their particular biological, psychological, and social characteristics—to develop successfully in their context. To attain the goal of peer acceptance and peer popularity, Jason had to understand his physical capacities (for football achievement), his psychological attributes (his ability to achieve academically), and his social context (what the students of Pathground High School expected of successful peers). He had to attain a self-definition, an identity, that fits his specific individual attributes and situational circumstances.

The actions adolescents take to meet the biological, psychological, and social challenges they confront determine whether or not they develop in a healthy, positive, or successful (that is, an "adaptive") manner (see Chapter 1). Explaining how adolescents select goals for their behaviors, how they

find the means or resources to achieve these goals (that is, to "optimize" their ability to attain their objectives), and what adolescents do to compensate for failures, that is, for the loss of opportunities, arguably are the essential tasks for theories of adolescence (Baltes, 1997; Baltes & Baltes, 1990; Freund & Baltes, 1998; Lerner et al., in press). Theories of adolescence must explain three different actions of young people, actions that may be summarized by the terms *selection, optimization,* and *compensation* (Lerner et al., 2001).

First, theories must explain how goals are *selected* and developed. For example, why did Jason, when confronted with the loss of his connections with the peers from his former high school, elect to try to gain acceptance and popularity with the students in his new high school rather than spend his free time with his parents? Why do adolescents in general elect to spend more and more time with peers and increasingly less time with their parents?

Adjusting to the requirements of college life may be a challenging experience.

ures or losses, to find other means (new resources) to reach goals, or to adopt new goals when original ones prove to be beyond one's biological, psychological, and social resources or capacities. Faced with the realization that he would never be outstanding in football, and that to try to achieve more in the sport would detract from his time (his resources) to attain academic success, Jason increased his efforts in academics. Thus Jason has learned how important it is to make choices and focus personal resources on a domain of functioning matching one's skills and potential when all options cannot be pursued.

To understand why adolescents act in the manner they do, to explain how their behaviors enable them to match their biological, psychological, and social characteristics with the challenges they confront in this period of life, theories must account for the selection, optimization, and compensation behaviors of youth (Baltes, 1997; Baltes & Baltes, 1990; M. Baltes & Carstensen, 1996, 1998; Freund & Baltes, 1998, in press; Lerner et al., 2001; Marsiske et al., 1995). Theories must explain how youth develop, structure, and commit to goals (**selection**), how they acquire and refine the means to reach goals (**optimization**), and what they do when the pathways they follow fail (**compensation**).

Explaining the actions of adolescents and their implications for adaptive outcomes is complicated because the life of adolescents is full of transitions. What makes sense to select as a goal changes across development. For example, the goal of peer relations in middle school might be sufficient popularity to be invited to desired parties, whereas the goal at the end of high school might be to establish a meaningful romantic relationship. The means to reach goals differs across adolescence. For instance, parents must be relied on for transportation to peer events in early adolescence but by the end of the adolescent period, reliance on parents for transportation to and from dates might be seen as humiliating. How a person compensates for failure or loss varies across adolescence. For instance, more sophisticated cognitive rationalizations for failure are available to older adolescents.

The selections youth make across the adolescent period involve changes in their relations with their contexts (e.g., "should I pursue more training in football or spend more time preparing for the SAT?"). Adolescents also consider anticipated

Second, theories of adolescent development must explain how youth develop the skills and/or find means to attain the goals they select. How do they learn to act in ways that *optimize* their opportunities to reach their goals? For example, why did Jason initially elect to reach his goal of peer status through high achievement in athletics and academics?

Third, to maintain a high level of functioning, losses must be compensated. The means we use to reach the goals we select do not always result in success. Failure is a normative experience for all people. However, healthy development rests on finding ways to *compensate* for fail-

Selection How youth develop, structure, and commit to their goals. Gives direction to development by directing and focusing resources on certain domains of functioning and preventing diffusion of resources.

Optimization How youth acquire and refine the means to reach their goals. Describes process geared toward achieving higher levels of functioning.

Compensation Investing additional resources or substituting or applying additional means, geared toward the maintenance of functioning when the pathways youth follow to reach their goals fail.

future contexts when making selections. Given what young people know of their physical and psychological strengths and weaknesses and the social world they wish to inhabit as an adult, they may ask, "What choices now will lead me to where I want to be when I am an adult?" (Oettingen, 1999). The selections made by adolescents can vary in their significance for life outcomes. Some selections can affect their entire life, such as decisions about substance use, unsafe sex, and college aspirations (J. S. Lerner, 1995).

When the adolescent understands his or her characteristics of biological, psychological, and social individuality and acts accordingly, successful development is promoted. Adaptive outcomes occur when actions involving selection, optimization, and compensation can foster diversity in the adolescent's behavioral repertoire. Jason can elect to spend more time in enhancing his academic abilities rather than devoting time to improving his football skills.

Theories of adolescence must explain how the individually distinct adolescent acts in relation to the particular context within which he or she is embedded. Theories must account for how the particular "context" of the adolescent provides feedback. Finally, theories must explain how the reciprocal nature of the adolescent and his or her context results in differences in adaptive development.

How successful are theories of adolescence in meeting these explanatory goals? Although earlier theories were perhaps less successful, *contemporary* theories of adolescence are in fact meeting these goals quite well. The next section of the chapter reviews past and current theories. The usefulness of contemporary theory lies in its stance in regard to a core, perhaps the core, conceptual issue in the study of human development: the **nature-nurture controversy**. The positions of current and past theories in regard to this controversy are discussed.

Understanding Adolescence: Contemporary Theory

Issues to Consider

- What are some concrete examples which illustrate that development has multiple levels of organization?
- How is the individual adolescent an "active agent" in his or her own development?

Nature-nurture controversy Debate about whether or how biology and/or environment provide the basis of human behavior and development.

Multiple levels of organization Idea that development occurs as a consequence of relations among biology, person, social groups, culture, history, and other levels in the ecology of human development.

The study of adolescence has provided a model for scholarship dedicated to the study of the life span. Today, theory and research in adolescence stresses that *development occurs as a consequence of relations among* **multiple levels of organization** (e.g., see Muuss, 1996). The levels considered in contemporary theory are typically the subject matter of different disciplines. For example, genes are one level and are the subject matter of biology. The adolescent and his or her behavior is another level and involves the discipline of psychology. Groups or institutions such as the family, peers, and schools are part of a level that is most often studied by sociology. Culture is a level studied most often by anthropologists.

A lot of adolescent social interactions occur in large groups.

Developmental systems theories stress that development occurs as a consequence of organized and mutually influential (or "systematic") relations among the levels. These theories emphasize that development occurs because of interconnections among biological, psychological, sociological, as well as other influences (for example, economics, historical events, and the occurrence of wars or disease epidemics). Changes at one level within the developmental system affect other levels. For example, parents' marital problems can affect a young person's psychological health (e.g., depression may arise as a consequence of witnessing parents arguing a lot). In turn, changes in the adolescent's psychological or behavioral characteristics (for instance, becoming involved in alcohol use) can place stress on parents and influence the quality of their marriage.

There are many versions of developmental systems models of human development (Baltes, 1987; Baltes, Reese, & Nesselroade, 1988; Brandtstädter, 1998; Bronfenbrenner & Morris, 1998; Elder, 1998; Featherman & Lerner, 1985, Ford & Lerner, 1992; Gottlieb, 1997; Gottlieb, Wahlstein, & Lickiter, 1998; Lerner, 1986, 1991b, 1995, 1998; Magnusson & Stattin, 1998; Overton, 1998; Sameroff, 1983; Thelen & Smith, 1998). One of these models—*developmental contextualism* (Lerner, 1982, 1986, 1998; Lerner & Kauffman, 1985)—is regarded by many scholars around the world as a general frame for studying adolescent development (e.g., Muuss, 1996) and, more broadly, for understanding the life-span perspective of human development.

The developmental contextual approach to life-span development suggests that to understand adolescence we must consider influences from multiple disciplines in an integrated manner. The theory emphasizes *the need to consider development as systematic change*. We must view the young person as a dynamic entity, the center of a network of influences involving his or her inner (biological, psychological) and outer (peer group, family, society) worlds. Developmental con-

textualism stresses that the individual is an active agent in his or her own development. The individual acts on the context just as the context acts on him or her, often in direct response to the actions (the selection, optimization, and compensation behaviors) of the individual (Brandtstädter, 1998, 1999; Lerner, 1982).

Theory, Method, and Application

Issues to Consider
- Why is multilevel, multivariate, longitudinal research effective in studying adolescence?
- What are some variables that might be relevant to intervention programs designed to support adolescents?

The developmental contextual approach to adolescence has specific implications for scientific methods used to study the multiple and changing connections between young people and their worlds (see Appendix 1). A life-span and developmental systems view of adolescence requires that several variables from different levels (e.g., biological ones relating to puberty, psychological ones relating to self-image or identity, and social ones relating to parent-child relations) be studied repeatedly (over time), in order to provide observations of the changes involved in development. Technically, this means that **multivariate** (many variables), **longitudinal** (repeated observations), and **multilevel** (e.g., biological, psychological, and social), and thus multidisciplinary, research should be used to study adolescence.

When we understand something about how adolescents' relationships with their peers, parents, schools, communities, and societies propel their development, we know how development might be improved in real-world settings. We may learn why some adolescents, despite growing up in poverty and in neighborhoods where there is a lot of crime, few social services, and poor schools, succeed academically, develop a strong commitment to a productive career, and end up having a healthy and positive life. We may also understand why other adolescents in these same circumstances succumb to the risks around them and do poorly in school, in their career or work life, and in their personal development (McAdoo, 1995; Spencer, 1990; Werner & Smith, 1992). Knowledge about the

Developmental systems theories Theories which stress that development occurs as a consequence of organized and mutually influential relations among different levels of organization (e.g., biology, society, culture, history).

Multivariate research/studies Research involving several variables.

Longitudinal research/studies Research composed of repeated observations.

Multilevel research/studies Research focusing on biological, psychological, and social facets of a phenomenon.

diversity (systematic differences) involving adolescents and their contexts provides information about how development occurs and suggests what *might* happen if relationships between young people and their settings were changed.

Basic knowledge about adolescent development may be used for purposes of designing or testing **interventions** (actions planned to reduce or prevent problems or to promote positive development). By focusing on development, diversity, and context we may interrelate basic and applied knowledge of adolescence and apply developmental science to promote policies and programs enhancing the life chances of youth (e.g., Fisher & Lerner, 1994). Applications Box 2.1 presents some of the key features of **applied developmental science** (ADS). In turn, Meet the Researcher Boxes 2.1 and 2.2 illustrate how the ideas associated with ADS are used in the scholarship of two prominent contributors to this field.

Conceptual Implications of Contemporary Theories of Adolescence

Issues to Consider
- Why might it be important to recognize the vast diversity within life pathways when designing intervention programs?
- Why might the developmental systems approach to supporting youth development be seen as an optimistic one?

Contemporary theories of adolescence have forwarded ideas that are also found in the life-span view of human development. The conceptual themes of development, diversity, context, and application highlight the individual differences and contextual variation that characterizes adolescent development, and they underscore the idea that development during this period is open-ended, malleable, or "plastic" (Lerner, 1984).

Because persons and contexts may change in unexpected ways, individuals' developmental pathways take unexpected courses. This potential for diversity does not mean an unlimited number of possible developmental pathways exists for each

person. Viewing development as open-ended and a product of current conditions means an adolescent's future is not prisoner to his or her past circumstances or conditions. Because of the relative plasticity of person-context interactions, future developmental pathways can deviate from previous pathways, be discontinuous as well as continuous (no changes from one period of life to the next).

Scholars disagree about what causes either continuity or discontinuity across life and whether the specifics of development are associated with our genetic inheritance or our experience. This disagreement is termed the nature-nurture controversy. Views about this controversy influence the theories of adolescent development. The features of this controversy organize our discussion of theories of adolescent development that differ from developmental systems theory in regard to the roles of nature and nurture in development, the bases and characteristics of plasticity in human development (and the extent to which adolescent behavior can be enhanced), and about how adolescents act to promote their own adaptive development (Brandtstädter, 1998).

The Nature-Nurture Issue

Issues to Consider
- What characterizes the theoretical debate of nature versus nurture?
- How does developmental contextualism differ from other theories of human development?
- How do developmental and contextual variables "dynamically" interact?

In its most basic form, the nature-nurture issue pertains to whether behavior and development derive from *nature* (heredity, maturation, and genes) or *nurture* (environment, experience, and learning). The issue raises questions about how inborn characteristics (e.g., genes)

Diversity In development, systematic differences among individuals, groups, or institutions of society.

Interventions Actions planned to reduce or to prevent problems or to promote positive development.

Applied developmental science Field of science that focuses on development, diversity, and context to interrelate basic and applied knowledge. Knowledge is applied to promote policies and programs to enhance the life chances of youth.

applications box 2.1

Characteristics of Applied Developmental Science

Applied developmental science (ADS) has been conceptualized by the National Task Force on ADS as scholarship that represents

> the programmatic synthesis of research and applications to describe, explain, intervene, and provide preventive and enhancing uses of knowledge about human development. . . . [It is] *applied* [because it has] direct implications for what individuals, practitioners, and policy makers do. . . . [It is] *developmental* [because it] focuses on systematic and successive changes within human systems that occur across the life span. [It is] *science* [because it is] grounded in a range of research methods designed to collect reliable and objective information that can be used to test the validity of theory and applications. (Fisher et al., 1993, p. 4)

As discussed by Fisher and her colleagues (e.g., Fisher & Lerner, 1994a, 1994b; Lerner & Fisher, 1994; Lerner, Fisher, & Weinberg, 1997, 2000a, 2000b), ADS, defined in terms of the convergence of application, development, and science, stresses the reciprocal relationship between theory and application, a relationship wherein:

- Empirically based theory not only guides intervention strategies, but also is influenced by the outcome of these interventions.

  Of equal import are the assumptions that valid applications of developmental science depend on:

- Recognition of the reciprocal nature of person-environment interactions;
- The influence of individual and cultural diversity on development;
- The importance of both within-person-change and differences between people in their respective within-person changes;
- The temporality (historical embeddedness) of change;

- An understanding of both normative and atypical developmental processes;
- Science-based knowledge and intervention strategies;
- Use of methodologically rigorous research designs, measures, and analyses that are developmentally and contextually sensitive; and
- A multidisciplinary perspective aimed at integrating information and skills drawn from relevant biological, social, and behavioral science disciplines.

Throughout this text, examples of applied development science are included in applications boxes such as this one. The ADS work described in these boxes illustrate how ADS scholars engage in one or more of the following activities:

- Conducting contextually sensitive research;
- Identifying developmental correlates of phenomena of social importance;
- Constructing and using developmental assessment instruments;
- Designing and evaluating developmental interventions; and
- Disseminating knowledge.

As do all scholars involved in the study of youth, applied developmental scientists follow strictly the canons of ethics involved with research with children and youth. These ethical principles are presented in the Appendix. In addition to these principles, ethics in ADS involve a commitment to:

- Beneficence and nonmalfeasance;
- Respect for the dignity of individuals;
- Social justice; and
- Civil society.

Source: Based on Fisher et al., 1993; Fisher & Lerner, 1994b; Lerner & Fisher, 1994; Lerner, Fisher, & Weinberg, 1997, 2000a, 2000b.

---

may contribute to development and/or how acquired characteristics (e.g., stimulus-response connections) may play a role in development. Table 2.1 lists some of the terms that pertain to nature and nurture contributions.

Theories of human development have stressed either nature as the primary basis for development, nurture as the major impetus for change across life, or some com-

bination or interaction of nature and nurture. However, when interaction was stressed, maturation and experience were regarded as separate sources of human development, ones that came together to cause development but that did not really affect each other.

Developmental contextualism stresses that nature *and* nurture are involved in development, but stresses that variables associated with a person's

MEET THE RESEARCHER BOX 2.1

CELIA B. FISHER

UNDERSTANDING HOW RACIAL DISCRIMINATION AFFECTS THE LIVES OF TEENAGERS LIVING IN OUR MULTICULTURAL SOCIETY

Young people growing up in the United States today have many more opportunities than their parents had to meet and get to know teenagers and adults from different ethnic groups. Although many of the old prejudices that were a part of U.S. history are fading away, racism and ethnic discrimination still exist and can be confusing and stressful for adolescents.

I am studying groups of African American, Hispanic, East and South Asian, and non-Hispanic white teenagers who live, shop, and go to school in the ethnically diverse city of New York. My collaborators in this research—Scyatta Wallace and Rose Fenton—and I have created two new scales to help us understand what types of discrimination are experienced by adolescents from different ethnic groups, how racial discrimination affects how they feel about themselves, and how their parents prepare them for the challenges of living in a multiethnic society.

One scale we created is called the Adolescent Discrimination Distress Index. It asks teenagers whether they have experienced different types of racial discrimination from teachers in school, from adults in stores or restaurants, or from other adolescents their age. Another scale we developed is called the Racial Bias Preparation Scale. This scale measures how often parents talk to their teenagers about race and what they say. For example, some parents feel they can best help their children deal with discrimination by making them aware that racism exists in this country. Other parents feel they can be most helpful to their children by encouraging them to be proud of their race. In creating these scales we relied on the work of other psychologists such as Harold Stevenson, Diane Hughes, Jean Phinney, and Claude Steele.

Celia B. Fisher is director of the Center for Ethics Education and professor of applied developmental psychology at Fordham University. She is a founding editor of the journal *Applied Developmental Science* and is chair of the American Psychological Association's (APA) Task Force to Revise the (APA) Ethics Code.

The results of our research suggest that teenagers from all ethnic backgrounds have experienced discrimination in stores and restaurants. As might be expected from recent news reports on racial profiling, some African American and Hispanic teenagers said they had been hassled by police just because of their race. In all racial groups, some high school students felt that teachers sometimes expected too much of them or too little from them based on racial prejudice and that they were excluded from peer activities because of their race. East Asian American (Korean, Chinese, Japanese) teenagers most often reported racial name-calling by other students. Many teenagers found being the target of discrimination very stressful. We also found that the more a teenager felt distressed about discrimination, the lower his or her feelings of self-worth.

Although more frequent in ethnic minority families, teenagers from all ethnic groups reported that their parents spoke about racial discrimination and ethnic pride. An interesting finding was that adolescents whose parents tried to help their children by warning them that they would face racial discrimination were more distressed when they had such an experience than teenagers whose parents talked about ethnic pride.

Researchers have just begun to study the effect of racial discrimination on teenagers' well-being, their ability to achieve in school, and their relationships with their peers. As we learn more about how adolescents and their parents prepare for and react to racial discrimination, we can begin to recommend programs aimed at reducing discrimination at school and in the community and at helping teenagers develop ways of confronting discrimination that strengthen their sense of self-worth.

---

biological characteristics **dynamically interact** (glossary term on p. 36) with variables from contextual levels. Dynamic interaction means that biological variables *both* influence and are influenced by contextual ones. In developmental contextualism, nature and nurture are not separate; they are completely integrated or fused, mutually shaping each other over the course of life.

Fused Influences on Development of Biology and Context

Issues to Consider

- In what ways, by what factors, are possible developmental outcomes constrained?
- How might genes be influenced by context and vice versa?

Table 2-1	Terms Associated with Nature or Nurture Conceptions of Development	
Nature Terms	**Nurture Terms**	
Genetic	Acquired	
Heredity	Education	
Inborn	Empiricism	
Innate	Environment	
Instinct	Experience	
Intrinsic	Learning	
Maturation	Socialization	
Nativism		
Preformed		

Source: Lerner, 1986, p. 8.

In developmental contextualism, influences of biology on human behavior and development are acknowledged, but are not seen to act independently of environment. Genes function neither as the primary nor as the ultimate causal influence on behavior. Instead, genes (heredity) and environment are seen as equal forces in the determination of development and as completely fused in life.

Genes are influenced by the specific characteristics of their context. Humans have genes, which, under normal human environmental conditions, are involved in the development of two arms and two legs. Under different conditions a different result might occur. Even a slight change in the chemicals in a baby's prenatal environment can result in an infant born without limbs, as illustrated by the unfortunate cases in the 1950s when scores of pregnant women took the fertility drug thalidomide.

The extent to which the environment influences behavior depends on the specific characteristics or hereditary makeups of the people who live within it. For instance, no known type of environmental intervention (be it medical or nutritional) can prevent the inheritance of Down syndrome in children. Nevertheless, medical and educational interventions can positively influence the health and development of children having this inheritance.

Dynamic interaction Interaction characterized by two different variables simultaneously influencing one another. For example, biological variables influence and are influenced by contextual variables.

Plasticity Potential for systematic change across life.

Monozygotic (MZ) twins Twins developed from one fertilized egg that splits after conception. In contrast, dizygotic (DZ) twins develop from separate fertilized eggs.

Zygote Fertilized egg.

Genotype Complement of genes transmitted to people at conception by the union of the sperm and ovum.

Meiosis Process of division resulting in formation of sex cells, sperm, and ova.

Relative Plasticity and Variability in Development

The thalidomide and Down syndrome examples in the previous section illustrate the relative **plasticity** of human development. Although different kinds of outcomes are possible depending on the specifics of gene-environment fusions, the diversity of possible outcomes is constrained by both the character of a person's genes and context. *No two people in the world have the same fusion of genes and environments across their lives.*

There are multiple levels of the environment or context of life and differences exist within each level. For example, within the physical environment are differences in noise, pollution, climate, and terrain. Even identical (**monozygotic**) twins, that is, twins who are born from one fertilized egg that has split into two separate fertilized eggs, or **zygotes**, after conception, do not share the same environments across life. Each twin meets different people, may eat different foods or suffer different accidents or illnesses, may have different teachers, and will fall in love with a different person. As such, even for identical twins, behavior and development are different.

Genotypes are also equally variable among people. The fusion of different genotypes and environments means that each person is distinct. The potential magnitude of individual differences among people underscores the gross errors we make when characterizing entire groups of people—racial, religious, or gender groups—as homogeneous and undifferentiated in significant ways.

Genetic Variability Our genetic endowment provides a basis for the uniqueness of each human life. Estimates of the number of gene pairs in humans typically range between 10,000 and 100,000. If we consider how many different combinations can be produced by the reshuffling process of **meiosis** (the division that forms sex cells—sperm and ova) occurring with this number of gene pairs, then the potential for genotypic variability is enormous. A conservative estimate is there are over 70 trillion potential human genotypes. In turn, geneticists have estimated that each human has the capacity to generate any one of 10^{3000} different eggs or sperm. By comparison, their estimate of the number of genotypes of all people who have ever lived is only 10^{24}. Thus "10^{3000} possible eggs being generated by

MEET THE RESEARCHER BOX 2.2

RICHARD A. WEINBERG
AFRICAN AMERICAN ADOLESCENTS GROWING UP IN CAUCASIAN FAMILES

The adoption of African American children into Caucasian homes (transracial adoption) has been a controversial practice for many decades. My collaborator, Sandra Scarr, and I initiated the Minnesota Transracial Adoption Study almost 30 years ago, at that time investigating 101 families who had adopted children (Caucasian, African American, interracial, Asian, or Indian), 4 years of age or older, and who also often had birth children of their own. Ten years later, in the mid-1980s, with funds from the National Science Foundation, we returned to study these same children who were then adolescents. The primary focus in this longitudinal study was to test the hypothesis that African American and interracial children reared in middle- to upper-middle-class families would perform better on measures of intellectual ability (IQ tests) and school achievement than would have ever been predicted. Growing up in the "culture of the tests and schools"—being exposed to more of the economic, health care, and social influences that promote higher performance on IQ and school achievement measures—did pay off and the hypothesis was affirmed.

Richard A. Weinberg is a university distinguished teaching professor of child psychology in the Institute of Child Development at the University of Minnesota. A former director of the institute, he is one of the founding editors of the journal *Applied Developmental Science.*

Recently, our interest has been renewed in the behavioral and emotional adjustment of members of these families (the adoptees as well as their siblings, adoptive moms, and adoptive dads), especially during adolescence when new challenges might emerge in the families' daily lives. We have returned to our rich database to study the parent interviews conducted about 15 years ago. These conversations with interviewers considered family characteristics; medical, educational, and occupational status of the children and their parents; family relationships; the children's adjustment to school/occupation; and the impact of transracial adoption on the family members. In particular, we are currently reviewing items dealing with school suspension and dropout, juvenile detention, referrals and professional treatment for behavioral and emotional problems, and the presence of disabilities and serious illnesses. We have not completed our work at this writing, but we hope to gain an understanding of the complex effects of transracial adoption on the lives of family members. Such knowledge could help guide policy making regarding the timing of placement of children in adoptive homes.

Identical (monozygotic) twins are born from one fertilized egg that splits after conception.

an individual woman and 10^{3000} possible sperm being generated by an individual man, the likelihood of anyone ever—in the past, present, or future—having the same genotype as anyone else (excepting multiple identical births, of course) becomes dismissibly small" (McClearn, 1981, p. 19).

Environmental Variability What makes this enormous genetic variability among humans all the more striking is that genes are fused with environments that have at least equal variation. As comparative psychologist Gilbert Gottlieb explained in 1991, the most significant feature of this fusion "is the explicit recognition that the genes are an integral part of a larger system, and genetic expression is affected by events at other levels of the system, including the environment of the organism" (Gottlieb, 1991, p. 5).

As emphasized by comparative psychologist Ethel Tobach (1971, 1972, 1981; Tobach & Schneirla, 1968), genes *must* be fused with the environment if they are to be involved in the development of *any* physical or behavioral characteristic of a person. Gottlieb explains,

> [G]enetic activity does not by itself produce finished traits such as blue eyes, arms, legs, or neurons. The problem of anatomical and physiological differentiation remains unsolved, but it is unanimously recognized as requiring influences above the strictly cellular level (i.e., cell-to-cell interactions, positional influences, and so forth). . . . Thus, the concept of the genetic determination of traits is truly outmoded. (Gottlieb, 1991, p. 5)

Examples of Gene-Environment Fusions How might gene-environment fusions influence human development? Consider again the case of a child born with **Down syndrome.** Genetic material (DNA) is arranged on stringlike structures present in the nucleus of each cell called chromosomes. The typical cells of the human body have 46 chromosomes, divided into 23 pairs. The only cells in the body that do not have 46 chromosomes are the gametes—the sex cells (sperm in males, ova in females). These cells carry only 23 chromosomes, one of each pair. This arrangement assures that when a sperm fertilizes an ovum to form a zygote, the new human will have the 46 chromosome pairs appropriate for the species. However, in a child born with Down syndrome, a genetic anomaly exists in that there is an extra chromosome in the 21st pair—three chromosomes are present instead of two.

Down syndrome Genetic anomaly characterized by extra chromosome in the 21st pair of chromosomes.

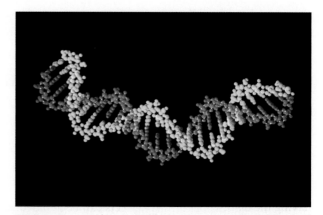

DNA is arranged in stringlike structures in the nucleus of each cell.

Children with Down syndrome have a specific genetic inheritance. Yet, even though the genotype has the same chromosomal anomaly, for all children with Down syndrome the developmental outcomes differ.

As recently as 40 to 50 years ago, children with Down syndrome were expected to have maximum life spans of about 12 years and to have low IQ scores. They were typically classified into a group of people who required custodial (usually institutional) care. Today, however, children with Down syndrome often live well beyond adolescence and tend to lead more self-reliant lives. Their average IQ is now higher, often falling in the range allowing for education, training, and, often, employment. Indeed, there is at least one quite striking instance of substantial intellectual accomplishment on the part of a person with Down syndrome. Nigel Hunt, a child born with Down syndrome, grew up to author his own autobiography (Hunt, 1967).

How did these vast differences come about? The chromosomal anomaly itself did not change. What changed was the environment of the children. Instead of being put into institutions that severely constrained the children's developmental possibilities, different and more advanced special education and training techniques were provided, often on an outpatient basis. These contrasts in environment led to patterns of individual development quite different from patterns displayed by children in previous years.

Heredity exerts its effects indirectly through environment in the development of physical characteristics as well as behavioral characteristics. To illustrate, the disorder **phenylketonuria** (PKU) involves an inability to metabolize fatty substances because of the absence of a particular digestive enzyme, and it leads to the development of distorted physical features and severe mental retardation in children. The lack of the necessary enzyme results from the absence of a particular gene. PKU is therefore another instance of a disease associated with a specific genotypic anomaly.

Today, however, many people have PKU without having either the physical or the behavioral deficits formerly associated with the disease. If the missing enzyme is put into the diets of newborns identified as having the disease, *all* negative effects can be avoided. Rather than the gene providing the enzyme, the environment does. A change in the environment changes the outcome, illustrating once again that when genes and environment interact dynamically, alternative outcomes, both physical and behavioral, can occur.

There would be no one *in* an environment without heredity, and there would be no place to see the effects of heredity without environment (Anastasi, 1958). Genes exert their influence on behavior in an environment having specific characteristics at each of several levels: physical, social, cultural, and so on. At the same time, if there were no genes (and consequently no heredity), the environment would not have an organism in it to influence. Nature and nurture are inextricably tied together, and they never exist independent of the other. Therefore, for *any* theory of human development to be logical and to reflect accurately life situations (that is, to have **ecological validity**), it must stress that nature and nurture are always interdependently involved in all behavior. It is simply not appropriate to ask which one is involved in a behavior because they are *both* necessary for any person's existence or for the existence of any behavior. The proper question to ask is, "How do nature and nurture interrelate to provide a basis for behavior?"

Nature, Nurture, and Theories of Adolescent Development

Across the history of the study of adolescence most theories have not taken the nature-nurture, fusion-type approach to development. Rather, they tend to take one of the three approaches described earlier,

Table 2-2	Theories of Adolescence Differ in Regard to Their Approach to the Nature-Nurture Issue
Nature theorists	G. Stanley Hall
Nurture theorists	Boyd R. McCandless
Weak nature-nurture interaction theories	Sigmund Freud Erik H. Erikson Anna Freud
Moderate nature-nurture interaction theories	Jean Piaget Lawrence Kohlberg
Strong nature-nurture interaction theories	Urie Bronfenbrenner Paul B. Baltes and Margret M. Baltes

emphasizing nature, nurture, or some "weak" interaction between the two. To provide an overview of the range of theories of human development it is useful to discuss how different theories are "located" in regard to their approach to the nature-nurture issue. Table 2.2 summarizes the theories reviewed in this chapter.

An Example of a Nature Theory: G. Stanley Hall and the Theory of Recapitulation

Issues to Consider

• What might Hall have meant by the statement "early adolescence is thus the infancy of man's higher nature"?
• How did Hall misinterpret Darwin's theory of human evolution?

G. Stanley Hall (1844–1924) was one of the most influential and prominent psychologists at the turn of the 20th century (Misiak & Sexton, 1966). He helped shape the nature and direction of the relatively new science of psychology. (The birthday of modern psychology is dated as 1879, with the opening of the first psychological laboratory in Leipzig, Germany, by Wilhelm Wundt.)

Hall organized the American Psychological Association and became its first president. He also started the first American journal of psychology (aptly

Phenylketonuria (PKU) Illness characterized by body's inability to metabolize fatty substances due to lack of a particular digestive enzyme.

Ecological validity A theory or an observation that reflects accurately real-life situations.

titled *The American Journal of Psychology*) and the first scientific journal devoted to human development (first titled *Pedagogical Seminary*, and then given its present name, *The Journal of Genetic Psychology*). Hall also authored the first psychological texts on adolescence (a two-volume work titled *Adolescence*, 1904) and old age (*Senescence*, 1922).

Hall had his most specific influence in shaping developmental psychology. As implied by the title of one of the journals he founded—*The Journal of Genetic Psychology*—Hall saw development from a nature point of view. Although not many people (including his influential former students, such as Arnold Gesell and Lewis Terman) adopted his specific nature-based theory of development, many did adhere to his general nature, or organismic, orientation. In devising his nature viewpoint, Hall saw himself as the "Darwin of the mind" (Dixon & Lerner, 1999; White, 1968), and he attempted to translate Darwin's phylogenetic evolutionary principles into conceptions relevant to **ontogeny**.

Features of Hall's Recapitulation Theory Hall believed that the changes characterizing the human life cycle are a repetition of the sequence of changes the species followed during its evolution. That is, Hall's theory specified a parallel between the evolution of humans and life-span changes, starting from conception and moving across prenatal (prebirth) and postnatal life. However, Hall believed that, during the years from birth through sexual maturity, the **recapitulation** was more limited than was the case for prenatal life (Gallatin, 1975). According to Gallatin (1975, pp. 26–27), Hall's recapitulation theory stated that:

> Rather than reflecting the entire sweep of evolution, childhood was supposed to proceed in stages, each of which mirrored a primitive stage of the human species. Very early childhood might correspond, Hall speculated, to a monkey-like ancestor of the human race that had reached sexual maturity around the age of six. The years between eight and twelve allegedly represented a reenactment of a more advanced, but still prehistoric form of mankind, possibly a species that had managed to survive by hunting and fishing.

Ontogeny Development, or life course, of an individual organism.

Recapitulation Developmental changes within the human life cycle that are the hypothetical repetition of the sequence of changes the species followed during evolution.

Hall believed that adolescence represents a specific period in ontogeny after childhood. Not only was Hall the first person to present a scientific theory of development that conceived of adolescence as a distinct portion of the life span (the term *adolescence* first appeared in the first half of the 15th century; Muuss, 1975), but he also did so in a manner consistent with a life-span view of development. Hall saw the capacities and changes of childhood continuing into adolescence *but* at a more rapid and heightened pace. He also saw adolescence as a period of transition between childhood and adulthood. The stages of life previous to adolescence stressed the innate characteristics of humans held "in common with animals," whereas the stage of life following adolescence was said to raise a human "above them and make him most distinctively human" (Hall, 1904, Vol. 1, p. 39). Adolescence is a period of transition from being beastlike to being humanlike (i.e., civilized and mature). This ontogenetic transition mirrored the evolutionary change involved when humans moved from being essentially like the apes to becoming civilized.

According to Hall, human evolution moved the person through this ontogenetic period and put the person in the position of being able to contribute to humans' highest level of evolutionary attainment: civilization. To quote Hall, "early adolescence is thus the infancy of man's higher nature, when he receives from the great all-mother his last capital of energy and evolutionary momentum" (1904, Vol. 2, p. 71).

Because of the acceleration and heightening of capacities in adolescence, and the difficulty in casting off the characteristics of animal-like behavior while attaining the characteristics of civilization, Hall perceived the adolescent period as stressful and difficult. Because adolescence was an ontogenetically and evolutionarily "betwixt and between" (Gallatin, 1975) phase of human development, it was, to Hall, a period of storm and stress.

Criticisms of Recapitulation Hall's recapitulationist ideas met criticism that severely diminished their usefulness. The application of Darwinian evolutionary ideas to ontogeny was based on a totally incorrect understanding of the meaning of evolution. Darwin's theory of evolution states that humans did not always exist as they presently do. Previous forms of being existed, and through natural selection some forms were adaptive and continued to evolve until eventually the human species as it is presently known came to exist. This evolutionary process occurs for all animals, not just humans, so all animals that exist today have an evolutionary history. They are as currently adaptive as is the human, albeit to their own environmental settings, or **ecological milieus.**

Thus a rat, monkey, or ape cannot be an ancestor of a human because all exist today. All are equal in evolutionary status—equally as evolved and as adaptive. When we look at a monkey embryo or at monkey behavior, we are not looking at humans as they existed in a former, lower evolutionary status (Hodos & Campbell, 1969). Although humans and monkeys may have had a common ancestor millions of years ago, that ancestor is long extinct because it was not fit to survive. Whatever exists today is, by definition, fit to survive and thus adaptive at this point in time (Hodos & Campbell, 1969). Hall did not appropriately understand the evolutionary process. Human ontogeny cannot repeat a phase of its evolutionary history if that phase never occurred.

Even as an analogy, a recapitulationist description of human ontogeny is inappropriate. As initially pointed out by Thorndike (1904), and reemphasized by Gallatin (1975), by 2 or 3 years of age a human child has already exceeded the capacities of monkeys, apes, or prehistoric humanlike organisms (e.g., the Neanderthals). Sensorimotor, verbal, and social behavior, for example, are all more advanced in the 3-year-old than in the "adults" of any of these other organisms. Additionally, no evidence whatsoever indicates that the events in adolescence are but a mirror of the history of evolution.

In short, Hall's theory that ontogeny recapitulates **phylogeny** is not correct. Although his work is historically quite important in that his is the first scientific theory of human development, and of adolescence in particular, his specific nature theory was not widely adopted. However, because of his influence and position in American psychology, his general nature orientation was often followed.

Nurture Theories of Human Development

Nurture theories of development stress the influence of experiential and environmental variables on behavioral change and view behavior as a response to stimulation. The explanation of why adolescent behavior develops in a particular manner (or direction) lies in the environment and not in the person. There are many different versions of nurture theories (White, 1970). McCandless's (1967, 1970) drive reduction theory was directed explicitly to understand adolescent development.

The Drive Reduction Theory of McCandless
Boyd R. McCandless (1970) proposed a "drive theory" of human behavior. He viewed a drive as an energizer of behavior and specified that several drives exist in the person (e.g., a hunger drive, a drive to avoid pain, and a sex drive). The nurture component of McCandless's theory involves the direction behavior takes as a consequence of being energized by a particular drive.

We learn in society that certain behaviors *reduce* **drive states** such as hunger, pain, or sexual arousal. McCandless asserts that drive-reducing behaviors are rewarded as a consequence of having the drive diminished and are thus repeated in comparable social situations. Behaviors that do not diminish a drive state are punished behaviors and are less likely to be repeated.

As a consequence of repeating behaviors, people form habits. When a particular drive state is aroused, it is probable an individual will emit the corresponding habit to reduce the internal state. To McCandless, although drive states need not be learned, and may be biologically based, what people do in response to the arousal of a drive is socially learned.

According to McCandless, a new drive emerges in adolescence: the sex drive. To reduce this drive in a way that will be rewarded, new social learning and habits must be formed. McCandless specifies that society does not reward males and females for the same sex drive–reducing habits. Males and females are channeled into developing habits that are socially prescribed as sex appropriate. Thus adolescence becomes a time of defining oneself in terms of new sex-specific habits, which are socially defined as rewarding for one or the other sex. McCandless argues that until new habits are formed, and new self-definitions attained, adolescence could be a period of undiminished drives, thus providing a nurture explanation of adolescent "storm and stress" (see Chapter 1).

Ecological milieu Particular environmental settings of a species/individual.
Phylogeny Evolutionary history of a species.
Drive state Energizer of behavior that exists within the individual.

Nature-Nurture Interaction Theories

Issues to Consider

- What are the differences among the three types of nature-nurture interaction theories?

A theory can be classified according to the type of stress it places on nature and nurture relations (Lerner & Spanier, 1978a). Although all interaction theories stress that both nature and nurture are involved in human development, not all such theories stress the fusion of nature and nurture. A **weak interaction theory** places primary stress on one source (usually nature) as the determiner of the sequence and character of development. A **moderate interaction theory** places equal stress on nature and nurture but sees the two sources as independent of each other. Although they interact to provide a basis for any and all development, one source does not change the quality of the other over the course of the interaction (Sameroff, 1975). A **strong interaction theory** is one that not only sees both nature and nurture as reciprocally related, but also sees the two as inextricably fused in all development. Examples of weak, moderate, and strong interaction theories are presented here. I discuss first the theories of Sigmund Freud, Erik Erikson, and Anna Freud.

Weak interaction theory Places primary stress on one source (usually nature) as the determinant of the sequence and character of development.

Moderate interaction theory Places equal stress on the influence of both nature and nurture but sees the two sources as independent of each other.

Strong interaction theory Sees nature and nurture as reciprocally related and inextricably fused in all development.

Libido Freudian term that defines the finite amount of energy that each human is born with which governs human mental life. Localization of the libido within the body changes over the course of development. Placement of the libido within the body determines what stimulation is appropriate and what stimulation is inappropriate to the developing individual.

Oral stage First psychosexual stage defined by Freud. Occurs during the first year of life when the libido is said to be located in the region of the mouth. Gratification is obtained through stimulation of this region through sucking and biting.

Fixation Freudian term to describe an arrest of the development of the libido; the person attempts to obtain missed gratification of a previous stage.

Anal stage Second psychosexual stage as defined by Freud. Occurs during second and third years of life, when the libido centers in the anal area. Gratification is obtained through exercising anal muscles, expelling or holding bowel movements.

Sigmund Freud and Psychoanalysis

Issues to Consider

- By focusing so extensively on the influence of the libido, what is Freud's theory of development missing?
- In what ways is Freud's work considered "biased"?
- What role does the libido play in adult emotional problems?

Sigmund Freud was born in Freiberg, Moravia, in 1856 and died in London, England, in 1939. He lived most of his life in Vienna, where in 1881 he obtained his medical degree.

Freud's theory represents an example of weak interaction because he sees experiences of people as acting only to support or hamper fixed and universal biologically based changes; experience cannot in any way influence the presence or sequence of these changes. Freud hypothesized that human mental life is governed by an energy, termed **libido.** Humans are born with a finite amount of libido. Its area of localization within the body changes over the course of development. Where the libido is concentrated determines what stimulation is appropriate, or gratifying, and what sort of stimulation is not appropriate.

Nature determines where and when libido moves. Experiences of the person may determine if appropriate stimulation is forthcoming, but does not alter the order of bodily concentration or, in Freud's terms, the stage of psychosexual development. Experience can only facilitate or hinder the development of certain feeling states. Freud specified five stages of psychosexual development: oral, anal, phallic, latent, and genital.

Stages of Psychosexual Development The first psychosexual stage is the **oral stage.** During the first year of life, gratifying stimulation occurs in the region of the mouth, and pleasure is obtained by sucking and biting. If the baby's attempts at oral gratification are frustrated often enough, some of the libido may become **fixated** (arrested) at this stage of development, and not free to progress to the next stage. Freud believed adult emotional problems result from fixation and involve attempts to obtain missed gratification of the oral stage. An example of a fixation in the oral stage might be overeating as an adult. However, fixation is a potential problem at any stage.

The next stage is the **anal stage,** which lasts from about ages 1 to 3 years and occurs when libido centers in the anal area. Children get pleasure through exercising their anal muscles, expelling or holding bowel movements. The anal stage corresponds to the period when children in many societies are toilet trained. Frustration resulting from severe toilet training can cause fixation in the anal stage. This fixation can lead to adult problems such as messiness and wastefulness or the holding back of everything, including emotions.

For both sexes, the **phallic stage** is the third stage, which to Freud spans the period from about the third through the fifth years. This stage involves the libido moving to the genital area. Because of structural differences in genitalia, this stage is different for males and females.

As the libido moves to a boy's genital area, gratification is obtained through stimulation of the genitals that may occur during bathing or dressing. Freud believed that the boy's mother is most likely to provide this stimulation, and he labeled the boy's emotional reaction to the mother the **Oedipus complex,** after a character in Greek mythology who unknowingly killed his father and then married his mother. Freud saw a parallel between this myth and events in the lives of boys.

Freud believed that when the boy realizes his father is the rival for his mother's affection, the boy comes to fear his father will punish him by castrating him, and he experiences **castration anxiety.** The power of this anxiety leads the boy to give up his desires for his mother and to identify with and model himself after his father. The boy forms a structure of his personality termed the **superego** by Freud, which has two components. The first component, the **ego ideal,** is the representation of the perfect, or ideal, man (the "father figure"). In modeling himself after his father, the boy becomes a "man" in his society. The second part of the superego is the **conscience,** the internalization of society's standards, ethics, and morals (Bronfenbrenner, 1960).

In regard to the female phallic stage, the libido moves to the genital area as with males. And, as also the case with males, gratification is obtained through stimulation of the genitals. The mother provides the major source of this stimulation for the girl, but the girl falls in love with her father (for reasons not perfectly clear even to Freud, and as a result, Freud himself was never satisfied with his formulation of this stage). Nevertheless, Freud said that, analogous to what occurs with boys, the girl has an incestuous desire to possess her father, but realizes that her mother stands in her way.

At this point, Freud's theory of female development becomes different from that of male development. In his theory, the female becomes afraid that the mother will punish her for her incestuous desires toward her father. Although it is possible that the girl first fears this punishment will take the form of castration, her awareness of her own genital structure causes her to realize that, in a sense, she already has been punished. The girl perceives that she does not have a penis, but only an inferior (to Freud) organ, a clitoris. Hence the girl experiences **penis envy** and this impels her to resolve her Oedipal conflict. She relinquishes her incestuous love for her father and identifies with her mother. The girl then forms a superego, as the boy does. Freud termed the reaction of girls to the events of this stage the **Electra complex** (Bronfenbrenner, 1960).

After the phallic stage, at about 5 years of age, the **latency stage** occurs. Freud said that the libido is not localized in any bodily zone and no erogenous zones emerge or exist. This stage continues until puberty occurs, at about 12 years of age. Here, the **genital stage** occurs. During this final stage, the libido reemerges in the genital area, but now in a mature or adult form. If the person has not been too severely restricted in psychosexual development in the first 5 years of life, adult sexuality can occur.

A Critique of Freud's Ideas Freud worked in Victorian Europe, a period of history noted for its repressive views about sexuality. As a practicing psychiatrist, Freud attempted to construct a theory

---

Phallic stage Third psychosexual stage as defined by Freud. Spans the period from about the third through fifth years when the libido moves to the genital area. Males and females experience this stage differently because their genitalia differ. See *Oedipal complex* and *Electra complex.*

Oedipus complex Boy's emotional reaction to his mother at the time when the libido has moved to the boy's genital area and when he obtains gratification through stimulation of the genitals. When the boy realizes his father is his rival for his mother's affection, the boy comes to fear his father will punish him by performing castration. The boy is so moved by his anxiety that he gives up desires for his mother and identifies with his father.

Castration anxiety Boy's fear that father will punish him for his affections for his mother by performing castration. Fear leads boy to alter affection and turn to identify with father.

Superego Freudian personality structure made up of two components: the ego ideal and the conscience. Formed as a result of the resolution of the Oedipal complex.

Ego ideal Component of the superego that represents the perfect, or ideal, person.

Conscience Component of the superego that represents the internalization of society's standards, ethics, and morals.

Penis envy Girl realizes she does not have a penis but, rather, an inferior (to Freud) organ, the clitoris. The girl experiences envy of the penis and this envy impels her to relinquish her incestuous love for her father and identify with her mother.

Electra complex For girls, the purported emotional crisis that occurs within the phallic stage of development in Freud's theory.

Latency stage Fourth psychosexual stage as defined by Freud. Occurs around the fifth year of life until puberty. The libido is said to be latent in this stage.

Genital stage Fifth psychosexual stage as defined by Freud. Occurs during puberty as the libido reemerges in the genital area, in an adult form.

of *early* development from the memories of adult neurotic patients from one particular historical period. Freud constructed a theory about early development without actually observing children.

Freud's adult patients reconstructed their long-gone past through **retrospection.** With Freud's help, they tried to remember what happened to them when they were 1, 2, or 3 years of age. Because it is quite possible that adults forget, distort, or misremember early memories and because his data were unchecked for failures of early memories, Freud likely obtained biased information.

We might question whether Freud's ideas represented all the possible developmental phenomena that could occur in each stage of life. Is latency actually a period of relative quiescence, a time when few significant events occur for the child? Is adolescence just a time when events in preceding life make themselves evident or are there characteristics of adolescence special to that period?

Although accepting most of Freud's ideas as correct, other psychoanalytically oriented thinkers led the way in showing that Freud was incomplete in his depiction of developmental phenomena within and across stages. Freud's theory emphasized the movement of the libido and focused on a structure of the personality, the id, which he believed innately contained this mental energy. Freud stressed also the idea that there was a primary process through which the id energized the person to gratify libidinal impulses. Erikson (1959, 1963), however, focused on societal demands placed on the individual—or, more precisely, the ego (which along with the superego and the id comprises the third of the structures of personality that Freud specified). Erikson emphasized that as the person developed, important phenomena related to the ego

Across history, relationships with parents have remained a key part of adolescence.

Retrospection Constructing the past through memories. A technique used by Freud.

Reality principle Ego develops only to deal with reality, to allow the person to adjust to demands of real world and hence survive.

Secondary process Functions (e.g., perception, reasoning) that enable ego to adjust to and deal with reality.

could be identified in latency, adolescence, and across the rest of the life span as well.

As compared to the id's primary process, which involves urges to gratify the libido in any way possible, even through fantasy, Freud believed that the ego develops only to deal with reality, to allow the person to adjust to the demands of the real world and hence survive. Accordingly, Freud said the ego functions in accordance with the **reality principle.** The ego has characteristics that enable it to adjust to and deal with reality. This **secondary process** involves such things as cognition and perception. Through the functioning of these processes, the ego is capable of perceiving and knowing the real world and hence adapting to it. Although Freud did not spend enough time discussing the implications of the ego, this focus was provided by Erikson (1963).

Erik Erikson and Psychosocial Development

Issues to Consider

• By focusing so extensively on the ego, what is Erikson's psychosexual theory of development missing?

• What might happen, according to Erikson, if and when an ego capability is not developed in a balanced manner?

Erikson also proposes a stage theory of development; however, unlike Freud's theory of psychosexual development, Erikson's theory speaks of **psychosocial development.** Whereas Freud focused primarily on the contributions of the id to development, Erikson focused on the role of the ego. Erikson emphasized the role of society in determining what the ego must do to fulfill its function of adapting to the demands of a reality textured and shaped by society.

Society does not expect the same things of all people at all times of their lives. We may expect a 1-year-old to do no more than eat and sleep, but we expect a 21-year-old to prepare for a career, and we expect a 31-year-old to be engaging in his or her career. To meet each of these successively different demands, the ego must develop different capabilities. The development of ego capabilities passes through eight stages of psychosocial development. Erikson believed that the time we have to spend at each stage is fixed by a maturational "ground plan" for development.

Within each stage a particular capability of the ego must be developed if the ego is to meet the adjustment demands placed on it by society. Each stage is thought of as a **critical period** in the life span (that is, it is a time in life when particular developments must occur if development is to proceed normally). Stage development proceeds whether the capability is developed or not. Even if a person does not develop a capability within the time limits imposed by the person's maturational ground plan, development proceeds. However, that part of the ego (that capability) does not have another chance for adequate development.

Within each stage of psychosocial development there is a crisis of development. For the person to feel he or she is progressing through the stages in an adaptive manner, the person must sense he or she has moved closer to rather than further away from developing the needed ego capability. Erikson delineated eight psychosocial stages and accompanying crises.

Within the first stage of psychosocial development, termed by Erikson **oral sensory** (what lasts from birth through about 1 year of age), a crisis exists between developing a sense of basic trust versus mistrust toward one's world. If favorable sensory experiences are encountered, the child develops toward the former feeling state. If unfavorable expe-

riences occur, a feeling closer to the latter state develops. In this stage, as well as in the seven others, a person typically develops somewhere in between the two extreme ends of the crisis state. In this first stage, where the crisis is between trust and mistrust, healthy ego development proceeds if the ratio of the trust to mistrust is greater than one. Unhealthy ego development proceeds if this ratio is less than one.

Stage 2 is termed **anal musculature** (which usually lasts for the second and third years of life), and here the crisis is between developing a sense of autonomy (e.g., being able to use one's muscles, to feed oneself) versus a sense of shame and doubt (e.g., not being able to feed oneself). Stage 3 is termed **genital locomotor** (and involves ordinarily the fourth and fifth years of life), and the crisis involved here is between developing initiative (e.g., being able to walk around and find your way, without having parents completely directing you) versus guilt (e.g., feeling you are inappropriately tied to your parents). In stage 4, **latency** (which spans from about the end of the fifth year through puberty), the crisis is between developing toward a sense of industry (e.g., learning how to read and write, in our society) versus a sense of inferiority (e.g., not being able to do what you feel others can do). In stage 5, **puberty and adolescence,** the crisis is between developing a sense of identity (e.g., knowing one's role in society, knowing what one believes in) versus role confusion or identity diffusion (e.g., not knowing what one believes in or what one can do with oneself in society).

The remaining three psychosocial stages occur during adulthood, and Erikson offers no precise ages for their onset or termination. In stage 6, **young adulthood,** there is a crisis between

Psychosocial development Emphasizes the role of the ego and, specifically, the role of society in determining what the ego must do to fulfill its function of adapting to the demands of reality.

Critical period Time in life when particular developments must occur if development is to proceed normally.

Oral sensory stage Stage 1 of Erikson's psychosocial theory. Involves a crisis between developing a sense of basic trust versus mistrust toward one's world.

Anal musculature stage Stage 2 of Erikson's psychosocial theory. Involves a crisis between developing toward a sense of autonomy versus a sense of shame and doubt.

Genital locomotor stage Stage 3 of Erikson's psychosocial theory. Involves a crisis between developing toward a sense of initiative versus guilt.

Latency Stage 4 of Erikson's psychosocial theory. Involves a crisis between developing toward a sense of industry versus inferiority.

Puberty and adolescence Stage 5 of Erikson's psychosocial theory. Involves a crisis between developing toward a sense of identity versus role confusion.

Young adulthood Stage 6 of Erikson's psychosocial theory. Involves a crisis between developing toward a sense of intimacy versus isolation.

developing toward a sense of intimacy (e.g., establishing a strong love relationship) versus a sense of isolation (e.g., feeling alone and unable to be close to anyone). In stage 7, **adulthood,** the crisis is between generativity (e.g., being able to produce those goods or services associated with one's role) versus stagnation (e.g., being unable to continue to produce what is associated with one's role). Stage 8, the final stage of psychosocial development, is **maturity.** Here the crisis is between ego integrity (e.g., feeling that one has led a full, rich life) and despair (e.g., feeling that one's life is ending before one has had a good life).

Erik Erikson's stage theory of psychosocial development offers descriptions of personality development consistent with a life-span perspective. Although Erikson's explanations of psychosocial development are limited for many of the same reasons that other psychoanalytic conceptions, such as Freud's, are, the descriptions of development Erikson provides have served as a major basis for research about human personality. Later chapters focus on Erikson's ideas.

Adulthood Stage 7 of Erikson's psychosocial theory. Involves a crisis between developing a sense of generativity versus stagnation.

Maturity Stage 8 of Erikson's psychosocial theory. Involves a crisis between developing toward a sense of ego integrity versus despair.

Id One of three structures of the mind in psychoanalytic theory. The initial source of the libido.

Ego One of three structures of the mind in psychoanalytic theory. Enables person to adapt to reality.

Defense mechanisms Developed by the ego to take the pressures imposed by the id and place them into the unconscious part of the mind.

Repression Ego defense mechanism by which unwanted desires and/or pressures are placed in the unconscious.

Rationalization Ego defense mechanism of applying plausible but untrue reasoning for behavior.

Substitution Process of replacing one goal for another.

Projection Process of attributing one's own feelings to other objects or people.

Anna Freud: Adolescence as a Developmental Disturbance

Issues to Consider

- Why does Anna Freud see adolescence as a unique period of time?
- What are the three specific roles of the structures of the personality in adolescent development?
- Based on what you have learned in Chapters 1 and 2, how might you critique the work of Anna Freud?

In agreement with her father, Anna Freud (1969) describes three structures of the personality. As we have noted, the **id** is the initial source of the libido, the **ego** is developed to deal with reality, and the **superego** is formed as a result of the resolution of the Oedipal complex and houses the child's conscience. Moreover, like her father, she believes all three of these structures are present by the end of the phallic stage, by about the end of the fifth year of life.

Both Freuds contend that when all structures are present, they present different directives to the person. As explained earlier, the id only "wants" pleasure (gratification) and is not concerned with either survival or morality. The superego, at the other extreme, contains the conscience and cares nothing for pleasure but cares only about morality. While the id might pressure the person for sexual gratification, the superego would condemn the person for such a desire. The ego has to balance these two conflicting types of pressures.

As emphasized by both her father and by Erikson, Anna Freud believed the ego's only function is survival. As a consequence, she emphasized that the ego must defend itself from dangers, whether those dangers are from within or without. The conflict between the id and the superego represents a danger to survival. If the person spent all of his or her time in conflict about action, no energy would be left to deal with the demands placed on the person from outside the self (for example, from society). Accordingly, the ego develops defense mechanisms, or ways to avoid dealing with at least one set of the conflicting demands imposed from within. Such avoidance rids the person of the internal conflict and frees up energy for external adaptive demands.

The **defense mechanisms** developed by the ego (mechanisms like **repression, rationalization, substitution,** and **projection**) involve taking the pressures imposed by the id and placing them in a particular area of the mind—the *unconscious*. This area contains material most difficult to bring into awareness—the *conscious*. Id pressures are defended against, but those of the superego are not. The superego's pressures represent the demands and rules of society. If we got rid of those demands and rules, we would have no morality. It would not be adaptive for the ego to put the superego in the unconscious because society would severely punish amoral behavior. As such, it is the id material that is placed in this area of the mind.

To both Freuds, the typical person establishes a balance among the id, ego, and superego by 5 years of age. By the time latency has been reached, ego defenses appropriate for dealing with all pressures or drives from the id have been established. The person is thus in equilibrium. However, although people may differ in regard to the character of this balance, depending on events in the first three stages of life, Anna Freud (1969) claimed that all people have their balance *destroyed* in adolescence.

Unlike her father, Anna Freud saw adolescence as a period in life presenting demands for the person that are not *just* those relating to earlier life. These demands involve new pressures on the ego that require adaptive solutions for the person. The new demands on the ego are universal, she contended, because the pressures that create them are universal. To understand this, it is necessary to consider the special alterations that Anna Freud (1969) associated with adolescence, alterations in drives, ego organization, object relations, and ideals and social relations.

With puberty comes an adult genital drive. Thus the balance among the id, ego, and superego is upset as this new feeling state comes to dominate the person's being. Because this alteration is an inevitable, universal one, Anna Freud argues that an inescapable imbalance in development occurs. As such, and as explained in Chapter 1, she believes that adolescence is necessarily a period of developmental disturbance.

Anna Freud claims that the new drive throws the person into upheaval. The adolescent tries out all the formerly useful defenses to deal with the new drive. This testing of the use of best defenses puts strain on the person because what would be adequate for one state may not be adequate for another, quantitatively greater and qualitatively different state. As such, not only does the adolescent try more of the same defenses, but also he or she eventually forms new types of mechanisms causing alterations in ego organization. For example, in relation to the new cognitive abilities that emerge in adolescence, the adolescent uses for the first time highly abstract, intellectual reasons to justify his or her behavior.

This new ego defense mechanism is termed **intellectualization**.

Despite the new ego defenses, the danger of inappropriately acting out the genital drive is so great that "nothing helps here except a complete discarding of the people who were the important love objects of the child, that is, the parents" (A. Freud, 1969, p. 8). Indeed, the new defenses are useful in helping the adolescent to alter the relations he or she has had with these "love objects." Defenses like intellectualization often involve elaborate rationales for why the parents are "stupid," "ineffective," or possess "useless . . . beliefs and conventions" (A. Freud, 1969, p. 8).

When the adolescent has broken the ties with the parents, he or she has also rejected the attitudes, values, and beliefs formerly shared with them. Anna Freud argues that the adolescent is thus left without social ties or ideals. Alterations in ideals and social relations are made with substitutes for both of these found in the peer group. Attachment to the peer group provides a mechanism wherein the new genital drive—which started all alterations initially—may be dealt with in a setting less dangerous to the adolescent's adaptation than the family setting.

A Critique of Anna Freud's Ideas By stressing the primary influence of biologically determined stages of development on psychological and social development, both Sigmund and Anna Freud are taking a weak interactionist stance in regard to the nature-nurture issue. Both Freuds describe human development in a manner inconsistent with what we know about the character of the transition that occurs from childhood to adolescence. Anna Freud described adolescence in terms that acknowledge little plasticity within people and few differences between people. She depicted adolescence as stormy and stressful.

Contrary to what she indicates, the research reviewed in Chapter 1 clearly indicates that most young people do not have stormy, stressful adolescent periods, do not break ties with parents, continue to share the ideals of their parents, and choose friends who have ideals consistent with those of their parents. Chapters 8 and 9 present additional research supporting these findings.

Intellectualization Ego defense mechanism of highly abstract, intellectual reasoning used to justify behavior.

Equilibration Individual's attempt to maintain cognitive balance between existing cognitive structures and what is encountered in the environment. Maintained through continuous process of assimilation and accommodation.

Assimilation Piagetian term to define process of changing external stimulation to fit already existing knowledge. With accommodation, part of the equilibration process.

Accommodation Piagetian term used to define process of changing already existing knowledge to fit external stimulation. With assimilation, part of the equilibration process.

Sensorimotor stage First stage of cognitive development as defined by Piaget. The child develops the knowledge that external stimulation continues to exist even when not sensed by the person.

Preoperational stage Second stage of cognitive development as defined by Piaget. The child can represent mentally absent objects and can use symbols to represent objects.

Jean Piaget and Cognitive Developmental (Structural) Theory

Issue to Consider

• How does the equilibration process, as defined and described by Piaget, account for his belief that environment and heredity are independent sources of developmental influence?

Swiss scientist Jean Piaget (1896–1980) presented a theory reflecting moderate nature-nurture interaction. Piaget considered both heredity and environment to be independent sources of cognitive (or knowledge) development. Piaget began writing in the 1920s, but because of his unique methods of observing and of describing his ideas, his work was not well regarded in the United States until the 1950s. Like Freud, Piaget believed that stages of development are universal and their sequence is invariant. Unlike Freud, Piaget believed that the stages unfold in response to both environmental and biological forces.

Cognitive development is said to arise from the action of the organism on the environment and from the action of the environment on the organism. Through this bidirectional process, Piaget proposed that cognition develops through four stages: sensorimotor, preoperational, concrete operational, and formal operational. Our progression through these stages involves our attempt to maintain a balance, an **equilibration,** between **assimilating** (changing external stimulation to fit already existing knowledge) and **accommodating** (changing already existing knowledge to fit external stimulation).

In the **sensorimotor stage,** the child develops the knowledge that objects continue to exist even when not sensed by the person. When the person can represent mentally (through images) absent objects and can use symbols (e.g., words) to represent objects, the major characteristics of the **preoperational stage**

are evident. Although thought about objects in the world is internalized mentally, it is not yet **reversible.** The child knows that a ball of clay can be rolled into a sausage, but he or she does not yet know that by reversing one's actions with the clay one can return the sausage to the original ball of clay.

Knowledge about the reversibility of actions occurs in the **concrete operational stage. Operations**—internalized actions that are reversible—now exist. The child can visualize or mentally represent that the ball of clay can be made into a sausage and vice versa. But thought is limited in that the person can think only about objects that have a concrete, real existence. Clay is real and can be thought about, but a substance that does not exist cannot be dealt with mentally. The child does not have the ability to deal adequately with counterfactual, hypothetical phenomena and does not recognize the subjective and arbitrary nature of thought. Such recognition characterizes the next stage, the stage most representative of adolescents and adults in modern Western society.

In the **formal operational stage** the person can think of all possible combinations of elements of a problem to find a solution, both real and imaginary. Because the person centers so much on this newly emerged thinking ability, some scientists believe the adolescent is characterized by a particular type of **egocentrism** (Elkind, 1967). An adolescent may believe others are as preoccupied with the object of his or her own thoughts—himself or herself—as he or she is (this is termed **imaginary audience**). Because of the attention, the adolescent comes to believe that he or she is a special, unique person (this is termed **personal fable**) (Elkind, 1967).

A Critique of Piaget's Ideas

Piaget's (1950, 1970) theory accepts a fuller role for experience in providing an interactive basis of stage progression and

Reversibility Ability to know that by reversing one's actions on an object one can return the object to its original state.

Concrete operational stage Third stage of cognitive development as defined by Piaget. The child is capable of internalized, reversible actions.

Operation Piagetian term referring to the internalized actions that are mentally reversible.

Formal operational stage Fourth stage of cognitive development as defined by Piaget. Most representative of adolescents and adults in modern Western society. The person is capable of thinking counterfactually and hypothetically. Can think of all possible combinations of elements of a problem to find a solution.

Egocentrism Cognitive focus on the self. Egocentrism changes as the child moves throughout Piagetian stages.

Imaginary audience Adolescents' belief that others are as preoccupied with the object of their own thoughts as they are.

Personal fable Due to attention of the imaginary audience, adolescents come to believe that they are special and/or unique.

may be seen as a more moderate stance in regard to the interaction between nature and nurture. However, there is not as full a consideration of environmental or experiential changes as there is of organism changes.

Although Piaget continually emphasized that developmental structural change arises from an interaction between organismic and environmental processes, it is only the organism that is seen as going through changes. Although the organism's *conception* of the environment changes, constant flux of the physical and social world was never systematically considered. In addition, the impact of these physical and social environmental changes on the character of the child's progression is viewed in a narrow way. That is, such environmentally based differences between people can only pertain to the rate of change and to the final stage of development reached; but any changes in the environment are irrelevant to the sequence and characteristics of the stages themselves. For Piaget, the organism changes but the environment does not (Riegel, 1976).

Lawrence Kohlberg and Cognitive Development in Moral Reasoning

Issue to Consider
• Why is Kohlberg's theory viewed as a moderate interaction theory?

Lawrence Kohlberg's (1927–1988) theory of the development of moral reasoning is derived from a cognitive developmental viewpoint, as represented in Piaget's theory. As such, it adopts the same moderate nature-nurture interaction view found in Piaget's theory. Kohlberg (1963a, 1963b, 1970) proposed a theory of moral development that has served as the impetus for much research and discussion. To study moral reasoning, Kohlberg presented children with a moral dilemma—a situation where there is no right or wrong answer—and asked them to give reasons for their particular responses to the situation.

Kohlberg described a progression in moral reasoning that involves **preconventional morality,** involving the stage of punishment and obedience reasoning and the stage of naive egoistic reasoning; **conventional morality,** involving the good-person orientation to morality and the stage of social order and institutional maintenance morality; and **postconventional morality,** involving the stage of contractual legalistic moral reasoning and the stage of conscience and principle orientation.

The work of Kohlberg and Piaget is discussed in later chapters (see Chapters 4 and 5). Note here, however, that by minimizing the impact on development of continual social and physical environmental changes, Piaget and Kohlberg did not sufficiently attend to the source of developmental progression: person-environment interactions. If only the person's changes are considered, and the environment's are not, then no variation in stages may be attributed to variation in the environment, and nothing can be related to environmental change. The only source of variation can be the person, the "organism," and only organism changes can predict organism changes.

Accordingly, Piaget's and Kohlberg's supposed interaction is reduced to an account of development that stresses primarily, if not exclusively, organism processes to the omission of environmental ones. Piaget and Kohlberg are left with only being able to account for organism changes on the basis of organism changes. A problem of circular logic is raised because of Piaget's and Kohlberg's failure to consider environmental changes as contributing to development as actively as do organism changes.

However, the last category of interaction theory, labeled strong interaction theory, regards nature and nurture processes as completely fused in life. Genes and contexts are interdependent, part of a unified, coherent system, wherein each influences the structure and function of the other (Ford & Lerner, 1992). Developmental contextualism illustrates well the strong interaction approach. Because it has been presented in some detail already, we discuss other key instances of such theoretical models.

Bronfenbrenner's Model of the Ecology of Human Development

Issue to Consider
• How does the social ecology of life play a role in a person's development?

Urie Bronfenbrenner (1977, 1979; Bronfenbrenner & Morris, 1998) argues that human

Preconventional morality First level of moral development as defined by Kohlberg. The individual is bound by issues of punishment and obedience and naïve and egoistic reasoning.

Conventional morality Second level of moral development as defined by Kohlberg. The individual is bound by issues of the good-person orientation and is concerned with upholding social order and the institutional maintenance of morality.

Postconventional morality Third level of moral development as defined by Kohlberg. The individual is concerned with legalistic reasoning oriented around principles and conscience.

development needs to be understood as it occurs in its real-world setting, or **ecology.** He believes the ecology of human development is composed of four distinct although interrelated systems or types of settings: the microsystem, mesosystem, exosystem, and macrosystem.

The **microsystem** is composed of "the complex of relations between the developing person and environment in an immediate setting containing the person" (Bronfenbrenner, 1977, p. 515). For example, the family is the major microsystem for youth development in our society (Belsky, Lerner, & Spanier, 1984). It involves interactions between the child, his or her parents, and any siblings present in the home. Other microsystems of youth include the school setting, involving both adolescent-teacher and adolescent-peer interactions, and athletic courts or fields, malls, or other neighborhood gathering places that most often involve just adolescent-peer interactions.

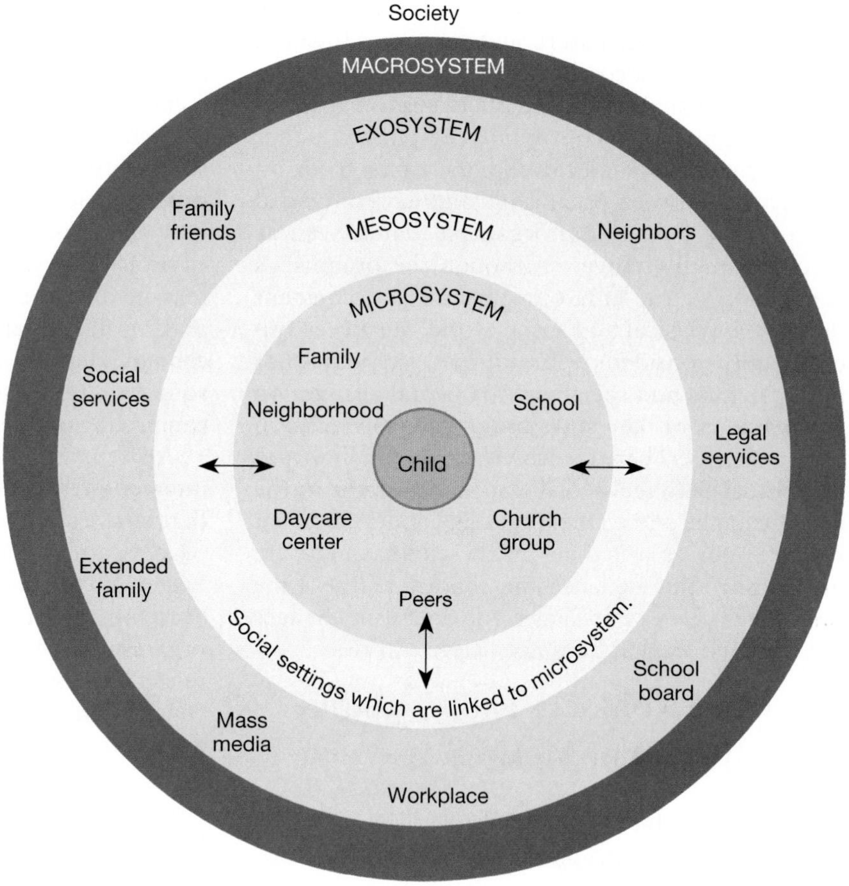

Figure 2-1 Bronfenbrenner's concentric circles representing human ecology.

Ecology Real-world setting(s) of the individual and/or species.

Microsystem As defined by Bronfenbrenner, the first of several interrelated systems whose composition defines the ecology of human development. Composed of relations between the developing person and the environment in the immediate setting within which the person exists.

Mesosystem As defined by Bronfenbrenner, the second of several interrelated systems whose composition defines the ecology of human development. Composed of interrelations among the major settings containing the individual, the developing person at a particular point in his or her life.

An adolescent's microsystems may be interrelated. What occurs in school may affect what happens in the family, and vice versa. Bronfenbrenner notes that such microsystem interrelations constitute a second ecological stratum, termed the **mesosystem.** He defines it as "the interrelations among major settings containing the developing person at a particular point in his or her life" (Bronfenbrenner, 1977, p. 515).

What happens in a microsystem (e.g., in an interaction between an adolescent and a parent within the family con-

text) may be influenced by events that occur in systems in which the adolescent takes no part. For example, an adult who is a parent also has other social roles, such as worker. The adolescent is probably not part of his or her parents' workplace interactions, but events that affect the parents at work can influence how they treat the youth. If a parent has a particularly good day at work, he or she may respond to adolescents more positively than otherwise by choosing to spend additional time with them in the evening.

The adolescent lives with people who interact in and are affected by contexts other than those containing the young person. The adolescent may be affected by settings in which he or she plays no direct role. Bronfenbrenner sees such influences as constituting a third system within the ecology of human development. He labels it the

exosystem and defines it as "an extension of the mesosystem embracing . . . specific social structures, both formal and informal, that do not themselves contain the developing person but impinge upon or encompass the immediate setting in which the person is found, and thereby delimit, influence, or even determine what goes on there" (Bronfenbrenner, 1977, p. 515).

Within the ecology of human development exists a fourth system, the **macrosystem**. This system is composed of cultural values and beliefs and historical events (e.g., wars, floods, famines), both of which may affect the other ecological systems. For instance, natural disasters may destroy the homes, schools, or other microsystems of a person or a group of people, and/or they may make certain necessities of life (e.g., food, fresh water) less available. Cultural values influence the developing person in many ways. In infancy, cultural beliefs about the appropriateness of breastfeeding and about when weaning from the breast should occur can affect not only the nutritional status of the infant but, because mother's milk may make some children less likely to develop allergies later in life, it can also affect their health status. In adolescence, values about child rearing, and indeed the value or role of youth in society, not only affect the behaviors developed by a young person (e.g., Baumrind, 1971, 1991) but can even have implications for whether the person survives adolescence (e.g., see Taylor, 1990, 1993).

Bronfenbrenner's model of the ecology of human development allows us to devise a means to represent the idea that the bidirectional socialization which occurs between adolescents and parents is embedded in a still more complex system of social networks and of societal, cultural, and historical influences.

The Baltes and Baltes Selection, Optimization, and Compensation (SOC) Model

Issue to Consider

• What are the different components of the SOC model, and how do they relate to adolescent development?

I have noted that theories of adolescent development need to explain three aspects of the actions of youth—those involved with selection, optimization,

and compensation. These are precisely the three processes discussed by Paul B. Baltes and Margret M. Baltes (1990) in their section, optimization, and compensation (SOC) model.

Baltes and Baltes (1990; Baltes, 1997; Freund & Baltes, 1998; Lerner et al., 2001) argue that selection, optimization, and compensation need to be considered simultaneously to adequately describe and understand development. The SOC model assumes there are constraints and limitations of internal and external resources in life (e.g., stamina, time, money, social support). As a consequence, a range of alternative developmental goals needs to be selected. Selection gives direction to development by directing and focusing resources (i.e., means to reach goals) on certain domains of functioning (e.g., academic achievement) and preventing diffusion of resources (e.g., trying to devote time to both academic achievement and athletic achievement).

In order to actually achieve higher levels of functioning in a selected area, optimization needs to take place. Optimization is the process of acquiring, refining, coordinating, and applying resources in the selected area or goal. Typical instances of optimization are acquiring specific goal-related skills (e.g., weight training to improve one's football stamina, SAT test-taking skills to improve one's scores on this exam) and persistence in the pursuit of a goal (e.g., never missing a football practice session, keeping up with homework, writing several drafts of a term paper until the best one is produced).

Optimization describes a process geared toward achieving higher levels of (or growth in) functioning. Throughout the life span, however, development can be characterized as multidirectional, that is, as encompassing both growth and decline, or loss and failure (P. Baltes, 1997; P. Baltes, Lindenberger, & Staudinger, 1998; Brandtstädter & Wentura, 1995; Labouvie-Vief, 1981). The SOC model addresses the decline and the management of loss by stressing the importance of compensation. When loss or decline in resources threatens our level of functioning, it is necessary to invest additional

Exosystem As defined by Bronfenbrenner, the third of several interrelated systems whose composition defines the ecology of human development. The formal and informal social structures that do not themselves contain the developing person but impinge on the setting within which the person exists.

Macrosystem As defined by Bronfenbrenner, the fourth of several interrelated systems whose composition defines the ecology of human development. Composed of cultural values and beliefs and historical events that affect the other ecological systems.

MEET THE RESEARCHER BOX 2.3

PAUL B. BALTES
THE PLASTICITY OF ADOLESCENT DEVELOPMENT

Adolescence is one of the critical periods in which the foundation of a successful life is laid down: intellectually, socially, motivationally, spiritually, and physically. If we grow successfully during the adolescent phase of life, the doors to a good life are open wide. At the same time, in my research on lifelong (life-span) development, I have been continuously impressed with the fact that the doors to a good life are never completely shut. We humans have the ability to come back and redirect our lives toward more desirable states and outcomes at later periods of life as well. This is called lifelong human plasticity. Three topics and research findings of my work are of special interest to young people.

First, there is the topic of the meaning of life. What makes life worthwhile? The key to a meaningful life is to have goals, to aspire to develop the means (cognitive, motivational, social, and economic) necessary to reach these goals, and in the face of obstacles to find ways for alternative ways to reach goals. When these three activities form a coalition we make progress in life. In technical terms, the theory behind those three modes of successful life management is called the "orchestration of selection, optimization, and compensation."

Second, and this insight owes much to my work in the Jacobs Foundation on Youth Research and Youth Policy, I have learned there are three general domains of "literacy" that adolescents—in addition to a concern with academic school knowledge and the ability to think critically—may want to focus on in order to achieve a good pool of resources and forward-looking perspective on life: (1) life skills literacy, (2) environmental or nature literacy, and (3) computer literacy. If adolescents move forward in knowing, for instance, how to take care of their bodies and how they can promote their own lives in cooperation with others (life skills literacy), in understanding and nurturing the conditions of their physical environment (environmental or nature literacy), and in using the information technology that the modern world offers (computer literacy), they possess the essential building blocks for becoming mature and future-oriented adults. These three types of literacy are the best insurance policy for moving forward in life and creating the potential to be a good citizen.

Paul B. Baltes is a professor of psychology and the director of the Center of Lifespan Psychology at the Max Planck Institute for Human Development in Berlin, Germany. In addition to being a researcher on all stages of life, for which he has received many prestigious awards, Baltes is a member of the board of trustees of the Jacobs Foundation. This Swiss foundation specializes in supporting international projects on youth research and youth policy.

The third topic of my research that is relevant to understanding how adolescents live their lives but at the same time prepare themselves for a good future deals with the more specific behavioral and cognitive elements that make us develop and use the best of our potential. With more specific elements, I mean the cognition and behaviors that pervade everything we do, for instance, as we select, optimize, and compensate or as we engage ourselves in the acquisition of the three literacies I described earlier.

Many of these insights about the specific elements involved I have gained from research on another stage of life, that is, aging. Adolescents often worry about their well-being and face what is called critical life events and challenging obstacles. The same is even more true for older people. Their everyday lives are full of challenges and losses. Thus studying the extreme conditions in the lives of older people helps scientists to better understand what happens in other stages of life, such as adolescence.

In this research with older adults we have identified some of the specific elements relevant for effective mastery in all sorts of domains of life. Among them are (1) a good self-esteem, (2) a solid but flexible self, (3) positive beliefs in one's potential (also called self-efficacy or agency), (4) a positive and optimistic orientation toward the future and the subsequent stages of life, and (5) the emergence of knowledge about such concepts as wisdom and moral behavior.

Each of these five components has its foundational origins in childhood and adolescence. It is possible to acquire and refine them later in life, but it makes for easier and earlier progress if they are built up early. What is occasionally difficult for adolescents is that they, in their wants to be independent and different from their parents or the current "establishment," see these components as parts of the conventional order of society and what parents want. It is later in life, however, that the insight arises that having these building blocks is in their own best interest as adolescents as well. What I as a researcher hope is that adolescents can do both: gain their autonomy including critical thinking but also the pool of resources that propels them forward to pursue their own and the common good.

resources or substitute or apply additional means geared toward the maintenance of functioning (Carstensen, Hanson, & Freund, 1995; Marsiske et al., 1995; Staudinger, Marsiske, & P. Baltes, 1995; see also Bäckman & Dixon, 1992). Typical instances of compensation are the substitution of means or the use of external aids (e.g., obtaining the help of an SAT tutor). When compensatory efforts fail or their costs outweigh their gains, the more adaptive response to loss or decline in resources might be to restructure our goal hierarchy (e.g., place academics ahead of football), to lower our standards (e.g., settle for being a second-string football player), or to look for new goals (**loss-based selection**; make academics a superordinate goal instead of a means).

To summarize, *selection* refers to the development of preferences or goals, the construction of a goal hierarchy, and the commitment to a set of goals or areas of preferred functioning. *Optimization* denotes the investment of goal-related resources in order to achieve higher levels of functioning. *Compensation* refers to the process involved in maintaining a given level of functioning in the face of loss or decline in goal-related resources.

Although it is possible to differentiate these components of SOC, successful development encompasses their coordinated integration (Freund & P. Baltes, 2000; Marsiske et al., 1995). For instance, optimization efforts most likely only lead to higher levels of functioning when they are focused on a small number of domains of functioning instead of diffused among many domains. Similarly, selection per se does not ensure high achievement if no goal-relevant resources are applied (e.g., wanting to have high peer status but using no means—neither athletic nor academic success—to attain it).

Finally, the adaptiveness of compensation needs to be seen in the context of the entire set of an adolescent's goals (e.g., how many other goals are there that need resources for optimization?, how important, relative to

other goals, is a threatened goal?) and the availability of resources. It does not appear to be adaptive to put a lot of one's resources into a relatively unimportant domain of functioning at the cost of having to neglect more important goals (Freund, Li, & P. Baltes, 1999). Meet the Researcher Box 2.3 discusses some of the other conceptual and empirical contributions of Paul B. Baltes to the understanding of adolescent development.

Conclusions

There exists a diverse array of theories with which to study development. Although these theories differ in regard to the way they approach the nature-nurture issue in the study of development, they are similar in one important respect. Each theory is an attempt to enhance understanding of the course of adolescence (i.e., how, across this period of life, youth act, why they act in particular ways, and the implications of these actions for healthy, adaptive development).

Although all theories have important uses for an advancing understanding of adolescence and, as well, even though *no* theory is free of limitations (Lerner, 2001), strong interaction theories such as those of Bronfenbrenner and of Baltes and Baltes appear most useful at this point in the history of the study of adolescence (Lerner, 1998a, 1998b). These theories integrate all levels of organization that are part of a young person's life (biology through society, culture, and history), stress the relative plasticity and diversity of development, and offer an active and optimistic approach to applications aimed at promoting healthy and successful adolescent development. Accordingly, as we consider the features of adolescent development in the following chapters, we find that strong interaction theories are useful for appreciating the diversity of development, the role of the context in adolescent development, and the several ways in which healthy development of youth can be furthered by positively integrating young people and their ecologies.

Loss-based selection When compensatory efforts fail or their costs outweigh their gains, individuals restructure their goal hierarchy, lower their standards, or look for new goals.

Summary

- The key challenge for adolescents is to discover what they can do to develop successfully in their context, given their biological, psychological, and social characteristics.

- An essential task for theories of adolescence is to understand adolescents' *selection* of goals, their *optimization* of their abilities to meet these goals, and their *compensation* for failures to meet their goals.

- Theories of adolescence must explain how an individual adolescent interacts with his or her context.

- Contemporary theories of adolescence stress that development occurs as a consequence of relation among "multiple levels of organization," such as biological, psychological, societal, and cultural.

- Developmental systems theories stress that development occurs as a result of organized and mutually influential relations among the various levels of organization.

- The developmental contextual approach to life-span development suggests that to understand adolescence, influences from multiple disciplines must be considered in an integrated manner, systematic change or development must be considered, and the individual must be seen as an active agent in his or her own development.

- To study adolescents, multivariate, longitudinal, and multilevel research should be used.

- The goal of applied developmental science is to use knowledge about adolescent development, diversity, and context to design interventions to prevent problems and to promote positive development.

- Person-context interactions are plastic (they show systematic change), and future developmental pathways can be constructed that are discontinuous from previous ones, as well as continuous.

- The nature-nurture controversy pertains to whether behavior and development derive from heredity, maturation, and genes (nature) or environment, experience, and learning (nurture).

- The developmental contextual approach stresses dynamic interaction between nature and nurture such that biological and contextual variables influence each other over the course of life.

- Genes and environment are equal forces in the determination of development and they are completely fused in life.

- The diversity of possible developmental outcomes is constrained by the individual's characteristics and context despite *relative* plasticity of human development.

- No two people have the same fusion of genes and environment across their lives.

- Differences in genotypes and environments, and the fusion of the two, underscores the error in making global characterizations of entire groups of people.

- The large number of potential human genotypes makes the possibility of any two people ever having the same genotype (excluding multiple, identical births) next to impossible.

- Genes must be fused with the environment if any human physical or behavioral characteristics are to be developed.

- Nature and nurture are inextricably linked and one cannot exist independently of the other.

- Although G. Stanley Hall's *specific* nature theory was not adopted, he had an influence in developing scientific concern with human development and a general nature perspective.

- Boyd R. McCandless's drive theory of human behavior states there are several drives in the person that are energizers of behavior. His theory is a nurture theory because he believes a person will learn from society that certain behaviors will reduce drive states, which is rewarding to the person.

- McCandless points to adolescence as a special time because of the emergence of the sex drive. Society does not reward males and females for the same sex-drive reducing behaviors. This could be a period of undiminished drives for the adolescent, and thus it is a nurture explanation of "storm and stress."

- A weak interaction theory places the stress primarily on nature *or* nurture as the source of development. A moderate interaction theory places equal stress on nature and nurture but sees them as independent of each other. A strong interaction theory places the stress on nature and nurture, and views them as reciprocally related.

- Sigmund Freud's theory of psychosexual development is a weak interaction theory. He believed human life is governed by the libido, which moves throughout the body over the course of development, determining what type of stimulation is gratifying.

- Freud proposed five stages of psychosexual development: oral, anal, phallic, latency, and genital. The stages correspond to localization in the body of the libido.

- Freud's ideas were critiqued because he worked with adult neurotic patients who were attempting to reconstruct their childhood. Freud did not check for memory lapses or distortions of early memories. He also worked at a time when views of sexuality were repressed. Other psychoanalytically oriented thinkers accepted most of Freud's ideas as correct, but incomplete.

- Erik Erikson created a weak interaction theory of psychosocial development focusing on the contributions of the ego to development, and on what the ego must do to adapt to reality.

- Erikson's theory proposes stages of psychosocial development that presents capabilities the ego must develop to meet societal demands. Development will proceed even if the capability is not achieved, but the ego will not be optimally developed.

- There are eight stages of psychosocial development and each presents a crisis of development.

- Erikson's stage theory is consistent with a life-span perspective, and although it has some of the same limitations as Freud's theory, it is a major basis for research about human development.

- Anna Freud and her father believed there were three structures of personality: the id (the initial source of libido), the ego (developed to deal with reality), and the superego (the conscience) that are present and balanced by the end of the phallic stage.

- The id only wants pleasure, the superego cares nothing of pleasure and is the conscience, and the ego is the balance between the two, caring only about survival.

- The unconscious contains material most difficult to bring into awareness. The ego uses defense mechanisms to take pressures imposed by the id and place them into the unconscious. The superego's pressures are not defended against because they represent the rules of society and placing this in the unconscious would mean losing morality.

- Anna Freud believes the balance among the superego, id, and ego is destroyed in adolescence because of new pressures on the ego.

- Anna Freud associated special alterations in adolescence, alterations in drives, ego organization, object relations, and ideals and social relations, that make adolescence a time of imbalance and upheaval.

- Anna Freud's theory was criticized because she did not acknowledge the plasticity within people and the differences between people and she characterized adolescence as inevitably stormy and stressful.

- Jean Piaget's theory of cognitive development is an example of a moderate interaction theory. He believed cognitive development arose from the action of the organism on the environment and from the action of the environment on the organism, but there is not as full a consideration of environmental or experiential changes as there is of organism changes.

- Piaget proposed that cognition develops through four universal stages in an unvarying sequence: sensorimotor, preoperational, concrete operational, and formal operational. Movement through these stages represents a person's attempt to maintain equilibrium using assimilation and accommodation.

- A special type of egocentrism characterizes adolescence. The adolescent believes that others are as preoccupied with him or her as he or she is (imaginary audience) and the adolescent comes to believe he or she is a special, unique person (personal fable).

- Lawrence Kohlberg developed a theory of moral development from a cognitive development viewpoint that has been the impetus for much research and discussion.

- Kohlberg described a progression of moral development starting with preconventional morality, moving to conventional morality, and ending with postconventional morality.

- Kohlberg's theory is a moderate interaction theory because it did not sufficiently deal with what is claimed to be the source of development, person-environment interactions. His theory focused almost exclusively on person processes to the exclusion of environmental processes.

- Urie Bronfenbrenner proposed a strong interaction theory of development, arguing that human development needs to be understood as it occurs in its real-world setting, or ecology.

- Bronfenbrenner believes that human development occurs in four distinct, although interrelated, settings: the microsystem, the mesosystem, the exosystem, and the macrosystem.

- There are many theories of adolescent development, which differ in regard to their treatment of the nature-nurture debate; however, they are all attempts to understand how and why youth act across adolescence, and what the implications of these actions are for adaptive development.

- These actions involve selection, optimization, and compensation and are discussed by Paul B. Baltes and Margret M. Baltes (1990) in their section, optimization, and compensation (SOC) model.

- In the SOC model, selection refers to the development of preferences or goals, the construction of a goal hierarchy, and the commitment to a set of goals or areas of preferred functioning. Optimization denotes the investment of goal-related resources in order to achieve higher levels of functioning. Compensation refers to the process involved in maintaining a given level of functioning in the face of loss or decline in goal-related resources.

Discussion Topics

1. Guided by developmental systems theory, how might you design efforts to support adolescents who exhibit problem and/or risky behaviors?

2. How do you think your particular genes and life contexts have determined your developmental outcome—the person you are today? Do you feel your genes or your life contexts have been more influential in that determination?

3. What might studies of fraternal and identical twins add to the nature-nurture debate?

4. Compare and contrast the theories of Hall and McCandless, focusing specifically on their conceptions of adolescence.

5. Why might the three psychoanalytic theories presented in the chapter be considered examples of weak nature-nurture interaction?

6. Why might Piaget's theory of cognitive development and Kohlberg's theory of moral reasoning be considered a moderate nature-nurture interaction theory?

7. Why might Bronfenbrenner's approach be considered a strong nature-nurture interaction theory?

8. Think of an example in your development to which you could apply the SOC model. What selections did you make? How did you optimize your chances of attaining, refining, and/or coordinating those selections? How did you compensate if and when you faced failure? Based on this example, would you describe the Baltes and Baltes model as a strong approach to the nature-nurture debate? Why?

Key Terms

accommodation (p. 48)

adulthood (p. 46)

anal stage (p. 42)

anal musculature stage (p. 45)

applied developmental
  science (p. 33)

assimilation (p. 48)

castration anxiety (p. 43)

compensation (p. 30)

concrete operational stage (p. 48)

conscience (p. 43)

conventional morality (p. 49)

critical period (p. 45)

defense mechanisms (p. 46)

developmental system
  theories (p. 32)

diversity (p. 33)

down syndrome (p. 38)

drive state (p. 41)

dynamic interaction (p. 36)

ecological milieu (p. 41)

ecological validity (p. 39)

ecology (p. 50)

ego (p. 46)

egocentrism (p. 48)

ego ideal (p. 43)

electra complex (p. 43)

equilibration (p. 48)

exosystem (p. 51)

fixation (p. 42)

formal operational stage (p. 48)

genital locomotor stage (p. 45)

genital stage (p. 43)

genotype (p. 36)

id (p. 46)

imaginary audience (p. 48)

intellectualization (p. 47)

interventions (p. 33)

latency (p. 45)

latency stage (p. 43)

libido (p. 42)

longitudinal research/studies (p. 31)

loss-based selection (p. 53)

macrosystem (p. 51)

maturity (p. 46)

meiosis (p. 36)

mesosystem (p. 50)

microsystem (p. 50)

moderate interaction theory (p. 42)

monozygotic (MZ) twins (p. 36)

multilevel research/studies (p. 32)

multiple levels of organization
  (p. 31)

multivariate research/studies (p. 32)

nature-nurture controversy (p. 31)

oedipus complex (p. 43)

ontogeny (p. 40)

operation (p. 48)

optimization (p. 30)

oral stage (p. 42)

oral sensory stage (p. 45)

penis envy (p. 43)

personal fable (p. 48)

phallic stage (p. 43)

phenylketonuria (PKU) (p. 39)

phylogeny (p. 41)

plasticity (p. 36)

postconventional morality (p. 49)

preconventional morality (p. 49)

preoperational stage (p. 48)

projection (p. 46)

psychosocial development (p. 45)

puberty and adolescence (p. 45)

rationalization (p. 46)

reality principle (p. 44)

recapitulation (p. 40)

repression (p. 46)

retrospection (p. 44)

reversibility (p. 48)

secondary process (p. 44)

selection (p. 30)

sensorimotor stage (p. 48)

strong interaction theory (p. 42)

substitution (p. 46)

superego (p. 43)

weak interaction theory (p. 42)

young adulthood (p. 45)

zygote (p. 36)

3

PUBERTY, PHYSICAL DEVELOPMENT, AND HEALTH

"Mom, I just can't go to the dance. I look so gross in a dress and heels!"

"Tina, you look lovely," her mother insisted. "I'm sure you'll look as nice as any of the other sixth-grade girls."

"No I won't," Tina pleaded. "I'm too tall already and these shoes make it worse. None of the boys will want to come close to me." Tears began to fill her eyes.

"Honey, at your age girls are often taller than boys. Believe me, I'm sure that a few inches won't stop them from asking you to dance. You're so pretty, you'll have a line of them asking you."

"Oh sure, and you're not biased. I'm so pretty and I just happen to be your daughter."

"Well dear, you are my daughter, but that does not mean I can't see that . . ."

"But Mom," Tina interrupted, "the boys already make fun of me. They make me feel so uncomfortable because I'm bigger than the other girls in my grade. This doesn't hide anything."

"Oh," her mother said softly, "I understand, but you know you can wear a shawl and . . ."

"No Mom, you don't understand! I feel ugly and wearing a dress makes me feel even worse. I just don't want to go any place where I have to wear one."

L E A R N I N G O B J E C T I V E S

1. To understand adolescents' perceptions of pubertal changes.
2. To define the three stages of adolescence and their corresponding ages.
3. To understand the three phases of pubertal maturation and what occurs during those stages.
4. To understand the role of hormones in pubertal maturation.
5. To define puberty and to understand the difference between puberty and pubertal maturation.
6. To understand the differences between primary and secondary sexual characteristics.
7. To understand the causes and effects of variations in the speed and timing of pubertal maturation and

how the effects are influenced by the social context, including history (the secular trend).
8. To understand how adolescents' behaviors influence their health.
9. To understand some of the physical problems related to pubertal changes.
10. To appreciate how adolescents' preoccupation with their bodily appearance can lead to eating behaviors that are detrimental to their health.
11. To name and describe some eating disorders and their implications.
12. To recognize how psychological and contextual influences affect eating disorders.

his interaction between Tina and her mother is all too typical during adolescence, especially during its early phases. The physical and physiological changes of adolescence involving **pubertal maturation** bring the young person from looking like a child to appearing like an adult.

Many adolescents report that they are not fully prepared for pubertal changes or fully informed about what will happen to them and how they should think and feel about these changes. In one study of about 150 ninth-grade girls, the participants reported a need to receive emotional support and assurance that menstruation is normal and healthy rather than bad, frightening, or embarrassing (Koff & Rierdan, 1995). The girls reported that they needed information about menstrual hygiene and about how they would actually feel across their menstrual cycles. The girls also noted that they talked about menstruation with their mothers but were unlikely to have similar discussions with their fathers. They were uncomfortable talking with their fathers about menstruation and many felt that their fathers should be supportive but silent (Koff & Rierdan, 1995).

Among younger (sixth-grade) girls from Australia, participants had only limited

Pubertal maturation *Process* through which the primary sexual characteristics develop into adult form and the secondary sexual characteristics associated with puberty emerge and develop.

Concerns about appearance and grooming are important parts of life for many adolescents.

knowledge about menarche and much of it was incorrect or reflective of negative myths (e.g., menarche is a source of shame and anxiety linked to periods of incapacity and illness) (Moore, 1995). The girls' attitudes about menstruation were characterized by embarrassment, discomfort, and ambivalence about growing up (Moore, 1995).

Both male and female adolescents find it useful to have accurate information about the nature and implications of pubertal change (Brooks-Gunn & Petersen, 1983). It is important to stress that emotions and thoughts often do not develop at the same pace as one's physical characteristics and that because of the relations among biological, psychological, and social functioning, **puberty** can have profound implications for both physical health and behavior. In this chapter we discuss both of these implications of puberty.

Characteristics of Pubertal Maturation

Issues to Consider
- What are the three stages of pubertal development, and what are their general characteristics?
- What is the physiological process that leads to pubertal maturation and bodily changes?
- What is puberty? How is it different from pubertal maturation?
- What are primary and secondary sexual characteristics?

The physical and physiological changes of adolescence typically span the second decade of life, involving early adolescence (around years 10 to14 or 15), middle adolescence (years 15 to17), and late adolescence (years 18 to 20). Although within these stages of adolescence, bodily and psychological changes do not proceed uniformly, a general sequence for these changes applies to most people (Katchadourian, 1977; Tanner, 1991).

The bodily changes of adolescence relate to both primary and secondary sexual characteristics. Bodily changes affect height, weight, fat and muscle distribution, glandular secretions, and both primary and secondary sexual characteristics. When some of the changes have begun, but most are yet to occur, the person is said to be in the **prepubescent phase** (Schonfeld, 1969). When most of these bodily changes have been initiated, the person is in the **pubescent phase.** Finally, when most of these changes have occurred, the person is in the **postpubescent phase.** This period ends when all bodily changes associated with adolescence are complete (Schonfeld, 1969).

The physical and physiological changes of adolescence involve alterations in the body. Most centrally, pubertal maturation and bodily changes involve changes in the particular chemicals released from certain organs within the body. These organs are **endocrine glands,** and the chemicals they release into the bloodstream are termed **hormones.**

The body has two types of glands. **Exocrine glands,** such as the salivary and mammary glands, have an opening (a duct) that allows their secretions to leave the body. Endocrine glands are ductless glands that secrete hormones directly into the bloodstream.

Pubertal maturation begins when a portion of the brain, the hypothalamus, produces "luteinizing hormone releasing hormone" (LHRH), a chemical that stimulates the secretion of hormones from the pituitary gland. These hormones are termed gonadotropins, luteinizing hormone (LH), and follicle-stimulating hormone (FSH). These hormones stimulate other endocrine glands, the gonads (ovaries in females, testes in males), to secrete sex **steroids**

Puberty period during which the primary sexual characteristics develop into adult form and the secondary sexual characteristics are emerging and developing and the capability to reproduce is attained.

Prepubescent phase Stage in pubertal maturation during which some of the bodily changes associated with adolescence (e.g., changes in height, weight, fat and muscle distribution, glandular secretions, or sexual characteristics) have begun.

Pubescent phase Stage in pubertal maturation during which most of the bodily changes associated with adolescence have been initiated.

Postpubescent phase Stage in pubertal maturation during which the bodily changes associated with adolescence are completed.

Endocrine glands Ductless glands, such as the pituitary gland, that secrete their content into the bloodstream.

Hormones Chemicals released into the bloodstream that have specific regulatory effects on the activity of certain organs.

Exocrine glands Glands with an opening (duct), such as salivary and mammary glands, that secrete their content directly into the environment.

Steroids Sex hormones (androgens in males and estrogens in females) that control development of physical and physiological changes associated with pubertal maturation.

(**estrogens** in females, **androgens** in males). It is these sex steroids that produce the physical and physiological changes of pubertal maturation.

Adolescence is a period during which the person reaches an adult level of reproductive maturity. However, puberty, the point at which the person can reproduce, is not synonymous with all maturational changes (Schonfeld, 1969). Puberty is not synonymous with menarche in females or with the first ejaculation (the release of semen) in males. Typically, the initial menstrual cycles of females are not accompanied by ovulation. Similarly, for males there is a gap between the first ejaculation, which usually occurs between 11 and 16 years of age (Kinsey, Pomeroy, & Martin, 1948), and the capability to fertilize.

Primary sexual characteristics are present at birth and involve the internal and external genitalia (e.g., the penis in males and the vagina in females). **Secondary sexual characteristics** are those attributes that develop during the prepubescent through postpubescent phases (e.g., breast development in females and pigmented facial hair in males).

Puberty is just one event within a series of changes that bring the adolescent from childhood to adulthood. Adjusting to these internal and external bodily changes represents a developmental task of adolescence. In order to understand the nature of this physiological developmental task, we discuss in more detail the three phases involved in adolescent physical maturation and present the specific changes associated with each phase. Given the vast number of bodily changes that adolescents must adjust to, we can appreciate the difficulty they face in formulating and maintaining a consistent sense of self.

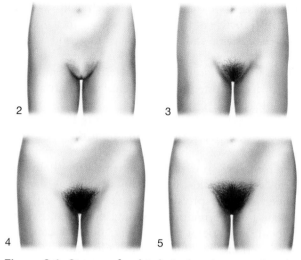

Figure 3.1 Stages of pubic hair development in adolescent girls.
(1) early pubescent (not shown) in which there is no true pubic hair; (2) late prepubescent/early pubescent in which sparse growth of downy hair is mainly at sides of labia; (3) pigmentation, coarsening, and curling with an increase in the amount of hair; (4) adult hair, but limited in area; (5) adult hair with horizontal upper border. (*Source:* Redrawn from J. M. Tanner, 1962.)

Estrogens Female sex hormones associated with the development of secondary sexual characteristics in girls.

Androgens Male sex hormones associated with the development of secondary sexual characteristics in boys.

Primary sexual characteristics Physical attributes present at birth that involve internal and external genitalia (e.g., the penis in males and the vagina in females).

Secondary sexual characteristics Physical attributes that develop during puberty (e.g., breast development in females and pigmented facial hair in males).

Prepubescence

Issue to Consider

- What are the characteristics of the prepubescent phase for males and females?

Prepubescence begins with the first indication of sexual maturation. It ends with the initial appearance of pubic hair. In females, prepubescent changes typically begin an average of 2 years earlier than in males. The first sign of female development in this period is the enlargement of the ovary and the ripening of its cells. In contrast with males, these changes in primary sexual characteristics are not visible. Changes involving secondary sex characteristics can be seen. There is a rounding of the hips and the first visible sign of breast development. This involves an elevation of the areola surrounding the nipple (Schonfeld, 1969) producing a small conelike growth, termed the breast *bud*. As with the male, there is no true pubic hair, although down may be present.

In males, there is a continuing enlargement of the testicles, an enlargement and reddening of the scrotal sac, and an increase in the length and circumference of the penis (Schonfeld, 1969). These changes all involve primary sexual characteristics. Insofar as secondary sexual characteristics are concerned, no true pubic hair is present, although the male may have downy hair.

Pubescence

Issue to Consider

• What are the major events that occur in the pubescence phase of development?

The onset of pubescence occurs with the appearance of pubic hair and ends when pubic hair development is complete (Schonfeld, 1969). Figure 3.1 shows the changes involved in pubic hair development for adolescent females, and Figure 3.2 shows these changes for adolescent males.

In pubescence a growth spurt occurs as well. The peak velocity (speed) of growth in height and weight occurs during this phase. The adolescent growth spurt occurs about 2 years earlier in females than in males. Menarche occurs in females about 18 months after the maximum height increase of the growth spurt (Schonfeld, 1969).

In regard to the primary sexual characteristics, the vulva and clitoris of the female enlarge, and the testes of the male continue to enlarge, the scrotum grows and becomes pigmented, and the penis becomes longer and increases in circumference (Schonfeld, 1969). The changes in males are illustrated in Figure 3.3.

In regard to secondary sexual characteristics in females, there is a change from having breast buds to having the areola and nipple elevated to form the pri-

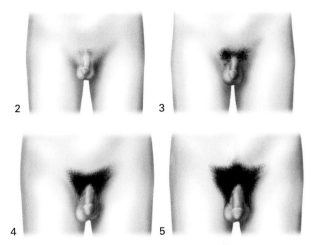

Figure 3.2 Stages of pubic hair development in boys.
(1) early prepubescent (not shown) in which there is no true pubic hair; (2) late prepubescent/early pubescent in which sparse growth of downy hair is mainly at base of penis; (3) pigmentation, coarsening, and curling, with an increase in amount of hair; (4) adult hair, but limited in area; (5) adult hair with horizontal upper border and spreading to thighs. (*Source:* Redrawn from Tanner, 1962.)

mary breast (Schonfeld, 1969). These changes are illustrated in Figure 3.4. In regard to males' secondary sexual characteristics, there is a deepening of the voice and pigmented axillary and facial hair appear, usually about 2 years after the emergence of pubic hair (Schonfeld, 1969).

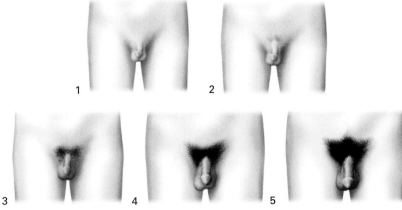

Figure 3.3 Stages of male genital development.
(1) prepubescence, in which the size of the testes and penis is like that in early childhood; (2) testes become larger, and scrotal skin reddens and coarsens; (3) continuation of Stage 2, with lengthening of penis; (4) penis enlarges in general size, and scrotal skin becomes pigmented; (5) adult genitalia. (*Source:* Redrawn from Tanner, 1962.)

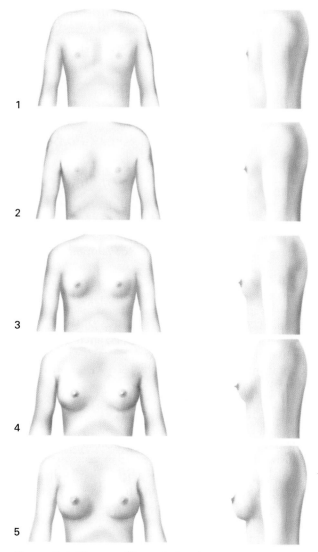

Figure 3.4 Stages of breast development in adolescent girls.
(1) prepubescent flat appearance; (2) small, raised breast bud; (3) general enlargement and raising of breast and areola; (4) areola and nipple form contour separate from that of breast; (5) adult breast—areola is in the same contour as breast. (*Source*: Redrawn from Tanner, 1962.)

Postpubescence

Issue to Consider

• What are the major bodily changes in the postpubescence phase?

Postpubescence starts when pubic hair growth is complete, when there is a decrease in the rate of growth in height, when there is completion of most of the changes in the primary and secondary sexual characteristics, and when the person is fertile and he or she can reproduce (Schonfeld, 1969). However, changes in the primary and secondary sexual characteristics continue. In males, the beard usually starts to grow in this phase, and in females there is further growth of axillary hair and breast development.

Conclusions About the Characteristics of Pubertal Maturation

Issue to Consider

• What are the limitations and variations in pubertal development?

The physical and physiological changes characterizing adolescence involve much more than just puberty. They include also changes spanning perhaps an entire decade of the life span and involving at least three phases of bodily change. It is important to recognize two points, however. First, the growth gains involved in pubertal maturation do not exist independently of limitations. Accompanying this growth is an increased risk for certain diseases. Eating disorders are a major example (discussed later in the chapter).

Second, although all males and females go through the changes of pubertal maturation in much the same sequence, people vary in the speed they mature. Some adolescents mature earlier than their peers; others mature later than the rest of their group. What is the basis of such differences? Does such variation matter for the individual's development? Does such variation complicate the nature of the physiological developmental task the adolescent must meet? If so, do the developments that occur correspond in any way to the stereotype that adolescence is a period of inevitable storm and stress (see Chapter 1), one linked (as hypothesized by Anna Freud, 1969; see Chapter 2) to the universal changes of puberty?

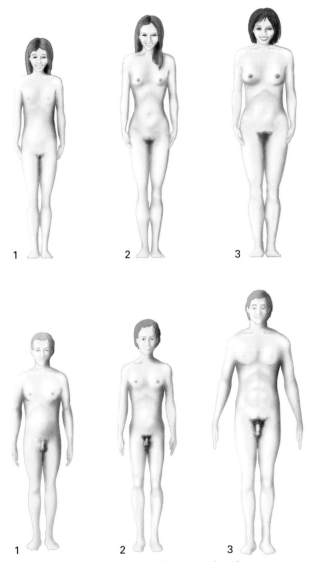

Figure 3.5 Variations in pubescent development. All three females are 12 3/4 years old, and all three males are 14 3/4 years old, but they are in different phases of change. (*Source:* Tanner, 1973.)

social implications of pubertal change, some negative and some positive. This variation is associated with the different peer group, familial, socioeconomic, and even historical contexts of the developing adolescent.

Social and Cultural Differences in the Timing of Pubertal Change

Issue to Consider
- What variables influence the timing and speed of pubertal maturation?

Early maturers develop faster than their same-age peers. They go through the periods of adolescent bodily change faster than average. **Late maturers** develop more slowly than do most of their same-age peers. They pass through the periods of adolescent bodily change slower than average. There are also youth who are **on-time maturers,** passing through the periods of bodily change at an average rate. In essence, then, although of the same age, the early maturer is accelerated in bodily growth and the late maturer is delayed.

Differences in rate of development lead to quite distinct differences in bodily appearance. As seen in Figure 3.5, all the females are of the same age, but "1" has the characteristics of prepubescence, "2" of pubescence, and "3" of postpubescence. Similar differences are seen with the three identically aged males shown in this figure.

Different rates of bodily change found in regard to pubertal maturation occur as a consequence of genetic differences (Comite et al., 1987) and in relation to social and cultural differences. To illustrate, consider one aspect of bodily change—**menarche.**

Early maturers Adolescents who attain the physical maturation characteristics of puberty earlier than the rest of their same-age peers.

Late maturers Adolescents who attain the physical maturation characteristics of puberty later than most of their same-age peers.

On-time maturers Adolescents who attain the physical maturation characteristics of puberty at the same time as most of their same-age peers.

Menarche Beginning of the first menstrual cycle.

The following sections address these questions. Consistent with the themes of diversity and context stressed in this book, there is little if any support for the stereotype of adolescence or for the view that pubertal change creates a necessary disruption in healthy psychological and social behavior. Instead, there are a range of behavioral and

Table 3-1	Median Age at Menarche in Several Populations		
Population or location	Median age, years	Population or location	Median age, years
Cuba		Tel Aviv, Israel	13.0
Negro	12.4	London, U.K.	13.1
White	12.4	Assam, India (city	
Mulatto	12.6	dwellers)	13.2
Cuba		Burma (city dwellers)	13.2
Negro	12.9	Uganda (wealthy Kampala)	13.4
White	13.0	Oslo, Norway	13.5
Mulatto	13.0	France	13.5
Hong Kong (wealthy		Nigeria (wealthy Ibo)	14.1
Chinese)	12.5	U.S.S.R. (rural Buriats)	15.0
Florence, Italy	12.5	South Africa (Transkei	
Wroclaw, Poland	12.6	Banfu)	15.0
Budapest, Hungary	12.8	Rwanda	
California, U.S.	12.8	Tutsi	16.5
Colombo, Ceylon	12.8	Hutu	17.1
Moscow, U.S.S.R.	13.0	New Guinea (Bundi)	18.8

Source: Jean Hiernaux, Ethnic Differences in Growth and Development, *Eugenics Quarterly,* 1968, 15. 12–21.

As shown in Table 3.1, there is a vast difference in the age of menarche in different cultures and in different social strata within a culture. The median age at menarche for Cuban blacks or whites is 12.4 years, the lowest age listed in Table 3.1, and the median age for people of the Bundi tribe of New Guinea is 18.8 years, the highest age shown.

These differences in age of menarche might relate to nutritional or health care differences associated with various social or cultural settings. For instance, differences in age of menarche within the same country are often seen between urban and rural areas. Tanner (1970, 1991) reports that in Romania the average age of menarche is 13.5 years in towns and 14.6 years in villages. Corresponding differences between town-reared and rural-reared children have been found in the former Soviet Union (13.0 and 14.3 years, respectively) and in India (12.8 and 14.2 years, respectively). In all of these countries, nutritional resources were less abundant in the rural setting.

The different availability of resources in different socioeconomic strata within a society is also associated with variation in the age of menarche. In Hong Kong, the age at menarche is 12.5 years for children of the rich, 12.8 years for those of average income levels, and 13.3 years for children of poor families (Tanner, 1970, 1991). In European countries, the range of socioeconomic status from rich to poor is associated with a range of about 2 to 4 months in age of menarche (Katchadourian, 1977). However, different studies of the relation between age of menarche and social class define social class differently. Although there is often a situation where the "poor" in one country may be starving while the poor in another society may have relatively adequate nutrition (Katchadourian, 1977), a relation between socioeconomic status and menarche is typically found.

The Role of Historical Differences in the Timing of Pubertal Change

Issue to Consider
• What is the secular trend, and what has the trend been in regard to adolescent bodily changes?

Adolescents of the same age may vary in their respective levels of physical maturity.

Adolescents seem to have matured at different rates in different historical periods. This relation between history and adolescent bodily changes is termed the **secular trend** (Garn, 1980; Katchadourian, 1977; Tanner, 1991). Since 1900, children of preschool age have been taller by an average of 1.0 centimeter and heavier by an average of 0.5 kilogram per decade (Katchadourian, 1977). The changes in height and weight occurring during the adolescent growth spurt have involved gains of 2.5 centimeters and 2.5 kilograms, respectively (Falkner, 1972; Katchadourian, 1977).

As shown in Figure 3.6, there has been a historical trend downward in the average age of menarche. Among European samples of youth there was a decrease of about 4 months per decade from about 1840 to about 1950 (Tanner, 1962, 1973, 1991). Although this rate of decrease seems to have slowed down, it has not stopped (Marshall & Tanner, 1986; Tanner, 1991). Within American samples, the decline in age of menarche seems to have stopped around 1940. Since that time, 12.5 years has been the expected age for menarche among European American, middle-class adolescents in the United States. In Japan, the most dramatic secular trend was evidenced. From the immediate post–

Secular trend Variation of adolescent bodily changes across history.

World War II years until about 1975, there was a decline of 11 months a decade in the average age of menarche (Marshall & Tanner, 1986). As suggested, the secular trend in menarche is generally ascribed to the improved health and nutrition of children and adolescents, influences moderated by historical, cultural, and socioeconomic variables affecting a given society or group.

The bodily changes of adolescence vary in relation to social, cultural, and historical settings. Given such variation, we may expect differences among adolescents in their rate of physical maturation. But if the pubertal changes of adolescence are so dependent on social, cultural, and historical conditions, may it also be the case that the implications of these biological changes for psychological and social development are also contextually influenced?

Figure 3.6 Historically declining age of menarche. (*Source*: Tanner, 1973.)

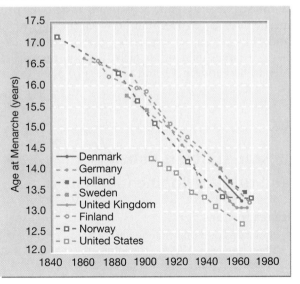

Implications of Differences Among Adolescents in Their Pubertal Maturation

Issue to Consider

- How is the influence of the hormonal changes of puberty consistent with the developmental systems idea?

The influence of the hormonal changes of puberty on psychological and social behavior and development during adolescence occurs in a manner consistent with the integrative developmental systems ideas we discussed in Chapters 1 and 2. The biological influences in adolescence occur in relation to physiological and social influences (Susman, 1997).

The research of Elizabeth J. Susman has been central in understanding these relations. Some of her recent research is presented in Meet the Researcher Box 3.1.

The findings of a study of a group of 75 premenarcheal European American middle- to upper-middle-class girls between the ages of 10 and 14 are consistent with Susman's relational perspective. Variables related to physical and physiological changes (breast development and weight), and variables related to psychological functioning (feelings of depression) and to social functioning (family relations) predicted age of menarche (Graber, Brooks-Gunn, & Warren, 1995). In turn, girls who become pregnant between the ages of 13 and 18 years do not experience menarche any earlier (or later) than other girls; that is, they reach menarche between 12 and 13 years of age (Ravert & Martin, 1997).

Research About Puberty and the Developmental System

Issues to Consider

- How does pubertal change and pubertal timing affect behavior? What is the interacting variable that causes pubertal influences on behavior?

- How does pubertal change and timing alter the relationship with the family?

Research aimed at understanding whether or how pubertal maturation influences an individual's development has taken one of two general approaches. First, studies have tried to determine whether pubertal change per se affects emotional and/or cognitive changes (Hill & Holmbeck, 1987; Hill et al., 1985a, 1985b; Papini & Datan, 1983; Steinberg, 1981) and, second, the effects of timing of pubertal maturation have been investigated (Brooks-Gunn, Petersen, & Eichorn, 1985). The second idea has been to determine if maturing earlier or later than is normative for one's sex-specific age group is associated with psychosocial functioning. One rationale for studying potential effects of pubertal timing is that, by assessing the extremes of normal variation, we may obtain a clearer view of more subtle effects associated with normative or on-time pubertal change.

One conclusion that can be drawn from these studies is that there exist few consistent (e.g., Nottelmann et al., 1987) direct effects of puberty or pubertal timing on emotional or cognitive functioning (e.g., Crockett & Petersen, 1987; Petersen, 1985, 1987) and certainly no strong effects (Linn & Petersen, 1985). Although some relationships between puberty and the development of problems such as depression, eating disorders, and norm-breaking behaviors have been identified (Alsaker, 1995), these associations have been linked to the developmental system of the adolescent.

To illustrate the nature of the links between puberty and psychological and social functioning, consider the findings of a study of over 400, mostly European American fifth through ninth graders living in the suburbs of Chicago. For girls, there was no relationship found between puberty and their moods or their mood changes (Richards & Larson, 1993). For boys, there were small relationships between being in a more advanced stage of puberty and positive mood, better attention, feelings of strength, and increased feelings of tension (Richards & Larson, 1993).

In contrast, in a sample of over 1,000 girls and over 1,200 boys from Bergen, Norway, adolescents' *perceptions* that they were early maturers (relative to their peers) were related in sixth-

MEET THE RESEARCHER BOX 3.1

ELIZABETH J. SUSMAN
SUCCESSFUL PASSAGES THROUGH PUBERTY AND PREGNANCY DURING ADOLESCENCE

The biological transitions that occur in development, like puberty and pregnancy, bring both opportunities for independence and new roles and risks for new problems. These changes may be welcomed by some adolescents but may lead to problems in other adolescents. In the case of puberty, rapid and pervasive changes occur in chemical messengers, called hormones, and in physical growth. For decades, scientists, parents, and adolescents have pondered over whether changes in hormones and growth, like increases in height, weight, and body proportions, are related to changes in moods and behavior, like depression and anxiety and aggressive behavior.

My colleagues and I have studied hormone change related to pubertal development and hormones secreted when adolescents are feeling stressed. The hormones that bring about pubertal development include estrogen and testosterone. The hormone secreted under stressful conditions is cortisol. When hormones were measured in adolescents during puberty, the hormones estrogen and testosterone were lower in boys with aggressive behavior than in boys who were not aggressive. In girls, estrogen was related to expressing anger toward parents, attempting to dominate parents, and other problem interactions with parents. In another aspect of the study, my colleagues and I showed that as testosterone levels increased, boys' ability to solve spatial problems also increased. To assess how the stress hormone cortisol changed during a challenging situation, it was measured at three different times when blood was being obtained for the hormones just mentioned. The stress of having blood drawn can change cortisol levels. Adolescents who increased in cortisol level during the challenging situation later developed more behavior problems and symptoms of depression than adolescents who showed no change in levels or who decreased in cortisol levels. An increase in cortisol levels during a stressful event is considered a risk factor for problems. In summary, the hormones that increase at puberty are related to aggressive behavior and emotions during adolescence. These findings do not mean that these behaviors or emotions are abnormal or that all adolescents have difficulty interacting with their parents during puberty. But hormones do appear to make a difference in the lives of adolescents at puberty.

Elizabeth J. Susman is the Jean Phillips Shibley Professor of Biobehavioral Health at The Pennsylvania State University. She was a co-editor of *Journal of Research on Adolescence* and participates in many government and foundation-sponsored activities related to health and development in adolescents.

My colleagues and I also have studied hormones and emotions in pregnant adolescents. As discussed for puberty, scientists and individuals responsible for the health care of adolescents have wondered whether the hormone changes that occur during pregnancy are related to moods in pregnant adolescents. The moods that adolescents sometimes experience, like depression, anger, and anxiety, are likely to become even more intense during pregnancy because of the hormone changes that occur as well as the changes that adolescents must make in their social lives while pregnant. Much to our surprise, the emotions of pregnant adolescents did not differ from emotions in adolescents of the same age who were not pregnant. As in the case of pubertal age adolescents, increases in cortisol levels in a challenging situation were related to emotions, in this case depression. Although change in cortisol level is considered a risk factor for problems, cortisol changes did not predict problems in the infants of these teens.

There is still much to be learned about how hormones affect emotions and behavior and even more to be learned about how behavior affects hormones and other physiological substances. Scientists from many different fields now are conducting research in the field of hormones, behavior, and brain development. This work is important and exciting as the findings will likely give insights into why some adolescents become depressed or aggressive whereas other adolescents experience no behavior problems or problematic changes in emotions.

through eighth-grade girls to poor body image and negative self-evaluation (Alsaker, 1992). In boys, the perception of late maturation was associated with negative self-evaluations, whereas early maturation was related to more positive self-evaluations (Alsaker, 1992). In a study of 52 young adolescent girls living in a midwestern suburban community, girls who felt they were experiencing pubertal change reported more negative moods and nervousness, and more variation in their negative moods, than did prepubertal girls (Buchanan, 1991).

Associations found between puberty level and change and emotional functioning vary from study to study for both boys and girls. Thus there is little if any support that emotional and cognitive changes are invariant, direct outcomes of puberty. To illustrate, consider some results of two major longitudinal studies of early adolescence, the Petersen Early Adolescence Study (EAS), an investigation of youth growing up in the suburbs of Chicago (Crockett & Petersen, 1987; Petersen, 1987), and the Lerner and Lerner Pennsylvania Early Adolescent Transitions Study (PEATS), an investigation of youth from a semirural area of northwestern Pennsylvania (Lenerz et al., 1987). Results of these studies are summarized in Table 3.2.

Similar variables were measured longitudinally in both studies. As you can see in this table, most relations studied were not significant. The few relations that are significant do not appear to be systematic or repeatable across studies. It might be concluded that pubertal change has little to do with an adolescent's psychological or social functioning, that the physiological developmental task is not so complicated after all, and, despite the vast number of bodily changes that occur in adolescence, there is little of importance to threaten or challenge the adolescent's sense of who he or she is.

Such conclusions would be incorrect. Pubertal change and pubertal timing do have fairly consistent and in many cases strong relationships with behavior. These relationships do not involve the *direct*, intrapsychic, inevitably stormy and stressful associations predicted in the stereotype of the period (A. Freud, 1969; Hall, 1904). The influence of an adolescent's pubertal characteristics on behavior involves interactions with his or her particular social context.

Influences of the Context on Puberty-Behavior Relations

Issue to Consider
- How does the social context influence the relation between puberty and adolescent behavior?

Several studies indicate that pubertal *change* can alter adolescents' social interactions and relationships with parents. Other studies suggest that pubertal *timing* may also influence young adolescents' relationships with parents (e.g., Clausen, 1975; Petersen, 1985; Savin-Williams & Small, 1986; Steinberg, 1987).

To illustrate these associations between puberty and family functioning, note that in some types of families more conflict and greater emotional distance is seen in relation to an adolescent's pubertal changes (e.g., Hill & Holmbeck, 1987; Hill et al., 1985a, 1985b; Papini & Datan, 1983; Steinberg, 1977, 1981, 1986; Steinberg & Hill, 1978). In a study of 85 mostly European American two-parent families with adolescents in grades 5 through 9, more advanced physical maturation in the youth was associated with the expression of *negative* affect by both mothers and fathers (Montemayor, Eberly, & Flannery, 1993). The level of parental and adolescent *positive* affect was not related to pubertal status.

These associations between adolescent pubertal change and relationships with parents may not necessarily be generalized to families of all racial/ethnic backgrounds. Among samples of primarily Mexican American boys and their families, pubertal maturation brought youth *closer* to their parents (Molina & Chassin, 1996). Puberty among these Latino youth is associated with greater parental social support and less intergenerational conflict than is the case for corresponding samples of European American samples of youth.

Steinberg (1981, 1988) found that increases in pubertal maturation were associated with different changes in "emotional distance" (that is, increased conflict and decreased closeness) between sons and their parents depending on the sex of the parent. Increased maturation in boys was associated with fewer interruptions of and more deference toward their fathers, with an increase in the tendency for boys to interrupt their mothers during conversa-

Table 3-2	Summary of the Relations Between Pubertal Status and Psychosocial Functioning in the Petersen Early Adolescent Study (EAS) and the Lerner and Lerner Pennsylvania Early Adolescent Transitions Study (PEATS)

	EAS						PEATS					
	Boys			Girls			Boys			Girls		
Psychosocial Variable	6th	7th	8th	6th	7th	8th	Time 1	Time 2	Time 3	Time 1	Time 2	Time 3
School achievement	NS	NS	NS	NS	NS	NS	*	*	*	NS	NS	NS
Standardized achievement	—	—	—	—	—	—	*	*	NS	NS	NS	NS
Cognitive ability/IA	NS	NS	NS	NSM	NSM	NS	*	NS	NS	NS	*	NS
Temperament (e.g., Mood)	NS	*	NSM	NS	NS	NSM	NS	NS	NS	NS	NS	NS
Self-perceived competence:												
Appearance	NS	NS	NS	NS	*	*	NS	NS	NS	NS	NS	NS
Scholastic	—	—	—	—	—	—	NS	NS	NS	NS	NS	NS
Social	—	—	—	—	—	—	NS	NS	NS	NS	NS	NS
Behavior/Conduct	—	—	—	—	—	—	NS	NS	*	NS	NS	NS
Physical	—	—	—	—	—	—	NS	NS	NS	NS	NS	*
Self-Worth	—	—	—	—	—	—	NS	NS	*	NS	NS	NS

Note: "—" = variable not measured; "NS" = Non significant result; "*" = Significant effect; "NSM" = Significant univariate effect in the absence of a significant multivariate effect. Time 1, Time 2, and Time 3 are the Beginning, Middle, and End of 6th grade, respectively.

tions and with a decrease in deference to their mothers.

Indicative of increased conflicts in the mother-son relationship during periods of pubertal growth, Steinberg found that mothers showed a tendency to increasingly interrupt their sons during conversations. However, mothers' deference to sons increased after the boys reached the height of their pubertal maturation (Grotevant, 1998; Steinberg, 1981, 1988). In contrast, among seventh-grade girls menarche was followed by a withdrawal of positive affect and a temporary period of conflict, especially between daughters and mothers (Holmbeck & Hill, 1988; Grotevant, 1998).

Despite such implications of pubertal maturation on adolescent-parent relationships, Grotevant (1998) notes that the relationship between the biological changes of adolescence and the relationships of youth with their parents often involves quite contradictory behaviors. Grotevant notes that there is both distancing from parents and a tendency for youth to use their parents as a "buffer" (as a source of support and protection)

Although adolescents may at times distance themselves from parents, they also typically remain attached to them.

against some of the potential social pressures that may be linked to looking and feeling more physically mature. For instance, among seventh-grade males and females, increases in pubertal maturation were generally associated with decreased attachments to mothers and fathers; however, higher levels of attachment to mothers and fathers were linked to lower levels of depression and to lessened social anxiety (Papini, Roggman, and Anderson, 1991).

There have been repeated demonstrations that the social context influences the relation between puberty and adolescent behavior and development in numerous ways. In regard to pubertal change, the research of Simmons and her colleagues (e.g., Simmons & Blyth, 1987; Simmons, Carlton-Ford, & Blyth, 1987) has shown that the relationship between pubertal changes in girls and their self-esteem involves the co-occurrence of contextual change, that is, the transition to junior high school (see Chapter 11 for a fuller discussion of the relations between school transitions and adolescent development). The research of Dornbusch and his colleagues (e.g., Dornbusch et al., 1981) indicates that the social context can moderate any potential effect of puberty on behavior. Social norms regarding the appropriate age for dating, rather than pubertal maturation, determined adolescents' heterosexual dating behaviors.

The research of Brooks-Gunn (1987) indicates that the particular social context within which an adolescent functions moderates the link between pubertal timing and behavior. Brooks-Gunn (1987) studied adolescent girls who were enrolled in highly competitive and physically strenuous schools for ballet and a comparison group of adolescent girls enrolled in a regular school setting. Within the ballet schools, extremely strong pressures existed for especially thin body builds, whereas no such intense pressures existed in the social contexts of the comparison group girls. Brooks-Gunn (1987) expected that in the com-

parison group, neither late nor on-time maturation would be related to a measure of body image, even though on-time maturation was related to high body weight in both groups. Brooks-Gunn also predicted that the pressures of the dancers' social context would mean that late maturation would be related to a better body image than would be the case with on-time maturation. As shown in Figure 3.7, these predictions were supported by Brooks-Gunn's findings.

Magnusson and his colleagues (e.g., Magnusson, Stattin, & Allen, 1986; Stattin & Magnusson, 1990) found that the relation between girls' early maturation and their problem behaviors was moderated by the specific characteristics of their peer context. Early maturing girls with older friends tend to break more norms (see Figure 3.8) and expect fewer sanctions from peers if they break norms than is the case for early maturing girls without older friends (see Figure 3.9). Meet the Researcher Box 3.2 presents more information about the work of David Magnusson.

In a 4-year longitudinal study of about 200 girls, early maturation was associated with more psychological distress than was the case in regard to on-time or late maturation (Ge, Conger, & Elder, 1996). The early maturing girls were more vulnerable to prior psychological problems, deviant peer

The pressures of competing, for example, in ballet, may complicate the ability of the adolescent to cope with the physical transitions of puberty.

pressures, and hostile feelings from their fathers. However, the association between maturational timing and distress was linked to the nature of the girls' peer groups. If early maturing girls had peer groups during the seventh through ninth grades composed of both boys and girls, they were more distressed in the tenth grade than were early maturing girls who had peer groups in earlier grades composed only of girls (Ge et al., 1996).

Conclusions About the Implications of Puberty for Psychological and Social Behavior

Adolescents vary in their rate of physical maturation. Although this variation influences their personality and social behavior, it is not a direct influence. Indirect, mediated, or interactive pubertal effects exist through their relation and moderation of the social context (Lerner, 1985, 1987; Petersen, 1985, 1987). The adolescent meets the developmental task of dealing with his or her changed body and physiology through interaction with the social context. Some of these interactions between puberty and psychological and social functioning may be adaptive, but others may cause problems for adolescents.

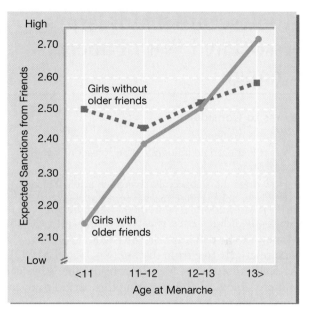

Figure 3.8
Relation between expected peer sanctions for norm-breaking and menarcheal age for girls with and without older friends. (*Source:* Magnusson et al., 1986.)

Figure 3.9
Relation between norm-breaking and menarcheal age for girls with and without older friends. (*Source:* Magnusson et al., 1986.)

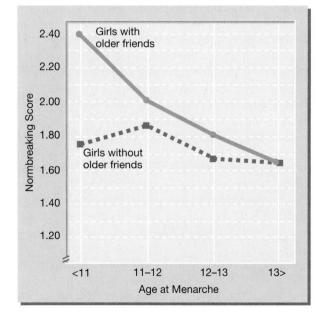

Figure 3.7
Mean body image score for dancer and comparison students by time of menarche. Note. Scale range is from 1 to 6. (*Source:* Brooks-Gunn, 1987.)

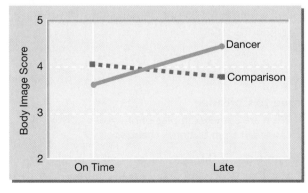

Adolescent Health Issues Associated With Pubertal Change

Issues to Consider

- What is resiliency?
- What is the prime influence on adolescent health problems?
- How does the sleep cycle change in adolescence, and how does it affect adolescent behavior?

Generally, adolescence is a period of health (Koch, Maney, & Susman, 1993; Pattishall, 1984). It is a time relatively free from disease (Koch et al., 1993). As well, adolescents possess considerable physical and physiological ability during this period to overcome adversity, or to be *resilient.*

Indeed, even chronically ill adolescents may show considerable **resiliency** to the stress of their disease. In fact, adolescents with chronic disease can be remarkably like their healthy peers. For instance, Italian adolescents with thalassemia major (a type of blood disorder) have normal psychological and social development and self-esteem as high if not better than their healthy peers (Zani, Di Palma, & Vullo, 1995). In turn, the experience of life stressors or of variation in social support by adolescents with juvenile rheumatic disease is unrelated to the outcomes of the disease on their health (Timko et al., 1995), although—as with healthy adolescents—increases in negative life events, life stressors, and problematic social support does impact their psychological and social functioning.

Moreover, adolescents may benefit psychologically when they pursue healthy lifestyles. For example, valuing health and positive health behavior was related to self-esteem among 12- to 13-year-old and 16- to 17-year-old Spanish youth (Torres, Fernandez, & Maceira, 1995). In turn, adolescents' views about health may be influenced by their families. For instance, adolescent self-reported physical health is linked to their parents' levels of education (Wickrama et al., 1998).

Of course, adolescents are also confronted with serious challenges to their health (Koch et al., 1993; Millstein,

Resiliency Presence of considerable physical and physiological ability to overcome adversities.

1989; Pattishall, 1984). The adolescent's own behavior is the major influence on these health problems. Consistent with the selection, optimization, and compensation (SOC) model (Baltes, 1987; Baltes and Baltes, 1990; Freund & Baltes, 1998) of adolescent behavior discussed in Chapter 2, youth select courses of action that influence their adaptation and health. Accidents (e.g., via motor vehicles), suicides, substance use and abuse, unsafe sexual behaviors, violence to and by adolescents, eating disorders, and even insufficient rest are examples of the problems of adolescent health affected by the behavior of youth. In later chapters, we discuss many of these problems (for example, in Chapter 10 we discuss problems relating to adolescent sexuality and in Chapter 13 we review problems linked to substance use and to crime and violence). Nevertheless, it is useful here to illustrate how adolescent behavior may influence adolescent health. In turn, it is important in the present chapter to discuss health problems linked to pubertal change.

To begin to illustrate, then, the association between adolescent behavior and health, it is useful to note that sleep and waking cycles change significantly during adolescence (Wolfson & Carskadon, 1998). Many of these changes are due to choices made by the adolescent. In a study of over 3,000 Rhode Island high school students, self-reported total sleep time on both school and weekend nights decreased by about 50 minutes from age 13 to age 19 (Wolfson & Carskadon, 1998). The decrease in sleep was associated with later bedtimes rather than earlier wake-up times. Students with better grades got, on average, more sleep and went to bed earlier than students who were doing poorly in school. However, all adolescents, despite their grades, did not get enough sleep, and this lack of sleep interfered with their daytime functioning (Wolfson & Carskadon, 1998).

Puberty and Health

Issue to Consider

- What are some examples of physical problems that can result from pubertal changes?

Beyond the influences of the behavioral choices made by adolescents, pubertal changes can also

MEET THE RESEARCHER BOX 3.2

DAVID MAGNUSSON
LONGITUDINAL STUDY OF PUBERTY AND ADOLESCENT DEVELOPMENT AND ADAPTATION

My own interest in research on adolescence has two roots. Substantively, it emanates from my experiences as an elementary school teacher and as a school psychologist responsible for a class of male and female problem youngsters in a Stockholm suburb in the mid-1950s. In terms of research strategy and methodology, my interest stems from my dissatisfaction with the kind of knowledge about adolescence that the literature offered at that time and from my experiences of teaching psychometrics at the university.

When I had to deal with and sometimes make decisions about young people in real-life situations—not as an observer in the lab—I asked myself, over and over again, questions like these: Why do some girls who mature earlier biologically than their age-mates often show what adults call norm-breaking behavior? Does this behavior have long-term effects on their life careers? What is the developmental background of deviant behaviors among male youngsters and what are the implications for the future? Why is it that most of the boys who come from so-called risky home environments do not become criminals and/or alcoholics? What are the protective factors that lead to a positive rather than a negative development?

In order to contribute empirical answers to these questions in the framework of knowledge about the processes involved in individual development in general, I initiated the longitudinal research program IDA (Individual Development and Adaptation), in which the first data were collected in 1965. The main cohort consisted of all boys and girls, about 1,300 at an average age of 10, attending the general school system in a community of reasonable size in central Sweden. The program is still active, since 1996 under the leadership of Lars R. Bergman.

Two issues pertaining to puberty and adolescence have been the foci of studies under the program in collaboration with colleagues and students. The first is the timing and synchronization of girls' mental, biological, and behavioral aspects and the sociocultural demands in terms of rules, regulations, and role expectations that a girl has to handle and master during this period and the long-term implications of the way these problems are solved. At present, female life careers, focusing on the developmental background of adult mental and physical health, are being studied after the collection of relevant data for the females at the age of 43–44. These data now provide a unique opportunity to study the role for the adult life situation of the girl's transformation from a girl into a woman during puberty and early adolescence.

The second focus was, for a long time, the role of psychological, biological, and social factors in the developmental background of deviant behaviors among male youngsters and young adults. Recently, my own interest has been extended to include the study of what promotes human strengths and positive development. In theoretical terms, the design, implementation, and interpretation of studies within the program have been guided by the proposition that an individual functions and develops as an integrated, indivisible organism, intentionally involved in reciprocal, dynamic interaction with the environment. At present I am concerned with the processes involved in the very early establishment of the integrated individual system of mental, biological, and behavioral aspects that form the platform for further developmental processes through childhood, puberty, adolescence, adulthood, and aging.

David Magnusson is Olof Eneroth professor emeritus of psychology at the Department of Psychology, Stockholm University. He is the author of *Individual Development from an Interactional Perspective* (1988). As vice president of the European Science Foundation, he initiated and chaired the European Network on Longitudinal Studies on individual Development, from which eight volumes on developmental issues were published during the years 1988 to 1993.

In planning the longitudinal program and in designing, implementing, and interpreting studies on specific developmental issues, I have gained from my early psychometric work and from teaching psychometrics at the university. My experiences of how psychometric methods were used and misused in experimental and applied settings taught me the importance of applying methods that match the character of the developmental processes in which we are interested. This issue has occupied much of my time and does so still. Good solutions to this matching issue are, to my mind, one of the most important tasks for further progress in research on puberty and adolescence.

impact adolescent health. Variations in the rate of bodily changes in adolescence can be sufficiently extreme to affect the health of the young person. For example, **delayed puberty** and **precocious puberty** are related to the insufficient production or the early production of hormones (Cutler, 1991). These disorders are elicited by early or late hormone production. However, although primarily biological in origin, whether they are treated or whether they cause long-term problems for the person, depends on the availability in society of the necessary medical treatments (Comite et al., 1987).

Initially, pubertal changes that cause physical problems may be known only to the adolescent. Painful menstruation, known as **dysmenorrhea,** and the failure to menstruate, known as **amenorrhea,** may have both medical and emotional causes. Other physical disorders are noticeable to others. Acne causes great concern to adolescents because it is visible to others. It is the most common medical condition during this period of life. About 85% of adolescents have acne at least some time during the adolescent period (Pattishall, 1984).

As a consequence of pubertal change, variations in height, weight, and muscle and fat distributions arise and adolescents often become preoccupied with their own bodies (Elkind, 1967; Lerner, 1987; McCandless, 1970; Perkins & Lerner, 1995). As illustrated by the conversation between Tina and her mother that opened this chapter, this preoccupation can result in particularly trying problems for parents. Changes in the adolescent's bodily appearance may puzzle and challenge a parent, particularly when their child(ren) are just beginning to undergo the changes of puberty. Implications for Parenting Box 3.1 describes these challenges for parents and suggests ways in which they may deal with their adolescents' bodily changes.

Eating Disorders

Issues to Consider
- What are some examples of eating disorders?
- What are the implications of having an eating disorder?
- What are some factors that may influence the existence of an eating disorder?

Adolescents' concerns with their own bodily changes can result in problems for youth. Adolescents are preoccupied with their weight and with controlling their appearance through their eating behaviors. In a sample of more than 1,200 male and female African American and European American high school students, about 50% of all males, about 66% of the African American females, and about 75% of the European American females reported that they had lost 5 or more pounds through dieting (Emmons, 1996). Although the dieting and the nondieting adolescents did not differ in their respective heights, the dieters were about 14 pounds heavier than the nondieters (Emmons, 1996). The majority of dieters were not overweight. In fact, some were underweight (Emmons, 1996).

Eating behaviors of adolescents involve not only unnecessary dieting but also problems of eating that are detrimental to their health and may even threaten their lives. Adolescent girls are more likely than adolescent boys to have eating disorders such as anorexia nervosa or bulimia. However, both sexes may show attitudes toward food and to eating behaviors that are dangerous. These problematic attitudes may exist even at elementary school levels and are often predictors of disordered eating. In a study of fourth-through sixth-grade youth from North Dakota, 3% to 4% of girls reported self-induced vomiting and/or secretly throwing away food to avoid gaining weight (Moreno & Thelen, 1995).

In a sample of over 500 adolescent 13- and 14-year-olds from Spain, 12.4% of the girls and 8.3% of the boys had risky attitudes toward eating (Canals et al., 1996). For both boys and girls, low self-esteem and high anxiety were related to problematic attitudes about eating. The attitudes of the girls, however, were more prototypic of pathological eating disorders than was the case for the boys' attitudes (Canals et al., 1996). Heavy and obese male and female adolescents were at high risk of having an actual eating disorder.

Obesity can be an outcome of a type of eating disorder that affects a significant

Delayed puberty Being behind schedule, for a given age group, in reaching puberty.

Precocious puberty Early or premature puberty.

Dysmenorrhea Difficult or painful menstruation.

Amenorrhea Failure to menstruate.

Obesity Condition characterized by an excessive accumulation of fat in the body.

minority of adolescents. When a person is 20% above the average weight associated with others of his or her height, he or she can be classified as obese (Katchadourian, 1977). There is no known cure for obesity, although increasing regular physical activity and following a moderately low-calorie diet may help an adolescent maintain normal body fat levels (Freedland & Dwyer, 1991). Unfortunately, many American youth, particularly females, follow rather sedentary lifestyles (Freedland & Dwyer, 1991).

Less frequent, but even more severe in its effects than overeating and not exercising are **anorexia nervosa** and **bulimia.** Girls are 10 times more likely to be affected by these disorders than are boys (Litt, 1991). In industrialized nations, the rates of anorexia nervosa and bulimia have increased about 400% over the last 20 years (Litt, 1991). Anorexia nervosa involves severe loss of weight (a 25% loss of normal weight is not unusual) with no known medical explanation. Today, anorexia nervosa may involve up to 3% of the total adolescent population. Bulimia, a disorder characterized by uncontrolled binge eating and purging behaviors, also has a reported prevalence among adolescent females of about 3%. But it may be even more widespread than anorexia nervosa (Leon, 1991) because bulimia is harder to detect. Bulimia is not typically accompanied by severe weight loss. It may not be until the problem has existed for some time, that is, at a point where binge-purge episodes may occur as often as 10 to 12 times a day (Leon, 1991), that signs (such as gastrointestinal problems and tooth decay) become evident. Both anorexia nervosa and bulimia can cause severe medical problems and result in death. In advanced anorexia nervosa, heart muscle tissue begins to metabolize, which can cause heart attacks. The mortality rate for anorexia nervosa is estimated to be between 5% and 23% (Leon, 1991).

There are both psychological and contextual influences on eating disorders. In addition to influences from attitudes and body appearance that were noted earlier, family variables can influence eating disorders in adolescence. Relationship and interaction patterns of the individuals within families of girls with bulimia show less attachment and less autonomy among family members than is the case within families with an adolescent daughter without bulimia (Ratti, Humphreys, & Lyons, 1996). Among adolescents with anorexia nervosa, as compared to normal adolescents, there is a greater likelihood of a history of family depression and alcohol or drug abuse or dependence and feelings of personal ineffectiveness than among adolescents without anorexia nervosa (Lyon et al., 1997).

Family influences on adolescents' eating problems occur in relation to the influences of peers. In a study of more than 800 Japanese adolescent girls in grades 7 through 11, influences of both parents and peers were found (Mukai, 1996). During earlier grades, maternal influences were greater than peer influences. At higher grade levels (grades 10 and 11), peer interactions had the most influence on girls' eating problems. Among 12- and 13-year-old girls, dating is associated with both dieting and disordered eating, especially among youth who recently experienced menarche (Cauffman & Steinberg, 1966).

> **Anorexia nervosa** Eating disorder characterized by low body weight due to a person's misperception of his or her body image and by the mistaken belief that he or she is overweight.
>
> **Bulimia** Eating disorder characterized by self-induced binge eating and purging behavior.

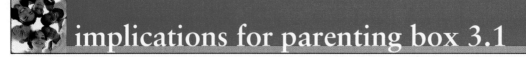

implications for parenting box 3.1

My Body Is So Ugly!

With the bathroom door locked, 12-year-old Anya carefully examines her still shower-damp body. She pokes disgustedly at her stomach. A year ago, her body felt comfortable and familiar. But the one in the mirror has new curves, and hair she isn't sure she likes. Maybe she should try that diet Becky told her about. Sighing, Anya pulls on her oversize black sweatshirt.

To their parents, it often seems as if young teenagers and preteens such as Anya are obsessed with their bodies, and that they are determined that their weight, height, and shape be regarded as desirable, or at least acceptable, to their peers. In fact, by age 7—if not sooner—children know which body shapes are considered best. By the early teens, the forms that children's bodies take become crucial to their sense of who they are.

All children this age will complain from time to time about being the wrong size or shape, even when they seemingly fit well within the norm for their peer group or their family. When a child becomes obsessed with appearance, however, there is genuine cause for concern. This is particularly true for young girls: because of the pressure they feel to remain slim in order to be considered attractive, they suffer from body-image problems more often than boys do.

In general, your best response to these complaints is to listen and then to reassure your child that everyone's body goes through awkward changes around this age. Make sure, though, that you don't supply your child with so much sympathy that you make the problem bigger than it is. For example, if your daughter is upset because she looks "dumpy" in a dress she likes, you can commiserate with her briefly by saying, "I remember how frustrating it was when my body was changing. We all grow out of it, though, thank goodness. In the meantime, let's try to find a dress that is better suited to your figure."

Girls' early maturity can cause anxieties

Much of the confusion preteens feel about their bodies has its origins, unsurprisingly, in puberty. On average, the first period for a girl arrives when she is between $11\frac{1}{2}$ and 12 years old, with changes in body hair and shape, including breast development, starting even earlier. Because girls typically reach puberty two years earlier than boys, most 10- or 11-year-old girls are bigger and taller than their male counterparts—ironically enough, just at the time when boys begin really wanting to be taller, and girls trimmer.

While the changes that come with puberty often make life difficult for girls, with boys the reverse is frequently true. Puberty, for them, means more weight and bigger muscles, in addition to sexual development—all physical qualities that we are taught to admire. Therefore, boys who mature early tend to be popular and are more likely to be seen as leaders by peers and adults.

Although these social advantages may last throughout life, it is also often the case that early maturers, by the time they're finished growing, are no bigger or stronger than the late bloomers; the seventh-grade sports hero isn't necessarily destined for the major leagues.

But how can you prepare your early-blooming athlete for a more competitive future without deflating his pride at his accomplishments? You might try saying something along the lines of, "I'm very proud of what a good football player you are. But you know, other boys are going to catch up to you in size eventually, so if you want to continue to be a strong competitor, you have to keep practicing."

Late-blooming boys need your reassurance

If your son is distressed because—for the time being, at least—he's shorter and less muscular than his peers, you can help him in several ways. First of all, you might tell him something like, "You know, it's normal for some boys to mature more slowly than others. I realize that it's hard to be patient sometimes, but your time will come, and if you practice and exercise now, it will really pay off later on."

Meanwhile, build your son's self-confidence by encouraging activities that set his intellectual or artistic abilities to good advantage while also promoting sports that are appropriate to his body build. Gymnastics and soccer are often well suited to shorter boys, whereas tall, slim boys often excel at track and field or basketball.

While puberty is often at the root of differences in body build among children this age, other factors such as obesity can play a harmful role. Research shows that pre-teens see being fat as a greater physical obstacle to popularity even than missing an arm or a leg. In one landmark study, youth were shown drawings of children who were disabled along with children who were obese: youth consistently chose the fat children as the ones they would least like to be, or to be friends with.

Unfortunately, although researchers aren't exactly sure why, a majority of preteen girls want their weight to be below average, and therefore are often unhappy with themselves for having what medical experts consider a normal, healthy weight. A University of Vermont study of 1,500 teenagers found that at any given time, two-thirds of girls between the ages of 13 and 18 were trying to lose weight. Most of these girls were considered to be of normal weight. (By contrast, many of the boys were trying to beef up.)

Diet-conscious girls need your attention

If your daugher is constantly dieting, chances are good that she's not getting the nutrients she needs for a body that is still growing. She may also be forming a pattern of dieting and binging that will carry into adulthood, with adverse long-term health consequences. Should she frequently complain of being overweight when she clearly is not, or should there be a sudden, unexplained shift in her eating habits accompanied by changes in her mood, then she may be having problems accepting her weight.

How can you help her? Start by examining your own attitudes and habits. Do you often complain of feeling fat, or compare your figure unfavorably with those of models in magazines or on television? Do you fluctuate between restricting your diet and indulging yourself? If so, without realizing it, you may be encouraging your child to dislike her postpuberty body.

Whether your child imagines that she is heavy or is genuinely overweight, you can best address the problem by focusing not on her eating habits but on your family's. Stick to a sensible, nutritious meal plan, and keep the emphasis on health rather than weight so that your daughter can think of changing her body in positive terms rather than negative ones. If you criticize her eating choices too often, or forbid her to eat certain foods, you'll only create power struggles that won't do either of you any good.

Finally, keep reminding your preteen that her body is still working toward its eventual shape, and that while her body's shape and size are hard to control at this time in her life, she still has control over something that's much more important—her good health.

Source: Lerner, R. M., & Olson, C. K. (1995, February). My body is so ugly! *Parents,* pp. 87–88.

Conclusions

In adolescence, people experience the physical and physiological changes of puberty. The timing of puberty is influenced by the social, cultural, economic, medical, and historical contexts of youth. The implications of pubertal change for the health of the adolescent and for his or her psychological and social functioning occurs in relation to the complex developmental system within which the young person is embedded. Puberty does affect psychological and social life, but the behavioral selections made by youth and the influences of their peers, parents, and culture also affect the presence and impact of puberty.

Summary

- Many adolescents feel unprepared for pubertal changes and report a need for more information about the nature and implications of pubertal change.
- Three stages of adolescence span the second decade of life: early adolescence (from 10 to 14 or 15 years of age), middle adolescence (from 15 to 17 years of age), and late adolescence (from 18 to 20 years of age).
- The prepubescent phase is when some of the physical and physiological changes of adolescence have begun, but most are yet to occur. The pubescent phase is when most of the bodily changes that will occur have been initiated. The postpubescent phase is when most of the bodily changes have already occurred.
- Pubertal maturation and bodily changes involve changes in hormones that are released from endocrine glands. When hormones are released, they stimulate the secretions of sex steroids, which results in the physical and physiological changes of pubertal maturation.
- Puberty is the point at which a person can reproduce, but it is only one event in the pubescent phase, which brings the person from childhood to adulthood.
- Primary sexual characteristics are present at birth and involve internal and external genitalia. Secondary sexual characteristics develop during the pre- through postpubescent phases.
- Prepubescence begins with the first indication of sexual maturation and ends with the first appearance of pubic hair. Pubescence occurs with the appearance of pubic hair and ends when pubic hair development is complete. Postpubescence starts when pubic hair growth is complete and ends when the person is fertile and can reproduce.

- There is variation in the speed of pubertal maturation. A person can be an early maturer, an on-time maturer, or a late maturer. The different rates of development occur because of genetic, social, and cultural differences.
- The secular trend is the relation between history and adolescent bodily changes.
- There are few, if any, consistent direct effects of puberty or pubertal timing on emotional or cognitive functioning. The effects of pubertal change and timing are influenced by the adolescent's social context.
- Adolescents as a group are resilient and have physical and physiological abilities to overcome adversity.
- Adolescents' behaviors are the major influence on their health problems. Sleep and waking cycles also change significantly during this period, and adolescents do not get enough sleep.
- Pubertal changes can lead to physical problems, such as dysmenorrhea (painful menstruation), amenorrhea (a failure to menstruate), and acne.
- Adolescents as a group are preoccupied with their bodily appearance, which can lead to eating behaviors detrimental to their health.
- Examples of eating disorders include overeating to the point of obesity, anorexia nervosa, and bulimia.
- Eating disorders can lead to severe medical problems, and even death.
- There are both psychological and contextual influences on eating disorders, such as attitudes, body appearance, and family variables.

Discussion Topics

1. Why is it important for adolescents to be better prepared for the changes associated with pubertal maturation? How can this preparation occur?

2. Why might the vast bodily changes associated with pubertal maturation create difficulty in meeting the developmental task of defining the self?

3. Do you think the effects of the variation in the speed and timing of pubertal maturation are the same for males and females? Do you think the differences are more difficult for one gender or the other?

4. What is the relationship between the social context of adolescents, pubertal maturation, and behavior? Give examples.

5. How might the knowledge that context influences the relation between pubertal maturation and behavior be used to help prepare adolescents and their parents for the many changes that can occur?

6. How does the adolescent's behavior affect his or her health? What interventions can be done to promote healthy development? Why should parents try to encourage adolescents to sleep more?

7. Pubertal changes can lead to physical problems that are known only to the person or that are noticeable to others. Do you think one is worse than the other? Why or why not?

8. What are some of the social/cultural contexts that lead to eating disorders?

9. In today's society, do you think males have similar issues with body image that are manifested in eating disorders? Do you think the issues might manifest themselves in a different way? Why is it more of a current issue?

10. Why do you think obesity as an outcome of an eating disorder gets less attention from the media?

11. What various selection, optimization, and compensation behaviors might an adolescent with an eating disorder go through?

Key Terms

amenorrhea (p. 76)
androgens (p. 62)
anorexia nervosa (p. 77)
bulimia (p. 77)
delayed puberty (p. 76)
dysmenorrhea (p. 76)
early maturers (p. 65)
endocrine glands (p. 61)
estrogens (p. 62)

exocrine glands (p. 61)
hormones (p. 61)
late maturers (p. 65)
menarche (p. 65)
obesity (p. 76)
on-time maturers (p. 65)
postpubescent phase (p. 61)
precocious puberty (p. 76)
prepubescent phase (p. 61)

primary sexual characteristics (p. 62)
pubertal maturation (p. 60)
puberty (p. 61)
pubescent phase (p. 61)
resiliency (p. 74)
secondary sexual characteristics (p. 62)
secular trend (p. 67)
steroids (p. 61)

4

COGNITIVE DEVELOPMENT

Mr. Stevens thought he had made a neutral observation. The arrangements his daughter Jennifer was making to get her and Shelia from the mall to Stefanie's house and then to the party at Gloria's that evening seemed unnecessarily complicated. There was no reason, he commented, that the girls had to stop first at Stefanie's. It would require that he do all sorts of criss-crossing around town. Why not just meet Stefanie at the party?

His daughter could not believe her father had interjected himself into the situation, with such an obtuse comment at that. "Dad, you just don't seem to understand," she sighed with exasperation.

"But Jennifer, honey, I . . ."

"Stop," Jennifer shouted. "You always do this. Why don't you just admit that you're wrong?" Jennifer turned away from her father and stomped angrily to her room.

Mr. Stevens sat there not understanding what had just happened.

In the early portions of adolescence, interactions between youth and their parents seem to be marked by disagreement and conflict. As illustrated by the interaction between Jennifer and her father, these types of exchanges involve adolescents' beliefs that what they know differs from what their parents know. These differences in knowledge, or cognition, are associated with often intense emotions on the part of the young person and with behaviors that reflect assertiveness and social independence.

The adolescent years involve intertwined changes in cognition and personality, and there exist important individual differences in key features of adolescent development. This variation is influenced by the social, cultural, and broader ecological context within which the adolescent lives.

Some of the diversity that exists in adolescence is associated with problems in development, especially when there are problems as well in the settings within which adolescents live. Programs that address problems associated with adolescent cognition and personality development have to be designed to be responsive to the particular contextual circumstances of the diverse youth that may participate in them. These emphases on diversity and context help frame a discussion of the cognitive processes involved in adolescent development.

LEARNING OBJECTIVES

1. To recognize that, in adolescence, cognition changes in two ways: Adolescents have more quantitative knowledge, and they think about their world in qualitatively different ways.

2. To understand that standardized tests and the IQ scores associated with them have been developed and widely used to assess intelligence quantitatively.

3. To identify the bases of the wide-held debates about what psychological characteristics are actually measured by intelligence tests.

4. To recognize that variation in quantitative intelligence is influenced by the social domain and that qualitative features of cognition constitute a key dimension of cognitive development.

5. To recognize that academic achievement is a factor that influences cognitive competence and academic achievement and is itself affected by multiple levels of the context of human development.

6. To appreciate that the academic achievements of youth from different cultural backgrounds differ due, primarily, to socialization experiences beginning in childhood and that, even within a cultural group, family and peer variables have an influence on academic achievement.

7. To understand that, in Piaget's theory, cognitive development involves the relation between the person and the context and that the person-context relation involves two processes: *assimilation* and *accommodation*.

8. To understand that, to Piaget, the goal of cognitive development is to create an *equilibration* between assimilation and accommodation.

9. To understand the basis of egocentrism and recognize that overcoming the egocentrism prototypic of each stage of cognitive development leads the person to attain the cognitive development most central to that stage and that the cognitive attainment of one stage leads the person to the egocentrism of the next stage.

10. To understand the defining characteristics of formal operational thinking, especially the INRC group.

11. To understand characteristics of adolescent egocentrism such as the *imaginary audience* and the *personal fable*.

12. To recognize that, across the formal operational stage, social thought becomes less egocentric and more responsive to societal conventions and the particular social audience or context to which it is directed and that it is increasingly more reflective of abstract principles of social organization.

13. To recognize that it is through interaction with peers and elders, and, most importantly, with the assumption of adult roles and responsibilities, that the adolescent decenters and the egocentrism of this stage diminishes.

Dimensions of Adolescent Cognitive Development

Issue to Consider

• How does cognition change during the adolescent period?

In adolescence, cognition changes in at least two ways. First, adolescents know *more* about their world. Increases in how much adolescents know, as measured by changes in their scores on tests of mathematics, reading, or spatial reasoning, reflect quantitative alterations in adolescents' knowledge. They may know more math, moving from algebra, to geometry, to calculus. Second, there are also *qualitative* changes in adolescents' cogni-

tion. Rather than being limited to concrete thinking, they begin to think abstractly. A problem of government (e.g., how to create a new law) may be decided by thinking about the particular system of representative democracy that exists in the United States; or it might be dealt with by imagining that a completely different form of government (e.g., a constitutional monarchy) could be used.

Both the quantitative and qualitative changes that occur in regard to adolescent cognition are discussed in this chapter. Both discussions highlight the importance of individual differences in cognitive development, the way that the context influences cognition, and the links between cognition and other individual characteristics of youth development.

The Quantitative Study of Adolescent Cognition

Issue to Consider
- What is an "intelligence quotient"? How is it measured?

A key means to assess cognition quantitatively is by administrating a standardized test such as the Stanford-Binet test or the Wechsler Intelligence Scale for Children. Intelligence tests quantify a person's knowledge relative to others of a similar age by computation of an intelligence quotient (**IQ**) score. To compute an IQ score, mental age (e.g., how much you know) is divided by chronological age (e.g., how much is known on average by others of your age) and multiplied by 100 (to eliminate fractions).

For at least half a century, researchers have studied the course of IQ changes from infancy through adolescence (e.g., Bloom, 1964). IQ scores remain fairly consistent across the adolescent period. The stability of IQ scores means that you can predict an 18-year-old person's IQ score with a good deal of accuracy by knowing his or her score in the early adolescent period. But what is being predicted when we predict IQ? What precisely is being measured by standardized intelligence tests and expressed as an IQ score?

Dimensions of Intelligence

Issues to Consider
- Why might a single IQ score not be useful?
- How does the social context influence cognition?

Across the 20th century there were debates about what psychological characteristics are actually measured by IQ tests (e.g., Gould, 1981; Lerner, 1976, 1986, 2002). Spearman (1927) hypothesized that one general intellectual factor—termed "**g**" (for "general intelligence")—was being measured, and Guilford (1967) theorized that over 100 different abilities could be measured by intelligence tests. Other scholars have also proposed that different aspects of cognition are assessed by intelligence tests (Fitzgerald, Nesselroade, & Baltes, 1973). To the extent that intelligence is expressed through multiple dimensions, the usefulness of a single score, such as IQ, is diminished.

Current research lends support to the multiple dimensions viewpoint. Among both normal adolescents and youth with psychiatric problems, three distinct intellectual factors (linguistic, logical mathematical, and social) are measured by the revised form of the Wechsler Intelligence Scale for Children (WISC-R; Anderson & Dixon, 1995). Additional evidence for the presence of three intellectual factors exists. Among about 120 gifted Canadian students in grades 6, 7, and 8, three factors also were identified (Matthews & Keating, 1995) and no evidence for "g" was found. Several different facets of both perceptual and reasoning ability were identified among about 850 eighth- and ninth-grade youth from the United States, Japan, and China (Li, Sano, & Merwin, 1996). Similarly, among samples of 10- to 16-year-old youth from India and Greece, there was evidence of several distinct dimensions of quantitative intelligence (Demetriou et al., 1996).

Moreover, the number of different intellectual abilities may remain consistent throughout the adolescent years. Studies of youth from grades 7 to 12 found the same number of mental abilities (four) to exist at all grade levels (Fitzgerald, Nesselroade, & Baltes, 1973). These abilities related to verbal intelligence, numeric intelligence, reasoning, and spatial ability.

This research underscores the importance of developing educational curricula to support the diverse dimensions of intellectual development among youth. Such findings, especially those of Matthews and Keating (1995), point to the significance of the social domain in the cognitive development of adolescents. In a longitudinal study of about 190 youth from late childhood/early adolescence (i.e., ages 8 to 12 years) through late adolescence/young adulthood (i.e., 17 to 23 years), cognitive competence was linked to three domains of functioning in the early developmental period: academic achievement, social competence, and conduct. Cognitive competence in the later developmental period was related to the three previously mentioned domains and to two other domains: romantic competence and job competence (Masten et al., 1995).

The social context is not only an important part of the content of cognitive functioning, but it also influences the course of cognitive

> **IQ** The intelligence quotient. A numerical scale measuring level of intelligence. For example, to compute an IQ score, mental age (i.e., how much you know) is divided by chronological age (i.e., how much is known on average by others of your age) and multiplied by 100 (to eliminate fractions).
>
> **"g"** General intelligence/ intellectual factor.

development. Among approximately 400 young adolescents from a predominantly poor rural area in the United States, both family and community factors influence academic achievement (Felner et al., 1995). As compared to adolescents from families in which adults were employed in semiskilled or skilled professional occupations, youth from families in which adults were employed in low-income unskilled jobs had lower school performance and academic achievement. When youth lived in families in which neither parent was a high school graduate, there was less likelihood of academic and socioemotional adjustment than when adolescents lived in families with parents who had higher educational levels (Felner et al., 1995).

In sum, studies of the quantitative features of adolescent cognition underscore the idea of multiple dimensions of adolescent cognitive development. Social functioning and the social context constitute significant domains of and important influences on cognitive development. Achievement in both academic and social arenas is an important part of cognitive development. Academic achievement and its relation to the context of human development is discussed next.

Academic Achievement: Diversity and Context

Issues to Consider

- How does culture influence academic achievement?
- How do peers influence academic achievement?
- What are their differences in achievement for adolescents with different self-perceptions?
- What other factors can lead to diversity in academic achievement? What can be done to raise achievement of adolescents?

Academic achievement is affected by multiple levels of the context of human development, ranging from the most macro cultural influences to micro interpersonal influences involving peers and family members. In an important series of studies, Harold W. Stevenson and his colleagues have identified key features of culture that influence adolescent achievement, particularly in mathematics.

In a study of approximately 600 grade 11 students from Minneapolis, Minnesota, Taipei, Taiwan, and Sendai, Japan, youth in all settings spent most of their time studying, interacting with friends, or

Formal operational thought involves scientific, logical thinking.

watching television (Fuligni & Stevenson, 1995). The distribution of time spent in these activities differed across groups. Chinese youth spent more time in academic activities (e.g., attending school, participation in after-school classes, and/or studying) than did their American counterparts. Although Japanese and American youth did not differ in regard to time spent studying or in after-school programs, Japanese adolescents did spend more time in school than did American youth (Fuligni & Stevenson, 1995). American youth spent more time than did adolescents in the other groups working or socializing with friends (Fuligni & Stevenson, 1995).

In another study examining the connection between culture and adolescent mathematics achievement, about 300 Asian American, 2,000 European American, 1,500 Taiwanese, and 1,100 Japanese 11th graders were studied (Chen & Stevenson, 1995). Achievement scores of the Asian Americans were higher than those of the European Americans but they were lower than those of Chinese or Japanese adolescents (Chen & Stevenson, 1995). Family and peer factors were associated with achievement among both the Asian American and the East Asian youth. Greater mathematics achievement was seen among adolescents whose parents and peers held high standards for, and positive attitudes about, academic effort and achievement. Achievement was better among youth who had fewer distractions from schoolwork caused by jobs or informal peer interactions (Chen & Stevenson, 1995).

Many of the academic achievements of youth from different cultural backgrounds may be based on socialization experiences beginning in childhood. In a longitudinal study of 475 American, Chinese, and Japanese youth from the first grade through middle adolescence, consistent relationships were found across time in all cultures among family socioeconomic status, cognitive abilities, and academic achievement (Chen, Lee, & Stevenson, 1996).

The cultural orientation toward academic achievement that youth experience may remain with them despite emigration to another country. In a study of about 1,100 Latino, East Asian, Filipino, and European adolescents from immigrant families, youth from both first- and second-generation immigrant backgrounds showed greater mathematics achievement than did peers whose families had lived in the United States for several generations (Fuligni, 1997). Socioeconomic factors were not primarily associated with these differences; rather, a common cultural stress on education, shared by the youth, their peers, and their families, seemed most important for their achievement (Fuligni, 1997).

Even within a cultural group, family and peer variables have an influence on academic achievement. In a study of rural African American 9- to 12-year-olds, maternal involvement with the adolescent's school, supportive and harmonious family interactions, and family financial resources were associated with academic competence (Brody, Stoneman, & Flor, 1995). Other research has found that living in either a single-parent family or a stepfamily has a negative influence on the mathematics and reading achievement of eighth graders, unless parental social relations are positive (Pong, 1997).

Peers can also have a facilitative influence on academic achievement. Working with peers when trying to solve a problem enhances the ability to succeed in such tasks (Dimant & Bearison, 1991).

Peers seem especially useful when the interactions with them are specifically relevant to the particular problem at hand, but even engaging in general games with peers or with interactive computers can facilitate cognitive performance. Playing video games, such as Tetris, can enhance an adolescent's ability to rotate figures mentally and to visualize objects in space (Okagaki & Frensch, 1994).

Although it may enhance peer popularity, spending a lot of time in informal peer interactions appears to have a negative impact on academic achievement. Research on ninth-grade inner-city youth (Luthar, 1995) finds that high sociability ratings from peers is linked to lower academic competence.

In a study of ethnically diverse young adolescents (Graham, Taylor, & Hudley, 1998), girls of all ethnic backgrounds and European American boys were found to value high-achieving female classmates, but ethnic minority boys place little value on high-achieving male peers. All youth believed that both academic disengagement and social deviance were associated with being male, a low achiever, and an ethnic minority (Graham et al., 1998).

It may be that some instances of low achievement are related to adolescents' own characterization of themselves. Their self-categorizations or labels of themselves may be self-handicapping in regard to their achievement. Girls who, across their adolescence, come to think of themselves in more masculine than feminine terms have better spatial abilities than girls who think of themselves as more feminine than masculine (Newcombe & Dubas, 1992).

Some youth use "self-handicapping strategies" (Midgley, Arunkumar, & Urdan, 1996) to account for their poor academic performance. Through engaging in procrastination, fooling around in class, and intentional reduction in effort, they provide for themselves causes for their poor academic achievement (Midgley et al., 1996). In a study of about 100 eighth graders, such handicapping strategies were associated with self-deprecation, negative attitudes toward education, and low grades (Midgley et al., 1996).

Adolescents can also develop self-enhancing strategies. Developing an ability to delay gratification, when still in preschool, facilitates cognitive and academic competence in adolescence (Shoda, Mischel, & Peake, 1990). Delay of gratification ability also enhances the capacity to cope with both frustration and stress (Shoda et al., 1990). Experiences

applications box 4.1

Building Programs to Counter Illiteracy and Its Associated Problems

Neither a country, its communities, nor its citizens can prosper unless they possess the knowledge and skills necessary to contribute to the global village and compete in the global marketplace. For these reasons programs are being developed around the world to counteract illiteracy and to diminish, or even prevent, the problems associated with it.

Here, two such programs are described, one from Dhaka, Bangladesh, and the other from Salvador, Bahia, Brazil.

Increasing Literacy Rates Among Rural Youth in Bangladesh: The "Non-Formal Primary Education Program" of Dhaka, Bangladesh

Equal access to education is a human right, reaffirmed by international acceptance at the United Nations Convention on the Rights of the Child. Yet almost 100 million children in the developing world were given no opportunity to attend school last year, a majority of which were girls.

In Bangladesh, the problem is especially severe with 35 percent of young people never learning how to read or write. In response to the educational needs of rural youth in particular, the Bangladesh Rural Advancement Committee (BRAC) created its Non-Formal Primary Education Program (NFPE) in 1985.

Through this program, BRAC recruits and trains paraprofessional teachers, 97 percent of which are women, and places them in one-room schoolhouses within their own community. These schools provide four years of primary education for 8- to 10-year-olds who have never attended school, or have dropped out. A similar program exists for older children providing the same curriculum but spread across three years of schooling. Special attention is paid to the needs of girls who make up 65% of those enrolled.

In the 15 years since its inception, BRAC has achieved remarkable success, expanding from a base of 22 schools to nearly 34,000. Dropout rates are less than 7%, compared with 35% in the overcrowded formal school system. Over 90% of students graduating from BRAC's fifth grade class have gained admission into formal government schools.

The BRAC experience is testimony to the fact that poor rural families want education for their children. It has also demonstrated that motivated paraprofessional teachers can be trained quickly and successfully.

Studies have shown repeatedly that on completion of BRAC's schooling, students from poor homes with illiterate parents are only marginally behind middle class families of government schools. Tests revealed that children from BRAC schools gained equal scores to their govern-

---

that provide knowledge about math problems and about strategies for addressing such problems are key influences on the performance of *both* adolescent boys and girls on the math subtest of the Scholastic Aptitude Test (Byrnes & Takahira, 1993).

Both IQ scores and academic performance are related to three aspects of social competence among 12- and 13-year-olds: showing socially responsible behavior; receiving positive appraisals by peers; and having the ability to regulate oneself socially, to set goals, solve problems, and elicit interpersonal trust (Wentzel, 1991). Adolescent girls who have high mastery of academic subjects also have the ability to seek and obtain appropriate help in solving a task (Nelson-Le Gall, 1990).

For some students, low achievement is related to a learning disability. Learning disabled youth encounter

difficulty in inhibiting incorrect responses in academic situations (Barrouillet, Fayol, & Lathulière, 1997). In such circumstances, family support such as parental expectations for the child's academic achievement and the young person's awareness of these expectations influence academic achievement among youth, even those varying along a learning disabled and non-learning disabled continuum (Patrikakou, 1996).

There are numerous interventions, beyond those associated with parental support, that can enhance academic achievement among youth. Many of these efforts involve community-based programs aimed at enhancing academic functioning and alleviating other interrelated problems of youth development (e.g., see Dryfoos, 1990, 1994, 1995, 1998).

In a report about the Chicago Longitudinal Study of the role of extended early childhood intervention

ment counterparts in reading and writing skills and slightly lower scores in mathematics and social studies.

A team of international education experts is currently evaluating the program to help improve its curriculum and teaching methods.

Increasing School Opportunities Among Brazilian Youth: The "Community Public Schools" (CECUP) Program of Salvador, Bahia, Brazil

In the 1970s, residents of poor neighborhoods in Bahia began organizing to secure land titles, electricity, water, and other basic services. Education was, and remains, a high priority due to their children's lack of access to basic education. Community organizing unfolded in an environment marked by sharp class distinctions, a skewed distribution of income, and racial discrimination. In Bahia, the state in which Salvador is located, an estimated 50% of school-age children are not enrolled in school and adult illiteracy (15 years and older) hovers around 50%. In Salvador alone, an estimated 220,000 school-age children are not in school. These statistics bode poorly for Brazilian children in terms of their health, future employability, income-earning capacity, and overall quality of life. In Brazil, the chief problems are low enroll-

ment and high attrition rates, particularly in the first years of primary school. Causal factors include poor teaching and weak curricula; parents' inability to provide books and uniforms; children's lack of readiness to learn when they enter first grade; inadequate educational materials and facilities; and lack of communication between schools and parents. In response to the absence of viable educational opportunities, associations of low-income residents throughout the city took matters into their own hands and established their own schools.

Over 10,000 low-income children and youth, ages 5 through 18, benefit from 62 community-built and community-run schools in poor neighborhoods of Salvador. To combat low levels of literacy among the city's poor, CECUP works closely with community organizations and teachers to improve the quality of education through teacher training, the development of curricula and educational materials, and cultural enrichment activities.

Using Freirean educational methods, CECUP and its teachers incorporate elements from the children's Afro-Brazilian culture and daily experience into the educational process. In bridging the gap between school and the children's living environment, parents support their children's education. The dropout rate among the community public school children is low.

Source: International Youth Foundation, 2001. <www.iyfnet.org> .

in school achievement (Reynolds & Temple, 1998), about 560 low-income inner-city African American youth were followed from early childhood to the seventh grade. Program participation for 2 or 3 years after preschool and kindergarten was associated with higher reading achievement through the seventh grade and with lower rates of grade retention and placement into special education classes. This study provides important longitudinal evidence of the benefits of a large-scale community-based program of extended early childhood intervention for adolescent academic achievement (Reynolds & Temple, 1998).

Being literate is a key requirement for academic achievement and success in life, especially in a world growing more dependent on technology and thus on the ability to speak, read, and write. Adolescents' literacy skills can affect not only their own life chances

but those of others in their social world. Among African American children of adolescent mothers from Baltimore, Maryland, differences in preschool cognition and behavior were related to literacy in late adolescence and young adulthood. Variations in maternal education, the size of the family during early childhood, the marital status of the mother, and family income in middle childhood and in early adolescence also influenced literacy (Baydar, Brooks-Gunn, & Furstenberg, 1993).

Given the developmental and generational significance of literacy, it is understandable that numerous programs exist worldwide designed to enhance literacy among youth. Applications Box 4.1 describes some of these programs. The programs typically have to attend simultaneously to several literacy-related problems to be effective.

Conclusions About Quantitative Features of Adolescent Cognitive Development

The quantitative characteristics of adolescent cognition show both consistency and change in patterns of development that are influenced by the context within which they occur. Such development in context provides the underpinnings of diversity in the course of cognitive development and promotes the link between cognition and other aspects of the individual's psychological and social functioning. These themes are not exclusive to the quantitative dimension of adolescent cognition. They apply as well to the qualitative one. There are important changes during adolescence in the quality of thinking.

The Qualitative Study of Adolescent Cognition

The way an adolescent thinks about the world differs from the type of thought shown by infants and children. Differences in "kind" or "type" are **qualitative differences.** Numerous scholars of human development in general, and adolescence in particu-

Qualitative differences (in cognition) Differences in "kind" or "type" of thought shown by a person.

lar, have studied the qualitative changes that characterize cognitive development (Overton, 1991, 1998). Historically, the most important approach to adolescent cognition was presented by Jean Piaget (1896–1980). Today, even though Piaget's (1970, 1972) approach is no longer the only one or even the central approach, most other perspectives take Piaget's views into account (e. g., Elkind, 1967, 1980; Feldman, 2000; Keating, 1991; Neimark, 1979; Overton, 1991; Overton & Byrnes, 1991). Because of this continuing salience, it is important to describe Piaget's ideas about adolescent cognition.

Adolescence and the Formal Operational Stage

Issues to Consider
- What are the achievements and limitations of the formal operational stage?
- Describe how knowledge is attained through the processes of assimilation, accommodation, and equilibration.
- According to David Elkind, what is egocentrism and why is it important?

As described in Chapter 2, the infancy and childhood portions of life are associated with the first three stages of Piaget's (1970) theory, and adolescence and adulthood are associated with the fourth. Table 4.1 presents the four stages of Piaget's theory:

Table 4-1	Stages of Cognitive Development in the Theory of Jean Piaget		
Stage	**Approx. Age Range**	**Major Cognitive Achievements**	**Major Cognitive Limitations**
Sensorimotor	0–1	Scheme of object permanency	Egocentrism: Lack of ability to differentiate between self and external stimulus world
Preoperational	2–6 or 7	Systems of representation. Symbolic functioning (e.g., language, symbolic play, delayed imitation)	Lack of conservation ability. Egocentrism: Lack of ability to differentiate between symbol and object
Concrete operational	6 or 7–12	Ability to show experience/ independent thought (reversible, internalized actions)	Egocentrism: Lack of ability to differentiate between thoughts about reality and actual experience of reality
Formal operational	12–	Ability to think hypothetically, counterfactually, and propositionally	Egocentrism: Imaginary audience, personal fable

Source: Adapted from Lerner, 1986.

Linguistic skills are important facets of the mental abilities assessed on intelligence tests.

the sensorimotor, the preoperational, the concrete operational, and the formal operational stages. The cognitive achievements and limitations involved in each of these stages within Piaget's theory are included in the table as well.

Note that in all periods of development within Piaget's (1970) theory, cognitive development involves the relation between the person and the context. The person-context relation discussed by Piaget involves two processes. First, knowledge is built by the person taking in information from the world around him or her and fitting it into his or her existing cognitive organization or structure. This changing of the world outside the person (the "object") to fit the structure of the person (the "subject") is termed **assimilation.** Second, knowledge is also built by the person (the "subject") changing his or her cognitive structure to adapt to new information ("object") in the world. This process is termed **accommodation.**

Piaget proposes that the goal of cognitive development is to create a balance (an equilibrium)

between assimilation and accommodation. Piaget calls the process of maintaining this balance **equilibration.** Piaget notes that equilibrium is hard to maintain. The world is constantly presenting new information and a person initially tries to deal with it by treating it as something he or she already knows and tries to assimilate it (a process that Piaget terms **reproductive assimilation**). When this attempt occurs, equilibrium is lost. Assimilation outweighs accommodation because there is more of a cognitive focus on the subject than the object. Eventually, the person needs to accommodate to bring his or her cognitive structure back into balance. This process of falling out of and moving into equilibration is the means through which the person moves from one level, or stage, of cognitive development to the next.

When the person is centered on his or her own cognitive structure, there is more of a concern with the perspective of the subject than with the actual details of the object, and the person is said to be egocentric (Elkind, 1967). As illustrated in Table 4.1, each stage of cognitive development within Piaget's theory has a type of **egocentrism** prototypic of it. According to David Elkind (1967), the scholar most instructive about the nature of cognitive egocentrism, overcoming the egocentrism prototypic of each stage of development leads the person to attain the cognitive development most central to that stage. At the same time, the cognitive attainment of one stage leads the person to the egocentrism of the next stage (Elkind, 1967).

The processes involving assimilation, accommodation, equilibration, reproductive assimilation, **disequilibration,** egocentrism, and eventual reequilibration leads eventually to the attainment of the last stage of Piaget's (1970, 1972) theory: formal operations. It leads to the emergence of a type of egocentrism prototypic to the adolescent

Assimilation Process during which a person modifies his or her external world to fit into the already existing cognitive schemas (structures) of the person (the subject).

Accommodation Process during which a person (the subject) modifies his or her cognitive schemas (structure) to conform with new information (the object) in the external world.

Equilibration Process of reaching a balanced relationship between assimilation and accommodation.

Reproductive assimilation When a person initially tries to deal with new information by treating it as something he or she already knows.

Egocentrism When the person is centered on his or her own cognitive structure/s and unable to differentiate between one's own point of view and the views of others; when there is more concern with the perspective of the subject than with the actual details of the object (i.e., the world surrounding the subject).

Disequilibration Cognitive process that occurs when our cognitive schemas (structures) are not in an agreement with one another, when there is an imbalance between assimilation and accommodation.

period. To understand this development, let's focus first on the characteristics of **formal operational thinking.**

Features of Formal Operational Thought

Issues to Consider
- What are the characteristics of formal operational thought?
- What is the INRC group? How is it important for formal operations?
- What does the *structural whole* in regard to formal operations mean? Does it exist?

When children attain the ability to see that reality and their thoughts about reality are different and can generate and recognize hypotheses about reality, they have reached the formal operational stage in Piaget's theory.

Formal operations begin at about 11 or 12 years of age and continue for the rest of life (Piaget, 1972). Because, in both theory and research, the lower age limit typically associated with this stage corresponds to the years associated with early adolescence (see Keating, 1991; Neimark, 1979; Overton, 1991; Overton & Byrnes, 1991), the study of the qualitative aspect of adolescent cognition is associated with the evaluation of formal operational development.

The concrete operational child can only form abstractions relevant to events or problems that exist. As a consequence, thoughts about a given topic cannot be integrated with potentially relevant but hypothetical aspects of the problem. The child cannot reach solutions to problems by means of general theories or by the postulation of all possible solutions to a problem (Overton &

Formal operational thought Fourth stage of Piaget's theory of cognitive development, when a person attains the ability to see that reality and his or her thoughts about reality are different, and when the person can generate and recognize hypotheses about reality.

INRC grouping Cognitive structure that characterizes formal operations and implies that all solutions to a problem may be obtained through the application of four components: *identity, negation, reciprocity,* and *correlation.*

Identity transformation Process of approaching a problem by recognizing the problem in terms of its singular attributes.

Negation operation Process of approaching a problem by canceling the existence of the problem.

Reciprocal transformation Process of approaching a problem by considering and taking its opposite.

Correlative transformation Process of thinking of all aspects of a problem by relating them to other problems.

Byrnes, 1991; Wadsworth, 1971). The formal operational child shows these attributes of thought.

In the formal operational stage, thought becomes hypothetical in emphasis (Overton & Byrnes, 1991). The child comes to recognize that his or her thoughts about reality have an element of arbitrariness about them, that they may not actually be real representations about the true nature of experience. The child's thoughts about reality take on a hypothetical characteristic. In forming hypotheses about the world, the child's thought can be seen to correspond, at least in part, to formal, scientific, logical thinking (Linn, 1991). Meet the Researcher Box 4.1 presents the work of Willis F. Overton in regard to adolescent thinking.

To be able to deal with all potentially relevant aspects of a problem, we must be able to transform the problem so as to contend with all its possible forms. The cognitive structure that characterizes formal operations, termed the **INRC group** by Piaget, allows such complete transformations (Inhelder & Piaget, 1958). All transformations of a problem may be obtained through the application of the components of this group: identity, negation, reciprocal, and correlative transformations. We can think of all aspects of a problem by recognizing the problem in terms of its singular attributes (an **identity transformation**), by canceling the existence of the problem (a **negation operation**), by taking its opposite (a **reciprocal transformation**), or by relating it to other problems (a **correlative transformation**). Only the coordinated use of all these transformations allows all potentially applicable aspects of a problem to be solved. Not until the INRC group is established do we possess a cognitive structure appropriate for dealing with pure abstractions.

To illustrate, Piaget and Inhelder (1969) describe a problem in which a youth is presented with five jars, each containing colorless liquids. Combining the liquids from three particular jars will produce a color; any use of the liquids from either of the other jars will not produce a color. The child is shown that a color can be produced but is not shown which combination will do this. Concrete operational children typically try to solve this problem by combining liquids two at a time, but after combining all pairs, or possibly trying to mix all five liquids together, their search for the workable combination usually stops. The formal operational adolescent explores all possible solutions and, typically,

MEET THE RESEARCHER BOX 4.1

WILLIS F. OVERTON
EXPLORING NEW FORMS OF THINKING AND REASONING FOUND IN ADOLESCENTS

As the person moves into adolescence, a new form of thinking and reasoning develops. Sometimes this new reasoning is called formal thought or reasoning, sometimes it is called abstract reasoning, and sometimes it is called deductive reasoning. The new type of thought permits the adolescent to think about his or her thinking in a systematically logical fashion. This opens all sorts of new possibilities for the adolescent, including the possibility of thinking logically and systematically about future plans and goals. Reasoning about the value of various perspectives, people take on many personal, social, and political issues, and take a scientific approach to the solution of scientific problems.

In my work I explore many features of this novel form of reasoning. In some of the studies that my colleagues and I conduct, we explore the development of this skill from late childhood through late adolescence. Here we are interested in knowing exactly when this skill develops, how it develops, and the detailed nature of the skill. So, for example, we know now that by the last year of high school 80% to 90% of people are showing clear signs of the ability to reason in a formal way, whereas in grade 6 fewer than half are able to reason in this way. Also, we find that the test we generally use to measure formal reasoning is closely related to other tests of deductive skills.

Willis F. Overton is professor of psychology in the Division of Developmental Psychology at Temple University. He is editor of the journal *Monographs of the Society for Research in Child Development.*

In other studies we are more interested in how this skill is related to other dimensions of the adolescent's life. For example, is the ability to reason formally a necessary precursor to establishing the kind of psychological identity that the theorist Erik Erikson talks about? One of our recent studies suggests that formal reasoning, adolescent self-identity, and the kind of worldview the adolescent takes are all closely related. We have also recently examined formal reasoning in relation to the style parents use in interacting with their children and in relation to the anxiety people feel when taking tests. We have found that the best adolescent formal reasoners have parents who use an authoritative parenting style, and that test anxiety is associated with lower scores on the test of formal reasoning.

We have also done some preliminary explorations of how formal reasoning, or the lack of formal reasoning skills, is related to adolescent emotional-behavioral problems. These studies involve comparing the reasoning skills of adolescents who have been hospitalized for various emotional-behavioral problems and nonhospitalized adolescents. At this point the findings suggest that adolescents who are admitted to a hospital for emotional-behavioral problems generally perform more poorly at formal reasoning when their admission occurs in later adolescence (i.e., after their 16th birthday), and poor reasoning is related to the specific diagnosed problem.

---

tests all possible combinations of two and three liquids until a color is produced.

As another example, consider the following verbal problem: "If Jane is taller than Doris and is shorter than Francine, who is the shortest of the three?" (Wadsworth, 1971). Concrete operational children may be able to solve an analogous problem, (e.g., one dealing with sticks of various lengths when the sticks are physically present). However, abstract verbal problems such as this one are usually not solved until formal operations have emerged.

Formal operational thinking increases substantially in early adolescence, between the sixth and eighth grades (Petersen, 1987). A central aspect of formal operational thinking, **conditional reasoning,** increases across adolescence (Overton, Byrnes, & O'Brien, 1985). This reasoning involves the idea that "if p, then q," and is the logical statement in scientific hypotheses. Also related to scientific reasoning is the ability to make valid inferences, for example, if and only if p, then q. The competence to make valid inferences emerges in and continues to develop throughout adolescence (Moshman & Franks, 1986). Strategies for remembering (Bray, Hersh,

> **Conditional reasoning** Type of deductive reasoning, characterized by "if p, then q" statements.

& Turner, 1985), particularly in familiar contexts (Ceci & Bronfenbrenner, 1985), develop in adolescence as well.

Formal operational development tends to occur in respect to certain cognitive competencies and not others (Keating, 1991; Kuhn, 1991; Kuhn, Amsel, & O'Loughlin, 1988; Leadbeater, 1991). It occurs for those competencies for which the person has a particular interest and/or specialized experience or training (Piaget, 1972). The essence of formal operations is abstract thought. This type of thought develops in a manner that includes both general and spe-

During adolescence thought changes from being predominantly concrete to being predominantly abstract.

cific components (Marini & Case, 1994). Similarly, understanding of particular topics, for instance, aspects of social roles such as job responsibility, develops in diverse ways (Warton & Goodnow, 1991). This research suggests that formal operations do not exist as a "structural whole" (Kuhn, 1991; Kuhn et al., 1988) and imply that universal stagelike structures may not likely be found (Keating, 1991).

In summary, formal operational thought is no longer dependent on concrete reality. The child can now think not only in the "if . . . then" manner, but also counterfactually and abstractly. These mental abilities continue to characterize thought in the adolescent years and beyond. However, several qualifications of these conclusions are necessary.

Development Across the Period of Formal Operations

Deductive reasoning Type of reasoning that begins with a set of statements (premises) used to infer if another statement (conclusion) is valid.

Inductive reasoning When reasoning inductively we use our observations and experiences to draw conclusions about the general truth of a particular statement.

Issue to Consider
- What change marks the movement from concrete operations to the formal reasoning ability of formal operations?

Willis F. Overton and his colleagues have conducted a series of studies investigating

the individual and contextual bases of the development of cognition during adolescence (e.g., Foltz, Overton, & Ricco, 1995; Reimer et al., 1996). Researchers hypothesized that the acquisition of competence in formal reasoning ability would be marked by a transition from inductive to **deductive reasoning** (Foltz et al., 1995). This hypothesis is based on the understanding that in the concrete operational stage youth are overly centered on existing phenomena, on the world as it was empirically given to them (Elkind, 1967), and use reasoning to confirm that their specific observations reflected the general state of affairs of the world. They therefore *induce* that what is observed is prototypic of the general nature of existence.

Foltz et al. (1995) conclude that a cognitive developmental progression exists, one that involves the adolescent moving from inductive to deductive reasoning strategies. By late adolescence, youth are highly efficient at using deduction to reduce or eliminate alternative solutions in problem-solving situations (Drumm & Jackson, 1996). This conclusion in based on the study where 100 adolescents were given both a problem-solving and a reasoning task (Foltz et al., 1995). They were given a toy wooden boat, were shown it could float on water, and were then asked to demonstrate that wooden boats, and only wooden boats, could float on water. Foltz et al. (1995) found that nonformal operational thinking was associated with **inductive reasoning** strategies, by attempts to verify their ideas through generating redundant information. Here, adolescents might place other wooden objects into the water to see if they too could float. However, formal reasoning was associated with attempts to prove one's ideas via "falsification" strategies, that is, by trying to identify information that would disconfirm one's ideas (Foltz et al., 1995). If the boat task was involved in an adolescent's attempts to use **falsification strategies,** for example, then the young person might attempt to place toys made of materials other than wood into the water to see if they could float.

Other research confirms that cognitive development during adolescence involves changes in the use of inductive reasoning. In a study of more than 2,000 Hungarian youth from grades 3, 5, 7, 9, and 11, six tests of inductive reasoning (number analogies, verbal analogies, number series, verbal series, coding, and exclusion) were administered (Csapó, 1997). The major increase in inductive reasoning occurred between the fifth and the ninth grades, with only small changes in such reasoning after ninth grade (Csapó, 1997), when deductive reasoning typically increases dramatically (Foltz et al., 1995).

During the portion of adolescence when deductive reasoning predominates there may not only be attempts to confirm existing beliefs, but also it may be the case that adolescents will evaluate arguments and evidence in a manner that maintains their already formed beliefs. For example, in one study, adolescents were presented with "scientific" information that either confirmed, disconfirmed, or was irrelevant to their existing religious beliefs (Klaczynski & Gordon, 1996); however, each presentation contained some problematic reasoning/ evidence that contradicted the information. Adolescents were most likely to detect problems in evidence that was inconsistent with their religious preferences. This bias in reasoning was not related to the intellectual ability of adolescents (Klaczynski & Gordon, 1996). Other research indicates that the development of formal operational thinking during adolescence is not related to quantitatively assessed intellectual abilities (Pulos, 1997).

Diversity and Context in Formal Operations

Issue to Consider

• Why can't generalizations be made about the emergence and course of formal operations?

Evidence indicates that the emergence of formal operational thought is not characteristic of all youth. Studies done with older adolescents and adults in Western cultures show that not all individuals attain formal operations (e.g., Kuhn, 1991; Kuhn et al., 1988). Estimates are that only about 40% to 60% of samples of college students from Western countries show appropriate performance on tasks requiring formal operational thinking (Neimark, 1979). Adolescents may be competent to reason formally, but they may not have developed the strategies to show this competence (Overton, 1990, 1991). Thus education is important for such cognitive performance (Kuhn et al., 1988).

Generalizations about the course of formal operations across the life span within a culture must be made with caution. Although evidence shows that some aspects of cognition (e.g., the ways in which youth justify their beliefs) are generalizable across cultural settings (Kitchener & Wood, 1987), people in many cultural settings do not attain formal operational abilities at the same average time in life that it occurs within Western cultural settings. For example, American adolescents (13- and 15-year-olds) are more advanced in formal operations than Hong Kong Chinese youth of corresponding ages (Douglas & Wong, 1977). In fact, in some non-Western groups there is a failure ever to attain such thinking ability. Piaget (1969, 1972) himself noted such failures.

Reasons for these differences have been suggested to lie in the different experiences of youth from rural and urban settings (Peluffo, 1962; Youniss & Dean, 1974), in type of school experiences (Goodnow, 1962; Goodnow & Bethon, 1966; Kuhn, 1991; Kuhn et al., 1988; Peluffo, 1962, 1967), and in the sorts of parent-child relations experienced (Jacobsen, Edelstein, & Hoffmann, 1994). For example, Icelandic youth with a secure attachment to their parents performed better on both concrete and formal operational tasks than did youth with insecure attachments (Jacobsen et al., 1994).

Although these explanations might lead us to expect socioeconomic or educational differences to be associated with formal operational attainment, the data do not support such a view. Neimark (1975, 1979) found that socioeconomic status had no effect on the development of formal thought, and only very

> **Falsification strategies**
> Proving one's ideas by trying to identify information that would disconfirm these ideas.

profound differences in education seemed to be associated with differences in the development of formal thought. IQ score differences do not relate to differences in formal operational development either (Kuhn, 1976). After some minimal level of psychometric intelligence is reached, variables other than those associated with IQ scores contribute to formal operational development (Neimark, 1975).

Formal operational thought does not represent a level of cognitive functioning reached universally by all people in all cultures. However, for many adolescents, formal operations represent a stage of thought that is reached. Although the abstract thinking associated with this type of thought is an asset to the young person, formal operational thinking also has limitations.

Adolescent Egocentrism

Issue to Consider

• What are the two components of adolescent egocentrism?

As noted earlier, the scholarship of David Elkind (1967) allows us to understand the special characteristics of the egocentrism of the formal operational period. Some of Elkind's recent work is featured in Meet the Researcher Box 4.2.

As Elkind (1967) explains, adolescent egocentrism is complicated by the physiological, emotional, and social changes involved in this period of life. Because anything and everything can become the object of adolescents' newly developed abstract and hypothetical cognitive ability, they may recognize their thoughts as only one possible interpretation of reality. Adolescents also may come to view reality as the only possible instance of a potentially unlimited number of possible realities. The concrete predomination of what is real is replaced in adolescence by the abstract and hypothetical predomination of what can be real. All things in experience are thought about hypothetical-

With the emergence of formal operations, many adolescents spend a lot of time immersed in their own thoughts.

> **Centration** In Piaget's theory, a focus on one's own point of view, which involves therefore a lack of balance between assimilation and accommodation.
>
> **Adolescent egocentrism** Term introduced by Elkind in 1967 to label problems in adolescents' thoughts; the belief that others are preoccupied with them and that they are unique individuals.
>
> **Imaginary audience** When adolescents become preoccupied with self, they come to believe that others are as preoccupied with their appearance and behavior as they are.

ly, and even adolescents' own thoughts can become an object of their hypothesizing.

In other words, adolescents can now think about their own thinking. Because young people spend a good deal of time using these new thought capabilities, their preoccupation, or **centration**, on self leads to egocentrism within the formal operational stage, a development that limits the newly developed formal operational thought. Elkind (1967) labels the egocentrism of this stage **adolescent egocentrism** and sees it as having two components.

First, because adolescents are preoccupied with their thinking, they fail to distinguish, or discriminate, between their thoughts and the thoughts of other people. Because adolescents are so preoccupied with their own appearance and behavior, and fail to make this discrimination, they come to believe that others are as preoccupied with their appearance and behavior as they are. Thus adolescents construct an **imaginary audience** (Elkind, 1967).

MEET THE RESEARCHER BOX 4.2

DAVID ELKIND
PERCEPTIONS OF ADOLESCENTS

The adolescent is a gift of nature, but our perception of adolescence is always a social construction. As a social construction, adolescence always reflects the values, roles, and perceptions of the prevailing society. When these values, roles, and perceptions change, so too does our manner of viewing adolescence. Much of my current research is an attempt to describe society that had its onset around mid-century.

Up until mid-century, our society was provincial in the sense that there was a great deal of ethnic, religious, and racial clannishness with many social taboos for dating and wedding outside of these rigid boundaries. In addition, male and female roles were sharply defined with little overlapping between what were regarded as appropriate activities for men and women. Finally, children were perceived as innocent and in need of protection and adolescents were perceived as immature and in need of adult guidance and protection. In turn, modern adolescents have been looked upon as needing to experiment, to try things out with a moratorium during which they were free from adult responsibilities. Starting with World War II, and followed by the women's movement, the civil rights movement, and the Vietnam War, there was a strong reaction against authority, particularly as it was exercised by white males. It resulted in a new cosmopolitanism in American society. For example, there is now much greater acceptance and val-

David Elkind is professor of child development in the Eliot-Pearson Department of Child Development at Tufts University. He is perhaps best known for his more popular books, *The Hurried Child, All Grown Up and No Place to Go,* and *Miseducation.*

uation of the achievements of different ethnic, racial, and religious groups as well as of women. Increased intermarriage among those of different racial and ethnic backgrounds reflects this cosmopolitanism. In the same way, gender roles have become more loose and overlapping and women now engage in many previously male occupations and males are now are free to show their more sensitive, nurturant sides. Finally, today's children are seen as more competent, ready, and able to deal with whatever our postmodern society has to throw at them. In their turn, adolescents are now viewed as sophisticated and knowledgeable about technology, drugs, and sex.

My own research has focused on how the postmodern perception of adolescence maps onto the biological and psychological characteristics of adolescents that have remained unchanged. Much of our work suggests that it is the mismatch between out new postmodern perception of adolescents and the real developing need of young people that helps account for at least a part of the disturbed behavior among them. As just one example, body piercing, tattooing, and hair dyeing are adolescent-created markers of their marginal status that replace societal markers, rites of passage, that have been taken away from them. Our task is to shape our postperceptions of adolescents in such a way that they reflect both the changes in society and the abiding needs, interests, and abilities of the young.

You can see an illustration of the functioning of the imaginary audience and of some emotional concomitants of this cognitive development if you think back to your days of early adolescence. Assuredly some new fad, perhaps in regard to a particular style of clothing, sprang up among your peers. Some adolescents you knew perhaps were stuck wearing the outdated style and were literally afraid to be seen in public. Because they were so aware of their absence of fitting in, they were equally sure that everyone was immediately aware of their shortcomings.

A second component of adolescent egocentrism also exists. The adolescent's thoughts and feelings are experienced as new and unique. Although to the adolescent they are in fact new and unique, the young person comes to believe that they are historically new and unique. The adolescent constructs a **personal fable,** the belief that he or she is a unique, one-of-a-kind individual, a person having singular feelings and thoughts.

Here too, it is easy to think of an illustration of the personal fable. We can think back to our early adolescent years and our first "love affair." No one ever loved as deeply, as totally . . . no one had ever felt such

> **Personal fable** Belief that one is a unique, one-of-a-kind individual; the idea that one is a singular person having singular feelings and thoughts.

implications for parenting box 4.1

Why Every Young Adolescent Sees Himself or Herself as the Center of the World

Thirteen-year-old Alexandra picks at her dinner, rolling the peas around her plate, not saying a word to anyone. Afterward, when her father invites her to join the rest of the family for a rental video and a bowl of popcorn, she instead barricades herself in her room.

There, overwhelmed by her feelings, she sulks and thinks about Sam, the guy who sits across from her in math class. How could he have ignored her sitting at the same table at lunch, especially when he *must* know how she feels about him? How could he *not* know? It doesn't occur to her that she has never said so much as "hello" to Sam.

Alexandra cannot imagine that anyone, ever, has felt so much or so deeply. Those who study adolescent behavior call this a "personal fable," the child's belief that she is, for better or worse, utterly different from everyone else. To a parent, such preteen—and even teenage—behavior appears self-centered, even grandiose. But it is absolutely normal, and quite different from being selfish or putting on airs.

But how can you help your child get through this period of egocentrism, especially when it is frequently so difficult to communicate with her? You can start by maintaining your patience and empathy—and a good memory of your own adolescence.

By the preadolescent years, a child's emotional and mental sophistication has grown to the point that she is quite comfortable with thinking abstractly. She asks new questions: "What if I try acting like this instead?" If I dress that way, what will happen?" Her sudden discovery of all these new alternatives is exhilarating, but with it

comes profound uncertainty about making the right choices.

Within your family, your child often displays this uncertainty by questioning the house rules. Although being challenged by your preteen can be trying, remember that the questioning comes not out of disrespect but because, for the first time, your child envisions a range of alternatives.

At the same time that they are moving rapidly toward maturity, young teens are still in many ways children. They have a tendency to focus almost exclusively on their own ideas, feelings, and behavior. Assuming that they are as central in the thoughts of others as they are in their own, children this age often feel as if an imaginary audience is continually observing and judging everything they say, do, feel, and wear.

That's why 13-year-old Tom flushes with embarrassment and fury when his mother volunteers to chaperone a school dance. Even if he doesn't attend, he'll be humiliated because everone will know that his mother is there. Reminded that there will be ten adult chaperones and, therefore, nine other classmates in the same boat, Tom responds, "Well, they don't care as much about what their parents do." As far as he is concerned, his own shame is uniquely awful.

Preteens tend to feel that their problems are more obvious and important than those of other people. Sally, 11, feels sure that everyone can tell she's wearing a tampon. And 12-year-old Richard sits at his desk, head tucked into his arm, convinced that the new pimple on his cheek is the object of everyone's disgusted gaze.

intense passion, devotion, the longing, the overwhelming fulfillment that we felt for this, our one true love. . . . Then remember a few days or week later when the relationship ended, when it was "over!" The pain, the depression, the agony . . . no one had ever suffered so deeply, no one had ever been so wrongfully abused, so thoroughly tortured, so spitefully crushed by unrequited love. . . . We sat in our rooms, unmoving, and our mothers would say, "What's wrong with you? Dinner is ready. Come and eat." Our inevitable answer:

"You don't understand. What do you know about love?"

Clearly, then, adolescent egocentrism is a feature of cognitive functioning that has both emotional and social components. Indeed, this may be especially true for girls. A heightened sense of imaginary audience is associated with depression among girls, but not boys (Schonert-Reichl, 1994). High egocentrism among girls is associated with their perceptions of being at high risk for problems (Dolcini et al., 1989).

The worst thing you can do when your child's outsize emotions are on display is to dismiss them. They may seem silly to you, but they are all too real to her. If she broods for days about whether she said the right thing to a boy she met at a party, or insists on a certain style of shirt, don't make fun of her or say that her worries aren't important. Doing so will only reinforce her sense that no one understands her.

Don't pooh-pooh a child's need to be accepted.

And be tolerant of the fact that, because your child feels so utterly different from everyone else, fitting in with his peers becomes a top priority in his life. Accept his need to be accepted. If he spurns your peck on his cheek as you're dropping him off at school and says, "You're embarrassing me in front of all my friends," it won't help for you to point out that no one can see inside the car.

Your wisest course of action in such cases is to talk about his concerns and to negotiate solutions that both of you can live with. For example, you might express your willingness not only to stop kissing him when you leave him at school but also to drop him off around the corner and out of sight—if he is willing to offer you a hug when he gets home. It should be added, however, that acknowledging your child's need to be part of the crowd does not require that you accept open rudeness or give in to demands for the most expensive sneakers in the store.

You can't banish your preteen's self-consciousness, but you can help him see that although others think and care about him, they also have other things on their minds. One way to accomplish this is to share your own adolescence with him. (This is where a good memory—or a high school yearbook—can come in handy.)

Think back to your own adolescent crises. In describing to your child how embarrassed you were the time you had to take a shower after gym class, or how hopelessly in love you were after your first date, you can help him understand that he is not alone in his feelings. Focus on how you felt at the time, not on how "everything worked out fine."

If your daughter is among the first girls in her class to start developing breasts, acknowledge how embarrassing that can be, and then talk about the ways that other kids in her class stand out. How might another girl feel about being the tallest or the only one with braces? Help your child see that all of her peers are different in some way, and that this difference is not necessarily bad.

Outside pursuits get kids outside themselves.

Another way that you can give your preteen a less egocentric perspective on the world is by encouraging her to be involved with a range of activities and people. Playing multiple roles in sports, joining arts groups, or even being with peers who share a hobby can shift your child's focus outside herself.

As your child gets older, she'll begin to realize that her thoughts and emotions are not as odd or unique as she once believed. Of course, most of us keep traces of our youthful egocentrism; we all feel that we're the ones who always get the parking ticket or pick the slowest line at the store. But adults have realized that their imaginary audience is just that—imaginary. Be patient; your preteen will realize it too.

Source: Lerner, R. M., & Olson, C. K. (1994, February). The imaginary audience. *Parents*, pp. 133–134.

From the perspective of the parent of an adolescent, having a young person in the midst of adolescent egocentrism presents a formidable challenge for child rearing. Implications for Parenting Box 4.1 describes the impact of adolescent egocentrism on parents and suggests ways for coping with a youth in this period of development.

Research about the nature and importance of adolescent egocentrism continues (e.g., Elkind & Bowen, 1979; Enright, Lapsley, & Shukla, 1979; Enright, Shukla, & Lapsley, 1980; Lapsley, 1991; Schonert-Reichl, 1994). There seem to be rich implications of adolescent egocentrism for adolescent cognitive, personality, and social development. For instance, adolescent egocentrism is highly related to **social cognition** (e.g., Vartanian & Powlishta, 1996). As discussed next, many of the features of the development of social cognition during adolescence are marked by egocentric thinking, especially at the beginning of this period.

> **Social cognition** Thinking about interpersonal relationships and the social world.

Social Cognition During Adolescence

Issues to Consider
- What are the characteristics of adolescent social cognition?
- How does social cognition differ between younger and older adolescents?

Formal operational thinking may be applied to any content area, including mathematics or the social world. This latter content area is termed social cognition. Such thought may involve virtually any aspect of the adolescent's social life. The development of social cognition occurs in a manner consistent with changes that are associated with formal operational development more generally.

Young adolescents, who are at the threshold of their formal operational period, may make decisions about social issues in a manner that is more egocentric than would be the case among youth at later points in their formal operational period. In a study of youth ranging in age from 6 through 18 years (Dyl & Wapner, 1996), younger individuals were more egocentric than older ones in their thoughts about cherished social objects (e.g., emphasizing the personal enjoyment provided by such possessions). Older youth thought about such valued possessions in a manner that reflected their understanding of the social relationships involved with one's possessions.

Social cognition among older youth typically involves the use of social principles. In a study of 120 Latino and European American fifth, eighth, and eleventh graders (Phinney & Cobb, 1996), youth were asked to respond to a dilemma in which a student from one ethnic group wished to join an exclusive club of the other ethnic group. Although three quarters of the participants made judgments to include the student, and neither ethnicity, grade, nor gender was related to these judgments of inclusion, older youth more often cited abstract social principles, as compared to individual welfare, as the basis for their decisions (Phinney & Cobb, 1996). In a study of the strategies 10-, 12-, and 14-year-olds use to present themselves socially, youth were asked about their willingness to portray themselves as diligent and as making a lot of effort to work hard in school (Juvonen & Murdock, 1995). Adolescents in

the two younger age groups wanted to present themselves as effortful to both teachers and peers. However, in light of a changing idea about the social value of achievement among one's peers and of the tactics one must use for successful self-presentation to friends, the older adolescents were more reluctant to convey to their popular peers that they were diligent students (Juvonen & Murdock, 1995).

Adolescents who are at the beginning of their formal operational period may not make decisions about social issues in as differentiated a manner as occurs later in their formal operational period. In a study of fourth, sixth, and eighth graders, youth were asked about the role a peer plays when the peer witnesses an act of aggression perpetrated by either a sibling or by a friend (Tisak & Tisak, 1996). The younger participants tended to think that bystanders should intervene and in fact would intervene. The older participants indicated that there is more of an expectation to intervene when the perpetrator is a sibling, and it would be more wrong not to intervene when the aggressor was a sibling than a friend (Tisak & Tisak, 1996).

Other evidence suggests that older adolescents possess a differentiated social cognitive structure. In two studies of about 350 late adolescents enrolled in college, evidence was found for several distinct components of social cognition (e.g., social perception, social knowledge, and social insight) (Wong et al., 1995). Other evidence indicates that such a differentiated intellectual orientation to the world is used when youth make social decisions. Adolescence is a time of choices involving self-definition and social roles (topics discussed in Chapters 6 and 7). Young people must make decisions about what sorts of activities they will undertake, both in the present and in the future. In one study of such decisions (Finken & Jacobs, 1996), 18- to 20-year-old adolescents were presented with four topic areas (abortion, medical issues, future plans, and interpersonal relations) and asked to select the people they would turn to for advice. Consistent with the presence of a differentiated cognitive structure, one in which different social issues are understood in their specific context, adolescents indicated they would consult with different groups for the different topics. For example, although abortion decisions may involve medical procedures, adolescents indicated they would prefer to consult with different people for advice about abortions than for advice about general medical issues (Finken & Jacobs, 1996). Similarly, with increasing development, individuals reason about gender roles, social conventions, and moral rules with greater flexibility (Levy, Taylor, & Gelman, 1995).

Social cognition develops across the formal operational stage in a manner reflective of other cognitive changes of this stage. Social thought becomes less egocentric and more responsive to societal conventions. It becomes more differentiated and more attuned to the particular social audience or context to which it is directed, and it is also increasingly more reflective of abstract principles of social organization.

The choices adolescents make are facilitated by their capacities for hypothetical and propositional thought.

Conclusions About Formal Operations

Egocentrism of the formal operational stage diminishes over the course of the person's subsequent cognitive functioning. According to Piaget (Inhelder & Piaget, 1958), the adolescent "decenters" through interaction with peers, elders, and, most importantly, with the assumption of adult roles and responsibilities: "The focal point of the decentering process is the entrance into the occupational world or the beginning of serious professional training. The adolescent becomes an adult when he or she undertakes a real job" (Inhelder & Piaget, 1958, p. 346).

Quite interestingly, Piaget sees the end point of adolescence as the adoption of a role in society, an idea consistent with what we will learn (in Chapter 6) is formulated by Erikson (1959, 1963). Thus within different theoretical perspectives the linkage of adolescents with their society through the processes of role search and attainment is a core component of development (Kahlbaugh & Haviland, 1991). Indeed, formal operations are related to adolescent identity resolution (Leadbeater &

Dionne, 1981). Some scholars (e.g., Wagner, 1987) have posited that formal operations are necessary for identity achievement in adolescence.

What, then, does the achievement of formal operations give adolescents? How does it help them deal with the developmental tasks imposed by their changed body? How does it help them find an appropriate niche in the social world? Being able to think hypothetically allows adolescents to imagine what their life would be like if they chose one or another life path: "Would I, given my physical characteristics, my beliefs, my values, and my hopes, be able to be a salesclerk, a day care worker, an athlete, or a parent? Would I be more happy doing one or the other of these things?" Formal operational thinking gives adolescents the ability to see themselves as workers, as parents, and as citizens. Given their understanding of their physical and psychological characteristics, formal thought enables adolescents to make plans and to establish goals and priorities.

For example, a tall, big-boned girl may understand that she would not do well in a career as a ballet dancer; but perhaps she would succeed in, and could plan for, sports such as basketball. In turn, a boy who understood that he liked helping others, enjoyed working with people, but did not prefer highly technical or scientific endeavors, could plan to enter the field of social work (as opposed to medicine or nursing).

Accordingly, formal thought allows adolescents to plan and to obtain the knowledge and skills for entry into the world of work, and to fit their individual characteristics with available or possible social roles. Formal thought allows adolescents to meet their psychological developmental tasks of understanding self and defining self appropriately and to move in the direction of becoming an independent adult. Adolescents will be able to be autonomous, self-governing people to the extent that they know who they are, know what they want, and can plan accordingly.

Conclusions

Formal thought allows people to demonstrate planful responsibility for their future, to plan to prepare themselves to merge with the social world as responsible partners in the enterprise of advancing self and their society. Such responsible partnership with the social world gives adolescents an important sense of morality (Kohlberg, 1978). It gives them a sense that an implicit, mutual contract exists between adolescents and their society. Society will provide a role that will allow adolescents to exercise their individuality, particular interests and abilities, and the opportunity to test this role. In turn, adolescents will responsibly perform these roles and be, for instance, productive workers, good parents, and participating citizens. In its most general sense, formal operations ability enables adolescents to organize a belief system involving self and society. It gives them a life plan, an ideology, and a moral code by which to live.

In short, a key contribution of cognitive development to adolescent functioning is the potential role it may play in allowing the young people to exist as moral members of society. We explore this potential contribution in the next chapter.

Summary

- The adolescent years involve changes in cognition and personality that influence each other and are influenced by the social, cultural, and broader ecological contexts.
- Cognitively, adolescents have more quantitative knowledge and think about their world in qualitatively different ways.
- There are debates about what psychological characteristics are actually measured by intelligence tests. Spearman hypothesized one general intellectual factor ("g") is being measured. Guilford theorized that over 100 different abilities can be measured by intelligence tests.
- Other scholars propose that different aspects of cognition are assessed by intelligence tests and the distinct dimensions of quantitative intelligence remain consistent across the adolescent years.
- Qualitative features of cognition constitute a key dimension of cognitive development.
- Academic achievement is affected by multiple levels of the context of human development, ranging from the most macro cultural influences to micro interpersonal influences involving peers and family members.
- The academic achievements of youth from different cultural backgrounds differ due, primarily, to socialization experiences beginning in childhood.
- Even within a cultural group, family and peer variables have an influence on academic achievement.
- Peers have a facilitative influence on academic achievement. The use of peers seems especially useful when the interactions with them are specifically relevant to the particular problem at hand. Spending a lot of time in informal peer interactions appears to have a negative impact on academic achievement—high sociability ratings from peers is linked to lower academic competence.
- Some instances of low achievement are related to adolescents' own characterization of themselves. "Self-handicapping strategies" are associated with self-deprecation, negative attitudes toward education, and low grades.
- Self-enhancing strategies such as the ability to delay gratification in preschool facilitates cognitive and academic competence in adolescence.

- There are numerous interventions that enhance academic achievement among youth and the interrelated problems of youth development.
- Adolescent literacy skills can affect their own life chances as well as others in their social world.
- In Piaget's theory, cognitive development involves the relation between the person and the context. The person-context relation involves two processes: *assimilation* and *accommodation*.
- Piaget proposes that the goal of cognitive development is to create an *equilibration* between assimilation and accommodation.
- When the person is more concerned with the perspective of the subject than with the actual details of the object the person is said to be *egocentric*.
- Overcoming the egocentrism prototypic of each stage leads the person to attain the cognitive development most central to that stage.
- In the formal operational stage, the child's thoughts about reality take on a hypothetical "if . . . then" characteristic.
- The cognitive structure that characterizes formal operations is termed the *INRC group* by Piaget. All transformations of a problem may be obtained through the application of the components of this group: identity, negation, reciprocal, and correlative transformations.
- Conditional reasoning increases across adolescence, involving the idea that "if *p*, then *q*"—the logical statement in scientific hypotheses.

- A cognitive developmental progression exists, one that involves the adolescent moving from inductive to deductive reasoning strategies.
- The emergence of formal operational thought is not a characteristic of all youth. Not all individuals attain formal operations.
- People in many cultural settings do not attain formal operational abilities at the average time in life that it occurs within Western cultural settings.
- Egocentrism coincides with the emergence of adolescence and is complicated by the physiological, emotional, and social changes involved in this period of life.
- With adolescent egocentrism, the adolescent's own thoughts come to predominate his or her thinking. The adolescent constructs an *imaginary audience*. The adolescent's thoughts and feelings are experienced as new and unique. The adolescent constructs a *personal fable*.
- Across the formal operational stage social thought becomes less egocentric and more responsive to societal conventions.
- Through interaction with peers, elders, and, most importantly, with the assumption of adult roles and responsibilities, the adolescent decenters and the egocentrism of this stage diminishes.
- Piaget sees the end point of adolescence as the adoption of a role in society. Formal operations enables the adolescent to organize a belief system involving self and society.

Discussion Topics

1. Think of some experiences from your own childhood. Do you remember having an argument or disagreement with your parent(s) that at the time was very important and relevant to your life but now seems to be what you might define now as typical teenage behavior. Why, at the time, were you so devoted to your side of the argument? Does your response include multiple life contexts and reasons? Why?
2. How does the fact that IQ remains relatively stable throughout life color your view on the value of standardized tests and the courses and curricula designed to "teach to the test"?
3. Give an example of how an elementary school child and a high school child think differently about a specific emotional situation and about a specific academic experience.
4. How have your ecological contexts impacted your academic achievement?
5. How might an adolescent's ability to think hypothetically add to his or her conflict resolution skills?
6. How has your specific cultural socialization impacted your academic achievement and cognitive competence?
7. Why is it important for educational institutions to recognize and appreciate the cultural variations inherent in approaches to academic achievement?
8. How have your peers helped or hindered your cognitive development?
9. Why do some adolescents adopt self-handicapping strategies and some self-enhancing? Are there certain individual and/or contextual assets or risks that lead some teens to adopt more harmful/less supportive learning traits?

10. Were the programs offered by your high school designed to support those with learning disabilities and/or life circumstances that compromise academic achievement? Why or why not?

11. Do you believe your literacy skills were predetermined by the literacy achievement of your parent(s)?

12. Give an example of a memory of a concept that went through the equilibration process—that was assimilated and accommodated to. For example, as a school-aged child you thought one way about a concept and as a teenager you were able to realize there were many more "sides to the coin."

13. How do you feel adolescent egocentrism limits and defines the thought processes of teenagers? Specifically, did the imaginary audience and personal fables of your life limit your experiences and understandings? How?

14. Why might a simple concept such as the "if . . . then" logic of thinking expand your world and cognitive competence?

15. Think of an example to which you could apply the INRC grouping to explain the characteristics of formal operational thought.

16. Cite evidence to prove that formal operations do not exist as a "structured whole." Can you be "advanced" in one content area and "behind" in others?

17. Why might not formal operational thought be universal? Can you make assumptions about those who do not attain formal operational thought? Are those assumptions qualified? Must you be cautious in making those assumptions? Why or why not?

18. How might formal operational thought prepare you to be a participating member of society?

19. How has interaction with peers, elders, and, most importantly, with the assumption of adult roles and responsibilities, helped to diminish any sense of egocentrism you may have experienced as an adolescent?

Key Terms

accommodation (p. 91)

adolescent egocentrism (p. 96)

assimilation (p. 91)

centration (p. 96)

conditional reasoning (p. 93)

correlative transformation (p. 92)

deductive reasoning (p. 94)

disequilibration (p. 91)

egocentrism (p. 91)

equilibration (p. 91)

falsification strategies (p. 95)

formal operational thought (p. 92)

"g" (p. 85)

identity transformation (p. 92)

imaginary audience (p. 96)

inductive reasoning (p. 94)

INRC grouping (p. 92)

IQ (p. 85)

negation operation (p. 92)

personal fable (p. 97)

qualitative differences (p. 90)

reciprocal transformation (p. 92)

reproductive assimilation (p. 91)

social cognition (p. 99)

5

MORAL DEVELOPMENT, BEHAVIOR, AND CIVIL SOCIETY

Scott thought Mr. Simpson was a terrific teacher, perhaps the best he had had in his four years at Pathground High. Mr. Simpson made the honors calculus course come alive. Even though it was really hard for Scott, and his grade in the course was still dependent on the final, Mr. Simpson's love for math was infectious. He conveyed enthusiasm to his students and generated in them an excitement for learning. He was also nice, approachable, and always willing to spend as much time as necessary to help his students. When Scott had asked him to write letters of recommendation for college, Mr. Simpson did not flinch—even when Scott said that he was applying to 10 colleges, each needing a letter.

Scott also thought Mr. Simpson was one of the most disorganized people he had ever known. He always seemed to misplace things and, because he never remembered to check his daily calendar or wear a watch, he was inevitably running late for appointments.

As Scott knocked on the door to the teacher's lounge, to meet Mr. Simpson and give him copies of the final two forms he needed to complete the letters of recommendation, Scott was not surprised to hear a frazzled-sounding Mr. Simpson tell him to come in. "Hi, Mr. Simpson," Scott said, as he saw Mr. Simpson rushing to gather papers off the table in front of him and balance them under his arm atop of the books and folders he was also carrying. "I've brought the two copies of the forms I need you to fill out for me."

"Thanks, Scott. Please just stick them on top of this pile here under my arm. I'll be sure not to lose them this time. I'll put them in a folder as soon as I get to my next class."

"Are you sure, Mr. Simpson?" Scott asked. "It looks like you have a lot of papers there and they might get mixed in with them. I could just follow you to class and help you get organized and then put the letters in the folder for you."

"No, that won't work, Scott. These are copies of the honors calculus final exam. My first section of the course takes the exam this next period. Since you won't be taking the exam until last period, I don't think it's a good idea for you to help me organize these papers."

"Oh, sure. I agree. I didn't know what you were carrying,"

"I know, Scott. No problem. I'll be careful with the letters this time. Just stick them under my arm . . . Thanks."

Scott placed the letters on top of the pile and Mr. Simpson hurried out of the door and down the hall. Scott followed him out and saw him start a sprint down the corridor. As the bell to start the period sounded, Mr. Simpson moved the books and papers under his arm to the front of his body in order to cradle them with two hands as he continued his run.

A paper flew out from the pile and landed behind the now rapidly receding Mr. Simpson. Scott ran to get the paper, certain that it must be one of his letters. The long hall was now empty as Scott caught up to the fallen paper. Scott picked the paper up. It was not one of his letters. Typed across the top of the paper was the title "Honors Calculus: Final Exam."

Mr. Simpson would never know that he had lost this one copy of the exam, and no one would know that Scott had found it. He could, unbeknownst to anyone else, spend the rest of the day preparing the answers to the exam, ace it, and be sure that a great grade in an honors course would be reported to college admissions' offices. Or, he could simply destroy the copy and not even look at it. Or, he could just give it back to Mr. Simpson, and hope he would believe Scott had not looked at it. What should he do?

LEARNING OBJECTIVES

1. To understand what civil society is and how it can be promoted.
2. To appreciate why the study of moral development is important.
3. To understand Lawrence Kohlberg's framework for studying moral development and to describe his levels and stages of moral development.
4. To recognize that individual and contextual factors influence levels of moral reasoning.
5. To understand how war and social conflict can influence moral reasoning.
6. To understand the development of prosocial behavior and the influences on it.

7. To appreciate the need for "youth charters" that create partnerships in the promotion of civil society.
8. To identify the 20 internal and 20 external developmental assets of youth and how these assets correlate with positive youth development.
9. To understand the model for promoting civil society through enhancing positive youth development and how this model may influence future generations.
10. To identify the "five Cs" related to positive developmental outcomes that can be attained from appropriate policies and programs.

Issues to Consider

- What is civil society? How is it maintained?
- What is the relation between civil society and adolescent moral development?

For any society to maintain and perpetuate itself over the course of generations, it must become committed to promoting the healthy, productive, and successful development of self, family, and society. Such a commitment by youth constitutes an allegiance to **civil society**, that is, to society's nongovernmental and governmental institutions (including cultural and political values) that provide rights to people and require responsibilities of individuals (Lerner, Fisher, & Weinberg, 2000a).

One key component of positive youth development is caring (or compassion) for others.

Civil society balances the rights "granted to individuals in free societies and the responsibilities required by citizens to maintain those rights" (O'Connell, 1999, pp. 10–11).

For civil society to exist, individuals must believe in and hold values that support a just, democratic social order. In both their personal lives and their roles as citizens, individuals must support justice and act to maintain governmental institutions and laws, and nongovernmental organizations, that promote social justice, equity, and democracy.

Within the context of civil society, morally developed youth think and behave in ways that maintain and enhance a just social order. Moral development involves thinking and behaving **prosocially**, in ways that allow society to create a just and equitable system. Given the crucial salience for the survival of a civil society, and for the quality of life of citizens within such a society, the study of moral development continues to be a central concern of scholars of human development and of adolescence in particular.

As noted in Chapter 2, Piaget (1932/1965), in *The Moral Judgment of the Child*, provided an important theoretical foundation for this topic. He discussed the development of moral reasoning and stressed that the child initially judges right and wrong solely on the basis of the objective outcomes of a behavior. For example, if the child's behavior resulted in a broken cup, the child is bad. At a subsequent point in development, the child makes judgments based on intentions. For example, if the child broke the cup intentionally, the child would be judged as bad; but if the act was an inadvertent mishap, no negative judgment would be made.

Building on Piaget's work, Lawrence Kohlberg (1958, 1963a, 1963b, 1976, 1978), Elliot Turiel (1969; Nucci & Turiel, 1993), Nancy Eisenberg (1986, 1991; Carlo, Eisenberg, & Knight, 1992), Paul Mussen (Eisenberg & Mussen, 1989; Mussen et al., 1970), William Damon (1997), and Anne Colby (1978; Colby et al., 1983) have extended the study of moral development in several significant ways. Today, the study of adolescent moral functioning focuses on both moral thinking or reasoning *and* moral behaviors, especially prosocial behaviors, that is, behaviors that *benefit* society. The study of moral development has also been extended to include an interest in how the strengths

> **Civil society** Society in which cultural and political values, as well as all nongovernmental and governmental institutions, both provide rights to people and require responsibilities of individuals.
>
> **Prosocial behavior** Behavior that allows society to create a just and equitable system; individuals act in a way that contributes to a just social order.

of the developing adolescent may be integrated with the assets of communities to enhance the likelihood that young people will develop the cognitive, emotional, and behavioral attributes requisite for contributing to civil society.

In this chapter we discuss all three of these foci: the development of moral reasoning, the character and bases of prosocial behavior, and the ways that youth and community assets may be combined to further civil society. Building on the discussion of cognitive development in adolescence (Chapter 4), we begin this presentation with a discussion of the development of moral reasoning.

Chapter 2 introduced the general characteristics of Kohlberg's theory of moral reasoning development. In the relatively recent history of the study of moral development, Kohlberg's theory and research has been most influential. We present more details of his work in order to provide a frame for discussing what is known about adolescent moral functioning.

Lawrence Kohlberg's Theory of the Development of Moral Reasoning

Issues to Consider
- What is the focus of Kohlberg's theory of moral development?
- What are Kohlberg's three levels and five stages of moral development?

Kohlberg (1958, 1963, 1978) proposed that a theory of moral development should focus on the reasons for moral behavior, rather than moral behavior itself. Two people could show similar moral behavior, but the reason for their behavior can be very different. One person could refuse to steal because he or she was afraid of being caught and punished. The second could say one should not steal because such behavior violates principles of mutual trust. Kohlberg devised a way to ascertain the reasons underlying moral behavior through the construction of a moral development interview. Information derived from

this interview provided the data for the theory he formulated.

Kohlberg's Method of Assessing Moral Reasoning

To understand the reasons for a person's moral behavior, Kohlberg devised a series of stories, each presenting an imaginary moral dilemma. Here is an example:

> One day air raid sirens began to sound. Everyone realized that a hydrogen bomb was going to be dropped on the city by the enemy, and that the only way to survive was to be in a bomb shelter. Not everyone had bomb shelters, but those who did ran quickly to them. Since Mr. and Mrs. Jones had built a shelter, they immediately went to it where they had enough air inside to last them for exactly five days. They knew that after five days the fallout would have diminished to the point where they could safely leave the shelter. If they left before that, they would die. There was enough air for the Joneses only. Their next-door neighbors had not built a shelter and were trying to get in. The Joneses knew that they would not have enough air if they let the neighbors in, and that they would all die if they came inside. So they refused to let them in.
>
> So now the neighbors were trying to break the door down in order to get in. Mr. Jones took his rifle and told them to go away or else he would shoot. They would not go away. So he either had to shoot them or let them come into the shelter.

This story is a moral dilemma because it presents a conflict to the listener. In this particular story the conflict involves the need for choice between two culturally unacceptable alternatives: killing others so that you might survive or allowing others and yourself and family to die. The story presents a dilemma because it puts the listener in a conflict situation such that any response is clearly not the only acceptable one. For Kohlberg, the particular response is irrelevant, but what is of concern is the reasoning used to resolve the conflict. Thus Kohlberg asks the listener not just to tell him what Mr. Jones should do but why Mr. Jones should do whatever the listener decides.

Kohlberg would first ask, "What should Mr. Jones do?" Next he would ask, "Does he have the

Table 5-1	Levels and Stages in Lawrence Kohlberg's Theory of Moral Reasoning

Level 1: Preconventional

Stage 1. Heteronomous morality. "Egocentric point of view." The person does not consider the interests of others or recognize that they differ from the actor's. The person does not relate two points of view. Actions are considered physically rather than in terms of the psychological interests of others. There is a confusion of authority's perspective with one's own.

Stage 2. Individualism, instrumental purpose, and exchange. "Concrete individualistic perspective." The person is aware that everybody has interests to pursue and that these can conflict. Right is relative (in the concrete individualistic sense).

Level 2: Conventional

Stage 3. Mutual interpersonal expectations, relationships, and interpersonal conformity. "Perspective of the individual in relationships with other individuals." The person is aware of shared feelings, agreements, and expectations, which take primacy over individual interests, and relates points of view through the concrete "golden rule," putting oneself "in the other guy's shoes." The person does not yet consider generalized system perspective.

Stage 4. Social system and conscience. "Differentiates societal point of view from interpersonal agreement or motives." At this stage, the person takes the point of view of the system that defines roles and rules and considers individual relations in terms of play in the system.

Level 3: Postconventional, or Principled

Stage 5. Social contract or utility and individual rights. "Prior-to-society perspective." The rational individual is aware of values and rights prior to social attachments and contracts. Such a person integrates perspectives by formal mechanisms of agreement, contract, objective impartiality, and due process; considers moral and legal points of view; and recognizes that they sometimes conflict and finds it difficult to integrate them.

Source: Adapted from Kohlberg, 1976.

right to shoot his neighbors if he feels they would all die if he let them in because there would not be enough air to last very long? Why?" Then, "Does he have the right to keep his neighbors out of his shelter even though he knows they will die if he keeps them out? Why?" And finally Kohlberg would ask, "Does he have the right to let them in if he knows they will all die? Why?"

On the basis of an elaborate and complicated system for scoring, the reasons people give to questions about this and other dilemmas (Kohlberg, 1958, 1963a; Kurtines & Greif, 1974) have evolved into a system that has undergone considerable revision (Colby, 1979). Kohlberg classifies people into different reasoning categories. This classification led him to formulate the idea that a sequence exists in the types of reasons people offer about their responses to moral dilemmas. He believed that the types of moral reasoning people use pass through a series of qualitatively different stages. Kohlberg (1976, 1978) and his collaborators (Colby, 1978, 1979) specify five stages of moral reasoning. The first and second stages, and the third and fourth stages, are associated with two distinct levels of moral thought, respectively. The fifth stage is asso-

ciated with a third level. These levels and stages are shown in Table 5.1.

Developmental Sequences in Moral Reasoning

Issue to Consider

• What evidence exists that there is a progression for the development of moral reasoning?

Kohlberg and his colleagues (e.g., Kohlberg, 1958, 1963a, 1963b, 1971, 1976; Colby et al., 1983) investigated whether moral reasoning progresses through a sequence akin to that suggested by his theory. Other researchers have also investigated how both moral reasoning and moral behaviors develop. This research indicates that there is some sequence to moral reasoning development.

Data collected in a longitudinal study by Kohlberg and his colleagues (Colby, 1979; Colby et al., 1983) provide the strongest support of the view that from

Heteronomous morality
Form of moral reasoning in which the person does not consider the interests of others or recognize that the interests of others differ from his or her own.

late childhood to the early part of the middle adult years, people go through the stages of moral reasoning in the manner Kohlberg specifies. Other data also suggest a developmental progression toward using principles or intentions to judge whether a person's behaviors are moral (Lourenço, 1990; Walker & Taylor, 1991). In a study of college freshman and college seniors about moral reasoning related to sexual behaviors that could result in the transmission of sexually transmitted diseases (STDs), the older group had a higher stage of moral reasoning (Jadack et al., 1995). In a longitudinal study of elementary and high school students' reasoning about moral dilemmas, elementary school children's reasoning tended to be pleasure oriented, stereotyped, approval oriented, and interpersonally oriented and/or it tended to involve labeling of others' needs (Eisenberg-Berg, 1979). Stereotyped images of persons and interpersonally oriented or approval-oriented reasoning were less evident among high school students and, alternatively, they used more emphatic considerations. Judgments reflecting internalized values increased with age.

Other studies indicate that adolescents use a variety of reasons to support their moral judgments. Early in adolescence, youth use reasons that reflect narrow or selfish concerns as well as concerns about care (wanting others not to suffer) and justice (using principles such as the "golden rule") (Perry & McIntire, 1995). Although all types of reasons are used by both males and females, boys were more likely than girls to use "narrow," selfish reasons (Perry & McIntire, 1995). Although, in early adolescence, girls are more advanced in their moral reasoning, by late adolescence and adulthood, sex differences in level of moral reasoning disappear (Basinger, Gibbs, & Fuller, 1995; Jadack et al., 1995).

Diversity and Context in Moral Development

Issue to Consider

- Why do individual differences and context need to be considered when studying moral development and behavior?

Moral development involves an orientation of a person toward others in his or her world. This relation underscores the social relational character of morality and why society deems morality so integral to maintaining the quality of life in a community. However, not all youth have similar levels of moral reasoning. This variation seems to be associated with gender and with different types of social experiences. Most of these experiences relate to interactions with models of moral behavior, including family members and people in the community (Camino, 1995). Individual differences and context need to be taken into account in understanding both the development of moral reasoning and of moral behavior.

Gender Differences

Issue to Consider

- What differences exist in moral reasoning and behavior between males and females?

There is some evidence of gender differences in the development of moral reasoning. Particularly during early adolescence, girls may be more advanced than boys. Carol Gilligan (1982) argues that approaches such as Kohlberg's stress the male "voice" of moral reasoning, a voice focused on "justice," rather than the female voice of reasoning, a voice focused on "care." Although not all research supports Gilligan's viewpoint (e.g., Brabeck, 1983; Walker, 1984), there are findings consistent with her perspective.

Adolescent girls, more so than adolescent boys, show a care-based morality that involves caring for other people (Skoe & Gooden, 1993). Girls also have more personal, real-life dilemmas, whereas boys have more impersonal ones. Girls' emotions are related to their interpersonal caring and their involvement in the problems of other significant people in their lives (Gore, Aseltine, & Colten, 1993). Girls are more concerned about hurting others and maintaining friendships; boys are concerned more about leisure activities and avoiding trouble (Skoe & Gooden, 1993).

Although not associated with Gilligan's (1982) ideas, other research does suggest gender differences in moral reasoning. From childhood through adolescence and into adulthood, women's overall prosocial moral reasoning increases more so than is the case for men (Eisenberg et al., 1995). However, for both women and men there are relations among prosocial reasoning, feelings of sympathy, the cognitive ability to take another person's perspective, and prosocial *behavior* (Eisenberg et al., 1995). The prosocial behavior of both men and women is related to having socially integrative goals, as compared to self-enhancing goals (Estrada, 1995).

There are also gender differences in ideas about punishments for violating behavioral rules. Young adolescent boys see disciplinary interventions for cheating as more acceptable than for breaking classroom rules for talking or getting out of one's seat (Bear & Stewart, 1990). Girls are more accepting of applying discipline for any infraction of rules.

There is diversity in moral reasoning, moral behavior, and in other morality-related thoughts and feelings (e.g., perspective taking, judging rule violations, empathy, and caring) linked to variation across development and to gender. This variation is also associated with contextual effects involving social interactions of several types.

Prosocial behavior in adolescence may involve caring for others.

Contextual "Models" of Moral Behavior

Issues to Consider

- How can modeling promote moral development in youth?
- What other contextual factors can influence moral functioning?

For more than 30 years, research has demonstrated that moral reasoning and behavior does not just naturally unfold. Rather, people to whom a youth is exposed shape his or her morality. The fact that modeling positive, or prosocial, moral behavior can

help develop it in others has resulted in several programs being designed worldwide to inculcate a prosocial orientation in youth. Given the investment all societies have in socializing the next generation to maintain and enhance the social fabric of their nation, and the increasing economic, technological, and ecological interdependence of all nations, it is likely that such programs will become even more important in the future. The programs discussed in Applications Box 5.1 illustrate the nature and scope of current efforts to foster moral leadership values and citizenship skills among today's youth.

The research associated with these programs indicates that both "experimentally created" and naturally occurring models (parents and peers) can promote moral thought and action. For instance, first- and second-grade children were shown either a model who made moral judgments on the basis of the motives underlying an act (intentions), a model who made judgments on the basis of the consequences of an act, or no model at all (Walker & Richards, 1976). Children exposed to the last model showed no changes in the type of moral judgments they offered; children exposed to the other two models showed changes in their moral reasoning in the direction of the particular model to which they were exposed. Third and

applications box 5.1

Creating Character, Caring, Competence, and Community Commitment Among Diverse Youth

Every society in the world needs a younger generation committed to and capable of moral, compassionate, intellectually sound, and productive leadership. The individuals, families, and communities of any nation will be healthier, and provide a more wholesome and higher quality of life, when its youth have such capacities.

Around the world, organizations and programs are striving to develop such youth community leadership. Two such programs, one involving over thirty nations around the globe, and the other centered in the United States, are described.

A School-Based Approach to Learning Life Skills: The Quest International "Skills for Growing, Skills for Adolescence and Skills for Action" Programs of Maryland, the United States

Founded in 1975, Quest International is an organization dedicated to the positive development of young people. Since its inception, Quest has recognized the need for children and youth to grow up and learn in healthy, safe, and nurturing environments. In its work with schools, community agencies, and youth-serving organizations worldwide, Quest has transmitted its belief that young people must be provided guidance so they may embrace positive values such as honesty, integrity, respect for self and family, and service to others.

As a youth advocacy organization, Quest has joined over the years with like-minded partners to ensure that our schools become caring and nurturing environments,

free of violence, weapons, and alcohol, tobacco, and other drugs. Joined in common purpose with its partners, Quest advocates a spirit of increased cooperation between families, schools, and other caring adults to meet the educational, physical, and emotional needs of youth. Throughout its existence, Quest has provided the tools and training to assist and empower parents, teachers, and community members in teaching children to make healthy decisions.

Lions Clubs International, an international service organization, has joined with Quest and other partners in the development of its programs aimed at positive youth development. These programs, *Skills for Growing*, designed for 5- to 10-year-old children, *Skills for Adolescence*, used with children 10 to 14 years of age, and *Skills for Action*, for 15 to 19 year olds, focus on the importance of acquiring key life skills such as decision making, goal setting, knowledge about the danger of alcohol and drugs, self-confidence, and problem solving necessary for success in adult life.

Quest's programs are designed to involve the home and community in assisting young people to make the necessary connections between knowledge and responsible behavior. In cooperation with its many partners representing service organizations, parent and community agencies, and professional societies, Quest's life skills programs are used by more than 300,000 educators in more than 30 countries. As a measure of its mission to serve youth worldwide, Quest affiliated partners in the United States, Canada, New Zealand, Sweden, Argentina, Denmark, Finland, Germany, Iceland, India, Italy,

---

fourth graders were exposed to empathic, normative, or neutral speeches, or "preachings," as the researchers termed them (Eisenberg-Berg & Geisheker, 1979). These preachings were delivered by a principal or teacher. Emphatic preachings significantly enhanced generosity in children's behavior.

Researchers study the effect of experimental models because they believe they simulate the actual influences that other people may have on the developing

person. Other researchers study the direct influence of such groups. For instance, young adolescent girls who show high levels of honesty and altruism have warm, intimate interactions with their mothers and high self-esteem (Mussen et al., 1970). For boys, honesty is negatively related to gratifying relationships with parents and peers and to self-esteem.

Other research indicates that parents' moral judgments are associated with adolescents' moral reasoning, especially for girls (Speicher, 1994). When they

Netherlands, Norway, Pakistan, South Africa, Sri Lanka, and Thailand.

In a world full of danger and challenges, Quest's programs have made a difference in the lives of millions of young people in communities around the globe.

Helping Youth Develop a Stronger Community: The "YouthBuild USA" Program of Massachusetts, the United States

In the United States, there are 5.4 million young people between 16 and 24 who either have dropped out of school without a diploma or completed high school but are nonetheless unemployed. There are approximately 2 million homeless people and countless government-owned properties in need of rehabilitation and construction. These are some of the grim facts that prompted the establishment of the YouthBuild program.

Founded in 1988, YouthBuild USA is committed to creating and sustaining a broad-based national movement to enable young people to assume leadership, rebuild their communities, gain an education, and lead responsible lives. YouthBuild is a comprehensive youth and community development program that has been designed by community activists with considerable contribution from young people over the past 22 years. In 2001, there were 165 YouthBuild programs operating in 43 states.

Young people interested in renewing their communities are trained in construction skills for 12 to 18 months. During their training, they rehabilitate abandoned buildings to provide affordable permanent housing for the homeless or very low-income people. In rural areas, because there are few abandoned buildings, they construct new housing. Besides weeks of on-site supervised construction work, they enrich their knowledge base with off-site academic and job skills training and counseling for half the program time. They receive a weekly stipend of US $150. Upon completion of the YouthBuild program, graduates usually pursue a college career or obtain unsubsidized jobs in the construction industry where they earn between US $6 and US $18 per hour.

YouthBuild USA acts as a catalyst for positive change in the larger community by creating affordable housing, responding to the needs of homeless people and various community needs; creating access to well-paying, long-term, substantive jobs for young people; advocating for expanded resources for low-income communities and youth; providing and developing visible role models; and stabilizing and strengthening the economic fabric of local communities by fostering entrepreneurship and individual residential home ownership.

The YouthBuild program is operating in both urban and rural communities throughout the United States. Statistics collected each year since 1993 show that an average of 60% of students complete the program, and 85% of these go on to college or jobs with wages averaging $7.60 an hour. This is especially noteworthy since 89% of the students had previously dropped out of school and most have enormous obstacles to overcome in their personal lives.

Source: International Youth Foundation, 2001. <www.ifynet.org>

are engaged with their youth in a morally relevant discussion, parents adjust their moral reasoning to the level of their adolescents (Walker & Taylor, 1991). When the parents' style of discussion involves Socratic questioning, supportive interactions, and use of moral reasons higher than those of their offspring, adolescent moral development is enhanced (Walker & Taylor, 1991).

The structure of the family, and the style of parent-child interaction, can influence moral func-

tioning among youth. Young adolescents living in a divorced family report more family-related moral dilemmas than youth living in intact families (Breen & Crosbie-Burnett, 1993).

Religiosity, perhaps especially in the home (McAdoo, 1995), can influence the development of moral reasoning and behavior. In a random sample of 13,250 adolescents, family religiosity was linked to a lessened likelihood of illicit drug use (Bahr et al., 1998). In longitudinal data from more than 1,500 adolescents, the expectation youth had of future religious activity was associated with a decreased risk of socially deviant behavior (Litchfield, Thomas, & Li, 1997). In data about adolescent religiosity and unsafe sexual behaviors derived from two national surveys (in 1982 and 1988), religious commitment was associated with a decreased likelihood of risk behaviors (Brewster et al., 1998).

The community surrounding the adolescent and his or her family is linked to moral functioning as well. For instance, youth from several different religious communities—Amish-Mennonite, Dutch Reform Calvinist, and Conservative and Orthodox Jewish—were found to differentiate between moral and nonmoral religious issues (Nucci & Turiel, 1993). Moral rules and some nonmoral ones were seen as not alterable by religious authorities. In all groups of youth, judgments regarding moral issues were justified in terms of justice and human welfare.

Social leadership in a community is also associated with morality. African American and Latino adolescents were nominated by community leaders for demonstrating high commitment to caring for others or for the community in general (Hart & Fegley, 1995). The youth community leaders described themselves as more moral and had more goals related to morality than youth not having such commitments. They also had better senses of the past and of their futures and believed their behaviors incorporated both their ideas and their images of their parents. Although they did not differ from the other youth in stage of moral reasoning, the youth leaders had ideas about themselves that stressed the importance of personal beliefs and of philosophy in governing one's life (Hart & Fegley, 1995).

Effects of War and Social Conflict on Moral Reasoning and Behavior

Issues to Consider

Post-traumatic stress disorder (PTSD) Psychological disorder experienced by individuals who have gone through some major traumatic experiences, such as a serious accident or war.

- How do war and social conflicts influence moral reasoning and behavior in youth?
- What can mediate the effects of war and social conflict on the development of moral behavior?

Not all community or broader social contexts can facilitate the development of moral reasoning and behavior. At some points in history and in some societal settings, the institutions of civil society may be so weak or so damaged that any potential positive contribution of community context to moral development is lost. Periods of war or of sustained social conflict may be such contexts. A growing body of research describes the risks to healthy youth development, and especially to the attainment of the moral orientation to contribute to civil society, that may occur in such contexts (e.g., Cairns & Dawes, 1996).

In a study of war experiences and psychosocial development of children in Lebanon (Macksoud & Aber, 1996), the traumas associated with growing up in a country torn by war were assessed among more than 200 10- to 16-year-olds. The more traumatic the war events, such as living through battles, kidnapping, torture, injury, mutilation, death of loved ones, separation from parents, or forced resettlement, the greater the likelihood of problems of adjustment and mental health, such as **post-traumatic stress disorder (PTSD)** or depression (Macksoud & Aber, 1996). In a sample of 170 Cambodian youth, an association between PTSD symptoms and war traumas was found (Sack, Clarke, & Seeley, 1996). In a study of 150 Palestinian youth living amid the Intifada in the West Bank, the number of risks present in the child's life due to the social strife of his or her context was related to the likelihood of the child having behavioral problems (Garbarino & Kostelny, 1996). Under conditions of high community risk (e.g., high level of political violence in the community), boys more than girls, and younger children more than older children, are at hightened behavioral risk (Garbarino & Kostelny, 1996). Among samples of youth living in South Africa during different periods of high violence, intracommunity violence was seen as the most significant problem for their adjustment (Straker et al., 1996). Finally, although, among a sample of Guatemalan Mayan Indian youth living in refugee camps in the Mexican state of Chiapas, depressive symptoms in girls were related to the poor health status of their mothers, positive maternal mental health was linked to good mental health among the youth (Miller, 1996).

Ideological or moral commitment to the political values involved in the conflict in one's society has been studied as a possible factor in moderating the effects of war on the behavioral development of youth (e.g., Covell, 1996; McLernon, Ferguson, & Cairns, 1997; Punamäki, 1996; Wainryb, 1995). For instance, in a study of 385 Israeli young adolescent girls and boys (Punamäki, 1996), exposure to political hardship and violence was associated with problems of anxiety, insecurity, depression, or with feelings of failure among youth with weak ideological commitment to the Israeli political cause. Among youth with a strong ideological commitment, these problems were not associated with the experience of political violence. That the buffering from the effects of war is due to political ideology, as contrasted to more general cultural differences between groups of youth in Israel, is supported by other research (Wainryb, 1995).

The specific national orientation to war can become a salient part of the ideology of youth. Canadian youth tend to possess attitudes reflective of the peacekeeping emphasis of Canada, whereas youth from the United States show attitudes prototypic of the interventionist policy orientation of the United States (Covell, 1996). In a study of about 100 14- to 15-year-olds from Northern Ireland, concepts of war as static and unchanging diminished after the country had committed itself to a cease-fire and to engagement in a peace process (McLernon et al., 1997).

Conclusions About the Individual and Contextual Bases of Moral Development

Considerable variation may exist in the development of moral reasoning and in behaviors that may reflect moral thought and support an order in society consistent with a moral stance reflective of social justice and civil society. By not affording young people the opportunity to develop in a community and societal context that supports the development of behaviors which advance the institutions of civil society, the positive development of children and society is risked. There is considerable social value to understanding the bases of the development of prosocial behavior among children.

The Development of Prosocial Behavior

Issues to Consider
- What developmental pattern exists for prosocial behavior?
- What factors influence the likelihood of prosocial behavior?

Nancy Eisenberg and her colleagues (e.g., Eisenberg et al., 1995; Eisenberg & Fabes, 1998) have studied extensively the development of prosocial reasoning and behavior. In a 15-year longitudinal follow-up of a study of the development of the reasons youth used for behaving in a prosocial manner, a complex pattern of prosocial moral reasoning was observed, one in which several distinct patterns of change were seen in regard to different types of prosocial reasoning (Eisenberg et al., 1995). Needs-oriented and stereotypic reasoning increased until mid-childhood/early adolescence and then declined in subsequent years. Hedonistic reasoning declined in use across childhood and into adolescence but then began to increase into early adulthood. Direct reciprocity and approval reasoning did not decline between mid-adolescence and early adulthood, but higher-level reasoning increased in use across adolescence and into early adulthood. Overall, females' prosocial reasoning was higher than that of males (Eisenberg et al., 1995).

Fabes and Eisenberg (1996) conducted an analysis of 179 studies of prosocial behavior. This analysis confirmed the general trend for higher prosocial moral reasoning across adolescence. The results also indicated that characteristics of the person in need of help influence the likelihood of prosocial behavior. For example, adolescents are more likely to act prosocially when the person in need is a child rather than an adult.

The general trend for higher prosocial moral reasoning across adolescence was confirmed in an analysis conducted by Fabes and Eisenberg (1996) of the results of 179 studies of prosocial behavior. This analysis indicated also that adolescents are particularly likely to act prosocially when the person in need of assistance is a child, as compared to an adult. Some of the recent work of Nancy Eisenberg is presented in Meet the Researcher Box 5.1.

Psychological and contextual characteristics also play roles in prosocial behavior (Eisenberg &

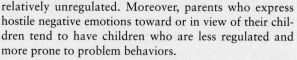

MEET THE RESEARCHER BOX 5.1

NANCY EISENBERG

EMOTION AND ITS REGULATION: CONTRIBUTORS TO DEVELOPMENT

Children and adolescents who get along with others and behave in a socially appropriate manner differ from their peers in a variety of ways. One important difference is in regard to how they express and handle their emotions. My interest is in the emotions children and youth express, the variety of ways they manage these emotions, and the factors that contribute to their success or failure at doing so.

In our work, which is supported by the National Institutes of Mental Health, we are following two samples of children from early school age into adolescence. We examine differences among the children in their tendencies to experience or express negative emotions such as sadness and anger, and their tendencies to regulate themselves by shifting their attention, focusing their attention, and inhibiting their behavior. For example, if a girl is angry, she can manage the anger by shifting her attention to other thoughts and control her facial and behavioral expression of anger (e.g., suppress facial expressions and aggressive responding). Children who are able to manage their attention and behavior in these ways tend to be socially competent and low in aggression and related problem behaviors, even if they are quick to anger. Moreover, they tend to be resilient to stress, sympathetic, and helpful to others. We are finding that differences in children's emotional responding and regulation predict how socially competent and adjusted they are, not only at the time, but years later.

Because of the importance of the regulation of emotions and emotionally driven behavior for children's development, we also are interested in why children differ in these aspects of their functioning. We believe that both socialization experiences and biologically based differences in temperament contribute to how children experience and manage emotions. Our data are consistent with the view that parents can help children learn ways to cope with their emotions and regulate their emotion-related behavior. For example, if parents respond punitively to children's expression of negative emotions such as sadness and embarrassment, their children tend to be

Nancy Eisenberg is Regents' Professor of Psychology at Arizona State University. She currently is editor of *Psychological Bulletin* and has been associate editor of *Personality and Social Psychology Bulletin* and *Merrill-Palmer Quarterly.*

relatively unregulated. Moreover, parents who express hostile negative emotions toward or in view of their children tend to have children who are less regulated and more prone to problem behaviors.

Currently, my colleagues Tracy Spinrad, Richard Fabes, and I, along with our students, are examining issues such as how differences in children's emotionality and regulation, and parents' expression and socialization of their children's emotional responding, relate to adolescents' adjustment, sympathy and social competence, and conflict with friends and parents. We also are examining stability and change in children's tendencies to express negative emotions and regulate themselves over 6 or more years. Findings from this work help us to understand stability and change in how children and youth deal with emotions and factors that contribute to healthy development. Moreover, in related work with Laurie Chassin funded by the National Institute of Drug Abuse, I am examining the relation of differences among children in their emotionality and regulation to familial risk for alcoholism (e.g., alcoholism in parent or grandparents) and behaviors associated with later alcoholism (e.g., antisocial behavior).

In addition to our work on emotion regulation, I study the development of sympathy and a prosocial orientation (i.e., the tendency to assist others). We have a longitudinal study in which a group of children have been studied from age 4 to 5 to age 25 to 26. We have found, for example, that children who spontaneously shared in preschool—that is, shared without being asked—were more helpful and sympathetic in childhood, adolescence, and even early adulthood. Their reasoning about why people help changed greatly over the years, and their thinking about this issue has been related to their tendencies to help and sympathize with others. In our view, prosocial development is an important aspect of successful social development. By studying a variety of factors contributing to social and emotional functioning, we hope to develop a richer, more nuanced picture of the complex process of social development.

Fabes, 1998). In a study of about 90 high school students, cognitive understanding of a situation, the ability to take the perspective of other people, and sympathy were related to prosocial behavior, in response to distress in friends (Estrada, 1995). Higher levels of prosocial behavior were associated with sympathy for one's friend as opposed to one's personal distress (Estrada, 1995).

Empathy, as well as sympathy, may be linked to prosocial behavior. For instance, among 5-, 9-, and 13-year-olds, empathy among boys was related to prosocial behavior (Roberts & Strayer, 1996), whereas in girls it was related to prosocial behavior with friends but not to cooperation with peers in general (Roberts & Strayer, 1996).

In addition to the peer group, the family, workplace, and school may provide contexts that influence the expression of prosocial behavior. In a study of 1,000 Minnesota youth, helpfulness in the home and in paid work settings was assessed (Call, Mortimer, & Shanahan, 1995). Helpfulness in the home was responsive to needs within the family, and helpfulness at work was related to behavioral competence among girls. For both boys and girls, the occurrence of helpfulness depended on the adolescent's motivation and on how meaningful the act of helping would be in the situation (Call et al., 1995).

Whether young adolescents did or did not cheat in a science class depended on whether the youth perceived their classrooms and schools as being extrinsically focused on performance and external rewards (Anderman et al., 1998). Such perceptions were associated with cheating, as were worries about school and the use of "self-handicapping" classroom behaviors (Anderman et al., 1998). Other, longitudinal research finds that either rule-breaking or rule-abiding conduct may remain relatively continuous from childhood through late adolescence, and that rule breaking undermines both academic achievement and job competence (Masten et al., 1995).

There is evidence that a youth's expression of prosocial behavior may be continuous, if not increasing across life (Fabes & Eisenberg, 1996). Such behavior may be applied across the key settings of life—peer group, family, school, and workplace—albeit in complex ways (Eisenberg & Fabes, 1998). The absence of prosocial behavior may mar a young person's behavioral repertoire

across childhood and adolescence (Masten et al., 1995), and competence in key contextual settings and the quality of these settings will be diminished. The nature of the development of prosocial behavior underscores the importance of moral development for civil society and the reason why communities find it crucial to invest their assets in the promotion of morally committed, competent youth.

Promoting Civil Society for Youth

Morally developed youth think and act in ways that maintain and enhance civil society (cf. O'Connell, 1999). Given the importance of moral development in support of civil society, at least two key questions suggest themselves as important. First, does adolescent cognitive development and/or moral reasoning development reflect attributes of thought pertinent to civil society? Second, is there any way in which the context of adolescents may foster the development of moral reasoning and prosocial behavioral orientations in support of civil society? Data suggest that the answer to both of these questions is "yes."

Moral Reasoning Development and Civil Society

Issue to Consider

- Are there data supporting the idea that adolescents' cognitive and moral development support civil society?

Several studies of American youth have investigated adolescents' concepts of the components of civil society. In a study of adolescents ranging in age from 12 to 19 years, civil liberties such as freedom of speech and religion were conceived of as universal rights (Helwig, 1995). In a study of about 170 youth, ranging in age from 8 to 16 years, the understanding of nurturance and of self-determination rights were investigated (Ruck, Abramovitch, & Keating, 1998). Younger children (8- to 12-year-olds) were less likely than older youth (14- to 16-year-olds) to see these rights as important. Whereas reasoning about nurturance did not show an age-related progression from concrete to abstract, reasoning about self-determination did show such a change.

In a study of 6- to 11-year-olds developing ideas about democratic and nondemocratic systems of government and freedom of speech (Helwig, 1998), notions of political fairness were present among all youth and were used to evaluate the range of political systems presented to them. These notions were used to reject the appropriateness of the nondemocratic alternatives. However, there were important age group differences among the youth (Helwig, 1998). The older children, more so than the younger, considered the pragmatic and moral consequences of the different systems of government presented to them. The older children were also more likely to use a broad set of rationales to justify the importance of freedom of speech (Helwig, 1998).

Additional data indicate that the growth of moral reasoning is consistent with the support of civil society. Adolescents enrolled in college demonstrate less of a capacity for interpersonal forgiveness than do their same-gender parents (Subkoviak et al., 1995). However, tolerance for people who transgress (if not their acts of transgression per se) does increase across age. In a study of 160 youth ranging in age from 7 to 10 years (Wainryb, Shaw, & Maianu, 1998), all participants were more tolerant of the holding of dissenting beliefs than of behaviors enacting such differences. They were also more tolerant of persons engaged in acts based on dissenting beliefs than they were of the acts themselves. Emblematic of an increase in the orientation to diversity of perspectives in society, tolerance of dissenting beliefs and speech increased with age (Wainryb et al., 1998).

Among adolescents developing within the United States and, one may speculate, for youth developing within other democratic societies, there are cognitive changes consistent with a greater understanding of the features of civil society. In the next section we consider how such developmental changes may become associated with the furthering of civil society.

Youth charters Community-organized groups that enable adolescents and adults to promote positive youth developmental outcomes systematically and create a system by which civil society can be maintained and perpetuated.

Enhancing Behavior That Promotes Civil Society

Issues to Consider

- What is the purpose of William Damon's "youth charter"? How does it work in a community?
- What is the relationship between positive youth development and the 40 developmental assets identified by Search Institute?

What is required for the promotion of civil society by our nation's young people? William Damon (1997) has envisioned the creation of a **youth charter** in each community in the United States and the world. The charter consists of a set of rules, guidelines, and plans of action that each community can adopt to provide their youth with a framework for developing in a healthy manner. Damon (1997) describes how youth and significant adults in their community (e.g., parents, teachers, clergy, coaches, police, and government and business leaders) can create partnerships to pursue a common ideal of positive moral development and intellectual achievement.

Embedding youth in a caring and developmentally facilitative community can promote their ability to develop morally and to contribute to civil society. In a study of about 130 African American parochial high school juniors, working at a soup kitchen for the homeless as part of a school-based community service program was associated with identity development and with the ability to reflect on society's political organization and moral order (Yates & Youniss, 1996).

In a study of over 3,100 high school seniors (Youniss, Yates, & Su, 1997), the activities engaged in by youth were categorized into (1) school-based, adult-endorsed norms; or (2) engagement in peer fun activities that excluded adults. Youth were then placed into groups that reflected orientations to (1) school-adult norms, but not peer fun (the "School" group); (2) peer fun but not school-adult norms (the "Party" group); or (3) both "1" and "2" (the "All-around" group). The School and the All-around seniors were both high in community service, religious orientation, and political awareness. In turn, the Party group seniors were more likely to use marijuana than were the School group (but not the All-around group) seniors (Youniss et al., 1997).

Furthermore, African American and Latino adolescents nominated by community leaders for having shown unusual commitments to caring for others or for contributions to the community were labeled "care exemplars" and compared to a matched group of youth not committed to the community (Hart & Fegley, 1995). The "care exemplars" were more likely than the comparison youth to describe themselves in terms reflective of moral characteristics, to show commitment to both their heritage and to the future of their community, to see themselves as reflecting the ideals of both themselves and their parents, and to stress the importance of personal philosophies and beliefs for their self-definitions (Hart & Fegley, 1995).

Adolescents' participation in democratically run organizations may facilitate the development of their moral reasoning abilities.

Damon (1997) envisions that by embedding youth in a community where service and responsible leadership are possible, the creation of community-specific youth charters can enable adolescents and adults, together, to promote systematically positive youth development. Youth charters can create opportunities to actualize both individual and community goals to eliminate risk behaviors among adolescents and promote in them the ability to contribute to high-quality individual and community life. Through community youth charters, youth and adults may work together to create a system in which civil society is maintained and perpetuated (Damon, 1997). Features of Damon's recent scholarship are presented in Meet the Researcher Box 5.2.

What, precisely, must be brought together by such charters to ensure the promotion of such positive youth development? Peter L. Benson and his colleagues at Search Institute in Minneapolis, Minnesota, believe that what is needed is the application of **assets** (Benson, 1997; Benson et al., 1998; Leffert et al., 1998; Scales & Leffert, 1999). That is, they stress that positive youth development is furthered when actions are taken to enhance the strengths of a person (e.g., a commitment to learning, a healthy sense of identity), a family (e.g., caring attitudes toward children, rearing styles that both empower youth and set boundaries and provide expectations for positive growth), and a community (e.g., social support, programs that provide access to the resources for education, safety, and mentorship available in a community) (Benson, 1997).

Accordingly, Benson and his colleagues believe there are both internal and external attributes that comprise the developmental assets needed by youth. Through their research they have identified 40 such assets, 20 internal ones and 20 external ones. These attributes are presented in Table 5.2.

Benson and his colleagues have found that the more developmental assets possessed by an adolescent, the greater is his or her likelihood of positive, healthy development. For instance, in a study of 99,462 youth in grades 6 through 12 in public and/or alternative schools from 213 U.S. cities and towns who were assessed during the 1996–1997 academic year for their possession of the 40 assets presented in Table 5.2,

Assets (Developmental assets) Resources of a person (e.g., commitment to learning), a family (e.g., caring attitudes toward children), and a community (e.g., social support) that are needed for positive youth development.

MEET THE RESEARCHER BOX 5.2

WILLIAM DAMON
ADOLESCENT MORAL IDENTITY

In the early part of my career, I spent years of trying to figure out—without much success—how a person's moral judgment (what the person would say when asked "what if" questions about right and wrong) was connected to the person's actual social conduct in real life. Then I came on the idea of "moral identity," and it occurred to me that this might be the key explanatory concept we had been missing.

Moral identity is how a person answers the question, "What difference does acting in a good rather than a bad way make to the kind of person I am, as well as to the kind of person I want to be?" It occurred to me that the way a person answers this question could be more indicative of how the person will behave in real life than any other measure that psychologists had been using.

And this is indeed what Anne Colby and I found when we conducted a study of extraordinary people who had spent their lives doing good work (Colby & Damon, 1992). We found that these people had a strong sense of themselves as moral people, indicating a high level of moral identity. They did *not* show a tendency to score especially high on standardized moral judgment measures. Colby and I concluded that "people who define themselves in terms of their moral goals are likely to . . . take responsibility for the actual solution of moral problems" (Colby & Damon, 1992, p. 282). In contrast to such people, those who do no more than mouth high-minded principles cannot be relied on to act in a moral manner when the chips are down.

Adolescence is a key time for the formation of moral identity. In studies with Dan Hart (Damon & Hart, 1988), we found that during adolescence, self-identity is marked by small gradual increases in the use of moral concepts such as "kind," "fair-minded," and "honest." Adolescents who describe themselves *primarily* in terms of moral goals are exceptionally committed to voluntary service and other prosocial activity. This is true even in the most disadvantaged communities (Hart & Fegley, 1995).

William Damon is professor of education and director of the Center on Adolescence at Stanford University. For the past 20 years, Damon has studied moral development at all ages of human life. Damon's books include *The Moral Child* (1990); *Greater Expectations* (1995); and *The Youth Charter* (1997). Damon is editor-in-chief of *New Directions for Child and Adolescent Development* and *The Handbook of Child Psychology* (1998).

In order to promote the development of adolescent moral identity, I have been helping schools and communities create youth charters. A youth charter is a consensus of clear expectations shared by a young person and all the important people in the young person's life. A youth charter evolves through discussions between young people and their parents, neighbors, teachers, friends, coaches, and other community members. It covers deep moral and spiritual issues such as the purpose of life. It also deals with practical problems such as cheating in school, alcohol and drug abuse, and hostile relations among peer groups.

In our beginning efforts with the youth charter approach (Damon & Gregory, 1997), we have led town meetings in a number of communities. In one place, parents were upset about an epidemic of binge drinking, especially at teen parties. They organized a townwide forum to create a community youth charter. The youth charter discussions led to many constructive actions, such as building a substance-free coffeehouse, run by the youth, where young people can have a good time without drugs or alcohol. Some other issues that were addressed included fostering a positive, character-building approach to youth sports; mitigating the pressures of academic competition; promoting spiritual understanding; and developing engaging service programs.

Youth charters are communication devices. They can help young people anticipate and understand the reactions of others to their behavior. When a teacher is disappointed in a student's performance, or when a neighbor calls the local police on a miscreant teenager, a youth charter can turn the youngster's shame or outrage into a constructive developmental experience. A youth charter can define high moral standards for adolescent conduct. It can provide a conduit for regular feedback between a young person, peers, and the adult world, thereby facilitating the formation of the young person's moral identity.

Table 5-2	The 40 Developmental Assets Proposed by Search Institute

External	Support	1. *Family support*—Family life provides high levels of love and support.
		2. *Positive family communication*—Young person and his or her parent(s) communicate positively, and young person is willing to seek advice and counsel from parent(s).
		3. *Other adult relationships*—Young person receives support from three or more non-parent adults.
		4. *Caring neighborhood*—Young person experiences caring neighbors.
		5. *Caring school climate*—School provides a caring, encouraging environment.
		6. *Parent involvement in schooling*—Parent(s) are actively involved in helping young person succeed in school.
	Empowerment	7. *Community values youth*—Young person perceives that adults in the community value youth.
		8. *Youth as resources*—Young people are given useful roles in the community.
		9. *Service to others*—Young person serves in the community one hour or more per week.
		10. *Safety*—Young person feels safe in home, at school, and in the neighborhood.
	Boundaries and Expectations	11. *Family boundaries*—Family has clear rules and consequences and monitors the young person's whereabouts.
		12. *School boundaries*—School provides clear rules and consequences.
		13. *Neighborhood boundaries*—Neighbors take responsibility for monitoring young people's behavior.
		14. *Adult role models*—Parent(s) and other adults model positive, responsible behavior.
		15. *Positive peer influence*—Young person's best friends model positive, responsible behavior.
		16. *High expectations*—Both parent(s) and teachers encourage the young person to do well.
	Constructive Use of Time	17. *Creative activities*—Young person spends three or more hours per week in lessons or practice in music, theater, or other arts.
		18. *Youth programs*—Young person spends three hours or more per week in sports, clubs, or organizations at school and/or in community organizations.
		19. *Religious community*—Young persons spends one or more hours per week in activities in a religious institution.
		20. *Time at home*—Young person is out with friends "with nothing special to do" two or fewer nights per week.
Internal	Commitment to Learning	21. *Achievement motivation*—Young person is motivated to do well in school.
		22. *School engagement*—Young person is actively engaged in learning.
		23. *Homework*—Young person reports doing at least one hour of homework every school day.
		24. *Bonding to school*—Young person cares about his or her school.
		25. *Reading for pleasure*—Young person reads for pleasure three or more hours per week.
	Positive Values	26. *Caring*—Young person places high value on helping other people.
		27. *Equality and social justice*—Young person places high value on promoting equality and reducing hunger and poverty.
		28. *Integrity*—Young person acts on convictions and stands up for his or her beliefs.
		29. *Honesty*—Young person "tells the truth even when it is not easy."
		30. *Responsibility*—Young person accepts and takes personal responsibility.
		31. *Restraint*—Young person believes it is important not to be sexually active or to use alcohol or other drugs.

(Continued)

Table 5-2	The 40 Developmental Assets Proposed by Search Institute (Continued)

Social Competencies	32.	*Planning and decision making*—Young person knows how to plan ahead and make choices.
	33.	*Interpersonal competence*—Young person has empathy, sensitivity, and friendship skills.
	34.	*Cultural competence*—Young person has knowledge of and comfort with people of different cultural/racial/ethnic backgrounds.
	35.	*Resistance skills*—Young person can resist negative peer pressure and dangerous situations.
	36.	*Peaceful conflict resolution*—Young person seeks to resolve conflict nonviolently.
Positive Identity	37.	*Personal power*—Young person feels he or she has control over "things that happen to me."
	38.	*Self-esteem*—Young person reports having high self-esteem.
	39.	*Sense of purpose*—Young person reports that "my life has a purpose."
	40.	*Positive view of personal future*—Young person is optimistic about her or his personal future.

Source: Benson et al., 1998.

Leffert et al. (in press) found that the more assets present among youth, the lower the likelihood of alcohol use, depression/suicide risk, and violence. Figures 5.1, 5.2, and 5.3, taken from the research of Leffert et al., present these findings.

For instance, Figure 5.1 displays the level of alcohol use risk for youth in grades 6 through 8 combined and for youth in grades 9 through 12 combined; as shown in this figure, in both grade groupings alcohol risk decreases with the possession of more assets. Youth with zero to 10 assets have the highest risk, followed by youth with 11 to 20 assets, youth with 21 to 30 assets, and youth with 31 to 40 assets. Thus, consistent with Benson's (1997) view of the salience of developmental assets for promoting healthy behavior among young people, both the trend lines represented in the figure and the fact that the last group has the lowest level of risk shows the importance of the asset approach in work aimed at promoting positive development in American children and adolescents. Moreover, the data summarized in both Figures 5.2 and 5.3

Figure 5.1

Changes in level of alcohol risk in relation to the possession of developmental assets. (*Source:* Leffert et al., 1998.)

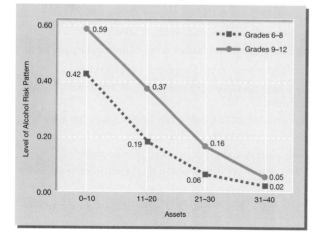

Figure 5.2

Changes in level of depression/suicide risk in relation to the possession of developmental assets. (*Source:* Leffert et al., 1998.)

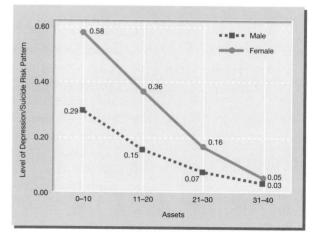

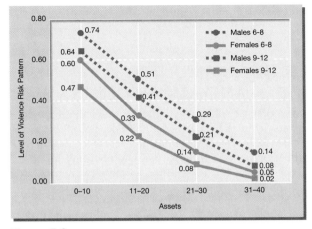

Figure 5.3
Changes in level of violence risk in relation to the possession of developmental assets. (*Source:* Leffert et al., 1998.)

replicate the trends seen in Figure 5.1—for males and females in regard to depression/suicide risk in the case of Figure 5.2 and for combinations of males and females in different grade groupings in regard to violence risk in the case of Figure 5.3. This congruence strengthens the argument for the critical significance of a focus on developmental assets in the promotion of positive youth development and, as such, in the enhancement of the capacity and commitment of young people to contribute to civil society.

Other data by Benson and his colleagues provide direct support for this argument. Scales et al. (2000) measured a concept termed **thriving** among 6,000 youth in grades 6 to 12, evenly divided across six ethnic groups (American Indian, African American, Asian American, Latino, European American, and multiracial). Thriving was defined as involving seven attributes: school success, leadership, valuing diversity, physical health, helping others, delay of gratification, and overcoming adversity. Most, if not all, of these attributes are linked to the presence of prosocial behavior (e.g., helping others, delay of gratification) and to the behaviors requisite for competently contributing to civil society (e.g., valuing diversity, leadership, overcoming adversity). The greater the number of developmental assets possessed by youth, the more likely they were to possess the attributes of thriving. Figures 5.4, 5.5, and 5.6 indicate that as developmental assets increase from level 1 to level 4, thriving in regard to helping others, valuing diversity, and leadership increases. (See Figs. 5.4 and 5.5 on page 127, Fig. 5.6 on page 128.) Peter

Civic engagement and contributions to the welfare of their communities are associated with positive youth development.

Benson's perspective about his work is presented in Meet the Researcher Box 5.3.

Other data support the importance of focusing on developmental assets both in understanding the bases of positive youth development and in using that knowledge to further civil society. Luster and McAdoo (1994) sought to identify the factors that contribute to individual differences in the cognitive competence of African American children in early elementary grades. Consistent with an asset-based approach to promoting the positive development of youth (Benson, 1997; Scales & Leffert, 1998), they found that favorable outcomes in cognitive and socioemotional development were associated with high scores on an **advantage index.** This index was formed by

Thriving Concept defined and measured by Scales et al. Thriving is defined as involving the following seven attributes: school success, leadership, valuing diversity, physical health, helping others, delay of gratification, and overcoming adversity.

Advantage index Index formed by scoring children on the basis of the absence of risk factors (such as factors pertinent to poverty) and the presence of more favorable circumstances in the children's lives.

MEET THE RESEARCHER BOX 5.3

PETER L. BENSON
UNLEASHING THE POWER OF COMMUNITIES
FOR RAISING HEALTHY CHILDREN AND ADOLESCENTS

Many of the efforts taken in the United States to improve the health and well-being of children and adolescents are organized to *reduce* the rate and incidence of health-compromising behaviors. For decades, the United States has invested people and resources in tackling such problems as alcohol, tobacco, illicit drugs, violence, teen pregnancy, and delinquency. These efforts are often orchestrated through federal and state initiatives and led by professionals trained in these areas.

In the late 1980s, I decided to go down a different path. Looking through a different lens, I asked this question: What opportunities, resources, and experiences do children and adolescents need in order to thrive? Asking the question in this way leads to a focus on the essential building blocks of human development that we need to *promote*.

I began to construct a taxonomy of positive building blocks by synthesizing decades of research. I also sought to identify those experiences and resources that were health promoting for all youth regardless of race, ethnicity, gender, or family income. This search for "universal" building blocks was fed by an instinct that naming a common core of experiences which are good for all youth would be helpful, ultimately, for uniting communities to take action on behalf of all youth.

This work led to the concept of developmental assets, a framework of 40 "molecules" of healthy development that communities have within their control. The assets are organized into 8 categories: support, empowerment, boundaries, structured time use, educational commitment, positive values, social competencies, and identity.

With my colleagues at Search Institute, we have developed a survey tool to help American cities understand

Peter L. Benson is president of Search Institute, Minneapolis, an independent applied research organization specializing in child and adolescent development. Trained as a social psychologist and the author of 10 books, he speaks and lectures widely about the natural and inherent power of communities in raising successful, competent, and caring youth. He is also the visiting scholar at the William T. Grant Foundation in New York City.

how they are doing in building these developmental assets. More than 1,000 cities have developed this profile of assets. A remarkable thing happens when local leaders and citizens look through the developmental asset lens. They rediscover a great deal of community capacity, often dormant in cities, to mobilize asset-building power. That's because inherent in the developmental asset model is the fact that developmental assets emerge significantly and powerfully from human relationships—from people, whether neighbors, teachers, employers, parents, youth leaders, coaches, members of congregations or just passersby on the street—attending deeply to knowing, naming, engaging, and connecting to the youth of a city.

We now do a great deal of publishing, speaking, training, and consulting to ignite communitywide asset-building initiatives. As of the end of 2000, about 625 cities have launched these efforts. Imagine the new challenge of learning the processes and dynamics of growing asset-building communities, with more than 600 "petri dishes." We've decided that the best way to grow knowledge about community change is to position ourselves as co-learners with all of these communities, asking them to teach us what they are learning about transforming neighborhoods, businesses, schools, families, congregations, and youth organizations into a vibrant, connected team of systems all seeking to build developmental strengths. Part of our scientific challenge now is to invite all of these communities to be part of the learning effort, synthesize the lay findings, feed back what we learn, and then loop through this process again and again, with the hope that all of us can become wiser about holding up and supporting the developmental journey of all children and adolescents.

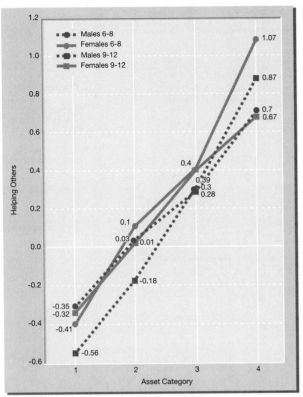

Figure 5.4
Changes in helping others in relation to the possession of developmental assets. (*Source*: Scales et al., 2000).

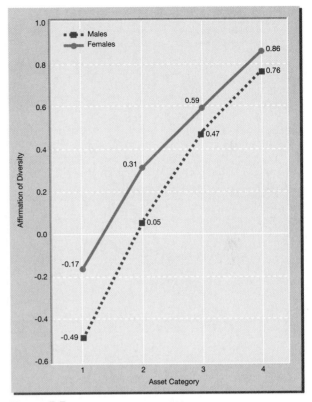

Figure 5.5
Changes in affirmation of diversity in relation to the possession of developmental assets. (*Source*: Scales et al., 2000).

scoring children on the basis of the absence of risk factors (e.g., pertaining to poverty or problems in the quality of the home environment) and the presence of more favorable circumstances in their lives.

Luster and McAdoo (1994) reported that, whereas only 4% of the children in their sample who scored low on the advantage index had high scores on a measure of vocabulary, 44% of the children who had high scores on the advantage index had high vocabulary scores. Similar contrasts between low and high scorers on the advantage index were found in regard to measures of math achievement (14% vs. 37%, respectively), word recognition (0% vs. 35%, respectively), and word meaning (7% and 46%, respectively).

Luster and McAdoo (1996) extended the findings of their 1994 research. Seeking to identify the factors that contribute to individual differences in the educational attainment of African American young adults from low socioeconomic status, Luster and McAdoo (1996) found that assets linked

with the individual (cognitive competence, academic motivation, and personal adjustment in kindergarten) and the context (parental involvement in schools) were associated longitudinally with academic achievement and educational attainment.

A Model for Promoting Civil Society Through Enhancing Positive Youth Development

Issues to Consider

- How can civil society be promoted by linking youth, families, and society?
- What should be the focus of public policies and programs in the promotion of civil society?
- What positive developmental effects should be seen from public programs?
- How does the promotion of civil society maintain itself over generations?

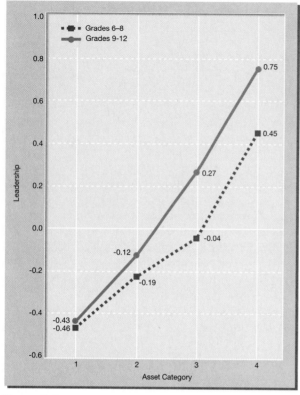

Figure 5.6
Changes in leadership in relation to the possession of developmental assets. (*Source:* Scales et al., 2000).

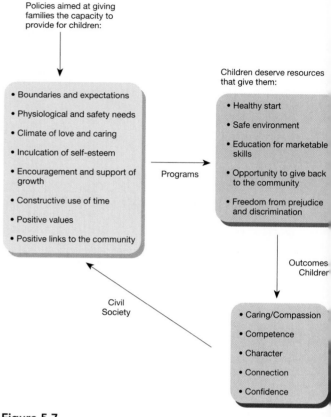

Figure 5.7
A model of a national youth policy: The integration of families, children, and civil society. (*Source:* Lerner et al., 2000b).

Consistent with the perspective forwarded by Benson (1997), and the data provided by Leffert et al. (1998) and by Luster and McAdoo (1994, 1996), the individual and contextual assets of youth are linked to their positive development. These data legitimate the idea that the enhancement of such assets will be associated with the promotion of positive youth development. How may such enhancement result in the promotion of civil society?

Figure 5.7 provides a model that links youth with the family and the community in ways that, over time, result in the promotion of civil society. Key to the model is the ability of the family to nurture and socialize youth effectively. The model summarizes the results of several studies and scholarly essays (e.g., Benson, 1997; Benson et al., 1998; Damon, 1997; Dryfoos, 1998; Leffert et al., 1998; Lerner et al. in press; Scales & Leffert, 1999; Scales

et al., 2000; Schorr, 1997). This literature describes the essential functions requisite for families to enact in order to promote positive development in their children, the resources necessary for families to transform their functional characteristics into valued child outcomes, and the elements of these positive youth outcomes.

As indicated in Figure 5.7, the enhancement of civil society feeds back to influence the family and the young people reared within it. As young people grow up in families providing the orientation to self and society, they take on the behaviors that the policies and associated programs were designed to inculcate. As the model indicates, through facilitating the nurturing and socialization of families, the growth of civil society occurs.

Figure 5.7 further indicates that **public policies** (discussed in more detail in Chapter 14) should be aimed at ensuring that families have the capacity to provide children with boundaries and expectations, fulfillment of physiological and safety needs, a climate of love and caring, the inculcation of self-esteem, the encouragement for growth, positive values, and positive links to the community. The programs that derive from these policies should ensure that the resources are available for families to nurture and socialize children in these ways. These resources would give children a healthy start, a safe environment, caring and reliable adults, an education resulting in marketable skills, and opportunities to "give back" to their communities by volunteering and serving.

If programs are effective, several positive developmental outcomes will accrue among children. These outcomes can be summarized by **Five Cs**: Competence, Connection, Character, Confidence, and Caring (or Compassion) (Carnegie Council on Adolescent Development, 1989; Lerner, 1995; Little, 1993). These five attributes represent five clusters of individual attributes, for example, intellectual ability and social and behavioral skills (competence), positive bonds with people and institutions (connection), integrity and moral centeredness (character), positive self-regard, a sense of self-efficacy, and courage (confidence), and humane values, empathy, and a sense of social justice (caring/compassion). When these five sets of outcomes are developed in youth, civil society is enhanced. Through the intergenerational effect these youth may initiate in rearing of their own children, these youth can positively affect the rearing of subsequent generations (Bornstein, 1995).

Conclusions

As with cognitive development, the development of moral reasoning and behavior is associated with other individual characteristics and with different instances of the social context surrounding the adolescent. These associations promote general characteristics of moral reasoning development and a change from judging a behavior based on the consequences of an act to judging whether an actor intended the consequences of the act to occur. These associations also foster diversity in moral functioning, especially those prosocial behaviors that with the community strengthen civil society.

The fact that the context, and specifically people in it, can model moral functioning, and promote moral commitments and behaviors among youth, is a key basis of applications aimed at developing a next generation of youth community leaders and citizens contributing to the maintenance and perpetuation of civil society.

Diversity and context are key themes useful in understanding moral development and behavior in adolescence. How adolescents through their singular combination of cognitive, emotional, behavioral, and contextual characteristics contribute in healthy ways to self and to society depends critically on understanding the individuality of their selves and of their contexts. This understanding involves adolescents' self-definitions and their attainment of personal identities. We consider the development of self-definition and identity in the next chapter.

> **Public policy** Standards, or rules, for the conduct of individuals, organizations, and institutions.
>
> **Five Cs** Five attributes (Competence, Connection, Character, Confidence, and Caring) representing positive developmental outcomes in youth.

Summary

- Moral development involves thinking and behaving *prosocially*. For any society to maintain and perpetuate itself over the course of generations, its youth must develop as individuals committed to promoting the healthy, productive, and successful development of self, family, and society.

- Although Kohlberg's work is widely used as the basis for most theories dedicated to moral development,

today the study of adolescent moral functioning focuses both on moral thinking or reasoning *and* on moral behaviors, especially those that *benefit* the society.

- Kohlberg proposed that a theory of moral development should focus on the reasons for moral behavior, rather than moral behavior. He devised a way to ascertain the reasons underlying moral behavior through the construction of a moral development interview. Kohlberg found that the types of moral reasoning people used passed through a series of five-qualitatively different stages.

- Overall, research indicates that individual differences and context need to be taken into account in understanding the development of both moral reasoning and moral behavior. Not all youth have similar levels of moral reasoning. Variation seems to be associated with gender (see, for example, Gilligan's work) and with different types of social experiences. Most of these experiences relate to interactions with models of moral behavior, including family members and people in the community.

- Modeling prosocial, moral behavior can help develop it in others. This information has resulted in several worldwide programs, designed to inculcate a prosocial orientation among youth. Both "experimentally created" and naturally occurring models (parents and peers) can promote moral thought and action.

- There are risks to healthy youth development, and especially to the attainment of the moral orientation to contribute to civil society in contexts, such as war, in which the institutions of civil society are weak and/or damaged. Society risks the generation of behaviorally and emotionally problematic children by not affording young people the opportunity to develop in a community and societal context that supports the development of behaviors which advance the institutions of civil society.

- In addition to the peer group, the family, workplace, and school may provide contexts that influence the expression of prosocial behavior. Prosocial behavior may be applied across the key settings of life. The absence of prosocial behavior may mar a young person's behavioral repertoire across childhood and adolescence. In such instances, competence in key contextual settings will be

decreased and the quality of these settings will likely be diminished.

- To promote civil society in young people, William Damon (1997) envisions the creation of a youth charter in every community. Living and working under the guidelines of a youth charter, communities can create partnerships to pursue a common ideal of positive moral development and intellectual achievement and, thereby, create a system wherein civil society is maintained and perpetuated.

- Positive youth development is furthered when actions are taken to enhance the strengths of a person, a family, and a community. Benson and his colleagues have identified 40 developmental assets, 20 internal ones and 20 external ones, that comprise the resources needed for the healthy development of youth.

- Because the individual and contextual assets of youth are linked to their positive development, it makes sense to assume the enhancement of such assets will be associated with the promotion of positive youth development. Key to models that link youth with family and the community in manners that result in the promotion of civil society is the ability of the family to nurture and socialize youth effectively.

- Public policies should be aimed at ensuring that families have the capacity to provide for children. If programs are effective in delivering resources to families, several positive developmental outcomes will accrue among children. When "five Cs," competence, connection, character, confidence, and caring (or compassion), are developed in youth, civil society is enhanced. As young people grow up in families providing the orientation to self and society, they may take on the behaviors that the policies and associated programs are designed to inculcate.

Discussion Topics

1. Within the context of civil society, morally developed youth think and behave in ways that maintain and enhance a just social order. Moral development involves thinking and behaving *prosocially*. What prosocial actions do you and/or your peers take to help maintain and support civil society?

2. Do you agree with the widely held belief that youth of today lack the moral principles practiced and promoted by your parents' and grandparents' generations? If so, why? If not, why not?

3. Based on your knowledge of the work of Jean Piaget, how does his conception of moral development mirror his theory of cognitive development? Give examples to back up your claims.

4. Look back on the Kohlberg moral dilemma story presented in the chapter. How would you resolve the dilemma? Is your response contingent on who you are culturally, ethnically, racially? Is it easy or difficult for you to resolve the dilemma? What is the basis behind your reasoning? Is it easy or hard for you to understand the reasoning of those who might solve the dilemma differently? Do you feel your gender may impact the way you resolve moral issues? If so, why? Does your age impact your resolution? Can you imagine that you would or will respond differently to the dilemma at different times in your life?

5. Individual differences and context need to be taken into account in understanding the development both of

moral reasoning and of moral behavior. Who in your life impacted your moral development? Is there a specific life context that was significant in this development? In what ways do you feel you have contributed to the moral development of your siblings and/or peers?

6. Carol Gilligan contends that there are important differences in moral reasoning and behavior among males and females and that certain approaches, such as Kohlberg's, stress the morality of "justice" rather than the morality of "care." The latter type of morality provides the "voice" of females' moral reasoning. What is she referring to in this distinction? Do you believe the moral reasoning of women is expressed in terms of relationships and responsibilities? Is the distinction between the moral reasoning of men and women all that clear and defined to you? Or can women, like men, resolve dilemmas based on issues of equity and justice? Why or why not?

7. Can you see the neighborhood in which you were raised creating a youth charter? What would it look like? Who would be involved (both individual members and businesses and institutions)? How would the charter support the moral development of its youth? What roadblocks might the community run into in establishing and maintaining the goals set forth by the charter?

8. With the asset model of Benson and colleagues as a guide, how much does socioeconomic status determine developmental outcome in American society? Race? Gender? Are there some assets you feel are more significant and important than others in promoting positive youth development? What are they, and why do you feel they are so significant?

9. With an understanding that positive youth development is furthered when actions are taken to enhance the assets of a person, a family, and a community, how might you design a youth charter that met the needs of the most impoverished communities in the United States?

10. What do you know about the policies and programs designed to support families in your state? Do they support the promotion of developmental assets and, in so doing, do they promote the moral development of the youth of your state?

11. In what ways did your parents promote in you the "five Cs" of competence, connection, character, confidence, and caring (or compassion)? Do you believe there are intergenerational effects inherent in this promotion—that civil society will be enhanced as youth initiate the positive moral behavior instilled in them by their parents in the rearing of subsequent generations of citizens?

Key Terms

advantage index (p. 125)

assets (p. 121)

civil society (p. 109)

five Cs (p. 129)

heteronomous morality (p. 111)

prosocial behavior (p. 109)

post-traumatic stress disorder (PSTD) (p. 116)

public policy (p. 129)

thriving (p. 125)

youth charters (p. 120)

6

IDENTITY:
THE SEARCH FOR SELF-DEFINITION
DURING ADOLESCENCE

CHAPTER OUTLINE

Garrett was nervous. The seventh-grade dance was starting in less than an hour and he still wasn't 100% sure if he was ready to go.

He wanted to look good but he didn't want to appear that he wanted to look good. When he walked into the gym he wanted people to look at him but he also wanted to fit in. He wanted his classmates to see him as special, but not in a bad way. Cool, but not different, was what he was after.

"Garrett, are you ready yet?" his dad shouted up the stairs to him. "I have to pick up two of your friends on the way and the traffic is going to be terrible tonight. I don't want to be stuck in it longer because we left late."

"Yeah, Dad, I'm coming in one more minute," Garrett called back. He turned from the door of his room to face the mirror over his dresser. One last check and he guessed he'd be ready to go. In any case, he knew he'd have to be.

His new sneakers were loosely laced. His pants were belted slightly below his waist and his extra-large flannel shirt was unbuttoned, its untucked tails hanging almost to his knees. It was opened wide enough so the logo on his T-shirt could be clearly seen. He was not sure his hair looked good but, as he placed his baseball cap carefully on his head, he decided it would not matter. He'd just keep his hat on all night.

"Garrett!" The tone of his Dad's voice told him that the time for self-reflection was over.

"Yes," he said to himself in the mirror, "you do look good." "I'm ready," he yelled out. He sprinted from his room and down the stairs. This was who he was and he and the kids at the dance would have to deal with it.

LEARNING OBJECTIVES

1. To define identity.
2. To learn what society expects from adolescents and how this relates to identity.
3. To understand the characteristics and importance of a role.
4. To understand what occurs if the adolescent does not resolve the identity crisis by early adulthood.
5. To understand the process of identity development through person-context interactions.
6. To describe Erik Erikson's theory of ego development.
7. To appreciate the role self-esteem plays in identity development.
8. To learn what self-regulation is and how identity is an instrument of self-regulation.
9. To appreciate the major instances of diversity in adolescent self-conception.
10. To understand the four identity statuses described by James Marcia.
11. To understand contextual influences on identity development.
12. To define ethnic identity and its importance to an adolescent's identity.
13. To understand there may be gender differences in identity development.

Parents often feel that each week they encounter a new person living in the body of their teenager. At least from the parents' perspective their adolescent's interests and emotions seem to rapidly change from one activity to another. Adolescence is a period of major change in body, mind, and behavior. The basis of adolescent self-definition lies in the combination of these major changes.

The combination of changes involved in adolescence leads to an alteration in how one looks, feels, and thinks. The **developmental task** involved in these alterations is to understand who one is in the face of these changes. If this task is dealt with successfully, it will result in a new definition of the self, as a particular individual with specific competencies, a personal life plan, and a niche in the world. This revised self-definition constitutes an alteration in personality. It represents a psychological and social adjustment to the physiological and psychological changes of adolescence. This adjustment is one based on the abstract self-understanding of the individual way these changes have affected the adolescent and the implications of the changes for the life directions he or she desires to take (Damon, 1991; Damon & Hart, 1988; Harter, 1986, 1988, 1998).

Accomplishing the task of self-understanding is not easy. The host of major biological, psychological, and social changes that characterize adolescence presents the young person with a serious emotional challenge. A young adolescent has developed a specific sense of self, as well as a sense of his or her self-competence and what he or she can do (e.g., in regard to school performance, social relationships, or athletics). At the beginning of adolescence this knowledge of self

Developmental task
Challenge to healthy or positive development that exists at a particular point in life; a challenge that must be met for development to proceed optimally.

Physical characteristics are often a key part of an adolescent's identity.

is challenged. The far-reaching bodily changes of this period (see Chapter 3) are accompanied by equally dramatic changes in thoughts (see Chapter 4). The assumptions adolescents held about their "selves" in the earlier stages of their lives may no longer be relevant to the new individuals they find themselves to be.

William Damon (1991; Damon & Hart, 1988) notes that prior to adolescence people view themselves in terms of their bodily characteristics (e.g., their height), their actions (e.g., playing video games, skateboarding), their membership in particular groups (e.g., their school class or 4-H or scouting group), or the state of their moods at a given moment. With the transition into the beginning of adolescence and the emergence of formal operational thinking (see Chapter 4), youth define themselves in enduring and general terms (Damon, 1991). They see themselves as possessing specific personality traits that apply across time and situations.

Young adolescents may apply contradictory traits to themselves, for instance, labeling themselves as both "smart" and "dumb" (Harter, 1988). It is not until the latter portion of adolescence, in fact, that a systematic and integrated sense of self develops (Damon, 1991; Harter, 1986). Often, youth use their moral ideas (see Chapter 5) in order to attain this integrated and coherent sense of self.

A coherent sense of self is necessary for functioning productively in society (Archer & Waterman, 1991; Erikson, 1968). As a consequence of their biological and psychological changes, and of society's pressure to have them make a useful contribution to the world, during adolescence young people ask themselves the crucial psychological question: "Who am I?" While trying to answer this question the adolescent may experience an **identity crisis** (Erikson, 1959). This crisis occurs because, at the same time adolescents feel unsure about who they are, society begins to ask them questions related to their self-definitions.

Social and behavioral scientists believe this crisis is the central issue in understanding personality and social development in adolescence. The need to resolve the crisis is another way to understand the key self-definitional developmental task of this period. To understand this issue, it is important to understand the meaning of the term *identity*.

Defining Identity

Issue to Consider
• How is identity defined?

Do you have a sense of your own attitudes and values? Do you know how you feel about things—about ideas (e.g., democracy, civil rights), people (your friends, parents, politicians, particular rock or movie stars), or activities (skiing, chatting online with friends, studying all night for exams)? Can you describe how you behave generally (e.g., in regard to how physically active you like to be, how much you enjoy being in social groups versus spending time alone, how much sleep you need) and in specific situations (e.g., when you are stuck for a long time in traffic, when you have too many things to do at one time, when you meet a particularly attractive person)? Would you guess that if you gave your best answers to these questions people who knew you well would agree you had described yourself accurately?

If your answers to all these questions are "yes," then you have described your identity. **Identity** is the "distinctive combination of personality characteristics and social style by which one defines him- or herself and by which one is recognized by others" (Grotevant, 1998, p. 1119). A person's identity is the set of the thoughts, feelings, values, attitudes, and behaviors that define his or her "self." It is the conception of who you are that you use to govern your present interactions with the world and navigate your life into the future. It is "one's subjective sense of coherence of personality and continuity over time" (Grotevant, 1998, p. 1119). Identity means accurately knowing one's attitudes and values, how one feels about things, and how one behaves generally and in specific situations.

Why Do Adolescents Need an Identity?

Issues to Consider
• Why is an identity necessary for adolescents?
• What does society expect from adolescents? How does this relate to identity?

Identity crisis Crisis between identity and role confusion elicited by the emotional upheaval provoked by the personal and social mandate to adopt a role in adolescence.

Identity Set of thoughts, feeling, values, attitudes, and behaviors that defines a person's self.

- What influence does the resolution of the identity crisis have on development during adulthood?

Much is asked of an adolescent by his or her family, teachers, and even friends that is not asked of children. Adolescents are expected to make the first steps toward career objectives (Castellino & Lerner, 1999; Vondracek, 1994; Vondracek, Lerner, & Schulenberg, 1986) by making educational choices that will lead them toward or away from particular vocational or professional objectives (Greenberger & Steinberg, 1986; Vondracek, 1999). Adolescents are also expected to develop intimate and/or romantic relationships (see Chapter 10), and they are given more responsibility for managing their time and finances.

Through such changed expectations, society is asking adolescents what roles they will play as adults. Society wants to know what socially prescribed set of behaviors adolescents will choose to adopt. In other words, a key aspect of the adolescent dilemma regarding self-definition or identity is that of finding a role. A general commitment to a role is taken to be the outward expression of an adolescent's identity.

A **role** provides a self-definition, which coordinates for the adolescent his or her biological and psychological characteristics with a set of activities deemed useful by society (Baumeister, 1986, 1991; Erikson, 1968). A role typically cannot be something that is self-destructive or socially disapproved (e.g., criminal behavior).

In the search for an identity, adolescents must discover what they believe and what their attitudes and ideas are. Commitment to a role entails commitment to a set of values (Erikson, 1959). An identity crisis may be elicited by the emotional upheaval provoked by this strong societal and personal mandate for role adoption, if it occurs at

a time in the person's life when he or she cannot find a role that fits (Baumeister, 1986; Erikson, 1959, 1968). In order to resolve this crisis and achieve a sense of identity, the adolescent must find an orientation to life that not only fulfills the changing biological and psychological attributes of the self but one that is also consistent with what society expects of a person.

Resolution of the adolescent identity crisis has a profound influence on development during later adulthood. If the identity crisis is not resolved by the time the adolescent enters adulthood, he or she will feel a sense of **role confusion** or **identity diffusion** (Archer & Waterman, 1991; Erikson, 1968). Some young adults waver between roles in a prolonged **moratorium** period in which they avoid commitment (Marcia, 1980). Others **foreclose** on a socially approved, easily available identity and avoid the crisis altogether (Marcia, 1980). Others resolve their crises by adopting an available but socially disapproved role or **ideology.** Called **negative identity formation,** it is often associated with delinquent behavior (Erikson, 1959; Kennedy, 1991).

Accordingly, for the person experiencing the changes of adolescence, the definitional challenge that must be met has implications for health and success for much of the rest of life. Thus it is crucial for the adolescent to deal adequately, and in many ways this means *integratively*, with the changes of biology, psychology, and the social world confronting him or her. For successful (healthy, or positive) development to occur, a role cannot be chosen that (1) ignores one's biological attributes, assets, or limitations (e.g., males cannot choose the role of "mother," and people of short stature would be ill-advised to aspire to a career in professional basketball); (2) does not consider one's psychological characteristics (e.g., people with high activity levels and who find themselves easily distracted would not fit well with the job demands of an air traffic controller); or (3) is independent of societal needs or constraints (e.g., the profile of socially proscribed roles differs between industrialized and preindustrialized nations; Whiting & Whiting, 1991). The adolescent must go through a process that allows him or her to develop a healthy identity and the capacities for interacting successfully with society.

Role Socially prescribed set of behaviors to which the person can show commitment.

Role confusion Feeling an adolescent gets if he or she cannot find a role that fits his or her biological, psychological, and social characteristics.

Identity diffusion Feeling an adolescent gets if he or she cannot resolve the identity crisis. The defining characteristic is a lack of commitment, about which the adolescent is not concerned.

Moratorium Period in which an adolescent avoids commitment.

Foreclosure Adopting a socially approved, easily available role and thereby avoiding the identity crisis.

Ideology Set of attitudes, beliefs, and values that serves to define a role.

Negative identity formation Resolving the identity crisis by adopting an available but socially disapproved role or ideology.

The Process of Identity Development

Issue to Consider

• How does identity develop through person-context interactions?

An identity allows you to explore your world in ways specific to your particular abilities, thoughts, feelings, and interests. It allows you to cull from your experiences with such interactions those "things" (e.g., activities, jobs, people) that fit with your self and that you will want to keep as a part of you in the future (e.g., "I seem to like skiing and will want to do more of this again"). In other words, identity develops through a process of person-context interactions in which you explore your world and evaluate and integrate the reactions you have to your explorations (Grotevant, 1998).

Given its person-context relational character, identity can change whenever there are significant alterations in the context (e.g., moving from elementary school to middle school; Simmons & Blyth, 1987) or in the person (e.g., involving puberty, and an ensuing spurt in height and weight that allows one to play basketball with a new ability; Graaffsma et al., 1994). Identity is a concept that reflects many of the theoretical ideas about person-context relations we discussed in other chapters, including the classical theory of Erik H. Erikson (see Chapter 2) as well as more contemporary approaches.

Erikson's Theory of Ego Development in Adolescence

Issues to Consider

• What is Erik Erikson's theory of ego development?
• How can the identity crisis be resolved?
• What is the relation between an ideology and identity development?
• What occurs if an adolescent cannot show commitment to a role?
• How does self-esteem relate to identity development?

Erik H. Erikson's (1959, 1964, 1968) richly evocative descriptions of the changes involved in adolescent ego development have fired the imaginations and empirical energies of many scientists studying adolescents, perhaps more so than any other theorist. As such, his ideas provide a useful frame for our discussion of the emotional and self-definitional changes of adolescence. Erikson (1959) proposed a theory of development that encompassed the entire human life span. As shown in Table 6.1, he divided the course of life into eight stages.

In each of the stages of development, Erikson saw development as involving the emergence of a new capability of the ego. However, such a gain in capacity comes at a price—there is the emergence of an emotional crisis and the risk of developing ego limitations as well. In fact, Erikson (1959, 1963) believes that within each stage of life, development involves a synthesis of a new ego capacity with a new type of incapacity. This synthesis of gain and

Table 6-1	Erikson's Theory of the Eight Stages of Ego Development		
	Bipolar emotional crisis		
Psychosocial stage	A sense of	versus	A sense of
1. Oral sensory	basic trust		mistrust
2. Anal musculature	autonomy		shame, doubt
3. Genital locomotor	initiative		guilt
4. Latency	industry		inferiority
5. Puberty and adolescence	identity		role confusion
6. Young adulthood	intimacy		isolation
7. Adulthood	generativity		stagnation
8. Maturity	ego integrity		despair

Source: Lerner, 1986, p. 353.

loss involves in adolescence the concepts of ego identity, on the one hand, and role confusion, on the other.

We introduced Erikson's theory of psychosocial development in Chapter 2. We noted that Erikson sees the changes of puberty as presenting the adolescent with serious problems. If development was successful throughout the stages leading to adolescence, an adolescent will have developed more trust than mistrust, more autonomy than shame and doubt, more initiative than guilt, and more industry than inferiority. All the feelings that have developed have given the youth a feeling about who he or she is and of what he or she can do. In adolescence, this knowledge is challenged. Adolescents now find themselves in a body that looks and feels different and find they are thinking about this body, and all things, in a new way.

It is at this time of life that a great disparity between the "real self," the person an adolescent believes himself or herself to be, and the "ideal self," the person he or she wants to be, may be felt (Harter, 1988; see too Damon, 1991). This disparity is greatest in the area of physical appearance (Harter, 1988), especially for young adolescent girls (Koff, Rierdan, & Stubbs, 1990; Simmons & Blyth, 1987), who are less secure than are boys of this age about their physical appearance. It may be for this reason that young adolescent girls tend to have lower self-esteem than young adolescent boys (Harter, 1988; see too Simmons & Blyth, 1987).

Because all past associations the adolescent has had about the self may now be irrelevant, the adolescent feels the need to develop a coherent and adaptive sense of self. The adolescent asks the crucial psychosocial question, "Who am I?"

As already noted, at precisely the time when the adolescent feels unsure about himself or herself, society begins to ask related questions about the adolescent. For instance, we have observed that in our society the adolescent must now begin to make the first definite steps toward career objectives (Vondracek, 1994, 1999; Vondracek et al., 1986). For example, students have to make a decision about whether or not they will enter into college preparatory courses.

Thus society asks adolescents what role they will play in society. Society wants to know how these soon-to-be-adult persons will contribute to its maintenance. Society wants to know what socially prescribed set of behaviors, useful for the effective maintenance of society, will be adopted. Yet how can one know what one can do, and what one wants to do, to contribute to society and meet its demands, if one does not know who one is?

In essence, then, the question Who am I? is basically a question of self-definition; it is necessitated by the emergence of all the new bodily changes, feelings, and capabilities arising during adolescence (e.g., the sex drive and formal thought), and by the new demands placed on the adolescent by society. The adaptive challenge to find a role one can be committed to, and thus to achieve an identity, is the most important task of adolescence. The emotional upheaval provoked by this crisis is termed by Erikson the *identity crisis*.

To achieve identity adolescents must, therefore, discover what they believe in, and what their attitudes and ideals are. Along with any role, there is an ideology, or set of attitudes, beliefs, and values, that serves to define it. These factors, which can be said to define our ideology, provide an important component of our role. When we know who we are, we know what we do, and when we know what we do, we know our role in society.

Along with any role (e.g., wife, father, student, teacher) goes a set of orientations toward the world that serves to define that role. These attitudes, beliefs, and values give us some idea of what a person engaged in a particular role in society thinks of and does. Thus an *ideology* serves to define a societal role. We know fairly well what the ideology of a Catholic priest is and how it is similar to and different from the ideology associated with a military general, or a professional artist, or a professional politician. The point is that along with any role goes a role-defining ideology. To solve our identity crisis, we must be committed to a role, which means showing commitment toward an ideology. Erikson (1963) terms such an emotional orientation **fidelity**.

If adolescents find their role in society, and show commitment to an ideology, they will have achieved a sense of identity. If adolescents do not find a role to play in society, they will remain in the identity crisis. In an attempt to resolve this crisis, adolescents might try many roles and, perhaps, be only temporarily successful investing the self in any one.

Erikson maintains that if adolescents are unable to show commitment to a role and thereby do not

Fidelity Emotional orientation toward showing commitment to a role and ideology.

resolve the identity crisis, they will feel a sense of role confusion, or identity diffusion. In short, the terms *crisis* and *commitment* become hallmarks of the fifth stage of psychosocial development in Erikson's theory.

Yet the adaptive struggle in this stage is not only preceded by events in earlier ones but also is influenced in its outcome by them. As Constantinople (1969, p. 358) pointed out,

> In order to achieve a positive resolution of the identity crisis, the adolescent must sift through all of the attitudes toward himself and the world which have occurred over the years with the resolution of earlier crises, and he must fashion for himself a sense of who he is that will remain constant across situations and that can be shared by others when they interact with him.

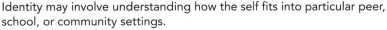

Identity may involve understanding how the self fits into particular peer, school, or community settings.

The identity the adolescent attains as a consequence of the psychosocial crises preceding and during adolescence influences the rest of the life span. To Erikson, **self-esteem** is a feeling about the self, which tends to remain constant across life and gives the person a coherent psychological basis for dealing with the demands of social reality. In one essay (1959) in which he cast the notion of identity in terms of self-esteem, Erikson says,

> Self-esteem, confirmed at the end of a major crisis, grows to be a conviction that one is learning effective steps toward a tangible future, that one is developing a defined personality within a social reality which one understands. (p. 89)

Constantinople (1969, p. 358) elaborates,

> This self-esteem is the end product of successful resolutions of each crisis; the fewer or the less satisfactory the successful resolutions, the less self-esteem on which to build at this stage of development, and the greater the likelihood of a prolonged sense of identity diffusion, of not being sure of who one is and where one is going.

Where we go from adolescence is the early portion of adulthood. During this period, we face another psychosocial crisis. Successful resolution of this crisis and the remaining crises of the adult years rests on the attainment of an adequate identity. Chapter 15 discusses the transition from adolescence to adulthood. Here, we turn to some concluding comments about Erikson's ideas about adolescence and then to a discussion of other theories of identity development.

Conclusions About Erikson's Theory Erikson believes the identity crisis of adolescence is provoked by individual and societal changes and can only be resolved through commitment to a role, which balances the individual and social demands raised by these changes. The crisis of this stage derives from the emotional turmoil precipitated by adolescent pubertal change, and the commitment of this stage arises due to the need to establish a new definition of the self that settles the emotional upheaval.

This viewpoint raises, however, what we have discussed as the "lore of adolescence" (Chapter 1). As epitomized in the theory of Anna Freud (1969; see Chapter 2), the changes of puberty are thought to initiate the alterations in body, emotions, and thought that precipitate this crisis of self-definition. Thus the identity

Self-esteem Degree of positive or negative feelings one holds about the self.

crisis, at least insofar as its initial stages are concerned, would seem to be a phenomenon of the early portions of the adolescent period. By the latter portion of adolescence, as we make the transition into early adulthood, we need to resolve the crisis of identity if successful transition to and development within young adulthood are to occur. Therefore, the portion of adolescence in which we would expect to see most ego identity development occurring is early adolescence. To determine if research evidence supports this type of development of identity, it is important to review other theories.

Contemporary Theoretical Views of Identity Development

Issues to Consider
- What is self-regulation? How does it relate to identity?
- How are assimilation and accommodation related to identity?

The work of Michael Berzonsky and his colleagues (1993, 1997; Berzonsky & Neimeyer, 1994) emphasizes that a person's developing identity is a feature of the individual that results from past, and contributes to future, person-context relations. As such, identity is an instrument of **self-regulation** (see Chapter 2). For example, it is the feature of adolescent psychological functioning and social life that allows the individual to *select* the paths he or she will pursue in life, to find the means to attain the goals that are chosen (*optimization*), and to cope with failures or losses in the means to reach goals (*compensation*).

As well, regulation of one's relations with the context involves construing how the context (e.g., the crowd of peers in one's high school) may be adapted or modified (e.g., through choosing a subset of peers with whom to form a clique) in order to fit or meet one's goals (e.g., the attainment of friendship or popularity). Assimilation (Chapter 4) may be seen to be involved in such selection and optimization actions. In turn, a youth may find that he or she cannot completely alter the context (e.g., the attitudes of the peer group about what looks "cool") while trying to reach a goal (e.g., popularity), and that one

Self-regulation Feature of adolescent psychological and social functioning that allows the individual to select goals, find the means to attain those goals, and cope with failures or losses to reach these goals.

must change the self (e.g., adopt a different style of dress to fit in better) in order to reach the goal. Thus accommodation (Chapter 4) is part of the process of compensation in such a situation (Berzonsky, 1993, 1997; Berzonsky & Neimeyer, 1994; Grotevant, 1997, 1998).

Other scholars also stress that identity development involves relations between the person and the social/cultural context (Adams & Marshall, 1996; Côté, 1996; Goossens & Phinney, 1996) and that it involves the regulation of these relations (Adams, 1997; Baumeister & Muraven, 1996; Berzonsky, 1997; Grotevant, 1987, 1997; Kerpelman, Pittmann, & Lamke, 1997). The ideas of one leading researcher, Gerald R. Adams, are presented in Meet the Researcher Box 6.1.

For instance, as we discussed in Chapter 2, the regulation of our relationship with the social world, through, for instance, the processes of selection, optimization, and compensation (Baltes & Baltes, 1990; Freund & Baltes, 1998), or through other attempts to control the relationships we have with the social context (e.g., Kerpelman et al., 1997), allows us to adapt to the context, and "adaptation may be the best way to conceptualize the complex, multilateral relationship between individual identity and sociocultural context, because it recognizes the causal importance of culture yet also recognizes individual choice and change" (Baumeister & Muraven, 1996, p. 405).

Several studies provide empirical support for the theoretical ideas describing the role of identity in regulating links between the adolescent and the sociocultural context. In a study of the influence of culture on adolescent coping behavior (Oláh, 1995), involving more than 700 male and female 17- and 18-year-olds from India, Italy, Hungary, Sweden, and Yemen, both cultural differences and similarities in regulative behavior were seen. When needing to cope with stresses from the context, youth from European countries were more likely to use assimilation as a strategy, whereas youth from India and Yemen preferred emotion-focused solutions. Youth from all cultural settings, if they possessed high levels of anxiety, coped with stresses by showing avoidance behaviors.

There are also cultural differences between youth within a geographic region related to regulation. German youth prefer a more active approach to reaching the developmental goals they select than Polish youth, and Polish youth

MEET THE RESEARCHER BOX 6.1

GERALD R. ADAMS
CONTEXTS THAT SUPPORT OR HINDER
ADOLESCENT IDENTITY DEVELOPMENT

Most teenagers grow up in supportive families, attend good schools, have a part-time job, date a little, or even have a serious girlfriend or boyfriend. So life is good for most teens. But for a few, life is less than kind. Some youth come from dysfunctional homes, live in poverty, and attend decaying and old schools where teachers are trying hard to work with little financial resources or operating money. The neighborhoods are often in rapid decline. The local role models are often involved in criminal or social deviance (drug dealers, prostitutes, etc.).

No matter if teens live in an advantaged or disadvantaged context, they share the same challenge of formulating a sense of self and constructing a sense of identity. For several years, I have been studying the patterns of identity development and the contexts that support or hinder identity formation.

As one example, our research team has been using the National Longitudinal Survey of Children and Youth, the first such study in Canada, to identify what family processes support children's academic success in school. Being a good or poor student in school is in part development of an identity as a student. We are observing a complex web of connections between family life and school success. Let me briefly describe for you one set of linkages. Higher income families have a wider number of family support systems. This is important because social support helps to diminish parent depression, where depression predicts higher family dysfunction (quarreling, fighting, disagreeing). So how does this relate to school success? Well, family dysfunction is associated with hostile and ineffective parenting behaviors that lower a child's academic interests and skills. And lower academic interest and skills result in lower academic

Gerald R. Adams is a professor of family relations and human development at the University of Guelph, Ontario, Canada. He is the current editor of the *Journal of Adolescent Research* and a senior editor of the *Advances in Adolescent Development* annual book series.

grades. So we are finding that income, family support, parental depression, family dysfunction, and hostile or ineffective parenting are important factors in predicting a teen's interest and success in school and their sense of academic identity. The web of interpersonal and social influences are complex and very interactive, as this book is demonstrating to you.

I have also been very interested in the role of identity in understanding problems like runaway behavior or bulimia. I believe that society sets certain expectations during the adolescent years to formulate a sense of self. With funding from the Social Science and Humanities Research Council of Canada, I have been able to study the nature and form of identity formation. Our research team is finding that we can identify three basic types of identity. The *empty self* is a teenager who avoids, procrastinates, and fails to make identity commitments, even in the face of societal pressure to do so. The *prefabricated self* involves using social conventions and parental role models to imitate and provide the structure and values that the teenager accepts is true of him or her. The *constructive self* includes teenagers who seek out information, analyze choices for work, values, and commitments, and select only those that fit the emerging construction of self-identity.

In our research programs we are finding the empty self is associated with many social problems, including running away, eating disorders, conduct disorders, and inattention in school settings. Escaping the developmental task of identity formation is diminishing the resources or human capital that teenagers should be making to help guide and direct them into adulthood. To this point in time, we are finding that escaping the self leaves an empty sense of identity that may make a teen and perhaps an adult susceptible to social deviance and identity disorders.

---

extend their goals for later in their development than German adolescents (Schönpflug & Jansen, 1995). There are within-national differences as well. Younger German youth (11- to 16-year-olds) use both behavioral approach and avoidance coping strategies, whereas older German adolescents (17- to 19-year-olds) show both behavioral and cognitive forms of approach (Kavsek & Seiffge-Krenke, 1996). In a longitudinal study of more than 3,200 Swiss adolescents, aged between 14 and 20 years, youth saw two general domains of the context over which they needed to exert control—the personal/social domain and the society domain (Grob, Flammer, & Wearing, 1995). Finally, in a sample of about 350 Korean adolescents in grade 12, problem-solving and information-seeking approaches to coping were associated with less of a likelihood of depression, and physical symptoms were associated with a coping style that involved discharge of emotions.

In short, the concept of identity is central to the understanding of adolescence and the theoretical ideas about the regulation of person-context relations. Given this centrality, it may be surprising to learn there are relatively few studies of the behavioral correlates or developmental consequences of identity development (Grotevant, 1998). Although Erikson (1968) emphasized that identity development is a process involving "*the core of the individual* and . . . *the core of his*[or her] *communal culture*" (p. 22), there have also been relatively few studies of the influence of the context on identity development (Goossens & Phinney, 1996). It is important to review what the research about identity development has focused on and what it says about the character of self and identity during adolescence.

How Does Identity Develop in Adolescence?: Research Directions

For at least the last 30 years scholars have conducted hundreds (and perhaps thousands) of investigations of identity during adolescence. This emphasis is not surprising, given the importance of this concept in (potentially at least) explaining how young people may or may not become healthy, contributing members of society. What may be surprising, however, is that still, after all this research, there remain relatively few sound studies that actually measure identity development across the span of the adolescent years (Grotevant, 1998).

Instead, beginning in the late 1970s and early 1980s, much of the research about identity focused on different statuses an adolescent may attain during the identity crisis—status that, as we discuss

later, may involve the attainment of an identity (in at least one of two different ways), remaining in a state of crisis, or being actively engaged in a search for identity (Marcia, 1980). In turn, research has also focused on the different domains within which identity may be expressed, for instance, in regard to one's ethnicity or gender and/or in relation to one's interpersonal relationships with family members and peers (Grotevant, 1998). Accordingly, in order to appreciate contemporary understanding of the nature of identity in adolescence it is important to discuss research that has tested Erikson's theory and, in turn, research about the developmental and contextual bases of identity development. This latter research involves also a consideration of the influence of characteristics such as ethnicity and gender on individual differences (diversity) in such development.

Research About Erikson's Theory of Ego Development

Issues to Consider
- During what period of adolescence should research on identity development focus on? Why?
- Does contemporary research support Erikson's theory of ego development?

Despite the theoretical importance attached to the emergence of the identity crisis in adolescence in Erikson's theory, little research has been reported about the study of ego identity in *early* adolescence. Most of the research activity has been directed at the late adolescent period, when we would expect most of the changes that should have occurred to have been completed (e.g., Archer & Waterman, 1991; Marcia, 1980, 1991; Schiedel & Marcia, 1985; Waterman, 1982). Meet the Researcher Boxes 6.2 and 6.3 present the work of two leading researchers in this area, Sally L. Archer and Alan S. Waterman, respectively.

This research has typically provided interesting and useful information about the search for a role (see Archer & Waterman, 1991; Marcia, 1991) and about how the family context and interactions with parents facilitate the exploration of roles (Adams & Jones, 1983; Grotevant, 1998; Grotevant & Cooper, 1985). However, this research has been focused too much on late adolescence.

MEET THE RESEARCHER BOX 6.2

SALLY L. ARCHER

DOES COMMITMENT GUARANTEE IMPLEMENTATION OF IDENTITY CHOICES: BARRIERS TO LIVING ONE'S CHOICES

As you have noted in this chapter, one of the ways we investigate the formation of one's identity is to examine the processes of exploration and commitment. Individuals who are knowledgeable, engaged in relevant activity, and can envision this choice as part of their future are seen as having a self-defined identity in this area of their life. As examples, one may have a committed identity pertaining to a career, religious beliefs, parenting, or so forth.

In earlier research, I documented the serious concern expressed by a majority of senior high school women regarding making their personal identity decisions about the priorities of career and family for their future. The next step in this dilemma was to investigate how one makes decisions regarding the implementation of these potentially conflicting choices. Toward that end I have developed a course on career decision making in psychology for college juniors and seniors. These students have made the commitment to their college major and are searching for a specific career and/or the continuance of study at the graduate level. "How do they proceed to implement their commitment to career, given their potential plans for family?" I have been using a variety of techniques to measure this process, such as identity interviews, a cognitive career block instrument, autobiographical lifelines of important events from birth to the present to retirement, professional autobiographical essays, and practical professional preparation. One of the challenges is to distinguish between issues of career implementation and family/career conflicts that block movement toward that implementation.

Sally L. Archer is a professor of developmental psychology at The College of New Jersey. She is on the editorial boards of *The Journal of Early Adolescence* and *Identity: An International Journal of Theory and Research.* She is a founding member of the society for research on adolescence and the society for research on identity formation.

The college men (of the 1990s) recognize the issue of conflict in the priorities of career and family to a far greater extent than did senior high school men (of the 1980s). But in common between the two age groups, there is little concern about how one might integrate the two major areas of career and family into their lives. They are comfortable making the self-definitional commitment to both identity areas and can envision both in their future, but they give little thought to their implementation. Thus plans for a family are not a barrier to plans for career implementation. College women, who make the commitment to both areas, attempt to visualize the implementation of the two in far greater detail than do the men. As a consequence, they experience major cognitive and emotional blocks to decisions regarding the implementation of the career component of their identities. This has serious implications for their ability to live the life that most fully expresses their potentials and sense of self. Do they choose careers that require major commitments in order to advance in or impact on their field? How much do they invest in graduate school, if they plan to have families and perhaps take time to remain home with their infants? These are not issues for the vast majority of these college men who also profess commitment to career and family and state that they believe in shared family responsibilities.

At the present, I am working on obtaining a more representative sample. My subsequent goal will be to address the implications of such findings for our college advisement process. Have you thought about these issues and spoken with your faculty about the impact of a "potential" family on career alternatives?

MEET THE RESEARCHER BOX 6.3

ALAN S. WATERMAN
FINDING SOMETHING TO DO OR SOMEONE TO BE: THE SEARCH FOR PERSONALLY EXPRESSIVE IDENTITY CHOICES

In my early research on identity formation I sought to document the patterns of movement among Marcia's identity statuses as college students made the transition from adolescence to adulthood. With increasing age, there was increasing concern with identity issues as evidenced by the active exploration of alternative identity possibilities. In the large majority of instances, this exploration was followed by the development of identity commitments. Despite the evident movement toward reflectively held identity commitments, there were also very substantial numbers of college students who either continued to hold commitments established relatively early in life through identification with parents or other model figures (commitments formed without exploration or reflection) or whose thoughts about identity issues were marked by vagueness and passivity.

After being involved in thousands of identity interviews with high school and college students, either as the interviewer or as a scorer, I concluded that I was not always impressed by the quality of the identity choices made by students who met all the criteria for being classed as "identity achievers." This view has led me in recent years to try to understand the differences between what can be considered as "better" and "poorer" identity choices and to search for the predictors of making better choices.

Alan S. Waterman is a professor of psychology at The College of New Jersey. He is North American editor for the *Journal of Adolescence*. He was a founding member of both the Society for Research on Adolescence and the Society for Research on Identity Formation. He is serving as a member of the Council of Representatives of the American Psychological Association.

In recent studies I have found it meaningful to distinguish between identity commitments that are personally expressive of the individual and those commitments that are instrumental; that is, they work for the person without being experienced as fully involving. Using an instrument entitled the Personally Expressive Activities Questionnaire (or PEAQ), my colleagues and I have been able to document that individuals in the Identity Achievement status are significantly more likely to have identified personally expressive activities than are those in the Identity Diffusion status.

In another series of four studies, linkages have been established between experiences of personal expressiveness and the constructs of intrinsic motivation and flow. Experiencing identity-related activities as personally expressive appears to be a function of (1) their involving the development of the individual's best potentials and (2) their furthering the individual's purposes in life. In a pair of current studies, I am using both a retrospective and a prospective (longitudinal) design to test the hypothesis that the progress college students make toward their stated goals can be predicted from the extent to which activities associated with those goals are experienced as personally expressive.

As a result, there is a lack of data pertinent to early adolescence.

Moreover, the findings which exist about ego identity in late adolescence indicate that theoretically surprising identity change rather than invariant stable identity achievement seems to be the rule (Archer & Waterman, 1991). For example, in a large and classic study involving an assessment of the presence of stagelike qualities in adolescent development, Constantinople (1969) tested more than 900 male and female college students from the University of Rochester. There were consistent increases in the successful resolution of identity from the freshman year to the senior year across participants and from one year to the next within groups of participants. However, only males showed consistent decreases in the scores for identity diffusion. Changes in scores for the other crises did not always decrease or increase in accordance with Erikson's theory. Thus Constantinople's (1969) data provide, at best, only partial support for Erikson's theory of ego development.

Other data also contradict Erikson's theory. For instance, by the end of their college experience, and the presumed beginning of their early adulthood stage of psychosocial development, college students do not invariably show stable identity achievement (Archer & Waterman, 1991; Waterman, 1982). Adolescents' feelings and ideas about themselves seem to change in several directions. In the Early Adolescence Study (Petersen, 1987), some aspects of self-esteem increase across early adolescence, others decrease, and still others show curvilinear changes across age.

Either the purported identity crisis of early adolescence does not develop until the late adolescent/young adult years or Erikson's theory and the lore of adolescence must be revised to encompass all of this period and the succeeding one as well. In either case, and as we have seen too in respect to the issue of storm and stress and to pubertal change (Chapters 1 and 3, respectively), and to cognitive development (Chapter 4), the lore of adolescence—as a period of upheaval, general maladjustment, and interpersonal conflict—finds no support.

Whether we view Erikson's theory as valid or not (e.g., see Lerner, 1986; Muuss, 1996), Erikson undoubtedly provided a service in directing the study of personality development in adolescence to a focus on the self, self-concept, and self-esteem. Much contemporary research, both consistent with and independent of Erikson's ideas, focuses on changes in the self during adolescence. This research demonstrates both the considerable diversity in the development of the self during adolescence and the important role of the social context in influencing this development. It is useful to consider first the diversity that exists in the development of the self.

Research on the Definition of Self During Adolescence

Issues to Consider
- What are the major instances of diversity in adolescent self-conception?
- What are two types of identity crises? How do they differ by gender?

Researchers concerned with the central issue of how adolescents define themselves have studied several variables related to the self, including self-concept, self-esteem, perceived self-competence, and ego devel-opment. Despite the particular variable of interest in a given study, research shows that major instances of diversity in adolescent self-conception occur in regard to differences in developmental pathways and contrasts between males and females.

In a longitudinal study of developmental changes in self-esteem from early adolescence through late adolescence to early adulthood, males and females were found to have distinct developmental trajectories (Block & Robins, 1993). The self-esteem of males tended to increase from early adolescence through early adulthood; that of females tended to decrease. In another longitudinal study of male and female adolescents, sex differences in using concepts of masculinity to define the self increased between the sixth and eighth grades (Galambos, Almeida, & Petersen, 1990); however, there were no sex differences in the use of concepts of femininity across this portion of adolescence.

Images of one's body and its capabilities are also part of the adolescent's sense of self (Perkins & Lerner, 1995), which differs between males and females. Females have more differentiated and males more global body images (Koff et al., 1990). That is, this research found that females' body images tend to involve ideas about many separate features or parts of their bodies, whereas males' body images tend to reflect a more general, overall impression of their bodies. The research found also that male adolescents are more positive about their bodies than are female adolescents.

The stress of searching for an identity may elicit emotional turmoil or a sense of crisis in an adolescent.

Other developmental differences occur in regard to self-development. Longitudinal research has found that children define themselves in regard to three dimensions of self-competence: academic achievement, social competence, and conduct (Masten et al., 1995). Adolescents, however, use these dimensions and two others—romantic competence and job competence—to define themselves. Similarly, from childhood through early and late adolescence, youth become more flexible in the roles they associate with the two genders (Katz & Ksansnak, 1994). Adolescents show more flexibility in regard to the particular roles they adopt—showing a greater willingness to adopt behaviors that may typically be associated with the gender other than their own (see Chapter 7 for a discussion of such gender role flexibility). In addition, they show greater tolerance about other people showing such flexibility (Katz & Ksansnak, 1994).

Diversity in the nature of the ego identity crisis has also been found by researchers (Archer & Waterman, 1991; Marcia, 1964, 1966, 1980, 1991), and, once again, gender differences are part of this diversity. For instance, Baumeister (1986; Baumeister, Shapiro, & Tice, 1985) found that at least two types of identity crisis exist. One type is labeled an **identity deficit**. Here the person cannot resolve his or her identity crisis because of an inability to make decisions (e.g., role choices). The second type of crisis is labeled **identity conflict**. In this type of crisis the person makes incompatible decisions (e.g., choosing roles that require different, almost mutually exclusive behaviors). For instance, the person might decide to be a parent who stays at home to raise children *and* a PhD-level scientist, a role that requires several years of postgraduate training. Baumeister (1991) reports that crises involving identity conflict seem to be an important part of the ego development of girls more so than boys.

Research on Identity "Status" During Adolescence

Issues to Consider

- What four identity statuses have been identified? What are some features of these identity statuses?

- Does gender play a role in the likelihood of being in any of the four ego identity status categories? How does gender play a role?

A series of provocative studies of different identity statuses among adolescents is related to research that focuses on differences between youth in how they define their selves during adolescence. James Marcia (1964, 1966, 1980, 1991) hypothesized that resolutions of the adolescent identity crisis involve more than just identity versus role confusion (or identity diffusion). Marcia believed that a more diverse pattern exists, and that to ascertain the adolescent's identity status accurately, a youth's feelings of both crisis and commitment to a role should be measured.

Marcia (1966) found evidence for four identity statuses (see Table 6.2). As Erikson (1959, 1963, 1968) said, two of these statuses are held by adolescents who achieve *identity* or those who are in a state of *identity diffusion*. The former group has a crisis period but then shows a commitment to an occupation and to an ideology. The latter group may or may not have a crisis, but their defining characteristic is their lack of commitment, a lack about which they are not concerned.

The third status Marcia identified is labeled *moratorium*. Although adolescents in moratorium are in a crisis and have, at best, a vague commitment to an occupation or to an ideology, they are actively trying to make commitments. The last identity status Marcia identified is termed *foreclosure*. Adolescents in this status never experience a crisis, yet are highly committed. Marcia found that they adopt the identities their parents want them to take, and they do so with little or no question and with no crisis.

Marcia (1991) summarized the evidence in support of the existence of the four identity status categories (e.g., from Marcia et al., 1985/1992). He notes that current research evidence indicates that Identity Achievers are cognitively flexible, have higher levels of moral reasoning, and are more capable of

Identity deficit Identity crisis in which the person fails to resolve the identity crisis because of an inability to make decisions.

Identity conflict Crisis in which the person is uncertain of how to define self and is not sure about the role he or she wants to play in society.

Table 6-2	Different Identity Statuses Identified by Marcia

Identity achievement
Identity diffusion
Moratorium
Foreclosure

Source: Marcia, 1980.

intimate relations than youth in the other ego identity status categories. These youth are also less neurotic and more extroverted and conscientious than those in other identity categories (Clancy & Dollinger, 1993). They are also more attached to their mothers (but not their fathers) than are other youth (Benson, Harris, & Rogers, 1992).

Youth in the moratorium category have conflicting needs to conform and to rebel, have ambivalent relationships with their parents, and are seen by other people as intense, often annoyingly so (Marcia, 1991). Adolescents who are actively engaged in identity exploration are likely to be characterized by self-doubt, confusion, and conflicts with parents (Kidwell et al., 1995).

Youth in the foreclosure category are high in authoritarianism, enmeshed in their families, and cognitively rigid (Marcia, 1991). They are also not open to new experiences (Clancy & Dollinger, 1993) and tend to have an extrinsic religious orientation (Markstrom-Adams & Smith, 1996). Youth who maintain their foreclosure status over a 2-year period of their late adolescence have been found to seek a lot of nurturance from others and to have many memories of seeking security early in their lives (Kroger, 1995).

Finally, people in the identity diffusion status have lower levels of moral reasoning than youth in other categories, feel alienated from their parents, and are less capable of intimate relations than are youth in the other categories. Both these youth and those in moratorium are more neurotic and less conscientious than youth in other identity categories (Clancy & Dollinger, 1993). Both moratorium and diffusion youth are less likely to be attached to their mothers and fathers (Benson et al., 1992).

Although the likelihood of being in any of the four ego identity status categories specified by Marcia (1991) does not differ between males and females (Archer, 1991), there are gender differences that occur in regard to the domains of social behavior that contribute to a person's identity status (Archer, 1985, 1989; Whitbourne & Tesch, 1985). Archer (1985) finds no gender differences in regard to the domains of vocational choice, religious beliefs, and sex role orientation, but in regard to political ideology, males are more likely to be in a foreclosed status and females in a diffusion status. In regard to family and career priorities and sexuality, females are more likely to be in either the iden-

tity achievement or the moratorium categories, whereas males are more likely to be in the foreclosure or the diffusion categories.

In short, then, differences in ego development are associated with differences between male and female adolescents and, as well, with variation in several domains of cognition, behavior, and personality. Similarly, differences in personality characteristics are associated with variation in dimensions of adolescent self-definition other than ego identity.

For instance, feelings of low self-worth are linked to feelings of depression among young adolescents (Harter & Jackson, 1993). Moreover, low ego development in adolescence is linked to anger and sadness (Hauser & Safyer, 1994); in turn, high ego development is associated with enthusiasm, affection, and low anxiety. Similarly, among Norwegian 10- to 15-year-olds, negative self-esteem is associated with high social anxiety (Alsaker & Olweus, 1986); in addition, negative self-esteem is related to peer harassment. Because self-esteem level remains relatively constant across the adolescent years for these Norwegian youth, especially among older adolescents (Alsaker & Olweus, 1992), these associations are likely to remain important parts of their development.

Conclusions: Diversity in Adolescent Self-Definition and Identity Status Constructs related to self-esteem, self-concept, perceived self-competence, body image, and ego identity vary across the adolescent years. This diversity, associated with gender, developmental change, and individual psychological characteristics pertinent to cognition and personality, is influenced by several features of the context within which the adolescent is embedded. The contextual influence on identity development is now discussed.

Identity Development: Diversity and Context

Issues to Consider
- What are some contextual influences on identity development?
- What research supports these contextual influences?

Considerable research links the general course of adolescent self-development to the context. Identity development is related to varying contexts, ranging from those general socialization experiences that vary across history and culture to quite specific effects of the family and the school setting.

The Historical Context of Adolescent Identity Development Perhaps the best example of how the changing historical context provides a basis of individual development is derived from a study by Elder (1974; see too Elder, 1980, 1998, 1999). Elder (1974, 1999) analyzed longitudinal data about the development of people who were children and adolescents between 1929 and 1941, the years of the Great Depression in the United States. He found that among a group of 84 males and 83 females born in 1920 and 1921, characteristics of the historical era produced alterations in the influence that education had on achievement (Elder, 1974, 1999).

The historical context of their adolescence continued to influence people in their subsequent, adult years. Later adult health was affected among youth from working-class families who suffered hardships during the Depression, and the importance of children in later adult marriages was enhanced among these youth (Elder, 1974, 1999).

Influences of the Sociocultural Context As suggested by the research just described that demonstrates a link between cultural context and processes of person-context regulation during adolescence, sociocultural context influences identity development (Nurmi, Poole, & Kalakoski, 1996). A study of 680 younger (13- to 14-year-old) and older (16- to 17-year-old) boys and girls from either urban or rural areas in Australia or Finland assessed the processes of identity exploration and commitment. Older youth living in Australian urban settings possessed higher levels of exploration and commitment in regard to both future occupation and education than did younger urban youth. There were no age differences among rural Australian adolescents or among the urban and rural Finnish youth (Nurmi et al., 1996).

In a study comparing identity development among approximately 200 American late adolescent youth and approximately 100 similarly aged Finnish youth (Nurmi et al., 1997), comparable relationships in both groups were found between identity and self-esteem. Youth with an identity style oriented to the acquisition of information had higher self-esteem than other individuals, whereas youth with diffuse or avoidant identity styles were most likely to be depressed (Nurmi et al., 1997).

Within a culture there are also important contextual influences on identity development. These influences are associated with family, peers, school, sports/athletics, social support, neighborhood/community, and the social, political, and economic structure of a society (e.g., DuBois et al., 1996; Grotevant & Bosma, 1994; Paschall & Hubbard, 1998).

Family Influences Parents and family can play a direct role in the socialization of differences in self-definition. For instance, in terms of gender differences, more girls than boys have parents who do not let them out of their homes after dark (Simmons & Blyth, 1987). Independent of the socialization of gender differences, parents and family provide contextual influences that influence self-development in adolescence. For example, among African American youth, high self-esteem is associated with the acceptance and warmth received from parents and other family members (Luster & McAdoo, 1995). Self-esteem among these youth is also linked to the completion of high school and to movement to economic independence.

As the research implies, family influences on adolescents' self-development appear most pronounced when specific types of parent-child interactions occur in the context of particular emotional exchanges in the family. For example, adolescent ego development and self-esteem increase when fathers challenge the autonomy and relatedness of their youth and when they express to them their feelings about the importance of being independent and involved in family life (Allen, Hauser, Bell, & O'Connor, 1994; Allen, Hauser, Eickholt, Bell, & O'Connor, 1994; Hauser et al., 1991; Powers et al., 1983).

Other research confirms the importance of the role for self-development of adolescents being urged to be both individuals and connected to the family (Cooper, Grotevant, & Condon, 1983; Grotevant, 1994; Grotevant & Cooper, 1983). The work of Harold Grotevant and Catherine Cooper (e.g., Cooper, 1994; Grotevant, 1998; Grotevant & Cooper, 1983, 1985, 1986, 1998) has been central in specifying that individuality and connection to parents are not opposing orientations in the world of adolescents. Rather, both of these orientations are important for healthy adolescent development. For some of the current work of Harold D. Grotevant, see Meet the Researcher Box 6.4.

HAROLD D. GROTEVANT
IDENTITY DEVELOPMENT IN ADOPTED ADOLESCENTS

All adolescents and young adults face the challenge of forming a sense of identity: answering the question, "Who am I?" in light of being both physically and cognitively mature. Identity development involves choices—about career possibilities, religious or political value systems, ideas about oneself in relationships. But there are also aspects of identity that we do not choose, such as our sex, our ethnic heritage, or whether we are an adopted person. My research seeks to understand how adolescents and young adults develop a sense of self which includes elements that are chosen as well as those that are givens.

Since the mid-1980s, Dr. Ruth McRoy, Piester Centennial Professor of Social Work at the University of Texas at Austin, and I have been studying adoptive families who vary in the contact they have with members of their child's birth family. Some of the adoptions are *confidential*: There is no contact between the child's families of birth and adoption, and the only information known by either party is very general (for example, height, interests, etc.). Other adoptions are *mediated*, meaning there is some contact, but it occurs through a person serving as a go-between, such as a social worker at the adoption agency. Family members are unable to contact each other directly. The third group includes families with *fully disclosed open adoptions*. Members of the child's adoptive and birth families know each other and contact each other directly.

Harold D. Grotevant is professor and director of graduate studies in the Department of Family Social Science, University of Minnesota, where he is also University Distinguished Teaching Professor and adjunct professor of child psychology. He is a fellow of the American Psychological Association and has received university awards for excellence in research and educational leadership.

We first interviewed our 190 adoptive families and 169 birth mothers when the children were in middle childhood, between ages 4 and 12. With funding from the William T. Grant Foundation, we just finished interviewing them a second time, now that the children are adolescents (ages 12–20). We interviewed the adolescents and their parents individually in their homes all across the United States in order to assess the degree to which they had explored possible futures in the areas of occupational choice, religion or spirituality, and friendships. The adolescents also talked about themselves as adopted persons—what adoption means to them, what kind of contact they have had with birth parents, and whether they think being adopted has influenced their thoughts about other aspects of their lives such as plans for marriage or parenting.

We are still in the process of analyzing the volumes of data we have gathered from the adolescents, their families, and their birth mothers. But we are focusing especially on each adolescent's narrative—the story that comprises his or her sense of identity. Some narratives are coherent: The aspects of the story tie together and make sense, just like they might in a good novel or movie. Other narratives are more disjointed, marked by gaps and inconsistencies. One question we are asking is whether adolescents from different adoption arrangements (confidential, mediated, fully disclosed) differ in how coherent their self narratives are. Do adolescents in fully disclosed adoptions, who know some members of their birth families, develop more coherent and consistent narratives than adolescents in confidential adoptions who know little or nothing about their birth families?

Why should we care about this? Although a narrative approach to identity is relatively new, the research literature leads us to hypothesize that narrative coherence is related to indicators of psychological well-being and mental health. If different openness arrangements are associated with different degrees of well-being and mental health, such findings could inform the national policy debate about the merits of open adoption and whether closed adoption records should be opened up. By studying the adolescents' families, we are also able to look at how families with complex arrangements (such as open adoptions) navigate the challenges of daily life. So far, we have found that the children do better when the adoptive and birth parents are able to work collaboratively, by understanding each other's needs and cooperating in their daily interactions. Relationships become problematic when the adults compete with each other for the child's affection or fail to take the other person's needs or life circumstances into account.

Understanding adolescent development in adoptive families will also give us hints about development in other types of families. As families become increasingly complex (second marriages, stepparents, gay or lesbian parents, grandparents serving as parents), we hope the information generated by our study will help us better understand the developmental challenges facing the adolescents in them, as they go about constructing their sense of identity, their life story.

Further information about this research project can be found at our Web site: http://fsos.che.umn.edu/mtarp/.

Youth who live in families in which there is an opportunity and the support for expressing and developing their own viewpoints show high levels of identity explorations (Grotevant, 1998; Grotevant & Cooper, 1998). Although emotional detachment from parents is detrimental to the psychological adjustment of adolescents when they live in such supportive families, such detachment is adaptive in less supportive families (Fuhrman & Holmbeck, 1995). Several characteristics of family interaction (enduring engagement of youth by parents, parental self-disclosure and sharing, tolerance of novelty and uncertainty, and tolerance of unwanted/unexpected emotions) is linked to enhanced ego development among youth (Hauser, Powers, & Noam, 1991).

Relations Between Family and Peer Influences
Of course, the family and other portions of the social context can interrelate in influencing self and identity development. Chapters 8 and 9 illustrate the combined contributions of the family and of peers, respectively. Here, we may note that these combined influences occur in regard to identity and self-development. For instance, Cooper (1994; Cooper et al., in press) has shown that close relationships—with peers as well as with family members—provide an important link in a causal chain between the broader sociocultural context (e.g., the structure of opportunities available to youth from particular ethnic, racial, or socioeconomic groups) and identity development.

Other studies find as well an influence of both parents and peers on identity development. For example, in a nationally representative study of Dutch adolescents, aged 12 to 14 years, both peers and parents contributed positively to identity development (Meeus & Dekovic, 1995).

In a study of young adolescents (Harter, Stocker, & Robinson, 1996), youth who based their self-worth on peer approval were more preoccupied with such approval than were adolescents who maintained that their self-worth existed prior to any approval they received from peers. The group preoccupied with peer approval was also more likely to be distract-ed from their schoolwork by peers, to show more fluctuations in both classmates' approval and their self-worth, and to have lower levels of classmate approval than the other group of youth (Harter et al., 1996). In a study of adolescent self-worth and relations to parents, teachers, male peers, and female peers, about 75% of youth reported differences in self-worth across the four contexts. High self-worth in one relational context was related to overall self-worth (Harter, Waters, & Whitesell, 1998).

Support from the social context in general may be linked to the development of a positive sense of self (e.g., Gray-Little & Carels, 1997). Adolescents' perceptions of approval from others, especially a general peer reference group such as classmates, is strongly related to self-worth among adolescents (Robinson, 1995). The school context is also important to consider as an influence on the development of self.

The Influence of the School Context The family and the peer group provide contexts that influence the development of the self in adolescence in often complex ways. Corresponding conclusions can be drawn about the influence of the school context. In a study of approximately 2,000 children and adolescents, young adolescents, in comparison to 8- to 11-year-old children, showed more self-consciousness, greater instability of self-image, and slightly lower self-esteem (Simmons, Rosenberg, & Rosenberg,

Social interactions in school can influence identity development in adolescence.

1973). However, context, rather than age, seemed to account for these findings (see too Simmons & Blyth, 1987). Upon completion of the sixth grade, one portion of the young adolescent group had moved to a new school, typically a local junior high school, and the remaining portion of the young adolescents stayed in the same school, which offered seventh- and eighth-grade classes. The group of young adolescents who changed their school setting showed a much greater incidence of the above-noted changes in self than did the group that remained in elementary school. Variables related to the school context, and to school transitions more specifically, therefore seem to influence self-development in adolescence.

Other research is consistent with this view. Although children's self-esteem does not seem to decrease during elementary school, it does show such change following the transition to junior high school (Wigfield & Eccles, 1994). In a study of almost 2,000 young adolescents, self-esteem declined across the transition to junior high school but increased during seventh grade (Wigfield et al., 1991). If an adolescent is young relative to classmates accompanying him or her in the transition to junior high or middle school, the detrimental effects on self-esteem seem to be increased (Fenzel, 1992).

The influence of school transition on self-esteem occurs in countries other than the United States. Japanese adolescents were more pessimistic and less optimistic about their future personal success in seventh grade (beginning of junior high school) than in sixth grade (the end of elementary school) (Kozumi, 1995).

School transition is not the only way the school context influences the development of self during adolescence. Adolescents' educational plans and self-image have been found to be lower among youth living and going to school in rural communities (Sarigiani et al., 1990). It may be that the quality of teaching the adolescent experiences can protect against such influences. For instance, adolescents enrolled in middle schools that provide interdisciplinary teaching teams have higher self-concepts than youth who attend schools where such instruction is not emphasized (Stefanich, Wills, & Buss, 1991). Youth with low self-esteem can show significant improvement in their self-regard if they have physical education instructors who are reinforcing and encouraging of their efforts at sports (Smith & Smoll, 1990). In fact, youth who experienced positive social interactions in their school have been shown to undergo marked enhancement in their perceived self-competence, and this influence can occur even among youth who are already quite advanced in their capacities (Kramer, 1991). Indeed, adolescent self-worth is predicted by social approval, especially from one's classmates (Robinson, 1995). In short, then, there may be features of the context that can have a positive effect on virtually any youth.

Conclusions About Diversity and Context in Adolescent Identity Development Multiple levels of the context are influential in the promotion of identity development during adolescence. If these contextual influences provide social support for young people, then they should be satisfied with who they are and who they are becoming. Such youths should develop a positive regard for their "self." If so, then, in a sense, they should find themselves "good company." They should enjoy spending time with themselves.

Research supports this possibility. About 500 European American adolescents in grades 5 through 9 reported on their feelings when alone (Larson, 1997). Time spent alone became more voluntary across this age period and, for the youth in grades 7 through 9, solitude had a positive effect on emotional state (Larson, 1997). This finding suggests that spending time alone has a useful influence in the development of the person during early adolescence.

Adolescents can typically decide if and when they want to be alone. To some extent they can make decisions about other contextual influences, such as peer groups, sport/athletic activities, and/or joining in on other community contexts (e.g., clubs or organizations). However, certain variables cannot be selected by the adolescent: Variables such as race, ethnicity, and gender are among such potential influences. It is important to understand their role in identity development.

Ethnic Identity in Adolescence

Issues to Consider
- What is ethnic identity? Why is it important to adolescent identity formation?
- What influences on ethnic identity exist?

Ethnic identity involves defining one's self in terms of one's membership in a particular racial group (e.g., African American) or as having a specific ethnic heritage (e.g., Italian American). A youth's racial or ethnic group membership often plays a central part in the formation of identity (Spencer, 1990, 1991; Spencer & Dornbusch, 1990; Spencer & Markstrom-Adams, 1990). Ethnic group membership provides a youth with a cultural identity, a sense of belonging and group pride, and a set of prescribed norms, values, and social behaviors. These attributes help give the youth a role to couple with his or her identity (Spencer, 1991). Racial pride acts to support the youth's self-respect, self-concept, and the ethnic or racial component of his or her identity and role.

Part of identity development involves understanding where one fits into one's society or culture.

Data indicate that ethnic identity increases with age. Among about 550 adolescents from three ethnic groups (African Americans, Latinos, and Asian Americans) such an age trend was noted (Phinney, Ferguson, & Tate, 1997). Increases in ethnic identity were associated with positive attitudes among the youth toward their ethnic group (Phinney et al., 1997). In a study of identity among African American young women ranging in age from 12 to 22 years (Shorter-Gooden & Washington, 1996), several domains of identity were found (race, gender, sexual orientation, relationships, career, religious beliefs, and political beliefs). The domain of racial identity was the most important to these women. In turn, however, among 14- to 18-year-old adolescents from Jamaica (Smith & Muenchen, 1995), gender and age were the major bases of differences in definitions of self in regard to domains such as morals, social relationships, sexual attitudes, mastery of the external world, vocational and educational goals, and emotional health.

It may be that the ethnic composition of the community within which youth live accounts for some of the above-noted differences across studies in the salience of ethnicity in the identities of youth. Research indicates that ethnic identity is influenced by community and family context. For an ethnic minority group in Norway, the Sami, having both parents of Sami background was associated with a Sami ethnic identity only among youth whose families lived in the highland areas of northern Norway (Kvernmo & Heyerdahl, 1996). When youth with two Sami parents lived in coastal communities, set-

tings characterized by great assimilation and integration, they identified themselves as either bicultural or as Norwegian. Youth with only one Sami parent identified themselves strongly as Norwegian when living on the coast and as bicultural when living in the highlands (Kvernmo & Heyerdahl, 1996).

Mexican American and African American adolescents showed three types of ethnic identity patterns in regard to their two reference groups, their ethnic one and their American one. These identity patterns were blended bicultural, alternating bicultural, and separated (Phinney & Devich-Navarro, 1997). In a study of about 100 Native American male and female ninth and twelfth graders, youth in a high school with a predominantly Native American student body demonstrated more ethnic identity exploration and commitment than did Native American youth in a high school with a predominantly European American student body (Lysne & Levy, 1997).

As with other aspects of identity, there are contextual influences on ethnic identity, and the family is one key context. The self-esteem of African American adolescents is associated with positive relationships with their parents and with the perceptions by the youth that their families approved of them and of what they were doing (Luster & McAdoo, 1995). In regard to such family influences, African American parents discuss prejudice with their adolescents more often than do Japanese American or Mexican American parents (Phinney & Chavira, 1995). However, Japanese American and African American parents emphasize adaptation to society more than Mexican American parents (Phinney & Chavira, 1995). Among about 200 Korean American youth living in California, about three quarters expressed a concern about their parents' limited English proficiency (Park, 1995). Although most of these youth were well adjusted to the way of life their parents presented at home and to the social patterns they encountered in their schools, more than half of them were concerned about their schoolwork and about a third were worried about their facility with the English language (Park, 1995).

An integrative approach to the understanding of the role of multiple levels of the context on ethnic identity has been undertaken by Margaret Beale Spencer and her colleagues (e.g., Cunningham & Spencer, 1996; Spencer, 1999; Spencer, Dupree, & Hartmann, 1997; Swanson, Spencer, & Petersen, 1998). They developed a "phenomenological variant of ecological systems theory" (PVEST) to study the identity development process among ethnically diverse youth. Much of this work has been directed to understanding identity development among African American male adolescents.

Spencer notes that a hypermasculine identity is often associated with African American male adolescents. Among these youth, this identity is linked to the enactment of aggressive coping responses to stressors. Although these adolescents possess the same values concerning school, religion, church attendance, and family caring found more generally in society, their aggressive coping style may be a way of dealing with a perceived high-risk environment (i.e., negative peer and teacher perceptions) and a lack of trust in the school, the learning context (Spencer, 1999).

Accordingly, the hypermasculine identity of African American male adolescents is a product of the regulation of their relationships with peer, family, teacher, school, and community contexts, contexts they perceive to be threatening and nonsupportive (Spencer, 1999). To reduce the amount of personal adjustment needed and school problems associated with the aggressive behaviors these youth use to cope with their context, Spencer (1999) recommends modifying the multiple levels of the ecology that seem to involve these behaviors. She also suggests introducing new socialization practices, including ones relating to school restructuring and to teacher training (Spencer,

1999). Some of the recent work of Margaret Beale Spencer is presented in Meet the Researcher Box 6.5.

Gender Differences

Issue to Consider
- What gender differences exist in identity development?

As highlighted in the scholarship of Spencer (1999), identity may develop in different ways for boys and girls. Several studies confirm this possibility. In a 4-year longitudinal study, which started with youth at the beginning of the ninth grade, of about 170 youth, girls had lower self-esteem than boys (Chubb, Fertman, & Ross, 1997). In a representative sample of 12-, 13-, and 14-year-old male and female adolescents from Lausanne, Switzerland (Bolognni et al., 1996), girls were found to have poorer self-esteems than boys across all domains of self-definition (e.g., in regard to appearance, scholastics, and athletic performance). These differences, and self-esteem in general, showed no major changes across the age range (Bolognni et al., 1996).

In a longitudinal study of Finnish males and females between 11 and 15 years of age (Lintunen et al., 1995), self-perceptions became increasingly fixed across the 4-year span, particularly for boys. Among girls, but not boys, there was a decrease in their perceptions of self-attractiveness with age (Lintunen et al., 1995). In a study of about 270 Turkish youth ranging in age from 14 to 17 years, symbolic items (e.g., relationships, happiness) and artistic and creative endeavors were more important in the identities of girls than boys, whereas material items (TV, sports equipment) and athletic activities were more salient to boys (Yildirim, 1997).

Of course, not all boys and girls embrace the general pattern of malelike or femalelike identity. Rather, there seem to be differences in adjustment associated with variation in gender identity. For instance, in a longitudinal study of about 160 adolescents, studied first between the ages of 13 and 18 years and then assessed again about 6 years later, males who showed coping behaviors associated with feminine gender roles showed poor adaptation in adulthood (Feldman et al., 1995). For females, coping behaviors associated with feminine gender roles was associated with good adaptation in adulthood (Feldman et al., 1995).

MEET THE RESEARCHER BOX 6.5

MARGARET BEALE SPENCER
IDENTIFYING MULTIPLE PATHWAYS TO RESILIENCY AMONG HIGH SCHOOL YOUTH

Having entered the field as a young researcher from a pharmacological and pharmaceutical background, I am now a scholar in the areas of social cognition, resiliency, and identity development among youth living in urban contexts. I have examined and identified developmental patterns of racial awareness among early and middle-childhood youth based on studies across three geographic regions in the United States. The scope of my work extends to addressing the impact of systematic victimization, following the Atlanta child murders, and the further development of a theoretical model to account for the unique experiences and adaptive responses of adolescents, particularly minority youth, and their families. This work has emerged with greater breadth in my current appointment as an endowed professor at the University of Pennsylvania and the director of the W.E.B. Du Bois Collective Research Institute and the Center for Health, Achievement, Neighborhood, Growth, and Ethnic Studies.

Margaret Beale Spencer is the Board of Overseers Professor of Education at the University of Pennsylvania Graduate School of Education and a professor of psychology in the School of Arts and Sciences Department of Psychology. Spencer serves as director of the Interdisciplinary Studies in Human Development Program at the Graduate School. She is also the director of the Center for Health, Achievement, Neighborhood, Growth, and Ethnic Studies (CHANGES) and the W.E.B. Du Bois Collective Research Institute.

Building on a theoretical foundation regarding the development of children, youth, and families in urban contexts, my program of research reflects an investment in conducting sound scientific investigations from a developmentally, contextually, and culturally sensitive framework in areas that had historically utilized a "deviance" or "deficit" perspective. My work, both as a scholar and mentor, demonstrates a responsibility to facilitate the bridging of research, practice, and policy implications for youth. I believe the combination of a rigorous approach to science and my commitment to youth has helped propel a greater sensitivity to context and culture in the scientific community and among young scholars and has shaped me as a scholar, a teacher, and a mentor.

My continuing and cumulative scholarly efforts seek to identify the multiple pathways to resiliency among high school youth at different levels of educational attainment while implementing intervention programs designed to provide youth with identity-enhancing experiences.

Conclusions About the Role of the Context: Promoting Positive Selves to Further Civil Society

People—parents, peers, and teachers, for instance—and institutions—for example, schools or the media—can influence the development of the self during adolescence. Such influences can promote either positive or negative changes among youth. Given the importance for society of having adolescents incorporate into their self-definitions commit-

ments to useful roles in society, numerous programs around the world are aimed at promoting positive identity among youth. As shown in Applications Box 6.1, these programs seek to instill in youth identities that involve a commitment to the institutions and organizations of civil society (see Chapter 5).

As illustrated by the programs described in Applications Box 6.1, the range of possible contextual influences on positive identity development among youth provides a reason for optimism about finding combinations of people and settings that can improve human development. At the same time, the combinations of individuals and contexts that will detract from healthy development must be identified and eliminated or prevented. As demonstrated by the

applications box 6.1

Promoting Self-Development, Promoting Civil Society

To maintain and perpetuate its institutions, society requires youth to develop in manners that reflect a commitment to civil society. For society to continue to function well in the present and the future it needs citizens committed to playing roles that are valued by society. Across the world, communities and governments create programs aimed at inculcating such identities among youth.

The programs described here represent a range of exemplary programs from the United States and internationally.

Boys' Society of Sierra Leone, Freetown, Sierra Leone

In the 1960s, increased urbanization and deteriorating economic conditions in Freetown, Sierra Leone, resulted in more and more young people living and working on the streets. Seeking to reduce the number of marginalized youth, an American professor convened a prominent group of area leaders to identify a solution. The result of their efforts is the Boys' Society of Sierra Leone, a multifaceted program providing youth from low-income families with vocational training, community service activities, and assistance with schoolwork.

The Boys' Society concentrates its efforts on boys (72%) and more recently girls (28%) between the ages of 8 and 18. Its offices and skills training program are housed in a downtown facility. The society also operates a working farm on 62 acres outside the city where young people help to raise pigs and grow rice and vegetables. The goal of the farm is to generate financial resources while providing youth with training in animal husbandry and small-scale production. A production and training center located in a former auto service station provides youth with hands-on training in mechanics, metal work, spray painting, body work, and electronics.

The society reaches young people throughout Freetown through the establishment of clubs or "zones." Today, more than 400 disadvantaged youth participate in club activities ranging from community betterment projects to vocational training. The zones function like surrogate extended families, generating a sense of comraderie, peer support, identity, and belonging.

In preparing youth to enter the work force, the society operates a Job Placement Program in which young people serve as apprentices to small businesses throughout Freetown. Of the 90% of young people who enroll and complete the program, 50% find jobs and 50% start their own businesses. Through this and other activities, the society fosters a feeling of "belonging" among youth who have grown alienated from their family and community.

With 44% of the population of Sierra Leone currently under the age of 15, the society's role is as vital today as ever.

Duke of Edinburgh's International Award Program, London, England

This program originated in a secondary school in Scotland, the brainchild of a headmaster with a belief in the importance of physical fitness in promoting confidence and the holistic development of young people. Officially launched in 1956, the Duke of Edinburgh's International Award Program encourages personal growth and discovery, self-reliance, responsibility, and community service among young people.

The Award Program is implemented by government agencies, nonprofit institutions, public and private schools, and independent groups of adult volunteers within individual countries. The program is based on individual development, not competition. To earn an award, young people,

Continued on next page

thought and richness of the youth programs discussed in the applications box, the combined challenge of "promotion" and "prevention" is being addressed around the globe. The potential for civil society can only be enhanced by these efforts.

To the extent that such initiatives are successful, youth will find roles in a society that enable them to contribute to their societies with enthusiasm and

skill. In such a society youth will find identities that seamlessly blend what they do with what they believe. Their roles will work for them and for their society. Conversely, their work will involve a role that is useful to them and to their social world. In Chapter 7 we consider the nature of the relationship in adolescence between role development and work.

ages 14 to 25, work with adult volunteers to build a personal development program that includes four distinct activities: service, expeditions, skills, and physical recreation. Medals are awarded to those who successfully complete all four sections over a set period of time—6 months designates a bronze medal, 12 months a silver, and 18 months a gold. The criteria for granting an award are individual effort and self-improvement.

Service activities can include helping an individual in need, learning first aid, conservation work, fund-raising for charity, or other activities that meet community needs. The expeditions section enourages the spirit of adventure and self-discovery. Participants plan, train for, and undertake a venture with a clearly defined purpose—whether on foot, cycle, horseback, or on water. The skills component is designed to develop personal interests and practical skills in fields such as agriculture, computer science, music, and arts and crafts. And finally, the physical recreation section encourages participation in athletic endeavors. Participants may choose from activities such as team sports, martial arts, swimming, yoga, and dance.

The Award Program has been successfully adapted to more than 100 countries, both developing and industrialized. Although the basic structure of the program remains the same, activities differ from country to country. In the past, local projects have included AIDS awareness programs in Uganda, fruit production and forestry in the Gambia, environmental protection in Sri Lanka, and Dragon Boat Teams in Hong Kong. In 1990–1991, there were 130,152 young people participating around the world, half girls and half boys.

Adolescent Development Program (Servol), Port-of-Spain, Trinidad

This program started in 1970 as a result of a widespread government protest against the desperate economic conditions of the poor in Trinidad. The uprising failed, but its message left a strong impression on Father Gerard Pantin. Father Pantin, a Roman Catholic priest, left his job as a schoolteacher and started talking to people about their problems and hopes for the future.

Rather than wait for change, Father Pantin soon realized that individuals and communities must take it upon themselves to create change. In bringing this theory to life, he founded "Service Volunteered for All," soon known as Servol. In the more than 30 years since it began, Servol has grown into an internationally recognized organization,

providing training for youth educators throughout the Caribbean and Central America, and even as far as South Africa, while working to empower citizens and communities in Trinidad and Tobago to help themselves.

In fostering positive attitudes among community members, Servol focuses much of its attention on the youngest members of society. To date, it has helped establish more than 184 preschools throughout Trinidad and Tobago. Teachers within the schools take part in an intensive preschool training program in which they are taught how to better interact with students and their parents. The schools are designed to encourage healthy youth development right from the start.

In addition, thousands of young people have benefited from participation in Servol's Adolescent Development Program (ADP). The program works to foster a positive self-image among teenagers. Classes include instruction on nutrition, health and sex education, sports and drama, drug prevention, craft-making, self-awareness, spirituality, and community service. They focus on spiritual, emotional, creative, intellectual, physical, and social development (SPICES). Parenting classes are also offered as a means of preparing young people to be better parents themselves.

In partnership with the national government, Servol has helped build more than 30 "Life Centres," providing young people with valuable skills training in such areas as welding, plumbing, woodwork, pottery, painting, and child care. Through training, young people develop marketable skills they can use to get jobs, or in some cases, to start their own small businesses. More importantly, however, they grow to have faith in themselves and their abilities.

Since 1994, Servol, with a grant from the InterAmerican Development Bank, has set up three technology centers providing training in computer literacy, electronics, computer repairs, and computer controlled electronics for its trainees. These courses are being complemented by an enhancement course preparing them for the world of work.

Since 1981, Servol has trained more than 450 early childhood educators, 33 field officers, and 125 adolescent instructors throughout Trinidad and Tobago. Its approach has been replicated in a number of countries throughout the region and in Ireland and South Africa.

Mobility International

An estimated 1 out of 10 people in the world have a disability of one form or another. Mobility International USA

(MIUSA) was founded in 1981 to expand opportunities for people with disabilities in international exchange, leadership, community service, and disability rights training.

Since it was started, MIUSA has helped young people from the U.S. and 80 other countries to develop leadership and organizational skills, gain a cross-cultural perspective, and experiment with independent living in foreign settings. As its name denotes, Mobility International USA works to eliminate the barriers that have traditionally prevented people with disabilities from participating in exchange programs and other cross-cultural learning experiences.

MIUSA's international exchange programs for youth last from 2 to 4 weeks and are held during the summer in the United States and abroad. Activities include living with homestay families, leadership seminars, disability rights workshops, cross-cultural learning, and team building activities such as river rafting and challenge courses. Participants develop strategies for making changes both within themselves and in their communities. MIUSA is able to offer Youth Leadership programs as funding is available.

MIUSA has received positive responses from participants, many of whom note that they were challenged in a positive way and were empowered to effect changes in their own lives and communities. Participation in the program has enabled many to overcome feelings of isolation and helplessness as they discover through sharing and their own actions what they are capable of. For some participants, the catalyst for empowerment is the simple act of using public transportation or boarding a jet for the first time. Others acquire confidence by learning to communicate in another culture. Still others grow by working together with other disabled youth to build a ramp, organize a public rally, or talk with local politicians about the rights of young people with disabilities.

MIUSA assists other organizations throughout the world to include youth with disabilities in all their existing and future programs. This is done through the National Clearinghouse on Disability and Exchange (NCDE) with its free information and referral services. NCDE is managed by MIUSA and sponsored by the Bureau of Educational and Cultural Affairs of the United States Department of State.

CelebrateYouth!, Albuquerque, New Mexico

The state of New Mexico has been found to have some of the highest rates of school attrition, poverty, unem-ployment, and youth substance abuse in the United States. The percentage of youth suffering the devastating effects of such problems is particularly high in minority areas. A 1991 study by the Center for the Study of Social Policy found New Mexico to be one of the worst places to raise a child in the United States, particularly with respect to its commitment of resources to children.

Added to this are the pervasive problems of alienation from learning and from self, racism and sexism, lack of integration between ages and between parents and children, between individuals and communities, and among various groups. Such problems create confusion and despair among children and youth of all classes and backgrounds.

To nurture the talents of the state's at-risk youth in particular, CelebrateYouth! was established in 1988. Although originally created as a drug prevention program, its focus shifted within a year to education and youth development. As such, its philosophy is based on promoting young people's strengths rather than overcoming their problems.

The focus of the program is on the pursuit of knowledge to foster personal and social development; the creation of new ways for young people to relate while recognizing their differences; and, most importantly, on building a human culture that places human development so high on its list of priorities that in any given exchange each person's dignity, integrity, and ethics come first in importance.

Through the program, young people, ages 9 to 18, work for a year with volunteer mentors on projects in dance, literature, theater, music, visual arts, history, chess, psychology, and other areas of interest. Each summer, their work is showcased during a 3-day festival attended by more than 1,000 people.

In 1992, over 450 young people, 200 mentors, and 150 other volunteers participated in the program. CelebrateYouth! reflects the region's rich ethnic diversity, including young people from the state's varied cultural and economic groups. More than 50% of program participants are from minority groups.

Outside studies of CelebrateYouth! have found the program to be successful in building self-esteem and promoting self-directed learning and meaningful sharing among diverse groups of young people, parents, and volunteers.

Source: International Youth Foundation, 2001. <www.iyfnet.org>

Summary

- Identity is the set of thoughts, feelings, values, attitudes, and behaviors that defines a person's self.
- Adolescents need an identity so they can coordinate their biological and psychological characteristics with a set of activities deemed useful by society.
- A commitment to a role is an outward expression of an adolescent's identity.
- If an adolescent cannot find a role that resolves the emotional upheaval which results from the strong societal and personal mandates for role adoption, an identity crisis may result.
- If the identity crisis is not resolved by the time adolescents enter adulthood, they will feel a sense of role confusion or identity diffusion.
- Some young adults waver between roles in a prolonged "moratorium" period, some "foreclose" on a socially approved, easily available identity and avoid the crisis, and others adopt an available but socially disapproved role or ideology or go through "negative identity formation."
- Identity develops through a process of person-context interactions in which adolescents evaluate and integrate reactions to the explorations of their world.
- Erikson sees the changes of puberty as presenting the adolescent with serious problems and bringing about the crisis between identity and role confusion. To resolve the crisis, it is necessary in Erikson's view to attain a complex synthesis between psychological processes and societal goals and directives.
- To resolve the identity crisis, the adolescent must be committed to a role and the accompanying ideology.
- Self-esteem grows out of the successful resolution of crises and is a confirmation that one is learning effective steps toward the future and developing a defined personality.
- Self-regulation allows the individual to select goals to pursue, to find means to attain those goals (optimization), and to cope with failures to reach goals (compensation).
- Erikson's theory predicted an invariant identity achievement in late adolescence, but research has shown that there continues to be important changes in ego identity throughout adolescence.
- Other data show that although Erikson would predict stable identity achievement by early adulthood, college students do not invariably show stable identity achievement.
- The major instances of diversity in adolescent self-conception occur in regard to differences in developmental pathways and gender differences.
- Baumeister found two types of identity crises: identity deficit, when a person cannot resolve the crisis because of an inability to make decisions, and identity conflict, when the person makes incompatible decisions when trying to resolve the identity crisis.
- Crises involving identity conflict are a more important part of ego development for girls than for boys.
- Marcia believed that the resolution of the identity crisis involves more than just identity versus role confusion, and a more diverse pattern exists of adolescent's identity status.
- The four statuses Marcia identified are identity achievement, having a crisis period but then showing a commitment to a role or ideology; identity diffusion, having or not having a crisis, but lacking commitment and not being concerned about it; moratorium, having a vague commitment but being in active search; and foreclosure, never experiencing a crisis, yet being highly committed.
- If contextual influences provide social support for young people, they should be satisfied with who they are or who they are becoming.
- Ethnic identity involves defining one's self in terms of one's membership in a particular racial group or as having a specific ethnic identity.
- Research indicates that identity may develop in different ways for boys and girls, and differences in adjustment are associated with variation in gender identity.

Discussion Topics

1. As a young adolescent do you remember how you felt emotionally as you began to experience changes in your body? Did you welcome those changes? How were your bodily changes regarded and responded to by those of your social world? Do you feel their reactions and involvement impacted your identity development? If so, how, and if not, why not?

2. Many adolescents experience an identity crisis as they attempt to answer the defining question, "Who am I?" Why are adolescents so self-reflective? What are the primary factors in an adolescent's life that may cause him or her to feel helpless in the face of this question?

3. How did you define your identity as a young adolescent? How would you define your identity today?

How and why are these two definitions similar and different? How have the ecological contexts of your life influenced these definitions?

4. How did the adults in your world, such as parents and school guidance counselors, impress on you the importance of selecting a role as an adolescent? Do you believe your social contexts were supportive of your quest to select a role or more harmful in the pressure they applied?

5. As adolescents, many of us are known to say, "When I grow up, I will be completely different from my parents." Now that you are a bit removed from the heart of the adolescent years, do you feel their involvement in your life was effective, appropriate, and supportive? What would you have done differently as a parent of an adolescent who was trying to select a role?

6. Do you feel the commitment you made to a role(s) as an adolescent enabled you to feel more at ease, stable, structured, and focused? Why or why not?

7. What ideology defined the role you chose as an adolescent? Are those attitudes, beliefs, and values still important to you today? Why do you believe they were important to you during your adolescent years? Do you feel they may change again if and when you decide to become a parent? Why is there often not complete fidelity to role ideologies throughout the life span?

8. Do you remember feeling as if your self-esteem increased throughout your high school years? If so, what factors influenced this change? Did your transition to college challenge your self-esteem? What have been some of the primary forces of your life that impact the self-esteem you have today?

9. What memories do you have of junior high and high school in which you had to assimilate or accommodate to your social contexts? Are you better able to adapt to your environment today? Why is adaptation generally less difficult as an adult?

10. What do you believe are some of the factors that might cause the developmental trajectories of adolescent self-esteem to differ for males and females?

11. What impact on development will the historical context of the years you spent as a child and adolescent have on you and the next generation? For example, do you believe that growing up in a generation when the "working mom" was an expected role will impact the way you parent?

12. Do you believe the way you were raised by your parents was heavily influenced by your gender? If so, in what ways? If not, do you believe they made conscious decisions to raise you in a gender-neutral fashion?

13. In what grades did your schools make the transitions from elementary to junior high and junior high to high school? What do you believe would be the ideal grades for schools to make these divisions and why?

14. How were your ethnic and racial identities supported or not supported in your social contexts as an adolescent? Do you believe the level of support you received influenced your personality development? If so, in what ways? How might schools do a better job of instilling ethnic and racial pride in their students?

Key Terms

developmental task (p. 134)

fidelity (p. 138)

foreclosure (p. 136)

identity (p. 135)

identity conflict (p. 146)

identity crisis (p. 135)

identity deficit (p. 146)

identity diffusion (p. 136)

ideology (p. 136)

moratorium (p. 136)

negative identity formation (p. 136)

role (p. 136)

role confusion (p. 136)

self-esteem (p. 139)

self-regulation (p. 140)

7

ROLE DEVELOPMENT AND WORK IN ADOLESCENCE

As John pulled his car carefully into the open space in front of the field house, he could not help but notice the wide-eyed stares of his teammates.

"Hey, man," Fred exclaimed with obvious admiration, "where did you get that car?"

"I bought it," John said. He carefully removed his helmet, pads, and cleats from the backseat. He wanted to be certain that he did not soil the new upholstery.

"Yeah, with what money?" Don asked with evident sarcasm. "Who'd you have to rob?"

"No one," John replied. "I earned the money this summer."

"If you worked this summer, what are you doing here at football practice?" Don asked. "I thought you had to make up two courses in summer school to be eligible for the team."

"Well, I took the classes and I got B's in both courses," John explained with obvious pride.

Fred became skeptical. "So you took classes all day, studied all night, and still found time to work enough to get money for this car? I guess that means you haven't slept since June," he said.

"Nope. I slept plenty *and* worked plenty. It's just that I was able to study while I worked," John explained.

"What were you, a night watchman or something like that?" Fred asked.

"Well, sort of . . . ," John replied.

"So what is it?" Fred asked. "What did you do to earn the money for the car?"

"Well," John explained, "when I knew I had to study every night and that I wouldn't be able to get a day job, I put up a poster in the community room of my apartment building. I advertised myself as a baby-sitter and said I would be available on any night, including weekends."

"From construction work last summer to baby-sitting this summer," Fred laughed. "So much for the rough, tough football player."

"Well, Fred," John said with a broad smile, "who is still taking the school bus and who is driving his own car? Maybe you should start thinking about becoming a baby-sitter yourself."

LEARNING OBJECTIVES

1. To understand the current patterns of work for adolescents.
2. To describe the positive impact work can have on adolescent development.
3. To be aware of the possible negative impact that work can have on an adolescent's life.
4. To understand differences in school performance between working and nonworking students.
5. To learn how gender is related to differences in the experience of a part-time job.

6. To understand gender role stereotypes and how they represent a significant influence on the social context and on youth development.
7. To understand why both flexibility and stereotypy exist in regard to work and gender roles.
8. To describe the gender intensification hypothesis and research about it.

Issues to Consider

- What are some of the ways in which socially and culturally defined gender roles may direct adolescents' selection of employment?
- How might adolescents' decision to be employed affect their identity development?

An important role transition in adolescence involves obtaining a driver's license.

The establishment of one's identity involves finding a **role**—a socially prescribed set of behaviors—to play in life (see Chapter 6). In actuality, a person's identity is a synthesis of several different roles. There are **gender roles**, a socially and culturally defined set of behaviors linked to being a male or a female in a given society. There are sets of behaviors linked to being a student, to being a student athlete, or to being a student leader (see Chapter 12). Of course, in addition, the type of work one does (e.g., being a sales clerk, a chef, or an auto mechanic) and/or the type of career one enters (e.g., lawyer, physician, engineer, teacher) are associated with specific sets of behaviors. Similarly, and on a more abstract level are roles such as "son," "daughter," or "citizen" that also have behavioral expectations associated with them, albeit perhaps less explicit ones than those linked to being a chef or a mechanic.

As a consequence of their search for identity (see Chapter 6), youth develop roles that have several components

(Vondracek, 1994; Vondracek et al., 1995). These components indicate to adolescents and to those with whom they interact what the adolescents will do in their world as workers, as men or women, and as members of the community.

Serious commitments to career are usually reserved until young adulthood (see Chapter 15) when, after high school or college, the adolescent chooses a specific occupation to pursue and makes choices regarding intimate relationships, marriage, and family. The selections made and the experiences that occur during the adolescent period shape and prepare young people to meet the challenges they will encounter when they make the transition from adolescence to young adulthood (see Chapter 15). For instance, in integrating their biological, psychological, and social characteristics, adolescents will

Role Socially prescribed set of behaviors.

Gender roles Socially and culturally defined set of behaviors linked to being a male or a female in a given society.

make decisions about the extent to which they feel comfortable with adult roles that are traditional or non-traditional for their genders. To illustrate, an electrical engineer or a preschool teacher are roles traditionally associated with males and females, respectively. Yet women may enter into electrical engineering as a career and men may become preschool teachers. What adolescents decide to do in regard to their role choices will, then, be influenced by their willingness to depart from traditional gender-linked roles (or, in turn, to be flexible in regard to the gender roles).

Several other factors influence how youth approach the world of work. Do they see themselves as involved in roles that require little or no education or training past high school or are they oriented to roles that require considerable postsecondary school education? Cognitive abilities, personality, family, and peers are important influences on role selections. Part-time work during adolescence is increasingly a key influence on the role choices of youth.

In this chapter we discuss the influences of work on adolescent development and role behaviors. The characteristics of gender role development are focused on, as are the nature and implications of traditional and nontraditional gender role selections during adolescence.

During high school, many adolescents have part-time jobs.

Work During Adolescence

Issues to Consider

- How frequent is part-time work during adolescence?
- What is the nature of racial differences in adolescent employment rate and adolescent school dropout rate in America?

Many adolescents in the United States work outside the home during their high school years and continue earning a salary during their college years. In fact, by the time they have completed high school, the majority of American adolescents have worked (Mortimer, Shanahan, & Ryus, 1994). Historically, such employment patterns are a relatively new phenomenon, at least in the United States: "In prior generations most adolescents in the United States did not work while school was in session, reserving paid employment for summer and other vacation periods. Now, however, simultaneous involvement in school and in the paid labor force has become the modal adolescent experience in the United States" (Mortimer et al., 1994, p. 304).

Among males and females aged 16 to 17 years who were in school, part-time employment rates were 35% in the mid-1980s (Mortimer, 1991). These rates represented a 37% increase from mid-1950s levels for males, and a 100% increase for females across this same time period (Mortimer, 1991). Self-reported rates of employment are even higher. During the 1980s and the 1990s, about 60% of high school sophomores and 75% of seniors indicated they were currently employed, and only about 7% of high school seniors reported they had never been employed (Greenberger & Steinberg, 1986; Mortimer, 1991).

There are racial differences in employment patterns. Among African American males, aged 16 to 19 years, employment rates dropped from 42% in 1960 to 36% in 1980. During the mid-1980s, about 50% of African American males, aged 16 to 24 years, were estimated to have never had regular employment (Taylor-Gibbs, 1991). Unemployment for African American males from urban areas is often coupled with dropping out of school. School dropout rates for African American adolescents, aged 18 to 19 years, *decreased* from 31.2% in 1970 to 17.3% in 1985, but across this same period, dropout rates for

African Americans living in the inner city *increased* to between 40% to 50% (Taylor-Gibbs, 1991).

Although working during adolescence is not as prevalent in other industrialized nations, such as Japan (Mortimer et al., 1994), considerable numbers of young people in these nations do work during their student years (e.g., Hagström & Gamberale, 1995; McKechnie et al., 1996; van der Velde, Feij, & van Emmerik, 1998). Evidence indicates that working during the adolescent years is linked to valuing work intrinsically (e.g., for its contributions to enhancing one's competence as a person) and not just for its extrinsic value (i.e., for its link to obtaining money). Youth from the Netherlands show increases in the intrinsic value of work across their late adolescent and young adult years (van der Velde et al., 1998) and, among Swedish youth, intrinsic work goals are seen as more important than are the economic benefits of employment (Hagström & Gamberale, 1995).

Thus, among contemporary youth, employment during the student years is a widespread phenomenon, especially in the United States. Moreover, there is some evidence that such activity is regarded by youth as primarily of importance because it helps make them better people—for instance, for giving them experiences and competencies that will enhance their future, adult lives. However, before concluding that work during adolescence is of unequivocal benefit to young people, note that some data suggest such benefits may not be certain, or that benefits of work can be outweighed by the negative influences of work on adolescent development. It is therefore important to understand the positive and negative impacts of work on adolescent development and under what conditions work may be beneficial to adolescents.

Positive and Negative Consequences of Adolescent Employment

Issues to Consider
- What characterizes employment opportunities most readily available to youth and why may these opportunities be considered a good challenge for identity development of youth?

- What are some of the positive and negative consequences of work for adolescents' academic and personal development?
- How does the intensity of employment interact with adolescents' intrinsic motivation for school?
- In what way may adolescents' employment influence their relationship with parents?

Adolescent employment may have several possible positive implications for youth development. Working may give adolescents a basis for new identities, new expectations of responsibility and independence from parents, and a new high status among peers (Mortimer et al., 1994). Working adolescents may encounter working peers and adults in their jobs, and these people may provide new models of adult behavior and new reference groups (Mortimer et al., 1994). Of course, these new groups may serve as either good or bad influences on the adolescent.

Therefore, working may not only offer positive benefits to adolescents. In fact, it can often have a negative impact on their lives. For example, working can take time away from school, diminishing the opportunity to participate in extracurricular activities or the time available for homework.

Moreover, the kinds of employment opportunities most readily available to youth are the same work activities that have the most negative consequences for adults. That is, most youth work in the retail and service sectors and are given jobs with high turnover, low pay, little authority, and low prestige (Mortimer et al., 1994). Adults in such jobs are often displeased by such roles because of these work characteristics and because such positions involve simple, repetitive tasks (e.g., "flipping burgers") that require very little or no special training or skills (e.g., "Here is the hamburger. Flip it over when it is brown. Don't touch the hot stove.").

It may be the case that such jobs are invariably boring and undesirable to most adults who, if they find themselves in such roles, will feel that their future prospects are dim. Nevertheless, it is possible that even such tasks may be new and challenging activities to a young person. Someone who has never worked outside the home, and never been asked to be productive for pay, may be more excited by the opportunity to be involved in the world of work than displeased by the particular activities he or she finds available in this setting (Mortimer et al., 1994).

Thus there is a range of possible positive and negative influences of work on adolescent development. It may be that the issue is not one of deciding whether work is or is not beneficial. Rather, it may be a matter of learning when, under what circumstances, work may have either a positive or a negative effect. Several major research projects have been conducted pertinent to the role of work in adolescent development.

In one major research project, Greenberger and Steinberg (1986) studied youth employment among students in four California high schools. The students reported that their employment was associated with their being punctual, dependable, and personally responsible.

By the tenth grade, a majority of adolescent girls work in part-time jobs.

Among girls, employment was also linked to reports of self-reliance (Greenberger, 1984). But employed adolescents were more frequently late for school and engaged in more deviant behavior than was the case with nonemployed youth (Greenberger & Steinberg, 1986). In related research, working students reported more school misconduct than did nonworking students, and working a moderate number of hours was linked to the highest rates of school misconduct (Steinberg & Dornbusch, 1991).

Another major study of the implications of work for youth development involved a longitudinal assessment of approximately 1,000 adolescents in the ninth and tenth grades conducted by Mortimer, Shanahan, and their colleagues (e.g., Mortimer et al., 1994, 1996). For about 90% of the adolescents, there was no formal association between school curriculum and work (for example, these youth were not involved in a work-study program and they did not receive credit for their work). Less than 20% of the adolescents indicated that their jobs provided them with knowledge about topics studied in school or reported that their work experiences gave them information they could contribute to class discussions.

Consistent with the earlier findings of Greenberger and Steinberg (1986), as well as those of other researchers (e.g., McKechnie et al., 1996; Mihalic & Elliott, 1997), Mortimer et al. (1994) found that working had some negative implications for the academic and personal development of

youth. For instance, 43% of the adolescents reported that working decreased the time they had available for their homework, and about 50% of the students reported that being a worker and a student simultaneously was stressful. Students who worked at high intensity engaged in more alcohol use (Mortimer et al., 1996).

Many students in this study also reported positive characteristics associated with working while being a high school student. For example, about 48% of the students indicated that their job taught them the importance of obtaining a good education, and approximately 33% of the students reported that working helped them identify the courses in high school they liked or did not like. About 36% of the students reported that what they learned at school facilitated their job performance.

By the tenth grade, 42% of the boys and 52% of the girls in this study were employed (Mortimer et al., 1994). Consistent with what was found when the students were in the ninth grade, no overall difference existed in tenth grade between working and nonworking students in time spent in schoolwork, in the time devoted to extracurricular activities, or in their grade point averages (GPAs) (Mortimer et al., 1994). Overall work status was not related to the incidence of school behavior problems (Mortimer et al., 1994). Working at a low intensity was linked to lower dropout rates (Mortimer et al., 1994). High school seniors who worked at a moderate intensity had higher grades than both nonworking students and students who worked more hours per week (Mortimer et al., 1996).

Furthermore, no difference was found between working and nonworking students in their *intrinsic* motivation for school, that is, in the degree to which they wanted to do well in school because of internal standards of excellence and personal values for achievement—as compared to wanting to achieve in school because such attainment is associated with rewards from parents, teachers, or society. Furthermore, the number of hours per week a student worked was also not systematically related to such motivation (Mortimer et al., 1994). For instance, the highest intrinsic motivation for school existed among students who worked relatively few hours a week (i.e., 1 to 5 hours) or, for girls, among youth who worked in excess of 25 hours a week. Similarly, among boys, the highest intrinsic motivation occurred when youth worked either at very low (1 to 5 hours a week) or at relatively high levels (i.e., 26 to 30 hours a week).

Accordingly, as compared to the conclusions associated with the research of Greenberger and Steinberg (1986), the findings reported by Mortimer et al. (1994) suggest no link between student employment—even when it exists at a high number of hours a week—and risk of poor school attitudes, diminished time devoted to homework, lessened involvement in extracurricular activities, or low school grades. Instead, for the youth in the Mortimer et al. (1994) study, evidence indicates that young people could "do it all," or—at least—could maintain their involvement and achievement in school and participate in the work force. Indeed, although work stress did have a negative impact on the schoolwork of these youth, the quality of the work environment (e.g., the menial nature of the roles youth were assigned at work) was not associated with their GPAs or their participation in extracurricular activities.

In addition to not negatively influencing activities in extracurricular contexts, work can have a beneficial influence on behavior in particular settings. For instance, in a longitudinal study of youth from rural Iowa between the seventh and tenth grades (Shanahan et al., 1996), earnings from paid labor, spent on nonleisure activities, was associated with more positive parent-adolescent relationships, with more time spent with the family, and with less parental monitoring of the youth. For girls, oppor-

tunities for skill development at work increased their intrinsic motivation for schoolwork (Mortimer et al., 1994). Girls' helpfulness at work increased their overall behavioral competence, and their increasing behavioral competence furthered the girls' tendencies to be helpful at work (Call, Mortimer, & Shanahan, 1995).

Work therefore has several beneficial effects for youth development in regard to personal abilities, school performance, and family relations. Some of these influences, including those pertinent to development into adulthood, are discussed by Jeylan Mortimer in Meet the Researcher Box 7.1.

There are important gender differences in the effects of work experiences on youth and, more generally, on the character of role development in adolescence. We discuss the dimensions and bases of these gender differences next.

Gender Differences in Work and Role Development

Issue to Consider
- How might gender affect the timing and the intensity of adolescent employment?

For most American adolescents, entry into the workplace begins in middle or late adolescence and usually involves experience with a part-time job (Camarena, Stemmler, & Petersen, 1994). However, there are usually gender differences in this experience (Camarena et al., 1994). For instance, boys are more likely to begin working at an earlier age and to work longer hours than girls (Greenberger & Steinberg, 1986).

Although both boys and girls are typically given jobs that involve little skill, training, or initiative, the precise assignments they are given often vary along gender-stereotypic lines (Camarena et al., 1994). For example, although boys and girls might both get a job in a department store, boys may be more likely to be assigned to duties in the stock room or mail room and girls may be more apt to be assigned duties as sales clerks.

The gender stereotypes reflected in such job assignments may signify societywide beliefs that males and females are fundamentally different in

MEET THE RESEARCHER BOX 7.1

JEYLAN MORTIMER
YOUTH WORK EXPERIENCE AND THE TRANSITION TO ADULTHOOD

Combining the roles of paid worker and student is very common in the United States. However, adolescent employment is a neglected context in the study of development. Some believe that extensive early work is detrimental because it imposes stressors and responsibilities for which the teenager is not yet ready. This "developmental readiness" or "stress sensitizing" hypothesis may be contrasted with a more sanguine "steeling" or "stress resilience" model. According to the second point of view, early work experience fosters coping skills that allow more effective response to subsequent stressors and better performance of adult roles. It has also been suggested that adolescents who have more work experience "grow up faster," acquiring adultlike identities and leisure time pursuits at an earlier age than those who invest less time in work while in high school, and make a more rapid transition to adulthood. Such "growing up" may take both negative—for example, alcohol use and smoking—and positive forms. Positive effects of employment on early adult development can be anticipated as a result of experiences in the work setting that develop both human and social capital.

Jeylan Mortimer is professor of Sociology, director of the Life Course Center, and principal investigator of the Youth Development Study at the University of Minnesota.

To address these questions, I initiated the Youth Development Study with my colleague Dr. Michael Finch in 1987. Because a large project like this requires the involvement of many people, we are joined by many other researchers, including Kathleen Call, Monica Johnson, Sabrina Oesterle, Michael Shanahan, and Christopher Uggen. We have followed 1,000 ninth graders through high school and into their late 20s (with support from the National Institute of Mental Health). This is the only longitudinal study in the country focused on part-time labor force participation (and other forms of work) during high school. With this data set, we can examine the effects of working on adjustment during high school, as well as the establishment of adult work and family roles.

We find that the quality of work experience, especially the rewards, opportunities, and stressors encountered in the work sphere, has important consequences for youth mental health (e.g., depressive affect, sense of mastery, or control orientation) and behavioral adjustment, as indicated by school problem behavior and substance use. Positive work experiences and supervisory relations buffer the effects of problems in the family, lessening depressive affect, declines in school achievement, and other negative responses to familial distress. Working during adolescence is also formative with respect to vocational development.

The "growing up faster" model is only partially confirmed. Youth's early involvement in the labor force is a precursor to earlier initiation of alcohol use, but not more use in the long term. Early investment in the labor force, as measured by hours of work, also precedes more rapid transition to full-time employment and higher earnings in the years following high school. However, attachment to work during high school appears to be associated with normative (not premature) timing of transition to family roles.

"Balanced early employment," work that is stable but limited in intensity to less than 20 hours per week, has advantages, in terms of postsecondary educational achievement, especially for youth who initially, when they entered high school, indicated little educational promise (e.g., they had little interest in school, poorer grades, and relatively low educational aspirations). In contrast, youth who worked at high intensity (more than 20 hours per week) obtained fewer months of postsecondary education and were less likely to receive BA degrees. Our future research will address the mechanisms through which early work produces such advantage and disadvantage, and longer term consequences that only become manifest after education is complete and occupational careers are established.

their capacities, behaviors, and interests. To understand gender differences in work and role development we must understand the nature of these gender role stereotypes and how they may represent a significant influence on the social context of youth development.

Gender Role Stereotypes

Issues to Consider
- In what way might societal gender-bound beliefs regarding a person's capacities, behaviors, and interest be reflected in a person's job assignment?

- How do stereotypical gender role attributes differ for males and females?
- How might an adolescent's flexible personal orientation to work defy a stereotyped view of gender roles?

Across history and, still, in contemporary society, men and women do not engage with equal frequency in the various social roles present in a given culture (Block, 1973; Camarena et al., 1994). Some roles are traditionally associated with men (e.g., working outside of the home in gainful, salaried employment) and some with women (e.g., being a homemaker and caring for children). These traditional divisions between the genders in the roles they play in society may, over time, become regarded as gender role stereotypes in a given society.

A *stereotype* is an overgeneralized belief. It is an *attitude*—that is, some combination of cognition and feeling—about a social stimulus, for instance, a person. A stereotype is an attitude that invariantly characterizes a person as possessing specific attributes. A stereotype allows for little exception (Allport, 1954). Because of this rigidity, a social stereotype is relatively resistant to change and, as such, may become accepted as always true in a given society. For more than a quarter century, scholars have indicated that gender role stereotypes exist in American society (Block, 1973; Worell, 1981).

A gender role may be defined as a socially defined set of prescriptions for behavior for people of a particular sex group. **Gender role behavior** may be defined as behavioral functioning in accordance with the prescriptions, and **gender role stereotypes** are the generalized beliefs that particular behaviors are characteristic of one sex group as opposed to the other (Lerner, 1986; Worell, 1981). Table 7.1 presents the findings of a well-known study (Broverman et al., 1972) of the gender role attributes associated stereotypically with males and females by male and female college students.

The findings summarized in this table indicate that males are stereotypically described as very aggressive, independent, dominant, active, skilled in business, and not at all dependent. Females are stereotyped to be very gentle, to be very aware of the feelings of others, to be very interested in appearance, and to have a very strong need for security.

Gender role behavior
Behavioral functioning in accordance with the prescriptions set by the society one lives in.

Gender role stereotypes
Generalized beliefs that particular behaviors are more characteristic of one sex group than the other.

Adolescent girls often engage in jobs that are not stereotypically associated with women.

These gender role stereotypes are held fairly consistently across sex, age, and educational levels within society (Broverman et al., 1972). In addition, other classic research indicates considerable cross-cultural consistency in these stereotypes. In a study of six countries (Norway, Sweden, Denmark, Finland, England, and the United States) cross-cultural consistency in these stereotypes was found to exist (Block, 1973).

In short, in American society and in comparisons among samples from other societies, stereotypes exist specifying that different sets of behaviors are expected from males and females. The male gender role is associated with individual effectiveness and independent competence. The female role is associated with interpersonal warmth and expressiveness.

Although the existence of these stereotypes means that people may believe males and females generally differ in these ways, the existence of the stereotypes does not necessarily mean males and females *actually* behave differently along these dimensions. Moreover, in regard to issues of work and role development in adolescence, although

Table 7-1	Gender Role Stereotypes of Male and Female American College Students

Competency cluster (masculine pole is more desirable)

Feminine	Masculine
Not at all aggressive	Very aggressive
Not at all independent	Very independent
Very emotional	Not at all emotional
Does not hide emotions at all	Almost always hides emotions
Very subjective	Very objective
Very easily influenced	Not at all easily influenced
Very submissive	Very dominant
Dislikes math and science very much	Likes math and science very much
Very excitable in a minor crisis	Not at all excitable in a minor crisis
Very passive	Very active
Not at all competitive	Very competitive
Very illogical	Very logical
Very home-oriented	Very worldly
Not at all skilled in business	Very skilled in business
Very sneaky	Very direct
Does not know the way of the world	Knows the way of the world
Feelings easily hurt	Feelings not easily hurt
Not at all adventurous	Very adventurous
Has difficulty making decisions	Can make decisions easily
Cries very easily	Never cries
Almost never acts as a leader	Almost always acts as a leader
Not at all self-confident	Very self-confident
Very uncomfortable about being aggressive	Not at all uncomfortable about being aggressive
Not at all ambitious	Very ambitious
Unable to separate feelings from ideas	Easily able to separate feelings from ideas
Very dependent	Not at all dependent
Very conceited about appearance	Never conceited about appearance
Thinks women are always superior to men	Thinks men are always superior to women
Does not talk freely about sex with men	Talks freely about sex with men

Warmth-expressiveness cluster (feminine pole is more desirable)

Feminine	Masculine
Doesn't use harsh language at all	Uses very harsh language
Very talkative	Not at all talkative
Very tactful	Very blunt
Very gentle	Very rough
Very aware of feelings of others	Not at all aware of feelings of others
Very religious	Not at all religious
Very interested in own appearance	Not at all interested in own appearance
Very neat in habits	Very sloppy in habits
Very quiet	Very loud
Very strong need for security	Very little need for security
Enjoys art and literature	Does not enjoy art and literature at all
Easily expresses tender feelings	Does not express tender feelings at all easily

Note: These results are based on the responses of 74 college men and 80 college women.

Source: Adapted from Broverman et al., 1972, p. 63.

Adolescent boys often engage in nontraditional male roles, such as child-care worker.

these stereotypes may represent sources of bias in the job opportunities made available to male and female youth, the existence of the stereotypes may not mean boys and girls actually take jobs during adolescence that are consistent with the stereotype.

Perhaps, most importantly, the presence of the stereotypes may not mean that adolescents plan to pursue jobs in later life that are gender stereotyped. Youth may hold a more flexible personal orientation to work. Counter to a fixed or stereotyped view about what males and females are capable of doing and about what they might be "allowed" by society to do, youth might believe that males and females can (in regard to capacities) and may (in regard to societal opportunities) pursue the same set of work roles. The nature of work orientation and gender differences in role development in adolescence is discussed next.

Gender Roles: Stereotypy or Flexibility?

Issues to Consider
- In what way may the nature of parental employment affect an adolescent's perception of different gender-bound roles at work and his or her flexibility to hold those roles?
- What characterizes the role strain experienced by an increasing number of adolescent females?

As the United States enters into the 21st century, there is evidence that although the gender role stereotypes of the 20th century are still very much a part of the landscape of American culture, the influence of the stereotypes is waning. The evidence indicates that society is at a point of historical transition from stereotypy to flexibility in the nature of the roles seen as appropriate, possible, and desirable for men and women. In almost every aspect of research pertinent to work and gender roles, both stereotypy and flexibility exist simultaneously.

Most youth in contemporary America are likely to have a parent or parents employed outside the home (Camarena et al., 1994; Hernandez, 1993; J. Lerner, 1994; see too Chapter 8). Although having a mother who works outside of the home is the typical experience for most American children and adolescents (Hernandez, 1993; J. Lerner, 1994), the meaning attached by youth to parental employment continues to show evidence of the influence of the gender stereotypes just described (Camarena et al., 1994).

Consistent with the stereotype, work outside the home (being the "breadwinner") is seen traditionally as the central domain of males, and family life is regarded as the central domain of females (who are regarded as the "homemakers") (Camarena et al., 1994). In this context, work is defined as earning a salary, whereas family is equated with housework (Camarena et al., 1994).

Consistent with a stereotyped division of labor between males (regarded as breadwinners) and females (regarded as homemakers), half of the high school seniors in the Monitoring the Future study (Johnston, Bachman, & O'Malley, 1991; see too Chapter 13) indicated that it is not acceptable for both parents to work when they have preschool-aged children. Contrary to the stereotyped breadwinner-homemaker division of labor between men and women, respectively, 79% of the female high school seniors and 67% of the male high school seniors said that even if they had the money to live as comfortably as they wished, they would still not want to give up paid work (Johnston et al., 1991).

Although an increasing numbers of adolescent females aspire to succeed in labor areas traditionally associated with males (Camarena et al., 1994), there has not been a corresponding investment in family work on the part of adolescent males (Camarena et al., 1994). Accordingly, for the older adolescent female, the need to integrate work and family may influence significantly the choice of her vocation or the timing of marriage. In addition, the more flexible role orientation of females—in regard to balancing family and work roles—may place more strain on them in regard to enactment of overall role behaviors than would be the case for men who opt to devote most of their effort to enacting their work roles (J. Lerner, 1994).

The findings of a longitudinal study of 147 youth between the sixth and eighth grades illustrates that the basis of role strain may begin in adolescence (Camarena et al., 1994). Although boys' attitudes toward women's roles changed more than did girls' attitudes to the work and family roles of men and women, across grades girls' attitudes were more positive and open than was the case with of boys (Camarena et al., 1994). In a 10-year follow-up of individuals first studied as adolescents, both men and women reported that they valued both work and family, but both groups also had highly stereotypic expectations for how work and family roles actually would be enacted (Camarena et al., 1994): Men would emphasize work for a salary and women would stress family roles.

Evidence exists for the presence of both stereotypy and flexibility in work and gender roles. Given this evidence, it may be reasonable to ask why these two contradictory trends exist. One hypothesis is that although society enunciates ideals about gender equality, and even promotes public policies and programs in support of such values, it also includes some countervailing influences. It may be that institutions of society, such as the family, socialize youth to become more gender stereotyped in their personal behaviors. Such socialization has been termed the **gender intensification hypothesis.** It is useful to consider whether there is evidence in support of this idea.

The Gender Intensification Hypothesis

Issues to Consider
- What are some of the examples in support of the gender intensification hypothesis?
- Why might it be important to understand conditions during adolescence under which gender intensification occurs?
- What might contribute to adolescents' development of flexible attitudes toward stereotypical gender role behaviors?

The gender intensification hypothesis rests on the idea that a key component of the social context of youth involves the socialization experiences an adolescent receives as a consequence of being male or female. That is, it is believed that adolescents experience quite different worlds by virtue of being either male or female. For instance, there may be increasing pressure by key socializing agents—for example, peers, media, and even family members and school personnel—for boys to act more masculine and for girls to act more feminine, that is, to show behaviors consistent with the stereotypes summarized in Table 7.1 (e.g., Bakan, 1966; Galambos, Almeida, & Petersen, 1990). For instance, it is believed that independence is encouraged in boys and compliance is encouraged in girls (Crouter, Manke, & McHale, 1995).

Such differential socialization is summarized around the concept of *gender intensification* (Hill & Lynch, 1983; Lynch, 1991), and the hypothesis associated with this concept is that these contrasting experiences will result in emerging or increasing differences between males and females during the early portion of adolescence. The belief is that, as the youth progresses through puberty, changes in physical appearance and in sexual maturity influence self-expectations and the expectations of other people about the adolescent (Lynch, 1991).

There are data consistent with such contextual effects. In addition, there are data that do not support the presence of gender intensification. As we discuss, and as was the case with stereotypy

> **Gender intensification hypothesis** Adolescents' socialization by institutions of society, such as the family, aimed at making the youth more gender stereotyped in their personal behavior. The hypothesis rests on the idea that adolescents experience quite different socialization by virtue of being either male or female.

versus flexibility in work and gender roles, the issue becomes one of understanding the conditions under which gender intensification occurs during adolescence.

To illustrate, then, the nature of the evidence pertinent to gender intensification, we may note that in a major longitudinal study of young adolescents, males and females showed increased concerns about gender roles, about body image, and about the perceived importance of popularity (Simmons & Blyth, 1987). Both boys and girls showed an increase after the sixth grade in feeling that it was important *not* to act like members of the opposite sex.

During the middle of the adolescent period both boys and girls engage in high levels of gender-typed activities and possess gender-typed interests (Ruble & Martin, 1998). There is also some evidence that girls show a relative preference for stereotypically feminine versus stereotypically masculine high school subjects (Archer, 1992).

Evidence shows that gender intensification occurs in regard to the incidence of psychiatric disorders among young adolescents (Brooks-Gunn, 1989). In girls, there was an increase in eating disorders (e.g., anorexia and bulimia; see Chapter 3) and in depression. In boys, there was an increase in conduct disorders.

But evidence also indicates that during the middle portion of adolescence there may be an increasing willingness for both boys and girls to depart, respectively, from stereotypically masculine or feminine role behaviors, and to adopt more flexible views of role behaviors. For instance, from middle childhood through early adolescence, gender preferences become less stereotyped and more flexible (Etaugh & Liss, 1992; Katz & Ksansnak, 1994).

It is not certain if boys and girls differ in regard to the flexibility of their gender preferences. Some evidence indicates that this increase in flexibility may occur primarily, or perhaps even only, for girls (Archer, 1984, 1992; Ruble & Martin, 1998). However, there is also research that shows an increase through late adolescence in the flexibility of gender role preferences among both males and females (Katz & Ksansnak, 1994) and that contemporary adolescents have a more flexible attitude toward female gender roles than do members of older generations (Mills & Mills, 1996).

In a longitudinal study of 144 adolescents between the ages of 9 and 11 years, three aspects of

the purported differential socialization for gender intensification were studied: (1) adolescents' participation in "feminine" or "masculine" household chores; (2) parental monitoring; and (3) adolescents' involvement in dyadic activities with mothers or fathers (Crouter et al., 1995). Evidence for socialization consistent with gender intensification occurred only in regard to the third aspect of family functioning. Over time girls became increasingly involved with their mothers and boys with their fathers, especially the case when the adolescents had a younger sibling of the opposite sex (Crouter et al., 1995).

To the extent that gender intensification occurs, it may be likely to take place in such one-to-one mother-daughter or father-son activities (Witt, 1997). In a longitudinal study of paternal involvement and gender role development among about 2,000 male and female youth, ongoing relationships with fathers were more important for sons' than for daughters' gender role development (Hardesty, Wenk, & Morgan, 1995).

Conclusions About Gender Role Development and the Importance of Work in Adolescence

Work represents an essential part of the life of all people. What we do to contribute to our own quality of life and to the health and prosperity of our family and community is vital to individual welfare and to societal maintenance and perpetuation. The vocation or career we select in life and the orientation to work we develop in youth are crucial parts of identity development and the transition to adulthood (Vondracek, 1994; Vondracek et al., 1995). The ideas of Fred W. Vondracek about these relations are presented in Meet the Researcher Box 7.2.

Although the data are not unequivocal, most information currently available indicates that work during adolescence has a beneficial influence on adolescent development. Work experiences during adolescence help prepare youth for successful adult careers—a point we emphasize

MEET THE RESEARCHER BOX 7.2

FRED W. VONDRACEK
VOCATIONAL DEVELOPMENT IN ADOLESCENCE: THE KEY TO SELF-REALIZATION IN ADULTHOOD

Some young people seem to know what they want to be when they enter the work force. Others have no idea, or they do not want to think that far ahead. Some decide to do what others in their family have done; still others want to explore the world of work and themselves before making any commitment to be or to do one thing or another. In the language of developmental psychology, they are all seeking to establish a vocational identity, which for most people becomes an important aspect of their overall identity.

Developing a vocational identity is a complex process that involves, for most adolescents, a great deal of exploration of the world around them, particularly the world of work. That, in turn, often leads to the capacity to make commitments to one course of action or another or to the choice of one occupation over others. When all goes well during this critical period, young people develop vocational interests, acquire skills necessary to make appropriate career decisions, acquire preferences for certain aspects of work and dislikes for others, and develop skills and knowledge necessary for the pursuit of their chosen career.

For the past two decades, my colleagues—Richard M. Lerner, John Schulenberg, and Vladimir Skorikov—and I have developed a conceptual framework, as well as a number of empirical studies for studying vocational development and the underlying processes in a sample of adolescents from a rural area of the northeastern United States. We discovered that adolescents who have a sense of curiosity about the world around them and willingness to be involved with others, and who are willing to put forth significant

Fred W. Vondracek is associate dean for outreach and professor of human development in the College of Health and Human Development at the Pennsylvania State University. He holds an honorary professorship in developmental psychology at the Friedrich Schiller University of Jena, Germany, and is a leading researcher on adolescent vocational development.

effort toward their goals, were better students, felt better about themselves, and were more likely to make good progress toward establishing a vocational identity.

Not all adolescents have the same opportunities to advance in their vocational development. It is known, for example, that minority youth and girls often find that their choices of occupational pathways are blocked because of race or gender stereotypes. In other cases it is the political and economic system or cultural stereotypes that compromise and constrict opportunities for vocational development. During the past decade, I have teamed up with collaborators—most notably Rainer K. Silbereisen, Matthias Reitzle, and Eva Schmitt-Rodermund—from the Friedrich Schiller University of Jena in Germany to study some of these factors in national samples from the formerly communist East Germany and from West Germany. Our findings have confirmed the profound impact of cultural and economic factors, as well as the significance of individual differences, in the vocational development of adolescents.

What are the factors that allow some to develop "dream careers" in which work is not experienced as work but as the expression of one's passion? What are the developmental processes and contextual circumstances that must combine for someone to experience a life of satisfaction and self-realization through work? How can we help adolescents to find a lifetime of pleasure and fulfillment in their work, and how can we help them to fit work meaningfully into their lives, rather than fitting their lives into work? These are the questions that my colleagues in vocational psychology and I will be addressing as we continue our work.

---

again in Chapter 15 when we consider the nature of the transition from adolescence to young adulthood.

Whereas in the past society has not maximized the potential contributions of its citizens because of the restrictions on equal role opportunities provided to men and women, there is more recent evidence of a greater presence of individual and social flexibility in gender roles. Even though evidence indicates that in adolescence socialization pressures exist for boys to engage in traditionally masculine roles and for girls to engage in

applications box 7.1

Overcoming Traditional Gender Role Restrictions in the Work and Careers of Women

Daughter's Education Program (DEP)

In the Northern province of Chiang Rai, Thailand, exploitation of girls is rampant. Poverty and the prevailing view of females as subservient encourage the sale of girls for commercial sex. The Daughter's Education Program (DEP) was established in 1989 to prevent elementary and high school aged girls from being forced into the sex trade. An internationally supported effort of the Development and Education Program for Daughters and Communities, DEP improves the employment prospects of girls through a residential education program that provides basic schooling and access to vocational training. Such training is offered in weaving, sewing, handicrafts, and computer operation. Equally important, the program reaches out to community members and educates them about alternatives to prostitution. Youth serve as spokespersons and role models and also work in the center in administrative roles. DEP is currently working with more than 250 elementary and high school girls in the region and, since its inception, has saved nearly 600 from sexual exploitation. The vast majority of those who complete the program find permanent employment, many becoming educators in the community.

Programa de Alfabetización Intergeneracional (Intergenerational Literacy Program)

Programa de Alfabetización Intergeneracional (Intergenerational Literacy Program) was begun in 1991 to improve the standard of living among Ecuador's villagers, primarily through greater literacy. The program uses the Total Language Approach that has been successfully tested in Australia and the United States. It trains mothers and youth to read to—and write stories and songs for—young children as a way of cultivating their own literacy skills. In the community's day care center, mothers and youth receive training in infant and child care and pre-

school development. Once trained, mothers work at the center where they read aloud books, folk tales, and other literature. Youth write and distribute a monthly newsletter. Employment skills are also strengthened through workshops on income-earning activities such as weaving, sewing, and electrical repair. Program results have been positive, including increased knowledge of child care, awareness of good nutrition, and enhancement of trade skills. To date, over 100 women and children have participated, and 60% of the mothers and youth report receiving economic benefits from skills learned in the program.

Junior Achievement International (JAI)

Junior Achievement International (JAI) was created to empower students with the knowledge, skills, and social awareness needed to participate in the global marketplace. The program aims to provide young people with skills in business management and economics as well as with self-confidence and the leadership skills required in the workplace. This is not done through job training or counseling, but through young people's exposure to business and economic concepts, their interactions with businesspeople, and the opportunity for them to run small businesses. JAI's approach is based on "learning by doing." As such, it is team-based, interactive, and practical. Enlisting volunteers in the business field, JAI teaches the fundamentals of business and applied economics, and fosters the development of democratic decision making and entrepreneurial skills through a variety of projects for youth, ages 5 to 22. The program's impact on youth includes better comprehension of business fundamentals, as well as greater self-esteem, increased job readiness, and teamwork. JAI has also shown effectiveness in adapting to various cultural contexts, operating in 108 countries; the materials are available in 36 languages.

Source: International Youth Foundation, 2001. <www.iyfnet.org>

traditionally feminine roles, there is also information indicating that gender intensification is far from a universal feature of adolescent development. Many of the aspects of family life do not socialize youth to become more stereotyped

in their gender role behavior (Crouter et al., 1995).

Because of the evidence for a growing flexibility among youth and their social worlds in regard to the work and career roles associated with males and females, there is optimism that future decades will bear witness to greater opportunities for male and female adolescents to explore and actualize the full range of the competencies and interests they possess. Due to the importance of such flexibility for the health of individual development and for the welfare of society, numerous programs in the United States and around the world are aimed at improving the life chances of young people and, especially in contexts where gender role stereotypes have been markedly prevalent, among women in particular. Applications Box 7.1 describes several of these programs.

Summary

- Historically, U.S. adolescents did not work while school was in session. Currently, many adolescents work outside the home during their high school years and continue to earn a salary during college.

- There are racial differences in employment patterns. For African American males, the rate of employment has decreased since the 1960s.

- Working can give adolescents a basis for new identities, new expectations of responsibility and independence, and a new high status among peers.

- Work can take time away from school, diminish the opportunity to participate in extracurricular activities, and limit the time available for homework.

- High turnover, low pay, little authority, and low prestige often characterize adolescent jobs.

- Working students have reported that their employment was associated with being more punctual, dependable, and personally responsible. However, working adolescents have been found to be more frequently late to school and engaged in more deviant behavior than their nonworking peers.

- Working status is not associated with differences in time spent in schoolwork, time spent in extracurricular activities, or grade point averages. It is also not related to incidence of school behavior problems. Working at a low or moderate intensity was also associated with lower dropout rates.

- There is no difference in intrinsic motivation for school between working and nonworking students and no systematic relation between intrinsic motivation and the number of hours worked.

- Male and female adolescents are both typically given jobs that require little skill or training, and precise job assignments often vary along gender-stereotypic lines.

- A gender role is a socially defined set of prescriptions for the behavior of a gender group. Gender role behavior is acting in accordance with this set of prescriptions.

- Research has shown that men and women hold gender stereotypes, with men typically being described as more aggressive and independent, and women being described as gentle, aware of others' feelings, and needing security.

- Gender role stereotypes are held fairly consistently across sex, age, educational levels, and cultures.

- The existence of gender role stereotypes may be a source of bias in the job opportunities made available to male and female adolescents.

- Despite the existence of gender stereotypes, youth may hold a flexible personal orientation to work and pursue jobs in later life that counter the stereotypes.

- Although an increasing number of females aspire to succeed in labor areas, there has not been a corresponding increase in male investment in family work.

- The gender intensification hypothesis rests on the idea that adolescents experience different socialization dependent on whether they are male or female.

- The differences in socialization result in emerging or increasing differences between males and females during the early portions of adolescence.

- To the extent that gender intensification occurs, it is likely to take place in mother-daughter or father-son activities.

Discussion Topics

1. What roles define(d) your life as an adolescent? Of these roles, are any of them considered by your culture to be stereotypical of your gender? Did the various social contexts (i.e., family, peers, school) of which you are/were a part influence which roles you adopted? If so, how?

2. What might be responsible for the high dropout rates of African American male adolescents who work? In an effort to promote positive development among its youth, how might society better support these adolescents in their efforts to pursue the benefits of both a working position and an education? What are the factors that may be unique to the position of African American adolescent males in American culture?

3. If you worked as an adolescent, in what ways did your position influence you—what were the positive and negative influences? Looking back on it now, did the intrinsic values you gained from the experience outweigh the extrinsic value of the job? Why or why not?

4. Do you believe that male and female adolescents suffer under societal gender stereotypy? What aspects of their lives are affected by gender biases?

Did your social world make efforts to offer gender-neutral opportunities to you throughout your development? If so, what efforts were made and how did the efforts impact your development? If not, how did gender stereotypes present during your adolescence impact the roles that now define you?

5. Do you think both mothers and fathers should work outside of the home? Why or why not? What if the family only needs to rely on one income—should the mother be the one to stay home with the child? Why or why not? Do you think the choices your parent(s) made in terms of working impacts the decisions you will make as a parent in terms of working or staying home to care for the children? If so, how?

6. In what ways did/do your peers and/or overall school environment intensify the pressure you felt/feel as an adolescent to hold to some gender stereotype?

7. If you worked or volunteered during high school, did your experience impact the career path you see yourself on at this time? If so, how?

Key Terms

gender intensification
  hypothesis (p. 171)
gender roles (p. 162)

gender role behavior (p. 168)
gender role stereotypes (p. 168)
role (p. 162)

8

ADOLESCENTS AND THEIR FAMILIES

"Jimmy, come out of your room. Dad and I are ready to go out to dinner."

There was no answer.

"Jimmy, I'm calling you . . . Jimmy. JIMMY!"

"What?" The reply came from inside Jimmy's room.

"Jimmy, I'm not going to shout through a door to you," she said, recognizing that this was precisely what she was doing.

"What, Mom? Do you want me?"

She caught her breath. If she didn't want him, why would she be calling? "Jimmy, your dad and I are ready to go out for dinner now. Are you ready?"

"Mom, I don't want to go. I thought I would have Paul and Norm over and we'd watch a movie. I'll just make a sandwich or something."

"Jimmy, I'd rather you went out with us. You can see your friends after dinner."

"Mom, I don't want to eat what you guys like. And I'd rather spend time with my friends."

LEARNING OBJECTIVES

1. To understand that the family is the most important component of an adolescent's social world.
2. To understand the changes that have occurred over time in regard to the typical family structure in the United States.
3. To name the eight revolutions across the last century in the lives of U.S. children described by Donald J. Hernandez and what they mean for parent-child relations.
4. To understand why diversity in family structure is important to adolescent development.
5. To understand how poverty, and economic hardship more generally, influence youth development, and how despite these influences, positive development can be promoted.
6. To understand the roles grandparents, marital quality, divorce, adoption, and maternal employment play in the social and emotional development of youth.
7. To realize that unsupervised time can promote problem behavior in youth and that parents can exert some control over the decisions youth make during this time and, as well, that effective and available community youth programs can offer youth rich experiences and promote fewer life problems.
8. To recognize that adults differ in the ways they enact their roles as a parent and that parenting style is associated with differences in adolescent behavior and development.
9. To recognize that cultures differ in what they determine to be a well-socialized individual and that parents can help to model and shape the cognitive, emotional, and behavioral attributes they hope to see develop in their adolescent.

The changes young people undergo during adolescence are linked to changes that occur in the context, particularly the family, the peer group, and the school. These three social institutions and the social relationships that occur within them provide the key contextual influences across adolescence. The diversity that characterizes the structure and function of these contexts is associated with diversity in developmental changes across adolescence.

In several ways, the social context of adolescence differs significantly from the context surrounding the person at earlier periods of development. The adolescent's social world is broader and more complex than that of the infant and the child. The most notable social phenomenon of adolescence is the emergence of the marked importance of peer groups (see Chapter 9 and, as well, Chapter 10, in regard to sexual relationships). The adolescent comes to rely heavily on the peer group for security and guidance. This is a time when the young person may feel that such peer support is urgently needed, perhaps because the adolescent thinks that only others experiencing the same transition can be relied on to understand what is being experienced. Nevertheless, the family still remains the most important component of the social world of adolescents.

The Function of the Family

Issues to Consider
- How is the family the most important influence on adolescents' social development?
- What is the key function of the family?

Contrary to the cultural stereotype about adolescence, the family is quite influential for adolescents (Adelson, 1970; Bengtson & Troll, 1978; Lerner, Sparks, & McCubbin, 2000; Steinberg, 1991). Families create caring people through modeling and establishing bonds of social and emotional attachment, through fostering healthy peer and other interpersonal relationships, and through inculcating in youth prosocial behavior and empathy (see Chapter 5), and agency and self-control (see Chapter 6). The family is the major institution of society that fosters the development of caring individuals (Chase-Lansdale, Wakschlag, & Brooks-Gunn, 1995), and promotes civil society (Lerner et al., 1999, 2000b; see also Chapter 5). This chapter discusses the diverse structure and function of families, both as they have changed historically and as they exist in contemporary society. The American family is used as a sample case of this variation.

The family context is often a setting for shared recreational activities.

Despite the diverse structures and functions of the family context, and the historical changes that have occurred in these attributes of the family (Hernandez, 1993), the essential point on which to focus is the continual influence of the family on the development of the young person. Due to this constancy of influence, the family is, and has always been, the key institution of society charged with creating a new generation of citizens committed to maintaining and furthering the social order (Chase-Lansdale et al., 1995; Elder, Modell, & Parke, 1993; Lerner et al., 2000b). As such, *parenting* is the core function of the family. The nature and effects on youth of child-rearing behavior is the focus of our discussion of the functions of the family. It is possible to evaluate the success of any particular family structure by ascertaining the quality of development of the youth living within it. Any family structure can be appraised in regard to how well it produces healthy, able, and productive youth.

After a discussion of the nature and diversity of family structures, we consider the differences in family functioning that influence an adolescent's development. This presentation involves a discussion of the different styles parents have of rearing children, and of how these styles relate to **socialization**—the process by which one generation (the parental one) influences another (the adolescent

one) to adopt the values, beliefs, and desired behaviors of society. In addition we discuss how the development of adolescents is influenced by the diversity of parent-child relations that exist as a consequence of parents' rearing styles and socialization patterns.

Family Structure in Adolescence

What is a family? Who are the people who comprise it? How does that structure relate to what a family does, how it functions, how parenting affects children? Across history, there has always been diversity in both family structure and parenting, and thus in the sort of parent-child relationships that occur within families. Understanding this historical and contemporary variation in family structure and function is important for appreciating ways in which parenting occurs, its influences, and the nature of parent-adolescent relationships. Understanding this diversity also helps us appreciate other family (e.g., sibling, grandparent) and nonfamily (e.g., peer) relationships associated with the developing adolescent. These relationships, and the family structures with which they are associated, shape adolescent development. Using the United States as a sample case of Western industrialized society, we describe contemporary and historical diversity in the structure of the family.

Examples of Contemporary Variation in Family Structure

Issue to Consider

- What changes have occurred in regard to U.S. family structure over time?

I grew up at a time when the stereotypic American family was an intact **nuclear family,** with two biological parents and two or three children (named either David and Ricky, or Bud, Kitten, and Princess, respectively). Yet,

Socialization Process by which one generation (the parental one) influences another (the adolescent one) to adopt the values, beliefs, and desired behaviors of society.

Nuclear family Intact family, characterized by the presence of both biological parents and one or more children.

today, only 1 in 5 married couples with children fits this still popular stereotype of living in what has been termed the "Ozzie and Harriet" family (i.e., the intact, never-divorced, two-parent-two-child family) (Ahlburg & De Vita, 1992; Hernandez, 1993). As shown in Table 8.1, at any one time children and parents may live in several quite different family contexts (see Allison, 1993).

The cross-sectional location of people in one of the family contexts noted in Table 8.1 is complicated by the fact that such settings may change longitudinally over the course of the lives of children and parents, and thus across generations (that is, over the course of history). This observation raises the need for a historically sensitive analysis of the social contexts within which youth find themselves (Allison, 1993; Featherman, Spenner, & Tsunematsu, 1988; Hernandez, 1993). Even within social class, a contextual variable seemingly constant over a child's life, only approximately 46% of American 6-year-olds remain in the social class within which they were born. In fact, about 22% of all children born in the United States change from their initial social class during their first year of life. During the first 6 years, about 54% of American children have lived in two or more social classes (Featherman et al., 1988).

Children and adolescents may find themselves in more than one family during their socialization. About 1 out of 5 children in the United States under the age of 18 does not live with two parents (Demos, Allen, & Fine, 2000). There are a substantial number of single-parent families, and many children and adolescents live in families with two adults, but only one biological parent. These variations in living arrangements and family status come about as a result of the high rates of marital dissolution found in the United States. Divorce and remarriage are common in the United States today, with about 2 out of every 5 marriages involving recently married persons expected to end in divorce (Demos et al., 2000).

About 75% of the persons involved in divorce eventually remarry, and those who remarry do so, on the average, about three years after the divorce. Perhaps 45% of children and adolescents can expect to live in a family setting without one of their natural parents for a period of time before they reach adulthood.

Longitudinal study Study that assesses a particular variable (e.g., sibling relationships) repeatedly over time.
Cross-sectional study Study that assesses a particular variable (e.g., youth-parent relations) at one point in time (e.g., during the year 2000). Often, different age groups are studied at this point in time.

Table 8-1	Examples of Contemporary "Family" Contexts of Children and Youth

Intact nuclear (and biological)
Single parent (biological)
Intact nuclear (adoptive)
Single parent (adoptive)
Intact (blended)
 {heterosexual; homosexual}
Single parent (step)
Intergenerational
Extended, without parent
 {e.g., child-aunt}
In loco parentis families/institutions
 Foster care homes
 Group homes
 Psychiatric hospitals
 Residential treatment facilities
 Juvenile detention facilities
Runaways
Street children/youth
 {e.g., adolescent prostitutes}
Homeless children

Source: From Lerner et al., 1995.

Social class and the financial resources differentially available to youth living in intact versus single-parent (e.g., divorced, widowed) homes (J. Lerner, 1994) structure the large majority of the societal resources and cultural values influencing families. The magnitude of change in regard to family social class and parental structure underscores the need to appraise the diversity of youth-family relations **longitudinally** (historically) as well as **cross-sectionally** (at any one point in time).

Historical Diversity in the Family: The Scholarship of Donald J. Hernandez

Issues to Consider

- What are the eight revolutions in the lives of America's children across the 20th century described by Donald J. Hernandez?
- What do the eight revolutions mean in terms of parent-child relations and history?

Across his career, Donald J. Hernandez (1993) has used census and survey data to understand past and current characteristics of American families. Some of his recent research is presented in Meet the Researcher Box 8.1. The research described in this box pertains to the impact on youth of a relatively recent change in public policy regarding welfare (see too Kalil & Eccles, 1998). However, Hernandez has identified several quite profound changes in the United States that have characterized the life courses of children and their families over the last 50 to 150 years.

Hernandez has adopted a perspective consistent with the stress in developmental contextualism on integrated relations between people and the multiple levels of the context within which they live. He argues that a person's life trajectory is constituted by, and differentiated from, those of others on the basis of (1) the specific order, duration, and timing of the particular events and resources experienced in life; and (2) by the number, characteristics, and activities of the family members with whom the person lives. Using this viewpoint as a frame, Hernandez describes what he labels as eight revolutions in the lives of U.S. children across the 20th century.

The Disappearance of the Two-Parent Farm Family and the Growth in the One-Parent Family

Between the late 18th century to almost the end of the 19th century, the majority of American children between the ages of birth to 17 years lived in two-parent farm families (Hernandez, 1993). At the beginning of the 20th century, about 40% of all children in this age range still lived in such family settings, with slightly more than an additional 40% living in nonfarm, two-parent families with the father as the breadwinner and the mother as the homemaker. At the beginning of the 20th century as well, the remaining children in this age range (slightly over 10%) lived in dual-earner nonfarm families, one-parent families, or in no-parent situations.

By 1950, only about 15% of American children lived, during their first 17 years of life, in two-parent farm families. Almost 60% of American children in this age range lived in two-parent, non-farm families, in which the father was the bread-winner and the mother was the homemaker. Most of the remaining American children within this age range lived in dual-earner nonfarm or one-parent families.

In 1990, fewer than 5% of America's children lived, during the first 17 years of their lives, in two-parent farm families. Fewer than 30% of children in this age range lived in intact nonfarm families in which the father was the breadwinner and the mother was the homemaker. Rather, about 70% of all American children in this age range lived in either dual-earner nonfarm families or in one-parent families. Indeed, about 25% lived in one-parent families.

The increase in one-parent families over the course of the 20th century was coupled with a decrease in the presence of a grandparent in the home. By 1990, about 80% of children in one-parent families did not live with a grandparent (U.S. Department of Commerce, 1993). Thus the parenting resources available from having two adults in the home are generally absent in contemporary American one-parent families. In the majority of such families no grandparent is present to replace the resources represented by the absent parent.

The Decrease in the Number of Siblings in the Family

As shown in Table 8.2, there have been dramatic changes over the last 100 or so years in the percentage of children living in families with large numbers of siblings. In 1890, 46% of America's children lived in families with eight or more siblings. An additional 30% lived in families with between five and seven siblings, and 16% lived in families with either three or four siblings. Only 7% of America's children lived in families having just one or two siblings (Hernandez, 1993).

By 1940, families in which a child had eight or more siblings accounted for only 10% of America's families. The percentages of American families in which a child had either between five and seven siblings, three or four siblings, or only one or two siblings were 21%, 38%, and 30%, respectively (Hernandez, 1993).

Table 8-2	A Century of Changes in the Percentage of America's Children Living in Families with Eight or More Siblings
Year	Percentage of Families
1890	46%
1840	10%
1990	1%

Source: Based on Hernandez, 1993.

MEET THE RESEARCHER BOX 8.1

DONALD J. HERNANDEZ
CONSEQUENCES OF WELFARE REFORM FOR CHILDREN, ADOLESCENTS, AND THEIR FAMILIES

The survival, comfort, and self-respect of children and adolescents depend on having access to adequate levels of nutrition, clothing, housing, health care, and other amenities of modern life. The market economy and government are the two societywide institutions that provide access to these essential goods and services. From the market economy, persons with jobs obtain income in return for work they perform in the labor market. From government, individuals can obtain access to essential goods and services through social welfare programs that provide economic resources in the form of cash, or in the form of quasi-cash benefits such as food stamps.

Children are legally barred from most jobs; few adolescents can earn enough from paid work to support themselves; and children and adolescents are usually not directly eligible for social welfare benefits. Therefore, children and adolescents depend mainly on parents to assure their economic well-being. But parents' economic resources are obtained, originally, from either the economy or government. A major goal of government welfare programs, historically, was to provide resources to families with low incomes. Welfare reform in 1996 introduced new goals that include forcing welfare recipients off of welfare and into the labor force and discouraging out-of-wedlock childbearing, especially among teens.

Proponents argue that children and adolescents will benefit from these reforms in several ways. Parents who are economically self-sufficient workers, instead of dependent on government welfare, will serve as better role models; their children will see work rather than welfare as a way of life. Working parents can obtain higher incomes for their families. Adolescents who do not bear children out of wedlock are less likely to drop out of school and more likely to become self-supporting. But, based on past research, critics argue that many parents who receive welfare are already working and are not qualified for jobs that pay well enough to lift them, and their families, out of poverty. They also argue that adolescents often drop out of school because of a lack of economic opportunities, and that adolescents and young adults who bear children out-of-wedlock do so because their potential spouses are not able to find work that would allow them to contribute significantly to the support of a family.

Donald J. Hernandez is a professor in the Department of Sociology and Center for Social and Demographic Analysis at the State University of New York in Albany. He is responsible for developing the Census Bureau's Survey of Program Dynamics, which is the federal survey for assessing the effects of welfare reform, particularly for children and adolescents, and he directed the study reported in *From Generation to Generation: The Health and Well-Being of Children in Immigrant Families* and in *Children of Immigrants: Health, Adjustment, and Public Assistance.*

I am using the U.S. Census Bureau's Survey of Program Dynamics, and other data sources, to study effects of welfare reform for children, adolescents, and their families. I am seeking answers to the following questions. Are parents working more, or less, as a result of welfare reform? Is self-esteem increasing among parents because they are becoming self-sufficient, or, alternatively, is stress increasing because of greater difficulties in juggling family responsibilities with additional hours of work? What are the consequences for the well-being of their children? Are children and adolescents experiencing increases in family income or increases in family poverty? Are children and adolescents receiving better care because their parents have more money to pay for higher quality child care and after-school learning opportunities, or are they receiving less attention because parents have less time to spend with them and to monitor their activities? What are the consequences of teen childbearing?

All children and adolescents share the same basic needs. But welfare reform is particularly significant for those in immigrant families, because the law has made them or their parents ineligible for many welfare benefits. Of all the children and adolescents in the United States, those in immigrant families are the fastest growing group. During the 7 years from 1990 to 1997, the number of children and adolescents in immigrant families grew by 47%, compared to only 7% for other children and adolescents. By 1997, 1 of every 5 children and adolescents under age 18 lived in an immigrant family. Because of these trends, children and adolescents in immigrant families are a major focus of my research.

Will the massive welfare reform initiated in 1996 lead to better or worse lives for children and adolescents? Preliminary results indicate that major social welfare programs acted to reduce child and adolescent poverty prior to welfare reform, but since welfare reform they are less effective in reducing poverty. But many additional consequences may flow from welfare reform, and we have only begun to measure these effects. Our hope is that this research will increase scientific knowledge about the effects of recent reforms and lead in the future to additional reforms that will increase the well-being of children and adolescents.

Across history, families have often included siblings of a wide age range.

In 1990, only 1% of U.S. children lived in families with eight or more siblings and only 5% of U.S. children lived in families with five to seven siblings. The rate of children who lived in families in which they had either three or four siblings remained steady at 38%, and about 57% of children lived in families with one or two siblings (Hernandez, 1993).

The Increase in Parents' Education In the 1920s, about 60% of the children in America had fathers with at least eight years of schooling, whereas about 15% had fathers with at least four years of high school education. The corresponding rates for mothers were a few percentage points higher than those for fathers (Hernandez, 1993).

By the 1950s, parental educational attainment had markedly increased. Approximately 90% of all mothers and about 87% of all fathers had eight or more years of schooling, and 60% of mothers and about 55% of fathers had at least four years of high school (Hernandez, 1993). By the end of the 1980s, about 96% of all mothers and fathers had eight or more years of schooling and about 80% of all mothers and about 85% of all fathers had at least four years of high school (Hernandez, 1993).

The Growth of Mothers in the Labor Force As shown in Table 8.3, the percentage of children with mothers in the labor force increased dramatically in the last half of the 20th century (Hernandez, 1993; J. Lerner, 1994).

Changes in Fathers' Full-Time Employment As shown in Table 8.4, the marked growth in maternal employment since 1940 has been coupled with the fact that between the 1940s and the

Table 8-3	Percentage of Children with Mothers in the Labor Force	
Year	Percentage
1940	10%
1950	16%
1960	26%
1970	36%
1980	49%
1990	59%

Source: Based on Hernandez, 1993.

Table 8-4	Percentage of America's Children Living with Fathers Not Employed Full Time Year Round	
Year		Percentage
1940		40%
1950		32%
1980		24%

Source: Based on Hernandez, 1993.

Table 8-5	Percentage of America's Children Living in Single-Parent, Female Head-of-Household Families	
Year		Percentage
1940		6.7%
1950		6.4%
1960		7.7%
1970		11.8%
1980		16.2%
1990		20.0%

Source: Based on Hernandez, 1993.

1980s many of America's children lived with fathers who were not employed full-time year round (Hernandez, 1993).

Between 1950 and 1980, the 8% decrease in children living with fathers who did not have full-time employment was offset by an 8% increase in children who did not have a father in the home (Hernandez, 1993). Given the percentage of American children that lived in such father-absent homes during this period, a phenomenon discussed later, from the 1950s to the 1980s only about 60% of America's children lived with fathers who worked full time throughout the year (Hernandez, 1993).

The Growth of Single-Parent, Female Head-of-Household Families

As noted, the last half of the 20th century saw a dramatic increase in the percentage of American children living in single-parent homes with their mothers (Hernandez, 1993) (see Table 8.5). As shown in the table, in 1940, 1950, and 1960 the proportion of children living in single-parent, female head-of-household families remained relatively steady. Between 1960 and 1990 the percentage of children living in such families almost tripled (Hernandez, 1993).

The Disappearance of the "Ozzie and Harriet" Family (the Intact, Never Divorced Two-Parent-Two-Child Family)

Over the course of the 20th century, America experienced a disappearance of the stereotypically predominant intact, two-parent family, in which the father is the breadwinner, the mother is the homemaker, and two to three children either spend their lives in socioeconomic and personal security or are faced with problems that require only about 30 minutes (the time of the typical American television situation comedy) to resolve. Not only are such stereotypic families largely absent in the United States, but, since the 1940s, a decreasing minority of

children have been born into such families (Hernandez, 1993).

The changing percentages of children born into "Ozzie and Harriet" type families are presented in Table 8.6. In addition to the trend illustrated in the table, few Americans spend their entire childhood and adolescent years in these family settings. In 1920, only 31% of children and youth lived their first 17 years in these types of families. This percentage fell to 16.3% by 1960, and estimates for succeeding decades have fallen to less than 10% (Hernandez, 1993).

The Reappearance of Widespread Child Poverty

A final revolution described by Hernandez (1993) pertains to the changing distribution of children across relative income levels and the growth of child poverty, especially during the 1980s. After the Great Depression the relative poverty rate among children dropped from 38% in 1939 to 27% in 1949 (Hernandez, 1993). During the 1950s this rate dropped further, to 24%, and by 1969 the rate was 23% (Hernandez, 1993). Between 1940 and 1990 there was a substantial increase in the proportion of adolescents living in demographically advantaged families (Cornwell, Eggebeen, & Meschke, 1996).

Between the end of the 1960s and the end of the 1980s this trend of decreasing relative poverty among children reversed, and in 1988 relative poverty among children had grown by 4% (Hernandez, 1993). During the 1980s, then, the percentage of children living in poor families returned to the comparatively high level seen in 1949 (Hernandez, 1993). The percentage of children living in "middle-class comfort" decreased between 1969 and 1988 from 43% to 37% (Hernandez, 1993).

Table 8-6	Percentage of Children Living in "Ozzie and Harriet" Type Families: Father Is the Breadwinner, Mother Is the Homemaker	
Year		Percentage
1940		40.8%
1950		44.5%
1960		43.1%
1970		37.3%
1980		27.4%

Source: Based on Hernandez, 1993.

Conclusions About Historical Changes in the Family

Hernandez (1993) embeds the child-parent relation within a changing set of variables involving family structure and function and other key institutions of society (e.g., the educational system and the economy). The import of Hernandez's scholarship is that, at any one point in time, parent-child relations and the diversity in these relations are products of multiple historical changes in the contexts of family life. In other words, historical variation provides a basis for the diversity of parent-child relations that exists at any point. In addition, the nature of the changes that characterize the family over time makes clear the contemporary diversity of family structures and functions that exist in society and the implications of this diversity for differences in family-child relations and adolescent development.

Families differ in their size. Some families consist of two parents in the home and others have one. Some may have one or two children and others may have many more. Some exist in densely populated urban centers and others are found in sparsely populated rural settings. How families function to rear youth varies also. In some families, adherence to rules of conduct is stressed for youth, and other families emphasize sports and/or academic achievement. In some families, parents' job responsibilities require a youngster to take on numerous household duties often assumed by adults (e.g., shopping for food for the family, preparation of dinner for the family); in other families, adolescents are assigned few tasks. In some families, parents and adolescents interact in warm and almost peerlike ways, whereas in other families the roles of parent and child are kept quite distinct.

The diversity in the structure and function of the family context fosters variation in parent-child relations and in adolescent development. To understand these influences let's begin by discussing the role of family structure in adolescent development.

Family Structure: Diversity and Its Importance for Adolescent Development

Issues to Consider

- How do the variations in family structure influence the way parents interact with youth and how the youth behaves?
- What impact does the relation between family diversity and other contextual factors have on adolescent development?

As shown in Table 8.1, adolescents live in different family structures. This variation influences both the way parents interact with youth and how the adolescent behaves. In a study of urban African American adolescents living in either single-mother, stepparent, dual-parent, mother-with-extended-family (e.g., grandparents, aunt, uncle), or extended-family-only settings (e.g., only an aunt is present), the social support provided to youth was generally the same across family types, with one exception: Youth living in single-mother families were given *more* support than the youth in the other four family types (Zimmerman, Salem, & Maton, 1995).

Support to mothers, especially when provided by relatives, can enhance adolescent and maternal adjustment and improve the mother's parenting skills (Taylor & Roberts, 1995). Among 14- to 19-year-old African American youth, social support from kin was related to self-reliance and good school grades. When kinship support was low, the youth experienced feelings of distress (Taylor, 1996). Although differences in regard to academic achievement and high school grades are slight among youth living in either intact, single-parent, or remarried families, large differences exist in regard to school dropout (Zimiles & Lee, 1991). Students from intact families are least likely to drop out. Youth from such families are also less likely to experiment with drugs than are adolescents from single-parent families (Turner, Irwin, & Millstein, 1991).

When variation in family structure occurs in relation to other contextual factors—relating to parental education, family social support, parental mental health, and poverty, for instance—influences on the adolescent may be more pronounced. IQ scores for youth are lower in larger families, in which mother's educational attainment and the family's social support are low and the family is of minority background and poor (Sameroff et al., 1993; Taylor, 1996).

Many youth enjoy the support provided by a large nuclear and extended family network.

Poverty Effects A family challenged by the economic stresses of poverty places its children at risk for problems of behavior and health (Farran & Margolis, 1987). These implications of financial stress on youth development exist for families living in both rural and urban areas. Parents from farm families report higher levels of family financial stress and of depression than do parents from nonfarm families (Clark-Lempers, Lempers, & Netusil, 1990). In both farm and nonfarm families, however, financial stress felt by parents is related to depression among adolescents. Youth living in poor, rural families have more social and emotional problems and poor academic adjustment and school performance than do adolescents living in less financially disadvantaged households (Felner et al., 1995). In a study of poor families who either did or did not receive welfare benefits (Kalil & Eccles, 1998), there was little evidence that welfare receipt has a negative impact on parent-child interactions (although mothers on welfare do show less effective strategies for managing the behavior of their youth).

The influence of economic hardship on youth development appears to occur through a process involving feelings of economic pressure by parents (e.g., the inability to pay monthly bills), which result in parents feeling depressed and demoralized. These feelings are associated with marital conflicts and disruptions of skillful parenting, which eventu-

ates in problems of adolescent behavior (Conger et al., 1992). Problematic outcomes of this process include the use of alcohol, antisocial behavior, depression, anxiety, and/or hostility among young adolescents (Conger et al., 1991; Ge et al., 1992).

Despite the negative outcomes of poverty (Schorr, 1988, 1997), parents in even the poorest families can promote positive outcomes in their children (McAdoo, 1998, 1999; Spencer, 1995). The scholarship of Harriette Pipes McAdoo (1995, 1998, 1999) has underscored the processes through which these positive influences of poor families occur. Her work is featured in Meet the Researcher Box 8.2.

Among poor African American families, social support to mothers from their kin was associated with adolescent and mother well-being and with higher quality parenting practices (e.g., firm control and monitoring) (Taylor & Roberts, 1995). Ronald D. Taylor has conducted research central to the understanding of how poor families living within economically disadvantaged communities can promote adolescent well-being. His work is presented in Meet the Researcher Box 8.3. Consistent with Taylor's research is a study of about 250 urban African American adolescent males. These youth, living in single-parent, female head-of-household homes, reported more parental support than did

MEET THE RESEARCHER BOX 8.2

HARRIETTE PIPES M^CADOO

FAMILY INFLUENCES ON SELF-ESTEEM AND EDUCATIONAL ATTAINMENT ON THE YOUTH OF THE HIGH/SCOPE PERRY PRESCHOOL STUDY

Throughout my career I have studied African American families, youth, and children. I wanted to see if the negative assessments that were in the literature were in fact reality in the everyday lives of these individuals. It appeared that the one-sided negative views were the result of continuing ethnocentrism. The reality of the black communities did not agree with the portrayal of families in the literature. And I knew from experience that most families did not really fit into these negative patterns. Many were poor; yet the majority of them were working every day, raising their children adequately, and were developing into functional adults.

I have studied family members at different stages of their lives and at different resource levels. Were these stereotyped patterns found in the nonpoor? Did families without a father really look as bad as the literature presented them? What were the patterns of social and economic mobility experienced by families? Is there something that could be done to enrich the lives of poor children that would enable them to make a better match later on of their expectations and their reality? Can we paint all of the persons who are of African descent with a negative brush? I did not think so, but I had to go out and collect data to support my hunches.

I conducted one of the few quantitative studies on middle-class blacks who had been upwardly mobile for up to three generations. Supported by the Office of Child Development, I found that the resources needed were often too difficult to have a family move up from being destitute to middle class in just one generation. It took the efforts of all of the family working together over two or three generations to be able to socialize their children and youth toward higher education. I found that the extended family social support system was responsible for the achievements that members had made.

With a Howard University Faculty Grant and later a NIHM grant, I looked at the adolescent pregnancy rate at a time when the level was getting higher. I found some of the tragic consequences that have been well documented. But I also saw parents of adolescents who supported the young parents and enabled them to have positive lives. Over a third of the young fathers were involved with the children, even when they did not get married. The father's parents were found to be active in supporting the young

mothers in many different ways, from buying diapers to babysitting while the mother was in school. In other words, I found a variety of situations and outcomes that were not often found in the literature. Why is that true? Maybe more sensitivity needed to be shown to their life experiences, but was not always shown by a researcher who is not of color. Or maybe it was the fact that I approached the families as regular people and did not hold to stereotyped preconceptions of their living situations.

Harriette Pipes McAdoo is a University Distinguished Professor in the Department of Family and Child Ecology in the College of Human Ecology at Michigan State University. She is the editor of *Black Families* (3rd ed.), *Black Children: Social, Environmental, and Parental Environments* (2nd ed.), and *Family Ethnicity: Strength in Diversity* (2nd ed.), all by Sage Publishers; plus *Women and Children: Alone and in Poverty*, with Diane Pierce.

When the resources of a rich environment are provided early to families and young children in a sensitive manner, it was hypothesized that there will be improvements in their attitudes, in their attainments, and in their overall life chances. Under a grant from the High/Scope Educational Research Foundation, we tested our hypotheses. The preschool experiences of children, who were poor and in destitute environments, were believed to have a positive impact on the children. It was a time when there was a rush to provide programs for children who lived in depressed communities around the country. The research that documented the effects on children many years later as youths and as young adults had not been done until this follow-up was made of the High/Scope Perry Preschool children.

These preschool children were followed as they went from the preschool level to adulthood. A great deal of effort was made to maintain contact with the children as they developed. As some went into the military services, some became married, and others settled down into jobs, researchers followed them all over the world to interview them. The positive experiences of early preschool were associated with favorable outcomes in elementary school and beyond. As adolescents they had higher self-esteems, and were self-supporting by the age of 19 years. We were intrigued by the longitudinal data that indicated that fewer of the girls were becoming pregnant as adolescents and that they tended to have fewer arrests. By age 27 years, those persons who had positive parental role models were found to have higher levels of education. Even though parents were all low income, many had helped their children to overcome obstacles associated with low SES and to achieve higher educations than the parents had. Again, the family support networks were fundamental in overcoming the paucity of their environments.

MEET THE RESEARCHER BOX 8.3

RONALD D. TAYLOR

ASSESSING THE LINKS TO THE POSITIVE ADJUSTMENTS OF ECONOMICALLY DISADVANTAGED AFRICAN AMERICAN ADOLESCENTS

Adolescents grow up in a variety of social and physical environments including family, school, peer group, and neighborhood. Some environments have an abundance of resources (social, financial, physical) and others suffer from a scarcity of even the basic necessities. Some adolescents thrive despite being raised in poor environments; others encounter many problems.

I am studying African American families living in Philadelphia. My research is aimed at understanding the factors associated with the positive adjustment of youngsters living in economically disadvantaged communities. My work—funded by the U.S. Department of Education—assesses parenting practices (emotional support, control and supervision, family organization) associated with positive development. In this work I want to understand whether there are practices in which parents engage that promote the healthy development of their adolescents. I also want to understand whether there are practices that appear to buffer adolescents from potential problems. In all of my work an underlying goal is to understand both the factors linked to the positive adjustment of adolescents and the experiences that shield or buffer them from problems. With this information policymakers and other people working for families may be able to reinforce or recreate relationships and experiences in the community that have been linked to the positive development of adolescents and their families.

I have also examined how parents and adolescents cope with some of the features of the neighborhood or

Ronald D. Taylor is an associate professor and the assistant director of the Center for Research in Human Development and Education at Temple University.

community in which they live (e.g., crime and safety, physical deterioration). For example, in this work I want to understand how adolescents are affected by the crime or safety in their neighborhood. Do adolescents who live in crime-ridden neighborhoods experience anxiety or depression, and are they more prone to engage in problem behavior? We also want to understand what practices in the family or what relationships adolescents may have that may shield or insulate them from problems in their community. Are adolescents who have social networks and relationships (e.g., social support from adult relatives) beyond their immediate family less likely to experience problems in an impoverished neighborhood?

Because most of the adolescents and families I study are poor, I also want to understand the processes through which poverty affects adolescents. In this work we are examining how the financial problems of the family influence the well-being of the youngsters. Are adolescents more prone toward depression or low self-esteem when their families have money problems? Do adolescents experience anxiety or depression in disadvantaged homes because they perceive that their parents are pessimistic about the future? Our hope is that this work will indicate areas (e.g., families' economic problems, parents' outlook and optimism, parents' emotional support, parents' depression) that when addressed through resources or assistance of some kind may be associated with positive adjustment in adolescents.

---

youth living in stepparent, dual-parent, mother-and-extended-family, and extended-family-only households (Zimmerman, Salem, & Maton, 1995).

Although family poverty is a significant structural variable affecting youth development, other structural characteristics of the family are important to note as well. Some of them are discussed next.

The Role of Grandparents Grandparents have always been important parts of families, especially for families living in rural areas (Hernandez, 1993).

Even today, grandchildren in farm families live closer to their grandparents, and have more contact with them, than is the case with nonfarm rural youth (King & Elder, 1995). Adolescents in farm families also have more positive relationships with paternal grandparents than do youth living in nonfarm families (King & Elder, 1995).

Grandparents play an important role in single-parent families, especially in those headed by a female adolescent. In such contexts, grandparents provide critical social support to the mother

(Spieker & Bensley, 1994). Grand-fathers, in particular, have been found to enhance the quality of life in such families (Clingempeel et al., 1992; Oyserman, Radin, & Benn, 1993).

Marital Quality Conflicts and dis-agreements are typical parts of life. All individuals, couples, and groups can expect to have negative interac-tions from time to time. Of course, it is possible to have an overall high-quality relationship despite occa-sional conflicts. However, when conflicts—arguments, fights, or even physical abuse—predominate in a relationship, the quality of the rela-tionship tends to be quite poor. There is a negative impact of such relationships on the people in them and on the people living within the context in which they observe such a relationship.

Grandparents are significant parts of contemporary family life.

When the parents of adolescents have a low-quality marriage, youth are adversely affected. In a longitudinal study of seventh-grade adolescents in the rural Midwest, marital conflict was related to the presence of what are termed **internalizing prob-lems** (e.g., depression or anxiety) and **externalizing problems** (e.g., aggression) among youth (Harold & Conger, 1997). Parents not only showed negative behaviors to each other, but also showed hostility toward their adolescent children (Harold & Conger, 1997). In another study of youth from Utah and Tennessee, parental conflict and hostility were associated with youth problem behaviors (Buehler et al., 1998).

In a study of Japanese youth and their families (Gjerde & Shimizu, 1995), parent disagreement in regard to how the adolescent should be socialized was related to adjustment problems among youth. In addition, boys who were more closely aligned with their mothers' points of view were most likely to have adjustment problems (Gjerde & Shimizu, 1995).

Whereas poor marital quality can negatively impact adolescents, good marital quality can be a positive influence. In a longitudinal study of adoles-cent boys, parents' satisfaction with their marriage was related to good peer relations (Feldman & Wentzel, 1995). When mothers and fathers share equal levels of family power, there are positive influ-ences on youth emotional adjustment (Wentzel & Feldman, 1996). However, for male adolescents, when mothers have more power in the marriage than do fathers, there is a likelihood that depression will occur in the adolescent (Wentzel & Feldman, 1996).

The positive benefits on adolescents of parental marital satisfaction may extend into adolescents' adulthood. In a longitudinal study of youth first studied when they were 13- to 18-year-olds and then again when they were between 18 and 25 years of age, marital satisfaction, especially for mothers, was related to the emotional and physical health of the young adults (Feldman, Fisher, & Seitel, 1997).

In sum, marital quality is associated with adolescent behavior and development. However, marital quality can have other ramifications. When the quality of a marriage is poor, parents may obtain a divorce, a transition that impacts youth behavior and development.

Influences of Divorce About 50% of all marriages that began over the last quarter century will end in divorce

Internalizing problems
Behavior problems not expressed toward one's envi-ronment but rather directed to one's mental or emoting functioning (e.g., depression or anxiety).

Externalizing problems
Behavior problems expressed through actions toward one's environment and, thereby, easily visible to others (e.g., aggression).

(Hetherington & Clingempeel, 1988; Sessa & Steinberg, 1991), and as many as 60% of children born in the 1990s will live for a time in a single-parent family (Bumpass & Sweet, 1989; Furstenberg & Cherlin, 1991; Simons et al., 1994). Some studies suggest that divorce may not have an influence on particular instances of adolescent development. For example, decisions made by adolescents or their parents about health and safety do not differ between intact and divorced families (Jacobs, Bennett, & Flanagan, 1993). Some studies of adolescents from divorced families find no difference in self-esteem (Clark & Barber, 1994), self-image, depression, or anxiety (Dunlop & Burns, 1995), although most research does find differences.

Divorce can have negative effects on an adolescent. Most research indicates that divorce is associated with social, academic, and personal adjustment problems, including those associated with early initiation of sexual behavior (e.g., Brody & Forehand, 1990; Carson, Madison, & Santrock, 1987; Demo & Acock, 1988; Doherty & Needle, 1991; Hetherington, 1991; Hetherington, Cox, & Cox, 1985; Simons et al., 1994; Whitbeck, Simons, & Kao, 1994; Zaslow, 1988, 1989). Parent-child relations in divorced families are less hierarchical and children are pushed to grow up faster (Smetana, 1993).

Whereas conflictual parent-child relations are not the norm in adolescence, such problematic interactions tend to occur more often in single-parent families and stepfamilies (Demo & Acock, 1996; Montemayor, 1986; Steinberg, 1991). Divorced families and stepfamilies have higher levels of mother-adolescent disagreement, lower levels of parental supervision, and lower levels of mother-adolescent interaction than do intact, first-married families or families headed by continuously single mothers (Demo & Acock, 1996).

The period following separation and divorce seems to be particularly stressful for youth (Doherty & Needle, 1991), especially if the adolescent is caught between divorced parents engaged in continuing, conflictual, and hostile interactions (Brody & Forehand, 1990; Buchanan, Maccoby, & Dornbusch, 1991). In the period immediately after a divorce, there are numerous instances of behavioral disruption and emotional upheaval (Hetherington, Anderson, & Hagan, 1991). Increases occur in aggression and noncompliance with rules, decreases occur in academic achievement and school adjustment, and there are problems that occur in peer interactions and in sexual behavior (Hetherington et al., 1991).

The effects of divorce seem to be more pervasive, problematic, and long lasting for boys than for girls (Beaty, 1995; Hetherington et al., 1991). Although girls tend to react more negatively than boys prior to the parents' separation, they also tend to adapt better than boys after the divorce (Doherty & Needle, 1991; Hetherington et al., 1985). Girls from single-mother, divorced homes have problematic sexual and heterosexual behaviors. They are more likely to marry early, be pregnant at the time of their marriage, and wed immature men (Hetherington, 1989). Given that, after divorce, 90% of children are in mother-custody homes (Hetherington et al., 1991), these problems related to girls may be quite widespread.

In a study following young adolescents into their young adulthood (Summers et al., 1998), individuals from divorced families had less secure romantic attachments in young adulthood than did youth from nondivorced families. Similarly, in a longitudinal study involving over 17,000 youth from Great Britain (Chase-Lansdale, Cherlin, & Kiernan, 1995), parental divorce was found to impact adult mental health. Although most individuals did not experience serious emotional disorders after divorce, the risk of having such problems did increase (Chase-Lansdale et al., 1995).

Remarriage can lead to additional problems for youth. There is evidence that both male and female adolescents may have difficulty interacting with stepfathers, although girls may have particular problems (Lee et al., 1994; Vuchinich et al., 1991). Both male and female adolescents show no improvement in their relationship with their stepfather or in behavior problems (e.g., regarding school grades) associated with the divorce 2 years or more after the remarriage (Hetherington, 1991; Lee et al., 1994). However, living with a stepfather, as compared to living with a stepmother, is associated with more positive self-esteem among both male and female adolescents (Fine & Kurdek, 1992).

In turn, living under the custody of one's natural father is linked to problems for both male and female adolescents (Lee et al., 1994). Adolescents living with their fathers adjust more poorly than youth living in other arrangements. This reaction seems to be due to the closeness they have with their father, and the monitoring provided by him (Buchanan, Maccoby, & Dornbusch, 1992). The risk of drug use is also increased among youth living in father-custody families (Hoffmann & Johnson, 1998).

Effects of Maternal Employment After divorce, most youth live with their mothers, often, for at least a period, in what becomes a single-parent household (Furstenberg & Cherlin, 1991). In fact, because of divorce, unwed pregnancies, or paternal death, almost one fourth of American families are headed by a single female (Center for the Study of Social Policy, 1995). Because these women must support themselves and their children, maternal employment is a virtual necessity.

Of course, women work outside the home even when they live in intact, two-parent families. Indeed, the majority of American mothers work outside the home. They do so for personal, social, and economic reasons (Hernandez, 1993; J. Lerner, 1994). Regardless of their reasons for working, maternal employment generally had not been found to have adverse effects on the personal or social development of youth (J. Lerner & Galambos, 1985, 1991).

Adolescents whose mothers work outside the home do not differ from youth with nonemployed mothers in regard to variables such as adjustment (Armistead, Wierson, & Forehand, 1990; Galambos & Maggs, 1990), the nature of the mother-adolescent relationship (Galambos & Maggs, 1990), adolescent responsibility and self-management (Keith et al., 1990), and adolescent sexual attitudes and behaviors (Wright, Peterson, & Barnes, 1990). There also does not appear to be a difference among adolescents with full-time, part-time, or nonemployed mothers in regard to conflict or social interactions (Laursen, 1995). However, and independent of employment status, youth in single-mother households do have more conflict with their mothers than is the case with youth in two-parent families (Laursen, 1995). Thus single parenthood, and not employment, predicts youth problems.

In turn, in a study of the relation between maternal employment and mathematics achievement among approximately 14,000 American youth, unsupervised time after school, rather than maternal employment, was the major determinant of achievement (Muller, 1995). Overall, youth with nonemployed mothers did slightly worse than did youth with mothers who worked either full time or part time.

Maternal employment can create a sense of **role strain** in some mothers. She may find it difficult to balance the demands of her role of worker with the demands of her role as mother, or she may feel dissatisfied with her role. Such role strain occurs when the mother feels there is a poor match between her aspirations or education and her job duties (Joebgen & Richards, 1990) or when she is in the midst of work transitions (Flanagan & Eccles, 1993). Because of the nature of her multiple roles, the mother feels stress, and when such stress or role strain is experienced, a negative influence on adolescent adjustment can occur (Galambos et al., 1995; J. Lerner, 1994; J. Lerner & Galambos, 1985, 1991). However, when mothers find they can handle the stress associated with their work overload, the influence on their adolescents' adjustment is improved (Galambos et al., 1995).

Parental Work and Adolescents in Self-Care For many youth, when their parents are at work, there is no adult in the home. Indeed, a mother's time at work is obviously associated with the amount of unsupervised time a youth experiences after, and sometimes before, school (Muller, 1995; Richards & Duckett, 1994). Unsupervised time, especially between the hours of 3 PM to 8 PM, represents a problem period for youth. During these times, they often do not spend their time profitably (e.g., they just "hang out"), or they engage in high risk and/or illegal behaviors (Carnegie Corporation of New York, 1992). The lack of supervision during this time and not maternal employment is the source of these difficulties for youth.

The problems associated with lack of supervision can be counteracted. When parents exert firm control over the way their youngsters spend time in self-care at home, problem behaviors can be reduced (Galambos & Maggs, 1991). Effective community programs for youth, such as 4-H or Boys and Girls Clubs, and community athletics, can provide youth with positive and productive ways to spend their time. Current opinion among leaders of youth-serving organizations is that if such community programs are strengthened, young adolescents will have richer experiences and fewer life problems (Carnegie Corporation of New York, 1992).

Role strain Often associated with maternal employment, the difficulty of balancing the demands of one's role as a worker and the demands of being a parent.

Families with Adopted Adolescents As is the case for other families, families with youth who had been adopted try to create strong and healthy connections between the adolescent and his or her family and the larger community (Grotevant, 1997). These families strive to regulate the adolescent's behavior in appropriate ways and to instill in him or her the capacity for autonomy and the basis for a healthy identity (see Chapter 6) (Grotevant, 1997).

Conflict is an inevitable part of family life.

In a study of about 700 adoptive families in the United States, comparisons were made among adoptive adolescents and "birth" adolescents (i.e., youth born into their families) (Sharma, McGue, & Benson, 1998). Scores of the adopted youth on various psychological tests were also compared to the norms (i.e., expected average scores) on these tests. The results of these comparisons indicated that in some cases adopted adolescents had higher adjustment scores than the comparison groups (e.g., for adopted boys in regard to withdrawn behaviors and for adopted girls in regard to withdrawn behaviors and social problems); in turn, in other cases the adopted youth had lower scores (e.g., for adopted girls in regard to delinquent behaviors and externalizing behaviors) (Sharma et al., 1998). A similar pattern of positive and negative differences was found in a study of adopted adolescents in the Netherlands (Hoksbergen, 1997).

Given the presence of these contrasting implications for adolescent adjustment, we should not make any generalization about whether adoption results in problems or benefits for adopted youth (Sharma et al., 1998). Instead, it is important to conduct additional research to discover how families of adopted youth can best pursue their goals of promoting positive development and preventing negative outcomes among these adolescents (Grotevant, 1997; Sharma et al., 1998).

Conclusions About Family Structure

Neither across history nor within contemporary society do we find one structure of the family. Families are diverse, and this diversity may be associated with either positive *or* negative developments in adolescence. It is simply not the case that one family structure is ideal for all people, living under all conditions, at all points in time.

The important issue for science is what sorts of family structures are associated with what types of family functions and how these links between structure and parenting influence adolescent development. The key issue for the application of developmental science is how to maximize the probability of healthy adolescent development, given the family structures and parenting experiences that youth encounter.

To address these key issues of science and application it is important to understand the central role of the family: parenting. Parents of adolescents use quite different styles of behavior to rear their offspring. This variation is associated with differences in the success of parents in socializing their youth and with diversity in the sorts of relationships parents have with their adolescent children. All this variation creates considerable diversity in adolescents' development.

Parenting: Child-Rearing Styles, Socialization, and Parent-Adolescent Relationships

Issue to Consider
• What are the key functions of parenting?

The key function of a child's family is to raise the young person in as healthy a manner as possible (e.g., see Bornstein, 1995). Although there is variation in different cultures in the family structures used to serve this function (e.g., Harrison et al., 1997), the caregiver's role is always to provide the child with a safe, secure, nurturant, loving, and supportive environment, one that allows the child to have a happy and healthy youth. This sort of experience allows youth to develop the knowledge, values, attitudes, and behaviors necessary to become an adult who makes a productive contribution to self, family, community, and society (Lerner et al., 1995).

What a parent does to fulfill these duties of his or her role is called *parenting,* a term that summarizes behaviors used by a person, usually, but not exclusively, the mother or father, to raise a child. Parenting is both a biological and a social process (Lerner et al., 1995; Tobach & Schneirla, 1968). Biologically, parenting summarizes the set of behaviors involved across life in the relations among organisms who are usually **conspecifics** (members of the same species), and typically members of different generations or, at the least, of different birth cohorts. Parenting interactions provide resources across the generational groups and function in regard to domains of survival, reproduction, nurturance, and socialization.

Parenting is a complex process, involving much more than a mother or father providing food, safety, and succor to an infant or child. Parenting involves bidirectional relationships between members of two or more generations and can extend through all or major parts of the respective life spans of these groups. It may engage all institutions within a culture (including educational, economic, political, and social ones), and is embedded in the history of a people, as that history occurs within the

natural and the designed setting within which the group lives (Ford & Lerner, 1992).

Adults differ in the ways in which they enact their role as parent. They show different styles of raising their children. Differences in child-rearing styles are associated with important variation in adolescent development.

Child-Rearing Styles in Adolescence

Issues to Consider
• What are the various parenting styles as defined by both Baumrind and Maccoby and Martin?
• How does specific parenting style impact adolescent development?

The classic research of Diana Baumrind (1967, 1971) resulted in the identification of three major types of child-rearing styles: **authoritative, authoritarian,** and **permissive.** The authoritative style of rearing is marked by parental warmth, the use of rules and reasoning (induction) to promote obedience and keep discipline, nonphysical punishment (e.g., using "time out" or "grounding" instead of physical punishment), and consistency between statements and actions and across time (Baumrind, 1971; Lamborn et al., 1991). Authoritarian parents are not warm, stress rigid adherence to the rules they set (obey—just because we, the parents, are setting the rules), emphasize the power of their role, and use physical (corporal) punishment for transgressions (Baumrind, 1971; Belsky et al., 1984). Permissive parents do not show consistency in their use of rules, they may have a laissez-faire attitude toward their child's behaviors (i.e., they may either not attend to the child or let him or her do whatever he or she wants), and they may give the child anything he or she requests; their style may be characterized as being either

Conspecifics Organisms that are members of the same species.

Authoritative parenting Parenting marked by parental warmth and the use of rules and reasoning to promote obedience and keep discipline. Authoritative parents use nonphysical punishment and maintain consistency between their statements and actions across time.

Authoritarian parenting Parenting marked by lack of warmth and rigid adherence to the rules set by parents. Authoritarian parents emphasize their power in the family and tend to use physical punishment.

Permissive parenting Parenting marked by lack of consistency in parents' use of rules. Permissive parents tend to have a laissez-faire attitude toward their child(ren)'s behaviors. The parents often overindulge their child(ren)'s requests and act more as a peer than as an independent observer.

more of a peer or, instead, an independent "observer" of their child. Indeed, because of the diversity of behavioral patterns that can characterize the permissive parenting style, Maccoby and Martin (1983) proposed that this approach to parenting can best be thought of as two distinct types: **indulgent** (e.g., "If my child wants something, I give it to her") and **neglectful** (e.g., "I really don't know what my child is up to. I don't really keep close tabs on her").

Whether the three categories of rearing style originally proposed by Baumrind (1967, 1971), the four categories suggested by Maccoby and Martin (1983), or other labels are employed, the use of different parenting styles is clearly associated with differences in adolescent behavior and development (Lamborn et al., 1991; Mboya, 1995; Smetana, 1995). In a study of over 4,000 14- to 18-year-olds, adolescents with authoritative parents had more social competence and fewer psychological and behavioral problems than youth with authoritarian, indulgent, or neglectful parents (Lamborn et al., 1991). Youth with neglectful parents were the least socially competent and had the most psychological and behavioral problems of any group of adolescents in the study. In turn, youth with authoritarian parents were obedient and conformed well to authority, but had poorer self-concepts than other adolescents. Youth with indulgent parents had high self-confidence, but they more often abused substances, misbehaved in school, and were less engaged in school.

In a study of about 10,000 high school students, adolescents whose parents were accepting, firm, and democratic achieved higher school grades, were more self-reliant, less anxious and depressed, and less likely to engage in delinquent behavior than were youth with parents using other rearing styles (Steinberg et al., 1991). This influence of authoritative parenting held for youth of different ethnic and socioeconomic backgrounds and regardless of whether the adolescent's family was intact. Adolescents with authoritative parents are also more likely to have well-rounded peer groups, that is, groups that admire both adult as well as youth values and norms (e.g., academic achievement/

Indulgent parenting
Parenting marked by overly permissive and condoning behavior toward one's child (e.g., "If my child wants something, I give it to him").

Neglectful parenting
Parenting marked by inattentive, careless behavior toward one's child (e.g., "I really don't know what my child is up to. I don't really keep close tabs on her").

school success and athletics/social popularity, respectively) (Durbin et al., 1993). Youth with uninvolved parents had peer groups that did not support adult norms or values, and boys with indulgent parents were in peer groups that stressed fun and partying (Durbin et al., 1993).

A great deal of research has assessed the link between parenting styles and school behaviors and achievements. In a longitudinal study of adolescents from California and Wisconsin, nonauthoritative parenting was associated with youth attributing academic outcomes to external causes or to low ability (Glasgow et al., 1997). Nonauthoritative parents, whose styles are either unengaged or authoritarian and directive, have youth who score poorly both in regard to measures of academic achievement in college and in respect to measures of personality, adjustment, and substance use (Weiss & Schwarz, 1996).

When parents are connected to and involved with their adolescents, better educational outcomes are seen (Herman et al., 1997). In a longitudinal study of about 350 seventh graders, parenting practices fostered change in adolescents' academic accomplishments (Melby & Conger, 1996). When mothers and fathers set and reinforced appropriate behaviors in their adolescent children, academic performance improved. If parents were hostile to their adolescents, academic performance decreased (Melby & Conger, 1996). In a longitudinal study of adolescents in the United Kingdom (Shucksmith, Hendry, & Glendinning, 1995), authoritative parenting was related to both school integration and mental well-being. Furthermore, in a study of 10,000 high school students, parental involvement in their adolescent's schooling was associated with better school performance among youth (Bogenschneider, 1997).

Monitoring by parents seems to be an especially important feature of authoritative parenting. Among approximately 900 African American youth living in Alabama or New York City and Latino youth living in Puerto Rico or New York City, higher levels of parental monitoring were related to lower levels of adolescent problem or deviant behaviors (Forehand et al., 1997). Among more than 600 pairs of European American mothers and adolescents and more than 500 pairs of European American fathers and adolescents, more parental monitoring and less parental psychological control was related to adolescent academic and psychosocial competence (Bogenschneider, Small, & Tsay, 1997).

Considerable additional research confirms the generally positive influence on adolescent development of authoritative parenting and the developmental problems that emerge in youth when parents are authoritarian, permissive, indulgent, or uninvolved (e.g., Almeida & Galambos, 1991; Baumrind, 1991; Brown et al., 1993; Feldman & Wood, 1994; Melby & Conger, 1996; Paulson, 1994; Simons, Johnson, & Conger, 1994; Wentzel, Feldman, & Weinberger, 1991). Poor parental discipline is linked to problems in adolescent adjustment among both rural Iowa youth and urban Oregon youth (Conger, Patterson, & Ge, 1995). In a longitudinal study of about 500 adolescents, harsh discipline by parents was associated with stress and depression among youth (Wagner, Cohen, & Brook, 1996). Warm parenting was linked to lower depression (Wagner et al., 1996). Among Australian adolescents, punitive discipline styles in parents is related to delinquency among boys (Peiser & Heaven, 1996), and authoritative (inductive) parenting is related to low levels of delinquency (Peiser & Heaven, 1996).

One especially problematic feature of ineffective parenting styles such as authoritarian ones appears to be the use of physical (corporal) punishment. In a nationally representative sample of 1,042 boys and 958 girls between the ages of 10 and 16 years, parental use of corporal punishment was related to adolescent depression and distress (Turner & Finkelhor, 1996). Because corporal punishment is used in over half of the families in the Unites States, such relationships between this type of punishment and adolescent outcomes is alarming (Straus & Yodanis, 1996). In a study of about 4,400 couples, corporal punishment was found to be linked to subsequent aggression in youth and to an increased likelihood of future, marital violence (Straus & Yodanis, 1996).

Finally, the research on parenting styles confirms that the positive influences of authoritative parenting extend to the adolescent's choice of and involvement with peers (e.g., Brown et al., 1993). As discussed in Chapter 9, the influence of parents is often highly consistent with the influence of peers among adolescents (Lerner & Galambos, 1998).

Socialization in Adolescence

Issues to Consider
- How do different cultures define a socially successful individual?
- What are the different ways of identifying if and how society has been successful in socializing youth?
- How do parents influence the socialization process?

Whatever style parents use to rear their adolescents, the goal of parenting is to raise a child who is healthy and successful in life, who can contribute to self and to society, who accepts and works to further the social order. The behaviors used over time to reach these goals is termed *socialization*. Although all societies socialize their youth (in order that, as future contributors to society, the society can survive and prosper), there are marked differences in what different societies, or groups within society, want to see in a youth who has been "successfully" socialized. Said another way, there is great diversity in the specific goals parents have in socializing their youth.

One way of illustrating this contextual variation and of judging whether parents and society at large have been successful in shaping youth to accept social values is to ask youth what it means to be a good or a bad child. In one study that took this approach, American, Japanese, and Chinese adolescents were asked, "What is a bad kid?" (Crystal & Stevenson, 1995). In the United States, youth answered that a lack of self-control and substance abuse were the marks of being bad. In China, a youth who engaged in acts against society was judged as bad. In Japan, a youth who created disruptions of interpersonal harmony was regarded as bad.

Another way of understanding the socialization process is to see how immigrants to a new country give up the values and customs of their country of origin and adopt to those of their new country—a set of changes termed **acculturation**. This approach was used in a series of studies involving youth of Chinese ancestry, who were either first-generation Americans (their parents were born in China and emigrated before the adolescent was born) or second-generation Americans

Acculturation Process of cultural change during which a member/group of one culture gives up his or her/their own values and customs and adopts those from a different culture.

(their grandparents were born in China, but their parents had been born in the United States). These youth were contrasted to Chinese adolescents from Hong Kong, youth of Chinese ancestry whose parents had emigrated to Australia, European American youth, and Anglo Australian youth. In one study in this series both first- and second-generation Chinese American youth were similar to the nonimmigrant youth groups in their levels of adolescent problems (Chiu, Feldman, & Rosenthal, 1992). However, immigration did result in lowered perceptions of parental control, but it was not related to views about their parents' warmth. In turn, Chinese American adolescents' value of the family as a residential unit changed across the generations (with younger generations placing less value on the family), and thus showed variation consistent with acculturation to both Anglo Australian and European American values (Feldman, Mont-Reynaud, & Rosenthal, 1992). The Chinese Americans still differed from these other groups in this value.

Another approach to understanding socialization is to appraise whether different groups within a society direct their youth to comparable developmental achievements. Research in Israel, for instance, suggests that youth from Arab Israeli families are raised to view the father as having more power than the mother. Conversely, Jewish Israeli youth see more maternal than paternal power (Weller, Florian, & Mikulincer, 1995). In Japan, problems of adolescent adjustment are most likely to occur for boys who are aligned with their mothers, but whose mothers and fathers disagree about socialization practices (Gjerde & Shimizo, 1995). Male and female adolescents who emigrated from developing countries to Norway differ in their attitudes toward acculturation (Sam, 1995). Although both groups place a lot of importance on maintaining their cultural heritage, boys favor acculturation more than girls.

Whereas in the United States there is evidence of consistency in some socialization practices across diverse groups (e.g., in regard to the development of mental health among Latino and European American youth; Knight, Virdin, & Roosa, 1994), there is also research indicating that practices vary in different American groups. For instance, African American parents more frequently discuss prejudice with their adolescent children than is the case for Japanese American or Mexican American parents

(Phinney & Chavira, 1995); in addition, both African American and Japanese American parents emphasize adaptation to society more so than is the case with Mexican American parents.

How successful are parents' attempts at socialization? By virtue of the fact that society continues to evolve and is not characterized by intergenerational warfare or revolution, and that the vast majority of youth become contributing adults to society, we can conclude that socialization "works," that the "apple does not fall far from the tree" (Adelson, 1970; Lerner, 1986). Indeed, during adolescence very few families—estimates are between 5% to 10%—experience a major deterioration in the parent-child relationship (Steinberg, 1991). Not only do parents expect to see change in their sons' and daughters' behaviors as they socialize them during adolescence (Freedman-Doan et al., 1993), but, through their interactions on a day-to-day basis, parents can also model and/or shape the cognitive, emotional, and behavioral attributes they desire to see in their offspring (e.g., Eisenberg & McNally, 1993; Grotevant, 1998; Larson & Richards, 1994; Simons, Finlay, & Yang, 1991; Whitbeck, 1987). It is through the relationships that parents and their adolescent children have that the most immediate bases are provided of youth behavior and development.

Parent-Child Relationships in Adolescence

Anyone who has ever been entertained by a stand-up comic knows that at some point in the performance, his or her parents will be blamed for one or even a host of psychological and social ills besetting the performer. However, you do not have to dig very deep under the surface of the monologue to realize that in addition to the comic's parents being a source of humor, they are also a source of love and admiration. The reason that such comic routines are so frequent and so popular is that they reflect a virtually universal reaction to our parents: ambivalence. We love and respect our parents and yet we often are frustrated by them and/or angry with or exasperated by them. Mark Twain's famous observation—that at age 14 he could not believe how stupid and embarrassing his father was but that, at age 21, he was amazed to see how much the old man had learned in just 7 years—perhaps captures for all of us the often mixed reactions we have about our parents.

Such reactions mirror the nature of research findings about parent-child relations in adolescence. A range of behaviors and associated emotions are exchanged between parents and their adolescent offspring. Some of these exchanges involve positive and healthy behaviors and others not. Some of the outcomes for adolescent development of these exchanges reflect good adjustment and individual and social success, whereas other outcomes reflect poor adjustment and problems of development. As is true for all facets of human development, there is diversity in the nature and implications of parent-child relations in adolescence.

Parent-child conflict may occur when adolescents try to exert their independence in ways unacceptable to parents.

Parent and Adolescent Expectations About Their Relationship Collins (1997; Collins et al., 1997) has noted that the relationships between adolescents and their parents involve the expectations that youth have about their parents (e.g., my parents will support my interest in sports; my parents will ground me for a week if I break my curfew) and the expectations that parents have about their adolescent children (e.g., I don't want to see your involvement in sports interfere with your doing your homework or your getting good grades; I expect that you will know enough not to go to a party where kids are drinking). Both youth and their parents expect that across the adolescent age period young people will become more autonomous, that is, able to make their own decisions about their behavior (e.g., when to go to bed, how long to talk on a phone, if and at what time a curfew should be set, and food choices).

Often, however, parents and youth disagree about the age at which such transitions from parent-determined behaviors to adolescent-determined behaviors should occur. For example, at what age should a parent allow his or her child to decide when to come home from a date? In a study of mothers and their 10- through 17-year-old adolescents, most discrepancies in opinions about the timing of these transitions to autonomous behavior occurred for 13- to 15-year-old youth (Collins et al., 1997).

There are often differences between what people expect others to do and how, in fact, others behave (Grotevant, 1998). During adolescence, such differences occur in relation to the young person's increasing maturation and changes in social relationships (e.g., involving greater participation in peer activities than family activities; despite parental expectations adolescents may attend peer gatherings where alcohol is being used) (Collins, 1997). These differences between expected and actual behaviors can result in conflicts between youth and their parents, can change expectations (e.g., "Son, I guess you can't be trusted to go to parties where no alcohol is being used"), and alter family relationships ("From now on, son, I will have to approve every party you go to." "Dad, you're just unreasonable. You can't control all the kids in my high school, and if you won't let me go out just because there is a chance someone might be there with beer, then I will never be able to go out!") (Collins, 1997; Grotevant, 1998).

Moreover, youth and their parents have different expectations about when during adolescence it is appropriate for particular transitions (e.g., staying home in the evening without parental supervision, going out on a date with one person instead of with a group) to occur (Collins et al., 1997). Nevertheless, decisions about what to do and when it is appropriate to do it are increasingly made by adolescents as opposed to their parents (Grotevant, 1998). Across the adolescent years the number of issues youth perceive as within their control, and not the control of their parents, increases (Smetana, 1988; Smetana & Asquith, 1994). As a consequence of these changes in expected control of their own behaviors, adolescents are often in a position of having to renegotiate the rules their parents ask them to live under (Smetana, 1995). In other words, part of parenting a child across adolescence is to have one's authority continually challenged (Grotevant, 1998; Smetana, 1995).

In sum, adolescents and their parents often have different expectations about youth behavior and, as well, their respective expectations vary across adolescence. In addition to expectations, there are behavioral components of parent-adolescent relationships. These components can involve either positive or negative behaviors.

Parent-Adolescent Relationships Involving Supportive Behaviors and Positive Emotions Life always presents challenges and obstacles. Healthy, adaptive development involves being able to solve the problems life presents, for example, by making wise decisions about how to spend our money, juggling multiple demands on our time, or resolving interpersonal conflicts.

For this reason, many researchers study family interaction patterns of youth and parents in the context of family problem solving or decision making (e.g., Jory et al., 1996; Lamborn, Dornbusch, & Steinberg, 1996); they try to determine the bases of successful and/or productive, or of unsuccessful or destructive, problem-solving styles.

Several studies have found that, among American youth, warm parental interactions are associated with effective problem-solving ability in both the adolescent and the family as a whole; however, hostile interactions are associated with destructive adolescent problem-solving behaviors (Ge, Best, Conger, & Simons, 1996; Rueter & Conger, 1995b). Moreover, problem solving is worse when adolescents do not join parents in the problem-solving process (Vuchinich, Angelelli, & Gatherum, 1996). In turn, among German adolescents, parental behaviors marked by approval and atten-

tion to the positive behavior of the youth is associated with an adolescent who feels he or she is capable of controlling events that can affect him or her (Krampen, 1989); however, when parental behaviors disparage the child and fail to attend to his or her specific behavior, the adolescent feels that chance determines what happens to him or her in life.

As illustrated by these studies, warmth, nonhostility, and closeness seem to be characteristics of parent-adolescent interaction associated with positive outcomes among youth. Indeed, adolescents who are in relationships with parents that are marked by good connections show less anxiety and depression than is the case among youth who are detached from their parents (Delaney, 1996). Other research confirms these linkages between the quality of parent-adolescent relationships and youth development (e.g., Lau & Lau, 1996; Phares & Renk, 1998). For example, in a study of about 3,400 Mexican adolescents, positive father-child and positive mother-child interactions are associated with lower levels of anxiety among youth (Hernandez-Guzman & Sanchez-Sosa, 1996).

Positive parent-adolescent relationships may be expected to involve feelings of attachment or closeness on the part of the young person to his or her parents. Such feelings may be beneficial to both parents and adolescents. For instance, feelings of closeness in the parent-adolescent relationship are related to parents' views of their parenting as satisfying to them and to the youth's self-esteem and to his or her participation in family activities (Paulson, Hill, & Holmbeck, 1991).

Similarly, when adolescents feel secure in their attachments to parents, they are more competent with peers, have fewer internalizing problems, and fewer deviant behaviors (Allen et al., 1998). Moreover, poor attachment (e.g., anger about their relationships with their parents) is associated with the adolescent showing internalizing problems and behavioral deviance (Allen et al., 1998). Moreover, parent-child relations marked by attachment are associated with high self-perceived competence among youth, especially across the transition to junior high school, and with low feelings of depression or anxiety (Papini & Roggman, 1992). In addition, attachment is linked to feeling cohesive with one's family (Papini, Roggman, & Anderson, 1991). Other research also has found relationships among attachment, a positive sense of self, and low levels of problematic behaviors/emotions, such as depression (Kenny et al., 1993).

Furthermore, adolescents who are close to their parents are more self-reliant and competent and have better self-esteem and school achievements, and fewer problem behaviors (e.g., drug use, depression, and deviant behavior) than is the case with adolescents who do not have close relations with their parents (Barnes, 1984; Maccoby & Martin, 1983; Montemayor & Flannery, 1991; Steinberg, 1991). Similarly, parents who encourage their adolescent children to express their own feelings and ideas have youngsters with high levels of ego development (Hauser et al., 1984).

Positive attachment involves in part warmth and acceptance by parents of their children, and there are other data indicating that nonhostile parent-adolescent relations are associated with better adjustment by the adolescent to the transition to middle school and greater peer popularity (Bronstein et al., 1993); in addition, nonhostility is related to a better self-concept for girls and better classroom behavior for boys. In addition, parent-youth relationships improve over the course of adolescence in warm supportive families, whereas relationships deteriorate in hostile and coercive families (Reuter & Conger, 1995a). Moreover, in the former (positive) type of parent-adolescent relationship problem-solving effectiveness improves, whereas the latter type of relationship is associated with destructive problem-solving styles (Reuter & Conger, 1995b).

In addition, when parents are attuned to their child's development and support his or her autonomy in decision making, the youth is better adjusted and *gains* in self-esteem across the junior high school transition (Lord, Eccles, & McCarthy, 1994). Similarly, parental support is associated with life satisfaction among youth (Young et al., 1995). Furthermore, parental religiosity, cohesive family relationships, and low interpersonal conflict are associated with low levels of problem behaviors and with self-regulation among rural African American youth (Brody, Stoneman, & Flor, 1996).

The characteristics of parent-child interaction associated with positive outcomes for the adolescent are similar in that they reflect support for and acceptance of the developing youth. Parental patterns of support and acceptance, as expressed for instance in their willingness to grant independence to their children, varies by family race/ethnicity and

by youth age and gender (Alnajjar, 1996; Bulcroft, Carmody, & Bulcroft, 1996). Nevertheless, in general, when parent-adolescent relationships provide support for the youth's behaviors, interests, and activities, numerous positive developmental outcomes are likely to occur. For instance, support has been associated with better school grades and scholastic self-concept (DuBois, Eitel, & Felner, 1994); with perceiving that social relationships could be more beneficial to one's development than risky (East, 1989); with being more satisfied with one's life (Young et al., 1995); and with a decreased likelihood of involvement in drinking, delinquency, and other problem behaviors (Barnes & Farrell, 1992).

Family relationships involving siblings are influential as well (Stocker & Dunn, 1991). Although 10- to 14-year-olds spend only about 5% of their time alone with their siblings—compared to about 20% alone with peers and about 6% alone with parents (Raffaelli & Larson, 1987)—77% of high school students report that their siblings are important influences in their lives (Blyth, Hill, & Thiel, 1982). However, if parents treat their children differently rather than similarly, then conflictual and rivalrous sibling relationships tend to occur (Hetherington, 1989, 1991; Stocker & Dunn, 1991).

In sum, then, parent-child relationships, and family relationships more generally, that are marked by behaviors supportive of the youth and by positive feelings connecting the generations are associated with psychologically and socially healthy developmental outcomes for the adolescent. However, some families do not have parent-child relations marked by support and positive emotions; and no family has such exchanges all the time. Families experience conflict and negative emotions. Such exchanges also influence the adolescent; but, as we might expect, the outcomes for youth of these influences differ from those associated with support and positive emotions.

Parent-Adolescent Relations Involving Conflict and Stress As noted, family conflicts are inevitable (Fisher & Johnson, 1990). At the least, conflicts are a ubiquitous part of all families at some times in their history. Just as the reasons for conflicts between individuals, on the one hand, or nations, on the others, vary, so too do the reasons for conflicts in families. For example, adolescents report that conflicts often arise because they feel parents are not providing the emotional support they want, or because youth or parents believe the other generation is not meeting the expectations held for them, or because of a lack of consensus about family or societal values (Fisher & Johnson, 1990). Moreover, when adolescents and parents have discrepancies in their perceptions of family functioning (e.g., regarding the cohesiveness or closeness in the family), there is a greater likelihood of adolescent depression or anxiety, particularly for girls (Ohannessian et al., 1995). In addition, adolescents' negative beliefs about their mothers is associated with negative communications with them (Reed & Dubow, 1997).

In turn, in a study of over 1,800 Latino, African American, and European American parents of adolescents, conflicts were said to occur in the main over everyday matters, such as chores and style of dress, rather than in regard to substantive issues, such as sex and drugs (Barber, 1994). Similarly, among Chinese youth living in Hong Kong, conflicts were primarily with mothers and also occurred in the main over everyday issues (Yau & Smetana, 1996). As discussed in Chapter 1, similar findings were reported in research conducted a generation earlier (Lerner & Knapp, 1975), suggesting that the nature of parents' views of reasons for arguing with their children may not change very much across time. Parents from all racial/ethnic groups reported arguing about the same issues; however, European American parents reported more conflict than parents from the other two groups (Barber, 1994).

Moreover, although other research reports that adolescents and their parents are in conflict about the same sorts of issues—chores, appearance, and politeness—there is a decrease in arguments about these issues as the adolescent develops (Galambos & Almeida, 1992); however, conflict over finances tend to increase at older age levels. In turn, as youth develop, they are less likely to concede an argument to parents; as a result conflicts may be left unresolved, especially it seems in families with boys (Smetana, Yau, & Hanson, 1991).

The presence of conflicts between youth and parents is, then, a fact of family life during adolescence. Arguments with their youngsters are events parents must learn to cope with. Parenting Box 8.1 presents letters sent to a colleague and me from parents. In these letters parents ask questions about the nature of the conflicts they have with their adolescents. In our responses to these questions, my col-

league and I provide suggestions about how parents may deal with these unpleasant interactions with their child.

Nevertheless, despite its developmental course, the presence of conflict at any point in the parent-adolescent relationship may influence the behavior and development of the youth. For instance, family conflicts may lead the adolescent to think negatively about himself or herself, and can even eventuate in his or her thinking about suicide (Shagle & Barber, 1993). In addition, conflict is associated with "externalizing" problems (e.g., such as hostility) among youth (Mason et al., 1996). In adolescent girls, the experience of menarche (see Chapter 3) is associated with increased conflict, especially in the mother-daughter relationship, and as a consequence less positive emotions and more negative ones characterize adolescent-parent exchanges (Holmbeck & Hill, 1991; Steinberg, 1987).

In addition, psychological control (e.g., exerting control through inducing guilt) by parents (and siblings) is associated with adjustment problems and lowered self-confidence among youth (Conger, Conger, & Scaramella, 1997). Moreover, in a study of about 3,200 young adolescents, lack of cohesion in the family was associated with depression (McKeown et al., 1997). In short, then, conflicts in the parent-adolescent relationship result in problems in youth development (Rubenstein & Feldman, 1993). A vicious cycle may be created in that, in turn, adolescent problems can increase parent-adolescent conflicts (Maggs & Galambos, 1993).

Moreover, the negative emotions exchanged between adolescents and their parents can themselves result in problems for the youth. For instance, fathers' feelings of stress are associated with adolescents' emotional and behavioral problems (Compas et al., 1989) and, as well, maternal stress is associated with "internalizing" problems (e.g., anxiety, depression) in adolescent boys and with poor school grades for adolescent girls.

The process through which parents' stress is linked to adolescent problems seems to involve the experience of depression in parents as a consequence of their stress, which, in turn, disrupts effective parental discipline and leads to adolescent problem behaviors (Conger, Patterson, & Ge, 1995). Other research finds that parental depression is associated with depression in youth (Gallimore & Kurdek, 1992), and that ineffective parenting behaviors (e.g., low self-restraint among fathers) eventuates in prob-

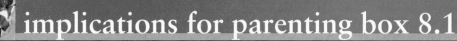

implications for parenting box 8.1

Teen and Tweens: Questions Parents Ask About Their Adolescents

Question: My 10-year-old daughter seems obsessed with *Beverly Hills, 90210* and has crushes on some of the characters. Should I be concerned?

Answer: In most cases crushes like your daughter's are perfectly normal. In fact, they may be a way for her to begin to act out her romantic notions in a safe, nonsexual way. Preteen crushes are like imaginary dates—unthreatening ones, since the preteenager will not have to deal with the consequences of her romantic feelings.

Question: Over the past year, our usually sweet 12-year-old son has started to argue with my wife and me about anything and everything. What's happening?

Answer: In the early part of the teen years, kids develop different ways of thinking about the world. They imagine new ways of behaving, question parental rules and wonder whether things could be different. Although they may test out their ideas on their friends, there is probably nobody safer to argue with than a parent. Kids know that by and large their parents will continue to accept and love them no matter how many arguments they have. Your child probably enjoys using his new thinking skills and has found that it is safe to argue with you. Use the best listening skills that you have, and let him know you are interested in hearing his ideas, although you don't always agree with him.

Question: Our 13-year-old insists on wearing old shirts hanging out over torn jeans. We can't get him to dress up without an all-out war. What can we do?

Answer: An important goal of adolescence is to understand who you are as an individual, and one of the easiest ways to declare who you are—especially as a person different from your parents—is through your clothing. Over

time your child will find other ways to define his identity. Until then, try to quietly tolerate some differences of opinion about dress standards. However, let your son know that while he can choose his everyday clothes, you have veto power over the choices for special occasions.

Question: My husband and I work full time. Our 15-year-old spends four to five hours alone before we get home. She says she likes it, but we're worried.

Answer: The issue is not about how much time your daughter spends by herself, but what she does with it. If she sits around watching television or engaging in aimless activities and doesn't do her homework, for example, then the time alone can be negative. First, leave numbers where you can be reached, and make it a practice to check in with her at regular times. Make it clear that you are checking in—not checking *up* on her. Talk to her about what you hope she will be accomplishing while you are gone. In addition, find out whether there is an after-school program for teens available in your community. This would provide your daughter with adult supervision and give her the opportunity to make new friends.

Question: My 10-year-old daughter is a bit chubby and she gets picked on at school. How can I help her feel good about herself and lose weight without making her too concerned about looks?

Answer: Work with your daughter to find things that she can be proud of about her appearance. Can she find a way to do her hair that she is excited about? Does she have some clothes that she thinks are really neat? Tell her that the whole family should and will find ways to eat well to maintain a healthy body. Don't *put* her on a diet, but provide healthful food that will promote weight control.

Source: From Lerner, R. M., & Hoopfer, L. C. (1993, October). Teens and tweens. *Family Circle*, p. 43.

lem behaviors in their offspring (Baumrind, 1991; D'Angelo, Weinberger, & Feldman, 1995; Feldman & Weinberger, 1994; Simons, Finlay, & Yang, 1991).

Furthermore, parents of tenth graders with conduct problems are more hostile than parents of tenth graders with depression (Ge, Best, et al., 1996); in addition, parents of tenth graders who are

both depressed and showing problem behaviors had high levels of hostility and low levels of warmth when their children were in grades 7, 8, and 9. Similarly, depression among both European American and Asian American adolescents is associated with family relations marked by low warmth and acceptance and high levels of conflict with mothers and fathers (Greenberger & Chen, 1996).

In turn, maternal depression adversely influences daughters' educational expectations (Silverberg, Marczak, & Gondoli, 1996). In addition, anger, hostility, coercion, and conflict shown by both parents and siblings have a detrimental effect on adolescent adjustment (Pike et al., 1996).

Clearly, then, parents' negative emotions can lead, through the creation of problematic parenting behaviors, to negative outcomes in adolescent development. Moreover, the presence of problem behaviors in parents per se is linked to problems in adolescent development. For instance, psychiatric disorders among parents are related to the occurrence of antisocial and hostile behaviors among adolescents (Ge, Conger, et al., 1996). In addition, problematic alcohol consumption—problem drinking or alcoholism—in parents is associated with alcohol use and abuse problems in their adolescent offspring, a relation that occurs in European American, African American, and Latino families (Barrera, Li, & Chassin, 1995; Hunt et al., 1995; Peterson et al., 1994). Similarly, parental drug use results in a host of behavioral, cognitive, and self-esteem problems in their offspring (Kandel, Rosenbaum, & Chen, 1994), maternal smoking is associated with smoking in their adolescent children (Kandel & Wu, 1995), and in fact parental substance use in general is linked to numerous problems, including experience with the substances (drugs, alcohol, cigarettes, etc.) used by parents (e.g., Andrews et al., 1993; Stice & Barrera, 1995). Moreover, when fathers have an emotionally distant relationship with their wives, and as a consequence turn to their adolescent daughters for intimacy and affection, the daughters show depression, anxiety, and low self-esteem (Jacobvitz & Bush, 1996).

Conclusions About the Family and Parenting

Parents are charged with an awesome responsibility by society. The role of parents is to develop future generations to carry society forward into the future. The children that the parents rear are the future. Society expects parents to do a good job in creating healthy and productive citizens. Although most parents fulfill this expectation, there are failures as well.

Parents vary in their rearing styles, the directions in which they socialize their youth and the types of relationships they have with, and behaviors and emotions they show to, their offspring. A good deal of this diversity is healthy and necessary to maintain the richness of culture and experience that enhances human life. But other levels of diversity involving, for instance, indulgent, neglectful, or authoritarian rearing styles, or hostile interactions marked by negative emotions, or the display of problem behaviors, can result in significant problems for youth.

The diversity in family functioning, coupled with the diversity in family structure, have pervasive implications for adolescent development. Families, in their structure and function, influence virtually all facets of the youth's psychological and social functioning, not only during adolescence but well into adulthood. The key social contexts affected by family structure and function are the peer group and the school. These contexts are discussed in Chapters 9 and 11.

Summary

- Families create caring young people through fostering healthy interpersonal relations and through promoting prosocial behavior, empathy, agency, and self-control in their children.
- The family is the major institution that fosters the development of caring individuals and promotes civil society and is charged with creating a new generation of citizens committed to maintaining and furthering the social order.

- In the 1950s, the typical family was a nuclear family, with two biological parents and two to three children. Today, only 1 in 5 families still fits this structure.
- Children and adolescents today may find themselves in more than one family structure during the course of their socialization.
- Hernandez describes what he labels the eight revolutions in the lives of America's children.

- The variation in family structures in which adolescents live influences both the way the parents interact with youth and how adolescents behave.
- A family under stress from poverty places its children at risk for problems of behavior and health. Parents may feel pressured, depressed, and demoralized by their financial situation.
- Parents can promote positive development in their children by receiving social support that promotes higher quality parenting practices.
- Grandparents are important in single-parent families, especially those headed by a female adolescent.
- When parents have a low-quality marriage, youth are adversely affected.
- Good marital quality can positively influence adolescent development and be related to positive peer relations and emotional adjustment.
- Most research finds that divorce has negative effects on adolescent development in social, academic, and personal adjustment realms.
- Gender differences are associated with the effects of divorce on adolescent development, the effects of remarriage on the adolescent, and the effects of living with the natural father after divorce.
- One fourth of American families are female-headed, single-parent families.
- Maternal employment does not have any direct adverse effects on the social and emotional development of youth.

- Adolescent adjustment may be related to having a mother who can adequately handle the stress of role strain.
- Unsupervised time can promote problem behaviors in youth.
- Research on adoptive families should concentrate on how the youth who are adopted and their families can best achieve goals and strategies that ensure positive development and prevent negative outcomes.
- Adults differ in the ways they enact their roles as a parent. Parenting style is associated with differences in adolescent behavior and development.
- Cultures differ in what they determine to be a well-socialized individual.
- In the United States, parents and adolescents expect that adolescents will become more autonomous across the adolescent period.
- Parents and youth often disagree about the age at which certain role transitions should occur.
- Warm parent-child relationships tend to foster effective problem-solving strategies and positive outcomes among youth.
- Adolescents often argue with their parents about everyday matters such as chores, appearance, and politeness. The number of conflicts tends to decrease over the course of adolescence.

Discussion Topics

1. In what ways are you significantly different from your close friends? How much of this variation is due to the influence of your family on your development?
2. Has the structure of your family changed throughout your life? How did the timing of these changes impact your development? For example, if you lived in a two-parent family until your parents divorced in adolescence, how did the timing of the divorce impact you?
3. What were the direct and indirect effects of being a member of the social class(es) to which you belong(ed)? For example, if you grew up in a lifestyle typical of the upper class in the United States, how did it impact your development? Did the social class with which your family identified change throughout your childhood? How were these changes experienced by you and your family?
4. What are some of the main causes and effects of the decline of the two-parent family?
5. How do you feel about mothers and fathers choosing to work soon after the birth of a baby? How do their decisions impact the development of their child? Do you believe one parent is more responsible for the caregiving and the other for the financial responsibilities of the family? Why or why not?
6. Do you believe American society will ever view the caregiving and breadwinning responsibilities of the family to be shared, 50/50, between two partners? Why or why not?
7. If a single, financially able woman came to you for advice on whether or not she should decide to have a baby on her own, what would you say? What are the bases for your advice?

8. What are some of the reasons behind the decrease in the birthrate in the United States over the course of the 20th century? How does the number of children in a family serve as both risk and protective factors to a family's welfare?

9. How has the increase of women in the work force impacted society?

10. Why might youth living in single-mother families be given more support than youth in the other non-nuclear family structures?

11. What are the potential reasons behind the finding that nonfarm poor adolescents suffer from fewer cases of depression than poor families who live on farms? What protective factors might influence the nonfarm youth as opposed to the farm youth?

12. How financially stable was your family throughout your childhood? How did your parent(s) influence your understanding of finances and its impact on your life? Were finances a significant issue of stress in your family, and, if so, how well did your parent(s) cope with those stresses?

13. Today, many grandparents are partially or fully responsible for raising children. What are some ways that society can better recognize and support their efforts? For example, how might schools and service organizations reach out to these grandparents?

14. How did the quality of your parents' marriage impact your development?

15. Why do you believe children of divorce tend to have higher rates of adjustment problems than children in two-parent families? How can parents who divorce support their child's social and emotional development?

16. If there were unsupervised blocks of time that you spent as an adolescent, how was that time spent? Why was there no adult monitoring your time? How do you feel this time impacted your development? How can communities better support adolescents and children who go home to empty houses after school and during the summer?

17. What is the sign of a successful parent? Is your answer culturally determined?

18. What parenting style defines your parent(s)? Using Bronfenbrenner's ecological model as a guide, how might your parents' life contexts impact their parenting style?

19. Many parents believe spanking is an effective discipline strategy. Based on what you have learned in this chapter and others, how would you advise these parents?

20. What socially derived expectations did your parent(s) have for you during your adolescence? What rules were set? What role did you have in creating these rules? How well did you follow those rules and live up to their expectations? Do you believe adolescents should have some say in the rules they live by? Why or why not?

21. How has the pattern of resolving conflicts established between you and members of your family impacted your social and emotional development?

Key Terms

acculturation (p. 197)

authoritarian parenting (p. 195)

authoritative parenting (p. 195)

conspecifics (p. 195)

cross-sectional study (p. 182)

externalizing problems (p. 191)

indulgent parenting (p. 196)

internalizing problems (p. 191)

longitudinal study (p. 182)

neglectful parenting (p. 196)

nuclear family (p. 181)

permissive parenting (p. 195)

role strain (p. 193)

socialization (p. 181)

9

THE ADOLESCENT
PEER GROUP

"Francisco, come inside," Mrs. Garcia called to her son.

Francisco stopped shooting the basketball at the hoop in the driveway long enough to answer. "Why, Mom?"

"First, because I said so, and second because your father just called. He'll be home in about 30 minutes and would like to go out tonight for a family dinner."

Francisco moaned. He carried the ball to the back door where his mother was standing. As he walked, he thought quickly. There were several reasons he did not need to go with his parents.

"Jaime is coming over and we were going to play basketball for a while. Can't you just take Rosita with you? It's Friday night, I have been in school all week, and I just want to do something with my friends."

"Well, your dad and I have worked all week and it would be nice to see you and your sister."

"Okay, I guess . . . " He paused for a moment until an idea came to him. "Why can't we eat at home? I don't really feel like going to a restaurant."

"Well, your parents don't feel like cooking, and if we eat at home you and your sister will disappear from the table in five minutes and so much for having a family dinner."

"But Mom, Jaime will be here in a minute."

"Good. Then after you wash up and change your shirt you and he can talk for a while until your father and I are ready to leave."

"But Mom," Francisco pleaded, "I'll be bored."

"Then you'll be bored. Now get in the house, get ready, and stop arguing."

Francisco knew he had lost the debate. He began to walk slowly into the house, but then he stopped and smiled.

"Okay, Mom, I'll go. But can we invite Jaime to come to dinner with us?"

1. To appreciate the different peer group structures that exist in adolescence and how they function.

2. To understand how peer reputations are determined, what types of peer reputations exist, and their effect on adolescent development.

3. To understand the components of friendship.

4. To appreciate how the nature of friendships changes across adolescence.

5. To learn how parents influence an adolescent's choice of friends.

6. To understand the broader peer context within which youth are embedded.

7. To define what a clique is and how it functions in adolescence.

8. To understand how peer status and peer relations are related to adolescent adjustment.

9. To learn the three dimensions of friendship that affect the course of adolescent development.

10. To appreciate the individual and contextual variables that shape the formation, and importance for development, of friendships in adolescence.

11. To learn how feelings of closeness to parents and peers develop across adolescence.

12. To understand how the amount of time spent with parents and peers changes across adolescence.

13. To understand how adolescent, parental, and peer values converge.

14. To learn how parents and peers can work together to promote positive youth development.

The adolescent's social world is broader and more complex than that of the infant or the child. The most notable social phenomenon of adolescence is the emergence of the marked importance of peer groups. The adolescent comes to rely heavily on the peer group for security and guidance. Adolescence is a time when such support is urgently needed, perhaps especially from others who are experiencing the same transition and can understand what is being experienced.

To understand adolescent development, it is important to review the nature and structure of peer relationships in adolescence, and to discuss the influence of peer relationships on adolescent behavior and development. Because of the continued importance of the family during adolescence (Adelson, 1970; Bengtson & Troll, 1978; Steinberg, 1991), it is also important to review the relationships an adolescent has with both parents and peers during this time, and the relative influence each has on the adolescent.

The Nature of Peer Relationships During Adolescence

Issues to Consider

- How are social interactions different from social relationships?
- What are social groups?

Consistent with developmental systems perspectives such as developmental contextualism, Rubin, Bukowski, and Parker (1998, p. 623) note that the experience of youth with peers "can best be understood by referring to several levels of social complexity: within individuals, within interactions, within relationships, and within groups." Rubin et al. (1998) explain that **interactions** integrate "the behaviors of two individuals into a social exchange of some duration"(p. 624). Social **relationships** rest on a commitment of the members of the relationship to each other and "involve a succession of interactions between two individuals known to each other. Importantly, because the individuals are known to each other, the nature and course of each interaction are influenced by the history of past interactions between the individuals as well as by their expectations for interactions in the future" (p. 625).

Rubin et al. (1998) note that a **group** "is a collection of interacting individuals who have some degree of reciprocal influence over one another. Groups often form spontaneously out of common interests or circumstances, but they are also established formally, the most ubiquitous example being the school class"

Interactions Integration of the behaviors of two individuals into a social exchange of some duration.

Relationships Succession of interactions between two individuals known to and committed to each other, which is influenced by the past interactions between the two individuals and by their expectations for the future.

Group Collection of interacting individuals who have influence over one another and who have relationships based on common interests or circumstances.

(p. 626). Different groups may have distinct rules or standards for behavior, that is, different norms for what is regarded as appropriate behavior (Rubin et al., 1998). Such norms may serve as a basis for identifying distinct crowds "within the network of relationships among children in high school" (Rubin et al., 1998, p. 626). Several different types of relationships may exist among the youth that comprise the peers of adolescents.

Table 9-1	Categories of Peer Reputation
Popular	
Rejected	
Neglected	
Controversial	
Average	

Peer Group Structures

Issues to Consider

- What different types of social networks exist during adolescence? How do they function?
- How are peer reputations determined? What does peer reputation mean for an adolescent?

Several types of peer groups exist in adolescence and these diverse structures are associated with important variations in adolescent behavior and development. Adolescents' peer relationships may be divided into several types of distinct groups of young people, or **social networks.** These groups include best friends, close friends, cliques (or friendship groups), social crowds, and sometimes romantic relationships (Urberg et al., 1995).

Although boys and girls possess all of these social networks, girls typically have more intimate relationships than boys (Urberg et al., 1995). Girls also have more positive network interactions and are bothered more by negative interactions than boys (Gavin & Furman, 1989). However, for both boys and girls there is "fluidity" in their social networks; that is, where a particular peer may be in the youth's set of networks (whether the peer is a best friend, a close friend, or an object of romance) may change relatively rapidly, over even a period of a few weeks (Cairns et al., 1995).

Nevertheless, the *reputations* youth have—for instance, as popular or unpopular—do remain relatively stable. These reputa-

tions not only reflect the social status of a youth in his or her broad peer group, but also mark the sorts of interactions he or she may have with peers. Perhaps most important, an adolescent's peer group reputation is related to both current and later life behavior and development.

Peer reputations can be determined for a particular youth by asking the members of his or her peer group to "nominate" or name people in their group (e.g., in their school or neighborhood) who have particular positive characteristics (e.g., well liked, chosen for games, would want at a party) and particular negative characteristics (e.g., disliked, left out of games, would not want to be with at a party). An adolescent's reputation can be determined by counting the number of positive and negative nominations he or she receives from the peer group.

> **Social networks** Distinct groups of relationships such as best friends, close friends, cliques, crowds, and romantic relationships.

Many adolescents spend time with their friends at shopping malls.

As shown in Table 9.1, various types of peer reputations exist. **Popular** youth are those adolescents who have a lot of positive nominations and few negative ones. **Rejected** adolescents have few positive nominations and a lot of negative ones. **Neglected** youth have very few nominations at all, either positive or negative, and **controversial** youth receive a lot of positive and a lot of negative nominations. Finally, **average** youth do not show extreme numbers of either type of nomination ("by definition," they have average numbers).

Despite his or her peer reputation, a given adolescent can have a certain type of peer relationship, a **friendship.** Just as youth having different reputations or status in their peer group differ in their personal and social behavior, youth with different patterns of friendship also show contrasting behavior.

The Nature of Friendships

Issues to Consider
- What are the components of a friendship?
- How does the nature of friendships change across adolescence?

Popular reputation Peer reputation characterized by receiving many positive nominations and few negative ones.

Rejected reputation Peer reputation characterized by receiving few positive nominations and many negative nominations.

Neglected reputation Peer reputation characterized by receiving very few nominations, either positive or negative.

Controversial reputation Peer reputation characterized by receiving a lot of positive nominations and a lot of negative nominations.

Average reputation Peer reputation characterized by not showing extreme numbers of either positive or negative nominations.

Friendship Voluntary and reciprocal relationship between individuals acknowledged by the people in it, with reciprocal affection and existing within a network of other relationships.

A friendship constitutes a special type of relationship within the groups formed by adolescents. According to Rubin et al. (1998, pp. 625–626), a friendship has at least four specific components:

1. A friendship involves a reciprocal relationship acknowledged by the people in it;
2. There is reciprocal affection in a friendship;
3. Friendships constitute voluntary associations between individuals; there is no obligation to be someone's friend; and
4. Friendships exist within a network of other relationships, for instance, involving peer cliques or crowds and family relations.

The nature of friendships develops during adolescence. Adolescents think about friendships differently than younger children (Selman & Schultz, 1990). Whereas young adolescents describe friends by noting their specific behavioral characteristics (e.g., "Ted is a terrific skateboarder" or "Anita sings great"), older adolescents depict their friends through descriptions of their personalities and values (Rubin et al., 1998).

There are also behavioral differences between adolescents and younger children in regard to the character of their respective friendships. In contrast to younger children, adolescents have fewer friends and same-sex friends become more important, friends equal or exceed parents as sources of social support and advice, friendships tend to be relatively stable, and intimacy and self-disclosure are the hallmarks of friendships (Rubin et al., 1998).

Parental Influences on Adolescent Friendships

Issue to Consider
- How do parents influence adolescent friendships?

Friendships are relationships predicated on personal choice (Hartup, 1996; Rubin et al., 1998), but parents still influence a youth's choice (Grotevant, 1998). Parents exercise great influence over their adolescent's peer relations in general and friendships more specifically (e.g., Parke et al., 1994). Through their socialization practices and child-rearing styles, parents inculcate in their children values and attitudes that influence their friendship selections.

Parents also supervise much of their adolescent's time, especially during the early portions of this period (Grotevant, 1998; Parke et al., 1994). They serve as chauffeurs to and from parties and trips to the mall, they organize play dates, and they may initiate their child's involvement in activities such as piano lessons, ballet classes, gymnastics, or soccer.

Friendships and Crowds

Issues to Consider
- What is the broader social context of the adolescent?

Parents may support their adolescents' social activities by attending their sporting events.

• What are the characteristics of a crowd?

The transformation across the adolescent period in what being or having a friend means to a person occurs in relation to the youth's broader peer context (Grotevant, 1998). For example, building on the scholarship of Brown (1990), Rubin et al. (1998) defined a **crowd** as "a reputation-based collective of similarly stereotyped individuals who may or may not spend much time together" (p. 643). Across adolescence, young people become enmeshed in crowds or "liaisons," that is, groups made up of often quite different youth (e.g., "jocks," "populars," and "brains") who are still in at least a loose sense affiliated with each other (England & Petro, 1998; Henrich et al., 2000). Crowds or liaisons may be identified on the basis of the attitudes or activities shared by their members (Rubin et al., 1998).

These attitudes and behaviors constitute the **stereotypes**—the overgeneralized beliefs—(Allport, 1954) that people viewing a crowd ascribe to them. For example, people may believe all the members of one crowd ("jocks") place a high (if not the highest) value on athletic participation and achievement and engage in behaviors (e.g., weight training) that facilitate their ability to perform in a manner consistent with this value. Numerous such crowds exist among American high school students. Brown and his colleagues (1990; Brown, Clasen, & Neiss, 1987) have identified some

of the labels associated with these different crowds. As indicated in Table 9.2, these labels include brains, burnouts, druggies, eggheads, greasers, grungers, jocks, loners, nerds, populars, and punksters.

Cliques

Issues to Consider

• What is a clique and how does it function in adolescence?

• How does an adolescent's social context develop across adolescence?

• How can crowds help adolescents understand the nature of social relationships?

Within a group there may be significant subdivisions. One key subdivision is a **clique**, a set of usually three or more young people who are in a tightly knit group. Clique members see themselves as mutual or reciprocating friends (Henrich et al., 2000) and are seen by others as having a key common

Crowd (liaison) Collective group of similarly stereotyped individuals who may or may not spend time together.

Stereotype Overgeneralized belief.

Clique Subdivision of a crowd in which a set of three or more people with a key common identity or interest form a tightly knit and often exclusive group.

Table 9-2	Examples of Adolescent Crowds or Liaisons
Brains	
Burnouts	
Druggies	
Eggheads	
Greasers	
Grungers	
Jocks	
Loners	
Nerds	
Populars	
Punksters	

Source: Based on Brown, 1990, and Brown et al., 1987.

identity or interest (e.g., athletics, socializing, music, academics). Cliques have a sort of impermeable "social membrane" around the youth in them. Youth within the clique hang out together and there is a degree of exclusivity of membership within a clique (cf. Rubin et al., 1998).

Cliques serve an important function in adolescence. Although membership in cliques decreases across the second decade of life, across adolescence membership in a clique is associated with psychological well-being and the capacity to cope with stress (Rubin et al., 1998).

Grotevant (1998) notes that the larger groups of crowds and cliques within which adolescent friendships exist develop across this period. During the early portions of adolescence, friendships are structured in regard to crowds (Urberg et al., 1995), and tend to be predominantly same-sex groups (Hartup, 1993). By the beginning of high school most youth are in friendship cliques, although there continue to be crowds and youth who are isolated and do not belong to any identifiable friendship group (Ennett & Bauman, 1996; Henrich et al., 2000).

All youth have one or another of these friendship types. For instance, hearing-impaired adolescents form friendships as do nonhearing-impaired youth; however, hearing-impaired youth tend to interact more with other hearing-impaired youth than with their hearing peers (Stinson, Whitmire, & Kluwin, 1996). Moreover, hearing-impaired youth tend to form emotional bonds with their hearing-impaired peers as opposed to their hearing peers.

The crowds within which adolescents exist may help the adolescent understand the nature of social relationships. For instance, building on the work of Brown, Mory, and Kinney (1994), Grotevant (1998, pp. 1115–1116) notes that "first, crowds and the stereotypes associated with them ("brains," "jocks," etc.) help adolescents understand alternative social identities available to them; second, crowd affiliations channel interaction such that relationships among some individuals are more likely than among others; third, crowds themselves vary in how relationships are structured in features such as closeness and endurance over time."

Functions of Peers During Adolescence

Issue to Consider

- How do peer relations influence adolescent development and behavior?

Adolescents' relationships with their peers have a profound influence on their behavior and development, second only perhaps to the significance in their lives of their family relationships. Good peer relationships are a mark of a youth's social competence (Morison & Masten, 1991); in addition, and underscoring the important connections that exist among the key contexts of adolescence, good peer relations are related as well to academic competence (Hartup, 1993; Morison & Masten, 1991).

Good peer relationships in adolescence are predictive of healthy development in adulthood (Parker & Asher, 1987). Adolescents who are disliked by peers, who are aggressive and disruptive, and who cannot establish good friendships are at risk for developing significant problems in adulthood. Youth with poor peer relationships are more likely to drop out of school, to engage in criminal behavior, and to experience mental or behavioral problems than are youth with good peer relationships (Morison & Masten, 1991; Parker & Asher, 1987).

Youth agree that a good peer group and strong friendships are valuable. For instance, when engaged in competitive activities (e.g., sports or games), friends are seen to offer supportive evaluations (e.g., to cheer you on, to say "you can do it"); in noncompetitive activities, they are seen to provide inclusion in a group, common interests, acceptance, and help with schoolwork (Zarbatany, Ghesquiere, & Mohr, 1992). Moreover, youth report that it is very valuable to them to be in a popular group (Gavin & Furman, 1989).

In turn, not only are peers perceived by the adolescent to be influential, they may in fact have an important influence on the adolescent's behavior. For instance, adolescents who report they have a good friend also tend to have good self-esteem and behavioral competence (e.g., Buhrmester, 1988; Bukowski & Newcomb, 1987). In turn, not being accepted by friends is related to school dropout, to delinquency and criminality, and to poor personal adjustment (Hartup & Overhauser, 1991; Parke &

Peer interactions often occur in the context of shared recreational or athletic activities.

Asher, 1987). Indeed, Coates (1991) notes that having a social network during adolescence has the primary purpose of providing social support, that is, a group of peers that may buffer the youth from experiencing the problems associated with lack of friendship (East, 1991).

Fortunately, at least insofar as it has been studied among middle-class youth, most adolescents (about 80%) have a "best friend" and five or more "good friends" (Hartup & Overhauser, 1991). In fact, fewer than 10% of youth have no contact with friends outside of school (Crockett, Lossoff, & Petersen, 1984).

Although, as I have noted, girls' friendships are more intimate than those found among boys (Bukowski & Kramer, 1986), adolescents of both sexes tend to choose friends of similar age and sex (Hartup & Overhauser, 1991). Moreover, in early adolescence, youth make friends with others who share their attitudes and values regarding schooling, drug use, and alcohol consumption (Epstein, 1983; Kandel, 1986).

In short, when an adolescent is popular with his or her peers, he or she is both sociable and has the ability to lead others (East, 1991). In addition, such youth tend to be physically attractive, intelligent, and successful in athletics (East, 1991). In turn, rejected youth tend to be physically and verbally aggressive and off-task and disruptive in the classroom (East, 1991). Understandably, these adolescents tend to perform poorly in school. Given this significance of peers in the lives of adolescents, it is useful to understand the function of these groups.

Peer Status, Peer Relations, and Adolescent Adjustment

Issue to Consider

• How are different peer status categories related to adolescent development and behavior?

Although positive peer relations are associated with healthy development in adolescence and later life (Hartup, 1993), not all youth have positive peer relations and not all youth are popular with other adolescents. Peer status influences development. Youth in different peer status categories behave differently, and these behavioral differences exist in comparable manners in different countries (Hatzichristou & Hopf, 1996; Luthar & McMahon, 1996). Peer status tends to remain fairly continuous across adolescence. Placement in a given status category (e.g., rejected) at one age by peers tends to be associated with being placed in that same category by peers at a later age (Merten, 1996).

Many different variables are associated with placement in a given peer category. Physical characteristics, as well as personality attributes and social skills, combine to influence peer rejection or acceptance (Brown, 1996). Youth who differ in physical attractiveness, especially facial attractiveness, enjoy different levels of peer acceptance. Higher physical attractiveness is linked to greater peer popularity (Adams, 1977; Perkins & Lerner, 1995).

Whatever physical, personality, or social attributes adolescents have that lead them to be placed in a given category tend to be repeated or carried over when youths enter a new setting. This carryover can be either negative (e.g., in the case of rejected youth) or positive (e.g., in the case of popular youth). For instance, adolescents who have best friendships characterized by positive features are accepted more readily in new groups they join (e.g., at a summer camp) than are youth whose best friendships are negative in character (Hanna & Berndt, 1995).

Differences in peer status category are associated with different behaviors and adjustment outcomes. This diversity in peer status category, behavior, and adjustment is influenced by individual and contextual factors. For example, popular youth show signs of good adjustment. Although there are a few studies that do not find such a link between peer group status and indicators of good adjustment, such as high self-esteem (e.g., Bishop & Inderbitzen, 1995), a great majority of studies do. Positive peer reputation is associated with good social and athletic competence, high academic performance, few symptoms of behavioral problems, and a positive sense of well-being (Morison & Masten, 1991).

Both neglected boys and neglected girls have been found to have good academic profiles, especially when compared to average status youth (Wentzel & Asher, 1995). They also have been shown to have greater motivation, higher levels of self-regulation as learners, more prosocial and compliant behavior, and were better liked by teachers (Wentzel & Asher, 1995). Among adolescent girls, both popular and neglected youth feel less stressed than controversial, rejected, or average girls.

Rejected youth have problematic academic records. Peer rejection and academic failure are not only closely related, but together they are associat-

ed with a youth becoming engaged with antisocial peers (Dishion et al., 1991). When rejected children are also aggressive, they do more poorly in the school context than do rejected but nonaggressive youth. Rejected youth also receive the least social support and have a higher rate of adjustment problems than do youth in other status categories (East, Hess, & Lerner, 1987), even though the levels of social support they receive can vary from time to time across all peer status groups (Munsch & Kinchen, 1995).

Finally, young adolescent girls who have a controversial status are most likely to become teenage mothers than are other girls (Underwood, Kupersmith, & Coie, 1996). In one study of 285 girls (Underwood et al., 1996), 50% of girls who were controversial in early adolescence eventually became adolescent mothers, whereas the base rate for teen motherhood in the sample was 26%. Similar finds occurred in regard to girls who had been aggressive in early adolescence. Controversial and aggressive girls both gave birth earlier in their adolescence than did girls in other status or behavioral groups (Underwood et al., 1996).

In sum, differences in adolescent peer status associated with a range of positive through negative personal and social characteristics are influenced by both individual and contextual variables. These influences on peer status and adjustment represent important potential sources for the application of knowledge about youth development. Knowledge about what influences peer status is vital in order to enhance the lives of youth though improving the quality of their peer relationships.

Youth who are rejected by their peers may engage in a range of problem behaviors.

Influences on Peer Status and Friendship

Issues to Consider
- What are the three dimensions of friendship that affect the course of adolescent development?
- What individual and contextual variables shape the formation of friendships in adolescence?
- What characteristics of a friendship can be linked to positive or negative development in adolescence?

Not a lot of theoretical attention has been paid to conceptualizing what individual and contextual variables enhance the quality of an adolescent's peer status, or how to help adolescents build healthy and supportive friendships (Furman, 1993). However, research does indicate that three dimensions of peer relationships, or friendships, affect the course of youth development: simply having friends, who one has as a friend, and the quality of the friendship (Hartup, 1983). Variation along all three of these dimensions is related to differences in the adjustment of youth (Bukowski, Hoza, & Borvin, 1993).

Adolescents form friendships more often with members of their own crowds than with members of other crowds (Urberg, Degirmencioglu, & Tolson, 1998; Urberg et al., 2000). The friendships formed within different types of adolescent groups—not only groups but, as well, cliques, dyads, or other instances of social networks—tend to be relatively stable, for example, a best friend in the fall of a school year is likely to remain a close friend (if not still a best friend) in the spring of the year (Degirmencioglu et al., 1998).

Unless one has a friend, the other influences of friendship on adolescent development cannot act. A diverse set of individual and contextual variables shapes the formation of friendships in adolescence.

Friendships are formed more readily by youth who are more age-mate oriented than family oriented in their attempts to establish new social relationships with peers (Takahashi & Majima, 1994). The ability to take the perspective of other people is important in establishing new friendships in adolescence (Vernberg et al., 1994). Knowledge of what are appropriate versus inappropriate strategies that can be used in making friends is important in establishing acceptance by peers (Wentzel & Erdley, 1993). Knowledge of such strategies as well as perspective-taking ability can be quite useful because being able to fit one's style of behavior to those desired by peers is a key basis of having positive peer relations (East et al., 1992).

Useful strategies in establishing friendships include managing conflicts in manners that avoid

Adolescents' interactions with their peers often occur in large groups or crowds.

any disruption in the relationship and using **display behaviors** to enhance one's attractiveness to others (Kolaric & Galambos, 1995). Because physical attractiveness is linked to better peer relations in both boys and girls (Lerner et al., 1991), each gender may use a set of behaviors they believe are associated with greater physical attractiveness. For instance, in order to try to appear more attractive, girls have been found to display chin strokes, hair flips, head tilts, coy looks, and movements to try to appear physically smaller (Kolaric & Galambos, 1995).

To the extent that these behaviors and characteristics are successful in forming a friendship, *and* if the adolescent can then become engaged in a friendship that is marked by the qualities of (1) stability (duration over time); (2) engagement (i.e., being involved in activities with a best or close friend); and (3) lack of deviance in the friend (that is, a friend who does not get into trouble; a friend who has behaviors and attitudes that are socially positive), then it is likely that positive self-esteem will develop in the youth (DuBois & Hirsch, 1993; Gillmore et al., 1992; Juvonen, 1991; Keefe & Berndt, 1996).

However, not all friendships are formed with youth who are engaged in positive behaviors and who avoid trouble and deviance. When friendships are formed with youth having such negative characteristics,

> **Display behaviors** Actions designed to enhance one's attractiveness to others.

the implications for adolescent development are not favorable. For instance, when a youth's friends engage in antisocial behavior or in disruptive behavior, it is likely the youth will follow course (Berndt & Keefe, 1995; Dishion, Andrews, & Crosby, 1995).

Moreover, there can be a congruence in the feelings of internal distress among youth and their friends (Hogue & Steinberg, 1995), and such personality characteristics can be associated with both adolescent and peer substance abuse (Dobkin et al., 1995). Indeed, involvement with deviant peers and feelings of depression increase the likelihood that the adolescent will use drugs (Simons, Finlay, & Yang, 1991). Moreover, changes in youths' grades and drug use are linked to these same changes in their friends (Mounts & Steinberg, 1995).

Such associations may develop through a process involving both hostile and low reciprocity relationships with a close friend, occurring in relation to feelings of depression and self-destructive behaviors in a youth (Windle, 1994). Such a process is related to high levels of alcohol use among adolescents.

A range of types of friendships exists in adolescence. As with peer relations in general, there are specific implications for youth behavior and development of the type of friendships they possess.

Friendship Quality and Behavior

Issues to Consider

- How does friendship quality influence adolescent development and later life?
- How do school friendships influence adolescent behavior and development?

Friendships are generally beneficial (Hartup, 1993; Henrich et al., 2000). For instance, "being liked" or "being disliked" by peers is related to an adolescent's social competence (Hartup, 1996). Also, who one has as a friend (e.g., a youth with positive attitudes to school and society vs. a youth who behaves in aggressive or delinquent manners) and the quality of that friendship (e.g., whether one enjoys continuous or stable support from one's friends, whether the friendship is marked by the reciprocal exchange of positive regard and cooperation) are significant as well (Hartup, 1996).

When friendships are marked by positive, healthy behaviors, they are associated with compa-

rable behavior and development in adolescence (Shulman & Knafo, 1997). When high-quality friendships are stable during adolescence, youth show positive self-esteem (Keefe & Berndt, 1996). Such close friendships are also related to an adolescent's social skills (Berndt & Keefe, 1995).

Positive friendships during adolescence can have beneficial effects during later life. In a study of young adults who either had a stable and reciprocal best friend during adolescence or who had been chumless during this period, friendship was associated with higher levels of feelings of self-worth in adulthood (Bagwell, Newcomb, & Bukowski, 1998). Unfortunately, not all adolescent friendships are stable. Especially in early adolescence, there may be great fluidity in whom young people regard as their friends (Cairns et al., 1995).

Friendships in school may be particularly useful in promoting positive development in adolescence. Positive school friendships can enhance a young person's academic performance and quality of school behaviors, including prosocial behaviors (Cairns & Cairns, 1994; Henrich et al., 2000; Wentzel & Caldwell, 1997).

Different types of school friendships are associated with differences in the behavior and development of youth. For instance, students aged 9 to 15 years who are more popular with the opposite sex hold attitudes about lifestyle (e.g., holding an after-school job or avoiding smoking) that differ from those held by youth less popular with the opposite sex (Harton & Latané, 1997). Membership in a clique in the sixth grade is associated with better grades in both the sixth and eighth grades (Wentzel & Caldwell, 1997).

However, because there is a great deal of consistency (homogeneity) in the behaviors of clique members, clique membership, as well as friendship per se, can be associated both with positive behaviors (good school grades, classroom involvement) and with negative behaviors (e.g., substance use, cognitive distortions, lower problem-solving ability, aggression, or delinquency) (Berndt & Keefe, 1995; Cairns & Cairns, 1994; Dishion, Andrews, & Crosby, 1995; Grotpeter & Crick, 1996; Henrich et al., 2000; Hunter, Vizelberg, & Berenson, 1991; Marcus, 1996; Vitaro et al., 1997). Being an isolate is also a potential basis of negative behaviors (e.g., substance use)(Ennett & Bauman, 1993; Henrich et al., 2000).

In a study of about 500 sixth- and seventh-grade European American, African American, and

Latino youth, isolation from school-based friends was associated with poor adjustment among both boys and girls (Henrich et al., 2000). For girls, membership in a clique or in a crowd was related to positive peer relationships, fewer behavior problems, and better school adjustment. Such associations were not present for boys (Henrich et al., 2000).

Conclusions About the Functions of Peers in Adolescence

As is also true of families, peer relationships can enhance or detract from healthy adolescent development. Despite the diversity that exists in the influence of the peer context, most youth peer relationships function to help bridge a successful path from adolescence to adulthood. This positive contribution of the peer group to adolescent development may occur because there is a great deal of consistency between the influence of peers and the influence of the family.

This congruence between the role of parents and peers is not a recent phenomenon. The consistency of the results of research conducted over the course of more than a quarter century suggests that such congruence may be a general feature of the relationships among generations.

Influences of Peers and Parents on Adolescent Development

No social institution has as great an influence throughout development as does the family (Lerner & Spanier, 1978). Studies across a 30-year period indicate that most adolescents have few, if any, serious disagreements with parents (e.g., Douvan & Adelson, 1966; Laursen, 1995; Laursen, Coy, & Collins, 1998; Lerner & Knapp, 1975). As noted earlier, during adolescence very few families—estimates are between 5% and 10%—experience a major deterioration in the quality of the parent-child relationship (Steinberg, 1991). In choosing their peers, adolescents typically gravitate toward those who exhibit attitudes and values consistent with those maintained by the parents. These attitudes and values are ultimately adopted by the adolescents themselves (Foster-Clark & Blyth, 1991; Guerney & Arthur, 1984; Kandel & Andrews, 1987).

Attitudes About and Emotions Expressed to Peers and Parents

Issues to Consider

- How do feelings of closeness to parents and peers develop across adolescence?
- How is this intimacy related to adolescent behavior?

Feelings of closeness to parents and peers develop in similar ways across adolescence, and these feelings are associated with the adolescent's behavior. From the eighth to the twelfth grades, male and female adolescents' feelings of intimacy with their parents tended to increase, but somewhat more so for boys than for girls (Rice & Mulkeen, 1995). Although both boys' and girls' intimacy with their best friends also increased across grades, the increases were greater for boys (Rice & Mulkeen, 1995). Adolescents who have high intimacy with both their mothers and fathers have higher self-esteem, lower depression, and lower scores for risk taking. Adolescents who have same-sex friends and greater intimacy with their mothers report greater interest in school (Field et al., 1995).

The attachment of adolescents to their parents remains strong in 16- and 17-year-old adolescents and is related to attachment to peers, particularly for girls (O'Koon, 1997). Attachment to parents is also associated with youth involvement in extracurricular peer group activities (Schneider & Younger, 1996). Harmonious relations between adolescent girls and their mothers are characterized by attributes (e.g., similar needs, needs being met) that correspond to the ones found in harmonious relationships between adolescent girls and their best friends (Gavin & Furman, 1996).

Time Spent with Parents and Peers

Issues to Consider

- How does the time adolescents spend with parents and peers change across adolescence?
- How does the provision of support change across adolescence?

Despite the high-quality relationships maintained between most adolescents and their parents, across the adolescent years there is a dramatic decline in the amount of time adolescents spend with parents and a marked increase in the time spent with peers, especially for girls (Larson & Richards, 1991). In order to study how adolescents spend their time, Csikszentmihalyi and Larson (1987) and Larson and Richards (1991, 1994) have ingeniously capitalized on adolescents' interest in electronic equipment and invented a new way of observing adolescent behavior. Termed the event sampling method (ESM), youth are given electronic pagers (beepers) to carry. Youth are paged from time to time and asked to respond to a short set of questions such as "Where are you?" "What are you doing?" "Who are you doing this with?" and "How do you feel right now?" Because they also carry a set of these questionnaires with them, they can respond to repeated beeps over the course of a day or week.

Using ESM, Larson and Richards (1991) found that across the 9- to 15-year-old age range, there was a decreasing likelihood that male and female adolescents would be in situations with their parents when paged. For boys, the tendency to spend time alone increased, and for girls, there was an increased tendency to spend time either alone or with friends.

Moreover, Larson, Richards, and their colleagues have traced longitudinally the changes in the distribution of time adolescents direct to peers and parents. For instance, 4 years after a group of fifth- through eighth-grade adolescents were initially studied, the now ninth through twelfth graders showed several changes in the way they apportioned their time with friends (Richards et al., 1998). Thinking about the opposite sex occurred before youth reported that they actually spent time with members of the opposite sex (Richards et al., 1998), and both thinking about the opposite sex and spending time with them increased over the course of adolescence. Girls spent more time with the opposite sex, and both girls and boys experienced time alone with the opposite sex as positive. As the youth developed, however, they regarded time spent thinking about the opposite sex as less positive (Richards et al., 1998).

Across time, there were also changes in same-sex relationships. Girls spent more time thinking about both same-sex and opposite-sex peers (Richard et al., 1998). In addition, in a study of about 2,000 seventh and ninth graders, girls reported spending more time alone or in conversation per week than did boys (Smith, 1997). Girls' conversations with friends tended to be more involved and friendly than their conversations with their mothers (Beaumont, 1996).

Given such developmental changes in time youth spend with their peers, it is not surprising that between early adolescence (about 10 years) through mid-adolescence (about 15 years) there is a decrease of about 50% in the time spent with parents (Larson & Richards, 1991). Between grade 5 and grade 12 the amount of time spent with the family decreases from 35% to 14% of waking hours (Larson et al., 1996). In addition, whereas mothers and fathers are seen as the most frequent providers of support in early adolescence, same-sex friends are regarded to be as supportive as parents in middle adolescence and as the most frequent providers of support by late adolescence (Furman & Buhrmester, 1992). The effects of mothers on daughters' sexual behavior is strongest in the ninth and tenth grades, whereas the influence of friends is higher starting in the eleventh grade and continuing into the college years (Treboux & Busch-Rossnagel, 1995).

Despite the greater attention paid to peers over the course of adolescence, considerable data indicate that the influence of parents not only remains strong but shapes and reinforces the effects of peers on youth development. Despite the decrease in the amount of total time adolescents spend with their parents, there are no changes in the proportion of time youth spend talking with parents about interpersonal issues, and this stability is especially true for girls (Larson et al., 1996).

Attitudes and Values

Issue to Consider

- How do adolescent, parent, and peer values converge?

As already emphasized, adolescents typically select peers who have attitudes and values consistent with those maintained by the parents. Perhaps not surprisingly, there is great concordance among adolescents in their attitudes and values. For instance, in one study involving about 3,500 youth from five nations (Israel, Costa Rica, the Philippines, Scotland, and the United States), youth showed significant agreement across both age and sex in their attitudes about the transition to adulthood (Seltzer & Waterman, 1996). Such high levels of agreement among adolescents do not gainsay the fact that there is also congruence between youth and their parents. All three groups, adolescents, adolescents' peers, and adolescents' parents, tend to have comparable attitudes and values.

Given this consistency, it is not surprising that the opinions of parents are the beliefs ultimately adopted by the adolescents themselves (Foster-Clark & Blyth, 1991; Guerney & Arthur, 1984; Kandel & Andrews, 1987). Adolescents' endorsement of conventional values (i.e., values pertinent to maintaining society, values about helping others) is associated with their identification with their parents and their parents' support of these values and with a lessened probability of selecting friends with socially deviant behaviors (Whitbeck et al., 1989).

Although peers affect adolescents in regard to such issues as educational aspirations and performance, in most cases there is convergence between family and peer influences (Brittain, 1963; Foster-Clark & Blyth, 1991; Kandel & Andrews, 1987). Adolescents and parents can have somewhat different attitudes about issues of contemporary social concern (drug use, sexuality, style of dress), but most of these differences reflect contrasts in attitude intensity rather than attitude direction. Rather than adolescents and parents standing on opposite sides of a particular issue, most generational differences simply involve different levels of support for the same position (Lerner & Knapp, 1975). For example, in regard to the statement, "Birth control devices and information should be made available to all who desire them," one study found that adolescents showed strong agreement with the item and their mothers showed moderate agreement with the item (Lerner & Knapp, 1975).

Adolescents tended to see their own attitudes as lying between those of others of their own generation and those of their parents' generation (Lerner et al., 1975). They placed their own positions between the "conservative" and the "liberal" end of a conservative-liberal attitude continuum. They put their parents toward the conservative end and their peers toward the liberal end. In reality, therefore, adolescents think their peers are more liberal than they actually are, which means, for example, that adolescents think their friends are using more drugs and having more sex than is actually the case.

If closeness and intimacy characterize adolescent peer relationships, there is correspondence between the educational aspirations of the adolescent and his or her peers (Kandel & Lesser, 1969), and most adolescents (57%) have educational plans that agree with both peers and parents. Among those adolescents who disagree with their parents, there is also a great likelihood (50%) that they disagree with peers as well. When there is a discrepancy between parent and peer orientations, it is most likely that the parental orientation will prevail (Kandel & Lesser, 1969).

Corresponding findings occur in other studies, including those conducted relatively recently (e.g., Laursen, 1995; Laursen et al., 1998). Brett Laursen's current work pertinent to adolescent-parent and adolescent-peer relations is discussed in Meet the Researcher Box 9.1.

Most adolescents perceive their parents as more influential than their peers in adjustment to school, and relatively few adolescents believe that peers are important at all in shaping school adjustment (Berndt, Miller, & Park, 1989). For other critical developmental issues such as deciding who to turn to for help when faced with a substance abuse problem, adolescents are more at risk if they turn to peers instead of to parents for help (Windle et al., 1991).

The data suggest that adolescents and their parents do not have many major differences in attitudes and values. Adolescents tend to perceive that their values lie between those of their parents and peers. Apparently, the impact of the intragenerational and intergenerational social contexts is often compatible.

Interactions Between Peer and Parent Contexts

Issues to Consider

- How can parents and peers work together to promote positive youth development?
- What are some programs that allow for facilitative contributions by peers?

Although peers gain in their influence on adolescence, their influence does not replace the influence of parents. Peer and parent contexts can work together to support healthy behavior and development. Both can be sources of positive interaction, and in supporting positive behavior, one context can compensate for the other when necessary.

MEET THE RESEARCHER BOX 9.1

BRETT LAURSEN

UNDERSTANDING HOW CLOSENESS AND CONFLICT IN PARENT-CHILD AND PEER RELATIONSHIPS INFLUENCES ADOLESCENT ADJUSTMENT

Closeness and conflict are part and parcel of all interdependent relationships. When it comes to the adolescent years, however, most of the research attention seems to focus on the downs rather than the ups. In the past, experts tended to reinforce the conventional wisdom about adolescence, namely, that it is an altogether disagreeable period of life. But is this really the case?

My research—supported by the U.S. National Institute of Child Health and Human Development and by the Johann Jacobs Foundation—is aimed at better understanding the positive and negative interchanges that adolescents have with their mothers, fathers, friends, and romantic partners. The ultimate goal of this work is to determine how relationship closeness and conflict shape the social and academic outcomes of individual adolescents.

It is important to remember that there is no such thing as an objective participant in the exchanges that take place in an interpersonal relationship. Two people can have completely different perceptions of the same interaction. In terms of effects, what may be gleaned by an observer is probably of less importance than what the participants themselves think and feel about the interaction. Simply put, if you want to know how experiences in a particular relationship affect an adolescent's well-being, then you have to ask the adolescent to recount the events and their consequences. In my research, we do this is by having participants describe all of their disagreements from the previous day. We ask them to tell us about every little quibble, not just about the major confrontations.

The findings may surprise you. On average, adolescents report between five and ten disagreements every day across all relationships. This may sound like a great deal, but it really isn't when you consider that youth spend around 12 hours a day in social interaction. That works out to something like one disagreement for every

Brett Laursen is a professor of psychology at Florida Atlantic University. He received his PhD in 1989 from the Institute of Child Development at the University of Minnesota. He is a member of the Steering Committee of the International Society for the Study of Behavioural Development and a consulting editor for *Child Development*, the *Merrill-Palmer Quarterly*, and the *Journal of Research on Adolescence*.

2 hours of interaction. Furthermore, the vast majority of these conflicts mean little or nothing to the adolescent. Angry feelings are reported in just 25% of the disputes. Few disagreements with family members are perceived to have any consequence for the relationship and, among friends, disagreements are as likely to make things better as make things worse. The *bottom line* is that most adolescents report only one or two substantive conflicts per day, typically one with their mother and perhaps another with a sibling or a friend.

These figures are averages, but we all know that there is no such thing as an average child. There are huge individual differences in interpersonal conflict. Some youth report no disagreements of any type with anyone; a few report 30 or 40 over the course of an average day! How do these different experiences impact development? Data from an ongoing longitudinal study suggest that the influence of conflict depends on the perceived closeness of the relationship in which it arises. When relationships with friends and parents are not close, more frequent conflicts are associated with lower school grades and more behavior problems. When relationships with friends and parents are close, the effect of perceived conflict is a little more complicated: Adolescents with no conflicts and those with many conflicts have worse school grades and more behavior problems than adolescents reporting just a few conflicts. Apparently, relationship closeness operates as a buffer that permits adolescents to explore some differences in a beneficial manner; those who have no conflicts miss this opportunity for growth, and those with many conflicts overload the system. Take away the closeness in a relationship, and conflict is an increasingly detrimental experience. These findings have important implications for our understanding of the role of relationships in development because they suggest that under conditions of closeness, disagreements can promote positive outcomes.

To illustrate how the contexts can contribute to similar outcomes, consider the findings of one longitudinal study, the Maryland Adolescent Growth in Context (MAGIC) study. This study of about 1,400 African American and European American adolescents and their families assessed the quality of social interaction in the home, in school, and in peer groups (Eccles et al., 1997). Youth with positive interactions in one context were also likely to have positive interactions in the other contexts (Eccles et al., 1997).

The power of peers to facilitate success of youth in the multiple contexts within which they function can be used as a basis for building programs to promote positive experiences among young people and the betterment of their contexts. Applications Box 9.1 illustrates these facilitative contributions of peers by describing three innovative programs. Children's Express involves youth and their peers in a nonprofit news service. The program uses 14- to 18-year-old editors in the training of 13-year-old or younger reporters, and provides youth with experiences and skill development in language use, writing, interpersonal relationships, and journalism. Youth as Resources enables groups of young people to form partnerships with institutions in their community (e.g., day care centers, nursing homes, community centers) in order to enhance the welfare of the community and to further civil society (see Chapter 5). Child to Child is based in Oaxaca, Mexico, and is a trainer program aimed at improving the health of youth and their communities. Youth community leaders train their younger peers to educate other young people and adults in their community in how to act to promote health and to prevent disease.

Given the role of peers in facilitating youth development and in making contributions to key contexts of their lives, it is not surprising that peers can enhance the functioning of youth in school. Among sixth graders, adjustment to school is related to quality of parenting (e.g., supervision, acceptance, and autonomy granting) *and* to peer group orientations (e.g., the presence of peer norms supporting academic excellence) (Kurdek, Fine, & Sinclair, 1995). Other studies confirm that peers and parents contribute to positive behavior among sixth-grade students. Among such students, peer support was associated with pursuing prosocial goals, and parent support was related to school-related interests and goals (Wentzel, 1998). In a study of African American, Latino, and European American families, the social support provided by peers emerged as salient in all groups during adolescence (Levitt, Guacci-Franco, & Levitt, 1993). This change was coupled with the significance of close family ties remaining strong from childhood through early adolescence within all the ethnic groups.

Other studies illustrate how one context can counteract the shortcomings of the other setting. In a study of 900 fifth and eighth graders, problems of social interaction and problems in the family, peer, or school contexts were compensated for by experiences in the other contexts (Barber & Olsen, 1997). In the families of African American adolescents, high-quality parenting can play a small but significant role in compensating for the negative influence on youth of having problematic peers (Mason et al., 1996). Maternal responsiveness and paternal monitoring have been found to decrease adolescents' orientation to substance-using peers and to result in reduced adolescent substance use (Bogenschneider et al., 1998).

As another illustration of compensating influences among contexts, when adolescents lack a close friend healthy adjustment can still occur if the adolescent has an adaptive and cohesive family (Gauze et al., 1996). In turn, if family adaptability and cohesion are low, healthy adolescent adjustment is associated with having a close friend (Gauze et al., 1996).

When parents show effective parenting practices—for example, authoritative child-rearing styles—the convergence between family and peer influences may be maximized. When parents' authoritative parenting extends to the youth's choice of peer network and his or her behavior in this network, several positive outcomes of youth development occur. These positive outcomes include lower levels of delinquency, substance use, and school misconduct for boys, and greater psychological and social competence and lower psychological distress for girls (Fletcher et al., 1995). Parenting practices that differ from authoritative ones (e.g., authoritarian styles) can create less positive outcomes for youth, and, in some cases, can result in adolescents being more oriented to peers than parents for support (Fuligni & Eccles, 1993).

Conclusions About Adolescent Peer Groups

The peer group context provides an important source of the person's behavior, both during adolescence and into adulthood. As is the case with the family, this influence of peers can be negative or positive. Much of this influence is shaped not by the peer group alone, but by how the family and peer group contexts combine to influence adolescent developmental outcomes.

applications box 9.1

Promoting Adolescents' Positive Contributions to Their Context Through Peer Relations

Peers are a key influence in the lives of youth. This influence can be used to promote positive development in young people. Numerous community-based programs throughout the world rely on the peers of adolescents to act as facilitators of their healthy development. Three exemplary instances of such programs are described here.

Providing Young People with Valuable Skills and a Voice on Issues Affecting Them
Children's Express Worldwide News Network, Washington, D.C.

Since it was founded in 1975, Children's Express (CE) has trained thousands of young people as reporters. More importantly, CE has given them a means through which to express their ideas and develop opinions on critical issues impacting their lives—from violence, divorce, and dropping out of school to national and international events.

Headquartered in Washington, D.C., but with offices in the United Kingdom and Japan, CE is a nonprofit, international news service run by student reporters 13 years of age and under who are assisted by teen editors ages 14 to 18. CE is based on the premise that young people not only understand but have valid perspectives on social, economic, and political issues. Through covering current events, CE promotes the written and verbal skills of participants, their critical thinking, and their awareness of national and international issues.

Currently, CE serves close to 1,000 youth annually from its ten bureaus and affiliated bureaus. In addition to its U.S. operations, CE has bureaus in Tokyo, Japan; CE United Kingdom operates bureaus in London, Newcastle, and Belfast, Northern Ireland, and satellite bureaus in a number of small towns in the U.K. Applicants are chosen on a first come, first served basis. CE reporters choose their own topics and which individuals to interview. Teenage editors then assist them in writing, editing, and producing their stories for publication.

In addition, participants and the young people they interview are urged to take part in roundtable discussions and workshops on specific social and political issues. Such meetings often include professional news anchors, educators, and policy analysts.

Through CE, young people gain skills in journalism and exposure to different views and ideas. The program has proven successful in promoting values such as patience, teamwork, tolerance, and compromise. A number of its graduates have gone on to pursue careers in professional journalism.

Involving Youth in the Design and Implementation of Community Service Projects
Youth as Resources, Washington, D.C.

Developed in 1987, Youth as Resources (YAR) views young people as valuable assets and provides youth with a means to contribute to the welfare of their communities. In the process, youth gain decision-making and other life and leadership skills.

The key components of the YAR model are youth-adult partnership in governance, youth as grantmakers, and youth-led service. YAR programs, governed by local youth-adult boards, award grants to youth volunteers to design and carry out community service projects.

YAR is unique because youth, not adults, research, plan, and lead the projects. Youth receiving grants require a sponsoring local nonprofit organization to serve as a conduit for grant funds and an adult volunteer to

As emphasized throughout this chapter and across this textbook, the developmental system within which youth exist must always be considered. We cannot fully understand the impact of peers on the development of youth without also understanding the impact of the family and the other components of the adolescent's social world (e.g., his or her school, the media, and technology). Outcomes of the relations between the developing person and his or

help with troubleshooting and general oversight of the project while still allowing the youth to be in charge.

Now in over 70 communities in the United States as well as Canada, New Zealand, and Poland, YAR programs have involved more than 200,000 youth ranging in age from 5 to 21 in contributing to positive change in their communities. YAR programs engage young people in a wide range of settings, including community-based organizations, faith-based institutions, public housing, schools, and juvenile justice facilities.

Projects can last anywhere from several days to months. Examples of YAR projects include middle school students who provided tutoring to 21 classmates for whom English was not a first language, high school students who performed puppet skits with an antidrug message, and other young people who offered companionship to seniors and assisted them with their chores.

An outside evaluation of the program found YAR participants to have developed more caring attitudes and a greater stake in the well-being of their communities. The Center for Youth as Resources in Washington, D.C. serves as the umbrella organization for YAR. Through instructional materials, technical assistance, and training conducted by experienced youth and adults, CYAR helps local YAR programs start, develop, and expand.

Youth Community Leaders Promoting Health Among Their Peers

Child to Child, Oaxaca, Mexico

The Child to Child program began in Oaxaca, Mexico, in 1989. The program is an instance of an international effort, begun in 1979 in London, England, as part of the celebration of the International Year of the Child, and has the goal of promoting health and preventive health care among youth.

The program is based on the philosophy that youth are a resource in the promotion of the health of other young people and of the community more generally. The program uses youth leaders in a community to attract children and adolescents to participate in an effort to learn to analyze health problems in the community, to study them, to act to solve them, and ultimately to evaluate the results of their actions.

Using youth leaders from the community (termed "guides"), groups of about 10 youth, usually ranging in age from 8 to 12 years, are formed. Using activities that are fun for young people and build on their creativity (for example, involving drawing, theater, and the construction and use of puppets in puppet shows), the groups participate in "train the trainer" programs. The youth leaders train the young people in their group to act as trainers of other youth and of adults in their community in regard to healthy behaviors.

For example, many youth and families in Oaxaca suffer from malnutrition, and the youth are trained to instruct their peers and the adults in the community in the principles of good diet and nutrition. Education is provided about how to develop a family garden in which nutritious foods are grown. In addition, the youth get trained in and then teach basic first aid skills. Other activities involve the cleaning up of the rivers and streams in a community.

Currently the Oaxaca Child to Child program involves about 380 youth and about 100 guides from almost 30 communities in its "train the trainer" groups. These groups are reaching approximately 1,500 youth in these communities. All youth who work in the program are volunteers, and all activities pursued by the youth groups use recyclable materials (cardboard, newspapers, and plastic) or materials indigenous to the communities (e.g., corn husks, clay, or dried flowers).

Source: International Youth Foundation, 2001. <www.iyfnet.org>

her context can show considerable diversity in relation to the particular set of individual and social variables encountered at a particular time in life. In the case of peer relations, it appears that characteristics of the individual's peer status or reputation, characteristics of the peer group, and characteristics of the family need to be considered to understand how relationships with peers influence developmental outcomes for youth.

Summary

- Peer experiences can be understood by referring to several levels of social complexity within individuals, within interactions involving social relationships, and within groups.

- *Interactions* integrate the behaviors of two people in a social interaction, *relationships* involve a succession of interactions between two individuals committed to each other, and *groups* are a collection of interacting individuals who influence one another.

- Adolescents' peer relationships can be divided into several distinct groups of social networks: best friends, close friends, cliques, social crowds, and romantic relationships.

- Peer reputations can be determined by asking adolescents to nominate peers for certain positive or negative characteristics. Various types of peer reputations include popular, rejected, neglected, controversial, and average.

- Peer reputations remain relatively stable across adolescence. Peer group reputation is related to current and later life behavior and development.

- A friendship involves a reciprocal relationship acknowledged by the people in it and with reciprocal affection. Friendships are voluntary and they exist within a network of other relationships.

- As compared to younger adolescents, older adolescents have fewer friends, same-sex friends become more important, and friends equal or exceed parents as sources of support and advice.

- Parents impart values and attitudes to their children that influence their friendship selections. Parents also provide supervision to their adolescents and peers through chauffeuring, organizing play dates, and involving their children in activities.

- Across adolescence, youth become involved in crowds, or liaisons, of loosely affiliated youth based on a similar stereotype.

- A clique is a set of usually three or more people in a tightly knit, somewhat exclusive, and mutually reciprocating friendship based on a key common interest or identity.

- During early adolescence, friendships are structured around crowds and tend to be predominantly same sex. By the beginning of high school, most youth are in cliques, although crowds still exist.

- Good peer relationships are a mark of social competence, related to academic competence, and predictive of healthy development in adulthood.

- Youth with poor peer relationships are more likely to drop out of school, engage in criminal activity, and experience mental or behavioral problems.

- Adolescents with good friends tend to have high self-esteem and good behavioral competence; not having good friends is related to school dropout, delinquency and criminality, and poor personal adjustment.

- The three dimensions of friendship are simply having friends, who one has as a friend, and the quality of the friendship.

- Friendships marked by stability, engagement, and lack of deviance allow positive self-esteem to develop in the adolescent.

- Friendships with youth who have negative characteristics and who engage in antisocial or disruptive behaviors often lead the adolescent to do the same.

- Feelings of closeness to parents and peers develop in similar ways across adolescence. Intimacy with both parents and peers increases across the high school years. High intimacy with parents can be related to higher self-esteem, lower depression, greater interest in school, and involvement in extracurricular activities.

- Across adolescence there is a large decrease in time spent with parents and a large increase in time spent with peers. Thinking about the opposite sex and spending time with them increases across adolescence.

- As adolescents typically select peers who have attitudes similar to those maintained by their parents, there is great concordance among adolescents in their attitudes and values. Most adolescents have educational plans that are consistent with both parents and peers.

- Parents and peers can work together to support healthy behavior and development, and when there is a problem in one context, the other can compensate.

Discussion Topics

1. Why do girls tend to have more intimate social relationships than boys? Why are girls more bothered by negative interactions with their peers than boys? Think back on your close friendships as a young adolescent. What traits were the most important and defining in terms of whom you became close to? Did those traits maintain their importance in late adolescence? Do they hold importance now? If you have experienced a change in the traits you value most, what factors and experiences in your life influenced that change?

2. Why do we so naturally define/limit people to one reputation or another? Can reputations be supportive of one's development? Or, alternatively, must reputations always be considered destructive? Why is it so difficult to change one's reputation in high school and why is it so common for one's high school reputation to influence behavior in later life?

3. What traits defined the popular adolescents in your high school? The rejected ones? The neglected? The average? At your fifth year high school reunion, do you believe those reputations will still be warranted? What influences your response? Did your reputation in high school fairly describe you or your status among your peers? Does it stand up to the image you hold of yourself now?

4. How did your parents influence whom you were friends with in high school? Did you respond well to their involvement? Why or why not? When you look back on it now, can you better appreciate their influence and input? How does their previous involvement in your friendship choices impact the choices you make now?

5. The term *clique* is often associated with negative, exclusive behaviors among adolescents. Despite this association, research finds that one's membership in a clique is actually related with psychological well-being and is, therefore, a positive attribute. If you were a member of a clique in high school, do you recall behaving in ways that may have been harmful to your classmates? What was the impetus behind this behavior? Did the feeling of membership you gained from your clique support your social and emotional development? If so, in what ways?

6. In light of the growing presence of violence in U.S. schools, school personnel need to make every effort to reach out to all students and make them feel welcome and accepted. Think back to your high school years and the students who were either rejected or neglected. How did their reputations influence their experiences at school? Were any attempts made by students or the school administration to reach out to these adolescents? If so, what efforts were made and were they successful? Based on what you know about the tendency and desire to identify with and rely on cliques and crowds in adolescents, what factors would you have to consider if you were to design a school mission statement that would empower and be accepted and practiced by all students?

7. What was your main focus in high school, academics or social relationships? How did one impact the other?

8. Did you ever have to alter your own behaviors to fit in with your peer group? How comfortable were you with those changes? Did your popularity increase among your peer group as a result of these changes? How did the changes impact your relationship with your parents? Your siblings? Do you at all regret altering your behavior patterns to fit in?

9. Of the friendships you shared in adolescence, how would you describe the nature of the friendship that most supported the development of your self-esteem? Did it have a positive or a negative impact? How, if at all, has that relationship impacted your later development and the relationships you presently seek to maintain?

10. How many close friends of the opposite sex did you have in high school? What about your personality, self-esteem, and life experiences determined your interactions with the opposite sex during those years? How do your experiences from adolescence impact your relationships that you currently share with the opposite sex?

11. During adolescence, how well did the attitudes your parent(s) held about adolescent high-risk behavior correspond with the attitudes of your friends? Whose attitudes were more influential in terms of impacting the daily decisions you made? Who did you typically turn to for advice? Did it depend on the topic you sought advice about? Why did you feel more comfortable seeking out one party (friend or parent) over the other? Given the chance, is there advice you would like to offer your parents now regarding their openness and ability to discuss certain topics?

12. If, during your adolescent years, there was a part of your social context that had a negative impact on your development, how well did your other social contexts compensate for these negative influences?

Key Terms

average reputation (p. 212)
clique (p. 213)
controversial reputation (p. 212)
crowd (liaison) (p. 213)
display behaviors (p. 217)

friendship (p. 212)
group (p. 210)
interactions (p. 210)
neglected reputation (p. 212)
popular reputation (p. 212)

rejected reputation (p. 212)
relationships (p. 210)
social networks (p. 211)
stereotype (p. 213)

10

SEXUALITY
IN ADOLESCENCE

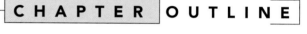

Beth looked at her reflection in the mirror. She turned her mouth up in a half smile and made sure her lipstick was evenly applied. Turning slightly she looked at her profile. She smoothed her shirt over her skirt and pulled at the sleeves.

"I have to look perfect for Steve," she said to herself.

Tonight was the first night Beth and Steve were going out and she wanted to make sure she looked nice. As Beth was putting away her lipstick the doorbell rang. Beth quickly flipped her hair, grabbed her coat, and ran down the stairs. She took a deep breath and opened the door to see Steve smiling at her.

"You look great. Ready to go?" he asked, giving her a big smile.

"Yep," she replied, blushing a little.

They got into his car and started driving. Beth was not sure where they were going, but she didn't really care. Steve reached over and placed his hand on her knee. Beth felt her stomach do a flip-flop. A few minutes later they pulled into a deserted park. Steve turned off the car and turned toward Beth. Beth's palms were sweating and she twitched nervously.

Steve reached over and lifted her face up to his. She looked at him and he moved in to kiss her. Beth moved away. This was not what she had thought her first date with Steve would be like. Steve moved in again, and this time they kissed and he put his hand on her chest. Beth pushed his hand away but he persisted.

"Aw come on," he whined.

"Please don't," she said quietly.

"You expect me to stop when you show up looking like that?" he retorted as he continued to kiss her.

Beth admitted to herself that she had dressed to get Steve's attention. But this was not the attention she wanted. She didn't know what to do.

LEARNING OBJECTIVES

1. To recognize the ways that male and female adolescents differ in their conception of romance and dating.

2. To understand what influences adolescents' styles of sexual behavior.

3. To understand why current research on adolescence should address the complexity of developmental contexts and issues experienced by homosexual youth.

4. To understand the ways in which heterosexism and homonegativity represent important obstacles to healthy development for homosexual youth.

5. To understand some of the sexual problems and risks faced by contemporary adolescents.

6. To learn the prevalence of STDs in the United States and the behaviors that increase adolescents' risk of contracting HIV infection and/or other STDs.

7. To understand what contributes to the effectiveness of AIDS intervention programs that address problem behaviors involved in contracting HIV infection.

8. To understand the conditions under which adolescent girls in the United States usually experience unwanted sex.

9. To understand how pubertal maturation, fantasies about sexual experiences, role expectations, attitudes regarding sex, and societal norms influence adolescents' sexual behavior.

10. To understand the characteristics of the community context that might influence adolescent attitudes toward sexual activity.

What do Beth and other adolescents in her situation do? What about Steve? What can be expected in regard to sexual behaviors among contemporary youth?

This chapter addresses these questions and explains why sexuality and dating are some of the greatest concerns of adolescents and of the adults who worry about them. Given the importance attached to sexuality in contemporary society, the attendant pleasures, and the danger ranging from sexual abuse and violence, exploitation, disease, and unwanted pregnancy and childbirth, it is obvious why there is so much concern about adolescent sexuality.

As noted in Chapter 3, the adolescent's hormonal balance changes throughout this period. The genitals develop to their nearly adult form. Both males and females begin to experience new feelings, including new bodily functions such as menstruation for females and ejaculation of seminal fluid for males. Perhaps more important than these physical changes are the social and psychological changes that accompany adolescence. Given the cognitive changes that occur during adolescence (see Chapter 4), it is not surprising that sexual behavior and sexual interaction take on new meanings as the adolescent begins to think about social events in school, parties outside of school, love, and dating.

Dating and Romance

Issue to Consider

• In what ways do male and female adolescents differ in their conception of romance and dating?

The character of romantic relationships changes across adolescence (Furman & Brown, 1999). A key facet of this development involves developing the skills to regulate the intense emotions associated with these relationships (Larson, Clore, & Wood, 1999). Support derived from other close, loving relationships, for instance with parents, may aid this regulation (Gray & Steinberg, 1999).

During adolescence, especially in its early and middle years (e.g., through about 11 years of age or so), most youth have dating experiences that are brief in duration but intense in regard to the frequency of contact (Feiring, 1996). Feelings of affiliation rather than attachment characterize young adolescents' conceptions of romance, with girls stressing the interpersonal qualities of those with whom they are romantically involved and boys emphasizing the importance of physical attraction (Feiring, 1996).

In a study of sexual behaviors and attitudes among high school students with a steady dating partner in the Kingdom of Swaziland, in southern

Africa, "traditional" gender differences were found (McLean, 1995). Although most youth were sexually active by the age of 16, girls stressed the importance of demonstrating affection more than boys and were less supportive of multiple sexual partners.

A study of American 12- to 19-year-olds indicates that the ages of acceptable dating partners among male and female adolescents range from partners who are about their own age (for girls dating boys) or slightly younger (for boys dating girls), to partners who are somewhat above their own ages (Kenrick et al., 1996). Males, however, reported that their ideal attractive partners would be several years older than themselves (Kenrick et al., 1996).

Dating and romantic relationships are important parts of adolescents' sexual development.

Across adolescence, especially during the early portions of this period, adolescents' romantic inclinations are not always directed exclusively to people they know personally. Adolescents often have relatively brief romantic attractions—crushes, if you will—to movie or music stars or to other people falling in the category of teenage idols. Parents often get concerned about such crushes, but, as explained in Parenting Box 10.1, attractions to teenage idols may serve very useful functions in the development of romantic emotions in adolescence.

Given this diversity in adolescents' ideas about dating and romance, it is not surprising to learn there are also differences among youth in the sorts of sexual behaviors in which they engage. These behaviors influence the person's emotions, social relationships, and often health throughout adolescence and may often have important implications for the rest of the adolescent's life, especially when problems of sexuality arise.

Adolescent Sexuality Today

The nature and extent of adolescent sexual activity clearly have changed in recent years. Several different patterns, or styles, of sexual behavior character-

ize contemporary adolescents. Many of these styles are linked to engagement in sexual behaviors that place the young person at risk of experiencing health, psychological, and social problems. The characteristics of contemporary adolescent sexual behavior and the nature and bases of the problems adolescents encounter in the expression of their sexuality are covered later. This discussion focuses on the diversity of patterns of sexual behavior that develop in adolescence, the role of the context in influencing this diversity, and the importance of the relations that adolescents have with their contexts in fostering both problems of sexual behavior *and* solutions to these problems.

Styles of Adolescent Sexual Behavior

Issue to Consider
• What influences adolescents' styles of sexual behavior?

Today, adolescents develop many different styles or patterns of sexual behaviors. For instance, Australian youth in grades 10 through 12 cluster into five different sexual style groups: sexually naïve, sexually unassured, sexually competent, sexually adventurous, and sexually driven (Buzwell &

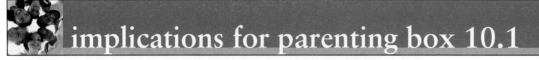

Teen Idols: Celebrity Crushes Actually Help Your Child Learn About Love

When 11-year-old Janet broke her arm, her parents' biggest worry was getting her to the hospital as fast as possible. Janet's greatest concern, however, was not the pain, nor even the disruption the injury would cause to her sports schedule. "Promise me you won't forget!" she pleaded with her parents in the emergency room. "You *have* to tape *Dawson's Creek!*"

How much does the show mean to Janet? Only everything. Its characters are central to the lives of her group of friends. Posters of the cast members cover much of the available space on their bedroom walls, and the girls pass along fan magazines offering glimpses into the actors' lives. They debate which of the guys is the cutest and fantasize about meeting them face-to-face.

All this can be tough for a parent to endure. If you've ever spent an evening listening to the stereo in your daughter's room play the same Backstreet Boys song over and over (and over), or if you've ever wished that your son spent more time studying and less time mooning over the *Sports Illustrated* swimsuit issue, you know what we mean. But your preteen's fixation on a teen idol is more than just a drain on the allowance; it provides a safe stepping stone on the path to adult feelings and roles.

Girls Develop Celebrity Crushes before Boys Do

You may notice your child's devotion to a certain pop-culture figure as early as 8 or 9; girls, who gener-

ally mature a couple of years sooner than boys, likewise tend to develop crushes earlier. However, it's generally not until the early teen years, when an interest in romantic relationships collides with a developing skill in abstract thought, that the swooning really begins.

Being infatuated with an idol offers a young teen a number of advantages over a relationship that involves actual dating. A real-life failure would be devastating to a child this age, but by imagining how attractive and witty she would be with her renowned crush, she boosts her self-esteem without risk of public deflation.

In addition, your child's fixation on a persona shaped by popular culture can offer her social benefits; if all your 13-year-old's friends like the same rock group or the cast of a particular television show, the conversation naturally turns to such hallowed questions as "Which one do you like best?" Chatting about their idols and acquiring photos, T-shirts, and tapes of them offers teens a common interest.

Talking about the doings of the cute and famous also allows the participants to share and test their values ("I heard he was arrested for drunk driving." "That *has* to be a lie! I *know* he doesn't drink!") And it gives a child the chance to assert that she's her own person. When The Beatles were popular in the 1960s, Paul McCartney was almost universally regarded as "the cute one;" announcing Ringo as her favorite was one way for a girl to show

---

Rosenthal, 1996). Youth in some of the style groups (e.g., adventurous, driven) take more risks in regard to sex with both casual and regular partners (e.g., in regard to the number of sexual partners they had in the last 6 months or the number of "one-night stands") (Buzwell & Rosenthal, 1996).

Youth in other nations and/or from diverse racial/ethnic backgrounds also develop particular styles of sexual behaviors. Among youth living in Norway, the development of sexuality is marked by slow growth and experimentation (Jakobsen, 1997), whereas Mexican adolescents working in factories are more sexually active and less likely to use contraception than are adolescents enrolled in schools

(Huerta-Franco, Diaz de Leon, & Malacara, 1996). Additionally, Asian American youth have fewer sexual partners than do European American youth (McLaughlin et al., 1997).

Adolescents' family relationships and family communication patterns are often associated with the sexual styles they develop. In a study of about 750 African American adolescents and their mothers, little agreement was found in regard to level of shared communication about sex, satisfaction with the parent-child relationship, maternal disapproval of adolescent sexual activity, and adolescent sexual behavior (Jaccard, Dittus, & Gordon, 1998). Mothers tended to underestimate the sexual activity

her independence. (It also meant less competition for her idol's imagined attention.)

Finally, a crush on an idol—like a crush on a "real" but unattainable person, such as a teacher or a popular older teen—helps prepare a teen for age-appropriate dating. She can rehearse how she might feel, act, and talk, as well as the responses she might get from her idealized date. (Of course, if she really met her idol, she'd be dumbstruck.)

All these are perfectly good reasons *not* to belittle your child's lovestruck extremes, no matter how patience-testing they become. Instead, acknowledge her feelings. Tell her about your own preteen crushes. ("I remember seeing *Bye Bye Birdie* 13 days in a row, just to see Ann-Margret.") Let her know how you felt ("She acted as if Bobby Rydell was so cool. I thought, 'Humph. She'd drop him in a minute for me.'")

Granted, it's harder to foster a sense of shared experience when your child's teen idol's hairstyle, behavior, or song lyrics are abhorrent to you. But saying, "How can you *like* someone like that?" won't get you anywhere. And, tempting as it might be, taking away the posters and CDs won't take away the fantasy. Instead, ask your child what she likes about her celebrity crush. If possible, mention something you like about him ("He *does* have a cute smile, and he's a good dancer") before mentioning specifics that concern you ("I really don't like the way he treats the women in his videos"). Again,

sharing your memories may help—perhaps you adored Mick Jagger, and felt betrayed after his arrest for drug possession.

Your child's choice of idols can be revealing

You might also ask your child how he'd feel if a girl he dated did some of the things his idol does on her show—a question that could lead to a discussion of what qualities he finds attractive in girls. Although you may not change his mind about his idol, you'll have given him food for thought. *And* you will have shown him that you respect his feelings and views. In general, infatuation with teen heartthrobs wanes as your child gets a social foothold in high school, although it's normal to maintain some fantasies about famous people into adulthood—witness the middle-aged Fabio fans. Although an occasional teenage crush is both common and healthy, you should be concerned if your preteen's infatuation is interfering with friendships or is leading to problems with schoolwork. If that's the case, your child may need some professional help in developing his social skills or addressing some other underlying problem.

Source: Lerner, R. M., & Olson, C. K. (1995, September). Teen idols. *Parents*, pp. 91–92.

of their daughters, and adolescents tended to underestimate their mothers' level of disapproval for engaging in sexual behaviors (Jaccard et al., 1998). Given these differences in communication and perception, it is perhaps understandable that the adolescents' reports, as compared to mothers' reports, were more associated with adolescent sexual behaviors (Jaccard et al., 1998). In a similar study among Mexicans, the communication pattern that 12- to 19-year-old adolescents had with their mothers was related to the initiation of sexual relations, contraceptive use, and pregnancy (Pick & Palos, 1995).

In another study of about 1,800 junior high school students in the United States, females saw par-

ents as less approving of sex than boys did, and yet girls were more likely than boys to discuss sex and dating practices with parents (De Gaston, Weed, & Jensen, 1966). Females reported more often than boys that parents had more rules, were more likely to believe that parents were unfair, and were more apt to report they had violated parental rules (De Gaston et al., 1996). In a related study of more than 8,300 youth raised in families that belong to the Seventh-Day Adventist religion, engagement by youth in behaviors discouraged by their family's religion (e.g., going to a movie theater or participating in competitive sports) was associated with early sexual activity (Weinbender & Rossignol, 1996).

In essence, adolescents show different patterns of sexual behavior. Some behaviors (e.g., early, unprotected sex) are linked to the problems and risks to their health and positive development more so than other behaviors (e.g., dating). These problems and risks are discussed later in this chapter.

Although, in terms of proportions, a logical assumption might be that most of the youth involved as participants in the just noted research on adolescent sexuality are heterosexual and that most of the styles of sexual expression among these youth involved members of the opposite sex, many adolescents have homosexual sexual orientations or are bisexual in their sexual orientation.

Homosexuality in Adolescence

Issue to Consider

• Why should current research on adolescence address the complexity of developmental contexts and issues experienced by homosexual youth?

Many of the studies of the development of sexuality during adolescence do not explicitly investigate whether the youth being studied are heterosexual or homosexual. As Grotevant (1998, p. 1116) has explained, many summaries of research knowledge about the development of adolescent sexuality

> generally carry the presumption that these emerging sexual relationships are heterosexual; yet awareness of gay, lesbian, and bisexual identities and relationships is growing in the popular culture and the research literature as well (D'Augelli & Patterson, 1995; Herdt, 1989; Oswald, 1994; Savin-Williams, 1990, 1994).
>
> Developmental challenges facing gay or lesbian youth are multifaceted and illustrate the need to understand adolescent development in context. Their erotic fantasies and experiences typically do not mesh with the messages they see portrayed in the media; they may feel isolated from peers and unable to discuss their feelings with family members; their sense of identity involves coming to terms not only with this sexual identity but also with how it relates to other identity domains; their emerging sexual orientation may clash with their racial, ethnic, or religious affiliations in such a way that they must hide their true feelings; and their behavior may put them at high risk for exposure to AIDS or drug use. Although there has been a significant increase in research activity relating to the development of homosexual behavior and identity, much work remains to be undertaken.

Romance and dating are significant features of relationships among gay and lesbian youth.

Savin-Williams (1999) agrees with the need for research and argues that both scholars and society must enhance their understanding of the complex developmental situation for gay, lesbian, and bisexual youth that Grotevant (1998) describes. He notes, "Investigators often explore the effects of gender, social class, religion, race, intelligence, and countless other human qualities in their empirical investigations, but rarely is sexual orientation or identity included" (Savin-Williams, 1999, pp. 151–152). He emphasizes,

> Few sexual minorities want special rights, only adequate rights. They want the right not to be psychologically and physically harmed. They want to lead their lives as we all do. They want to see the murders of young people stopped, regardless of the victim's sexuality, race-ethnicity, social class, or sex. Gay activists alone cannot fulfill these aspirations. As professionals, we are afforded an invaluable opportunity to contribute to the struggle for justice by the way we conduct research, teach courses, and confront heterosexism and homonegativity. (Savin-Williams, 1999, p. 154)

Ritch Savin-Williams continues his research on gay, lesbian, and bisexual youth. His recent work is presented in Meet the Researcher Box 10.1.

MEET THE RESEARCHER BOX 10.1

RITCH SAVIN WILLIAMS
THE DEVELOPMENT OF YOUTH WHO EXPERIENCE SAME-SEX ATTRACTIONS

In my research, teaching, and clinical practice during the last two decades I have explored the developmental milestones of youths with physical and romantic attractions for members of their own sex. It should be understood that many youths who experience same-sex attractions and sexual behavior never identify as a sexual minority. Indeed, fewer than 2% of all adolescents classify themselves as lesbian, gay, or bisexual, although far more might were it not for negative societal stereotypes and discrimination.

Ritch Savin-Williams is a professor in the Department of Human Development and Family Studies in the College of Human Ecology at Cornell University.

Through in-depth interviews conducted during the last decade, these youths have shared with me their first awareness that they might be different from other youths because they have sexual desires toward their own sex. This early awareness can begin with first memories that average third grade and proceeds through self-recognition, self-labeling, disclosure of this information to friends and family, sexual and romantic encounters, and a sense of resolution. This process can occur over a few years or a lifetime. When these milestones are reached and how they are negotiated differ based on a youth's gender, personality, family history, and life experiences.

One of the most striking changes that has occurred during the past few years is the earlier age of reaching these milestones, including disclosing to family members, often while still living at home. This contrasts markedly with earlier cohorts of youths, most of whom remained safely hidden and tightly closeted until they moved into their own apartment or dorm room. Thus adolescents are coping with family reactions earlier, more immediately, and for longer periods of time than those who grew up during any previous generation. A second noteworthy lesson from the youths' narratives is that many of the developmental issues they face as sexual-minority adolescents are the same ones faced by other youths regardless of their sexual orientation: concern with being popular, having an early curfew, engaging in sexual relations, relating to parents, and selecting a college. A third discovery is that their lives are diverse and complex. There is no one way "to be gay" or to have a "gay lifestyle." Some youths are troubled and some are resilient, but most are ordinary. This full spectrum of sexual-minority youths has seldom been acknowledged or celebrated. I have written about these issues in the lives of youths in *". . . And Then I Became Gay": Young Men's Stories* (1998, Routledge) and *"Mom, Dad, I'm gay." How Families Negotiate Coming Out* (2001, APA Press). The third book in this trilogy will focus on the life stories of young women. The experiences of girls appear to differ markedly from most boys. For example, many young women first recognize their same-sex attractions through crushes and infatuations with other girls, and not through physical cues, and tell a best friend as soon as they become aware of their romantic attractions.

I am equally fascinated by the ways in which sexual-minority youths cope with peer victimization and harassment, societal condemnation, and family disappointment to become healthy, resilient individuals who develop romantic relationships, raise children, and become major contributors to our culture. Sexual-minority youths are fabulously successful navigating the terrains of their sexuality to become healthy, well-functioning adults. This resiliency—a necessary adaptation to living in heterocentric and homonegative environments—is generally not recognized in the popular media, which tend to emphasize the "doom and gloom" of gay youths. The visibility given to same-sex attracted individuals, however, has helped by giving adolescents positive role models to emulate and pride with being associated with such individuals. They thus learn to refute societal and religious stereotypes to experience the joy and diversity of life.

Nearly every junior high school student today knows what homosexuality is and most families have a sexual-minority member or know someone who is. It is nearly impossible not to see homosexuality portrayed on television or in the movies or written about in magazines or newspapers. Individuals might attempt to deny its existence, but this is becoming increasingly difficult with each gay pride march held or denied, each law passed or rejected, or each adoption granted or refused. Indeed, it is now possible to be young, gay, and proud and to live an ordinary life as someone who falls in love with someone of his or her own gender.

Homosexuality in Adolescence: Definitions and Prevalence Scholars who define homosexuality refer to one or more components of sexual orientation, that is, emotional attraction, behavior, self-definitions, targets of sexual fantasies, and affiliation in a given social community (Remafedi, 1985, 1991). **Homosexuality** may be defined as the orientation of such components to people of the same gender as oneself (Remafedi, 1991). The classic interviews conducted by Kinsey and his colleagues (Kinsey, Pomeroy, & Martin, 1948; with Gebhard, 1953) are still useful in providing estimates of the incidence of homosexuality. Kinsey et al. report that about 37% of males and 13% of females have had at least one homosexual experience that has resulted in orgasm. In turn, 8% of men and about 1% to 3% of women were reported to be exclusively homosexual. Because an awareness of same-sex attraction and arousal usually starts during early adolescence, typically after pubertal changes have begun to occur (Savin-Williams, 1991), it makes sense that these estimates of prevalence have been applied to adolescent populations (Remafedi, 1991).

Homosexuality and Individual and Social Development During Adolescence There is variation in the implications of homosexuality for adolescent psychosocial development (Remafedi, 1991). As with all youth, the sense of self for homosexual youth is influenced by many factors. In a study of 85 lesbian adolescents and 87 gay male adolescents, variables important for the males' identities included political ideology, socioeconomic status, heterosexual friends, and gender nonconformity (Waldner-Haugrud & Magruder, 1996). For females, key variables were religion and the importance of school (Waldner-Haugrud & Magruder, 1996). In a related study of African American adolescent male homosexuals, ranging in age from 16 to 21 years, all participants reported that they understood their sexual minority status and were comfortable with their sexual identities (Edwards, 1996). Despite the fact that, at the time of the study, all participants were living their lives as heterosexuals

Homosexuality Sexual orientation to people of the same gender as oneself.

Heterosexism Sexual orientation to people of the opposite gender as oneself.

Homonegativity Expressing negative attitudes toward homosexuals.

(Edwards, 1996), the youth had positive perceptions of themselves (Edwards, 1996).

Homosexual adolescents may face obstacles to healthy development as a consequence of their sexual orientations. As Savin-Williams (1999) has explained, key bases of these obstacles are **heterosexism** and **homonegativity.** In a study of more than 1,000 youth in grades 10 through 12 from Newfoundland and Labrador, Canada, male adolescents were more likely than female adolescents to possess homonegative attitudes, as well as gender-stereotypic attitudes and erroneous beliefs about sexual coercion (Morrison et al., 1997). Better grades for both male and female adolescents were associated with less homonegativity.

Homonegative attitudes are all too often translated into violence against gay and lesbian youth (Savin-Williams, 1999; Van de Ven, 1995). Adolescent perpetrators of such violence have attitudes toward gays and lesbians that, in addition to their homonegativity, may be characterized by ambivalence, defensiveness, and adherence to myths and stereotypes about gay and lesbian lifestyle (Van de Ven, 1995).

Across the adolescent age range there are some indications of poor adjustment (e.g., suicide attempts; Hershberger, Pilkington, & D'Augelli, 1997) that occur more among homosexual youth than among heterosexual youth (Remafedi, 1991). In addition, when the obstacles to healthy development affect gay, lesbian, and bisexual youth, younger adolescents may be particularly at risk for problems of psychosocial adjustment (Remafedi, 1991).

In a study of about 200 gay, lesbian, and bisexual youth aged 15 to 21 years (Hershberger et al., 1997), youth who had made suicide attempts were more likely than youth who had not made suicide attempts to have disclosed their sexual orientations to others in a more complete manner. The former group of youth had lost more friends due to their disclosures and had experienced more victimization due to their sexual orientation (Hershberger et al., 1997). The suicide attempters also had lower self-esteem and more mental health problems than did the youth who had not attempted suicide (Hershberger et al., 1997). Substance use and abuse had been found to be prevalent among gay, lesbian, and bisexual youth, with lesbian youth particularly at risk for substance abuse (Rosario, Hunter, & Gwadz, 1997).

As discussed in further detail later, substance abuse, particularly intravenous drug use (Rotheram-Borus & Koopman, 1991), is linked to other risks during adolescence. Although a risk to all adolescents practicing unsafe sex and/or drug practices, particularly for gay, lesbian, and bisexual youth, a major risk during adolescence is **AIDS (Acquired Immune Deficiency Syndrome)**. During the 1980s and 1990s AIDS became a major problem among homosexual youth (Sussman & Duffy, 1996), with about 80% of AIDS cases in homosexual youth due to unsafe sexual practices (Remafedi, 1988, 1991). As a consequence, preventive educational interventions, as well as testing for the **HIV** antibody, are recommended for all youth, but particularly for homosexual youth who engage in unsafe sexual practices and substance abuse involving intravenous drug use (Remafedi, 1991; Rotherman-Borus & Koopman, 1991; Sussman & Duffy, 1996).

Unfortunately, homonegativity and heterosexism are associated with barriers to the receipt of effective services by gay and lesbian youth (Travers & Schneider, 1996). Youth attempting to receive treatment for addictions report feeling marginalized, harassed, and misinformed by treatment facility staff (Travers & Schneider, 1996). Youth say that these agencies avoid gay and lesbian issues, give them early discharge, or participate in revealing their sexual orientations (Travers & Schneider, 1996).

Teenage pregnancy is a significant life event for many adolescents.

Conclusions About Contemporary Adolescent Sexuality

Today's adolescents express their sexuality in diverse ways. Many of these styles of expression are associated with positive engagement with peers, dating, romance, and the building of a foundation for later adult sexuality. Some of the ways in which youth express their sexuality involve risky sexual behaviors (e.g., adventurous sexual actions, early initiation of sexual intercourse) as well as other types of behavioral risks (e.g., substance use and abuse). Because contemporary adolescence is fraught with problems associated with sexual behavior, we discuss the nature and extent of these relationships next.

Contemporary Problems of Adolescent Sexual Behavior

Issue to Consider

- What are some of the sexual problems and risks faced by contemporary adolescents?

Depending on personal values, the definition of what constitutes a sexual problem may vary from person to person. Most researchers who study adolescent sexuality would, however, now agree on at least one fact: A greater number of adolescents have sexual intercourse before reaching adulthood than at any previous time in U.S. history. Most agree that when adolescents are forced to have sex they do not want, have unwanted pregnancies, bear children they

AIDS (Acquired Immune Deficiency Syndrome) Condition of acquired deficiency of the immune system caused by the presence of a retrovirus.

HIV Type of retrovirus (human immunodeficiency virus) responsible for AIDS.

are neither emotionally nor financially capable of supporting, or contract sexually transmitted diseases, their sexuality is associated with problems and risk for their future healthy development.

Numerous illustrations indicate the presence of such sexual problems and risks among contemporary adolescents. These include the following:

- Each year, 1 million adolescents become pregnant (di Mauro, 1995); about half have babies. Indeed, about every minute, an American adolescent has a baby (Children's Defense Fund, 1995).

- Of adolescents who give birth, 46% go on welfare within 4 years; of *unmarried* adolescents who give birth, 73% go on welfare within 4 years (Lerner, 1995).

- By age 18, 25% of American females have been pregnant at least once (Coates & Van Widenfelt, 1991).

- Over the last three decades, the age of first intercourse has declined. Higher proportions of adolescent girls and boys reported being sexually experienced at each age between the ages of 15 and 20 in 1988 than in the early 1970s. In 1988, 27% of girls and 33% of boys had intercourse by their fifteenth birthday (Carnegie Corporation of New York, 1995).

- Pregnancy rates for girls younger than 15 years of age rose 4.1% between 1980 and 1988, a rate higher than for any other teenage age group (Carnegie Corporation of New York, 1995).

- In 1993 the proportion of all births to teenagers who were unmarried was 71.8%. This rate represents an increase of 399% since 1963 (Children's Defense Fund, 1996).

- By the end of adolescence about 80% of males and about 70% of females have become sexually active. As shown in Figure 10.1 these rates represent significant increases across a 15 year period (Alan Guttmacher Institute, 1994; Carnegie Corporation of New York, 1995).

- Among sexually active female adolescents, 27% of 15- to 17-year-olds and 16% of 18- to 19-year-olds use no method of contraception. Among Latino, African American, and European American adolescents, the percentage of females not using contraception is 35%, 23%, and 19%, respectively (U.S. Department of Health and Human Services, 1996).

- Among sexually active male adolescents in 1991, 21% reported using no contraception at their last intercourse. An additional 56% of males used a condom and 23% relied on their female partner to use contraception (U.S. Department of Health and Human Services, 1996).

- By age 20, 74% of males and 57% of females who became sexually active by age 14 or younger have had six or more sexual partners (U.S. Department of Health and Human Services, 1996).

- In 1991, 38% of the pregnancies among 15- to 19-year-olds ended in abortion (U.S. Department of Health and Human Services, 1996).

- By age 19, 15% of African American males have fathered a child; the corresponding rates for Latinos and European Americans is 11% and 7%, respectively (Coates & Van Widenfelt, 1991). Moreover, 74% of European American youth, 76% of Latino youth, and 95% of African American youth are unmarried at the birth of their first child (Marsiglio, 1987). Teenage fathers are often absentee fathers (Neville & Parke, 1991). Among 14- to 21-year-old fathers, about 40% were absentee (Lerman, 1985).

- Thirty-nine percent of children born to 15-year-olds and 47% of children born to 16-year-olds have fathers older than 20 years of age (U.S. Department of Health and Human Services, 1996). Between 30% to 40% of adolescent mothers have been impregnated by males who have not yet reached their 20th birthday (Elster, 1991).

- Women who become mothers as teenagers are more likely to live in poverty later in their lives than women who delay childbearing. Although 28% of women who gave birth as teenagers were poor in their 20s and 30s, only 7% of women who gave birth after adolescence were living in poverty in their 20s and 30s (Carnegie Corporation of New York, 1995).

- About $25 billion in federal money is spent annually to provide social, health, and welfare services to families begun by teenagers (di Mauro, 1995).

- In 1992, the federal government spent nearly $34 billion on Aid to Families with Dependent Children, Medicaid, and food stamps for families begun by adolescents (Carnegie Corporation of New York, 1995).

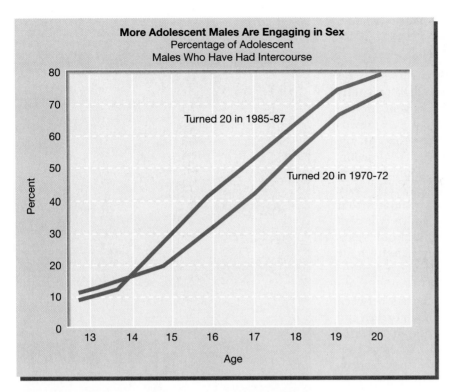

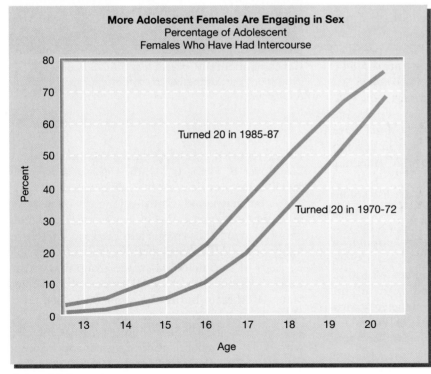

Figure 10.1
Current cohorts of adolescents are more sexually active than cohorts of just 15 years ago: percentages of adolescent males and adolescent females who have had intercourse by age and in relation to the dates in which they reached their twentieth birthdays. (*Source*: Carnegie Corporation of New York, 1995.)

The scope and variation of the problems just noted pertinent to contemporary adolescent sexual behavior is staggering. The magnitude and diversity of the manifestation of these problems is challenging U.S. educational, health care, and social service systems.

A full appreciation of the breadth and complexity of any of these problems of adolescent sexuality requires greater depth of discussion. In all cases, such discussion indicates that the adolescent's relations to his or her context is both a basis of the problems of adolescent sexuality and a potential route to addressing the problems.

Accordingly, to illustrate the person-context relational character of the problems of adolescent sexuality, we discuss two key problems. One, involving AIDS and other sexually transmitted diseases, cannot only diminish the adolescent's life chances but can also eliminate his or her chances of even *having* a life. The other key problem is sexual abuse, involving unwanted sex and date rape in particular. Sexual abuse may profoundly impact the safety and self-esteem of the young people involved in this problem.

AIDS and Other Sexually Transmitted Diseases (STDs)

Issues to Consider

- How prevalent are STDs in the United States?

• Why must we take into account the latency period for HIV when talking about the prevalence of AIDS among adolescents?

The **CDC (Centers for Disease Control)** estimates that about 12 million cases of **STDs (sexually transmitted diseases)** occur each year in the Unites States, and approximately two thirds involve people younger than 25 years of age (Boyer, Shafer, & Tschann, 1997). Adolescents between 15 and 19 years of age account for 25% of the sexually transmitted disease (STD) cases each year. In addition, the CDC estimates that about 25% of all sexually active youth will contract an STD during their high school years (Boyer et al., 1997). Adolescents usually have higher rates of STDs than all other age groups (St. Lawrence et al., 1995a).

U.S. cases are estimated to comprise between 24% to 30% of all reported cases of gonorrhea and between 10% to 12% of all reported cases of syphilis (St. Lawrence et al., 1995a). Whereas gonorrhea rates in older age groups have been decreasing, rates among adolescents have either stayed the same or increased (St. Lawrence et al., 1995a). Inner-city ethnic minority adolescents have a particularly high risk for STD contraction.

The best current predictor of the spread of AIDS among adolescents is their rate of STD infection (St. Lawrence et al., 1995a). AIDS was first recognized as a separate disease in 1981 (Boyer & Hein, 1991). Over the past two decades AIDS has become an epidemic in the United States and throughout the world, particularly in developing nations (e.g., in Africa; Araoye & Adegoke, 1996).

Concerns about HIV infection and AIDS are a prominent part of the world of contemporary adolescents.

Because no precise studies have examined the prevalence of AIDS across the general adolescent population (St. Lawrence et al., 1995a), the exact number of adolescents infected with the human immunodeficiency virus (HIV) causing AIDS is unknown (Rotheram-Borus & Koopman, 1991). Although the relative number of reported cases of AIDS among adolescents is small (e.g., only about 1% of the total num-ber of reported cases falls in the second decade of life; Boyer & Hein, 1991), the disease is probably much more prevalent during adolescence. HIV has a long **latency period** (that is, a long period between infection and appearance of symptoms), averaging about 8 years (Boyer & Hein, 1991). Therefore, many of the AIDS cases that appear among people 20 years of age and older, an age group that constitutes about one fifth of all AIDS cases in the United States (Rotheram-Borus & Koopman, 1991), probably involve infection during adolescence (St. Lawrence et al., 1995a). Moreover, as is the case with STDs in general, there are disproportionate rates of HIV infection among African American and Latino youth (Sigelman et al., 1996).

Preventing HIV Infection and AIDS Medical advances continue to be made in the treatment of

HIV infection and AIDS. However, because, at this writing, there is still no cure for the disease, the prevention of infection remains the best way to avoid the spread of AIDS (Boyer & Hein, 1991).

HIV infection, as well as the contraction of STDs, occur in relation to other behaviors that place the adolescent at risk. Chapter 13 focuses on the nature of and interrelation among risk behaviors in adolescence. Note that HIV infection is related to engagement in unsafe sexual practices (e.g., failure to use a condom during intercourse), intravenous drug use, and delinquent behaviors such as running away from home (Rotheram-Borus & Koopman, 1991; St. Lawrence et al., 1995b). Of the 750,000 to 1 million adolescent youth in the United States who run away from home *each year,* 6.4% have positive serum tests for HIV (Rotheram-Borus & Koopman, 1991). These runaway youth often engage in unsafe sex, prostitution, and intravenous drug use. Thus each year up to 64,000 "time bombs" are going out onto the streets of U.S. towns and cities and spreading a disease that will kill them and the other people with whom they engage in unsafe sexual and drug use–related behaviors.

Programs that seek to prevent AIDS need to direct their efforts to the cluster of problem behaviors involved in HIV infection, and not just to AIDS prevention per se (Boyer & Hein, 1991; Dryfoos, 1990; Lerner, 1998). When these intervention programs involve attempts to promote multiple changes in youth, such as better knowledge *and* more skills, they appear to be more effective than efforts directed to changing only one feature of adolescent behavior and development. Skill training appears to be especially useful. Applications Box 10.1 describes the results of several intervention programs aimed at changing risky behavior and knowledge about HIV and AIDS through education or skill training.

Sexual Violence: Unwanted Sex and Date Rape

Issues to Consider

- How is the experience of sexual abuse related to later behavior problems?
- Under what conditions do adolescent girls in the United States usually experience unwanted sex?
- In what way may family and peer contexts increase a girl's likelihood of experiencing unwanted sexual activity?

Sexual abuse of and violence toward youth is all too common in America. There were 150,000 substantiated cases of sexual abuse of youth in the United States in 1993 and perhaps as many as an additional 350,000 instances of such assaults (Finkelhor, 1994). In fact, sexual abuse during childhood and adolescence involves about 20% of all females and between 5% and 10% of all males (Finkelhor, 1994; Luster & Small, 1997). About 20% of adolescent girls in grades 8 through 11 are subjected to sexual harassment, and 75% of girls under the age of 14 who have had sexual relations are victims of rape (di Mauro, 1995). Thus sex is usually forced among young adolescent girls (Carnegie Corporation of New York, 1995).

These experiences have profound impacts on the behavior and development of young people. In a study of about 45,500 adolescents, the experience of sexual abuse, especially when coupled with physical abuse, was linked to problems such as binge drinking and suicidal ideation (Luster & Small, 1997). The negative outcomes of sexual abuse were lessened by high levels of parental monitoring and of support from at least one parent (Luster & Small, 1997).

Given the widespread nature of sexual abuse in American society, it is perhaps not surprising that many adolescent girls experience unwanted sexual activity by dates or boyfriends. For instance, the rate of rape among youth aged 16 to 19 years is 1.9 per 1,000 girls and, from 1973 and 1987, 11% of female rape victims were between 12 and 15 years old and 25% were between 16 and 19 years of age (Kershner, 1996). Adolescent males between the ages of 12 and 20 years were involved in 17% of single-offender rapes for the years 1973 to 1982 (Kershner, 1996).

Given these patterns of sexual violence involving youth, it may be expected that many adolescent girls experience unwanted sex or even date rape. Data support this conjecture. For example, in a 4-year longitudinal study of young, rural adolescent girls (Vicary, Klingaman, & Harkness, 1995), 23% had such experiences by the end of the 4-year period. Instances included forced touching, intercourse, and oral sex. Fifteen percent of the girls had been raped by their dates. Girls who had been early maturers, who already had been sexually active, who had

applications box 10.1

Preventing HIV Infection and AIDS Through Intervention Programs Involving Education or Skill Training

Numerous programs have been developed to use education as a means to increase knowledge about HIV/AIDS and to reduce behaviors that place an adolescent at risk for contracting HIV (Grunseit et al., 1997). Providing youth with accurate information about AIDS is obviously important. For instance, in a study involving primarily Mexican American youth from grades 3, 5, and 7, provision of a coherent, scientifically accurate account of how risk behaviors lead to AIDS resulted both immediately and at a follow-up 10 to 11 months later in greater knowledge of AIDS, better understanding of its causes, and more willingness to interact with people who had AIDS (Sigelman et al., 1996).

Although there has been criticism that education programs actually increase the sexual behaviors they are intended to prevent (e.g., some people claim that educating youth about safe sex "puts ideas in their heads" about sexuality that they would otherwise not have), there is little evidence of such an influence (Grunseit et al., 1997). In fact, an analysis of the effectiveness of 47 HIV/AIDS and sexuality education programs indicated that more than half of them (25 of 47) neither decreased sexual activity nor rates of STDs or pregnancy (Grunseit et al., 1997). Although three programs did report that education was associated with an increase in sexual behavior, about a third (17) reported that education delayed the onset of sexual activity, resulted in a reduction in the number of adolescents' sexual partners, and reduced STD and unplanned pregnancy rates (Grunseit et al., 1997).

Programs that employ just education as their mode of intervention have not met with overwhelming success. In response, many people trying to prevent HIV infection and AIDS have sought to combine education that enhances knowledge with education that improves the behavioral skills of youth regarding unsafe sexual practices. For example, a group of substance-dependent youth who received training in skills to avoid HIV risk behaviors showed greater knowledge about HIV-AIDS, more favorable attitudes about condom use, a greater sense of internal control and self-efficacy, increased recognition of HIV risks, and decreased high-risk sexual behaviors than did substance-dependent youth who received only education about HIV risks (St. Lawrence et al., 1995b).

Similarly, in a study of about 240 African American youth randomly assigned either to an 8-week education program or to a program that combined education with behavioral skills training (involving, for instance, correct condom use, sexual assertion, refusal, information provision, self-management, problem solving, and risk recognition), skilled-trained youth showed several positive outcomes in comparison to the "education only" group (St. Lawrence et al., 1995a). There was a reduction in unprotected intercourse and increased condom use during intercourse and greater improvement in behavioral skills (St. Lawrence et al., 1995a). In addition, the skill-trained youth maintained their advantages in reduced risk behavior when assessed 1 year later. For example, 31.1% of the youth in the education-only program who were abstinent when the program began had become sexually active 1 year later, whereas the corresponding figure for the skills-trained youth was 11.5% (St. Lawrence et al., 1995a). Other evaluations of interventions that integrate both education and skills also show that such programs increase knowledge and skills related to prevention of risky behaviors, although actual behavioral changes in risk behaviors may not always be evident (e.g., Slonim-Nevo et al., 1996).

sexually active friends, who had poor peer relations, and/or who had emotional problems were more likely to have these experiences.

Family and peer contexts also influence the likelihood that adolescent girls will experience an incident of unwanted sexual activity (Small & Kerns, 1993). About 20% of girls report that unwanted sexual experiences have occurred within the past year. Approximately one third of these encounters involved forced sexual intercourse; the other two thirds of the events involved unwanted touching. Most of these experiences were initiated by boyfriends, dates, friends, or acquaintances (in this order). A girl's history of sexual abuse, a tendency to conform to peers, and having parents whose rearing style was either authoritarian or reflective of low monitoring were predictive of her being a target of an unwanted sexual advance. Similarly, in divorced families, a mother's dating behavior and her possession of sexually permissive attitudes influences the sexual activity of both daughters and sons (Whitbeck, Simons, & Kao, 1994).

Youth do not feel helpless in the face of unwanted sex. Although both adolescent girls and boys find it easier to encourage than to discourage sex (Rosenthal & Peart, 1996), in a study of about 2,400 European American, African American, and Latino(a) tenth graders, adolescent girls were more likely than adolescent boys to believe they could say no to unwanted sex (Zimmerman et al., 1995). In addition, youth who had a less permissive attitude toward sex and who placed less importance on peer influence were also more likely to believe they could decline unwanted sex (Zimmerman et al., 1995). For girls, a sense of self-efficacy was particularly important in regard to their believing they could say no to sex (Zimmerman et al., 1995). Girls report that the presence of others is a useful strategy to avoid engaging in unwanted sexual behavior (Rosenthal, Lewis, & Cohen, 1996).

As illustrated by the vignette about Beth and Steve that opened this chapter, there exist tendencies in American society to blame the victim in cases of sexual assault. These tendencies can be found among male and female youth. Adolescent girls may take actions that place them "in harm's way" in regard to experiencing unwanted sex and/or in being blamed for it if it in fact occurs. For example, evidence shows that both male and female adolescents perceive a girl who experiences date rape when dressed provocatively as more responsible for her assailant's behavior than a girl who dresses conservatively (Cassidy & Hurrell, 1995). In addition, provocative dressing was associated with youth believing the male's behavior was justified or that the unwanted sexual intercourse was not rape (Cassidy & Hurrell, 1995).

Many adolescents are victims of unwanted sexual advances.

Conclusions About Problems of Adolescent Sexuality

The problems adolescents experience in regard to their sexual behaviors are complex. This complexity is due, at least in part, to the connection of these problems to other risk behaviors in adolescence and to the numerous individual and contextual influences on adolescents, such as their peers, families, and communities (Small & Luster, 1994). Whether we seek to understand the bases of problems of sexuality or of the adolescent's resilience to such problems, we need to appreciate the diversity of adolescent sexual behavior and of the contextual influences on it.

Diversity of, and Contextual Influences on, Sexual Behaviors

Individual variables involving biology, cognitions, emotions, and behavioral characteristics, and contextual variables, linked to peers, family, and the community, influence adolescent sexual behaviors and the problems associated with these behaviors. Although it is useful to introduce the influence of these individual and contextual variables separately, a clear theme evident in the research is that these individual and contextual variables act together within the developmental system to affect adolescent development.

Both individual and contextual variables often coincide not only with the presence or absence of problematic sexual behaviors but also with other risks or problem behaviors. When the developmental system involves multiple risks, the likelihood of problematic sexual behaviors increases (Jessor, 1987, 1992; Jessor, Donovan, & Costa, 1991; Jessor & Jessor, 1977; Ketterlinus & Lamb, 1994; Lerner, 1998). Accordingly, we discuss sexual behaviors in a special context: the context of multiple risks and problem behaviors.

Individual Influences

Issues to Consider

- In what way are adolescents' attitudes regarding sex and societal norms associated with the adolescents' sexual behavior?
- How is pubertal maturation linked to adolescents' sexual behavior?
- What role do expectations and fantasies about sexual experiences play in the adolescents' sexual behavior?
- What are some of the individual characteristics associated with teenage parenting?

Attitudes are mental structures that have both an emotional component (e.g., attitudes reflect one's likes and dislikes about some topic, thing, or person) and a cognitive component (e.g., attitudes involve beliefs about and/or some knowledge of the topic, thing, or person in question). Ambivalent attitudes toward childbearing, contraception, contraceptive efficacy, and abortions are related to adolescent childbearing (Zabin, Astone, & Emerson, 1993). Similarly, when combined with nonconforming behavior, possession of attitudes that reject societal norms is associated with early initiation of sexual intercourse among both African American and European American adolescents (Costa et al., 1995). Among both male and female adolescents, poor psychological adjustment is linked to early initiation of sexual intercourse (Bingham & Crockett, 1996).

Attitudes Mental structures that have both an emotional and a cognitive component.

Pubertal maturation may also be related to adolescents' sexual behaviors. Among gay and bisexual male adolescents, pubertal maturation is associated with age of first orgasm and first homosexual activity and with frequency of orgasms during junior high school (Savin-Williams, 1995). It should be stressed that gay and heterosexual male adolescents did not differ in their levels of self-esteem.

Other individual variables, if shown by gay adolescents, may not bode well for their adjustment. Among African American and Latino gay and bisexual adolescent males, sexually risky attitudes, coupled with substance abuse, conduct problems, and emotional distress, are associated with the likelihood that this set of problems will remain stable for the youth (Borus et al., 1995). In fact, across a 2-year period only about 20% to 30% of youth change their pattern of problem behaviors.

Expectations and fantasies about sexual experiences also play a role in the adolescent's sexual behavior. Adolescents who have not yet initiated sexual activity may have expectations about how it will make them feel that are unrealistic. The adolescents may, for example, overestimate how positive they will feel about sexual activity. In a study of about 1,300 high school students from Miami, Florida, the degree to which virgins predicted they would feel better after first experiencing sexual intercourse was much *less* than that which nonvirgins reported actually feeling about the event (Langer, Zimmerman, & Katz, 1995). Male nonvirgins felt better about their first sexual experience than did female nonvirgins, and the more sexual partners youth had, the more positive were their reported feelings (Langer et al., 1995).

There are also behavioral characteristics of youth whose sexuality has resulted in childbearing that appear to be associated specifically with their status as teenage parents. Adolescent mothers, for instance, are less verbally interactive with their infants (Osofsky & Eberhart-Wright, 1988) and, perhaps not surprisingly, maternal youth is associated with lower IQ scores in later childhood (e.g., Broman, 1979), even when the socioeconomic status of the mother is taken into consideration (Field, 1991). Similarly, preschool children of teenage mothers are more active, aggressive, and less self-controlled than children of older mothers (Brooks-Gunn & Chase-Lansdale, 1995; Brooks-Gunn & Furstenberg, 1986). By the time these children of teenage mothers reach adolescence themselves, their academic achievement is much lower than the achievement of youth of older mothers (Brooks-Gunn & Furstenberg, 1987).

In regard to teenage fathers, youth who father a child during adolescence are less likely than non-teenage fathers to complete high school and they attain fewer years of education than do nonteenage fathers (Pirog-Good, 1996). European American youth who become fathers tend to have low self-esteem, a belief that factors external to themselves are responsible for their behaviors, and conservative sex role attitudes (Pirog-Good, 1995). These attributes are not seen among African American teenage fathers (Pirog-Good, 1995).

Overall, teenage fathers are more likely to use drugs, engage in crime, and initiate these problems at earlier ages than youth who are not teenage fathers (Pirog-Good, 1996). Teenage fathers are more likely than nonteenage fathers to come from minority, poor, and single-parent households (Pirog-Good, 1996; Thornberry, Smith, & Howard, 1997). Moreover, the members of the households of teenage fathers are less educated than family members of nonteenage fathers (Pirog-Good, 1995).

In sum, the individual characteristics associated with adolescent sexuality and with teenage parenting combine with contextual variables to shape the implications of the adolescent's sexuality for his or her contemporaneous behavior and later development. As we consider contextual influences on the adolescent's sexuality, the continued combined impact of individual variables is apparent as well.

Contextual Influences

Issues to Consider
- In what ways do family and peers represent contextual variables that influence adolescents' sexual behavior?
- How might the presence of an older sibling impact younger siblings' adolescent sexuality?
- What characteristics of community context might influence adolescent attitudes toward sexual activity?

The families and peers of adolescents influence their sexuality. For instance, although adolescents' reports of their age at first intercourse are not particularly reliable (Capaldi, 1996), several contextual variables—and some individual ones as well—influence whether youth (report that they) initiate sexual intercourse (coital activity) early or late in adoles-

cence (Murray, 1996). Among African American females, girls who lived in two-parent households, had talked with their parents about sexual issues, and had greater knowledge of sexuality were more likely to delay age of first coitus until 18 years or beyond (Murray, 1996). In turn, among about 270 low-income urban African American youth aged 11 to 14 years, coital activity was associated with conflict with parents and with having peers who were sexually active (Black, Ricardo, & Stanton, 1997).

Other studies also link peers with sexual activity. In a longitudinal study of about 75 boys from grade 6 through grade 10 (Feldman et al., 1995), both peer rejection *and* peer acceptance were associated with the number of sexual partners a youth had 4 years later. Rejected youth were low in self-restraint and were involved in misconduct. This pattern of behavior was linked to the number of sexual partners a youth had 4 years later (Feldman et al., 1995). Popular boys were more likely to date extensively and to drink alcohol at parties. These behaviors were associated with capitalized on opportunities for sexual intercourse with multiple partners (Feldman et al., 1995).

Peers are also important influences in the lives of adolescents whose sexual activity has resulted in pregnancy and childbirth. Peers provide more emotional support to adolescent mothers than do family members and interfere less than family members do in the life of the teenage mother (Richardson, Barbour, & Butenzer, 1995). Within the family, mothers provide more support to pregnant and parenting female African American adolescents than fathers (Davis, Rhodes, & Hamilton-Leaks, 1997). Although the provision of support from both mothers and fathers was associated with lower levels of depression among these adolescents, the teenagers also had relationship problems with both parents (Davis et al., 1997).

Siblings are both peers and family members, and they have important influences on adolescent sexuality. Having an older sister who is a teenage mother is associated with childbearing among younger sisters (East, 1996). Younger sisters of childbearing adolescents differ from younger sisters of nonchildbearing youth in that they are more accepting of nonmarital adolescent childbearing, more pessimistic about their school and career chances, and more likely to have engaged in problem behaviors such as smoking cigarettes and skipping school (East, 1996). In addition, these younger sisters were likely to be nonvirgins (East, 1996). Moreover, the number of sexually active girlfriends that an adolescent female has, as well as the number of her sexually active sisters, and whether she has an adolescent childbearing sister, are linked to her possessing permissive sexual attitudes, having positive intentions for future sex, and being more likely a nonvirgin (East, Felice, & Morgan, 1993). Some of the recent work of Patricia L. East is presented in Meet the Researcher Box 10.2.

Siblings as well as teachers, but not, it seems, parents, are cited by youth as major sources of accurate information about sexuality (Ansuini, Fiddler-Woite, & Woite, 1996). Reliance on siblings for accurate knowledge may at times be appropriate because, in some cases, mothers have been found unable to define sexual development terms adequately (e.g., ejaculation, hormones, menstruation, ovulation, puberty, semen, and wet dreams) to their adolescent children (Hockenberry-Eaton et al., 1996).

Thus both peer and family contexts can combine to influence adolescent sexuality. This point is underscored by other research. Among African American and European American males and females, possession of a girlfriend or a boyfriend, respectively, one's educational expectations, and the educational background of one's mother were associated with being sexually active (Scott-Jones & White, 1990). Although these associations did not differ across the groups of African Americans and European Americans, the former group of youth was less likely to use contraception than the latter group.

The community context also influences adolescent sexuality. In poor communities, youth have higher rates of abortion and lower rates of marriage (Sullivan, 1993). Among both African American and European American female adolescents, living in a socially disorganized, low-income community (one in which family planning services are not readily available) is associated with the initiation of sexual intercourse and with the young women's subsequent sexual activity.

In sum, sexual behaviors are related to several different individual and contextual variables. There are conditions under which the expression of an adolescent's sexuality in the context of particular individual or contextual variables will involve either healthy sexual behaviors (e.g., avoidance of early initiation of coital activity) or risky ones (e.g., early initiation of sexual intercourse). However, when sexuality is expressed in the context of other behavior risks, it is very likely that problems in sexual behavior will be seen.

Influences of Other Risk Behaviors

Issue to Consider
• What are some additional individual and contextual risk factors influencing adolescent sexual activity?

Some of the individual and contextual variables linked to adolescent sexual activity involve risk or problem behaviors other than sexual ones (Fortenberry et al., 1997). For instance, in a study of about 1,000 high school students, sexually active males used alcohol more often, had higher stress levels, were less likely to use seat belts, were more likely to engage in physical fights, and (understandably) were more likely to worry about AIDS than were males who had never engaged in intercourse (Harvey & Spigner, 1995). In turn, sexually active females used more alcohol and cigarettes and had higher stress levels than did females who had never had sexual intercourse (Harvey & Spigner, 1995).

Engaging in unconventional behavior (e.g., rejecting social norms, showing nonconformist behaviors) is also linked to sexual activity in youth (Costa et al., 1995). For instance, in a longitudinal study of more than 1,300 urban European American, Latino(a), and African American male and female middle school and high school students, unconventionality was associated with early initiation of sexual intercourse, especially among European American and Latino(a) youth (Costa et al., 1995). Although this research does demonstrate a differential association between unconventionality and sexual activity across racial/ethnic groups, most research indicates that the risk factors predicting sexual activity do not differ among ethnic groups (Perkins et al., 1998).

Additional risk factors influencing sexuality are antisocial and delinquent behavior. These behaviors, as well as pubertal maturation and substance use, were associated with early initiation of sexual intercourse among Oregon youth in grades 7 through 12 (Capaldi, Crosby, & Stoolmiller, 1996). In turn, anxiety was associated with the delay of first intercourse (Capaldi et al., 1996). Other studies (e.g., Tubman, Windle, & Windle, 1996) also find a link between delinquency and early onset of sexual intercourse, as well as with such behavior problems as poor school grades, early alcohol use, and antisocial behavior. Repeat pregnancies among adolescent mothers are associated with many of the same variables in what appears to be a "cluster" of problem behaviors (Jessor, 1987, 1992; Jessor,

MEET THE RESEARCHER BOX 10.2

PATRICIA L. EAST
THE SISTERS OF PREGNANT AND PARENTING TEENS AT HIGH RISK FOR EARLY PREGNANCY

In the late 1980s, my colleagues and I noticed that in the UCSD Medical Center adolescent health clinic, many of our current pregnant teenage patients were the *younger sisters* of our *former* pregnant teenage patients. Although many doctors across the country had also recognized this as a clinical phenomenon, research on the younger sisters of pregnant teens, at that point, was very sparse.

In 1992 Dr. Marianne Felice and I published a literature review of the studies that had been done on the sisters of pregnant and parenting teens. These studies showed that, when compared to same-age women of comparable race, ethnicity, and economic status, the sisters of teenage mothers had as much as 6 times higher teenage childbearing rates, 4 times higher teenage sexual activity rates, were significantly younger at their first pregnancy, and were significantly more likely to be sexually active during early adolescence, or by age 12 or 13.

Why would the sisters of pregnant and parenting teens be especially vulnerable to an early pregnancy? We believe two general sets of factors predispose the sisters of pregnant and parenting teens to early pregnancy. The first set of factors derive from the sisters' shared background. These factors include sisters' shared economic situation, their shared race and ethnicity, living within the same family and neighborhood, and being parented by the same parents. Much research has shown that these kinds of factors increase one's risk for a teenage pregnancy.

The second set of factors, we think, result directly from the teen's pregnancy and birth and the impact they have for the teen's family and siblings. Close to 80% of teenagers continue to live with their families one year after they give birth. So it is very likely that a teenager's childbearing would have a profound impact on all of the siblings within the household.

How does a teen's childbearing alter her family and siblings? Unfortunately, not much research has been done on this subject, but findings from a few recent studies are beginning to provide some answers. For example, I studied a group of pregnant teenagers and their mothers and followed them until about a year after the teenager had her baby. In all of these families, no other child had ever been pregnant, so the teen's family had not been previ-

Patricia East is an associate research scientist in the Department of Pediatrics at the University of California, San Diego Medical Center. She has been on the editorial boards of the *Journal of Research on Adolescence*, the *Journal of Youth and Adolescence*, *Developmental Psychology*, and the *International Journal of Behavioral Development*, and on several grant review committees for the National Institutes of Health.

ously "exposed to" a teen's birth. Results showed that, after the teen gave birth, the mothers reported being less strict with their other children, talking less with their other children, and monitoring their other children less carefully. Mothers also reported being more accepting of teenage sex after the older daughter gave birth. These findings are important because they show how a teen's pregnancy and birth affect her mother and, consequently, how they impact the other children in the household. The particular changes that the mothers in the study underwent are important because they indicate that the teen's family may be changed in ways that make siblings in the household more susceptible to early sexual activity and, thus, early pregnancy.

There are many other plausible ways that a teenager having a baby could affect her brothers and sisters. For example, it could expose the girls in the family to a role model of "mother" that appears attractive because of its associated status, femininity, and attention. Teenagers who are mothers often receive a lot of attention and are sometimes treated as adults, both within the immediate family and within the community. Thus mimicking their sister's pregnancy may be very seductive for girls because they see their sisters achieve adult status and recognition through motherhood instead of through school or job achievements.

One of the most positive things that has been accomplished by my research was that a new program was started in California called the Adolescent Sibling Pregnancy Prevention Program. This program started in 1996 and it has provided pregnancy prevention services to approximately 4,000 siblings of pregnant and parenting teens throughout California. This is a very important program because it serves a group known to be at high risk for teen pregnancy. This is also a unique program, being the only one of its kind to focus specifically and exclusively on the siblings of pregnant and parenting teens. It is hoped that this program will be permanently legislated within California, as well as serve as a model program for other states that wish to launch similar pregnancy prevention initiatives. In the meantime, continued research on the siblings of pregnant and parenting teens will help us understand how these siblings are affected by their sisters' giving birth and how they themselves become at risk for early pregnancy.

Donovan, & Costa, 1991; Jessor & Jessor, 1977), that is, school problems, substance use and abuse, and violence/delinquency (Gillmore et al., 1997).

Given that teenage coital activity, pregnancy, and childbearing occur in the context of other problem behaviors, interventions that are most effective in preventing the problems of adolescent sexuality focus on these clusters of behaviors and not just on sexual behavior alone (e.g., Allen et al., 1997). Chapter 14 presents a fuller discussion of the importance of a multiproblem focus on interventions aimed at preventing unhealthy/undesirable behaviors in adolescence.

Conclusions About Adolescent Sexuality

The breadth and depth of the problems associated with the sexual behavior of today's youth exist at historically unprecedented levels. Not only do these problems arise from a diverse set of individual and contextual influences but they also impact the adolescent's social world (e.g., his or her peers, family of origin, and, with increasing probability, own children).

To address the problems of adolescent sexuality requires an approach that considers the entire system of influences involved in the youth's development. This need to devise programs that bridge sexual and other risk behaviors in manners that are sensitive to the diverse contexts of youth is no less true in other nations than it is in the United States. Issues of youth sexuality are present and pressing ones around the world. Applications Box 10.2 provides details about three effective programs in other nations—in Gaborone, Botswana, in Recife, Brazil, and in Jamaica, West Indies—and illustrates the common need for all effective youth programs to address the complex system of individual and contextual variables affecting youth development.

The influences on problems of adolescent sexuality and the sorts of systems change needed to address them are not dissimilar from those found in regard to other problems of adolescent development. In Chapters 8 and 9 we discussed the multiple individual and contextual bases associated with both negative and positive development in the family and peer contexts. These themes will be evident again in Chapter 11 in a discussion of adolescence and school and the nature, bases, and implications of school underachievement, failure, and dropout.

applications box 10.2

Addressing the Complex Problems of Adolescent Sexuality Around the World

Problems of teenage sexuality exist in all nations of the world. These problems may be manifested through issues of emotional distress in sexually active youth; in health problems, such as sexually transmitted diseases and AIDS; in teenage prostitution; in teenage childbearing; in losses to the educational and economic system, arising because teenage parents cannot go to school or prepare for jobs; and in weakened families, arising when a generation of children themselves have and rear children. Even when only a subset of issues applies in a country, these problems nevertheless involve multiple facets of the young person's individual, interpersonal, and institutional (family, community) world.

Successful programs effecting positive changes in adolescents' sexuality engage as many of the relations between youth and their contexts as possible, given their available financial and personnel resources (Benson, 1997; Dryfoos, 1990; Lerner, Sparks, & McCubbin, 2000). The three programs described here are illustrative of this attempt to change the system of influences within which youth are embedded.

Increasing Opportunities for Pregnant Teenagers

The Educational Center for Adolescent Women/Peer Counseling by Teens Program, Gaborone, Botswana

Since gaining independence from Britain in 1966, Botswana has experienced rapid development and social change, including advances in education, health, and communications. Traditional family and community structures no longer control sexuality and reproduction. Youth are sexually active from a very early age, often have multiple sex partners, and frequently use no protection against pregnancy and sexually transmitted diseases.

In response to high rates of teenage pregnancy in Botswana, the YWCA initiated two programs aimed at educating teen mothers and adolescents at risk of becoming pregnant. Established in 1989, the Educational Center for Adolescent Women (ECAW) provides pregnant women and new mothers with a place they can go to continue their education and learn about motherhood. It fills a critical gap in services for pregnant teens in that many are forced to leave school for at least a year after becoming pregnant and find it difficult to return due to lack of space and other reasons. ECAW courses include

family and sexuality education, baby and child care, individual and group counseling, and academic subjects. A craft component was introduced in 1990 whereby teen mothers learn sewing, dressmaking, and knitting skills so that those who do not continue with their education can be self-supporting.

The Peer Counseling by Teens (PACT) program is based on the notion that young people are more apt to trust and listen to each other concerning their sexuality than older, authority figures. PACT trains youth to act as peer counselors to their friends and classmates. Each year, the program trains 5 boys and 5 girls from each of Gaborone's nine secondary schools to be Peer Counselors. These 90 students, ages 12 through 19, meet regularly to learn about human sexuality, HIV, AIDS, and other sexually transmitted diseases and receive training aimed at increasing their self-esteem, confidence, and communication skills. Afterward, each is expected to share the information they have learned with their friends and classmates.

Both programs build on one another's efforts. Through ECAW, PACT counselors learn the circumstances and influences behind teenage pregnancies. By focusing on preventive efforts, PACT aims to reduce the number of teenage pregnancies in Gaborone in the future. Because of its impact on behavioral change and self-assurance among young people, PACT is in demand and has spread countrywide.

Providing Street-Based Girls with Health Care Education and Training

The "Casa de Passagem" Program, Recife, Brazil

In Recife, the capital of Northeast Brazil, the poorest region in the country, more than 700 children and adolescents live on the streets. Many of these children and adolescents maintain contact with their families, but poverty does not permit them to live as a family unit. To survive, many girls become involved in prostitution, leading them to a world of drugs and often death. In addition to the sexual violence that they suffer in the streets, many of these girls also suffer sexual abuse in their families.

Founded in 1989, Casa de Passagem (Passage House) works through an educational process so that the girls recognize themselves as people with rights. For this, it is necessary to work on their self-esteem, to help them see themselves as citizens—with rights—and to help them see

continued on next page

applications box 10.2

continued from page 251

their individual talents and develop other strategies for survival. In the 10 years since it began, Casa de Passagem has served 10,000 girls directly and, through them, around 60,000 others indirectly.

Casa de Passagem has become so well known that the street girls come to the center to participate in the programs of their own accord. Casa de Passagem's services are delivered through three basic programs that include self-esteem building and counseling, community training and assessment, and job placement. The program also offers a primary health clinic.

In addition, Casa de Passagem trains young girls and adolescents to serve as peer educators that reach out to other adolescents and community members. The peer educators work on issues ranging from family planning to drug prevention to prevention of STDs.

Casa de Passagem also plays an important advocacy role, working with other institutions to advocate for improved policies benefiting young girls, particularly in the areas of preventing domestic violence, sexual abuse, and the imprisonment of girls by the police.

Providing Teens with Life Skills Training and Sex Education

The YWCA NEET Project, Jamaica, West Indies

Teenage pregnancy is a serious problem in Jamaica, where in 1988 23% of all births were to teenage mothers. With 40% of the country's population currently under the age of 15, the problem is expected to worsen. Factors contributing to the rise in teenage pregnancies include poverty, high school dropout rates, few employment opportunities, and an increase in single-parent, female-headed households.

In an effort to reverse this trend, the YWCA initiated the NEET ("teen" spelled backward) program in 1980. The goals of the program are to reduce the incidence of teenage pregnancy and help teens prepare for the responsibilities they will face in adulthood.

NEET provides education and services to young men and women ages 12 to 19. Regular educational sessions are conducted in participating schools following a curriculum developed by NEET. The curriculum includes discussion topics on physical and emotional growth and development, conception and contraception, health, and social issues.

In addition, NEET offers workshops on family life and sex education and a peer counseling training program in which young people are instructed in how to provide other young people with accurate sex information. With many young people hesitant or fearful to discuss personal issues with adult authority figures, NEET's peer counseling program provides them with support and a much needed outlet. To date, more than 250 young people have been trained through NEET as peer counselors.

Between 1987 and 1991, over 26,500 young people received instruction and training through NEET in their schools or through youth groups. Participating schools report improved discipline and fewer dropouts due to pregnancy. Student participants report a better understanding of reproduction, heightened awareness of themselves, enhanced self-esteem, and increased ability to perform leadership roles.

Source: International Youth Foundation, 2001. <www.iyfnet.org>

Summary

- Girls stress the interpersonal qualities of their romantic partners, and boys emphasize the importance of physical attraction. Girls also stress the importance of demonstrating affection and are less supportive of multiple sexual partners.

- Diversity in racial/ethnic backgrounds, adolescents' family relationships and communication patterns, and religion all influence the development of particular styles of adolescent sexual behaviors.

- Because of the complex and multifaceted developmental challenges facing gay and lesbian youth, there is a great need to understand adolescent development in context and to explicitly investigate through research the developmental situation for gay, lesbian, and bisexual youth.

- About 37% of males and 13% of females have had at least one homosexual encounter that has resulted in orgasm, and estimates are that 8% of men and about 1% to 3% of women are exclusively homosexual.

- Political ideology, socioeconomic status, heterosexual friends, and gender nonconformity for males, and religion and the importance of school for females influence a homosexual adolescent's sense of self.

- Homonegative attitudes can lead to violence against homosexuals, and the perpetrators of such violence often have attitudes characterized by ambivalence, defensiveness, and adherence to myths about homosexual lifestyles. Homonegativity and heterosexism are obstacles to healthy development and lead homosexual youth to be at greater risk for psychosocial adjustment problems.

- Some of the sexual problems facing adolescents today include forced sex, unwanted pregnancies and the birth of children that cannot be supported, and sexually transmitted diseases.

- The Centers for Disease Control estimates 3 million cases of sexually transmitted diseases occur each year within the United States to adolescents between the ages of 15 and 19. In addition, about 25% of all sexually active youth will contract an STD during their high school years.

- AIDS is probably more prevalent in adolescence than statistics might show because there is a long latency period for HIV.

- Programs that focus on the cluster of problem behaviors involved in HIV infection and attempt to promote multiple changes in youth are most effective in preventing HIV and AIDS.

- Sexual abuse, especially when combined with physical abuse, is linked to problems such as binge drinking and suicidal ideation.

- A girl's history of sexual abuse, a tendency to conform to peers, and having parents whose rearing style was authoritarian or reflective of low monitoring raise her likelihood of being a victim of an unwanted sexual advance.

- Teenage mothers are less verbally interactive with their infants and teenage fathers are less likely to complete high school than nonteenage fathers. Teenage fathers can also have low self-esteem, external locus of control, and conservative sex role attitudes, and are more likely to use drugs and engage in crime.

- Family and peers have a great influence on adolescent sexuality, for instance, in regard to time of first intercourse and the number of sexual partners per year. Peers are also important influences in the lives of teenage parents.

- Living in poor communities is linked to higher rates of abortion and lower rates of marriage, as well as to the initiation and continuance of sexual activity.

- Adolescent sexual behavior is associated with the use of alcohol and tobacco, levels of stress, involvement in physical fights, and worrying about AIDS.

- Antisocial and delinquent behavior, as well as pubertal maturation and substance abuse, are linked to early initiation of sexual intercourse.

Discussion Topics

1. Do you remember when your age-mates started to first express romantic interests in others? How old were you? Were you a leader in being one of the first to express these emotions or did these feelings take longer to develop in you than in your friends? How did the timing of your romantic and/or sexual emotions impact you and your friendships? When you first started having these feelings, did you share them with anyone? If you could describe now the feelings you felt then, what would you describe? Were those feelings typical for your gender and age?

2. What was it about the people you were romantically attracted to or involved with as an adolescent that drew you to them? Are you still attracted to those same qualities? If not, what caused your change in interests and/or what determined your interests as an adolescent?

3. Did your parent(s) ever sit down with you and have the "birds and the bees" discussion? If so, how did this discussion impact you and the decisions you made and make about sexual involvement? If not, do you think such a discussion would have made a difference in the decisions you make? Why or why not?

4. How accepting was your high school of individuals whose life experiences and expressions were outside of the so-called norm? Were there any homosexuals at your school? Were they open with their sexuality? Was there a gay/lesbian support group at your school? How were their experiences different from those of heterosexual students in terms of feeling and expressing emotions for their same-gendered classmates?

5. Look back over the illustrations of risks and problems related to adolescent sexual experience. Which findings are the most surprising to you? What factors have led to the increase in the last decades in the rate of sexual intercourse among adolescents?

6. Did you know any teenage mothers as an adolescent? How were their lives impacted by this life change? Can you identify any contextual variables that might have been potential risk factors leading to their early pregnancies? How were they supported (by their families, friends, communities) once their babies were born?

7. What reasoning and rationales do teenagers tend to employ when discussing the use of contraceptives? What information were you supplied with as a teenager? Was this information available from parents, siblings, peers, and/or school? How open were you to this information? Why do so many adolescents believe they will not be affected by high-risk sexual behaviors?

8. Data show that 1 in 5 adolescent girls are victims of unwanted sex. Despite the fact that sexual experimentation during adolescence is often experienced by youth as occurring too early and therefore as lacking in pleasure and enjoyment, there is still great pressure on adolescents to become sexually experienced. Why? How might one's peer group influence the occurrence of unwanted sex? When an adolescent is a victim of unwanted sex, he or she often has no one to turn to. Why is being a victim such a taboo?

9. Think back on the adolescents in your high school and, specifically, those teenagers you believed were involved in high-risk sexual behaviors. What about these teenagers made you think they were sexually active? What was their overall reputation in school? How do you think their sexual behaviors impacted this reputation? Can you identify any commonalities in the contexts of these youth that might stand out in terms of being predictors for unwanted sex and/or teenage pregnancy?

10. If you were ever in a situation where you found yourself needing to discourage sexual activity, what strategies did you employ? How well did those strategies work? Looking back on the experience now, how might the situation have been avoided? Did you change your behaviors and interactions once this experience occurred? In what ways?

11. Do you believe girls who dress provocatively and behave flirtatiously deserve the potential unwanted attention they get? Why or why not? Is your answer influenced by your gender or by your own experiences or the experiences of those close to you?

12. Research shows that individual and contextual influences predict sexual activity. What personal characteristics and environmental factors influenced the choices you made about sexual behavior?

13. How would you describe your generation's attitude about sex? How has the media impacted that attitude? How has the prevalence of AIDS impacted that attitude?

14. What makes someone ready to have sexual intercourse? Is your response different now from what it would have been in high school? Do your personal experiences with sex impact your response?

Key Terms

AIDS (acquired immune deficiency syndrome) (p. 237)

attitudes (p. 244)

CDC (Centers for Disease Control) (p. 240)

heterosexism (p. 236)

HIV (p. 237)

homonegativity (p. 236)

homosexuality (p. 236)

latency period (p. 240)

STD (sexually transmitted disease) (p. 240)

11

SCHOOLS AND EDUCATION DURING ADOLESCENCE

Hector had not seen Louis for a long time, not since they had been in gym class together during sophomore year. Now, as Hector entered the tuxedo rental store, there was Louis standing behind the counter.

"Hey, Louis, what's up?" Hector said, extending his hand in greeting. The two young men shook hands warmly.

"Hey, man, good to see you. Nothing much. Are you here to rent a tux?"

"Yes, I am renting one for the senior prom. I'm taking Gloria Ruben. You remember her, don't you?"

"No. No, I don't think so," Louis responded matter-of-factly.

Hector sensed a bit of unease creeping into Louis's demeanor. "Oh, well, anyway, you must be able to get a great deal on tux rentals since you work here."

"Yeah, I suppose," Louis shrugged. "But I don't really ever rent them."

"I don't much either, just for the prom. You'll need one for the prom too though, I guess."

"No, no I won't," Louis explained. "I'm not going to the prom."

"Why not?" Hector blurted out. But as soon as the question left his mouth he saw that it pained Louis. He regretted asking him.

"Hey, man, don't you know? I'm not a senior. I dropped out of school at the end of last year."

LEARNING OBJECTIVES

1. To understand the types of functions that schools perform.
2. To appreciate how the structure of the school can influence youth.
3. To understand how teachers' attitudes, expectations, and behaviors can influence adolescent development and behavior.
4. To understand the factors associated with the achievement of diverse students.
5. To appreciate how parents, peers, and the neighborhood or community can affect the academic performance of youth.
6. To learn how extracurricular activities are associated with school-related behaviors.
7. To understand the individual and contextual variables linked to school dropout and to other school problems and risks related to youth development.
8. To learn the approach that effective school dropout prevention programs take.
9. To understand the individual bases of school problems in adolescence.
10. To appreciate how a return to school affects teenage mothers.
11. To learn why schools are being charged with providing services that were previously provided by other social institutions.
12. To understand why schools are failing to provide a goodness of fit with the social, health, and cognitive needs of adolescents.
13. To understand different kinds of classroom and school organizations (e.g., full-service schools) and the effects they have.
14. To understand how school transition affects adolescents.
15. To understand how pubertal change and school transition are related.

At the beginning of adolescence, virtually all boys and girls in the United States attend school. This enrollment can be attributed to the high value placed on education and the compulsory laws of school attendance. In most states, however, a student is no longer compelled to attend school upon reaching his or her sixteenth or seventeenth birthday. As a consequence, by the end of the high school years, many adolescents have dropped out. Discontinuing school attendance does not necessarily mean a young person becomes gainfully employed. Between 1994 and 1996 about 10% of all 16- to 19-year-old youth in the United States were not attending school or working, and only about half of American males and females go on to college (Sherrod, Haggerty, & Featherman, 1993).

This chapter discusses the bases and implications of failure to complete high school and the successful outcomes for adolescents of their educational experiences. Again we emphasize the connections between the development of adolescents and their key contexts. This chapter focuses on the school and other contexts in influencing adolescent development and in fostering either academic success or academic problems.

The School Context and Adolescent Development

A lot of development occurs in schools. Growth in academic abilities is a key instance of this development. The capacity of the young person to be socially competent with peers and with adults develops, and athletic and health-maintaining abilities can advance. Self-esteem and personal perceptions of competence also develop by virtue of changes in all these facets of academic, social, and physical growth.

Variables from the school context as well as from the family and the peer group are linked to a diversity of developmental outcomes. The school functions alone and in combination with other key contexts of adolescence to affect adolescent development.

Functions of the School

Issues to Consider

- What types of functions do schools perform?
- How can social status be earned through school attendance?

- How can the structure of school be nonbeneficial to some youth?
- How do teachers' behaviors, attitudes, and expectations influence adolescent behavior and development?

Schools perform many functions. A long tradition views schools as training institutions (e.g., Ausubel, Montemayor, and Svajian, 1977; McCandless, 1970), as agents of cultural transmission designed to perpetuate and improve a given way of life, and as a means to inculcate both knowledge and values. In addition, schools have been regarded traditionally as fulfilling a **maintenance-actualization** role, representing a way in which the adolescent can be happy and yet challenged. Schools are a place to develop optimal personal and interpersonal attributes and the ability to contribute to society (Dryfoos, 1994, 1995; Lerner, 1994; McCandless, 1970).

Schools also provide a context for social interactions and relationship development (Ausubel et al., 1977; Dryfoos, 1994, 1995). They can facilitate the adolescent's emancipation from parents through giving youth an opportunity to earn their own social status. Status may be earned concurrently with school attendance by demonstrating a mastery of the curriculum, by attaining high class standing, and by nonacademic interactions with the peer group in school activities such as organized athletics or clubs (Ausubel et al., 1977; Lerner, 1994, 1995). In addition, social status may be earned in the future through the training and education attained in school (Johnston & Bachman, 1976; Lerner, 1994, 1995). The school also serves a custodial role in society, in that a system of **compulsory education,** such as that found in the United States, highly structures the time and activity of students (Villarruel & Lerner, 1994).

The structure provided by schools is not necessarily beneficial for all youth. In a study comparing about 350 Native American youth with about 1,000 European American ones, the Native Americans tended to perceive that the structure of the school created barriers to their success. This perception was associated with lessened school performance among the Native Americans (Wood & Clay, 1996).

Teachers are obviously a critical part of the school context, and their behaviors, attitudes, and expectations apart from their skills as instructors can influence youth behavior and development. In a longitudinal study of about 250 sixth- to eighth-

Parents and teachers may work together to support the school achievement of youth.

grade students, perceptions by the adolescents that their teachers cared about them were associated with enhanced motivation to achieve positive academic and social outcomes (Wentzel, 1997). Teachers who cared were described as having attributes akin to those associated with authoritative parents (Baumrind, 1971; see too Chapter 8). They showed democratic interaction styles, developed expectations for their students that were based on the individual characteristics of the adolescents, and provided constructive feedback (Wentzel, 1997).

Relations Between the School and Other Contexts

Issues to Consider

- How can support from the family context enhance school performance?
- What factors are associated with the achievement of Asian and Asian American students?
- How can parents and peers have a negative effect on school performance?
- How does the neighborhood or community context of the school influence the academic performance of youth?

Schools exist in relation to the other key contexts of adolescent development. The family,

Maintenance-actualization
Function of schools in which students are both made happy about their current status and yet challenged to do better.

Compulsory education
System mandating that children and adolescents attend school up to a certain age.

peer, and community contexts either enable or detract from the ability of schools to function as society intends.

Support from the family context can enhance school performance. In a study of African American, European American, and Latino students, social support from the family was associated with higher students' grades, scores on a standardized achievement test, and teacher ratings (Levitt, Guacci-Franco, & Levitt, 1994). In addition, the students' self-esteem was enhanced by the support they received. Among middle school girls who had the ability and motivation to do well in mathematics, those whose grades increased had mothers who possessed positive attitudes toward the subject (Klebanou & Brooks-Gunn, 1992).

In a longitudinal study of the offspring of African American teenage mothers, family support was among the key factors reducing the likelihood of high school dropout (Brooks-Gunn, Gus, & Furstenberg, 1993). The decrease in the chances of discontinuing school were related to high maternal educational aspirations for the child in early life, number of years the father was present, being prepared for school, and not repeating an elementary school grade.

The culture transmitted through socialization by the family and by peers influences school performance. Positive family climate and peer group norms supporting positive behaviors for youth have been found to be associated with school achievement (Kurdek, Fine, & Sinclair, 1995). Social support by parents has been found to be related to youth feeling open to, excited by, and involved in school-related activities. A family climate that challenged the young person to succeed was related to an adolescent focusing on important goals (Rathunde, 1996). Youth who lived in families where both support and challenge were present had the best school experiences (Rathunde, 1996).

Mathematics scores of Asian American students are higher than those of European American students, but lower than those of Chinese and Japanese students (Chen & Stevenson, 1995). Factors associated with the achievement of Asian and Asian American students include having parents and peers who hold high standards, believe that one succeeds through effort, have positive attitudes about achievement, study diligently, and are less apt to distract youth from studying. The psy-

chological adjustment of both Asian American and European American students is not different, suggesting that the higher performances and family and peer influences on the former group do not interfere with positive psychological functioning. The better academic performance of Asian American youth has been confirmed by other research (e.g., Rosenthal & Feldman, 1991). This achievement is linked to the presence of a demanding but nonconflictual family environment.

Parents and peers can also have negative effects on school performance. For example, when parents react negatively to school performance, youth show negative performance (Rosenthal & Feldman, 1991). In another study, low parental academic achievement and ineffective child-rearing practices were linked to antisocial behavior among adolescent boys in the sixth grade, to decreases in the engagement with academic course work in the seventh grade, and to poor achievement in the eighth grade (Debaryshe, Patterson, & Capaldi, 1993). African American students' awareness of the discrimination toward people of their race was associated with their perceptions that academic achievement was not important (Taylor et al., 1994). However, when ethnic identity was high, students showed both school engagement and school achievement.

In addition to family and peer influences, the neighborhood or community context of the school influences the academic performance of youth. For instance, African American youth attending neighborhood schools report feeling "stuck" in a setting in which they perceive they have little access to community culture and to the wider society (Miron & Lauria, 1995). When African American youth from the same neighborhood attend a citywide school, they perceive that they possess such access (Miron & Lauria, 1995).

In a study of 202 census tracts in the Chicago metropolitan region (Ensminger, Lomkin, & Jacobson, 1996), African American males were more likely to graduate from high school if they lived in middle-class neighborhoods or in neighborhoods having a high percentage of residents working in white-collar occupations. No neighborhood effects were found for females (Ensminger et al., 1996). Other research also has found that African American males from less poor neighborhoods are more likely to stay in school (Connell et al., 1995).

MEET THE RESEARCHER BOX 11.1

CYNTHIA GARCIA COLL
CHILDREN OF IMMIGRANTS: UNDERSTANDING THEIR EDUCATIONAL AND DEVELOPMENTAL NEEDS

The number of immigrants in the United States continues to grow. As a result, the number of children born to immigrant parents also continues to increase. These children may be faced with multiple challenges as they enter school. For example, many attend urban school systems that have inadequate resources and do not have extra money or teachers to address their unique educational needs sufficiently. These include high-quality ESL (English as a Second Language) or bilingual classes for children who do not speak English or having translators readily available to speak with parents who do not speak English. Another challenge of being the child of an immigrant is growing up negotiating between two worlds—the world of their parent(s)' place of birth and the world of the United States.

Despite the challenges these children face, not all of them do poorly in school. In fact, some researchers have found that children of immigrants do better in school than their U.S.-born peers. In my research I am trying to understand why some children of immigrants are very successful in school and why some are not. I also study how the children's racial, ethnic, and national identification may affect their attitudes about and/or success in school. Further, I am trying to understand how being the child of an immigrant affects the way a child is treated by peers and teachers, how they view other children who are different from them, and the coping mechanisms they use to deal with real or perceived prejudice.

My research uses a multimethod approach to investigate the lives of these children. I am focusing on 450 elementary school-aged children in the Providence, Rhode Island, area who have at least one parent born in Portugal, the Dominican Republic, or Cambodia. I try to determine how the many factors affecting immigrant children influence their success in school. As a result, we are interviewing children, parents, and teachers and observing classrooms to better understand the children's daily lives.

In my longitudinal study, I am following the same group of children for 3 years; right now I am in the third year of the study. By following the same children over time, I also hope to understand how children's attitudes about school, race, ethnicity, and nationality change developmentally. How do the ways they identify themselves in terms of race, ethnicity, and nationality change over time? Do their feelings about school, teachers, and friends vary as they get older?

Cynthia Garcia Coll is a professor and the Mittleman Family Director of the Center for the Study of Human Development at Brown University.

Because we are still collecting data, I cannot tell yet what factors lead children of immigrants to be successful or unsuccessful in school. Based on our data, I hope to be able to make recommendations to educators and policymakers about the needs of children of immigrants and their families to help ensure that all children are successful in school.

Other studies support the link between the type of occupations present in a community and high school dropout. In a study of youth from Virginia (Stallmann & Johnson, 1996), a higher percentage of service occupations in a community was associated with increased rates of dropout. A higher percentage of managerial/professional occupations was associated both with a lowered dropout rate and a greater likelihood that high school graduates would continue their education.

The immigrant status of an adolescent's family is another contextual variable that may relate to school performance. The work of Cynthia Garcia Coll, presented in Meet the Researcher Box 11.1, discusses this relation.

Variation in the key contexts of youth is related to differential outcomes of school experiences, but individual differences among adolescents in their psychological and behavioral characteristics may moderate the potential influences of the school on youth development.

Adolescent Diversity and School Functions

Issues to Consider

- What factors influence academic achievement?
- How are self-handicapping behaviors linked to academic achievement?
- How does orientation to peers affect school performance?
- How are extracurricular activities associated with school-related behaviors?

Psychological characteristics of youth, such as self-regard, motivation, and identity, interrelate with contextual influences to influence development and achievement in schools. For instance, differences among youth in their academic motivation to succeed in school have been identified as a key basis of academic achievement (e.g., Eccles, 1991).

Being motivated to master a subject and to be socially responsible, and expectancies about one's success, are associated with good grades among young adolescents (Wentzel, 1993). Expectancies for success were the major predictors of middle school students' class effort and grades (Goodenow, 1993). Support from teachers enhanced this motivation, especially for girls. Positive motivational beliefs, such as success expectancies, are associated with the ability of youth to regulate their learning in classrooms and to take more control over their knowledge acquisition (Pintrich, Roeser, & DeGroot, 1994).

Self-regard variables are also associated with academic achievement. Positive self-image is linked to academic achievement as measured through grade point average among young adolescents (Roberts & Petersen, 1992). This association varies across the school years. The relation between self-image and achievement decreases for girls and increases for boys as they move from the sixth to the seventh grade (Roberts et al., 1990). This trend reverses itself for girls, but remains stable for boys, between the seventh and the eighth grade.

A key dimension of diversity related to school performance involves differences among students in their tendencies to do immediately and efficiently the schoolwork assigned to them. In a study of about 250 eighth graders (Midgley & Urdan, 1995), students who procrastinated, allowed

Self-handicapping behaviors Actions of procrastination and not studying that lead to low achievement.

Community service is a prominent part of many adolescents' school experiences.

other youth to keep them from studying, or deliberately did not try to do the work given to them were prototypic of low-achieving students. Boys, more so than girls, showed these **self-handicapping behaviors** (Midgley & Urdan, 1995). Feelings of self-consciousness, low self-worth, and associations with friends who had a negative orientation to academics were among the other variables linked to self-handicapping behaviors (Midgley & Urdan, 1995). Some of Carol Midgley's recent work on school, motivation, and achievement is presented in Meet the Researcher Box 11.2.

Being oriented to peers is not in itself an indicator of problematic school performance. Volunteering in school to help other students is associated with better self-esteem, less depression, and fewer problem behaviors, particularly among male adolescents (Switzer et al., 1995). In a longitudinal study of more than 200 youth between grades 6 and 8, pursuit of social goals

MEET THE RESEARCHER BOX 11.2

CAROL MIDGLEY

INVESTIGATING HOW THE LEARNING ENVIRONMENT INFLUENCES ADOLESCENTS' MOTIVATION AND ACHIEVEMENT

My colleagues and I use goal orientation theory as the lens through which we examine the effect of the middle school learning environment on adolescents' motivation and achievement. In some schools the message is conveyed to students that they should *demonstrate* their ability. Competition, social comparison, and relative ability are emphasized. We call this a "performance" goal structure. In other schools, the message conveyed to students is that they should *develop* their ability. Mastery, effort, and improvement are emphasized. We call this a "mastery" goal structure. Research provides evidence of the negative effect on students of a performance goal structure and the positive effects of a mastery goal structure.

Because our studies have included many participants, we are able to examine the effect of schools and classrooms on students' motivation and achievement. For example, in a recent study undertaken with my colleagues Avi Kaplan and Margaret Gheen, we found that students reported engaging in disruptive behavior significantly more in some classrooms than in others. When students, on average, perceived an emphasis on mastery goals in the classroom, the average level of disruptive behavior was lower. In contrast, when students perceived an emphasis on performance goals in the classroom, the average level of disruptive behavior was higher. In a study conducted with my colleagues Tim Urdan and Eric Anderman, we found that student reports of self-handicapping (withdrawing effort to protect self-worth) were significantly higher in some classrooms than in others. Students used handicapping strategies more in classrooms in which teachers reported using approaches to instruction that emphasized performance goals.

In 1970 Charles Silberman called the junior high school the "cesspool" of American education. Many

Carol Midgley is a research scientist in the Combined Program in Education and Psychology at the University of Michigan. She has directed several large-scale longitudinal research studies using achievement goal theory as the motivational framework. This work is summarized in a soon-to-be-published book titled *Goals, Goal Structures, and Patterns of Adaptive Learning.*

teachers, parents, and adolescents agreed. Since that time, many middle-level schools have initiated reforms. Ten years ago we asked elementary and middle school students about the goals emphasized in their schools. Middle school students said their schools emphasized performance goals more and mastery goals less than did elementary schools. The schools in this study had adopted the middle school grade configuration but had not implemented the recommended reforms. Recently we replicated this study in three school districts in which middle school reforms had been undertaken. Middle school students no longer perceived an increase in the emphasis on performance goals. However, they still perceived a decrease in mastery goals.

It is a cause for concern that the emphasis on mastery goals still declines when students move to reformed middle schools. In a recent study, we found that students who perceived a decline in the emphasis on mastery goals during the transition to middle school also reported a decline in their feelings of academic efficacy, their use of self-regulation strategies, and their positive feelings toward school. Their negative feelings toward school increased, and their grades declined.

Now there is a backlash against the middle school reform movement. In a recent book by Tucker and Codding, middle schools were labeled "the wasteland of our primary and secondary landscape," reminiscent of Silberman's comments three decades ago. This is unfortunate, in that many of the middle school reforms have had a positive effect on students. We hope that our research will provide information to educators and policymakers about the need to increase the emphasis on mastery goals in middle-level schools, without increasing the emphasis on performance goals.

was associated with efforts to perform well in English classes (Wentzel, 1996). Proficiency in English classes may be a good indicator of more general academic attainment. In a study of more than 1,600 Mexican American eighth graders (Singh & Hernandez-Gantes, 1996), English language proficiency was related to educational aspirations and academic achievements.

Another way in which youth differ in regard to school-related behaviors is in respect to their involvement in nonschool **extracurricular activities.** Males in middle school gain in status through participation in extracurricular activities more so than do females (Eder & Kinney, 1995). The majority of youth enrolled in high school full time also work part time, and therefore the workplace is a significant context for youth behavior and development (Steinberg, 1983; Vondracek, 1999; Vondracek, Lerner, & Schulenberg, 1986, and see Chapter 7 for a discussion of the impacts of work on adolescent development). Teachers express considerable concern about how their students' employment is related to their academic performance (Bills, Helms, & Ozcan, 1995). Nevertheless, there is little evidence that teachers adjust their classroom behavior to accommodate the possible needs of working students (Bills et al., 1995).

The individual's behavioral, motivational, affective, and self-regulatory characteristics all play a role in academic performance during adolescence (Wentzel et al., 1990). When coupled with socially competent behavior, significant enhancement of school achievement occurs (Wentzel, 1991). Some of the recent work of Kathryn R. Wentzel on social behavior in school is presented in Meet the Researcher Box 11.3.

Other individual characteristics such as spatial ability, content knowledge, knowledge about problem-solving strategies, temperamental style, and physical attractiveness are also associated with academic achievement (Byrnes & Takahara, 1993; Casey et al., 1995; Guerin et al., 1994; Jovanovic & Lerner, 1994; Lerner et al., 1990).

Conclusions About the Functions of Schools

Together, the associations among schools, other contexts of youth development, and adolescent diversity underscore the fact that a diverse array of individual and contextual variables combine to pro-

Extracurricular activities
Events and activities that take place outside the academic realm of school.

vide the bases of the range of different outcomes for youth developing in the context of schools. Given this significance of the school context for adolescent development, it is understandable that when school problems occur they can have broad impact on the lives of young people.

School Underachievement, Failure, and Dropout

Issues to Consider
- What statistics support the idea that a large number of youth are ill prepared to function in society?
- What is the single most important action youth can take to improve their future economic prospects?

About 25% of the approximately 40 million children and adolescents enrolled in 82,000 public U.S. elementary and secondary schools are at risk for school failure (Dryfoos, 1994). Each year about 700,000

Not all young people are equally engaged in classroom activities.

MEET THE RESEARCHER BOX 11.3

KATHRYN R. WENTZEL
SOCIAL BEHAVIORS IN SCHOOLS

Each day at school, most adolescents work to maintain and establish interpersonal relationships, they strive to develop social identities and a sense of belongingness, observe and model standards for performance displayed by others, and are rewarded for behaving in ways that are valued by teachers and peers. Quite often, children who succeed at these activities are also the most successful students.

My research addresses two broad questions of relevance for understanding the role of these various social endeavors in young adolescents' lives at school: (1) What must adolescents do to be successful at school and (2) what motivates them to be successful? In addressing these questions, I have concentrated on identifying ways in which interpersonal relationships with parents, peers, and teachers might influence the development of young adolescents' social and emotional adjustment and, in turn, how these aspects of young adolescents' functioning are related to their social and academic successes in middle school.

Recently, I have begun to study the influence of teacher-student relationships on young adolescents' adjustment to school. This line of inquiry is based on the notion

Kathryn R. Wentzel is a professor of human development in the Department of Human Development/Institute for Child Study at the University of Maryland, College Park.

that mechanisms by which parents influence their children's development might be generalizable to the classroom. In other words, it is clear that parents promote the development of social and emotional skills that can influence how well their children do in school. However, it might also be true that teachers can promote further development of these skills by behaving in ways that are characteristic of effective parents.

To begin work in this area, I conducted several studies of teacher characteristics and student motivation and performance in the classroom. My initial findings indicated that perceived support from teachers is related to positive changes in student motivation over time, that social support from teachers contributes to student motivation over and above support from parents and peers, and that students

ascribe specific characteristics to caring and supportive teachers that match the characteristics of effective parents.

My current work has extended this research by utilizing models of parenting to identify specific teacher characteristics related to student motivation. It appears that for African American as well as European American middle-class children, characteristics of effective parents, including consistent rule setting, high expectations and demands for maturity, democratic communication, and nurturance, also describe effective teachers. These characteristics also appear to explain levels of student motivation and performance, with high expectations being the most consistent positive predictor of students' school-related goals and interests, and low levels of nurturance being the most consistent negative predictor of academic performance and social behavior.

I am also continuing research on the relative contribution of teachers and peers to adolescents' school adjustment. My graduate students and I are looking at teacher and peer contributions to four dimensions of classroom climate: emotional support, safety, instrumental help, and values for social and academic competence. Our preliminary findings suggest that teachers have a far more pervasive influence on students' adjustment than do classmates. Moreover, the strongest influence on student outcomes, such as classroom grades, behavior, and interest, appears to be the degree to which students believe their teachers to be emotionally supportive.

We hope that our research will promote further understanding of why some teachers are so effective with young adolescent students when others are not. In particular, we hope to increase knowledge concerning how teachers can contribute to the overall social and emotional climate of their classrooms, including how adolescents relate to each other, and to identify ways to help students themselves contribute to the development of socially supportive school environments.

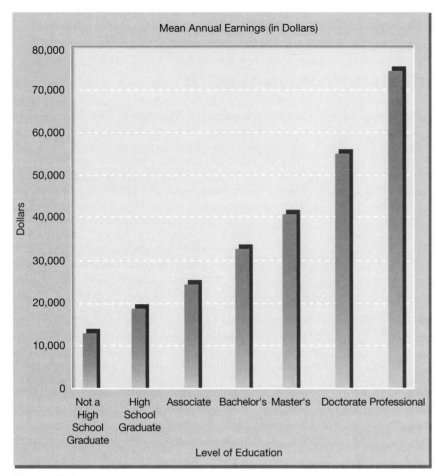

Figure 11.1
Higher levels of education are linked to higher annual earnings (data are for incomes in 1992). (*Source*: Carnegie Corporation of New York, 1995.)

degree added $40,000 to the average annual income of college graduates (Carnegie Corporation of New York, 1995).

Despite the advantages to a youth's life chances and to the quality of life of his or her more proximal (e.g., family) and more distal (e.g., community) context, youth continue to drop out of school. Even for those who remain in school, growing evidence indicates that many young people do not achieve at levels expected of them.

There are numerous indicators of the seriousness of the problems of underachievement, and of school failure and dropout, among today's youth. As illustrations, consider the following:

- Only 28% of eighth graders scored at or above their expected proficiency level in reading in 1994. Two percent read at or above an advanced level (Carnegie Corporation of New York, 1995).

- In 1990, 7% of the eighth-grade class of 1988 (most of whom were then 15 and 16 years old) were dropouts. By their senior year (1992), 12% of this class were dropouts. Dropout rates vary by students' race/ethnicity: European American (9.4%); African American (14.5%); Latino (18.3%); Asian/Pacific Islander (7.0%); and Native American (25.4%) (Carnegie Corporation of New York, 1995). Figure 11.2 presents further details about racial and ethnic differences in the United States in the nature of dropping out of school.

- At any point in time, about 18% of all 18- to 24-year-old dropouts, and 30% of 25–34 year old dropouts, are under supervision of the criminal justice system. Among African Americans the corresponding percentages are about 50% and 75% (Mincy, 1994; National Research Council, 1993).

youth drop out of school, and about 25% of all 18- and 19-year-olds have not graduated from high school (Center for the Study of Social Policy, 1992, 1993; Dryfoos, 1990; Simons, Finlay, & Yang, 1991). The costs to society in having large numbers of youth ill prepared to contribute productively to society and the costs to youth themselves are enormous.

Remaining in school is the single most important action youth can take to improve their future economic prospects (see Figure 11.1). In 1992 a high school graduate earned almost $6,000 per year more than a high school dropout (Carnegie Corporation of New York, 1995). College graduates in 1992 had a mean annual income of $32,629, whereas high school graduates had a mean annual income of $18,737. Earning a professional

- During the 1980s, school dropout rates for African Americans living in inner cities were between 40% and 50% (Mincy, 1994; National Research Council, 1993).

- High school dropout rates are 300% higher among poor young adults, of all race or ethnic backgrounds, than they are among non-poor young adults (National Research Council, 1993; Simons et al., 1991).

- African American youth graduate from high school at about the same rate as do European American youth. Across the nation the percentage of European American and African American males, aged 18 to 24 years, who have not completed high school is about 24% and 32%, respectively. However, the number of years needed to graduate from high school is greater among African Americans (National Research Council, 1993).

- About 4.5 million 10- to 14-year-olds are one or more years behind in their modal grade level (Simons et al., 1991).

- Each added year of secondary education reduces the probability of public welfare dependency in adulthood by 35% (National Research Council, 1993).

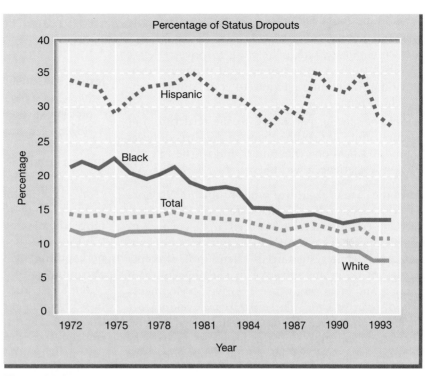

Figure 11.2
Disparities exist in dropout rates among ethnic groups, 1972–1992. (*Source:* Carnegie Corporation of New York, 1995.)

Bases and Implications of School Problems: Diversity and Context

Issues to Consider
- What are the individual and contextual variables linked to school problems and other risks related to youth development?

- What approach do effective dropout prevention programs take?

The problems of school underachievement, failure, and dropout are linked to other key problems and risks associated with youth development, including unsafe sex, teenage pregnancy and teenage parenting, delinquency and often violent crime, and substance use and abuse (Dryfoos, 1990; Lerner, 1995; Lerner & Galambos, 1998). School problems as well as the other problems and risks related to youth development are associated with both individual and contextual variables. These include the following:

- *Individual variables*, relating to cognitive abilities, motivation, personality, and self.

- *Peer variables*, pertaining to peer reputation or status, and to the nature of the social or antisocial behaviors shown by one's peers.

- *Family variables*, pertaining to the nature of parental child-rearing style, socialization practices, and types of behavioral interactions between the youth and his or her parents.

- *Community variables*, relating to poverty level, social support for learning, and programs providing wholesome activities to youth during non-school hours.
- *School setting*, pertaining to the structure and curriculum of the school and to the sorts of peers and teachers one encounters and to the interactions experienced with them.

As is the case in regard to other problem behaviors of adolescence, the entire system of individual-through-contextual relations needs to be engaged to understand the source of adolescents' school problems. This same system needs attention in attempts to design programs effective in keeping youth in schools and in promoting the positive developments schools can provide. These positive developments include knowledge, abilities and skills, self-esteem, social relationships, and the opportunity to contribute productively to self, family, community, and society.

Effective dropout prevention programs take a **systems approach.** They deal simultaneously with the set of risks facing youth, including poverty, substance use, unsafe sex, and delinquency. They engage all levels of the context including the school, businesses, governmental bodies, religious institutions, and youth-serving organizations in building a setting that not only prevents dropout but through such a collaborative setting promotes the positive development of youth.

Applications Box 11.1 describes an exemplary program of this sort. Although centered in Virginia, the program Cities in Schools has been adopted across the United States and throughout the world.

As illustrated by the Cities in Schools program, adequate understanding of youth academic problems involves an integrated focus on individual and contextual influences on adolescent school behaviors. Although many researchers and educators may focus initially on either individual or institutional factors, most end up appreciating the interrelation of these levels. This integration is illustrated in the following sections that discuss individual and institutional bases of school problems.

Systems approach Approach to programs that deals with multiple problems simultaneously and engages all levels of the context to prevent problems and to promote the positive development of youth.

Equivalency degrees Degrees equivalent to a high school diploma.

Individual Bases of School Problems in Adolescence

Issues to Consider
- What are some of the individual bases of school problems in adolescence?
- How does a return to school affect teenage mothers?

In a longitudinal study of about 440 urban African American adolescents across grades 7 to 9 (Connell et al., 1995), students who avoided risk behaviors in junior high school and reported themselves as more engaged in school were likely to remain in school. School engagement was associated with perceptions of self-competence and feelings of autonomy and relatedness to the school setting (Connell et al., 1995). Males from more advantaged families reported less support from adults in the school, and females from poorer families experienced less support from adults in the home (Connell et al., 1995).

In a study of the characteristics of about 550 high school students from a working-class community in South Africa (Flisher & Chalton, 1995), engagement in risk behaviors was associated with dropout. Substance abuse, and, for girls, sexual intercourse, were linked to dropout (Flisher & Chalton, 1995).

Other research confirms the findings of Connell et al. (1995) regarding the association between school engagement and dropout. In a nationally representative sample of American high school youth (Jordan, Lara, & McPartland, 1966), European American adolescents, more so than African American or Latino youth, cited alienation from school as the reason for dropping out. The major reason given by African American males for dropping out was suspension or expulsion from school; Latinas and African American females tended to cite family-related reasons for dropping out (Jordan et al., 1996).

Across all ethnic/racial groups, most youth reported that they had plans to resume their education (Jordan et al., 1996). Eventually, about 95% of American males and females who go on to parenthood do graduate from high school or obtain **equivalency degrees** (Hernandez, 1993). Among African American and Puerto Rican teenage mothers who do return to school, there are fewer repeat pregnancies and a greater tendency to seek postsecondary

applications box 11.1

Preventing Youth from Dropping Out of School

School dropout results in the loss of a great part of a young person's chances for a productive and healthy life. Dropout is a loss for society too—of the human and social capital it needs to prosper and grow, and thus to continue to offer a quality life to all of its citizens. Given the enormous potential costs of school dropout and, in turn, of the several other risks associated with it, a broad community approach is warranted. All portions of the community with a stake in keeping youth in schools—and this constitutes virtually everyone in a community—and all people with expertise in helping youth with the diverse problems they face must be brought together.

This comprehensive integration is a key feature of one of the most successful dropout prevention programs. Centered in Virginia, it has been adopted throughout the United States and has been influential around the world as well.

Encouraging Young People to Stay in School: The "Communities in Schools" Program

Each day nearly 3,000 young people drop out of school in the United States. The reasons are complex and can range from family crises, drug and alcohol abuse, and homelessness to teenage pregnancy and a belief that "no one cares." This educational crisis is creating a new underclass of untrained and unemployable citizens.

Well before the dropout crisis registered in the national consciousness, Communities in Schools (CIS), which was founded in 1977 and is considered one of the nation's leading community-based organizations, has been helping kids succeed in school and prepare for life. With its national headquarters based in Alexandria, Virginia, CIS reaches out across the nation with 154 independently incorporated programs in 32 states, all working to ensure America's underserved youth receive the additional support necessary to succeed in life. Today, more than 1 million students and their families in 243 school districts around the country have access to services through CIS.

CIS works by empowering communities to meet the needs of its young people. It begins by teaching individual communities how to establish a coalition of business, education, social service, and government leaders. Each local CIS program has its own board of directors and is autonomous from the Communities In Schools National organization. Moreover, these local public/private partnerships connect the appropriate social services with at-risk youth.

Once a public/private partnership is established, CIS' mission is to create a CIS program within the public school system. Local CIS staff identify those students most in need of assistance. By working with various youth-serving agencies in the community, including tutors, social workers, employment counselors, recreation workers, and health care professionals, necessary personnel are repositioned to work on-site in the identified schools. The result is a coordinated, personalized, safe environment for youth. Outcomes have been impressive: grades have risen as have school attendance and overall scholastic achievement.

Source: International Youth Foundation, 2001. <www.iyfnet.org>

---

education (Leadbeater, 1996). Returning to school was associated with fewer stressful life events, more family support, fewer depressive symptoms, and greater commitment to a career (Leadbeater, 1996).

Institutional Bases of School Problems in Adolescence

Issues to Consider
- What are the goals of schools?
- Why are schools being charged with providing services that were previously supplied by other social institutions?

- Why are schools failing to provide a goodness of fit with the social, health, and cognitive needs of adolescents?

Given that the entire developmental system is involved in both the bases of school problems and in the solution to them, it is crucial to understand how any component of the system is involved in positive or negative outcomes. Individual, peer group, and family variables may influence positive or negative developments in school, and schools in their structure and function may contribute to the problems experienced by adolescent students (Dryfoos, 1994, 1995).

U.S. schools are intended to promote the intellectual and social development of students. Schools are also supposed to be contexts for the socialization of cultural values and for the development of citizens competent to pursue healthy individual and family lives and to contribute productively to our society. Simply, the goals of schools are the development of intellectually reflective, healthy, caring, and ethical people who are good citizens on the path to lifetimes of meaningful work (Carnegie Council on Adolescent Development, 1989).

Because of changes in the nature of the American family across this century (Hernandez, 1993) and the growth of youth poverty and of violent crime and other risk behaviors among adolescents (Dryfoos, 1990; Huston, 1991; Lerner, 1995, Schorr, 1988), schools are increasingly charged with providing services that were previously the aegis of other social institutions (Dryfoos, 1994). That is, "Until recently and for centuries, young generations were integrated into society via their families. During this century, school experiences became the *conditio sine qua non* to participate in the benefits of social life in most places in the world" (Alvarez, 1992, p. 1).

All too often, schools are not fulfilling these functions. School programs and school structures frequently fail to provide a **goodness of fit** with the complex health, social, and cognitive needs of youth (Ames & Ames, 1989; Dryfoos, 1994; Eccles & Midgley, 1989). This failure is derived in part from at least three interrelated problems (Dryfoos, 1994; Lerner, 1994).

First, schools are not adequately addressing the problems presented by the large proportions of U.S. youth engaging in one, and often several, of the other major high-risk behaviors of adolescence. The risk of school failure is interrelated with the three other types of major risk behaviors in adolescence: unsafe sex, drug and alcohol use and abuse, and delinquency (Dryfoos, 1990). Other community-based organizations may have to help address these problems and "today, thousands of youth programs

Goodness of fit Degree to which two individuals and/or groups match in goals or styles.

Safety issues have become a prominent part of the school experiences of many youth.

are complementing, and in some cases supplementing, the role of families and schools" (Alvarez, 1992, p. 1).

Second, the increasing prevalence of youth poverty is challenging the resources of schools and diminishing the relevance and utility of current portfolios of school-based programs (e.g., Pungello et al., 1996). Youth poverty exacerbates the risk behaviors of adolescents. Poverty is associated with early school failure as well as with unemployability, violent crime, and feelings of hopelessness and despair (McLoyd & Wilson, 1992; Schorr, 1988). Accordingly, "Schools cannot educate children who are too 'stressed-out' to concentrate. Teachers are not trained as social workers, and cannot possibly attend to their jobs if they must spend all of their time trying to remedy problems" (Dryfoos, 1995, p. 149).

Last and perhaps most important, failure is occurring because of the absence of a thorough integration of the school into the community, an integration involving the services of other youth-serving institutions, parents, and youth themselves. As one scholar has described this point,

Educational experts have excellent ideas about how to improve the educational outcomes of disadvantaged children, with extensive research and demonstration models that work in low-income communities (Comer, 1989; Slavin, Karweit, & Wasik, 1994; Wehlage et al.,

1989). Consensus is building among educators about the importance of bringing support services into schools that will strengthen their efforts at restructuring (U.S. Government Accounting Office, 1993; Usdan, 1994). Organizations such as the National Association of State Boards of Education, the National Association of School Boards, and the Council of Chief State School Officers have been in the vanguard of task forces and commissions that call for comprehensive school-based service programs. (Dryfoos, 1995, p. 150)

Addressing School Failures: Understanding the Influence of Schools on Adolescents

Considerable evidence indicates the need to restructure schools innovatively in a manner that involves the inclusion of comprehensive, integrative services. A key illustration of this need is that approximately one fourth of the 40 million children and adolescents enrolled in U.S. public elementary and secondary schools are at risk for school failure (Dryfoos, 1994).

Nevertheless, in the midst of this challenge, youth still attend schools and are affected by their structure and function. Therefore, we must understand the influence of schools on youth development. Two general approaches have been taken to understand these influences on adolescents. First, researchers study how the school as an institution influences youth behavior and development through its organization or curriculum. Second, researchers examine the nature and bases of adolescent behavior and development within the school context. We consider both of these approaches.

Reorganizing and Reforming Schools

Issues to Consider
- Through what procedures can schools better address the problems of youth in schools?
- What kind of classroom and school organizations are there, and what effects do they have?
- What are full-service schools and how do they deal with the multiple problems facing adolescent students?

One way to address the problems of the youth enrolled in schools is **school restructuring.** Schools may be organized differently and the functions of schools may be altered. These latter changes may be termed **school reforms.** Reorganization and reform are related in the actual practice of trying to change schools to serve youth better. These linkages are illustrated in the following discussion of some ways in which reorganization and reform have been approached.

Schools may group students on the basis of their academic ability. Both positive and negative effects on development occur in relation to **ability grouping.** For students with low mathematics ability, grouping at the beginning of junior high school has some negative and no positive effects on tenth-grade math achievement (Fuligni, Eccles, & Barber, 1995). For students with medium and high levels of ability, grouping at the beginning of junior high has a positive influence on tenth-grade performance.

Given these differential effects of groupings on youth, it is vital to have as much information about a student as possible when deciding if and how to group him or her. Parents input would seem valuable here. Although in most school districts parents do have some influence over the process by which their children are ability grouped and/or placed in particular courses, the degree to which such parent participation is welcomed, restricted, or even thwarted varies across school systems (Useem, 1991).

One innovation in grouping provides separate schools for African American male adolescents, a group of youth at particular risk for school problems and dropout (Lerner, 1995; Mincy, 1994). In such settings the youth receive an instructional program designed specifically for them. As compared to African American male youth enrolled within a typical school structure, youth in this specialized context perceive themselves as more academically competent, rate their teachers and classmates as more supportive, and attend school more regularly (Hudley, 1995). Although more evaluation of such an innovation is needed, such a school organization might constitute an effective intervention for youth at risk for school problems.

Other variations in classroom organization also influence youth with a diversity of outcomes associated with these differences. Classrooms can be organized in regard to the formats of teacher-student

School restructuring Altering the organization of a school.

School reform Altering the functions of a school.

Ability grouping Placing students in a classroom based on their academic ability.

interactions that take place within them. Lectures, question and answer sessions, provision of discussion activities, and encouraging student participation in shaping the content of the course are examples of different formats that can be used. All of these formats have been found to enhance eighth graders' achievement in both English and social studies classes (Gamoran & Nystrand, 1991).

However, schools by themselves are unable to deal adequately with the multiple problems facing many of their adolescent students. One tactic addresses the problem that schools are not part of communitywide, multiagency, collaborative efforts to stem the tide of adolescent educational failure coupled with other risk behaviors. The leading spokesperson for the creation of schools involved collaboratively with the community in this manner is Joy G. Dryfoos. She terms schools that are collaborative with the community **full-service schools** (Dryfoos, 1994, 1995). Applications Box 11.2 describes the vision Dryfoos has developed for such schools.

Dryfoos's (1994) call for the creation of full-service schools constitutes an appeal to reorganize and reform the structure and function of these institutions. Research, although still in its initial stages, suggests that such revisions have positive influences on youth. When middle schools undertook reforms that included building school-community partnerships, enabling teachers of different subject areas to work together on interdisciplinary teams, and bringing community volunteers into the school to help the students discuss connections between social studies and art, students' awareness of art increased, they developed attitudes and preferences of particular styles of art, and their movement from concrete to abstract thinking was enhanced (Epstein & Dauber, 1995). Changing a school's organization, in the direction of the reforms described by Dryfoos (1995), can be beneficial to youth.

Full-service schools Schools that are part of a communitywide, multiagency, collaborative effort to prevent adolescent educational failure coupled with other risk behaviors.

Teachers may create a classroom climate that effectively engages students in academic work.

The School as a Context for Development

Issues to Consider

- What facets of adolescent development need to be understood in relation to school transitions?
- How do school transitions affect adolescents?
- How does the change from a focus on mastery to a focus on performance influence adolescents?
- How are pubertal changes and school transitions related?

The second general approach to understanding the influence of schools on adolescent behavior involves studying the school as a developmental setting. Here the focus is on the experiences that occur within school. These experiences involve stresses on adjustment that may occur when youth make a transition from one school level or setting (e.g., elementary school) to another (e.g., middle school), problems that may exist when school changes are linked to other developmental changes experienced by the adolescent, or how achievement may be facilitated when there is a goodness of fit (Lerner & Lerner, 1989) between the adolescent's characteristics of individuality and the demands placed on the adolescent in the classroom.

Instances of all these facets of adolescent development within the school context have been studied in relation to the transitions youth make into and out of middle school/junior high school and into and out of high school.

The Potential Role of Full-Service Schools

Joy Dryfoos (1990, 1994, 1995) believes that enhancing the role of schools in child and adolescent development rests on the creation of full-service schools. The state of Florida, in 1991 legislation to support comprehensive school-based programs, has defined a full-service school as one that

> integrates education, medical, social and/or human services that are beneficial to meeting the needs of children and youth and their families on school grounds or in locations with which are easily accessible. Full Service Schools provide the types of prevention, treatment, and support services children and families need to succeed . . . services that are high quality and comprehensive and are built on interagency partnerships . . . among state and local and public and private entities . . . [including] education, health care, transportation, job training, child care, housing, employment, and social services. (Dryfoos, 1994, p. 142)

Such schools involve, then, in a fully integrated manner: (1) communitywide, multiagency collaborations, and (2) a full range of social services (e.g., health centers, vocational guidance and career development programs, and counseling services) that are (3) embedded within schools but are administered by the collaborating nonschool agencies and use (4) citizen input and volunteerism.

These components of the full-service school concept are congruent with Dryfoos's (1995) vision for these schools. In her view, the full-service school "integrates the best of school reform with all other services that children, youth, and their families need, most of which can be located in a school building" (p. 152).

Given the comprehensive and integrative character of full-service schools, it is clear that such institutions engage children, adolescents, and their families across the life span. Emphasizing a preventive and capacity-building orientation to address the co-occurrence of child and adolescent problems, such schools provide integrated services for both, or even prenatally, through the point that the person is launched successfully on a path involving a productive and healthy adult life. Dryfoos (1994, 1995) finds that, to accomplish these ends, full-service schools typically incorporate several components of service (as distinguished from components pertinent to educational restructuring). These service components include the following.

A Planning Process

This process begins with assessing the capacities and needs of the community, a step aimed at ensuring that the structure and function of the full-service school use the resources and meet the specific needs of the children and families of the community (cf. Kretzmann & McKnight, 1993). Here it is critical that the school and community

agencies overcome turf issues and create a vision of a new type of joint institution. Thus this planning process must yield "an efficient design, utilizing the contributions of each party to building strong and durable full service schools" (Dryfoos, 1995, p. 42).

A Service Design Process

This process integrates new services with those health, social, and counseling services already present in the school. Thus, rather than replace existing programs, services are designed in the supplementary manner (Alvarez, 1992).

A Collaborative Governance Structure

This governance structure often takes the form of an advisory board, one that involves personnel from the school and from service agencies and parents, community leaders, and children and adolescents as well. This governance structure is based on an agreement among all collaborators to "pursue a shared vision and have common goals, expect to share resources, participate in joint decision-making, and use their personal and institutional power to change systems" (Dryfoos, 1995, pp. 26–27).

A System to Use Space for Primary Health Care and/or Other Services

If primary health care is provided, then an area in or near the school building is used. As noted by Dryfoos (1994, 1995), this space should be used for examination rooms, a laboratory, confidential counseling rooms, and an office for referrals and files. When primary health care is not provided in or near the school, school space should nevertheless be dedicated for individual and group counseling, parent education, and case management and referrals. Furthermore, space should be allocated for career information, play, clothing and food distribution, and food preparation. In addition to providing the space for these functions, the school provides maintenance and security. Moreover, classrooms, gyms, and computer facilities remain open for use by the community, and the doors of the school remain open before and after school, on weekends, and during the summer (Dryfoos, 1994, 1995).

Opportunities for Building Leadership

The building principal is instrumental in implementing the programs of the full-service school and in maintaining the programs' effective operation. A program director is responsible for the conduct of the services provided in the school and functions collaboratively with the governance structure.

School Transitions in Adolescence

For adolescents, perhaps the key school organizational influence on their development is encountered when they make the transition from elementary school to junior high school or middle school. Many youth look forward to the transition.

For example, students' perceptions of junior high school tend to be positive (Berndt & Mekos, 1995), perhaps because the transition to this more advanced school is associated with their feeling more mature. For instance, in a longitudinal study of about 100 adolescents from the spring of their sixth-grade school year to the end of their seventh-grade year, youth reported more positive than negative reactions to junior high school (Berndt & Mekos, 1995). However, although misbehaving sixth graders showed little concern about moving to junior high school, after the transition they perceived the junior high school less positively than did other students; in turn, high-achieving sixth graders expressed a lot of concern about moving to junior high school, but, after a year there, they felt more positive about it than the other students (Berndt & Mekos, 1995).

In turn, however, when the transition to junior high school or to middle school entails moving from a small school to a large one, initial optimism, prior to the transition, is often transformed into anxiety about it after the move (Cotterell, 1992). Any effects of the transition on students' academic performance or on their academic feelings and motivation may be due in part to the organization and curriculum of the junior high/middle school. In fact, the transition from elementary school to middle school *is* linked to negative changes in academic motivation and academic performance (Eccles & Midgley, 1989; Midgley, Anderman, & Hicks, 1995; Simmons & Blyth, 1987; Wigfield et al., 1991).

The transition to middle school is hard for youth for many reasons (Urdan, Midgley, & Wood, 1995). Changes in the adolescent's travel schedule to and from school, alterations in sleep and waking cycles to accommodate the middle school class schedule, altered parental expectations about independence in completing homework, homework load, and a new set of youth comprising the "crowd" (see Chapter 9) of youth in the school can all be difficult for adolescents. Adjusting to any of these changes could impact the motivation and achievement of a young person. However, one key basis for the change in motivation and achievement across the transition to middle school may be the different goals for students stressed in elementary school versus middle school (Midgley et al., 1995).

Middle schools place more stress on a student's relative ability (to other students), and less stress on how the student masters a given task, than is the case in elementary school (Midgley et al., 1995). In other words, middle schools emphasize the goal of performing well *on* a task, and not the goal of learning how *to do* a task (independent of how well one performs on the task). Both middle school teachers and students perceive (correctly) that this stress is present in the middle school classroom (Midgley et al., 1995).

This change in emphasis from elementary school (where learning how to do a task is important) to middle school (where performing well on that task is important) is associated with lessened motivation in mathematics (Mac Iver & Reuman, 1988; Midgley et al., 1995; Midgley, Feldlaufer, & Eccles, 1989a, 1989b). In turn, when there continues to be a stress on task goals in middle school, both students and teachers show self-efficacy. However, when stress on performance is present there is no connection to self-efficacy in either group (Midgley et al., 1995).

Other research has confirmed these relations between task goals and feelings of academic efficacy (Roeser, Midgley, & Urdan, 1996). Moreover, this research has been extended by demonstrating an association between perceived self-efficacy and the actual grades earned by middle school students.

School can be a stressful context for many adolescents.

Given, then, the changes in academic motivation found across the transition to middle school or junior high school, it is not surprising to learn that the transition is associated also with changes among adolescents in their optimism or pessimism about their future life successes. For instance, in a study of about 580 Japanese fifth through ninth graders (Koizumi, 1995), optimism scores were lower and pessimism scores were higher after the transition to junior high school (in the seventh grade). Greater pessimism was associated with less interest in school and with more negative academic performance and peer relationships (Koizumi, 1995).

In essence, then, the change in the middle school culture to a focus on performance, as opposed to one on learning activities or tasks, may contribute to students' perception that the middle school is a context that does not match, or fit with, their preferred style of making decisions about their learning. For instance, in a study of middle school mathematics classrooms, students saw fewer student decision-making opportunities in middle school as compared to elementary school (Midgley & Feldlaufer, 1987); teachers agree that this difference exists. More important, perhaps, students have a preference for more decision-making opportunities, whereas middle school teachers believe they should have *fewer* opportunities. This lack of congruence between students and teachers may be one source of the influence of middle school transition on the academic performance of youth.

Moreover, school transitions can have other effects on adolescent development. Simmons and Blyth (e.g., Simmons & Blyth, 1987; Simmons, Carlton-Ford, & Blyth, 1987) find that a decrease in self-esteem is most likely when a young adolescent female is experiencing simultaneously the changes associated with menarche and the contextual alterations associated with the transition from elementary school to middle or junior high school. Thus the work of Simmons, Blyth, and their colleagues illustrates that changes in both the adolescent and her school context contribute to developments in school.

In sum, the school as an institution—its organization, "culture," and curriculum—influences youth academic and personal development in several ways. Some of these linkages result in positive outcomes for youth, whereas others result in problematic ones. It is precisely because of this diversity of developmental outcomes that the school context is a key setting for youth development.

Conclusions About the Role of School in Adolescence

Today, schools are in a state of crisis. They are charged by society with doing more than just educating youth but faced with diminishing resources and challenged by the complex and serious problems shown by the young people they encounter. Important school reforms are being initiated to increase schools' capacities to fulfill their mission, and effective youth-serving programs are available to assist the efforts of schools to enhance the life chances of all youth, but schools must continue on a day-to-day basis to serve youth.

Schools, through their organization and curriculum, and by virtue of providing a key context for youth development, are having an ongoing influence on youth. Some of these contributions result in positive outcomes for adolescents and others are linked to negative ones. In both cases, this diversity of influence occurs because of the interconnections among the school, family, and peer contexts and, in turn, through the contribution made by characteristics of the developing person to the social relationships encountered in the school, the peer group, and the family.

Accordingly, to address the problems faced by schools and, in a more positive view, to enhance the contributions schools can make to healthy youth development, schools must seek more integration with the community, and thus must build bridges to the other key contexts affecting the developing adolescent. Such innovation will require school *policy changes*, will require the school to make *revisions* in its *programs*, and will necessitate that the school take steps to *assess* how well it is doing in implementing these altered approaches to its role in youth development. Table 11.1 presents the key policy, programmatic, and assessment issues faced by schools. Implementing the changes outlined in Table 11.1 will enable schools—and families and the broader community as well—to play a new and needed role in addressing the problems not just of schools but, more significantly, of the youth they serve.

Table 11-1	Reforming Schools to Address the Problems of Youth Development: Policy, Programmatic, and Assessment Issues

Policy Issues

Full-service schools should be created. Schools should become centers for the coordinated delivery of medical, mental health, and social service programs. These school-based centers should be (a) administered collaboratively by community agencies and youth-serving organizations; (b) focused on prevention and on enhancement; and (c) evaluated in both formative and summative terms that are reflective of community values and goals and engage the community in both the evaluation process and in the centers themselves.

The services provided by schools should be integrated. Comprehensiveness by itself is not sufficient to support the adolescent, his or her family, and the community.

School structures and programs should be reorganized to better meet the developmental needs of youth. Use of "team" or "house" organizations (i.e., of "schools within schools") can ease the middle school transition; students should be allowed to share control of assignments and of the evaluation of these tasks.

The focus of teacher education should be revised. Teaching should move from a subject matter emphasis to a holistic focus on the adolescent, and thus on his or her relations with peers, family members, and the community.

Programmatic Issues

Schools should offer a full range of integrated programs—those spanning the educational, medical, mental health, developmental, and social service needs of adolescents.

The design and administration of these integrated school programs must involve collaborations with the community, parents, and youths themselves. A focus on capacity building and on prevention should be maintained.

School policies, organization, and programs must be culturally competent (i.e., attuned to the values and traditions of the community within which the school exists). They also must be designed in light of the developmental and social needs of youth.

Teacher education and professional development programs should focus teachers' efforts primarily on building competent citizens and not on building subject matter competence per se. The latter focus is only a vehicle to produce the former, and thus greater emphasis on competency for life is warranted.

Assessment Issues

Schools must assess whether policies, structures, and programs are meeting the holistic needs of adolescents.

Barriers to the development and implementation of full-service schools must be identified and culturally competent means used to put such schools in place.

The active involvement of students, parents, school personnel, and the community must be ascertained. Means to enhance their collaborative involvement in the policies and programs of the school must be devised.

Source: Adapted from Lerner, R. M. (1994). Schools and adolescents. In P. C. McKenry & S. M. Gavazzi (Eds.), *Visions 2010: Families and adolescents*, 2(1), (pp. 14–15, 42–43). Minneapolis: National Council on Family Relations.

Summary

- Schools are training institutions, agents of cultural transmission, and a means to inculcate knowledge and values. Schools fulfill a maintenance-actualization role and are a place to develop optimal personal and interpersonal attributes and the ability to contribute to society.

- Schools provide a context for social interactions and relationship development and can facilitate an adolescent's independence from his or her parents. Schools also provide the adolescent with an opportunity to gain social status. Status can be earned at school through demonstrating a mastery over the curriculum, attaining high class standing, and by nonacademic interactions with peers. Future status can be earned through the training and education attained in school.

- Native American adolescents perceive that the structure of the school creates a barrier to their academic success. This perception is associated with their lessened school performance.

- Perceptions by adolescents that their teachers care about them can be associated with enhanced motivation to achieve positive academic and social outcomes.

- For African American, European American, and Latino students, social support from the family is associated with students' grades, scores on a standardized achievement test, and teacher ratings and enhanced self-esteem.

- The factors associated with the achievement of Asian and Asian American students include having parents and peers who hold high standards, holding a belief that one succeeds through effort, having positive attitudes about achievement, studying diligently, and being less apt to distract youth from studying.

- When parents react negatively to school performance, youth show negative performance.

- African American students' awareness of discrimination toward people of their race is associated with their perception that academic achievement is not important. High ethnic identity, however, is associated with school engagement and achievement.

- A higher percentage of service occupations in a community is associated with increased dropout; an increased percentage of managerial/professional occupations is associated with lowered dropout and a greater likelihood that high school graduates would continue their education.

- Self-handicapping behaviors such as procrastination, allowing other youth to keep one from studying, or deliberately not trying to do work are associated with low-achieving students. Boys show more self-handicapping behaviors than girls do.

- Volunteering in school to help other students is linked to better self-esteem, less depression, and fewer problem behaviors, particularly for male adolescents.

- Males in middle school gain status through participation in extracurricular activities more so than females do.

- Work is a significant extracurricular activity for adolescents but there is little evidence that teachers adjust their classroom behaviors to accommodate the possible needs of working students.

- About one fourth of the 40 million children and adolescents enrolled in U.S. public schools are at risk for school failure.

- Remaining in school is the single most important thing a youth can do to improve his or her future economic prospects. The costs of dropping out of school are enormous for society and for the quality of life of the young person.

- School problems, as well as other problems of adolescence, are associated with individual variables related to cognitive abilities, motivation, personality, and self; peer variables related to reputation and to the nature of behaviors shown by peers; family variables, relating to parental practices and parent-child interactions; community variables, relating to poverty level, social support, and the availability of programs; and school variables pertaining to structure and curriculum and to peer and teacher interactions.

- Effective dropout prevention programs take a systems approach that deals simultaneously with the set of risks facing youth and engages all levels of their contexts.

- Engagement in adolescent risk behaviors has been related to school dropout.

- European American students cite alienation, African American male students cite suspension or expulsion, and African American and Latina female students cite family-related reasons as explanations for dropping out of school.

- Returning to school is associated with fewer life stressful events, more family support, fewer depressive symptoms, and greater commitment to a career.

- Schools are a context for the socialization of cultural values and for the development of citizens competent to pursue goals and to contribute productively to and maintain civil society.

- The risk of school failure is interrelated with three other major risk behaviors: unsafe sex, drug and alcohol use and abuse, and delinquency. Schools are not adequately addressing the multiple problems facing a large proportion of U.S. youth engaged in high-risk behaviors.

- School restructuring involves organizing the school differently; school reform involves changing the functions of the school.

- Schools' use of ability grouping has positive effects for students with medium and high mathematics ability but not for students with low ability.

- Classrooms can be organized in regard to the formats of teacher-student interactions that take place, including lectures, question and answer sessions, provision of discussion topics, and encouragement of student participation in shaping curricular content.

- Full-service schools are involved collaboratively with the community to deal with the multiple problems facing adolescent students; they have been shown to have positive benefits for youth.

- Youth report more positive than negative reactions relating to the transition to junior high school. The transition is linked to negative changes in academic motivation and performance. It alters adolescents' perceptions of future life successes. There is lower optimism and higher pessimism after the transition.

- Both middle school teachers and students perceive a stress on performing well on a task rather than just learning how to do the task, which is associated with lessened motivation in mathematics.

- A decrease in self-esteem is most likely when an adolescent female is experiencing school transition and the changes associated with menarche at the same time.

Discussion Topics

1. How well did the structure of your high school support your development? Many school systems are questioning the schedules they employ. Did the early start of the day, timing of the lunch hour, time allowed for extracurricular activities, and number of days spent in school during the year impact your learning and/or your attitude about school in general? If so, in what ways?

2. Who were your favorite teachers in high school? What about them attracted you? Were they better able to interact socially with the students than were other teachers? Alternatively, was it the depth of their knowledge about certain topics that drew you to them? Or was it both? Did they show their admiration and respect in ways that other teachers did not? In what ways were they involved in the school? How did they make their presence known?

3. Did your ethnicity, race, socioeconomic status, and/or gender determine the general expectations for school success placed *on* you *by* others? How well did you meet those expectations? Did your ability to meet those expectations impact your eventual school success and your attitude about school? Do you think it will impact the career path you choose? Why or why not?

4. Did you have a job while in high school? If so, how did it impact your ability to meet the day-to-day expectations of your teachers and the social expectations of your peers? How did your experiences at your job positively impact your development? How might schools be more supportive of those students who need to work after school in order to support their families and/or begin to save money for college?

5. Do you know anyone who dropped out of high school? What became of him or her? What are some of the main factors that cause an adolescent to drop out of school? What can be done to decrease the dropout rate in the United States? Would this strategy work in other nations? If not, why not? How effective are the intervention programs and multifaceted approaches that we now employ to keep students interested and motivated to learn?

6. Do you think that schools and teachers have too much responsibility in raising today's youth? Why or why not? Do you think it is a necessary responsibility for them to take on? How well do schools live up to this responsibility?

7. What effect does grouping by ability have on student motivation, self-esteem, and school success?

8. Look over Applications Box 11.2. What do you think of Dryfoos's idea? How feasible is the idea of implementing full-service schools in your community? What needs would be met that are lacking now?

9. Think back on your transitions from elementary school to middle school and middle school/junior high to high school. How well prepared were you for these transitions? If you experienced any anxiety, what was the major focus of this anxiety? How well did the school you transitioned into address the anxieties of their new students? What could the school administration have done to make the students feel more at ease?

Key Terms

ability grouping (p. 269)

compulsory education (p. 257)

equivalency degrees (p. 266)

extracurricular activities (p. 262)

full-service schools (p. 270)

goodness of fit (p. 268)

maintenance-actualization (p. 257)

school reform (p. 269)

school restructuring (p. 269)

self-handicapping behaviors (p. 260)

systems approach (p. 266)

12

THE WORLD
OF CONTEMPORARY
ADOLESCENTS

Mr. Spence turned the handle of the door, pushed it open, and shoved his brief-case and suitcase quickly in ahead of him. "I'm home," he shouted. There was no answer. It had been a long business trip—five cities in six days—and he had eagerly anticipated coming home to his family.

He shouted again, "Hey, everyone. I'm here." But again there was no answer. He hung up his overcoat in the hall closet. Undoing his tie he walked slowly into the kitchen. There was a note from his wife on the counter. "Hi, Hon," it read, "I had to drive Karen to the mall for some clothes she needs for her class dance. There is a salad in the fridge. Max is home and you can call out for pizza. See you right after the mall closes."

"Welcome home, Steve," Mr. Spence thought to himself. Well, at least his son was home, he reasoned. He was glad that 12-year-old boys didn't like to go clothes shopping with their older sisters. "The poor kid," Mr. Spence observed. "Home alone with nothing to do." At least he and Max could now spend a few hours together, eating dinner and just hanging out.

He walked to the bottom of the stairs. "Max," he called. Still no answer. "Perhaps he's fallen asleep," Mr. Spence thought. He bounded up the stairs. At the end of the hall, he saw a light coming from behind Max's door. As he came closer he heard music playing. He knocked on his son's door. There was again no answer and so he opened it.

There was Max, seated at his desk in front of his computer, with his hand on the mouse. Mr. Spence saw that Max was talking online with his friends. However, at the same time his phone was cradled on his shoulder and he was immersed in a con-versation with someone. Max's voice was raised because a CD player was playing on his stereo system and his TV was on and tuned to a rock video station.

Max saw his father enter the room. He nodded in recognition. "Hey Max, how are you doing?" Mr. Spence asked. "Mom thought we should order some pizza. What would you like?"

"Nothing now, Dad. I'm busy now. I'll speak to you later . . . and please close the door when you go out."

LEARNING OBJECTIVES

1. To understand how the world changed in regard to media during the 20th century.
2. To recognize how a youth's use of media changes across adolescence.
3. To learn the effects of media, such as television, on youth.
4. To understand how the organization and function of the school are designed to provide youth with a context for social life.
5. To recognize how an exclusive focus on school activities puts a youth in a dilemma when applying to college.
6. To understand the key elements of what is developed among youth by virtue of their participation in a community-based organization.
7. To understand why it is important for young people to interact with caring adults and how such interactions can be promoted.
8. To learn how the positive experiences and developmental outcomes of youth in community sports activities can be maximized.
9. To understand how the niches selected by youth change across the adolescent years.
10. To understand how and why the contexts of adolescents must cooperate to enable them to develop in a positive manner.

Max is not an unusual adolescent. Today, the world of adolescents is a world of **media**. As discussed in prior chapters, family members, peers, teachers, and schools also populate the world of adolescents. These parts of the world of adolescents are perennial ones. They are influences on adolescent behavior and development that exist across historical eras.

There are also influences on adolescent behavior and development that are products of the contemporary historical moment. People, events, and inventions make a particular time in history different than others. To understand adolescence, we must appreciate both types of historical influences (Baltes et al., 1998, 1999).

One of the most striking features of the contemporary world of adolescents is the proliferation and ubiquitous presence of different forms of media. It is useful in a discussion of the world of contemporary adolescents to focus first on this facet of the world of today's youth.

The Media and Adolescent Behavior and Development

Technology has become a prominent means through which adolescents interact.

Media Means through which information or entertainment is passed such as television, radio, movies, magazines, computers, pagers, cell phones, and video games.

Issue to Consider
• How did the world change in regard to media during the 20th century?

Although Max and his peers perhaps cannot imagine a world without television, radio, the movies, magazines, computers, pagers, and cell phones, the invention and spread of these media were largely phenomena of the 20th century. As Huston and Wright (1998) comment,

It was this period that witnessed a radical transformation of the media environment. In less than 100 years, radio, movies, comic books, television, video games, CD-ROM, and audiotapes and videotapes have become a routine part of most children's environments. Digital television, the Internet, and virtual reality are spreading rapidly. In the United States, mass media have typically been commercial enterprises for which the primary purpose was entertainment. (p. 999)

One third of American homes have video game equipment (Greenfield, 1994). Although there is almost no published research on the effects of adolescents' use of "on-line networks to communicate on e-mails; to visit sites on the World Wide Web; or to post their own work, play games, or 'chat' in real time . . . there is no doubt that they are becoming active in all these formats" (Huston & Wright, 1998, p. 1027).

Arcade games are popular activities for many youth.

Age Changes in Media Use

Issue to Consider

• How does the use of media change across adolescence?

Youth do not use different media with the same frequency. At some points in their lives one instance of media is used more than others are. The total amount of time children or adolescents spend watching television increases from infancy to early adolescence (Huston & Wright, 1998), and then declines throughout the rest of adolescence. At the high point in this series of age changes (i.e., in early adolescence), youth average 3 to 4 hours a day in television watching (Huston & Wright, 1998). Young male German adolescents watch television about 2 hours a day, viewing mostly entertainment and action programs (Myrtek et al., 1996). As television viewing decreases during the middle to late years of adolescence, radio listening, primarily to music, increases (Huston & Wright, 1998). However, in a longitudinal study of sixth- through twelfth-grade youth, the time spent listening to the radio or viewing movies decreased (Mutz, Roberts, & van Vuuren, 1993).

Adolescents frequently use other media. In a study of about 400 male and about 400 female 11- to 16-year-old adolescents from the United Kingdom, 77% reported playing video games, typically daily for between 30 minutes to an hour (Phillips et al., 1995). In another study of 460 11- to 16-year-olds from the United Kingdom, the major leisure activity was visiting arcades (Fisher, 1995). Adolescents reported that their motivation for frequenting arcades was to hang out or to meet friends (Fisher, 1995).

There do not appear to be any consistent differences between male and female adolescents in their respective frequency of use of television (Huston & Wright, 1998). In addition, it is not clear whether parents act to increase or decrease the television watching of their adolescent children. Some research indicates that children watch less television when their mothers do not work, presumably because mothers monitor and limit the time adolescents spend watching television (Huston & Wright, 1998). Other research indicates that the television watching of youth increases when their mothers are home, presumably because youngsters and their mothers watch television together (Huston & Wright, 1998).

Effects of Media Use

Issues to Consider

• What are the effects of media on the vast majority of youth?

- What effects can high levels of television viewing have on adolescent development?

Although the influence of media on youth behavior and development continues to be a topic attracting social and political debate, the data indicate that for most forms of media that have been studied there are no major, enduring effects on the vast majority of youth. Current information indicates that only some youth, under specific circumstances, are influenced by exposure to the media.

Across all youth, there are, at most, only small influences of television viewing on adolescents' leisure reading, completion of homework assignments, school achievement, or physical and social activities (Huston & Wright, 1998). However, high levels of viewing can have some dramatic influences on these activities. For example, extensive television viewing is associated with obesity (Huston & Wright, 1998). Although findings from about two dozen studies of the association between television watching and school achievement indicate virtually no overall relation between these two domains of youth behavior, lowered achievement does occur when adolescents spend 30 hours a week or more watching television (Huston & Wright, 1998). This frequency of television watching approaches the time devoted to many full-time jobs. In a longitudinal study of youth, first in childhood and then in adolescence, early life television viewing was linked in adolescence to increased obesity (Dietz & Gortmaker, 1985). Between the sixth to the eighth grades, high levels of television viewing are related to lower participation in organized school and community groups. Among German youth, boys who watched a lot of television read fewer books, showed diminished activities outside the home, did less homework, and had less interest in hobbies (Myrtek et al., 1996).

Problematic levels of media use can be associated with other problematic features of adolescent behavior. Among male and female 12- to 19-year-old Australian adolescents, engagement in **passive leisure activities** (e.g., watching television) is greater than participation in **active leisure activities** (e.g., playing a sport) (Gordon & Caltabiano, 1996). Among these youth, boredom in regard to their leisure time activities (in other words, being bored by watching television) is asso-

Passive leisure activities Free time events that require little expenditure of energy on the part of the participant.

Active leisure activities Free time events that require a large expenditure of energy by the participant.

Sports events offer important opportunities for adolescents to participate in the social world of their schools.

ciated with drug use and delinquency (Gordon & Caltabiano, 1996). In a study of about 200 youth from the midwestern United States, watching rock music videos was related to permissive sexual attitudes and behaviors, especially among girls and, in particular, among girls with problematic family relationships (Strouse, Buerkel-Rothfus, & Long, 1995). Among about 1,200 high school students from the northeastern United States, television viewing was associated with being socially and politically authoritarian, especially among youth from higher socioeconomic levels (Shanahan, 1995).

Conclusions About Media and Adolescent Development

Media are a major part of the life of most youth. Although high levels of media use can be associated with problems in adolescent behavior and development, for the vast majority of youth there are no pervasive or long-term detrimental influences of media. It will be important, however, to revisit this conclusion as more research is conducted about the possible influences of new and emerging media, such as interactive television, on youth development.

Research about the influence of contemporary features of the adolescent's world on behavior and development will also have to focus on topics other than the media. Adolescents do more than spend time in their rooms chatting online, watching television, or listening to music. Formal and informal areas of activities texture the world of adolescents. These contexts, or niches, within the ecology of youth are places populated by other adolescents, locations where young people pursue hobbies, engage in sports, see or are seen by friends, or merely hang out.

The Community Niches of Adolescents

Portions of the world of adolescents are shaped by youth themselves. Selecting an area of town in which to hang out, such as a shopping mall or a street corner, are instances of such adolescent-shaped contexts or niches. There are also portions of the world of adolescents influenced by adults. A prime instance of such a niche is the school, where in addition to academic experiences, a range of social interaction opportunities and extracurricular activities are offered to youth. Adult-influenced settings also take the form of youth clubs, organizations, or programs (see Chapter 14). Let's first consider the two types of adult-shaped niches for youth, school, and community-based youth organizations, and then look at youth-selected niches.

The Social Life of the School

Issues to Consider
- How is the organization and function of the school designed to provide youth with a context for social life?
- How does an exclusive focus on school activities put a youth in a dilemma when applying to college?

- What evidence exists that traditional differences in school careers are changing?

Although media and electronic technology are ubiquitous parts of the world of contemporary adolescents, they are not the only features of it. For many youth, the school constitutes their social world as well as their academic one. In many ways, the organization and function of the school is designed to provide for youth a context for social life. A culture is developed within schools that in the extreme channels young people into focusing their social life within the calendar of events that occur each year within the school. These events can include sports events and rallies, homecoming weekends, and social events such as dances, class trips, proms, class plays, and awards ceremonies. In other words,

> The school year is built around a relatively unchanging sequence of activities designed to enhance the social atmosphere of the school and the school's competitiveness with other schools. . . . Students are expected to be motivated by loyalty to their own school and by competition with other schools.

Many adolescents participate in extracurricular activities such as drama clubs, student government, or sport teams.

Loyalty dictates confining one's network and activities to the school at the expense of involvement in the local community and in other communities or organizations that would take time away from school activities. (Eckert, 1995, p. 180)

Such exclusive focus on building one's social life by participation in the sets of activities available within the school (e.g., student government, the school newspaper or yearbook, varsity teams, cheerleading, academic interest clubs, and honor societies), to the exclusion of any form of community involvement, may put youth in a dilemma when they begin to apply to colleges and universities. Today, many higher educational institutions want applicants who have broad and varied profiles of credentials that include good grades and standardized test scores, participation in school extracurricular activities, and community service. Youth may need to find a balance between a social life that involves investing time exclusively in the school and one that involves investing time in the community, to gain entrance into a desirable college or university.

Many youth do just this (Eckert, 1995). They opt to invest in both the social world of the school and in the life of the community. Although significant proportions of youth choose to live almost exclusively in the school or the community, many young people intentionally select an **in-between existence.** In a study of several high schools populated almost exclusively by European American students in the suburbs of Detroit, Eckert (1995) found that many students built their lives exclusively through participating in the social roles available in schools. These roles amounted to **social careers,** for instance, election as a member or officer of student council, selection as a varsity cheerleader or varsity team athlete, election or selection as a captain of such a squad, or election to the presidency of a school honor society. Students who

Team sports are a prominent part of the school experiences of many youth.

based their lives and identities in the school's extracurricular arena were labeled in the high schools as **jocks** (Eckert, 1995). Other students, labeled **burnouts,** rejected the school as a center for social life (Eckert, 1995). These youth focused their lives and pursued identities within their neighborhood or the local community. They stayed at the fringe of school activities. However, the majority of the students in these schools did not fall into either of these two categories. Most youth saw themselves in the in-between category (Eckert, 1995).

Youth from different socioeconomic levels were differentially distributed in the three categories. As shown in Table 12.1, the social category that youth from working-class backgrounds were most likely to be in was burnouts, whereas lower middle-class youth and upper middle-class youth were most likely to be in the social categories of in-betweens and jocks, respectively (Eckert, 1995). At least as operationalized by having a school career that will make one competitive for admission into selective colleges and universities, there were also high percentages of lower middle-class and upper middle-class youth in the jocks and in the in-between categories, respectively. This distribution arises perhaps in recognizing the need to live in both school and community contexts for success in later life.

Not only do most youth merge the school-focused and the nonschool-focused worlds of the jocks and the burnouts into their personal array of interests and activities, but some evidence suggests that traditional gender differences in school careers

In-between existence
Balance between investing time in the social world of the school and the life in the community.

Social careers Life built exclusively around participating in a particular social role.

Jocks Students who use the school's extracurricular arena as a center for their social life.

Burnouts Students who reject the school as a center for their social life.

Table 12-1	**Distribution of Adolescents from Different Socioeconomic Backgrounds into Types of Students: Jocks, In-Betweens, and Burnouts**		
	Percentage of Youth in the Social Category		
Socioeconomic Category	Jocks	In-Betweens	Burnouts
Working class	16	16	50
Lower middle class	34	42	22
Upper middle class	50	42	23

Source: Eckert, 1995, p. 180.

are changing. Girls are increasingly seeking prestige in school through sports and are placing decreased emphasis on activities such as cheerleading (Suitor & Reavis, 1995). Nevertheless, remnants of traditional divisions between boys and girls in the routes to school success persist. Boys continue to seek prestige through sports and achievement, and girls attempt to acquire status through physical appearance, sociability, and achievement (Suitor & Reavis, 1995).

Schools, at least in part by adult design, are centers of youth social development. Most youth take advantage of the opportunities for honing their academic, athletic, and social interests and skills provided by schools. The majority of youth combine their school-centered lives with activities in their communities. When they move from school to community they also find numerous adult-designed opportunities for pursuing their social, athletic, intellectual, and cultural interests.

Community-Based Youth Organizations

Issues to Consider

- How can different meanings of citizenship lead to quite different developmental outcomes for youth?
- What key elements do youth develop by virtue of their participation in a community-based organization?

Just as much as the world of media that exists for contemporary adolescents is a product of inventions of the 20th century, many features of the community context provided for youth arose during this period:

In the late 19th century social reformers invented a new set of contexts intended specifically to foster adolescents' development. These reformers initiated and promoted hobbies, youth organizations, and sports as valuable and healthful parts of adolescents' lives. In the United States the Boy and Girl Scouts, 4-H, the YMCA and the YWCA, Little League, and numerous recreational centers, hobby clubs, and eventually in school extracurricular activities were launched by community activists who wanted to improve the lot of developing youth. These activists believed that, with proper adult guidance, such organized activities could promote initiative, build character, discourage delinquency, and provide "laboratories for training in citizenship." (Larson, 1994, p. 46)

The clear intent of the founders of many of the community-based youth organizations was to develop a means to instill in the future generations of adult leaders a commitment to civil society (see Chapter 5), and to imbue youth with the moral foundation to be engaged and productive citizens.

Citizenship can mean different things in different societies. In the United States Little League is intended to teach fair play and teamwork and in Scotland, jazz bands for girls are used to provide a stabilizing influence in their lives (Larson, 1994). However, the goal of the Soviet Pioneer youth groups in the former USSR was to make good communists and the Hitler Youth groups in Germany in the 1930s and 1940s was to create good Nazis (Larson, 1994).

Thus it is possible to subvert the energy and potential commitment of youth to community engagement and create citizens who embrace ideas antithetical to civil society. This danger was explained by Erik Erikson (1950), more than a half century ago, when he described how the Hitler Youth movement capitalized on the striving of German adolescents for an identity (see Chapter 6) and on the orientation of all youth to show fidelity toward an ideology associated with their identity. Hitler offered German youth an identity as a Nazi and an ideology that was antidemocratic and linked to dehumanizing, subjugating, and even murdering other people (Lerner, 1992).

It is not automatic that a community organization for youth will build citizens promoting civil society (Damon, 1997; Larson, 1994). The moral values of the community are key elements of what is developed among youth by virtue of their participation in a community-based youth organization. Within those countries such as the United States, in which good citizenship is linked to democratic ideas, the value of civil society, and the promotion of social justice, it is important to know whether the vision of the founders of community organizations for youth is being actualized. Does participation in such organizations enhance the positive development of youth?

Benefits of Community-Based Youth Organizations Participation in community-based youth organizations can be effective in promoting values and positive developments and in preventing undesirable values and development among adolescents. For instance, 4-H participation is associated with increased understanding and communication in families (Larson, 1994). In a longitudinal study of extracurricular participation, delinquency and sports participation were found to exist together in the junior high school grades (Larson, 1994). By grades 11 and 12, however, there was an inverse relation with higher levels of sports participation associated with lower levels of delinquency (Larson, 1994). Nevertheless, sports participation did not appear to increase prosocial behavior (see Chapter 5) or to decrease antisocial behavior (Larson, 1994).

However, while adolescents' engagement in arts or hobbies (e.g., coin or stamp collecting, model airplane construction) and their participation in youth organizations (e.g., 4-H, YMCA; see Chapter 14) are also not inversely related to delinquency, participation in these activities does appear to decrease delinquency in the high school years (Larson, 1994). These beneficial influences of organizational membership and engagement in the arts or in hobbies continue to play a role in the positive development of people into their adult years (Larson, 1994). Among Australian high school students, being involved in organizations that enable them to perform at exceptional or elite levels in such activities as dance, music, and drama is associated with a self-concept as an artist and with positive self-esteem (Marsh & Roche, 1996).

Reed W. Larson (2000) continues to investigate the nature of the experiences of adolescents. For some of his recent work, see Meet the Researcher Box 12.1.

Because of the benefits for positive youth development of involving youth in leisure activities that engage their interests in the arts and in hobbies, numerous programs have been developed to offer young people a range of such experiences. Applications Box 12.1 presents examples of programs from around the world.

A key feature of the programs described in Applications Box 12.1, and in community-based youth organizations in general, is the opportunity provided for young people to interact in positive ways with caring adults who model the sorts of citizenship behaviors that community organizations seek to inculcate in young people. Contemporary adolescents have relatively few opportunities to interact with adults other than family members or teachers (Larson, 1994). Extracurricular activities offer a chance to get to know and learn from other adults (e.g., coaches and leaders of community organizations) (Larson, 1994).

Youth sports organizations represent an important instance of such an opportunity for beneficial youth-adult interactions. Each year in the United States millions of young people engage in formal, organized, community-based athletic activities involving sports such as baseball (e.g., the Little League), football (e.g., Pop Warner Leagues), basketball, soccer, ice hockey, field hockey, track and field, swimming, diving, bicycling, and gymnastics. When we consider the additional millions of youth who participate in informal, but adult-supervised athletic activities as well, it is clear that in America, there is enormous potential for sports to provide a route to positive adult-youth relations and healthy adolescent development.

Unfortunately, the potential benefits of sports participation are not being fully realized. As explained by William Damon in his book *The Youth Charter: How Communities Can Work Together to Raise Standards for All Our Children* (1997) (see Chapter 5), many coaches and parents have lost sight of the founding purpose of such athletic activities, which is to build moral character and promote citizenship (Larson, 1994). Very few

MEET THE RESEARCHER BOX 12.1

REED W. LARSON

CAPTURING EXPERIENCE AND UNDERSTANDING ITS MEANING

*E*xperience is a word that sends tingles up my spine like few other words. Experience is the stuff of which human existence is made: events, encounters, thoughts, and emotions that register in consciousness in the stream of daily life. Developmental scientists often speak of experience as in "Children are shaped by their experience." But we often know little about what we mean. What is experience? What about it matters? How does it "shape"? Do we even know what range of experiences make up the ordinary lives of children, adolescents, and adults? I don't have answers to these questions, but I am very intrigued by them.

As a college student, I was attracted to existentialists, like Rollo May and Jean-Paul Sartre, who argued that experiences are unique and irreducible. In the research I have done since then on adolescent experience, I try to keep attuned to this uniqueness: for example, to the fusillade of feelings a person might meet in a first romantic encounter, or the strange mixture of emotions triggered when a father fails to show understanding at a key moment.

As a now middle-aged researcher, I have also been interested in understanding some of the shared features and patterns of adolescents' daily experiences. Along with Maryse Richards and other collaborators, I have asked, How much time do teenagers spend in different "experiential contexts"? What are

Reed W. Larson is a professor at the University of Illinois, Urbana-Champaign, in the departments of human and community development, psychology, educational psychology, kinesiology, and leisure studies. He is author of *Being Adolescent* (with Mihaly Csikszentmihalyi) and *Divergent Realties: The Daily Lives of Mothers, Fathers and Adolescents* (with Maryse Richards).

the typical emotions they encounter in these contexts? How does the daily round of experience change with age and vary by gender, culture, and other factors?

I have discovered, for example, that as American children move into adolescence, they begin spending more time alone, often in their bedrooms. They listen to music, read, do homework, draw, and sometimes just lie on their beds and think. What is curious is that the emotions they experience during this time are not particularly positive; loneliness is common, yet they appear to seek it out. Thus we know there is a new set of experiences in adolescents' lives and they are not choosing it to have a good time, but much is to be learned about what these experiences are and how they change kids.

In my current research I am interested in the types of experiences that adolescents have in extracurricular activities and community organizations. In prior studies I have found that it is the one consistent place in daily life when teenagers both concentrate deeply and want to be doing what they are doing. They are genuinely engaged and challenged in a way that doesn't often happen elsewhere. I believe this deep psychological engagement creates conditions for special kinds of developmental experiences. I am hoping to learn more about what they are, both in their general patterns and in their unique varieties.

---

of the youth involved in the sports activities go on to have careers as professional athletes. However, all of the young people will be expected, and needed, to contribute to the future of a just and civil society. Damon (1997) explains how a youth charter can be developed to maximize the positive experiences and long-term desired developmental outcomes of youth in community sports activities (see Applications Box 12.2).

Conclusions About the Role of Adult-Organized Youth Niches Adults care about, and have an investment in, the healthy development of young people. The niches provided by adults to foster such

development have met with considerable successes; but significant challenges remain in order to maximize the life chances of all young people. Community-based initiatives such as those envisioned by Damon (1997) through the youth charter constitute a potentially productive means to enhance the contributions of adults to the positive development of youth.

Enhancement through such endeavors as a communitywide charter for the welfare of youth has the added benefit of helping create a seamless safety net for young people no matter where they may go in their communities. Such a safety net is important in that not all the niches within which contemporary

applications box 12.1

Using Leisure Activities, Culture, Media, and the Theater Arts to Promote Positive Youth Development

Vicaria Zona Norte (The North Zone Vicarship)
Santiago, Chile.

In Chile, many children are forced by circumstance to work at an early age. Others may be left at home with little developmental stimulation. Established in 1981 by an outreach office of the Catholic Church, Vicaria Zona Norte (The North Zone Vicarship) unites communities to improve the quality of life for such children through recreational and cultural activities. Community organizations known as "Urban Colonies" (Colonias Urbanas) train youth as monitors to work with children. The program annually coordinates activities of community groups in over 30 neighborhoods in northern Santiago. During the school year, at each Urban Colony between 10 to 50 youth monitors, aged 14 to 20 years old, work with 100 to 200 children, between 3 and 12 years old. The older youth address social problems and prevent risky behaviors among children, and organize weekly meetings for cultural, urban camps, where children receive meals, basic assistance and recreation. To date, the program has served over 65,000 children and trained more than 700 youth monitors. Studies of adults who were formerly youth counselors reveal that they have enhanced leadership skills, increased awareness of children's rights, and a heightened sense of civic responsibility.

The Mirror Art Group (MAG)
Manila, Philippines.

Established in 1989 by the Philippine Educational Theater Association, the Theatre in Education Program (TIE) develops the creative and analytical skills of young people through theater. TIE has two components: the Children's Theater Collective and the Metropolitan Teen Theater League. Together they organize children and youth collectives in schools and organizations, providing a curriculum and assistance in theater training. In addition to students, TIE works with street children, refugees, and dropouts. Indeed, it has succeeded in joining children from disparate backgrounds in theater training and productions. Children view, plan, and participate in plays and evaluate their activities at the end of performances. Some teen members have even gone on to assume positions in the organization as program directors, project coordinators, music directors, and playwrights. In its first five years, TIE reached more than 60,000 children as audiences of its mobile theater performances and trained more than 5,000 in newly formed theater collectives. Impressively, the TIE program has given birth to more than 350 theater guilds throughout the Philippines.

Source: International Youth Foundation, 2001. <www.iyfnet.org>

youth interact are ones organized by adults. Youth select and shape their own niches, and some of these contexts may not be ones linked to positive development. These niches are a product of the lifestyles of contemporary youth.

Youth-Selected Niches and Lifestyles

Issues to Consider

Lifestyle Preferences and behaviors of adolescents regarding what they want to do, how and where they will spend their time, and with whom they want to interact.

- How do the niches selected by youth change across the adolescent years?
- What is the pattern of change in lifestyle that occurs with developmental change for adolescents?

- How and why must the contexts of adolescents cooperate to enable them to develop in a positive manner?

Adolescents have their own ideas about what they want to do, about how and where they spend their time, and about the sorts of people they interact with (e.g., Larson, Gillman, & Richards, 1997). These preferences and the behaviors associated with them constitute the **lifestyle** of adolescents. At any one point in adolescence, youth differ in regard to their lifestyles and thus in respect to the niches they choose to frequent. For instance, in early adolescence, some youth may elect to spend their leisure time in shopping malls, others may elect to stay at home, and still others may opt to just hang out on the street. Across the adolescent years, the lifestyles and the niches selected by adolescents may alter

(Hendry et al., 1994). A shopping mall may be replaced by a youth dance club or, although it may not be legal, by a bar. Similarly, whereas younger adolescents may have their choices of niches and activities constrained because of not being licensed to drive, a broader set of possibilities is available to older adolescents who can drive a car.

Developmental changes in the lifestyles of youth create a pattern of change that appears to move the person from a youth-centered world, where hanging out and recreation are central, to a lifestyle marked by concern with the imminent entry into the world of young adulthood (see Chapter 15) (Hendry et al., 1994). Developmental changes in lifestyles were assessed in a longitudinal study of about 300 British male and female adolescents between the times when they were 15 to 16 years and when they were 17 to 18 years (Hendry et al., 1994). When they were between 15 and 16 years, the lifestyles of girls were characterized by visiting friends or being visited by them, spending a lot of time with their best friend, or hanging out on the street with friends, by going dancing and to clubs, by working at a job, and by engaging in sports. When they were between 17 and 18 years of age, these girls' lifestyles were characterized first by being involved full time in pursuing their education, but going to bars and clubs with friends was also a key focus of their lives (Hendry et al., 1994).

The focus on education seen among the 17- and 18-year-old girls was present among boys at a younger age. When they were between 15 and 16 years of age, educational goals were most important for the boys. In addition, the lifestyles of the boys were characterized by having hobbies, by staying away from drugs and tobacco, and by sports participation (Hendry et al., 1994). However, although the boys' focus on educational goals continued to characterize their lifestyles when they were between 17 and 18 years of age, their world was also characterized by going to bars and clubs with friends and by using tobacco (Hendry et al., 1994).

In a longitudinal study comparing adolescents from Berlin, Germany, with adolescents from War-

Many older adolescents spend time at dance clubs.

saw, Poland (Silbereisen, Noack, & Schönpflug, 1994), the most frequent leisure contexts among 12- through 15-year-olds from both nations were home, sports areas, streets, cultural settings (e.g., museums), nightclubs, youth clubs, and nature (e.g., woods, lakes, mountains) (Silbereisen et al., 1994). Adolescents used these settings to promote their social contacts with same-sex peers and with romantic friends (Silbereisen et al., 1994).

Among older German adolescents, and akin to the British youth studied by Hendry et al. (1994), a niche preference that differed from the ones of younger adolescents was found (Todt, Drewes, & Heils, 1994). As with the British youth, this difference involved an emphasis on education. Specifically, these youth said that the most significant feature of their lives was an emphasis on specialization in school and the selection of a life path involving either vocational training or a college education (Todt et al., 1994). Other significant features of their lives were identified as involving an interest in having satisfying free time and friendships, by working to develop their identities and especially their gender identities (see Chapters 6 and 7), and by striving to enhance further their cognitive competencies (see Chapter 4) (Todt et al., 1994).

To live in a world marked by such activities, the context of adolescents must cooperate (Todt et al., 1994). To enable adolescents to develop in a healthy manner, families, peers, schools, and the residential and recreational areas of communities

Sports: A "Youth Charter" to Promote Positive Adolescent Development

Participation in sports is a significant part of the lives of many contemporary adolescents. Damon (1997) points out the many important benefits of such participation. Young people enhance their physical fitness, learn athletic and physical skills, and, through sports, they experience lessons pertinent to the development of their character (for example, they learn about the importance of diligence, motivation, teamwork, balancing cooperation versus competition, balancing winning and losing, and the importance of fair play) (Damon, 1997). Sports can be a context for positive parent-child relations, and such interactions can further the adolescent's successful involvement in sports. For instance, parental support of their male and female adolescents' participation in tennis is associated with the enjoyment of the sport by the youth and with an objective measure of their performance (Hoyle & Leff, 1997).

Damon (1997) notes that organized and even informal opportunities for sports participation for youth, such as Little League, soccer, or pickup games in school yards, often fall short of providing these benefits for young people. He points out that in modern American society, sports participation is often imbued with a "win at any cost" orientation among coaches and their young players. Parents may also have this attitude. Together, a value is conveyed that winning is not only the main goal of competition, it is the *only* thing (Damon, 1997, p. 210).

Damon believes that this orientation corrupts the purposes of youth participation in sports. Parents and

coaches often forget that most of the young people on these teams will not become professional athletes. Even if they were to make sports a career, they, as well as the majority of young people involved in sports, need moral modeling and guidance about sportsmanship (Damon, 1997).

In order to enable youth sports to make these contributions to positive adolescent development, Damon (1997) proposes a youth charter (see too Chapter 5) that constitutes a set of guidelines for the design and conduct of youth sports programs. Adherence to the principles of the charter will enable communities to realize the several assets for young people provided by youth participation in sports. Components of the charter include the following commitments:

1. Make youth sports a priority for public funding and other forms of community support (space, facilities, volunteer coaches);
2. Emphasize standards of conduct as a primary goal of youth sports;
3. Provide young people with opportunities to participate in individual as well as team sports;
4. Encourage broad participation by ordinary players as well as stars; and
5. Carefully coordinate sports programs for youth with other community events for young people. (Damon, 1997, pp. 123–125)

need to provide structures and values supporting the competent development of youth in regard to the significant features of their world (Todt et al., 1994). As we discussed in Chapter 5, creating a

healthy world for adolescent development involves providing them with ecological resources or assets (Benson, 1997; Scales & Leffert, 1999; Scales et al., 2000).

Conclusions: Issues and Assets of the World of Modern Youth

Contemporary youth occupy a world that is in some respects just like the one their parents experienced when they were adolescents. As was true for their parents, family, peers, schools, and community play a significant part in their lives. They share with their parents an adolescence marked by the availability of technological achievements in communication and entertainment. Movies, television, radio, books and magazines, and even VCRs, were present during the adolescence of the parents of many of today's youth.

However, parts of the modern adolescents' world were not part of their parents' adolescent world. Fax machines in the office and home, cell phones, and electronic mailing to friends through home or laptop computers were not part of their parents' adolescent world; yet they are an ordinary part of the world of contemporary youth.

In addition, modern adolescents live in a world that in still other respects is totally unlike the one of their parents. Today, shopping for almost anything in any part of the world can be done through a home computer. Almost all of the world's knowledge is readily accessible through the same technology. Breakthroughs in the speed of travel, in medicine, and in use of machines to conduct many of the routine tasks of life (from banking to residential climate control) have given contemporary youth more options for pursuing their interests and for realizing their aspirations.

For most youth living in contemporary society the innovations and opportunities available to them are not diminishing the likelihood of their healthy development. In many cases the interaction of youth with modern media and with the community niches of their world are enhancing their chances for positive development.

Nevertheless, the modern world also presents unique challenges to youth. The parents of today's youth grew up in a world that was not beset by the AIDS epidemic (see Chapter 10). Youth of past eras were not faced with an increase in problems of adolescent health and behavior such as burgeoning crises of drug and alcohol use and abuse and of youth violence, or with a growing tendency for such problems to occur together in the lives of young people.

The special challenges of modern youth find both their sources and their solutions in the perennial components of the world of adolescents—family, peers, schools, and communities. As we turn to key dilemmas of youth development (Chapter 13) and to the policies and programs that may effectively address these issues (Chapter 14), we acknowledge the individual strengths of youth, when coupled with the assets of the traditionally key contexts of their lives, as the link to overcoming the unique constellation of problems besetting modern youth.

Summary

- The invention and spread of television, radio, movies, magazines, computers, pagers, cell phones, and video games are largely 20th-century phenomena.
- At certain points in the life span, the use of certain types of media is different from that of other points in the life span. For example, television viewing increases from infancy to early adolescence, and then decreases throughout the rest of adolescence.
- Data indicate that most forms of media have no major, enduring effects on adolescents. Only certain youth, under specific circumstances, are influenced by exposure to media.
- A culture of loyalty and competitiveness is developed within schools that channels young people into focusing their social life around events that occur within the school during the school year.
- Today, universities and colleges want students with good academic credentials who also demonstrate participation in school extracurricular activities and community service.
- Girls are increasingly seeking social status through sports and placing a decreased emphasis on activities such as cheerleading. However, boys continue to seek prestige through sports and achievement and girls through physical appearance, sociability, and achievement.
- The moral values of a community are the key elements of what is developed in youth by virtue of their participation in community-based youth organizations.
- Caring adults can model positive citizenship behaviors for young people, and extracurricular activities offer young people a chance to get to know and learn from other adults.

- A youth charter containing commitments for the design and conduct of sports programs can be developed to maximize the positive experiences and the long-term developmental outcomes of participation in sports activities.

- In early adolescence, youth may spend leisure time at the mall, at home, or hanging out on the street. By late adolescence, the niches may change so that a dance club or, illegally, a bar replaces the mall. Older adolescents have a broader set of possibilities for finding niches by virtue of having a driver's license.

- The family, peer, school, and community contexts of adolescents must provide structures and values supporting the competent development of youth in regard to civil society and the promotion of assets.

Discussion Topics

1. How much television did you watch as a high school student? Were there specific shows you tried not to miss? What about these shows attracted you? What purposes did these shows serve? Were there specific lessons/morals/experiences you were able to apply to your life? Were you more attracted to real-life dramas or fantastical story lines?

2. Has any media experience (i.e., television show, movie, newspaper) made such an impression on you that you changed your way of thinking about or approaching some topic or situation? Describe that experience and explain what made that experience so powerful.

3. What do you think about the recent associations made between certain rock videos and lyrics and high-risk behavior among adolescents? Why are some youth so much more drawn to media that promotes negative behavior? What about the messages they hear in the lyrics and see on the videos is so powerful? Should adults and peers be concerned about teens who are attracted to these powerful negative images and the behaviors they espouse?

4. How has the Internet affected your life? What role do parents play in terms of monitoring the use of the Internet by their adolescents? What role do the Internet providers play? Do you feel that adolescents are mature enough to make their own decisions about appropriate and healthy use of the Internet? Why or why not?

5. Where did you and your friends hang out in high school? When you visit your hometown now, are teens still frequenting this spot? Why or why not? What characteristics define a healthy and supportive environment for adolescents to hang out in? How much adult interaction/involvement needs to be included in these environments? Does your response depend on the group of adolescents in question and their specific character traits?

6. How knowledgeable were you and your friends about available community resources in which you could spend your free time? Did you make use of these resources? Why or why not?

7. How involved were you with student activities at school? How proactive were the teachers and administration in your school at involving all students in extracurricular activities? Did your involvement require you to manage your time more effectively? In terms of prioritizing, how important was watching your favorite television shows or spending time surfing the Web? What, if anything, did you sacrifice/give up, because there just was not enough time in the day?

8. What, if any, were the different expectations of teachers, parents, and peers for males and females in terms of the route to school success? Do you feel these expectations impacted the decisions you made or the goals you set for yourself? In what ways?

9. Were you involved in extracurricular activities? How did your involvement support your development? Was there a specific club you were interested in but never joined? What about that club and its members attracted you? Why do some youth choose not to become involved in any extracurricular activities? What are they missing out on?

10. Think back on the various adult role models you encountered in school and in the extracurricular activities you were involved in both in and out of school. What did you learn from these people that you might not have learned from your parents?

11. How well did your immediate community support your changing interests in terms of where and how you chose to spend your time? When your interests and needs were not met, did you ever search for entertainment outside of your environs? Did you ever have to partake in risky behavior to satisfy these interests? Was part of the attraction stepping outside of environments that were familiar? How could your community better meet its adolescents' interests?

Key Terms

active leisure activities (p. 282)

burnouts (p. 284)

in-between existence (p. 284)

jocks (p. 284)

lifestyle (p. 288)

media (p. 280)

passive leisure activities (p. 282)

social careers (p. 284)

13

PROBLEM BEHAVIORS IN ADOLESCENCE

It was my first visit to Flint, Michigan. I had heard a lot about how the city had deteriorated as a consequence of the downsizing of the auto industry, which had been the lifeblood of Flint for generations. I had seen *Roger and Me*, the documentary that illustrated the problems that had grown in Flint in relation to General Motors laying off thousands of workers in the auto plant. Yet, as I drove through the rows of burned-out buildings, of boarded-up houses and stores, and of streets empty at midday, I was not prepared for the desolation that characterized every inch of my path.

I arrived at Mott Children's Health Center, a large, community-based, family-oriented health facility. The center provided medical, dental, and mental health services to the poor and largely minority youth living in the neighborhoods surrounding the center. I was there to meet with a group of youth workers and the young people they served. The purpose of the meeting was to discuss how the university where I worked, the Health Center, and the community could work together to promote positive development among youth in Flint.

After enjoying some refreshments, we began the meeting by getting acquainted. I found myself sitting next to Ray, an African American adolescent. "Hi, I'm Richard Lerner," I said, and offered my hand. He took it, but not strongly. He looked down at the table as we shook. "You about 14?" I asked. He said he was.

At first I tried to make small talk with Ray. I asked if he was a Detroit Lions fan and what he thought of their prospects for the season. Ray appeared uncomfortable. I guessed that he was not used to just jumping into a conversation with a stranger—a middle-aged white guy in a suit and tie at that. I decided to change the topic and try to talk about him.

"So what did you do this summer?"

A brief pause, and then, "I worked in McDonald's . . . just tried to stay out of trouble."

I asked him to elaborate. Ray's voice raised a bit. "A few weeks ago my two friends and I were walking over to the school yard to play basketball. These guys drove by and thought we were these dudes who ripped them off for some drugs. But it wasn't us. We're not into that stuff. They shot at us and my two friends were killed . . . " Ray paused. "I'm just trying now to stay out of trouble. I'm trying not to get killed."

Fourteen years old. Walking in his neighborhood to play basketball with two friends. A moment later his friends are dead. Now all he hopes for is that he won't be killed also.

It has been about 10 years since I met Ray. Although I worked in Flint for several years, I never saw him after that day. I've asked about him, but to no avail. My conversation with him has stayed with me, a so-called expert on adolescent development who knew nothing of what life was like on a day-to-day basis for Ray, or for the millions of other young adolescents who live every moment with the potential that there is trouble, and possibly death, driving down the block toward them.

LEARNING OBJECTIVES

1. To learn some of the major categories of adolescent risk behavior and the dangers of engaging in them.
2. To define the two general dimensions of problem behaviors: internalizing and externalizing; to understand the attributes of adolescents and of the contexts associated with these behaviors.
3. To understand the nature of poverty among youth and its relation to the behavioral risks of adolescence.
4. To understand the individual and social bases of delinquency, and the relationship between violence toward the self and others.

5. To understand adolescent substance abuse in terms of the adolescent's individual characteristics and relationships with parents and peers.
6. To appreciate gender differences in internalizing problem behaviors.
7. To understand the development of adolescent internalizing behaviors in terms of multiple individual characteristics, including gender and social contexts, such as family life.
8. To recognize that understanding the relation between developing adolescents and their social contexts may help design policies and programs to address adolescent problem behaviors.

Across America and indeed across the world, adolescents are dying every day. They are dying from violence, drug and alcohol use and abuse, unsafe sex, poor nutrition, and the consequences of persistent and pervasive poverty (Annie E. Casey Foundation, 1999; Children's Defense Fund, 1996; Dryfoos, 1990, 1998; Hamburg, 1992; Huston, 1991; Lerner, 1995; Lerner & Galambos, 1998; Little, 1993; McKinney et al., 1994; Schorr, 1988, 1997; World Health Organization, 1993).

Even if our youth are not dying, their life chances are being squandered. They experience school failure, underachievement, and dropout, crime, teenage pregnancy and parenting, lack of job preparedness, and health risks, such as lack of immunizations, inadequate screening for disabilities, insufficient prenatal care, and insufficient infant and childhood medical services. They often experience despair and hopelessness as they see their parents struggle with poverty and realize they have little opportunity for a life marked by societal respect, achievement, and opportunity (Annie E. Casey Foundation, 1999; Carnegie Corporation of New York, 1995; Children's Defense Fund, 1996; di Mauro, 1995; Dryfoos, 1990, 1998; Huston, 1991; Huston, McLoyd, & Garcia Coll, 1994; Johnston, Bachman, & O'Malley, 1999; U.S. Department of Health and Human Services, 1996).

Dimensions of Youth Problem Behaviors

Issues to Consider

• Despite improving trends in several categories relating to quality of life in America, why are statistics still alarming?

• What are some of the major categories of adolescent risk behaviors?

• What are the dangers of risk behaviors and, in particular, comorbidity of risk behaviors?

Numerous examples illustrate the severity and breadth of the problems besetting the youth, families, and communities of our nation and our world. For instance, Table 13.1 displays the frequency of risks and problems affecting America's children and youth.

The trends are also instructive. Table 13.2 contrasts the status of indicators of the quality of life for children and youth in 1990 with the status of the indicators in 1997. In several categories, trends show improvement across this 7-year period. Despite such trends, however, the absolute levels of these indicators remain poor. For instance, despite an improvement in the infant mortality rate between 1990 and 1997, the United States ranks 18th among all industrialized nations of the world in infant mortality. Similarly, although the 1990s saw fluctuations in the overall percentage of children living in poverty, about 20% of America's youth remain poor (*Kids Count Data Book*, Annie E. Casey Foundation, 2000).

Given these trends, it is perhaps not surprising to learn that the quality of life America provides its children and youth compares poorly to that provided by other modern industrialized countries. Although the United States leads other industrialized nations in productivity related to military and defense expenditures, health technology, and the number of individuals who attain very substantial personal wealth, it falls far behind other nations in indicators of child health and welfare (Children's Defense Fund, 1996). Among the major 18 industrialized countries, the United States ranks highest in the poverty rate for children (Children's Defense Fund, 1996).

Several of the indicators displayed in Table 13.2 involve problems of adolescence. Despite some positive trends, the levels of these indicators of well-being suggest that American youth in the second

decade of life may be in particular peril. To illustrate, consider four major categories of risk behaviors in late childhood and adolescence: (1) drug and alcohol use and abuse; (2) unsafe sex, teenage pregnancy, and teenage parenting; (3) school underachievement, school failure, and dropout; and (4) delinquency, crime, and violence (Dryfoos, 1990). Participation in any one of these behaviors could diminish a youth's life chances. Involvement in some of these behaviors could eliminate the young

Table 13-1	Moments in America for All Children
Every second	a public school student is suspended.*
Every 9 seconds	a high school student drops out.*
Every 10 seconds	a public school student is corporally punished.*
Every 20 seconds	a child is arrested.
Every 24 seconds	a baby is born to an unmarried mother.
Every 44 seconds	a baby is born into poverty.
Every minute	a baby is born to a teen mother.
Every 2 minutes	a baby is born at low birthweight (less than 5 lbs., 8 oz.).
Every 4 minutes	a baby is born to a mother who had late or no prenatal care.
Every 4 minutes	a child is arrested for drug abuse.
Every 8 minutes	a child is arrested for a violent crime.
Every 9 minutes	a baby is born at very low birthweight (less than 3 lbs., 4 oz.).
Every 11 minutes	a child is reported abused or neglected.
Every 19 minutes	a baby dies.
Every 37 minutes	a baby is born to a mother who is not a high school graduate.
Every 42 minutes	a child or youth under 20 dies from an accident.
Every 2 hours 20 minutes	a child or youth under 20 is killed by a firearm.
Every 3 hours	a child or youth under 20 is a homicide victim.
Every 4 hours	a child or youth under 20 commits suicide.
Every day	a young person under 25 dies from HIV infection.

*Based on calculations per school day (180 days of seven hours each).

Source: Children's Defense Fund, 2001.

| Table 13-2 | Kids Count Data for the United States: 2000 |

Indicators of Child Well-Being		Trend Data	
		1990	1997
Percentage of low birth-weight babies	U.S.	7.0%	7.5%
Infant mortality rate (deaths per 1,000 live births)	U.S.	9.2	7.2
Child death rate (deaths per 100,000 children ages 1–14)	U.S.	31.0	25.0
Rate of teen deaths rate by accident, homicide, and suicide (deaths per 100,000 teens ages 15–19)	U.S.	71.0	58.0
Teen birthrate (births per 1,000 females ages 15–17)	U.S.	37.0	32.0
Percentage of teens who are high school dropouts (ages 16–19)	U.S.	10.0%	10.0%
Percentage of teens not attending school and not working (ages 16–19)	U.S.	10.0%	9.0%
Percentage of children living with parents who do not have full-time, year-round employment	U.S.	30.0%	27.0%
Percentage of children in poverty	U.S.	20.0%	21.0%
Percentage of families with children headed by a single parent	U.S.	24.0%	27.0%

Source: Annie E. Casey Foundation, 2000.

person's chances of even having a life. Unfortunately, the risks to the life chances of American children and adolescents are occurring at historically unprecedented levels.

There are about 39.4 million American youth between the ages of 10 and 19 years (Yax, 1999). Approximately 50% of these adolescents engage in *two or more* of the categories of risk behaviors just noted, and approximately 10% of U.S. youth engage in *all* of the four categories of risk behaviors (Dryfoos, 1990). These data suggest that risk behaviors are highly interrelated among adolescents. Dryfoos (1990, p. 3) describes this situation:

> Many children are growing up in the United States today without a hope of enjoying the benefits that come with adulthood. They are not learning the skills necessary to participate in the educational system or to make the transition into the labor force. They cannot become responsible parents because they have limited experience in family life and lack the resources to raise their own children. The gap between achievers and nonachievers is expanding. A new class of "untouchables" is emerging in our inner cities, on the social fringes of suburbia, and in some rural areas: young people who are functionally illiterate, disconnected from school, depressed, prone to drug abuse and early criminal activity, and eventually parents of unplanned and unwanted babies. These are the children who are at high risk of never becoming responsible adults.

Comorbidity Simultaneous occurrence of two or more problem or risk behaviors or symptoms (e.g., violence and substance abuse often occur together).

Table 13.3 summarizes recent information about the **comorbidity** of risk behaviors among youth. Comorbidity refers to the simultaneous occurrence of problem behaviors among adolescents. The level of comorbidity among adolescent risk behaviors suggests that risk is a typical, or normally occurring, feature of the lives of many, if not most, adolescents. Meet the Researcher Box 13.1, which focuses on the work of Lisa J. Crockett, discusses the nature of risk in normal adolescent development.

To grasp the full magnitude of the problems facing U.S. youth and the challenges we as a society face in addressing these problems, let's examine more closely some of the risks besetting America's youth and discuss their diverse individual and contextual bases.

Individual and Contextual Bases of Adolescent Problem Behaviors

Issues to Consider

- What are the two general dimensions of problem behaviors? How do they differ? How do they overlap?
- Which attributes of adolescents are associated with the occurrence of problem behaviors?

Table 13-3	Examples of the Co-Occurrence of Sex-Related and Nonsex-Related Problem Behaviors in Adolescence	
Sex-Related Problem of the Adolescent	**Nonsex-Related Problem**	**References**
Unsafe sexual practices	Peer relations and alcohol use	Feldman et al., 1995
	Sexually active peers and siblings	East, Felice, & Morgan, 1993
	Friends with low educational expectations	Scott-Jones & White, 1990
	Parenting style and parental marital status	Whitbeck, Simons, & Kao, 1994
	Substance abuse, conduct problems, and emotional distress	Borus et al., 1995
	Living in poverty settings	East & Felice, 1996; Sullivan, 1993
Initiation of sexual behavior	Attitudes that reject social norms, nonconforming behavior	Costa et al., 1995
	Poor psychological adjustment	Bingham & Crockett, 1996
	Pubertal maturation	Savin-Williams, 1995; Stattin & Magnusson, 1990
Teenage parenting	Welfare dependency	Carnegie Corporation of New York, 1995; di Mauro, 1995
	Ambivalent attitudes about childbearing, contraception, and abortion	Zabin, Astone, & Emerson, 1996
Sex-related crimes (abuse, rape)	Parent characteristics, peer relations	Blaske et al., 1989; Small & Kerns, 1993
	Personality problems	Henry et al., 1996

Source: Lerner, 1998.

Problem behaviors may be associated with several attributes of the individual young person, for example cognitive, personality, and behavioral characteristics. They are also associated with numerous features of the individual's context, for example culture, community, family, school, and peers. The diversity of individual and contextual influences on problem behaviors is associated with both externalizing problems and internalizing problems. **Externalizing problems** are directed to other people or, more generally, to the social context (e.g., aggression, arson, disruptive behaviors in school, or inordinate family conflict). **Internalizing problems** are directed to the person himself or herself and affect his or her mental, cognitive, and emotional functioning (e.g., **depression** or **anxiety**).

Some problem behaviors involve both externalizing problems and internalizing problems. For example, substance use and abuse or unsafe sex can have features that involve both externalizing behaviors such as engaging in drug trafficking or in unprotected sex. These behaviors can also involve internalizing features such as becoming addicted to drugs or contracting a sexually transmitted disease. In such cases, both diverse individual and contextual characteristics are associated with these behaviors.

Certain components of the context of human development affect the incidence and development of internalizing and externalizing behaviors. Across history, culture is always such an ecological influence (Shweder et al., 1998). In the contemporary world of adolescents, poverty is another key ecological basis of problem behaviors (Hernandez, 1993). To help frame the discussion of the two domains of problem behaviors in adolescence, we discuss these two key features of the human development system next.

Externalizing problems Problems directed to other people or, more generally, to the social context, for example, aggression, arson, disruptive or conflictual behavior in the school or in the home.

Internalizing problems Problems directed inward to the individual and that affect his or her mental, cognitive, or emotional functioning, such as depression or anxiety.

Depression Emotional problem characterized by listlessness, lethargy, a blunting of affect, and disengagement from social activity.

Anxiety Unpleasant feeling state associated with such reactions as dread, fear, general uneasiness, or panic.

MEET THE RESEARCHER BOX 13.1

LISA J. CROCKETT
NORMAL RISKY BEHAVIOR AND ADOLESCENT DEVELOPMENT

Most adolescents in the United States engage in some amount of risky behavior during their teenage years. For example, they experiment with sex, drinking, and other forms of drug use; they may drink and drive, or ride with others who have been drinking. Clearly, these behaviors can increase the risk of such problems as sexually transmitted infections, pregnancy, substance abuse, and serious accidents. However, some adolescents seem to be able to experiment with risk behaviors without experiencing lasting negative consequences, whereas others may not be so lucky. Which adolescents experience negative consequences and why? Also, are there certain characteristics of adolescents or their experiences that help us predict who will continue risky behaviors in adulthood?

I am studying a group of adolescents that my colleagues and I have followed since they were in junior high school—they are now adults in their mid to late 20s. These adolescents all grew up in the same rural community. In adolescence, we surveyed them every year about their feelings, relationships with family and friends, and activities, including participation in risky behaviors. We have also surveyed them twice since they left high school. The goal of this research is to understand the role that risk behaviors play in adolescents' lives, both during adolescence and later as they move into adulthood.

With funding from the Office of Adolescent Pregnancy Programs and the National Institute on Alcohol Abuse and Alcoholism, my collaborator, Judith Vicary, and I have examined the changes in risk behaviors these young people exhibit as they move through adolescence. For example, as they get older, more teenagers report some experience with having sex, getting drunk, and getting high. Moreover, the frequency of these behaviors tends to increase with age, although the frequency of drug use declines in adulthood and heavy drinking levels off. Focusing on drinking specifically, we find that heavy drinking decreases in early adulthood for

Lisa J. Crockett is professor of psychology and associate dean of arts and sciences at the University of Nebraska-Lincoln. She is associate editor of the *Journal of Research on Adolescence* and serves on the editorial board of the *Journal of Early Adolescence* and the *Journal of Adolescent Research*.

some youth but not others. Youth who reported high levels of misconduct as adolescents and those who delay marriage and parenthood continue to drink more heavily and are also more likely to initiate heavy drinking in adulthood if they did not do so in adolescence. On a related note, we have asked whether the age at which adolescents begin to experiment matters for their future psychological adjustment. What we find is sometimes surprising. For example, although adolescents who start to have sex at young ages also engage in other risky behaviors and show poorer adjustment in other ways, having sex early does not appear to cause these outcomes. Rather, adolescents who initiate sex early are already on a path that involves greater risk. Finally, we have asked what family characteristics and adolescent behaviors predict early versus late initiation of intercourse. Family background (for example, having a sister who became pregnant as a teenager or not living with both parents), academic investment, and involvement in other risky behaviors all appear to predict early initiation of intercourse.

What puts children on a path to engage in risky behavior as adolescents? Are some young people attracted to risk? Are they unable to resist the lure of risky behavior because they lack self-control? In a new research project, funded by the National Institute of Mental Health, Marcela Raffaelli and I will explore these questions. Using data from a national sample, the National Longitudinal Survey of Youth, we plan to study the development of self-regulation (the regulation of attention, affect, and behavior) in middle childhood to learn whether young people's capacity to self-regulate helps them refrain from early intercourse and unprotected sex when they reach adolescence. We will also identify individual characteristics, such as temperament, and contextual variables, such as maternal characteristics and parenting practices, that play a role in the development of self-regulation and risky sexual behavior.

Culture and Problem Behaviors

Issue to Consider

- What are some of the effects of cultural context on problem behaviors and on attitudes about their presence?

Culture provides a frame for the definition of behavior problems. Youth have distinct ideas about the nature of adolescent problem behaviors, and these conceptions vary in relation to cultural context. One study of high school students from the United States, China, and Japan assessed the perceptions of the behaviors and personality characteristics associated with a "bad kid" (Crystal & Stevenson, 1995). Among youth from the United States, the behavior most frequently associated with a "bad kid" was lack of self-control. In China, the key problem behaviors defining a "bad kid" were acts against society, and in Japan the most significant behaviors of a "bad kid" were disruptions of interpersonal harmony. In addition, the perception that substance abuse is a mark of a "bad kid" was more prevalent among American youth than among the Chinese or Japanese adolescents (Crystal & Stevenson, 1995).

For a group of 120 inner-city African American fifth and sixth graders, orientation to African American culture or to European American culture was differentially related to problem behaviors (Jagers, 1996). The African American cultural orientation was not associated with problem behaviors, but the European American orientation was, especially when it was associated with ideas about minority youth being embedded in a culture that involves school rejection and gang activity (Jagers, 1996).

Other studies support the conclusion that the presence of behavioral problems among youth is linked to culture and cognition, for example, perceptions or ideas about problem behaviors. Among about 2,800 15- and 16-year-olds from the Netherlands, youth with behavioral problems had negative perceptions of their families, school, and peers (Garnefski & Okma, 1996). Among boys, problems in school were the most important predictors of behavioral problems. For girls, problems at home were most associated with problem behaviors. In a study of about 220 African American youth in grades 9 through 12, lack of perceived support from friends and the experience of stressful life events were associated with problem behaviors such as drug and alcohol use and delinquent acts (McCreary, Slavin, & Berry, 1996).

In a longitudinal study of about 100 Canadian youth, beginning when they were between 11 and 12 years of age and continuing for 3.5 years, disobedience to parents, school misconduct, and substance use increased with age (Maggs, Almeida, & Galambos, 1995). These increases in problem behaviors were associated with decreases in positive self-images and increases in peer acceptance and involvement and were linked to beliefs among the youth that engaging in risk behaviors was fun (Maggs et al., 1995). Similarly, among 650 Australian male and female adolescents, both peer approval and ideas about pleasure and risk were associated with perceptions about risk behaviors (Smith & Rosenthal, 1995).

In short, culture constitutes a key contextual influence on youth problem behavior. Another factor, poverty, also exerts a strong influence. As illustrated in Table 13.2, poverty is a part of the contemporary context of one fifth of youth living in the United States.

Poverty and Youth Development

Issues to Consider

- What is the most striking distinction between youth who experience poverty as chronic and youth who experience poverty as transitory?
- What are some of the "rotten outcomes" of poverty?
- What issues should be considered when designing interventions against youth poverty and the associated "rotten outcomes"?

Poverty is a key structural issue in American society that impacts all behavioral risks engaged in by youth (e.g. Huston, 1991; McLoyd, 1994; Schorr, 1988, 1997). In 1993 the poverty line for a family of four was $14,763 (Center for the Study of Social Policy, 1995), a figure that is quite low, given that families earning 150% or even 200% of this amount still struggle financially. In 1996 the poverty line for a family of four rose only to $16,036 (Annie E. Casey Foundation, 1998). During the last two decades of the 20th century at least 20% of the 78.3 million

About one fifth of American youth live in poverty.

youth (people in the first two decades of life) in the United States, or 15.6 million youth, were poor (Annie E. Casey Foundation, 1999; Yax, 1999).

Racial and Ethnic Differences Although poverty disproportionately affects minority youth, it occurs across all racial and ethnic groups and in all geographic regions of the United States. The rates of poverty in rural areas are as high as those in the inner cities, although poor families in rural areas receive fewer welfare benefits (Huston, 1991; Jensen, 1988).

African American, Latino, and Native American youth are more likely than their European American age-mates to be among the poor (Annie E. Casey Foundation, 1997; Center for the Study of Social Policy, 1992, 1993; Huston, 1991; McLoyd, 1994; Simons et al., 1991). In 1989, 44% of African American children were poor, a rate four times greater than the corresponding rate for European American children (Center for the Study of Social Policy, 1993). Among Latino children, the 1989 rate of child poverty was 38%, and the increase in poverty across the 1980s for these youth was 25%, the greatest increase for any of America's racial/ethnic groups (Center for the Study of Social Policy, 1993).

In terms of absolute numbers, data from the 1990 census indicate that 5.9 million European American children lived in poverty. The corresponding numbers of African Americans, Asian Americans,

"Rotten outcomes" Problems of youth development associated with poverty.

Native Americans, and Latinos were 3.7 million, 346,000, 260,000, and 2.4 million, respectively (Annie E. Casey Foundation, 1996; Children's Defense Fund, 1992).

Race is the most striking distinction between youth whose poverty is chronic and youth whose poverty is transitory (Huston, 1991). African Americans spend a significantly larger portion of their childhood years in poverty than non–African Americans (Duncan, 1991). The average African American child spends 5.5 years in poverty; the average non–African American child spends only 0.9 years in poverty (Duncan, 1991).

"Rotten Outcomes" of Poverty
The trends involving youth poverty are associated with problems of youth development. Schorr (1988) has described these relations as the **"rotten outcomes"** of poverty. They include early school failure, unemployability, long-term welfare dependency, violent crime, and feelings of hopelessness and despair (Schorr, 1991; Simons et al., 1991). Poor youth are also at high risk for low self-confidence, conduct problems, depression, and peer conflict, and for encountering severe health problems (for example, infant mortality, lack of immunization against common childhood diseases), physical or mental disabilities, and physical abuse, neglect, and unintended injury (Carnegie Corporation of New York, 1994; Klerman, 1991; McLoyd & Wilson, 1991; Simons et al., 1991). Female adolescents from the most disadvantaged backgrounds are the most likely to drop out of schools and/or become teenage mothers (Upchurch, 1993).

Youth living in poverty are at high risk of dying from violence. Between 1985 and 1992 the rate of violent deaths for 15- to 19-year-olds increased by 13%. For European American youth, this rate increase was 10%, whereas for African American 15- to 19-year-olds the rate increase was 78% (Center for the Study of Social Policy, 1993).

Societal and cultural conditions have created and maintained poverty in America. The breadth and impact of youth poverty represents a formidable challenge for intervention programs. Ideally, efforts should be designed to be sensitive to the diverse conditions of poverty. Many poor youth are homeless or live in diverse families or family-type settings such as foster care homes, institutions, shelters, and other types of placements (Allison, 1993; Huston, 1991). Lack of attention to this contextual variation may lead to an inadequate appreciation of the diverse role of "the family" in poor children's development. Inattention to this contextual variation may lead to insufficiently differentiated policies and programs related to the family life of poor children. Programs that are successful in addressing the several risks and "rotten outcomes" linked to youth poverty adopt diverse strategies and approaches. Some of these are illustrated in Application Box 13.1.

In sum, individual-psychological variables associated with cognition, personality, and health are linked to cultural context and to poverty in the development of adolescent problem behaviors. The diversity of individual and contextual influences is involved in both externalizing and internalizing problem behaviors. To illustrate the links among diverse individual and contextual characteristics and problem behaviors, we first discuss associations with externalizing behaviors.

Externalizing Problems in Adolescence

The role of diverse individual and contextual characteristics in the development of externalizing problems among youth may be discussed in relation to problem behaviors generally and in respect to those problem behaviors that result in a youth being labeled as delinquent.

Delinquency, Crime, and Violence

Issues to Consider

• How might different psychological and behavioral attributes of adolescents and varied social contexts influence the development of problem behaviors?

• In what way might the values and goals of an adolescent and his or her culture be linked to delinquent behavior?

Of all the problems confronting contemporary youth, no set of issues has attracted as much public concern *and* public alarm as youth delinquency and violent crimes. People point in fear to the growth of **youth gangs** (Taylor, 1990) and to territorial battles, drug trafficking violence, random street violence, and the seemingly younger and younger ages of violent criminals.

Adolescents are the perpetrators of and also the victims of a disproportionately large share of the crime in the United States. During the mid-1980s, youth aged 13 to 21 years accounted for 35.5% of all nontraffic-related arrests in the United States, despite representing only 14.3% of the population during this time period (Kennedy, 1991). From 1995 to 2000, there was a decrease in the juvenile crime rate (Schwartz, 1999). Nevertheless, as shown in Figures 13.1 and 13.2, between 1981 and 1997, the juvenile arrest rates for aggravated assault and robbery remained high.

Although the rates of adolescent delinquency and violence remain high, we must emphasize that youth who are arrested represent only a small proportion of the nation's children and adolescents. As noted by Schwartz (1999), 95% of American youth are never

Youth gangs Groups of youth potentially involved in criminal activity.

Figure 13.1
Arrests for aggravated assault per 100,000 juveniles, ages 10–17, during the 1980s and 1990s. (*Source:* Schwartz, 1999.)

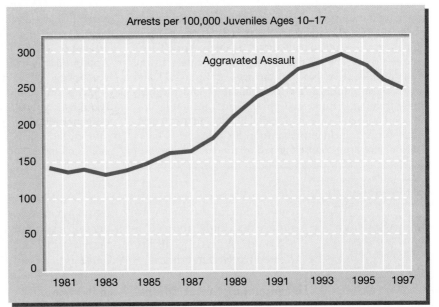

applications box 13.1

Designing Programs to Reduce or Prevent the "Rotten Outcomes" of Youth Poverty

Youth poverty is the single most important predictor of problems in youth development (Huston, 1991). The "rotten outcomes" (Schorr, 1988) linked to poverty include early school failure, unemployability, prolonged welfare dependency, delinquency and (often violent) crime, and feelings of hopelessness and despair.

Given the many negative impacts of poverty, effective programs must address the whole child and his or her community in both integrative and innovative ways. Three outstanding, effective, but quite different programs have had impacts across the United States and the world. These programs are summarized here—two local programs in New York City and one national program in Washington, D.C.

A Comprehensive Approach to Youth Needs: "The Door" Program of New York City

In an old converted warehouse in downtown New York City, some 300 teenagers a day enter a four-level complex to share in programs designed to rebuild their faith in the future. Some of them, like Carla and Yvonne, came to "The Door," as it is known, feeling disconnected from the community and life around them. Both girls were in high school when they learned of the program and both were mothers. "I felt like a nobody," said Carla. "The feeling of togetherness here has changed that. It's a homey feeling. It's like a family."

The Door was founded in 1972 to provide services and a community gathering place for young people whose needs and circumstances cover the vast spectrum of opportunity and disadvantage in New York City's unique urban melting pot. The program caters to the needs of both sexes between the ages of 12 and 21 and covers social and legal services, education and prevocational training, creative and physical arts, mental health, pre- and postnatal care, and sexual health and awareness. Other services include preparation for jobs, crisis intervention, and drug counseling and treatment. All activities

are integrated to help develop the potential of young people to be well-rounded individuals.

The Door offers educational services for both in-school and out-of-school youth, including an alternative high school program that provides graduates with a diploma. Reflecting the rich cultural diversity of New York City, the Door also teaches English as a Second Language.

The Door works with hundreds of agencies and institutions in New York City and offers more services to young people than any other program in the United States. More than 7,000 young people draw on its staff and facilities each year, and since April 1989, more than 1,000 youth experts from more than 80 countries have visited its facility. The Door has 17 city, state, and federal contracts to provide services to young people, and it draws its financial support from a wide variety of individual foundations and corporate sponsors. It also has a growing list of individual donors and volunteers. The Door model has been adapted and replicated in many other cities and countries in Europe and Latin America.

Providing At-Risk Youth with Educational, Cultural, and Sporting Opportunities: The "Jackie Robinson Center for Physical Culture" Program of New York City

Like many U.S. cities, Brooklyn, New York, has experienced a sharp decline in living standards. Forty-one percent of the population is on some form of public assistance due to joblessness or low-wage employment. Approximately 45% of the area's inhabitants are under 21 years of age.

With limited opportunities and underdeveloped skills, Brooklyn's youth face high levels of unemployment. An estimated 60% of area youth are ill prepared to secure jobs due to low educational achievement and/or limited skills and experience.

Juvenile delinquency Violation of a law committed by a person prior to his or her 18th birthday, a violation that would have been a crime if committed by an adult.

Status offense Violation of the law involving a behavior that would not be illegal if engaged in by an adult.

arrested and, of the ones who are arrested, only about 6% to 8% in a given year are arrested for violent crimes.

Delinquency, Status Offenses, and Gangs Juvenile de-

linquency is the violation of a law committed by a person less than 18 years of age that would have been a crime if committed by an adult. A **status offense** is a violation of the law which involves a behavior that would not have been illegal if engaged in by an adult.

In adolescence, delinquency and status offenses

Founded in 1987, the Jackie Robinson Center for Physical Culture (JRC) is a comprehensive program targeting at-risk youth in Brooklyn. The program provides education, sports, and counseling services to youth ages 8 to 18.

Currently, the Jackie Robinson Program serves approximately 4,000 students at 15 sites throughout Brooklyn. The focus of JRC's services can be seen through 4 of the program's 11 components. A sports and cultural program stresses positive growth and development and personal achievement. Young people typically spend 3 hours a week engaged in sports or cultural activities ranging from playing in bands to drama, chorus, dance, double dutch, cheerleading, basketball, softball, track, or soccer. The educational component, offered for 3 hours each week, involves classes in reading, writing, science, and math. The social services section provides instruction in employment preparation, health, decision-making and interpersonal relations, as well as legal services. In addition, special events are offered each month and range from artistic performances to visits by local celebrities.

JRC is recognized by the General Accounting Office in Washington, D.C., as one of the 10 best preventive programs in the nation. In the brief period of time it has been in existence, JRC has helped foster community solidarity and improved the math and science scores of its participants.

Providing "At Risk" Youth with Job Training and Career Services: Job Corps: Washington, D.C.

The typical youth enrolled in the Job Corps is an 18-year-old high school dropout who reads at the seventh-grade level, comes from an economically disadvantaged family, belongs to a minority group, and has never had a full-time job. Established in 1964, Job Corps traces its beginnings to President Lyndon B. Johnson's War on Poverty programs and his vision of a Great Society. The program was designed to relieve youth unemployment, particularly in inner-city areas where jobs were scarce due to urban decay, widespread poverty, and the transfer of people and jobs to the suburbs.

Today, over 118 Job Corps centers across the country are working in partnership with government, labor, and the private sector. Seventy-seven of the centers are managed and operated by corporations and nonprofit organizations; the remainder are run by the Departments of Agriculture and the Interior.

Job Corps, whose budget was approximately $1.3 billion in 1999, is funded wholly through government appropriations. In order to reduce its heavy reliance on government funding and expand its services, the Corps is now exploring private sector funding alternatives.

Job Corps takes the form of a residential learning program providing participants with basic education, vocational skills training, work experience, counseling, health care, and related support services. A compulsory World of Work program provides students with job information and emphasizes work and behavior attitudes, sources of job information, employment applications, preparation for job interviews, and consumer education. Vocational training programs focus on specific business skills, training in the automotive trade, construction, welding, health occupations, information technology, culinary arts, building and apartment maintenance, and others.

In the nearly 37 years it has been in existence, Job Corps has established a successful track record. Seventy-five percent of graduates become employed (or move on to higher education), earning approximately 15% more than their counterparts who were not enrolled. In addition, Job Corps members are one third less likely to be arrested, according to Department of Labor statistics.

Source: International Youth Foundation, YouthNet International, 2001. <www.iyfnet.org>

often occur in gangs. Gangs are an outgrowth of the importance of peer groups in the social behavior of adolescence. These groups of youth probably come into existence because they meet certain needs for the individuals who participate. They may create security, status, and belonging, provide a way to pass idle time, and offer a way to gain new experiences (Taylor, 1990, 1993). Carl S. Taylor's continuing research with gangs and the cultural context within which they live is discussed in Meet the Researcher Box 13.2.

Some of the problems of adolescence classified as delinquent really signify more an issue of poor social relationships than of criminality. Running

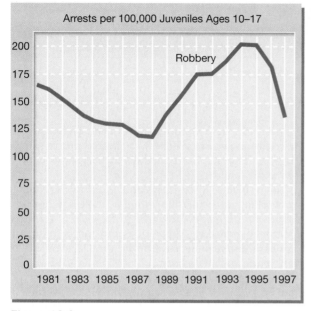

Arrests per 100,000 Juveniles Ages 10–17

Robbery

Figure 13.2
Arrests for robbery per 100,000 juveniles, ages 10–17, during the 1980s and 1990s. (*Source*: Schwartz, 1999.)

Developmental and Contextual Bases of Delinquency The development of problem behaviors among delinquent youth has been associated with several different psychological and behavioral attributes of youth and numerous levels of the context. It is not surprising to learn that aggressive conduct is strongly associated with aggressive youth (Cairns & Cairns, 1994; Pakiz, Reinherz, & Frost, 1992), feelings of anger among incarcerated male adolescents are associated with both verbal and physical aggression (Cornell, Peterson, & Richards, 1999), and, among youth offenders, violent and nonviolent offenses are associated with alcohol use more strongly and consistently than with either marijuana or heroin use (Dawkins, 1997).

It may be surprising to learn that certain styles of thought are associated with delinquency. Delinquent youth appear to use particular cognitive strategies to solve social problems (Kuperminc, Allen, & Arthur, 1996). In a study of 80 African Americans and European Americans age 11 through 18 at high risk for delinquency, acts of delinquency were more frequent among youth whose problem-solving strategies were not based on trying to form relations with others (Kuperminc et al., 1996). Among about 300 male 14- to 18-year-olds who were committed to a state training school for hard-core youth offenders, treatment to decrease externalizing behaviors such as aggression were successful if youth conceptualized treatment success as due to their own behavior and when

away from home technically is considered a delinquent act, but it is really more than that. Whatever its classification, running away represents a large and significant problem in adolescence (Adams, 1991).

Other problematic behaviors also skirt the borderlines between status offenses, social relationship issues, and actual illegality. Problems of teenage sexuality—unsafe sex, pregnancy, and childbearing—pertain to both status offenses and social relationships. Issues of tobacco, alcohol, and drug use cross the border between status offenses and illegality.

A range of behaviors may involve delinquency, status offenses, or some combination of these two categories of problem behaviors. Despite the categorization of a given instance of such behavior, the presence of such acts within the adolescent population raises a serious challenge for the quality of civil society in America (see Chapter 5).

It is important to appreciate not only the incidence of problems of delinquency but the bases of their development. Such understanding is crucial for the design of intervention programs and public policies to prevent these problems and promote positive alternatives among youth.

During adolescence, delinquency often occurs in gangs.

MEET THE RESEARCHER BOX 13.2

CARL S. TAYLOR
STUDIES OF YOUTH CULTURE

As an ethnographer, I take my work and research directly to the source. I have worked in some of the most isolated and distressed communities in the nation. As a criminologist and ecologist, I have successfully merged the two disciplines to give a unique viewpoint on emerging social issues.

A lot of my focus and work has been with gangs, but I am now stressing the issues pertaining to youth culture. You might ask what youth culture is and what issues youth culture deals with. I have identified youth culture as ever changing. Youth culture is reflective of young ideas and attitudes, and it will always counteract adult society. Youth culture has its own language, and to work with youth culture, one must understand their language. Youth culture believes it is invincible, and the glue that sticks youth culture together is technology. While youth culture fights to fit in among themselves, they face the pressures of the larger society. These pressures include teen pregnancy, drugs and alcohol, and AIDS.

What I am finding when working with youth culture is that violence fits in their realm. They are exposed to violence on a daily basis, from the video games they play to the movies they watch. All these accounts of violence are desensitizing our youth. This leads to more and more children and youth committing violent acts. They rarely see consequences, and many see violence as the only way to resolve conflict.

Carl S. Taylor is director of community and youth development programs at the Institute for Children, Youth, and Families and a professor of family and child ecology at Michigan State University. Currently he is the principal investigator in the newly launched Michigan Gang Research Project. Taylor also serves on the Michigan Juvenile Justice Committee and advises various projects concerning youth throughout America today.

The evolution of violence has taken it to the global level. Two years ago, while conducting research in Germany, I encountered several young men. Most of them were white; however, they came from various ethnic backgrounds: French, German, Serbian, and some that were biracial with one parent in the U.S. military. All these young men had one thing in common: They were members of the Crips, the same Crips that are out of south central Los Angeles. I was amazed. Here were these children of modern-day Europe telling me that they identify themselves with icons such as Tupac Shakur. I had traveled across the Atlantic Ocean, and I was finding youth culture in Europe identifying itself with the same things as American youth culture. From the boys in the Middle East to the young men in New York City, global violence has reached an all-time high.

As interesting as all this information is, it is also very frightening. What do future generations of youth have to prepare for? What can we do to change the direction that youth culture is traveling in? We need to invest in human capital. Early investment, intervention, and education create strong homes, families, and communities. Communities need to provide the assets that some homes are unable to provide. We need to reach out to youth culture and give youth the resources that can aid them into becoming productive members of society.

they perceived themselves as worried or anxious (Swenson & Kennedy, 1995). When youth with these problems perceived themselves as happy, treatment tended not to be successful. Treatment was also not successful among these youth if they perceived themselves as highly physically competent or if they saw problems as being of their own making (Swenson & Kennedy, 1995). It is useful to note that some of these youth in this study had internalizing problems as well, for example anxiety or depression.

Poor judgment may also be associated with

aggression by delinquent youth (Graham, Hudley, & Williams, 1992). In situations where negative outcomes of a social interaction are unintentional, aggressive African American male adolescents make more extreme judgments of the other person and of the situation than comparable groups of nonaggressive youth (Graham & Hudley, 1994). Other beliefs about aggression may influence youth violence. African American and Latino urban adolescents believe that their parents would disapprove more if they retaliated against their siblings than against peers (Herzberger & Hall, 1993).

Values and goals are other psychological attributes that have been linked to delinquency. In a study comparing Caucasian and Asian high school students living in Hong Kong (Stewart et al., 1998), valuing tradition and conformity was associated with fewer disciplinary violations in both groups. In a study of 80 delinquent youth, 90 youth at risk for delinquency, and 90 not-at-risk youth (Carroll et al., 1997), members of the first two groups placed more importance on goals associated with developing a social image linked to both delinquency and to freedom/autonomy than youth in the latter group. The goals of youth not at risk were associated with developing an academic image (Carroll et al., 1997).

Bullying behavior also seems to be prototypic of delinquents. In a study of young male offenders incarcerated in Ontario, Canada, 70% reported being involved in bullying at least several times a week, either as perpetrators (45%) or as victims (25%) (Connell & Farrington, 1996).

In addition to the psychological and behavioral attributes of delinquent youth, several components of their social context are linked to their problem behaviors. The type of peer group a youth is in influences the probability of his or her behaving in a delinquent manner. In a study of more than 860 young adolescent males, moderately disruptive 11- and 12-year-old youth who had peers who were aggressively disturbing to others showed higher levels of delinquency at age 13 years than did mildly disruptive youth with other types of friends (Vitaro et al., 1997).

Early maturing girls are at greater risk for delinquency when they are involved in mixed-sex social settings (Caspi et al., 1993). In a longitudinal study of Swedish youth, girls' early maturation was related to norm breaking and delinquent behavior when the girls were part of a peer group of older girls (Stattin & Magnusson, 1990). When early maturing girls had a same-age peer group, no association was found between delinquency and maturational status.

Peer context acts in conjunction with family variables to influence delinquency. Male delinquents who have committed assault offenses have family relations characterized by rigidity and low cohesion and peers who are highly aggressive (Blaske, Borduin, Henggelen, & Mann, 1989). In the face of the youth offenses, the offenders and their mothers show little anxiety or interpersonal discomfort. Male delinquents who have committed sexual offenses have high levels of neurotic symptoms. Their mothers show such problems as well (Blaske et al., 1989). Sexually offending youth also have low-level emotional bonds with their peers.

Multiple family factors are associated with conviction by age 18 for both violent and nonviolent criminal offenses. These factors include authoritarian parenting, deviant mother-child interactions, number of parent changes experienced by a child, having a single-parent family, quality of family relationships, mother's reading level, and socioeconomic level (Henry et al., 1996). In a study of 15- and 16-year-olds from London, England, the youth who had been repeatedly arrested by the police showed high levels of family disruption (Hagell & Newburn, 1996). Although these youth reported good relationships with their mothers and strong ties to their friends, they also frequently said they lacked social support. In addition, they reported they had few constructive daily activities and used a lot of drugs and alcohol.

It is possible, however, that the community setting within which a youth lives can counteract negative influences from parents or peers. In one intriguing study (Sampson, 1997), 80 different neighborhoods in Chicago were assessed in regard to the presence of informal social control provided by the citizens living in the community. When such control was high, the incidence of adolescent delinquency in the neighborhood was lessened.

A diversity of individual and contextual variables are linked to the incidence of a range of delinquent behaviors. Such influence by both individual and ecological components of the developmental system is also evident when we consider specific instances of delinquency, such as running away and violence.

Runaways and Homeless Youth Running away from home is an act of delinquency for adolescents. It is often a sign of the youth's inability to tolerate the social setting in which he or she resides. Leaving home may be a way to tell parents that the home situation has become seriously negative, and/or it may be a way to indicate that the individual needs and wants help.

Each year, between 750,000 and 1 million young people engage in runaway behavior (Adams, 1991).

Many runaway adolescents are homeless and live on the streets.

Although regional variations in the magnitude of the problems are associated with running away (Zimet et al., 1995), runaways often become involved with other acts of delinquency, such as prostitution and illicit drug use (Adams, 1991; Rohr, 1996). Moreover, they are more likely than other adolescents to become HIV positive (Rotherman-Borus & Koopman, 1991; see also Chapter 10). These youth are also likely to become targets of aggravated assault and/or sexual assault (Terrell, 1997), because of their frequent status of being homeless and living on the streets.

As with other instances of delinquency, running away is associated with diverse individual and contextual attributes. Runaway and homeless street youth have high rates of disability in reading, arithmetic, and writing (Barwick & Siegel, 1996). Also associated with adolescents' running away are home environments that involve rejection, neglect, disinterest, hostile control, parent-child conflict, inadequate supervision, and lack of family organization (Adams, 1991). Although some runaway and homeless youth characterize their parents as supportive and emotionally available, the majority do not characterize their parents in such positive terms (Kipke et al., 1997). Terms such as *intrusive, unavailable, detached,* or *having problems with drugs and/or the law* are prototypic of the way

these youth describe their parents (Kipke et al., 1997).

The problems of runaway and/or homeless youth are not limited to one geographic area, either within or among countries. Rather, they are global problems. Applications Box 13.2 describes programs used in different nations to address the problems faced by runaway and homeless youth.

Violence Delinquent youth are often violent, although violence is a major problem for all adolescents whether or not they are delinquent. Youth are often the targets of violent delinquent acts. This tragic circumstance has been illustrated all too often in America by the occurrences of youth shooting their classmates and teachers. Nationwide, 4% of all students report that they missed 1 or more days within the last 30 days of school because they had felt unsafe at school or unsafe when traveling to and from school (Centers for Disease Control and Prevention, 1998).

Violence breeds violence as well as other risk behaviors. Growing up in a neighborhood replete with violence is associated with enactment of risk behaviors linked to substance use and abuse. Youth living in violent communities often become involved with illicit drug use (Taylor, 1990, 1993), they are more likely to smoke than other adolescents (Fick & Thomas, 1995), and they are more likely to behave in ways that may make violence more likely, for example, carrying a gun.

In a study of more than 200 African American males and females, 11 to 19 years old, living in a high-poverty, high violent crime community in Augusta, Georgia (DuRant et al., 1995), certain behaviors were associated with previous exposure to violence and with having been a victim of violent crime. These behaviors included carrying a weapon during the previous 30 days and carrying a hidden weapon during the last year. Weapon carrying was related as well to other contextual and individual characteristics, such as family conflict and depression (DuRant et al., 1995). Nationally, 8.5% of youth reported carrying a weapon on school property on at least 1 of the prior 30 days of school, and boys (12.5%) were more likely than girls (3.7%) to have carried a weapon (Centers for Disease Control and Prevention, 1998).

Although most youth exposed to violence do not become murderers, exposure to violence can result in

applications box 13.2

Enhancing the Life Chances of Street Children

Youth run away from home and/or are forced to live on the streets for many reasons. Homelessness and street life in general can affect the immediate health and safety of youth and have long-term negative influences on their development. Street children exist throughout both the industrialized and the developing world. Programs have arisen around the globe to address the problems faced by these youth. Several exemplary ones from around the world are described here.

Proyecto Alternativas, Tegucigalpa, Honduras

Honduras is one of the poorest countries in Latin America, with an economy that is highly dependent upon export crops such as bananas, coffee, sugar, and timber. During the last decade the economic situation has deteriorated as production in both the manufacturing and agricultural sectors has declined.

The decline in the nation's economy has had a dramatic impact on its youth, 65% of whom currently live in poverty. Of those, more than half work at jobs ranging from construction and transportation to vending and domestic labor. An estimated 40% of young people are not enrolled in school.

Established in 1990, Proyecto Alternativas is directed at the more than 1,400 children who live or work on the streets of Tegucigalpa. Its principal goal is to protect the rights of children and youth and reduce the multiple risks associated with unprotected labor and life on the streets. In addition, the program aims to provide young people who have assumed adult responsibilities with a sense of what it is like to be young—through games and cultural and sporting activities.

Proyecto Alternativas also provides youth with health education, educational support, and counseling. The program's integrated health and social services reach more than 2,000 children and youth. Those at risk of poor nutrition are selected for a special supplementation program. More than 100 youth participate in the program daily, most of whom work and scavenge for food while collecting and sorting garbage.

Hundreds of parents and relatives are formally enrolled in the program with others involved informally at the community level. In recent months there has been a 25% increase in adult/family involvement.

Young people are also actively involved in decision making as evidenced by the fact that all but one of the project's 14 staff members are under the age of 30. Most of its street educators are in their late teens or early 20s.

The program has had a positive impact on the nutritional status of young people throughout the city and has contributed to a decline in death rates among the city's marginalized youth.

Movimento Nacional de Meninos e Meninas de Rua, Brasilia, Brazil

Brazil has the largest population of street-based and working children in the world, with 1 in every 8 children under the age of 15 spending the majority of their time on the streets. Most of such children have either no schooling or dropped out of school after the first grade. Many work in low-paying jobs ranging from selling candies and lottery tickets to washing cars, shining shoes, and running errands.

In response to growing violence and abuse against street-based children and youth, Movimento Nacional de Meninos e Meninas de Rua (MNMMR) was founded in 1985. Today, MNMMR, a national movement of street children and adult educators, coordinates the activities of 40 organizations reaching out to 900,000 youth nationwide.

MNMMR is a multifaceted program offering youth and youth service providers with training, education, research, materials development, and public policy advocacy. Through regularly scheduled workshops, courses, and conferences, MNMMR provides educators with professional training in child psychology and family counseling and allows them to share ideas and approaches with others in the field. One of its main priorities is to detect, document, and denounce the widespread and often fatal violence committed against street children.

Since its inception, MNMMR has had a tremendous impact on the way Brazilian society views street-based children. In the past, such children were viewed with suspicion, fear, and were often abused. Society traditionally labeled them as "delinquent," putting them away in jails or juvenile institutions. As a result of MNMMR's public education campaigns the needs of such children and their reasons for being on the street are now far better understood. MNMMR was instrumental in introducing advanced laws on family welfare and children's rights into the Brazilian constitution. Both the Philippines and India have used its model to lobby their own governments for the more humane treatment of street-based children.

Don Bosco Homes for Street Children, Buenos Aires, Argentina

Between 1940 and 1970, industrial growth in Buenos Aires attracted poor families from rural areas and the neighboring countries of Bolivia and Paraguay in search of jobs and opportunity. As a result, underemployment and unemployment in the area soared. This, coupled with the economic crisis of the 1980s and 1990s, contributed to making the region a major center of poverty in Argentina.

Children and youth are the greatest victims of poverty and related problems such as alcoholism, violence, and family crises. Such problems often result in the increased marginalization, neglect, and abuse or abandonment of children—and consequently, in a rise in the number of street and working children.

To help meet the needs of the city's growing population of street-based youth, the first Don Bosco home for street children was founded in 1985. An outgrowth of the Salesian Institution in Argentina, the Don Bosco Homes and Day Centers now reach out to 150 young boys and girls between the ages of 7 and 17.

The Don Bosco approach is based on a fourfold process of prevention. Initially, former street children who have received training visit street-based children and youth in their home environment. Following, children are invited to visit Day Centers where they may come to take a bath, wash their clothes, receive health care, eat, and sleep. The Centers also offer recreational and artistic activities such as music, theater, and handicraft production.

During the next stage children are invited to live within one of Don Bosco's six homes. From the home, children attend local schools and engage in recreational activities with other children from the neighborhood. At these "little homes" children receive a variety of services including health care, psychological counseling, school follow-up, and contacts with courts, judges, social workers, police, and national or regional children's institutes.

The most difficult and complex task faced by children at the "little home" is the search for his or her family. Don Bosco attempts to return each child to their original home wherever possible. Periodic studies conducted by the Salesians have found that approximately 70% of the children at the Homes return to their original families.

Bosconia/La Florida, Bogota, Colombia

Rapid urbanization in Colombia and widespread poverty have contributed to a dramatic increase in the number of street-based youth. At any one time there are between 7,000 and 10,000 street-based youth, or "gamines," in Bogota alone.

In response to the growing numbers of young people living and working on the streets, Bosconia/La Florida was established in 1971. Its aim is to enable Bogota's street children to become responsible, productive members of society. Over the past 20 years, Bosconia has expanded from a small, experimental program to a complex system of classrooms, group homes, farms, vocational training, and productive activities. Currently, it serves approximately 5,400 boys and girls, ages 8 through 22.

Program participants move through its various phases at their own pace. Most are first introduced to the program through its outreach activities known as Operation Friendship. Two nights each week, dedicated educators visit the gamines where they live on the streets. Through direct contact on the street or by word of mouth, "gamines" find their way to one of the six program-operated "patios" around the city. The patios are drop-in centers where young people may come to take a shower, wash their clothes, get a meal, receive medical attention, and play games.

Those young people who choose to leave the streets participate in a 30-day motivation and detoxification program. Following, both boys and girls are given the opportunity to enter group homes, providing them with a more structured learning and living environment.

To date, more than 17,000 young people have graduated from the program. The majority of graduates become successfully integrated into society as productive adults. A substantial number continue on with the program as educators, or work in other youth programs. Fifty graduates have received fellowships for study abroad.

As a result of the success of Bosconia/La Florida, the Colombian government has reduced the number of juvenile detention homes and opted for alternative education programs. The program has served as a model to many nongovernmental groups working to reduce the number of street-based youth in their communities. Bosconia/La Florida's approach has been successfully adapted to other Colombian cities as well as in Ecuador, Paraguay, the Dominican Republic, Mexico, Brazil, and Venezuela.

Undugu Society, Nairobi, Kenya

The rapid growth of Kenyan cities over the last 20 years has resulted in escalating numbers of street-based

continued on next page

children and youth. Currently, 60,000 street children are estimated to live in the capital city of Nairobi with national estimates exceeding 150,000.

In response to the growing number of street-based young people (or "parking boys" as they are known in Nairobi), the Undugu Society was formed in 1972. Today, it is the largest and most established nongovernmental organization (NGO) working with street and working children in the country.

Initially a series of youth centers, the Society was consolidated into a single organization in 1975. Today, it operates a variety of interrelated programs for young girls and boys, ages 6 to 18. The program aims to prevent young people from choosing a life on the streets through addressing the underlying causes of poverty.

Its Basic Education Program provides young people with a 4-year curriculum aimed at giving them the literacy and numeracy skills they will need to navigate through life. The Undugu Basic Education Curriculum has been certified by the Kenyan government. Recently the government announced plans to start a national programme on non-formal education. In addition, a Part-time Informal Skills Training Program offers skills training to graduates of the Undugu Basic Education Programme and other disadvantaged boys and girls with hands-on training in valuable trades such as carpentry, tailoring, auto mechanics, and metal working. This programme has a flexible schedule modeled on the apprenticeship system. The programme assists the youth in identifying a local artisan with whom they are attached for a period of time, usually one year, in order to gain further training and experience.

Other programs operated by the Society include Community Homes/Centers providing cultural, recreational, and sporting activities and a Community Health Care Program. These are transit homes where children who have been weaned from the streets temporarily live as they attend school or training.

The Society's strong community-based approach has empowered the residents of some of the poorest neighborhoods in Nairobi to improve the conditions of their families and community. Not only have numerous businesses been started with Undugu's financial and technical support, but the Society has achieved about 48% self-reliance through profitable income-generating activities and proceeds from the Undugu Craft units.

Source: International Youth Foundation, 2001. <www.ifynet.org>

---

the commission of violent acts. For example, homicidal youth from Great Britain were likely to have witnessed serious violence and to have experienced neglect and deprivation (Hardwick & Rowton-Lee, 1996). These youth also showed signs of poor impulse control and had learning difficulties. Living in an environment where one is exposed to violence and may even often be the target of violence can have profoundly negative effects (Garbarino, 1995, 1999). Such an environment is known as a "**socially toxic**" environment. James Garbarino's continuing research about these contexts is presented in Meet the Researcher Box 13.3.

Unfortunately, evidence shows that such a harmful context is becoming wide-spread in the United States and these negative effects are growing in prevalence. In a national sample of 10- to 16-year-old youth, one third reported having been the victims of an assault (Boney-McCoy & Finkelhor, 1995b). Compared to nonvictimized youth, these youth victims showed more problem behaviors and emotions, such as **posttraumatic stress disorders,** feelings of sadness, and school difficulties (Boney-McCoy & Finkelhor, 1995b).

Sexual assault is associated with particularly high levels of the problems linked to the experience of assault (Boney-McCoy & Finkelhor, 1995a,b). The rates of sexual violence are unfortunately quite high. In a study of over 1,000 girls from Alberta, Canada, in grades 7 through 12, 23% reported experiencing at least one event of assault, for example sexual touching, sexual threats or remarks, or an incidence of indecent exposure. And 4% of these

"Socially toxic" environment Environment in which one is exposed to multiple high-risk factors.

Posttraumatic stress disorder Set of emotional and behavioral problems that occur after experiencing a severe stress, for example an assault.

Adolescents may inflict injuries upon themselves, such as lacerations or burns.

girls reported they had experienced such events often (Bagley, Bolitho, & Bertrand, 1997). The girls who had experienced a high number of assaults were more likely than other girls to have emotional disorders. Experiencing violence may also lead to violence toward one's self in the form of attempting or enacting suicide or other forms of self-directed violence. Fifteen percent of the girls who had experienced frequent, unwanted sexual touching had attempted suicide in the previous 6 months. Such attempts occurred among only 2% of the girls who had no experience of sexual assault (Bagley et al., 1997).

Self-Injury and Suicide Many adolescents think about hurting themselves, and a large number act on such thoughts. During a typical year, 20% of high school students seriously consider attempting suicide, and 7.7% actually attempt suicide one or more times (Centers for Disease Control and Prevention, 1998). Between 1980 and 1992, the rate of suicide among young adolescents increased 120%. The increase was most dramatic among young African American males (300%) and young European American females (233%) (Carnegie Corporation of New York, 1995). Suicide rates among 10- to 14-year-old Native Americans were four times higher than those for 10- to 14-year-olds of all other races (Carnegie Corporation of New York, 1995).

Feelings of hopelessness and depression are associated with self-harm in adolescence (McLaughlin, Miller, & Warwick, 1996). Such behaviors may involve cutting, burning, or self-mutilation (Solomon & Farrand, 1996). Problems with social relationships are also associated with both self-harm and suicide (e.g., Adam, Sheldon-Keller, & West, 1996). In American youth, lack of cohesion in the family is associated with thinking about suicide (Zhang & Jin, 1996). Among Canadian youth, suicide is linked to family disruption, for example, parental divorce (Leenaars & Lester, 1995).

Whether inflicted on the self or others, violence is not an isolated problem. Rather, violence occurs often in relation to other adolescent problem behaviors such as substance use and abuse.

Substance Use and Abuse

Issue to Consider

- How might different psychological attributes and varied social contexts influence adolescent substance use and abuse?

Overall, cigarette smoking and illicit drug use has been decreasing among youth (Johnston, Bachman, & O'Malley, 1998). For instance, in the *Monitoring the Future Study* (Johnston et al., 1998), which has been tracking this behavior among high school students since the 1970s, smoking rates among eighth, tenth, and twelfth graders, encompassing youth between ages 13 and 18, decreased slightly between 1997 and 1998. The proportion of students who indicated they smoked at all during the 30 days prior to the survey had decreased by 1.9% over the previous 2 years among eighth graders (to 19.1%), by 2.8% among tenth graders (to 27.6%), and by 1.4% among twelfth graders (to 35.1%) (Johnston et al., 1998).

Similarly, the youth showed some decline in using illicit drugs during the 12-month period prior to the *Monitoring the Future Study* (Johnston et al., 1998). Marijuana continued to be the most widely used illicit drug, but its use was found to be decreasing. In 1998, 22% of all eighth graders said they had used marijuana and 49% of all twelfth graders reported they had done so (Johnston et al., 1998). The study found that the use of stimulants, hallucinogens (e.g., lysergic acid diethylamide, or LSD), inhalants, heroin, cocaine, tranquilizers, and alcohol either

MEET THE RESEARCHER BOX 13.3

JAMES GARBARINO
UNDERSTANDING VIOLENT YOUTH

For the past 25 years I have been searching for answers to three questions: "Why do human beings hurt each other?" "What effect does this hurt have on the development of children and adolescents?" and "How can we transform our lives to heal the hurt?" This work has taken me to war zones around the world to understand the impact of political violence. It has taken me all over the world, from Yugoslavia to Mozambique, from Cambodia to Nicaragua, from Israel and Palestine to Northern Ireland. For example, in the wake of the Gulf War. I was sent to Kuwait and Iraq on behalf of UNICEF to assess the impact of the violence on children there.

In my work here at home as a psychologist and a researcher, I go to neighborhoods, schools, courtrooms, and prisons all over North America, where I try to understand how violence at home compares with violence abroad and what lessons we can learn from the one to help us deal with the other. For the last 5 years I have been focusing my work on the problem of lethal youth violence in America: kids who kill. This means that I sit down hour after hour with violent boys and young men to hear their stories. I have learned a great deal from these hours spent listening. I have learned to see beyond the outside toughness so many violent youth project to glimpse their inner sadness and pain. And I have come to see the central importance of spiritual development in understanding and dealing with the issue of youth violence—preventing it and curing it. This is what *Lost Boys* is all about.

I think it has something to offer to every adult who cares about kids—as the parent, grandparent, aunt, uncle, friend, or neighbor of a particular boy or in some general way as a teacher, a counselor, a coach, a police officer, a lawyer, or a therapist. I hope readers will come away from *Lost Boys* with a renewed sense of hope and

James Garbarino is the Elizabeth Lee Vincent Professor of Human Development and co-director of the Family Life Development Center at Cornell University. He is the author of 17 books, most recently *Lost Boys: Why Our Sons Turn Violent and How We Can Save Them* (New York: Free Press, 1999; paperback: Anchor Books, 2000).

sympathy for the difficulties many boys face in growing up in our society and the devastating costs to all of us when boys grow up hurt and sad, costs that take the form of violence directed at self or others. Remember that about the same number of boys kill themselves as kill other people in our society.

In many ways *Lost Boys* is a work of love. It reflects my love for the boys in my life—my son, my stepson, and my nephews. Learning how to love them has taught me a great deal. And it reflects my love for the girls in my life—my daughter and my niece—because the quality of the lives "my girls" will live depends to a great extent on the relationships they will have with the boys of today who will become the men of tomorrow.

Lost Boys is also a work of love in that it reflects the love I have found in my own spiritual life. This recognition of the central importance of spirituality runs through the book as a complement to all the psychology, sociology, biology, and anthropology I use to make sense of violence in the lives of boys.

Currently, I am working on a research project we call "The Secret Lives of Teenagers." This project grew out of my understanding of the families of the two boys in Littleton, Colorado, who attacked their school on April 20, 1999. They killed 13 before killing themselves. In the wake of this terrible event many people assumed the two boys' parents must have been negligent. I have set out to explore how common and how "normal" it is for "good" parents to be unaware of the secret lives of their teenage offspring. This research sets the stage for further explorations of the difficulties parents face when raising temperamentally vulnerable children in today's socially toxic society. My colleague Claire Bedard and I are working on a new book based on these explorations entitled *Parents Under Siege*.

declined slightly or showed no increase (Johnston et al., 1998).

Unfortunately, the overall rate of substance use and abuse is high. For instance, 33% of all high

school seniors reported being drunk at least once in the 30 days prior to the *Monitoring the Future Study* (Johnston et al., 1998). Similarly, data compiled by the Centers for Disease Control and

Prevention (1998) also report high levels of substance use. In a nationally representative sample of students in grades 9 to 12, the study found that 70.2% of all students had tried cigarette smoking and 36.4% had smoked on 1 or more days in the 30-day period prior to the survey; 9.5% of students had used smokeless tobacco on 1 or more days prior to the survey; 79.1% of students had initiated alcohol use, and 50.8% had at least one drink on 1 or more days in the 30-day period prior to the survey (Centers for Disease Control and Prevention, 1998).

Consistent with the prevalence rate reported in the *Monitoring the Future Study,* the Centers for Disease Control and Prevention (1998) found that 47.1% of students nationwide had initiated marijuana use and that 26.2% had used it on 1 or more days in the 30-day period prior to the survey. The study also reported that 8.2% of students had used some form of cocaine and that 3.3% had used cocaine on 1 or more days in the 30-day period prior to the survey, that 17.0% of students had used other illegal drugs (e.g., LSD or heroin), and that 16.0% had used inhalants.

The breadth of the use and abuse of alcohol, tobacco, and illicit drugs is substantial among contemporary youth. As with the behaviors associated with delinquency and violence, there exists a diverse range of individual and contextual influences on substance use and abuse.

Developmental and Contextual Bases of Substance Use and Abuse

The use and abuse of substances among adolescents is associated with the individual's personality as well as with relationships with parents and peers. Adolescent substance abuse is associated with maternal substance use (Stephenson, Henry, & Robinson, 1996) and the perception that parents approve of using substances (McMaster & Wintre, 1996). In a study of young adolescents and their mothers and fathers, maternal smoking was highly associated with smoking among youth, especially daughters (Kandel & Wu, 1995).

Parenting style has been found to correlate with adolescent substance use. In a study of more than 1,000 12- to 16-year-old youth, males who perceived their families as "authoritarian" or "neglecting" (see Chapter 8) used more alcohol, cigarettes, stimulants, or sedatives (Foxcroft & Lowe, 1995). In contrast, females who saw their families as warm and directive used less alcohol, but were more likely to use sedatives or stimulants and to report they would use cigarettes to cope with a problem.

Parental supervision and support are also linked to adolescent substance use (Bogenschneider et al., 1998a). In a study of about 200 European American and about 150 European mother-adolescent dyads, in which all youth reported regular alcohol use, only one third of the mothers were aware of their adolescents' drinking (Bogenschneider et al., 1998b). In a study assessing the association between single-mother households and heavy drinking and illicit drug use, rates of substance use among 600 African American and European American youth were associated with the role of the nonresident father (Thomas, Farrell, & Barnes, 1996). When the father provided no support to the youth, European American male adolescents showed rates of substance problems higher than those in any other racial and gender group. However, when the father did support the adolescent, the rate of substance problems among the European American males was comparatively

There are several different illicit substances that are used or abused by some adolescents.

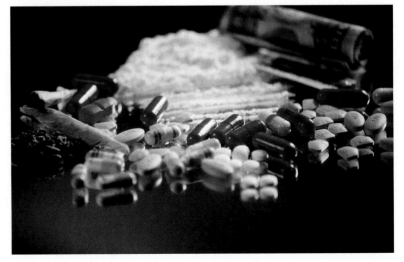

lower. In contrast, African American males had fewer substance problems when their nonresident fathers were not involved in the family (Thomas et al., 1996). However, when peer pressure for drug use was high, substance abuse increased in these families (Farrell & White, 1998).

Parental religiosity is also associated with adolescent substance use. In a longitudinal study of about 1,550 12- through 14-year-olds, higher maternal religiosity was linked to lower levels of adolescent alcohol use (Foshee & Hollinger, 1996).

The impact of peers on adolescent substance use and abuse may be significant. In a study of about 5,200 eighth graders and 4,700 eleventh graders from South Korea, perceived peer smoking was the major influence on smoking among both boys and girls (Juon, Shin, & Nam, 1995). In a study of approximately 500 German adolescents, intensity of peer relations was related to substance use (Maggs & Hurrelmann, 1998). Among African American tenth graders from an urban school, peer pressure was associated with drug use, especially among girls (Farrell & White, 1998). In a study of 2,200 randomly selected eighth-, tenth-, and twelfth-grade students from Ohio, the strongest correlate of drug use was affiliation with drug-using friends (Jenkins, 1996). Among about 1,000 sixth-through tenth-grade American adolescents studied longitudinally, use of cigarettes by one's friendship group was associated with transition into smoking, and use of alcohol by close friends was associated with the start of drinking (Urberg, Degirmencioglu, & Pilgrim, 1998). Changes in adolescent drug use seem to occur in relation to increases in peer drug use as well (Curran, Stice, & Chassin, 1997).

In addition, the quality of peer relations may differ between substance-abusing and nonsubstance-abusing youth. For instance, among Icelandic youth, frequent drug and alcohol use was linked to lower social ability (Sigurdsson & Gudjonsson, 1996).

Substance abuse is also associated with individual characteristics related to adjustment. In a study of about 1,000 sixth- and seventh-grade European American and Latino youth, poor adjustment to the school context was associated with substance use (Flannery, Vazsonyi, & Rowe, 1996). Alcohol use by adolescents is associated with self-destructive thoughts and behaviors—thinking about suicide, attempting suicide, and engaging more frequently in risky behaviors such as taking someone else's medication (Windle, Miller-Tutzauer, & Domenico, 1992). Low self-esteem is linked to substance use among high school students (Moore, Laflin, & Weis, 1996) and, perhaps in particular, to smoking among adolescent females (Abernathy, Massad, & Romano-Dwyer, 1995). Some of the recent work of Michael Windle on the influences on developing substance use among adolescents is presented in Meet the Researcher Box 13.4.

In a study of more than 2,000 Native American high school students, the quantity and frequency of alcohol use was associated with psychological adjustment, for example, depression and antisocial behavior. (Mitchell et al., 1996). Among adolescents hospitalized for psychiatric problems, those youth who abused drugs had personality characteristics different from other hospitalized youth (Hart, 1995). They had negative attitudes toward their family and toward authority figures in general, and they showed personalities marked by aggression, low conscientiousness, lack of academic confidence, and impulsiveness. In a longitudinal study of about 750 boys between the ages of 6 and 13, substance abuse was associated with individual characteristics linked to aggression, hyperactivity, and oppositional behavior (Dobkin et al., 1995).

Substance-abusing youth are also more likely than nonsubstance-abusing youth to have problems with gambling (Vitaro, Ladouceur, & Bujold, 1996). It may be that the arousal associated with the risks of gambling is in some way associated with drinking. In addition, among more than 2,300 youth from grades 3, 6, 9, and 12, higher levels of drinking were associated with the tendency to see alcohol as positive and arousing (Dunn & Goldman, 1998).

There are also individual-psychological characteristics and contextual resources related to a lessened probability of substance use and abuse. In general, such protective factors involve personal and social controls against the occurrence of problem behaviors. Personal controls include religious beliefs and good self-concepts. Social controls include social support and authoritative parenting (Jessor et al., 1995). As suggested earlier by the findings pertinent to the role of family (maternal) religiosity in protecting youth from alcohol use, religious commitments and beliefs protect African American adolescents against the use of

MEET THE RESEARCHER BOX 13.4

MICHAEL WINDLE

INVESTIGATING INFLUENCES ON POSITIVE AND DISRUPTED DEVELOPMENT AMONG ADOLESCENTS USING ALCOHOL AND OTHER SUBSTANCES

The use of alcohol and other substances such as marijuana is common among many young people. This is the case even though it is widely recognized that the use of these substances is highly associated with the three major causes of mortality in adolescence: accidental deaths (e.g., fatal automobile or boating accidents), homicides, and suicides. In addition, the use of alcohol and other substances is commonly associated with many other risky behaviors such as sexual activity that may pose risks for teen pregnancy, sexually transmitted diseases, and human immunodeficiency virus (HIV). Although most adolescents will use alcohol and other substances during adolescence, not all will engage in high levels of use, persist in their use across time, or develop serious problems related to their use. Two important health issues for adolescents are which influences contribute to experimental versus heavy use, and how does the timing of events (e.g., age of initiation of alcohol use) impact biological, cognitive, and social development?

In a study supported by the National Institute of Alcohol Abuse and Alcoholism, I am using a longitudinal research design that involves the repeated measurement of over 1,200 adolescents who reside in Buffalo, New York, to study changes in their levels of alcohol and substance use, and the predictors of those changes. The goal of my research is to identify factors that contribute to our understanding of why some adolescents experiment with alcohol and other substances but do not escalate or persist in their use, and why some adolescents maintain or increase high levels of use across time. We need to understand and draw on the experiences of adolescents in both the experimenter and heavier user adolescent groups to assist in identifying individual, family, and community resources that may be used to enhance the prospects for positive development.

Our findings have indicated that some identifiable characteristics distinguish experimental users from persistent heavier users. Specifically, persistent heavier users were more likely to come from homes in which their father was an alcoholic. Children raised in homes in which fathers (and/or mothers) are alcoholics have both an increased genetic risk for subsequent alcohol problems and a more chaotic home environment that may undermine healthy family and peer socialization processes. We have also found that adolescents who are persistent heavy substance users have also initiated alcohol use earlier, perform more poorly in school, engage in higher levels of violence and general delinquency, have poorer family relations, and are more likely to affiliate with alcohol- and drug-using peers. In addition, adolescents who experiment with alcohol and other substances, but then cycle out of this experimentation phase, are more committed to attaining higher education, place a higher value on religion and attend church more frequently, and tend to maintain stronger emotional bonds with their family.

In our ongoing data collection with this sample, we are now studying the impact of adolescent alcohol and substance use practices on functioning in young adulthood. We are investigating the quality of their interpersonal relationships, their satisfaction with their job, their alcohol and substance use practices, and their mental health. A question of interest is whether those adolescents who were heavy substance users in adolescence will be experiencing a range of difficulties in adjusting to the demands of young adulthood (e.g., occupational and parenting roles), or will many of them have adjusted to these demands. If they have adjusted, what individual, family, peer, and community influences contributed to such positive adaptation. The identification of influences that impact positive changes across time may serve as a platform for needed interventions that are designed to optimize development.

Michael Windle is a professor of psychology and pediatrics in the Department of Psychology at the University of Alabama at Birmingham. He is the director of both the Center for Research on Child and Adolescent Development and the Comprehensive Youth Violence Center. Windle received a prestigious MERIT Award from the National Institutes on Health for the research he has conducted on adolescent alcohol use.

alcohol (Barnes, Farrell, & Banerjee, 1994). Among Latino adolescents, attitudes about both alcohol use and positive self-concepts are associated with a decreased likelihood of alcohol use (Alva & Jones, 1994).

Conclusions About Externalizing Behavior Problems in Adolescence

The externalizing problems common in adolescence may influence the context, for example in regard to violence toward peers. These problems also may be influenced by the context, for example in regard to parental effects on substance use (Bogenschneider et al., 1998a). In addition, any one externalizing problem can and often does occur together with other such problems—for instance, violence and substance use occur together, that is, they are *comorbid*. Externalizing problems are also comorbid with internalizing problems that express themselves primarily in regard to the adolescent's psychological or behavioral functioning.

Internalizing Problems in Adolescence

Issue to Consider
• What influences the expression of internalizing behaviors in adolescence?

Just as adolescents exhibit several instances of externalizing problems, they also exhibit numerous types of internalizing problems. These problems can be somewhat benign, for example negative self-esteem, which can often be bolstered with assistance from parents, teachers, or friends or may improve over the course of typical developmental changes. The problems can also be more serious, involving the individual's mental health.

Psychosis Severe mental disorder, characterized by problematic behaviors and thoughts that reflect a disengagement from reality.

Psychopathology Serious problems of mental health that require professional treatment, for example, sustained pervasive feelings of depression, anxiety, or the existence of a psychotic

All mental health problems require professional intervention. These include sustained and pervasive feelings of depression or anxiety or the occurrence of a **psychotic** disorder—all examples of common adolescent **psychopathology**.

Instances of Internalizing Problems

Psychopathology can occur among all youth. In a nationwide sample of 1,400 5- to 17-year-old American youth, psychopathology was found to be distributed proportionally across race and class (McDermott & Spencer, 1997). Moreover, in a study of 220 sixth and twelfth graders, 57% reported at least some experience of depression and one third indicated they had thought of suicide (Culp, Clyman, & Culp, 1995); 6% of the participants reported they had attempted suicide (Culp et al., 1995).

In a study of about 900 Irish high school youth, approximately 12% had serious levels of depression, and females were more likely than males (16% to 7%, respectively) to have serious levels of depression (Donnelly, 1995). Several other studies find gender differences in the incidence and correlates of internalizing problems among youth.

Gender Differences

Issue to Consider
• How are the internalizing problems differently expressed in male and female adolescents?

Female adolescents show more internalizing problems and fewer externalizing problems than male adolescents (Leadbeater, Blatt, & Quinlan, 1995). Adolescent girls are often found to report more psychological and physical symptoms than boys (Eiser, Havermans, & Eiser, 1995). In particular, girls have more symptoms of depression than adolescent boys do (e.g., Compas et al., 1997; Hart & Thompson, 1996). Girls are more vulnerable to becoming depressed about interpersonal issues than boys, and they show greater vulnerability to stress (Garton & Pratt, 1995) and higher reactivity to stressful events involving other people (Leadbeater et al., 1995).

Depression is a serious internalizing problem that may affect adolescents.

Contextual Influences

As with externalizing behaviors, internalizing problems are associated with variation in both contextual and individual characteristics. In regard to the family, maternal acceptance decreases the likelihood of depression among young adolescents (Garber, Robinson, & Valentiner, 1997). However, maternal psychological control is associated with increases in depression. Such control includes attempting to govern the behavior of the child through techniques such as inducing guilt (Garber et al., 1997). In a study of about 450 adolescents, depression was associated with less intimate relations with parents and with less social support (Lasko et al., 1996).

In a longitudinal study of Albanian youth beginning when they were 12 years old, depression and antisocial behavior among girls was associated with parental economic problems and value differences, low marital happiness, low nurturance by parents, and parental hostility toward and value differences with the daughter (Kloep, 1995). Adolescents hospitalized for psychopathological problems report less marital satisfaction between parents than non-hospitalized youth (King et al., 1995). Marital con-flict over child rearing and a weak father-adolescent relationship were associated with severe behavior problems in school and in spare time (King et al., 1995).

The nature of the involvement with or attachment to the parent can affect the presence of internalizing problems in adolescents. In a longitudinal study of youth between the ages of 14 and 25 years, those who had been hospitalized for severe psychopathology had insecure attachments with their parents (Allen, Hauser, & Borman-Spurrell, 1996). Similarly, adolescents hospitalized for psychiatric reasons who have problems of attachment are also likely to suffer from conduct or substance abuse disorders, antisocial problems, and paranoid personality characteristics (Rosenstein & Horowitz, 1996). For sixth- through eighth-grade adolescents, problems of attachment to the father were highly associated with the presence of antisocial behavior among both boys and girls (Marcus & Betzer, 1996).

Individual-Psychological Influences

Contextual influences on internalizing problems exist along with influences associated with psychological and behavioral characteristics of the adolescent. Boys who are depressed also possess feelings of antagonism toward other people, and girls who are depressed also show an overly introspective concern with the self and an overly high concern with the rules of socialization (Gjerde, 1995). In a longitudinal study of 330 young adolescents, feelings of depression are associated with feelings of anxiety (Cole et al., 1998). The more anxious the youth became over time, the higher the resulting level of depression (Cole et al., 1998). Moreover, covariation between anxiety and depression is associated with delinquent behaviors (Hinden, et al., 1997).

Other psychological characteristics are involved in the occurrence of internalizing problems. In a study comparing middle school students from the United States and Japan (King, Akiyama, & Elling, 1996), feelings of depression among American youth were associated with problematic self-perceptions regarding physical attractiveness and social acceptance and with problematic behavioral conduct. Among the Japanese adolescents, feelings of depression were related to problematic self-perceptions involving interpersonal connectedness, peer social acceptance, and physical attractiveness and to problems of behavioral conduct (King et al., 1996).

A longitudinal study of 800 youth between the ages of 3 and 18 found that youth who had problems controlling their behavior were also highly impulsive, danger seeking, and aggressive, and they felt alienated from others (Caspi & Silva, 1995). However, youth who were inhibited had low levels of impulsivity, danger seeking, aggression, and social ability (Caspi & Silva, 1995). Perhaps not surprisingly, youth who lacked control had more externalizing problems than other adolescents (Caspi et al., 1995).

Conclusions About Internalizing Behavior Problems in Adolescence

As with adolescent externalizing problems, several contextual and individual variables create diversity in the development of internalizing problems in adolescence. Although girls show a higher incidence of internalizing problems than boys, the development of psychopathology in adolescence for both males and females is significantly influenced by social relationships, particularly with parents. There are also high degrees of comorbidity between internalizing and externalizing problems, and the individual and contextual variables associated with one domain of problems are linked to the other domain as well.

Thus the domains of externalizing and internalizing problems are related to the diversity of the individual and contextual variables comprising the ecology of human development. To address these problems, it is important to capitalize on this person-context developmental system.

Positive youth development may result from youth activities that involve the support from and trust of peers: A young girl falls into the arms of fellow campers and counselors from a four foot high perch, an exercise in building trust and group conclusion.

From Problem Behaviors to Prevention and the Promotion of Positive Development in Adolescence

Issues to Consider
- What explains the failure of so many policies and programs designed to support adolescents with problems?
- What are leading factors that contribute to the success of some intervention programs designed to support adolescents?

To rephrase an old metaphor, the glass of American adolescence is both half full and half empty. About 50% of America's youth are at moderate or greater levels of risk for engaging in unhealthy, unproductive, and even life-threatening behaviors. These behaviors arise because of the unfortunate confluence of sets of individual and contextual factors. Given the diversity of behaviors that a youth can exhibit over the course of adolescence, parents can hope for the best but should be ready to deal with problematic and/or risky behavior. Implications for Parenting Box 13.1 on page 322 may provide some assistance.

Many people have argued that the solution to the problems of adolescence, and perhaps especially those that involve delinquency, is to build more and/or different sorts of institutions (more psychiatric hospitals or special types of youth prisons, e.g., "boot camps"; Taylor, 1996). These policy prescriptions are often made with little understanding of, and almost no research evidence about, the influence of youth institutionalization or incarceration on youth development (Schwartz, 1999; Taylor, 1996). These policy ideas are often predicated on the belief that delinquent youth, and troubled adolescents more generally, cannot be helped, nor can their problems be diminished or prevented. With such a perspective, there is little, if any, consideration that positive development could be promoted among these adolescents (Schwartz, 1999).

Rather than pursue policies and programs untested by systematic research, a more useful approach to the problems of youth is one that reflects the developmental contextual/developmental systems perspective. This approach deals with all facets of the developing person and his or her context and is committed to integrating these facets in treatment. In this manner, all the people with a stake in the youth's positive development, including the youth themselves, can pool their resources to protect the adolescents and to promote positive outcomes in their lives.

Current thinking about public policy and youth-serving programs supports pursuing paths of application that emphasize the potential of young people for positive development and healthy lives. The presentation in Chapter 14 is framed by stressing the importance for reducing or eliminating youth problems through a systematic integration of individual and contextual characteristics of adolescents. Chapter 14 also addresses how this system may be used to devise intervention programs and public policies aimed at both preventing the development of problems in adolescence and in promoting healthy and positive lives among them.

implications for parenting box 13.1

Why Smart Kids Do Risky Things

Despite the fact that they are more sophisticated thinkers than they were a few years earlier, one of the paradoxes of child development is that teenagers do thoughtless and dangerous things. They are not quite thinking with the sophistication and insight of an adult. Understanding differences in levels of thinking, and the other developmental issues facing teenagers, can be helpful in keeping them out of trouble.

Adolescents see themselves as the center of the universe. They're not as simplistic in their egocentric view as toddlers, although the similarities can at times be striking. At some level many adolescents believe that other people are as interested in them as they are in themselves. They believe they are special and the ordinary rules and consequences that adults (rightfully) worry about need not apply to them.

This egocentric, invulnerable attitude can lead them into risky situations. A true story: A police officer pulls over a car late at night for speeding. The driver is a 17-year-old boy who is wearing sunglasses. Several other teens are in the car with him, giggling. From the smell of the driver's breath and the stagger in his gait, it is clear he has been drinking heavily. The officer tells him he is lucky—people get killed when they drink and drive. The teenager replies, "Hey, you can't kill The Kid!"

Because adolescents see themselves as invulnerable, they often cannot conceive of the world existing without them living. Although they will tell you in one breath that drinking and driving is dangerous, they still may brag about doing it. Probate judges say that over 90% of the traffic violations involving teenagers are alcohol related.

Another factor that can lead to risky behavior is your teenager's need to forge an independent self. A major task of adolescence is coming up with a new and separate identity. Your teenager is going through the physical changes of puberty, changes in thinking abilities, social changes in school, and often the new experience of part-time employment. When everything about an adolescent is changing inside and outside, he or she wonders, who am I?

To deal with all the changes in their lives, adolescents turn to their peer group. In trying their best to differentiate from their parents, they put significant efforts into assimilating into a peer group. To get peer approval,

young people will often do things that intellectually they know are risky (e.g., playing "chicken" with speeding cars, chugging beers until they are sick).

It is unrealistic for any of us to say, "It won't happen to my child!" It's not that you should not trust your teenager, but you need to understand that there is often an intense pressure to get acceptance from peers.

This does not mean parents should give up trying and hope simply for the best. One thing you can do is pay more attention to how your teenagers spend their time—not in a punitive or suspicious way, just monitoring what they're up to. Even as teenagers push for more independence, they want and need clear and consistent supervision.

Rules work best when the adolescents' perspective is brought in and when they try to develop their own point of view of why they should behave in a particular way. Although only one of you is the parent, when you supply reasons for rules beyond "Because I say so!" it shows respect for your teenagers' new thinking skills. Encourage them to participate in generating household rules. If teenagers take part in discussing and setting rules, those rules will more likely become part of their own set of standards and, therefore, be adhered to. Supportive and open communication increases likelihood that your child will end up having values consistent with your own and will choose friends with similar values.

Remember, your teenager will spend more time with peers than with you. Try to get a sense of what your child's friends are like. Chat with them and build trust over time. Strive for a home atmosphere where your child's friends feel welcome. (An extra few dollars per week for pretzels and frozen pizza may be a good investment.) Take care not to be too intrusive and not to embarrass your teenagers, or they will not bring their friends home to meet you.

Such home-based socializing also provides opportunities to know the friends' parents, as you coordinate schedules. Try to find out their standards for acceptable teenage behavior and agree to help each other monitor activities. Many risky activities, such as sexual intercourse, happen most often not in motels or cars, but in the homes of adolescents' friends or relatives. If you and other parents can present a united front to the peer group, it helps your children understand that widely agreed-on standards exist, and it is not just you who are "impossible." Peers' parents can also reinforce common values by befriending your child. As teenagers strive to be different from their own parents, they may find it easier to talk over some concerns with other adults.

If you know that some of your child's peers engage in potentially high-risk behaviors, share your concerns with him or her. Try to provide alternative less risky experiences. Perhaps your teenager would enjoy ice skating, horseback riding, computer workshops, or a youth club. Additional activities are likely to expose teenagers to more potential friends. Look into ways your adolescents can volunteer to work with younger kids. For example, they can teach younger kids about the consequences of high-risk behaviors. This benefits both sides: Teenagers tend to have great credibility with younger children, and the exposure to the naïveté and misinformation others have about risky behaviors reduces teenagers' own egocentric feelings of invulnerability.

Finally, even though your child pretends to "know it all," and probably does know a great deal about life's dangers, keep talking. Your child is more likely to listen to you if you do not preach and if you focus on the short-term risks (e.g., smoking gives you bad breath and hurts your athletic performance).

Ideas About Talking to Your Teenager About Risk

Most parents feel uncomfortable talking about issues such as drinking and driving or sexual behavior. Unfortunately, these topics can literally be matters of life and death. Here are several things parents might need to do to be helpful to their adolescents:

- Try to be as direct and open with your adolescent as possible, even about your own discomfort.
- As you listen to your teenager's perceptions and idea, resist the urge to say, "I went through exactly the same thing!" That works against your child's need to establish a separate identity from you. Instead, you might say you've heard from other teens' parents that their children feel the same.

- Go from general to specific. You might start a conversation by saying, "I want to talk about drinking and driving. I've been hearing from other parents (or at the PTA meeting) that there's a lot of drinking and driving among kids at your school. What kinds of things would you say go on at your school?" By keeping the subject distant from your teenager and his friends, at least at first, you are not seen as accusing him or her. Next, you might ask, "How do your friends deal with it?" Or, "You must confront this all the time. How do you handle it?"
- Talk about alternatives. Research has shown time and again that knowledge is not enough to change behavior. Adolescents need skills and resources to get out of risky situations without losing face. For example, you might say, "The person who drives you to a party may not be the person you want to go back with. I'll give you a quarter to call me, and $20 for a cab. Keep it in a separate part of your wallet, and use it only for that. If I'm out, and you're out, I'll give you the number where I am." This lets your child know that even if you are going out, you are still the parent, and you are there if he or she needs you.
- Try rehearsing possible scenarios and realistic responses, and generate ideas together. Ask your child, "What else can I do to help you deal with this kind of situation?"
- Share your values. Make sure your child is clear on what your values are and why you believe those values are appropriate and useful. For example, "Even if nothing happens, I'd be very upset if you rode in a car with a driver who'd been drinking. That's like giving your okay to behavior that could get you or someone else seriously hurt."

The issue of sex can be particularly uncomfortable and confusing. For example, although you may feel strongly that your 15-year-old should abstain from sex, do you mean from intercourse or any sort of sensual touching? Try to offer your teenager realistic alternatives to engaging in unsafe or too-early sex, ones that are compatible with your values.

Source: Adapted from Lerner & Olson, 1996.

Summary

- Despite improvements in some indicators, the overall rate of quality of life for adolescents in the United States remains poor in comparison to other industrialized countries.

- Four major categories of risk behaviors in adolescence are drug and alcohol use and abuse; unsafe sex and teenage pregnancy and parenting; school underachievement, failure and dropout; and delinquency, crime, and violence.

- Engagement in risk behaviors diminishes life chances, and evidence indicates that risk behaviors are highly interrelated; that is, adolescents often participate in more than one risk behavior.

- There are two general dimensions of problem behaviors among youth. Internalizing problems are directed inward to the individual and affect cognitive, mental, and emotional functioning. Externalizing problems are directed outward toward other people or the social context. Some problem behaviors involve both internalizing and externalizing features.

- Poverty is a pervasive problem in the United States and it impacts all behavioral risks engaged in by youth.

- Poverty disproportionately affects minority youth, and race is the most striking distinction between chronic poverty versus transitory poverty.

- Poverty is associated with "rotten outcomes," or problems with youth development, in all domains of individual and social behavior and development.

- Effective interventions for poverty and the associated "rotten outcomes" must take into account the diverse contextual conditions of youth, for example, family, peers, neighborhood, and culture.

- Problem behaviors of adolescence occur in clusters; for example, runaways are at a high risk for substance abuse.

- Adolescent girls show more internalizing problems and fewer externalizing problems compared to adolescent boys.

- There is a high degree of comorbidity between internalizing and externalizing problems.

- Many policies and programs fail to support adolescents. In order to deal successfully with the multiple problems of adolescence, policies and programs should focus on the relations between the individual's development and the specifics of his or her social context.

Discussion Topics

1. Are all teenagers equally at risk for engaging in a single risk behavior? Why or why not? Are all teenagers equally at risk for engaging in multiple risk behaviors? Why or why not?

2. Name some problem behaviors common in adolescence and decide whether they are internalizing, externalizing, or both. How do you know?

3. Why does culture influence attitudes about problem behaviors?

4. Recognizing the pervasiveness and implications of poverty in the United States, what are the first issues to consider when designing a program to promote positive youth development?

5. How do the individual and social contexts influence adolescent development? What are potential risk factors that may lead to delinquency in teen youth?

How might a limited view of contextual influences contribute to social prejudices?

6. Why is there such a high level of violence in American high schools? How might you lead a youth group discussion about how to prevent violence in high schools?

7. Understanding the influence of social context, how might the media meaningfully support and encourage teens to avoid peer pressure to use and/or abuse substances?

8. Why do adolescent girls tend to have more internalizing problems than adolescent boys?

9. What are some characteristics of a program that would successfully promote positive adolescent development?

Key Terms

anxiety (p. 299)

comorbidity (p. 298)

depression (p. 299)

externalizing problems (p. 299)

internalizing problems (p. 299)

juvenile delinquency (p. 304)

posttraumatic stress disorder (p. 312)

psychopathology (p. 318)

psychosis (p. 318)

"rotten outcomes" (p. 302)

"socially toxic" environment (p. 312)

status offense (p. 304)

youth gangs (p. 303)

14

POTENTIALS OF ADOLESCENTS: COMMUNITY PROGRAMS AND PUBLIC POLICY

CHAPTER OUTLINE

Elizabeth was nervous. She hoped Mrs. McKinney couldn't tell.

"So, Elizabeth, is this your first college interview?"

Elizabeth felt that Mrs. McKinney knew the answer just by the way she had asked the question. "Yes it is, Mrs. McKinney."

"Well, don't be nervous . . . "

"Oh sure," Elizabeth thought. "Your future doesn't hang on this conversation."

"I only want to chat with you about some of the things you listed on your application. Your academic record is certainly strong. I can tell you that it is competitive in our early decision pool."

"That's good to hear." Elizabeth tried to stifle a deep sigh of relief.

"So, then," Mrs. McKinney went on, "what I'd like to chat about is you. What makes Elizabeth special, what makes her different from the other students with terrific grades and SAT scores?"

"Oh no," Elizabeth thought, "she is telling me that my grades are competitive but I may not be unless I can make her believe I'm different." Elizabeth felt defeated. She really didn't think she was different than anyone else. Most of her friends had grades as good or better than hers, and her SAT scores, although good, were not that great, and she had to take the test three times to get them up to where they were. She decided the only thing she could do was to be honest with Mrs. McKinney and own up to her ordinariness.

"I don't know, Mrs. McKinney," Elizabeth began. "I am afraid I am not really very different from anyone else. I have good friends, I want to be accepted by the people I meet, and . . . "

"Well, yes, of course, I understand that, Elizabeth. We're all like other people in some ways. But we're also different in some ways. Let me see . . . " Mrs. McKinney scanned Elizabeth's application. "You've been involved in a lot of school activities. Are any of them particularly important to you?"

"Sure." Elizabeth answered without any hesitation. "I am part of the Student Awareness Initiative, the SAI. I guess that means the most to me."

"Good. Tell me about it, then," Mrs. McKinney asked. "What is the program and why do you like it so much?"

"Well, like I said," Elizabeth began, "I am just like the other kids in my school. I want to be popular. I want to go to parties and have dates and things like that. But in my high school the major way that kids seem to get this acceptance is to go to parties every weekend, drink, and then they see what happens. What happens is they get drunk, sometimes they get involved in drugs, and—at least sometimes—they have sex that they did not really want. I saw this wrecking the minds and bodies of a lot of my friends, and I knew I just couldn't get involved in all of that. I knew it would have been easy for me to do it, but I also knew that I wouldn't be happy about it. I just don't believe that drinking at my age or taking drugs is right or responsible. And, to be honest, I was scared of the consequences of doing these things. So I knew I couldn't do them, but I didn't know what I could do."

"Where does the Student Awareness Initiative come in?" Mrs. McKinney asked.

"Well, sometime during my junior year I heard about the SAI program, and it made me decide that being popular was not as important as acting on what I thought was right. SAI is a really selective service program in my school. It involves being trained to serve as an advocate and a role model for drug and alcohol abstinence among middle school and high school students. Sixty students applied to participate in SAI. I was one of fourteen who was chosen. I wanted to be a part of this group because I felt this was a way I could help myself and others eliminate the use and abuse of drugs and alcohol in my school."

Mrs. McKinney smiled. "What does being in the program mean for you?"

"Well, I guess I knew that joining this group could damage my social acceptance. Many kids in my school regard SAI kids as members of a spy team who are out to get anyone that drinks. But that's not true, of course. We're trying to be positive role models, not spies. Anyway, being the target of such remarks is not very pleasant, and it makes it difficult to believe you are popular. But I guess it doesn't matter. I learned I have the ability to stand up to social pressure and that my beliefs are what matter most to me."

"Did you learn anything else?" Mrs. McKinney asked.

"I realize now how good it can feel to help other kids make healthy choices in life."

Mrs. McKinney's smile now beamed across her face. "Thank you, Elizabeth. This was a very helpful conversation. I think you'll be a great addition to our college."

LEARNING OBJECTIVES

1. To define youth programs and what they attempt to do.
2. To learn Stephen Hamilton's definition of positive youth development.
3. To learn about the three key issues of youth programs.
4. To gain knowledge of the need for evaluations, the different types of evaluations, and their goals.
5. To learn what needs to be done to determine the appropriate scale for a program.
6. To understand why many youth programs are not sustainable.
7. To understand the difference between efficacy research and outreach research.
8. To understand how universities and communities can collaborate effectively in support of positive youth development.
9. To understand what "prevention does not equal provision" means for the future of youth programs.
10. To learn what must be done to develop effective youth programs and what influences must be engaged.
11. To gain knowledge of the features of a positive youth development program that are needed for best practice.
12. To define public policies and to understand the need for a national youth policy.
13. To understand how assets can be promoted through existing community youth-serving organizations.
14. To understand the importance of mentoring programs and how they are most effective.

In Chapter 13 we discussed the problems faced by contemporary adolescents. The breadth and severity of these externalizing and internalizing problems and the added challenges of poverty make it clear that our communities need to have greater access to existing, effective family- and youth-serving programs (e.g., Dryfoos, 1998; Hamburg, 1992; Lerner, 1995; Schorr, 1997). New programs must also be devised, evaluated, and, if effective, sustained (Lerner, 1995, Lerner & Galambos, 1998).

In the United States more than 17,500 organizations report that they are delivering youth-serving programs (Roth et al., 1997). These organizations are involved in sets of actions aimed at addressing the significant challenges affecting contemporary youth. However, what precisely is being provided to youth in such programs? Are such programs actually helping youth lead better lives? To address these questions we need to both define youth programs and understand how their effectiveness may be ascertained.

Defining and Evaluating Youth Programs

Issues to Consider

• What are youth programs? What do they attempt to do?

• What is Stephen Hamilton's three-part definition of positive youth development?

• What is an intervention program?

Programs are planned and systematic attempts to reduce the presence of an emotional, behavioral, or social problem, prevent such problems from occurring, or promote positive, healthy behaviors among people. As we discussed in Chapter 5, key attributes of positive youth development are competence, confidence, character, connection, and caring/compassion (Lerner, Fisher, & Weinberg, 2000b; Lerner, Sparks, & McCubbin, 1999; Little, 1993).

Programs that seek to develop these attributes of positive development in young people constitute attempts to optimize the lives of individuals by building up their strengths. Such programs reflect an abiding concern for youth well-being, employ principles of effective youth programs, and are committed to going beyond traditional preventative or remedial interventions, instead stressing skill and competency development (Roth et al., 1997). Jodie L. Roth and her colleagues have studied how youth programs may contribute to positive development (see Meet the Researcher Box 14.1).

Stephen F. Hamilton (1999) has provided a comprehensive definition of positive youth development programs that reflects three interrelated facets of such programs: (1) the conception of the process of youth development used by proponents of such

MEET THE RESEARCHER BOX 14.1

JODIE L. ROTH

HELPING CREATE POSITIVE SPACES FOR POSITIVE DEVELOPMENT

D rive through different communities at 3:00 P.M., when school is over for the day, and you are likely to see dissimilar scenes. In one, athletic fields are teeming with youth practicing soccer, football, field hockey, or for the marching band. Inside a school building or community center, other youth are gathered for meetings of a variety of after-school activities—from drama to model airplane building. In another, the streets are empty. Youth are at home, by themselves, watching television, playing video games, or online. In still another, adolescents are hanging out on the streets or in the malls with their friends, looking for something to do.

What adolescents do after school offers another avenue for understanding adolescent development. That is, it represents one more environment affecting their lives. Unlike school or family, this environment has not been the focus of much research. In my research, my colleague Jeanne Brooks-Gunn and I look at how the choices adolescents have, and the choices they make, for what to do during this time contributes to their development. In doing so, we hope to identify common positive elements from seemingly diverse after-school experiences. These elements can then serve as the basis for developing new programs or strengthening existing ones, particularly in communities with few after-school opportunities for youth.

We are reviewing evaluations of community-based and school-based after-school programs to identify common program elements that foster positive development in youth. Unfortunately, most of the thousands of programs that aim to promote positive outcomes for their

Jodie L. Roth is a research scientist at the Center for Children and Families, a research center at Teachers College, Columbia University. She studies how different settings, such as after-school programs, contribute to how adolescents think and act.

adolescent participants do not get evaluated using rigorous methods.

From our review of those that have been evaluated thus far, we have identified three common elements. First, positive youth development programs promote positive behaviors and competencies. They strive to prepare youth for their futures by building their competence in academic, social, and vocational areas and fostering positive traits such as caring, compassion, confidence, and character. Second, these programs have a positive atmosphere. Youth are viewed as resources to be developed rather than as problems to be managed. Often this is done through the relationship between the youth and staff. The staff creates an atmosphere in which youth feel safe, supported, and challenged. Third, positive youth development programs offer challenging, authentic activities, with an emphasis on active participation. Numerous types of activities—athletic, academic, or artistic—can be offered in such a way.

Programs that share these elements go a long way in helping promote positive development for youth. Of course, one program is not going to be right for all youth in a community. We still need to better understand how youth use the array of opportunities in their community to best meet their needs for positive spaces. Furthermore, after-school activities are just one of the many environments influencing adolescents' development. A next step in our research is to better understand how the after-school program environment interacts and influences the other spheres of adolescents' worlds. In doing so, we hope we can help families and communities provide more positive spaces for their youth.

programs; (2) the approach to programming associated with this conception, and (3) the characteristics of programs or organizations that use such an approach. Hamilton's (1999) three-part definition of positive youth development programs is presented in Table 14.1.

In programs of problem reduction, problem prevention, and positive development promotion, the work undertaken constitutes attempts to *intervene* into the course of a person's develop-

ment by changing the person's life for the better. **Intervention programs** may be conducted by professionals trained to use particular methods (e.g., psychotherapy, group interactions) or they may be presented to youth through community-based clubs or organizations (e.g., YMCA, 4-H, Boys and Girls Clubs, or scouting).

Intervention program
Program conducted by professionals or through community-based organizations that attempts to change a person's life for the better.

| Table 14-1 | **Positive Youth Development: Hamilton's Three-Part Definition** |

Hamilton (1999) envisions positive youth development as a process, as a philosophy of or an approach to youth programming, and as a specific type of organization or program.

1. **A natural process: The growing capacity of a young person to understand and act on the environment.**

   Youth development (synonymous in this sense with child and adolescent development) is the natural unfolding of the potential inherent in the human organism in relation to the challenges and supports of the physical and social environment. People can actively shape their own development through their choices and interpretations. Development lasts as long as life, but youth development enables individuals to lead a healthy, satisfying, and productive life, as youth and later as adults, because they gain the competence to earn a living, to engage in civic activities, to nurture others, and to participate in social relations and cultural activities. The five C's are a useful summary of the goals of youth development: caring/compassion, competence, character, connection, and confidence. The process of development may be divided into age-related stages (infancy, childhood, adolescence, and smaller divisions of these stages) and into domains (notably physical, cognitive, social, emotional, and moral).

2. **A philosophy of or an approach to programming: Active support for the growing capacity of young people by individuals, organizations, and institutions, especially at the community level.**

   The youth development approach is rooted in a commitment to enabling all young people to achieve their potential. It is characterized by a positive, asset-building orientation, building on strengths rather than categorizing youth according to their deficits. However, it also recognizes the need to identify and respond to specific problems faced by some youth (e.g., substance abuse, involvement in violence, premature parenthood). The most important manifestation of youth development as a philosophy or approach is the goal of making communities better places for young people to grow up. Youth participation is essential to the achievement of that goal.

3. **Programs and organizations: A planned set of activities that foster young people's growing capacity.**

   Youth development programs are inclusive. Participation is not limited to those identified as at risk or in need. They give young people the chance to make decisions about their own participation and about the program's operation, and to assume responsible roles. They engage young people in constructive and challenging activities that build their competence and foster supportive relationships with peers and with adults. They are developmentally appropriate and endure over time, which requires them to be adaptable enough to change as participants' needs change. Youth development is done with and by youth. Something done to or for youth is not youth development, even though it may be necessary and valuable. Youth development organizations exist specifically for the purpose of promoting youth development. Some other organizations operate youth development programs but have other functions as well. Programs to prevent or treat specific problems stand in contrast to youth development programs. However, problem-oriented programs may incorporate youth development principles by acknowledging participants' strengths and the wider range of issues they must cope with and by giving participants a strong voice in the choice to participate and in the operation of the program.

Source: Hamilton, 1999.

Representative Focal Issues of Youth Programs

Issues to Consider

- What are examples of the target behaviors of youth programs?
- What are the three key issues of youth programs?

The target behaviors of youth programs vary. Interventions may be aimed at externalizing and/or internalizing problems and may focus primarily on the individual or on the developmental system within which the youth is embedded; that is, in addition to the individual adolescent the program may involve his or her peer group, family, school, or community. For example, for externalizing behaviors, interventions focus primarily on the individual in regard to problems of alcohol use and abuse (e.g., Marlatt et al., 1998), smoking (e.g., Prince, 1995), conduct disorders (e.g., Ansari et al., 1996; Mann-Feder, 1996), social skills (e.g., Thompson, Bundy, & Broncheau, 1995), and delinquency (e.g., Richards & Sullivan, 1996). Interventions that involve the developmental system exist in regard to such problems as juvenile delinquency (e.g., Battistich et al.,

1996; Chamberlain & Reid, 1998; Henggeler et al., 1997), alcohol use and abuse (e.g., Hohlman & LeCroy, 1996; Johnson et al., 1996; Richards-Colocino, McKenzie, & Newton, 1996), violence (e.g., Corvo, 1997; Henggeler et al., 1996), and drug use (e.g., Battistich et al., 1996; Gottfredson, Gottfredson, & Skroban, 1996; Johnson et al., 1996; LoSciuto et al., 1996; Richards-Colocino et al., 1996).

In regard to internalizing behaviors, interventions focus primarily on the individual for such problems as depression (e.g., Field et al., 1996), anger (e.g., Kellner & Tutin, 1995), and suicide (e.g., Cotgrove et al.,

Many young people participate in community-based scouting programs.

1995; Kerfoot, Harrington, & Dyer, 1995). Interventions that involve the developmental system focus on such problems as anxiety (e.g., Kendall & Southam-Gerow, 1996), conduct disorders (e.g., Mann-Feder, 1996), or multiple "emotional problems" (e.g., Wassef et al., 1996). Some systems-level efforts focus on multiple internalizing and externalizing problems such as several health needs (Gullotta & Noyes, 1995) or emotional and behavioral problems (e.g., Dolan, 1995; Wassef et al., 1995a).

Moreover, in programs that seek to promote positive development there may be efforts that focus either on the individual level (for instance, attempts to enhance cognitive and ego development may adopt such an orientation; e.g., Faubert et al., 1996) or on the developmental system. Examples here include programs that seek to enhance self-esteem (e.g., Jurich & Collins, 1996), adolescent-parent relations, family strength (e.g., Gavazzi, 1995), or health (e.g., Brack, Brack, & Orr, 1996; Emshoff et al., 1996).

Whatever the focus of an intervention program might be—whether it is an individual adolescent or includes features of his or her developmental system, or whether the interest is on reducing or preventing one or more internalizing and/or externalizing behaviors or in promoting one or several

> **Program effectiveness**
> Concept indicating whether a program is accomplishing its goals by achieving what it attended to achieve.

facets of positive development—every program must in some way consider three key issues: effectiveness, scale, and sustainability (Little, 1993). To understand these issues let's focus first on the issue of effectiveness.

Program Effectiveness and the Role of Program Evaluation

Issues to Consider
- Why is program effectiveness difficult to determine?
- What can be done to determine if a program is effective?
- What are some types of evaluations, and what are their purposes?

Does a program accomplish its aims? For example, does it reduce youth violence? Does it prevent unsafe sexual behaviors? Does it enhance self-esteem among adolescents? If a program achieves what it is intended to achieve it is effective. It is a program that is valid for its intended purpose.

But **program effectiveness** is often difficult to determine (Jacobs, 1988; Jacobs & Kapuscik, 2000). Young people are not randomly assigned to programs; rather they enter a program for particular reasons based on their past and/or current life experiences. For instance, adolescents are in a drug reduction program because they use drugs, in a violence prevention program because there is a risk they will engage in violence, or in a positive youth development program because they live in a community that has the resources to provide a potentially beneficial experience to its young people. Because of the reasons youth enter into a program, it may not be possible to determine if any changes that occur during their participation are due to who they were when they started the program or to the program itself.

Procedures—termed **evaluations**—are used to ascertain if changes in participants are due to the program, if programs are effective, and if programs attain their goals (Connell et al., 1995; Fetterman, Kaftarian, & Wadersman, 1996; Jacobs, 1988; Millett, 1996; Lerner, Ostrom, & Freel, 1995; Ostrom, Lerner, & Freel, 1995). Evaluations try to *prove* that any changes youth experience over the course of their participation in a program are due to the program itself and not due to the factors that involved them in drugs, that lead them to be at risk for violence, or that gave them the opportunity to live in a community that provides programs promoting positive development. Evaluations aimed at proving that a program is effective are often termed **outcome** or **summative evaluations.**

Evaluations also try to *improve* the quality of a program as it is being conducted. Here, the evaluator tries to ascertain if the program can be improved, if midcourse corrections can be made to the program so better efforts at promoting self-esteem or preventing violence can be made. For instance, if the theory of developmental change used by program planners involves the idea that more police need to be on the streets to reduce youth violence, the evaluator may monitor whether such presence is in fact increasing. If not, then he or she may work with the community to create conditions that would allow greater community policing. The evaluator would not wait for a final determination of violence reduction to be made prior to taking the step of involving more police in the community. Before any outcomes are seen, efforts would be made to improve the work

In attempts to reduce or prevent problems such as drug and alcohol use and abuse, some community-based programs engage the peer group.

involved in the delivery of the program. Evaluations that seek to improve programs are often called **formative evaluations.** Because they seek to enhance the process through which a program provides its services, such evaluations may also be termed **process evaluations.**

Evaluations try to *empower* the people who are delivering the program and the young people and/or families who are participating in it. A key goal of evaluators of contemporary youth programs—especially those programs located in communities and begun and continued through the efforts of members of the community (as compared to trained professionals, such as psychologists, social workers, nurses, or physicians)—is to increase capacity among community members to both prove and improve the program (Connell et al., 1995; Fetterman et al., 1996; Jacobs, 1988; Jacobs & Kapuscik, 2000; Millett, 1996; Ostrom et al., 1995). These **empowerment evaluations** (Fetterman et al., 1996) are seen as critical to enact if the community is to use evidence of program

Evaluations Procedures used to ascertain if changes in program participants are due to the program.

Outcome or summative evaluation Procedures used to determine if a program is effective.

Formative evaluation Procedures that seek to improve programs.

Process evaluation Procedures that seek to improve programs through enhancing the process through which the program provides its services.

Empowerment evaluation Procedures used to increase the ability of community members to prove the effectiveness of the program and to improve it.

effectiveness to bring the program to all youth who need it and to maintain the program over time. Such goals for a program pertain to the issues of scale and sustainability, respectively.

Program Scale

Issues to Consider

- Why is determining appropriate program scale important?
- What factors might contribute to a youth program not reaching all eligible youth?

As we discuss later, we know a good deal about the characteristics of effective youth programs. We know how to prove programs are effective and how to improve their quality while they are in process. In addition, researchers are studying how to empower communities through evaluation (Connell et al., 1995; Fetterman et al., 1996; Jacobs, 1988; Millett, 1996; Ostrom et al., 1995). However, even if programs are known to be effective, they may not be reaching all the youth for whom they are appropriate, for whom they could have positive benefits. This is a problem of **program scale.** Often the number of youth that would be appropriate for a given program is not known. For instance, if a YMCA modern dance program or an after-school basketball program involves a dozen youth, it may not be known if greater skill attainment could be developed in the participants if the maximum number of youth in the program were 8 or if equivalent skill attainment could be achieved among youth if the program size were increased to 20 youth.

In turn, we may have information that more people could benefit from a program; for instance, we might know a program that sends visitors to the homes of adolescent mothers to help improve their skills as parents is effective, but that only 50% of the youth eligible for the program participate in it. We might not know, however, why we cannot involve all eligible youth in the program. What are the psychological, social, economic, and political reasons that keep youth from participating in the program? Alternatively, we might understand the

Program scale Concept indicating whether a program is reaching the appropriate number of people for whom it could have positive benefits.

Program sustainability Concept indicating whether a program is maintained over time.

economic reasons that keep adolescents mothers out of home visiting programs (e.g., they have to work and are not available when the program is offered), but we may not know how to change the social system (e.g., by developing labor law policies regarding flexible working hours or time off from work for program participation) in a manner that would enable the program to be brought to scale.

Program Sustainability

Issues to Consider

- Why are many youth programs not sustained?
- What is Francine Jacob's five-tier model of evaluation?

If there is a lot of scholarship to conduct about program scale, there is even more to learn about **program sustainability.** A sustained program is one maintained over time. Most programs, especially community-based ones, are not sustained over long periods of time. Many programs are initiated through start-up grants made by government agencies or private, philanthropic foundations or by university faculty who have obtained a grant to demonstrate that a particular intervention they have invented is effective. In either case, after the start-up funds have run out or the demonstration project is completed, the project usually ends either immediately or after a relatively short period (e.g., Dryfoos, 1998; Hamburg, 1992; Lerner, Sparks, & McCubbin, 1999; Little, 1993; Schorr, 1988, 1997). This lack of sustainability occurs even for programs that have been proven through evaluations to be effective (Little, 1993).

Typically, after start-up funds end or the expertise possessed by university faculty has left the community, members of the community do not have the capacity to identify new resources to sustain the program. They may not have the skills to conduct the program, especially in ways that will enable them to both continue to improve the program and to prove to potential funders that they are effectively changing youth for the better (Jacobs, 1988; Jacobs & Kapuscik, 2000; Lerner, Ostrom, & Freel, 1995, 1997; Ostrom et al., 1995; Weiss & Greene, 1992).

Because of the need to assist community program leaders to develop such capacities, increasingly greater attention has been paid in recent years to the empowerment approach to evaluation (Fetterman et al., 1996). Arguably, the most useful of these approaches has been developed by Francine Jacobs (Jacobs, 1988; Jacobs & Kapuscik, 2000). In her five-tier model of evaluation, Jacobs provides means for a community to develop a stronger program in regard to both the proving and improving dimensions of evaluation. Applications Box 14.1 summarizes Jacobs's five-tier model.

Toward a New Research Model for Youth Programs

Issues to Consider

- What is the difference between efficacy research and outreach research?
- Why should more effort be focused on outreach research?
- How can universities and communities collaborate to support positive youth development?

The National Institute of Mental Health (NIMH) is a federal government agency that has funded many demonstration projects pertinent to reducing or preventing problems of youth development. Recently, some of the leaders of NIMH have suggested that the predominant research model used to conduct evaluations may be flawed and that its use may be the reason effective youth programs have not been sustained (Jensen, Hoagwood, & Trickett, 1999).

Jensen et al. (1999) describe two distinct models of research pertinent to the promotion of positive youth development that have been pursued through grants provided by units within the National Institutes of Health (NIH), such as the National Institute of Mental Health (NIMH), and the National Institute of Child Health and Human Development (NICHD). The first model has been predominant in American social and behavioral science and is termed by Jensen et al. (1999) the **"efficacy research"** model. Research conducted within the frame of this model addresses this key question: "What works under optimal, university-based research conditions?"

Studies using this model try to determine what is maximally effective under "optimal," that is, university-designed as opposed to real-world conditions, in regard to preventing the onset of behavioral or emotional problems, ameliorating the course of problems after their onset, and treating problems that have reached clinical severity. Jensen et al. (1999) note that the results of the studies con-

ducted within this model indicate that effective preventive interventions for several high-risk behaviors and/or outcomes are possible.

However, a second model of research exists, although it has not received the literally hundreds of millions of dollars of NIH support given to efficacy research. Indeed, this second model has been rarely used and poorly funded. It is one of **outreach research**; it is research conducted in real-world community settings.

This model addresses this key question: "What works that is also (1) palatable; (2) feasible; (3) durable; (4) affordable; and (5) sustainable in real-world settings?" Jensen et al. (1999) conclude that when this question is asked, the answer in regard to prevention or to positive youth development programs is "Very few (if any), indeed."

Jensen et al. (1999) argue that the federal government must move, and is in fact now moving, to support outreach research, to change the answer to the last-noted question to "Many, if not most." To create this sea change in the way scholars conduct their research, Jensen et al. (1999) recognize that universities and communities must create new, more effective partnerships. Jensen et al. (1999) believe there must be a qualitative change in the way universities interact with communities in regard to identifying ways to promote positive youth development (see, too, Eccles, 1996; McHale & Lerner, 1996). Table 14.2 presents the ideas suggested by Jensen et al. (1999) and others (e.g., Chibucos & Lerner, 1999; Eccles, 1996; McHale & Lerner, 1996) about how universities and communities can collaborate in sustaining effective youth-serving programs.

Conclusions About Defining and Evaluating Youth Programs

Youth programs vary in numerous ways. They differ in their emphasis on problem reduction or prevention or in their attempts to promote positive development. They also differ in their emphasis on changing an individual versus changing the developmental system, or changing both the individual and some portion of his or her developmental system. Finally, they differ in regard

"Efficacy research" Model of research conducted under optimal, university-based research conditions.

Outreach research Model of research conducted in real-world, community-based settings.

applications box 14.1

Francine Jacobs's Five-Tier Model of Program Evaluation

Level/Title	Purposes of Evaluation	Audiences	Tasks	Kinds of Data to Collect/Analyze
TIER ONE Needs Assessment	1. To document the size and nature of a public problem 2. To determine unmet need for services in a community 3. To propose program and policy options to meet needs 4. To set a data baseline from which later progress can be measured 5. To broaden the base of support for a proposed program	1. Policymakers 2. Funders 3. Community stakeholders	1. Review existing community, county and state data 2. Determine additional data needed to describe problem and potential service users 3. Conduct "environmental scan" of available resources 4. Identify resource gaps and unmet need 5. Set goals and objectives for interventions 6. Recommend one program model from range of options	1. Extant data on target population; services currently available 2. Interviews with community leaders 3. Interviews or survey data from prospective participants 4. Information about similar programs in other locations
TIER TWO Monitoring and Accountability	1. To monitor program performance 2. To meet demands for accountability 3. To build a constituency 4. To aid in program planning and decision making 5. To provide a groundwork for later evaluation activities	1. Program staff and administrators 2. Policymakers 3. Funders 4. Community stakeholders 5. Media	1. Determine needs and capacities for data collection and management 2. Develop clear and consistent procedures for collecting essential data elements 3. Gather and analyze data to describe program along dimensions of *clients, services, staff,* and *costs*	1. MIS (management information system) data; collected at program, county and/or state level 2. Case material; obtained through record reviews, program contact forms, etc.
TIER THREE Quality Review and Program Clarification	1. To develop a more detailed picture of the program as it is being implemented	1. Program staff and administrators 2. Policymakers 3. Community stakeholders	1. Review monitoring data 2 Expand on program description using information about participants' views	1. MIS monitoring data 2. Case material

Level/Title	Purposes of Evaluation	Audiences	Tasks	Kinds of Data to Collect/Analyze
TIER THREE (*continued*)	2. To assess the quality and consistency of the intervention 3. To provide information to staff for program improvement		3. Compare program with standards and expectations 4 Examine participants' perceptions about effects of program 5. Clarify program goals and design	3. Other qualitative and quantitative data on program operations, customer satisfaction, and perceived effects; obtained using questionaires, interviews, observations, and focus groups
TIER FOUR Achieving Outcomes	1. To determine what changes, if any, have occurred among beneficiaries 2. To attribute changes to the program 3. To provide information to staff for program improvement	1. Program staff and administrators 2. Policymakers 3. Community stakeholders 4. Funders 5. Other programs	1. Choose short-term objectives to be examined 2. Choose appropriate research design, given constraints and capacities 3. Determine measurable indicators of success for outcome objectives 4. Collect and analyze information about effects on beneficiaries	1. Client-specific data; obtained using questionnaires, interviews, goal attainment scaling, observations, and functional indicators 2. Client and community social indicators 3. MIS data
TIER FIVE Establishing Impact	1. To contribute to knowledge development in the field 2. To produce evidence of differential effectiveness of treatments 3. To identify models worthy of replication	1. Academic and research communities 2. Policymakers 3. Funders 4. General public	1. Decide on impact objectives based on results of Tier Four evaluation efforts 2. Choose appropriately rigorous research design and comparison group 3. Identify techniques and tools to measure effects in treatment and comparison groups 4. Analyze information to identify program impacts	1. Client-specific data; obtained using questionnaires, interviews, goal attainment scaling, observations, and functional indicators 2. Client and community social indicators 3. MIS data 4. Comparable data for control group

Source: Jacobs, 1988; Jacobs & Kapuscik, 2000.

Table 14-2	Sustaining Effective Youth-Serving Programs: Ideas for Building University-Community Collaborations

Jensen et al. (1999) point out that effective university-community collaborations in support of positive youth development should be based on several specific principles:

1. An enhanced focus on the relevance of research to the actual ecology of youth (Bronfenbrenner, 1979; Bronfenbrenner & Morris, 1998; Hultsch & Hickey, 1978). Youth must be studied in the actual settings in which they live as opposed to contrived, laboratory-type studies.

2. Incorporating the values and needs of community collaborators within research activities (Kellogg Commission on the Future of State and Land-Grant Colleges, 1999; Richardson, 1996; Spanier, 1997, 1999).

3. Understanding and measuring both the intended and the unintended outcomes of an intervention program for youth and their context.

4. Flexibility to fit local needs and circumstances and an orientation to adjust the design or procedures of the research to the vicissitudes of the community within which the work is enacted (Jacobs, 1988; Jacobs & Kapuscik, 2000).

5. Accordingly, a willingness to make modifications to research methods in order to fit the circumstances of the local community.

6. Embracing long-term perspectives and the commitment of the university to remain in the community for a time period sufficient to see the realization of community-valued developmental goals for its youth.

Chibucos and Lerner (1999), Ebata (1996), Eccles (1996), Fitzgerald et al. (1996), Lerner and Simon (1998), McHale et al. (1996), McHale and Lerner (1996), Peterson (1995), Small (1996), Weinberg and Erikson (1996), Zeldin (1995), and Zeldin & Price (1995) proposed ideas that allow several other principles to be forwarded, including:

7. A commitment by both the university and the community to learn from each other (to co-learn) what is required to enhance the lives of particular youth.

8. Humility on the part of the university and its faculty, so (a) true co-learning and collaboration among equals can occur; and (b) cultural integration is achieved and, through this, the university and the community recognize and appreciate each other's perspective.

to their approach to the issues of evaluation, effectiveness, scale, and sustainability. Together, these variations make the picture of contemporary youth programs quite complex.

Themes of Contemporary Youth Programs There are some themes that characterize contemporary discussions of youth programs. Focus on these themes allows the complexity involved in understanding youth programs to be reduced to a few key concepts. First, most scholars and practitioners want to prevent problems before they occur. Although the plasticity of human development (see Chapter 2) means there is always optimism about finding some intervention to reduce problem behaviors, it is both more humane and more cost effective to prevent problems from occurring than to wait for them to develop.

Second, although steps need to be taken to ensure effective preventive programs are being developed, the focus should shift to promoting positive development rather than preventing negative outcomes (e.g., Furstenberg & Hughes, 1995;

Lerner, 1993, 1995; Moore & Glei, 1995; Oden, 1995). Several scholars (e.g., Benson, 1997; Lerner et al., 1999; Pittman, 1996) have emphasized that prevention is not the same as provision. *Preventing a problem from occurring does not guarantee that youth are being provided with the assets they need for positive development.*

As we noted in Chapter 5, in the discussion of the individual and ecological assets for positive development identified by the Search Institute (Benson, 1997; Benson et al., 1998; Blyth & Leffert, 1995; Leffert et al., 1998; Scales et al., 2000; Scales & Leffert, 1999), communities need to provide resources proactively to youth to ensure that they develop the "five C's" of positive youth development and thus thrive across their lives.

Preventing problems does not provide these assets, but effective programs do. Researchers from the Search Institute report the following:

> Time spent in youth programs appeared to have the most pervasive positive influence [predicting] thriving outcomes . . . [G]ood youth programs provide young people with access to caring adults and responsible

peers, as well as skill-building activities that can reinforce the values and skills that are associated with doing well in school and maintaining good physical health (Scales et al., 2000 p. 43).

Developing Effective Programs for Youth

Issues to Consider

- What must be done to develop effective youth programs?
- Why is it important to engage both individual and contextual influences?
- What are protective factors, and what is their role in positive youth development?

If programs are to succeed in addressing the combined individual and contextual influences on youth problems and if they are to be associated with positive youth development, programs must engage both of these levels (individual and context) (Benson, 1997; Lerner, 1995; Pittman, 1996; Pittman & Irby, 1995; Pittman, Irby, & Cahill, 1995; Trickett, Barone, & Buchanan, 1996; Wassef et al., 1995b; Whalen & Wynn, 1995). Whether aimed at drug use (e.g., Rohrback et al., 1994), alcohol use (e.g., Maguin, Zucker, & Fitzgerald, 1994; Wagenaar & Peery, 1994), aggression and delinquency (Guerra & Slaby, 1990), school problems (Switzer et al., 1995), or socioeconomic disadvantage (Furstenberg & Hughes, 1995), effective programs engage the system of individual and contextual variables affecting youth development.

By involving multiple characteristics of the young person—for instance, his or her developmental level, knowledge of risk taking, intrapersonal resources (e.g., self-esteem, self-competence, beliefs, and values), interpersonal management skills (e.g., being able to engage useful social support and prosocial behaviors from peers)—successful risk prevention programs may be developed (Levitt, Selman, & Richmond, 1991). However, the programs described here are more than ones focusing on diminishing risk. They emphasize the strengths and assets of young people and their capacities for positive development. These capacities are their possession of attributes, or **protective factors**, that

keep them moving forward in a positive developmental path. Protective factors are individual attributes (such as self-esteem, spiritual values, and knowledge, skills, and motivation to do well), and contextual attributes (such as the experience of having authoritative parents and a socially supportive, prosocial peer group) that researchers have identified as integral in the healthy development of young people (e.g., Browne & Rife, 1991; Feldman, 1995; Jessor et al., 1995; Stiffman, Church, & Earls, 1992). These protective factors are the assets for healthy development described by the Search Institute (Benson, 1997; Scales & Leffert, 1999; see Chapter 5).

A Vision for Youth Development Programs

Issues to Consider

- What are some of the basic needs of youth?
- How can these needs be met?

Promoting the role of assets, or protective factors, in youth programs is associated with healthy adolescent development. As summarized in the report of the Carnegie Council on Adolescent Development, *Great Transitions: Preparing Adolescents for a New Century* (Carnegie Corporation of New York, 1995), programs that build on the assets of positive youth development help adolescents meet the enduring needs of youth. If they are to develop into healthy and productive adults, all youth need to do the following:

> (1) Find a valued place in a constructive group; (2) Learn how to form close, durable human relationships; (3) Feel a sense of worth as a person; (4) Achieve a reliable basis for making informed choices; (5) Know how to use the support systems available to them; (6) Express constructive curiosity and exploratory behavior; (7) Find ways of being useful to others; and (8) Believe in a promising future with real opportunities.
>
> [The report goes on to note that] [m]eeting these requirements has been essential for human survival into adulthood for millennia. But in a technologically advanced democratic society—one that places an increasingly high premium on competence in many

Protective factors Strengths and assets of young people that keep them on a positive developmental path.

domains—adolescents themselves face a further set of challenges. They must (1) Master social skills, including the ability to manage conflict peacefully; (2) Cultivate the inquiring and problem-solving habits of mind for lifelong learning; (3) Acquire the technical and analytic capabilities to participate in a world-class economy; (4) Become ethical persons; (5) Learn the requirements of responsible citizenship; and (6) Respect diversity in our pluralistic society. (Carnegie Corporation of New York, 1995, pp. 10–11)

There are programs that meet these needs. These youth-serving programs include key features that make them effective, which we discuss next.

Faith-based programs may make important contributions to positive youth development.

Key Features of Effective Youth Programs

Issues to Consider

- What are the features of a positive youth development program that are needed for "best practice"?
- What are some examples of community-based positive youth development programs?

Numerous scholars, practitioners, advocates for youth, and policymakers have studied and discussed effective youth programs (e.g., Benson, 1997; Carnegie Corporation of New York, 1995; Damon, 1997; Dryfoos, 1990, 1998; Hamilton & Hamilton, 1999; Lerner, 1993, 1995; Lerner & Galambos, 1998; Little, 1993; Pittman, 1996; Roth et al., 1997; Schorr, 1988, 1997). Although all contributors to this discussion may have their own ways of phrasing their conclusions, it is possible to provide an overview of the **best practices** that should be integrated into effective positive youth development programs. These features of best practice involve coordinated attention to the youth's characteristics of individuality and to the specifics of his or her social context. Programs that are effective in promoting positive youth development incorporate the following ideas:

Best practice Set of procedures or program attributes believed to be most effective in constituting a good program.

1. They are predicated on a vision of positive youth development (for exam-

ple, the "Five C's" of positive youth development; Hamilton, 1999; Lerner et al., 1999) and have clear aims (goals) for the program.
2. They focus on the assets of youth and on the importance of their participation in every facet of the program—including its design, conduct, and evaluation.
3. They pay attention to the diversity of youth and family, community, and cultural context. Both the special strengths and the particular needs of youth and their contexts are of central concern.
4. They assure that the program represents a safe space and is accessible to them. Such a setting should also provide a context within which youth can use their time constructively.
5. In recognition of the interrelated challenges facing youth, they integrate the assets for positive youth development that exist within the community. Such integration involves collaborations (partnerships) among all youth-serving organizations and contributions by families, peers, and schools.
6. Through the presence of safety, accessibility, and collaboration, they provide broad, sustained, and integrated services to youth and a seamless social support system across the community.

7. In recognition of the importance of caring adult-youth relations in healthy adolescent development, they provide training to adult leaders. Useful training may involve enhancing sensitivity to diversity and providing information about the principles of positive youth development.

8. They act to develop life skills, competency, caring, civic responsibility, and community service, or the "Five C's" of positive youth development.

9. They are committed to program evaluation and to strengthening the use of research in the design, delivery, and evaluation of the program. The role of university-community partnerships is important here.

10. They advocate for youth. Although programs are not (and should not) be partisan, they should provide a clear voice to policymakers across the political spectrum about the importance of investing in positive youth development.

Multiple features of person and context must be combined to design and deliver a program that effectively promotes positive youth development. Building on the general developmental characteristics of the period—involving identity and family, peer, and institutional (e.g., school and workplace) contextual levels—these programs, when attuned to the specific characteristics and needs of the youth and his or her setting, will help the adolescent not just avoid the development of risk behaviors, but will also promote positive youth development.

There are numerous examples of how the elements of effective positive youth development programs have been successfully combined in a community-based effort. Applications Box 14.2 provides examples of programs that reflect the presence of these elements.

Conclusions About Effective Youth Programs

We should be optimistic about the likely success of prevention efforts if they are designed and delivered while keeping in mind that no single or isolated effort is apt to succeed, given the multiple interrelated challenges facing youth (Dryfoos, 1990; Roth et al., 1997). A coordinated set of community-based programs, aimed at both individuals and their contexts, is required for success. These programs should begin early and be maintained for as much of the adolescent years as possible. No one effort, even a comprehensive one, can continue to prevent the appearance of risk across all of this period.

Clearly, then, means may be found to capitalize on the potentials and strengths of all youth, their families, and communities. By meeting their developmental needs, their positive development is promoted. However, if the hope is to reach the maximum number of youth possible in a sustained manner, the resources of society need to be organized. To attain this end, scholars of youth development must engage policymakers in the support of effective programs (Lerner, 1995; Lipsitz, 1991; Ralston et al., 1999; Takanishi & Hamburg, 1996).

Public Policy for Youth Development Programs

Issue to Consider
- What are public policies, and what do they mean for society?

Public policies represent standards, or rules, for the conduct of individuals, organizations, and institutions (Lerner, 1995; Lerner et al., 1999). As such, policies structure our actions; they let others know how they may expect us to function in regard to particular substantive issues. In addition, policies reflect what we value, what we believe, and what we think is in our best interests. Simply, policies indicate the things we are invested in and care about.

If we value our youth, we will promote public policies that enable effective programs to be designed and sustained for all youth that need them. We know how to design effective programs. Our task now is to formulate a set of social rules—policies—that will enable our values about youth to be translated into effective actions. But why, specifically, do we need a **youth policy**? What will happen if we continue to be without such a policy?

Public policy Standards or values for the conduct of individuals, organizations, and institutions that structure actions and indicate appropriate investment of resources.

Youth policy Set of social policies that will enable the values of positive youth development to be translated into effective actions.

applications box 14.2

Community Programs That Promote the Positive Development of Youth

The Carnegie Council for Adolescent Development, as well as scholars of youth development (Dryfoos, 1990; Lerner, 1995; Little, 1993; Roth et al., 1997; Schorr, 1988), have outlined the elements of community programs key to effectively promoting positive youth development. Numerous programs exist throughout the United States and the world that employ these program elements. Two identified by the Carnegie Council involve the Boys and Girls Clubs and Project SPIRIT.

Collaborating for Youth: Boys and Girls Clubs Programs in Public Housing Projects Across the United States

Low-income neighborhoods often lack safe places for young adolescents to congregate and to participate in recreational or educational activities. Meeting the needs of adolescents living in these areas is the mission of the Boys and Girls Clubs of America, a national federation of independent local clubs.

Opening their doors to all young people, ages 6 to 18, clubs offer a wide variety of activities. Grouped in six core areas, these include health and physical education, personal and educational development, citizenship and leadership development, cultural enrichment, recreation, and outdoor environmental education. Through these activities, the clubs hope to instill such values as good work habits, self-reliance, perseverance, teamwork, and consideration of others. Club programs are designed to provide girls and boys with responsible adult guidance, encourage-

ment, and support that are frequently not available at home, in school, or elsewhere in the community.

Each year, Boys and Girls Clubs serve 2 million young people. More than half of these youth come from minority groups, single-parent households, or low-income families. To reach even more young people in need, Boys and Girls Clubs launched an ambitious new initiative in 1987. At the heart of the plan was the decision to expand its efforts in public housing projects. Today, with the ongoing support of the U.S. Department of Housing and Urban Development and several key federal agencies and private foundations, 270 clubs are located in housing projects nationwide and in Puerto Rico. They are the only national youth-serving agency with a major presence in public housing. Through this public-private collaboration, thousands of young people have a positive alternative to hopelessness and lives frequently filled with violence.

Boys and Girls Clubs in public housing are significant for two key reasons. They are responsible for bringing about many broad-based and dramatic social changes, and they provide a self-sustaining program of assistance. Research conducted over a 3-year period in 15 public housing projects has shown that these clubs have a positive impact on parental involvement and school performance and their presence encourages residents to organize and improve their community. The clubs also have had positive effects on reducing drug use, juvenile crime, and the presence of crack in housing projects compared to housing projects without them.

Why Is a Youth Policy Needed?

Youth constitute 100% of the future human and social capital on which our society depends. The healthy rearing of children has often been identified as the essential function of the family (Bowman & Spanier, 1978; Lerner & Spanier, 1980). As such, although family policy is not isomorphic with child or youth policy (e.g., family policies may involve aged adults living in retirement and without children or grandchildren), it is arguably the case that

no policy issues are of greater concern to America's families than those that pertain to the health and welfare of their children (cf. Kalil & Eccles, 1998).

Indeed, in Chapter 8 we stressed the view that society has charged the family with the primary responsibility for rearing children; we maintained that the family was "invented" as the institution that could best raise children in a safe, healthy, and effective manner (Johanson & Edey, 1981; Lerner, 1984; Lerner & Spanier, 1978, 1980) and as the setting best able to produce citizens committed to

Black Churches Supporting Youth Development: The Project SPIRIT Program Centered in Washington, D.C.

Since 1978, the Congress of National Black Churches (CNBC) has worked to build on and strengthen the black church's ministry by serving as an organizational umbrella for the eight major black American religious denominations. Headquartered in Washington, D.C., CNBC represents approximately 19 million African Americans in more than 65,000 local churches.

CNBC seeks to harness the historical mission of black churches to respond not only to the spiritual but also to the economic and social needs of the black community. The organization launched its first major national demonstration effort, Project SPIRIT, in 1986. Project SPIRIT, which stands for Strength, Perseverance, Imagination, Responsibility, Integrity, and Talent, aims to instill those very qualities in African American youth, ages 6 to 12. Goals of the project are to provide constructive after-school activities for young people growing up in low-income communities, expand their network of relationships with caring adults, support academic achievement, and teach practical life skills. The project focuses on three target populations: children and young adolescents, parents, and African American pastors. Project SPIRIT is currently operating in 65 churches in Arkansas, California, Florida, Georgia, Indiana, New York, and Minnesota—and in the District of Columbia.

The CNBC youth component revolves around daily after-school programs conducted in church facilities. Project SPIRIT generally enrolls young people who are underachievers, bored with the traditional school setting, earning low grades, and experiencing discipline problems. For 3 hours every school day after school, they concentrate on their homework under the supervision of retired or active teachers and other professionals, who are recruited into the program and trained in providing motivation and support. They then receive supplementary tutoring from workbooks and curricular materials. A portion of the afternoon is devoted to developing African American cultural and ethnic pride, improved self-concepts, and practical living skills through games, skits, and role-playing real-life situations. Project SPIRIT also organizes Saturday programs for parents and children and provides parent education programs focused on child and adolescent development, parent-child communication, discipline, and financial management. The program has served more than 2,000 children with tutorials aimed at strengthening their skills in reading, writing, and arithmetic and in building their self-esteem.

The Pastoral Counseling Training Component of Project SPIRIT provides pastors of participating churches with a 15-session workshop designed to help them become more effective in the care, education, and guidance of African American youth. Because this type of training is missing from most seminaries and in-service education programs for black ministers, it is a critical component of Project SPIRIT.

Source: Carnegie Corporation of New York, 1995, pp. 108, 112.

---

maintaining and perpetuating society. Thus, as we noted in the discussion of civil society in Chapter 5, the family is the key institution contributing to civil society (Lerner, 1984; Lerner & Spanier, 1978, 1980; Lerner, Sparks, & McCubbin, 1999), and—in this sense—*family policies represent societal principles or strategies for furthering civil society through the nurturance and socialization of children by families.* If families are effective institutions, children will become productive and committed members of society.

Despite the crucial connection between families, children, and civil society, all too many Americans today still do not see the need for a comprehensive and integrated national policy pertinent to all of the nation's children. To the contrary, many Americans associate youth problems with other people's children. Their stereotyped image of the at-risk or poor child is of a minority youth living in the inner city. Yet the probability that an American child or adolescent will be poor—and thus experience the several "rotten outcomes"

(Schorr, 1988) of poverty—is the same whether that youth lives in an urban or a rural setting (Huston, 1991). Poverty, then, is a major issue that needs to be addressed in the discussions of programs and policies pertinent to children and youth in America. Meet the Researcher Box 14.2 presents some of the recent work of Aletha C. Huston on this topic.

However, complicating the problems of poverty is the high incidence of risk behaviors among youth (Dryfoos, 1990, 1994). The breadth of these risks extends the problems of America's children and adolescents far beyond the bounds associated with the numbers of the nation's poor or minority children.

These reasons alone make the development of a national youth policy pertinent to all of America's children and adolescents. However, there are additional reasons. Just as we may be concerned with developing better policies for sustaining and/or enhancing American agricultural, industrial, manufacturing, and business interests, we must not lose sight of the need to sustain the communities—and the people—involved in the production, distribution, *and* the consumption of the products of our economy.

Still, we often neglect the fact that problems of rural and urban youth—problems that are similarly structured, similarly debilitating, and similarly destructive of America's human capital—diminish significantly the nation's present and future ability to sustain and enhance economic productivity. Clearly, then, both from the standpoint of the problems of children and adolescents and from the perspective of enlightened self-interest within America's industrial, agricultural, business, and consumer communities, policies need to be directed to enhancing youth development, to preventing the loss of human capital associated with the breadth and depth of the problems confronting children and youth.

Problems Resulting from the Absence of a National Youth Policy

Despite the historically unprecedented growth in the magnitude of the problems of America's youth, and of the contextual conditions that exacerbate these problems (e.g., changes in family structure

and function and in youth poverty rates—described in Chapters 8 and 13, respectively), few major policy initiatives have been taken to address these increasingly more dire circumstances. Indeed, as Hamburg (1992, p. 13) noted,

> During the past three decades, as all these remarkable changes increasingly jeopardized healthy child development, the nation took little notice. One arcane but important manifestation of this neglect was the low research priority and inadequate science policy for this field. As a result, the nature of this new generation of problems was poorly understood; emerging trends were insufficiently recognized; and authority tended to substitute for evidence, and ideology for analysis. Until the past few years, political, business, and professional leaders had very little to say about the problems of children and youth. Presidents have tended to pass the responsibility to the states and the private sector. State leaders often passed the responsibility back to the federal government on the one hand or over to the cities on the other. And so it goes.

As a result of this treatment of social policy, the United States has no national youth policy (Hahn, 1994). Rather, policies, and the programs associated with them, tend to be focused on the family (e.g., Aid for Dependent Children, or AFDC; or the Personal Responsibility and Work Opportunity Reconciliation Act, or PRWORA) and not on the youth themselves (Corbett, 1995; Huston, 1991; Morelli & Verhoef, in press; Zaslow et al., 1998). Although these policies may influence the financial status of the family, they fail to emphasize, and they may not readily impact on, youth development. That is, these policies do not focus on the enhancement of the capacities and the potentials of America's children and adolescents. For instance, a policy or program that provides a job for an unemployed single mother, but results in the placement of her child in an inadequate after-school care environment for extended periods of time, may enhance the financial resources of the family, but it may do so at the cost of placing the child in an unstimulating and possibly detrimental environment (Lerner et al., 1999).

If the current waste of human potential caused by the problems confronting contemporary American youth is to be substantially reduced, we must pursue new policy options that focus on children and adolescents and emphasize positive youth development and not just amelioration, remediation, and/or

MEET THE RESEARCHER BOX 14.2

ALETHA C. HUSTON
ALLEVIATING POVERTY FOR FAMILIES WITH CHILDREN

Poverty among families with children in the United States has been a persistent problem. After the longest period of unparalleled prosperity in the history of the United States, about 1 in every 6 children lives in a family with an income below the poverty threshold. Children in poor families are at risk for school failure, behavior problems, and psychological distress. Many poor families receive welfare (e.g., cash payments, food stamps) for some periods in their lives. We are in an era of welfare reform in which programs are designed to move parents receiving welfare into jobs.

In the research I am conducting with colleagues from Manpower Demonstration Research Corporation and several universities, we are investigating how welfare-to-work programs affect children and family life. Our goal is to identify the features of programs that can help children and to learn whether some programs are harmful to children. The first step was to study the New Hope Project, a 3-year demonstration in Milwaukee, Wisconsin, designed to test the effectiveness of an employment-based antipoverty program for families who are economically poor. Unlike many welfare-to-work interventions in the United States, its goal was to reduce family poverty as well as to induce employment.

For adults who worked 30 hours a week or more, New Hope provided a package of benefits including job-search assistance, wage supplements designed to raise total family income above the poverty threshold, subsidies for health insurance, child care subsidies, and project representatives who provided information and advice to participants. The study used a random assignment experimental design—applicants for the program were randomly assigned to be in the program or in a control group. This type of design assures that differences between the two groups are due to the program, not to personality, job skills, or other qualities of the people. We interviewed parents and their children 2 years after they entered the program, and we collected information from the children's teachers as well.

Overall, the New Hope program had significant and sizable positive impacts on children's educational progress and aspirations and on their social behavior in

Aletha C. Huston is the Priscilla Pond Flawn Regents Professor in Child Development in the Department of Human Ecology at the University of Texas-Austin.

school. These impacts were much larger and more consistent for boys than for girls. Children in New Hope families scored higher than those in control families on teachers' ratings of academic performance and classroom behavior and on teacher's ratings of positive social behavior (e.g. getting along with others, cooperating). The New Hope boys had fewer behavior problems and were less likely to be disciplined in school. And, finally, when asked about their future occupations and educational plans, boys in New Hope families had higher aspirations than did boys in the control group. The differences were large, suggesting that New Hope children were on a path toward better educational attainment and fewer deviant behaviors in the future.

Why did parents' participation in New Hope have positive effects on their children? Two factors appear to be important. First, many families had higher income. Second, because of the child care subsidies, younger children in New Hope families were likely to attend center-based child care rather than home-based care. Older children spent more time in lessons, clubs, and community centers that provide adult supervision and opportunities to gain many skills. When parents spend time working away from home, the activities and support systems for their children are likely to play an important role in determining the impacts on the children.

Our team of investigators is now examining the results of several welfare-to-work experiments in a project called the Next Generation. All of the programs promote employment for parents, but merely changing welfare for work generally does not leave families any better off financially, and there are not positive effects on their children. When programs include financial incentives, such as wage supplements, subsides for child care, or opportunities to keep part of the welfare grant while earning, the consequences for children are more likely to be positive. Children show better school achievement and often improved social behavior as well. The basic purpose of welfare in this country is to protect children from severe poverty. As states design new welfare systems, we hope this research can provide information about what programs help the children in the families served.

deterrence of problems. As argued by Pittman and Zeldin (1994, p. 53), "The reduction of problem behaviors among young people is a necessary policy goal. But it is not enough. We must be equally committed to articulating and nurturing those attributes that we wish adolescents to develop and demonstrate."

Possible Features of a National Youth Policy

Issues to Consider
- What are key features of a national youth policy?
- How can the media be involved in promoting the message of a national youth policy?

The Carnegie Council of New York (1995, pp. 13–14) has elucidated key features of a national youth policy. In the *Great Transitions* report they offer five policy directions that will marshal the resources needed to enhance the lives of the youth of America if followed. These are the recommendations: "(1) Reengage families with their adolescent children; (2) Create developmentally appropriate schools for adolescents; (3) Develop health promotion strategies for young adolescents; (4) Strengthen communities with young adolescents; and (5) Promote the constructive potential of the media."

This last recommendation is crucial. A chapter in a textbook may broaden understanding of the nature of youth problems and of effective means that exist to address them. But other ways of disseminating this information must also be found. Most people in the United States do not study adolescent development. Most get their information about youth development not from science or scholarship, but from their personal experience and the media. U.S. citizens must be convinced that resources will not be wasted if invested in youth-serving programs. The media can help convey this story of hope and potential to all segments of society.

Other ideas exist about the important features of youth policy. Benson (1997) and Pittman and Zeldin (1994) emphasize that policy must focus on promoting positive features of youth development and not the deterrence of negative characteristics. The vision of Karen Johnson Pittman for youth pol-

icy in the United States is presented in Meet the Researcher Box 14.3.

How might Pittman's vision be pursued? As described by Benson (1997), and reviewed in Chapter 5, assets must be marshaled to promote the competencies and potentials of youth and to develop and evaluate programs designed to promote these positive attributes. Policy must go beyond the two necessary but not sufficient goals of "meeting basic human needs [through ensuring] economic security, food, shelter, good and useful work, and safety" (Benson, 1997, p. xiii) and reducing or even eliminating "the risks and deficits that diminish or thwart the healthy development of children and adolescents. Guns, unsafe streets, predatory adults, abuse, family violence, exclusion, alcohol and other drugs, racism, and sexism are among the threats" (Benson, 1997, pp. xiii–xiv). Policy must add a third component—of assets—that is crucial for building a strong young person supported through positive relationships with his or her family and community. As Benson et al. (1998, p. 156) note,

> Ultimately, the most critical question is how communities can be supported to integrate and simultaneously pursue strength-building in three community infrastructures—economic, service delivery, and development. The goal of this integration is to develop a combination of policy, resources, and actions which will meet basic human needs, reduce threats to human development, provide humane and effective access to services, and promote healthy development.

Implementing Policy: The Potential of Community-Collaborative Programs

Issues to Consider
- How might existing community youth organizations be used to promote positive youth development?
- What are some examples of community-based organizations?

How might a system be developed to implement the policy objective of delivering these assets to youth in their communities? There are numerous answers to this question, but an obvious principle is to build on existing assets, such as the youth-serving

MEET THE RESEARCHER BOX 14.3

KAREN JOHNSON PITTMAN
BEYOND PREVENTION:
PROMOTING YOUTH PREPARATION AND PARTICIPATION

"Problem free is not fully prepared." This is a catch phrase that I coined more than a decade ago to convey the need for practitioners, policymakers, and the public to be as deliberate and precise about expectations of what young people should do/be/know as they are about what they should not do/be/know. Beyond educational achievement, there are few functional outcome areas in which policymakers are willing to stake out positive goals for youth. There is much more public consensus on the negatives (e.g., no young people should drop out, use drugs, join gangs, become parents outside of marriage) than there is on the positives (e.g., all young people should get postsecondary education, join organized youth groups, contribute to their communities, delay marriage and parenthood until their mid-20s). Concomitantly, there are few positive indicators of youth attitudes, values, knowledge, or behaviors beyond the education arena. Data books like *Kids Count*, funded by the Annie E. Casey Foundation, continue to gauge child and youth well-being predominantly by the absence of negatives (e.g., child abuse, illiteracy, teen births).

Yet common sense tells us that problem-free really is not fully prepared. The two states are clearly correlated. Young people with the requisite skills, knowledge, and experiences for further education, employment, and civic participation are more likely to be those who have avoided, or at least not been fully consumed by, drugs, gang participation, or early parenthood. But it is erroneous to assume that (1) every young person with problems is unprepared, (2) every young person without problems is well prepared, or (3) positive values and behaviors cannot be defined and measured.

Ten years ago, I had the opportunity to prepare a commissioned paper for the Carnegie Council on Adolescent Development and to sit on its Task Force on Youth Development and Community Programs. The paper afforded me an opportunity to take a comprehensive look at academic and practice-based theory and research on

Karen Johnson Pittman is senior vice president of the International Youth Foundation and executive director of the Forum for Youth Investors, an IYF Initiative dedicated to helping organizations that invest in youth invest in change. A sociologist by training, she was the founding director of the Center for Youth Development and Policy Research at the Academy for Educational Development and director of the President's Crime Prevention Council in the Clinton administration. She is a regular speaker and a columnist for *Youth Today*.

adolescent development and youth outcomes. This synthesizing work reinforced my original assertion—which grew out of my work at the Children's Defense Fund—and generated several more. Developmental theories strongly reinforce the first assertion that problem-free is not fully prepared. And these, combined with evidence from an array of surveys, program evaluations, and longitudinal studies, clearly suggest two more:

• *Academic competence, although critical, is not enough.* There are a range of functional domains in which young people need to achieve and sustain competence—vocational, physical, moral, social, civic.

• *Competence, although critical, is not enough.* There are a range of outcomes that young people need to achieve beyond competence, particularly if measured narrowly as the demonstration of skills and knowledge. To function as adolescents and adults, young people need to be *confident* (have a sense of safety, security, mastery, and self-worth), *connected* (have strong personal relationships and a sense of community), have good *character* (morals, ethics, a sense of responsibility), and have a sense of industry and civic connection, a need to *contribute* to family, community, society.

Equally important, the literature review yielded fairly consistent lists of resources or inputs that young people need if they are to achieve these outcomes (e.g., basic care and services, caring adults, high expectations, challenging opportunities), and reinforced the roles that key settings and institutions such as schools, families, nonformal community-based organizations, faith-based institutions, and the media play in providing or threatening these supports. The message, then, to policymakers: Broaden the outcomes (beyond prevention and academic competence), broaden the inputs (beyond basic services and education), broaden the settings (beyond schools).

In one way or another, I have spent the years since this report was issued promoting these basic ideas: sometimes

continued on next page

deepening the research, but more often moving the concepts (with footnotes) within the spheres of policy, practice, philanthropy, and research and across issues such as education, adolescent health, out-of-school programming, and violence prevention. In the past year, for example, the Forum for Youth Investors has brought researchers, planners, and policy advocates together to advise measurement specialists developing a taxonomy of human strengths on the applicability of their work to youth programming and youth indicators, and to discuss ways to better link prevention and development approaches in policy and practice.

But some of the most important work we have done is to document the voices of young people themselves and help bring them and their recommendations into policy discussions with public officials and chief state school officers about school reform and youth leadership. This work has convinced us to add a fourth assertion: "Fully prepared is not fully engaged." Preparation is accelerated when young people, even those declared "high risk," are full participants in designing the structures and defining the purposes of their work.

organizations and programs that exist in virtually all communities in America.

Whether programs in a particular community are associated with national organizations such as 4-H or with the thousands of existing community-specific grassroots organizations, many scholars and advocates for youth stress the important role of these organizations in building a system to deliver assets that enhance the life chances of youth (cf. Carnegie Corporation of New York, 1992; Dryfoos, 1990; National Research Council, 1993; Schorr, 1988). Advocates for the support and sustainability of youth-serving programs argue that policies must promote the financial health and broad acceptance of community-based youth organizations (Pittman & Zeldin, 1994). In so doing, policies support the socialization experiences and youth services provided by these organizations.

As we noted earlier, across the United States, more than 17,500 organizations have the mission of providing community-based, comprehensive, and/or integrated programs for youth (Roth et al., 1997). These organizations represent a rich and diverse array of institutions aspiring to be assets in the lives of America's young people. Applications Box 14.3 illustrates the potential contribution to positive youth development of such organizations. The box provides examples of three of the larger instances of such organizations, drawn from different sectors of civil society: a scholarly organization, a nongovernmental organization (NGO), and a governmental organization.

How College Students May Collaborate with Youth Development Organizations

Issues to Consider

- How might college students become involved in the promotion of positive youth development?
- Why are mentoring programs important, and how are they most effective?

Organizations serving the interests of youth are open to being contacted in regard to accessing their resources. Akin to the thousands of other organizations like those outlined in Applications Box 14.3, they are collaborative institutions.

Youth and their families can work with these organizations in numerous ways. One way is to contact local NGOs or the state, regional, or national affiliates. For instance, every county in the nation has a 4-H program and each state has an office (usually located at the site of the land-grant university). One may direct inquiries about possible routes to collaboration to the National 4-H Council in Chevy Chase, Maryland.

Similar collaborations can be made with organizations such as **Cooperative Extension System** (CES) offices, with locations in almost every county. Every state has a director who is open to inquiries about

> **Cooperative Extension System (CES) offices** Offices, usually located in each county in a state, that coordinate the community-based programs of the land-grant university in that state; these programs pertain to youth , families, community and economic development, and agricultural issues.

applications box 14.3

Promoting Positive Youth Development: Examples of the Role of Three U.S. Organizations

Organizations that include within their mission the promotion of positive youth development range in size and scope. Some are local grassroots entities that involve one or a few leaders or organizers. At the other end of the range are organizations that have a national focus and/or may have programs in most if not all communities in the nation. In order to illustrate the scope of activities present across all sectors of civil society to promote positive youth development, we focus here on the latter type of organization.

A Scholarly Organization: The American Association of Family and Consumer Sciences (AAFCS)

AAFCS is one of the oldest professional societies in the United States. Founded in 1909, its purpose is to improve the quality and standards of individual and family life through programs that educate, influence public policy, disseminate information, and result in published research findings. The 14,000 members of AAFCS work to empower individuals, strengthen families, and enable communities. Members include elementary, secondary, postsecondary, and Cooperative Extension System educators and administrators, other professionals in government, business, and nonprofit sectors, and students preparing for the field.

AAFCS is the only national organization representing family and consumer science professionals across practice areas and content specializations. These professionals develop, integrate, and provide practical knowledge about such topics as human growth and development, personal behavior, housing and environment, food and nutrition, apparel and textiles, and resource management. Such knowledge is necessary to make sound decisions that contribute to a healthy, productive, and more fulfilling life. The association provides leadership in improving individual, family, and community well-being; impacting the development, delivery, and evaluation of consumer goods and services; influencing the creation of policy; and shaping societal change.

The nature of family and consumer sciences, as well as the association's programs, have evolved because of changes in the family, culture, and resources, new knowledge in the basic disciplines, and applied research. To reflect the breadth and scope of the profession more accurately, in June 1994 the organization changed its name

from the American Home Economics Association to the American Association of Family and Consumer Sciences.

AAFCS continues to be deeply committed to many of the issues initially identified by Ellen S. Richards, the association's founder and first president. Richards, the first female graduate and professor of the Massachusetts Institute of Technology, was concerned with consumer education, nutrition, child protection, industrial safety, public health, career education, women's rights, purity of air, food, and water, and the application of scientific and management principles to the family. Historians credit Richards with originating the concept of ecology as well as formalizing the profession of family and consumer sciences (Bubolz & Sontag, 1993).

Thus its history and current orientation to scholarship suggests that AAFCS will be an excellent partner for applied developmental scientists in collaborative endeavors aimed at enhancing the context and life trajectory of youth. Indeed, the AAFCS "Investment in Youth" initiative is predicated on the recognition that increases in violent crimes on and by youth, juvenile delinquency, adolescent suicide, substance abuse, pregnancies, abortions, and out-of-wedlock births to youth all signal a decline in the well-being of American children and adolescents. The association supports and promotes efforts that assure an optimal future for all young people and their families, utilizing the unique potential and abilities each possess. Accordingly, AAFCS is poised and professional, structured to work—by itself and in a multidisciplinary alliance—to promote positive youth development.

Non-Governmental Organizations (NGOs): The Sample Case of the National 4-H Council

The promotion of positive youth development is also a central goal of America's largest youth-serving NGO, 4-H. Through the leadership of the National 4-H Council, 4-H organizations across the nation are building community-based partnerships to serve youth.

The National 4-H Council is a not-for-profit educational organization that focuses on the issues of America's youth. The council offers programs and assistance to youth workers in state and county 4-H or Cooperative Extension System offices, which assist youth in finding solutions to the challenges they face. National 4-H Council envisions a renewed society in which youth and adults take action together as equal partners.

continued on next page

National 4-H Council creates partnerships with corporations, foundations, the Cooperative Extension System, and others to bring together the resources for meeting the needs of young people. These partnerships and resources include training, developing curricula, offering technical assistance, and conducting youth forums and seminars.

In the early 1900s, 4-H programs began throughout the country in response to young people and their need for a better agricultural education. Most states organized clubs outside of schools with parents serving as volunteer leaders and Cooperative Extension System agents providing appropriate educational materials.

Through the years, the overall objective of 4-H programs has remained the development of youth as individuals and as responsible and productive citizens. 4-H serves youth through a variety of methods including community service activities, organized clubs, school enrichment programs, and instructional television. Universally recognized by its four-leaf clover emblem, representing head, heart, hands, and health, 4-H conducts such programs in all 3,150 counties of the United States, the District of Columbia, Puerto Rico, the Virgin Islands, Guam, American Somoa, Micronesia, and the Northern Mariana Islands.

The alumni of 4-H total about 45 million people, and more than 6 million youth currently participate in 4-H programs. Today, 52% of 4-H youth live in towns and cities with populations of 10,000 to 50,000 plus, and 26% are minorities. 4-H reaches out to young people across ideological and demographic spectrums and designs programs to respond to the needs of local youth. The National 4-H Council, in fostering this vast involvement, dedicates itself to building an environment throughout the nation in which youth and adults work together as equal partners in ways that result in responsible and positive community change.

The Council believes that if today's youth are to survive and prosper, then all of society must support them, engage them in civic life, and help them develop the necessary life skills to meet challenges they face (Sauer, 1998). Because of its history, vision, and values and the scope and diversity of the programs and youth involved in 4-H, this NGO represents a collaborative opportunity that may result in outreach scholarship that has vast impact on America. The potential influence is present in part because 4-H has as one of its key partners the Cooperative Extension System. This organization itself represents an important potential source of collaborative opportunities for all sectors of society interested in enhancing the lives of youth.

A Governmental Organization: The Sample Case of the Cooperative Extension System

Through a partnership between the U.S. Department of Agriculture and America's land-grant universities, the Cooperative Extension System (CES) provides educational and youth-, family-, and community-serving programs in all of the nation's 3,150 counties. Although many developmental scientists work at land-grant institutions the collaboration that exists with CES is quite minimal, and there are relatively few instances of developmental scientists joining community-based coalitions promoting positive youth development (Snider & Miller, 1993).

Given the reach of the Cooperative Extension System, the potential impact of such collaboration would be enormous. Contributions by developmental scientists would help further the mandate the Extension received when the federal legislation that created it was enacted.

participation (volunteering to take part in or to lead a program) or other forms of collaboration.

Finally, potential resources exist in the colleges or schools of family and consumer sciences, home economics, and child development, human development, or human ecology in public and private institutions across the country. Crossing your campus may result in both new academic understanding and new resources for the youth of your community. You may become involved, for instance, in opportunities to integrate the information you are learning in classes (e.g., about adolescent development) with

This legislation is unfamiliar to many developmental scientists, so we summarize it next.

As explained by the National Association of State Universities and Land-Grant Colleges (Enarson, 1989), the American land-grant university system was created through the Morrill Act, which was signed into federal law by President Abraham Lincoln on July 2, 1862. The act provided 17.4 million acres of land to the states in order that each might have at least one college whose purpose was to "promote the liberal and practical education of the industrial classes in the several pursuits and professions of life."

A second Morrill Act was signed into law by President Benjamin Harrison on August 30, 1890, in order that the states provide a "just and equitable division of the fund to be received under this act between one college for white students and one institution for colored students." The enactment of this law was an impetus for the creation of 17 historically black land-grant colleges in southern and border states (Enarson, 1989). The Hatch Act was then approved by Congress on March 2, 1887. It mandated the creation of agricultural experiment stations "to aid in acquiring and diffusing among the people of the United States useful and practical information on subjects connected with agriculture and to promote scientific investigation and experiment respecting the principles and applications of agricultural science."

The Smith-Lever Act was signed into law by President Woodrow Wilson in 1914. This law was intended to allow land-grant institutions to extend instruction beyond the boundaries of campuses. This was the act that established the CES. The purpose of the extension service created by Smith-Lever was to "aid in the diffusing among the people of the United States useful and practical information on subjects relating to agriculture

and home economics, and to encourage the applications of the same." The act further specified that the cooperative extension work of land-grant institutions "shall consist of the giving of instruction and practical demonstrations in agriculture and home economics to persons not attending or resident in said colleges in the several communities, and imparting to such persons information on said subjects through field demonstrations, publications, and otherwise."

Program areas within which such activities occur often focus on parenting, child care, youth development, nutrition, family management, community development, and policy (Lerner et al., 1995). All these CES educational programs have been directed traditionally to child and family audiences whose resources are limited. Such programs have significant potential in addressing the issues of youth development.

In regard to low-income youth and families, CES has developed curricular resources that include parenting education aimed at inculcating practices that have a long-term positive impact on children's well-being, child care selection and decision making; youth development, focusing on programs targeted to improve healthy outcomes for young people; nutrition education, delivered through the EFNEP and the Family Nutrition Program; financial management, aiding families to move beyond government dependency; housing, focusing on landlord/tenant issues, home maintenance, and first-time home buying; community development, providing educational programs, recreation services, and social support systems to families; and policy formation, aiding policymakers, whether staff at state or federal agencies or elected officials, to understand how policies will affect families and how to improve service delivery practices.

opportunities for community service organized by your university (Kenny & Gallagher, 2000; Kenny et al., in press). This is termed **service learning.**

Service learning may take many forms. You may serve at various community-based youth-serving organizations, by volunteering at community hot

lines that provide services to youth through telephone referrals (e.g., Dolan, 1995; Schondel et al., 1995), or by working at your local 4-H Clubs or CES offices. As a college student you may also be a

> **Service learning** Integration of classroom learning with the opportunity to perform community service.

mentor to a younger person (e.g., Grossman & Rhodes, 1999; Rhodes & Davis, 1996; Turner & Scherman, 1996). Mentoring is a significant way to promote positive youth development.

Promoting Positive Youth Development Through Mentoring The National Mentoring Partnership "One to One" describes **mentoring** programs for youth as involving a structured, one-to-one relationship or partnership that focuses on the needs of the mentored participant. A responsible mentoring program fosters caring and supportive relationships, encourages individuals to develop to their fullest potential, helps an individual develop his or her own vision for the future, and represents a strategy to develop active community partnerships.

The scholarship of Jean E. Rhodes and her colleagues provides considerable evidence that mentoring programs having these characteristics can effectively promote the positive development of youth. Among pregnant and parenting African American adolescents, the support of a natural mentor lowers depression and increases optimism, career activities, and beliefs about opportunity (Klaw & Rhodes, 1995; Rhodes, Ebert, & Fischer, 1992). Latina adolescent mothers with natural mentors have lower levels of depression and anxiety, are more satisfied with their support resources, and are more able to cope effectively with relationship problems (Rhodes, Contreras, & Mangelsdorf, 1994). Only 20% of urban adolescent girls with mentors continue to show sexual- and school-related risk behaviors (Rhodes & Davis, 1996). Urban youth involved in Big Brother/Big Sister mentor relationships for a year or longer show the largest number of improvements.

Mentoring appears to work best when it is extended for specific lengths of time, and some people profit more from mentoring than others. Among youth who are in mentoring relationships that terminate earlier, progressively fewer positive effects occur. Adolescents in relationships that terminate after a very short period of time show decrements in behavior. Older adolescents, adolescents referred for having experienced sustained emotional, sexual, or physical abuse, married volunteers aged 26 to 30 years, and volunteers with low incomes are most likely to be in early terminating relationships (Grossman & Rhodes, 1999).

Particular levels of mentoring seem most effective.

Mentoring One-on-one relationship that is structured and focuses on the needs of the person being mentored.

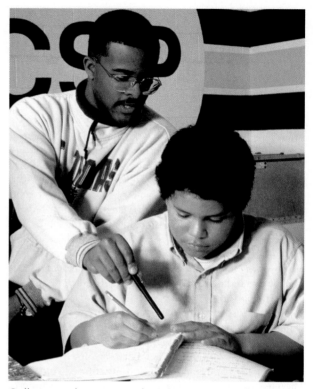

College students can make important contributions to the positive development of younger people.

Among 10- to 16-year-old youth involved in Big Brother/Big Sister programs, mentoring relationships that involve moderate levels of both support and structure are associated with improvements in parent and peer relationships, in personal development, and in academic performance (Langhout et al., 1999). The positive effects of mentoring relationships on academic performance are mediated primarily through improvements in the parent-child relationships and associated with reductions in unexcused absences and improvements in academic perceived competence (Rhodes, Grossman, & Resch, 1999).

Evidence indicates that mentoring programs can also be effective with youth in difficult family circumstances. Among foster care youth involved in Big Brother/Big Sister programs, mentoring relationships are associated with improved social skills, greater trust and comfort in social interactions, stable peer relationships, prosocial behavior, and self-esteem (Rhodes, Haight, & Briggs, 1999). Jean Rhodes continues to study youth mentoring programs, and her ideas about her scholarship are presented in Meet the Researcher Box 14.4.

MEET THE RESEARCHER BOX 14.4

JEAN E. RHODES
RISKS AND REWARDS IN YOUTH MENTORING

Adolescents who develop into competent adults, despite the profound stress associated with urban poverty, often demonstrate an ability to locate a positive, nonparent role model. Anecdotal reports of mentors' protective qualities are corroborated by a growing body of literature that has underscored the positive influence of nonparent adults in the lives of adolescents. Despite the promise of mentoring, as well as the recent growth in volunteer programs, many questions remain concerning the nature and influence of mentor relationships.

My research is designed to uncover the processes by which mentors promote resilience, the extent to which protective relationships can be arranged through mentoring interventions, and the conditions under which such interventions are most effective. In a series of investigations—supported by the William T. Grant Foundation, the National Institute of Child Health and Human Development, and the Spencer Foundation—my students and I have examined the role of both natural and assigned mentors in the lives of minority adolescent mothers. We have found, for example, that adolescents with natural mentors exhibit better vocational and educational outcomes and lower levels of alcohol consumption during pregnancy.

Unfortunately, families, schools, and communities have changed in ways that have dramatically reduced the availability of caring adults. To address the needs of adolescents who lack close attention from prosocial adults, volunteer mentoring programs have been increasingly advocated in such diverse areas as welfare reform, education, violence prevention, school-to-work transition, and national service. An estimated 5 million American youth are currently involved in school- and community-based volunteer mentoring programs nationwide, including more than 100,000 participants in Big Brothers Big Sisters of America programs.

For the past several years, I have been working with colleagues to analyze longitudinal data collected from over 1,000 urban adolescents who participated in a national study of Big Brothers Big Sisters. We have explored the predictors and effects of relationship duration and the mediators of the interventions' effects on adolescents' academic, emotional, and behavioral outcomes. In addition, we have empirically distinguished a range of mentor relationships and evaluated their influence on youth outcomes, tested the differential benefits of mentor relationships on foster versus nonfoster youth, and examined the role of youth characteristics on outcomes.

The findings that have emerged from these other studies have provided ample evidence of the extraordinary potential that exists within mentoring relationships. They have also exposed the rarely acknowledged risk for harm that unsuccessful relationships can render. It is true that one good relationship can transform a life, becoming the means by which youth connect with themselves, others, their schools, and their futures. Yet because a close relationship is at the heart of this intervention, a careless approach can do tremendous damage to a child's sense of self and faith in others. My strong contention—which is clearly supported by data—is that vulnerable children would be better left alone than paired with mentors who do not fully recognize and, in a sense, honor the responsibility they have been given. It is my hope that a deeper understanding of these important relationships will lead to interventions and policies that better address the needs of youth.

Jean E. Rhodes is director of Gender Studies and visiting associate professor in the Harvard University Graduate School of Education. She has written a book and over 20 chapters and articles on the topic of youth mentoring and is serving as guest editor of the *American Journal of Community Psychology* special issue on mentoring.

Conclusions

Given the evidence about the outcomes of positive youth development programs, it is reasonable to conclude that public policy must move from a focus on just building effective programs to also building cohesive and effective communities (National Research Council, 1993; Pittman & Zeldin, 1994). Hamburg (1992) suggests three policy initiatives that together would enhance the capacity of communities to (1) provide comprehensive and integrated services that (2) promote positive youth development through (3) the provision of effective programs delivered by a well-trained staff. Thus Hamburg (1992, p. 166) would:

> First, use federal and state mechanisms to provide funding to local communities in ways that encourage the provision of coherent, comprehensive services. State and federal funding should provide incentives to encourage collaboration and should be adaptable to local circumstances.
>
> Second, provide training programs to equip professional staff and managers with the necessary skills. Such programs would include training for collaboration among professionals in health, mental health, education, and social services, and would instill a respectful, sensitive attitude toward working with clients, patients, parents, and students from different backgrounds. Three, use widespread evaluation to determine what intervention is useful for whom, how funds are being spent, and whether the services are altogether useful.

A report by the National Research Council (1993) makes a similar argument, noting that building supportive communities for youth faced with the destruction of their life chances "will require a major commitment from federal and state governments and the private sector, including support for housing, transportation, economic development, and the social services required by poor and low-income residents" (p. 239).

Furthermore, Pittman and Zeldin (1994) emphasize that for youth development programs to attain sustained successes—across the span of individual lives and across multiple generations—issues of individual and economic diversity must

be clearly and directly confronted. Specifically, poverty and racism must be a continued, core focus of social policy. We must continue to be vigilant about the pernicious sequelae of poverty among children and adolescents, about the vast overrepresentation of minority youth among the ranks of the nation's poor, and about the greater probability that minority youth will be involved in the several problem behaviors besetting their generation.

The policy recommendations forwarded by Pittman and Zeldin (1994), Hamburg (1992), Benson (1997), Lerner et al. (1999), and the National Research Council (1993) stress the importance of comprehensive and integrative actions linking youth, families, programs, evaluation research, and policymakers. These actions involve both proximal community participation and the contributions of broader segments of the public and private sectors, community-based evaluations, diversity, and the promotion of positive development across the life span (Damon, 1997).

Adolescence is a double-edged sword. It is a period in which myriad individual and social problems may exist; yet the scientific evidence indicates that individual differences are prominent throughout adolescence, and conditions exist or can be created to allow most youth to pass through this period with few, if any, problems. Youth are very resilient (Werner & Smith, 1982), and for most adolescents the period is or can be one of quite favorable physical and mental health.

Most youth can successfully meet the challenges of this transition period. They integrate the biological, cognitive, emotional, and social changes they experience and can form a useful self-definition. A sense of self allows most youth to make decisions and commitments which result in adopting social roles that keep society moving forward effectively into the future. Parents, educators, and other caregivers can be confident that if the social context is attuned to the individuality and developmental changes of youth, healthy and successful people will emerge from the adolescent period. Policies and programs focused on positive youth development can make this happen.

Summary

- Youth-serving programs are involved in *reducing* the presence of an emotional, behavioral, or social problem, *preventing* such problems from occurring, and/or *promoting* positive, healthy behaviors among people.

- Three interrelated facets define the programs aimed at the *promotion* of the key positive attributes of youth: (1) the conception that the programs hold about the process of youth development, (2) the approach to programming associated with this conception, and (3) the specific characteristics of the approach these programs use. Programs that seek to promote positive development tend to focus on the individual and/or on the developmental system.

- Every program must in some way consider issues of *effectiveness, scale,* and *sustainability.*

- Effectiveness exists if a program achieves what it is intended to achieve; an effective program produces the effects it is designed to create.

- Program evaluations are used to ascertain if changes in participants are due to the program, if programs are effective, and if programs attain their goals. Evaluations try to *prove* that any changes youth experience are due to the program itself. Evaluations also try to *improve* the quality of the program as it is being conducted. Evaluations also try to *empower* the people participating in a program.

- Even if programs are known to be effective, they may not be reaching all the youth for whom they are appropriate, a problem of program *scale.* Research needs to examine why some programs fail to involve all eligible youth and how the social system might be changed to enable the program to be brought to scale.

- A sustained program is maintained over time. For reasons typically related to funding, most programs are not sustained over long periods of time.

- Studies using the "efficacy research" model try to determine what is maximally effective under "optimal" conditions, in regard to (1) preventing the onset of behavioral or emotional problems; (2) ameliorating the course of problems after their onset; and (3) treating problems that have reached clinical severity.

- Studies using the "outreach" model address this question: "What works that is also (1) palatable, (2) feasible, (3) durable, (4) affordable, and (5) sustainable in real-world settings?"

- To assist communities in developing effective community-university collaborations, greater attention has been paid to empowerment approaches to evaluation. Jacobs's five-tier model of evaluation provides a means for communities to develop stronger programs in regard to both the proving and improving dimensions of evaluation and to empowering program participants.

- Although it is both more humane and cost effective to prevent problems before they occur, the primary focus of programs should be on promoting positive development. Preventing a problem from occurring does not guarantee that youth are being provided with the assets needed for positive development.

- Youth policies must be created that enable the values about positive youth development to be translated into effective actions.

- Existing assets such as the youth-serving organizations and programs that exist in virtually all U.S. communities are good building blocks for positive youth development programs.

- Service learning involves combining classroom work and information with opportunities for participation in community programs.

- A responsible mentoring program fosters caring and supportive relationships, encourages individuals to develop to their fullest potential, helps an individual to develop his or her own vision for the future, and represents a strategy to develop active community partnerships. Mentoring appears to work best when it is extended for specific lengths of time, and some people get more benefits from mentoring than others do.

- Hamburg suggested policy initiatives that can enhance the capacity of communities to provide comprehensive and integrated services, which promote positive youth development.

Discussion Topics

1. Were you ever involved in a youth-serving organization and/or are there such programs in your community you are familiar with? What do you believe is the mission or goal of the organization(s) in terms of serving youth? Is the mission focused more on internalizing problems, externalizing

problems, equally focused on both, or focused mainly on promoting positive attributes?

2. If you were to conduct your own outcome evaluation on the program discussed in number 1, how effective would you say it is in meeting its mission? If you were to conduct your own formative evaluation, how might you improve on the efforts of this organization in how it strives to promote the 5 C's of positive youth development?

3. What steps would you take in your evaluations to determine if a program is operating at an appropriate scale? For example, if you were evaluating a program, run by only two staff members, designed to offer parenting skills to teen mothers, what would be an appropriate number of teens to work with to promote their parenting skills effectively? What issues must you consider in determining this scale?

4. Look back at Francine Jacobs's five-tier model. Why is such an empowerment evaluation necessary for the long-term sustainability of programs?

5. What might be some arguments for approaching youth problems from a prevention perspective or from a promotion perspective? In some cases, it is difficult to know whether financial support should be directed toward immediate concerns or if the money would be better spent on long-term asset promotion. What would you do if you were in a position to decide where to direct funding in countries that have extremely high rates of disease such as AIDS and whose children are infected and dying at alarming rates?

6. Knowing that time spent in a youth-serving program is the asset that has the most positive influence on youth behavior, what are some ways your community could attract youth to participate in such programs?

7. Youth face multiple and interrelated challenges. To be successful in their attempts to promote positive youth development, community-based programs must work together, coordinating their aims to meet both the individual and contextual needs of youth. Brainstorm some ideas about how different service organizations within your community could volunteer time and support to take responsibility for developing assets in its youth.

8. Why is a national youth policy needed? Why has it been so difficult to get such a policy accepted? How have children been viewed historically in the United States? Does society see them as assets to support and nurture? Do you believe that the country has begun the 21st century ready and willing to make changes in public policy that are more supportive of America's children and their future? Why or why not?

9. How might racism and/or classism impact the development of community-based service organizations, specifically the funding of these organizations? What steps can be taken to combat such destructive mindsets?

10. What organizations are available to the students at your school and how do they support the promotion of assets? What other services are needed? How might departments collaborate to ensure that the needs of all students are addressed?

11. How might mentoring a student from a nearby community impact your life? What do you think you might be able to offer this young person?

Key Terms

best practice (p. 340)

Cooperative Extension System (CES) offices (p. 348)

"efficacy research" (p. 335)

empowerment evaluation (p. 333)

evaluations (p. 333)

formative evaluation (p. 333)

intervention program (p. 330)

mentoring (p. 352)

outcome or summative evaluation (p. 333)

outreach research (p. 335)

process evaluation (p. 333)

program effectiveness (p. 332)

program scale (p. 334)

program sustainability (p. 334)

protective factors (p. 339)

public policy (p. 341)

service learning (p. 351)

youth policy (p. 341)

15

BEYOND ADOLESCENCE:
LAUNCHING THE YOUNG ADULT YEARS

It seemed to have all happened too quickly. Mrs. Brown felt like it had been just a short while ago that she and her husband had taken the 75-mile trip from their home to Andrea's freshman dorm. They had unpacked the car, gone to an Entering Freshman Parents' orientation, had a terrific dinner together, and then made the 90-minute trip back home.

The tears that filled Mrs. Brown's eyes that evening, as Andrea waved good-bye from the front steps of her dormitory, were diminished then by the recognition that, in just 4 weeks, she and her husband would return for Parents' Weekend and then, only a few weeks after that, Andrea would be home for Thanksgiving. And after Thanksgiving the long winter recess would quickly follow. "It's as if she is going to summer camp," Mrs. Brown recalled thinking.

But now, as she and her husband sat in the warm May sun, listened to the recessional music, and watched her daughter and the other graduates file out of the football stadium, she knew that things would now be different.

"Mom, I've got the job! I've got the job!" Andrea had exclaimed as she had hung up the phone a week ago. "They want me to start right after graduation. I can't believe it. I'm so excited!"

Mrs. Brown was proud of her daughter. And happy for her. But this job was 2,000 miles away. This would change everything. No more quick trips to campus or home. No more weekends and term breaks spent together. Now, with her daughter beginning her career, Mrs. Brown knew that their time together would be measured in days per year, not weeks or months.

Mr. and Mrs. Brown came out of the stadium onto the sidewalk. After a moment they saw Andrea standing among several friends. Her graduation gown was folded and draped over her arm; her cap was in her hand. It seemed symbolic to Mrs. Brown. Andrea had taken off the mantle of being a student. She was now a young adult with her own career and an independent life about to begin. Mrs. Brown rushed through the crowd to congratulate the young women who stood before her and also to kiss good-bye the little girl she loved so much.

LEARNING OBJECTIVES

1. To understand why choice and commitment constitute the key developmental tasks of young adulthood.

2. To understand the theoretical models of Erik Erikson and of Daniel Levinson about young adult development.

3. To understand the concept of being "off time" in achieving the tasks of young adulthood.

4. To understand why young adulthood may be a safe haven for testing out possible adult roles and an opportunity to get back on a positive developmental track.

5. To understand the childhood and adolescent antecedents and the consequences for adulthood of getting back on track during young adulthood.

6. To understand the ways in which the family influences the young person's development during and after the transition to young adulthood.

7. To recognize the strong connection in the United States between school and work.

8. To learn why, in Stephen F. Hamilton studies of the transition from school to work in the United States and internationally, the concepts of transparency and permeability describe the link between school and work.

9. To recognize why the apprenticeship system created in the United States by the 1994 School-to-Work Opportunities Act is useful in promoting positive transitions from school to work.

10. To understand the essential characteristics of a youth apprenticeship system.

11. To recognize the importance for civil society of enhancing the school-to-work transition for all youth within a nation.

Often, as we recount our lives to ourselves and others, meaningful events or entire periods may seem to have moved by quite fast. Perhaps, metaphorically, we can view the life course as a train moving rapidly across the tracks of time and space. If so, then each period of life, each stop along the tracks, may be regarded as a "life station" (Cohler & Musick, 1996, p. 204). In the stop labeled "Young Adulthood" we may ask what is present when we get off at this station. What fills the world of the young adult?

Lerner and Hultsch (1983) described young adulthood as a time of serious choice and relatively permanent commitment. Individuals make their first major (that is, potentially enduring) selections related to marriage, children, occupation, and lifestyle.

Other scientists agree with these descriptions. They see young adulthood as a time when "many individuals try out their first adult life structures by committing to their first careers. Educational and occupational decisions, at this juncture, represent major developmental tasks" (Bell et al., 1996, p. 346). Indeed, pursuing postsecondary education and initiating a career are key challenges for the young adult, ones related to both attaining autonomy from one's family while, at the same time, retaining sufficient connection with parents so as to maintain their continued support (Bell et al., 1996).

Although agreeing that the transition from the end of adolescence to the beginning of adulthood is a time of choice and commitment, several scholars have presented theories of development which emphasize that the commitments of young adults serve both individual and societal ends.

Theories of the Young Adult Period

Issues to Consider
- Why is young adulthood a period of choice and commitment?
- What are the tasks of young adulthood envisioned by Erikson?
- What are the tasks of young adulthood envisioned by Levinson?

Several theorists supplement the descriptions of the young adult period by stressing that the choices made by individuals at this time of life contribute to both the quality of the individual life span and to the maintenance and perpetuation of society. For instance, Erik H. Erikson (1959, 1968; see too Chapter 6) believed that young adulthood is a period within which the individual must make commitments that ensure the institutions of society (e.g., the family, the economy, the structure of civil society) will continue into the future. For example, Erikson

(1968) discusses the importance for youth within this portion of life to form an intimate relationship with another person so a stable family may be formed and so that, as a consequence, the next generation of children—of society's citizens—will be reared in an institutional context reflecting and conveying the values and mores of the culture.

Other theories of young adulthood exist as well. A key one has been proposed by Levinson (1978).

The transition to the world of work involves such tasks as preparing a resume, completing applications for employment, and going on job interviews.

Levinson's Theory of the Tasks of Young Adulthood

An interesting theory of young adulthood was proposed a quarter century ago by Daniel Levinson (1978). Although Levinson's theory, and the research he conducted in relation to it, were focused on the nature of young adulthood among men, to the extent the theory is useful, it can also apply to women. Nevertheless, in the years since Levinson (1978) proposed his theory, no definitive research pertinent to the relation of his ideas to young adult women has been presented.

Levinson believed that males must accomplish four tasks during young adulthood: (1) forming a dream, (2) finding an occupation, (3) establishing a relationship with a mentor, and (4) establishing love relationships, marriage, and a family. To Levinson, the dream is a vague sense of the self in an adult world. The dream can take on a dramatic form, for example, the great scientist, the world-acclaimed artist, or the record-setting professional athlete. In turn, the dream can be more modest, for example, the skilled craftsman, the effective father, or the respected community member (Lerner & Hultsch, 1983).

The task of the young man is to define the dream and to find ways to live it out. In many cases, the realization of the dream involves identifying an occupation. This occupation will define the set of activities the young adult will pursue to attain the dream.

Levinson (1978) argues that forming a relationship with a mentor is critical in actualizing the dream and, perhaps especially, to attaining it in the context of an occupational choice. The **mentor** serves as a teacher, guide, or counselor to the young adult. The mentor is usually several years older than the young adult and often in the work setting (for example, it may be a senior colleague). However, neighbors, friends, or relatives may play this role. The mentor enables the young adult to see how all the tasks of this period can be woven together to realize the life dream and to do so in a manner that allows integration with others (through love, marriage, and family).

The Timing of the Tasks of Young Adulthood

Issue to Consider
• What are the implications of being "off time" in accomplishing the tasks of young adulthood?

Whether one embraces the theory of Levinson (1978) or of Erikson (1968), or the general descriptions of the period provided by Lerner

> **Mentor** Teacher, guide, or counselor to another person. The mentor is usually several years older than the person he or she mentors.

and Hultsch (1983), Cohler and Musick (1996), or Bell et al. (1996), specific socially defined tasks involving choice and commitment clearly define the life station of young adulthood. But the time allotted in life for the completion of these tasks is not infinite (Cohler & Musick, 1996). Spending one's 20s looking for an occupation may be accepted by modern, industrialized society. However, if one is still not committed during one's 30s or, certainly, during one's 40s, not only will there be a lack of societal acceptance, but social approbation (e.g., "He/she is a failure!" or "His or her life is meaningless.") will almost certainly follow.

Many youth gain knowledge of the adult world through receiving mentoring from an older adult.

Thus the train leaves the life station after some period of time or, at the least, it is expected to move on (Cohler & Musick, 1996). In other words, young adulthood is a socially defined life period. Although this definition takes into account biology (e.g., young adulthood and, for women, especially the 20s is associated with the task of reproduction), society maintains conceptions of how much time is appropriate to devote to accomplishing the tasks associated with the young adult period (Cohler & Musick, 1996; Hagestad & Neugarten, 1985; Neugarten & Moore, 1968).

Life changes taking place too late—or too early for that matter (e.g., becoming a mother not in young adulthood but, instead, at age 13)—are regarded as problems by society. Indeed, events taking place too early (for example, becoming a widow in young adulthood) have greater negative impacts than those taking place too late (Cohler & Musick, 1996). This is perhaps the case because being early off time is not only unexpected, but it is typically the case that there is no preparation for this occurrence and, by definition, few people of one's age share this situation (Cohler & Musick, 1996).

In any case, not only is being off time in regard to the life tasks of young adulthood a problem as seen by society but, in addition, the person experiences it as a problem. Being off time diminishes feelings of psychological well-being and morale (Cohler & Musick, 1996).

Challenges During the Transition of Young Adulthood: Contemporary Dimensions

Issues to Consider
- In contemporary society, what is the relation between attaining physical maturity and adultlike independence?
- In what ways is college a safe haven for young adult development?

As evidenced by the ideas just described regarding young adulthood, this period of life is a significant one for the individual and for society, which requires competent and committed young people to maintain and perpetuate its institutions. The challenges for the person, then, are to make choices about aspirations, careers, and relationships that serve both individual and societal needs, and to do so within the temporal boundaries imposed by his or her culture.

However, the transition from late adolescence to young adulthood may be especially problematic for contemporary young people. In modern society, there is an "increasing delay between the acquisition of physical maturity and the assumption of adult responsibilities" (Sherrod, Haggerty, & Featherman, 1993, p. 218). This gap creates a change in the period of dependency of youth on adults. Moreover, modern society is marked by a diversity of developmental paths (e.g., involving different career possibilities, some of which—such as software designer, e-commerce specialist, or manufacturer of digital television equipment—did not exist in earlier historical periods), and this variation makes achieving of adult independence more complicated. Different adult responsibilities (completion of career training, establishing an intimate adult relationship, establishing a home, paying off educational loans) are increasingly segmented and separated across chronological periods (Sherrod, Haggerty, & Featherman, 1993).

Lonnie R. Sherrod's work is concerned with understanding the bases of and outcomes of adolescents' transition to young adulthood, both for young people themselves and for the society in which they are becoming adult citizens (see Meet the Researcher Box 15.1).

Complicating the transition to young adulthood still further is the relative lack of funding, public support, or public policies and programs facilitating the transition to adulthood for the half of the adolescent population that moves directly from secondary school to full-time work, that is, the half of the population of youth that does not go on to college from high school (Sherrod et al., 1993). College gives youth a slower transition to adulthood; that is, it provides a "safe haven to experiment with a variety of adult behaviors, values, and life styles; the developmental opportunities provided by this privilege are not well explored, but half of the population not attending college may be missing more than continued academic achievement" (Sherrod et al., 1993, p. 219).

The Transition to Young Adulthood as a Means to Reestablish a Healthy Developmental Path

Issues to Consider
- How may young adulthood offer opportunities for young people to get back on track after high school?

- What problems may emerge for the young adult as he or she explores life options?

The presence of a safe haven may be quite useful for adolescents making the transition to young adulthood. If there were problems of personal adjustment and/or of social relationships in high school, the transition to adulthood might provide an opportunity to get back on track (Sherrod et al., 1993).

For example, in a study of 920 students randomly selected from three public schools in the Boston, Massachusetts, area, relations with parents improved across the transition to adulthood, and these enhanced relations were associated with lower depressed mood and less delinquency among the youth (Aseltine & Gore, 1993). In addition, and also suggestive of using the transition to adulthood to get back on a healthy developmental track, among high school graduates prior mental health and behavior problems were not substantially related to post-transition mental and behavior functioning, suggesting that graduation from high school may have given youth the chance to break away from the troubles of their past (Aseltine & Gore, 1993).

However, not all explorations of possible life tracks during the transition to young adulthood might be beneficial to youth. For instance, the nature of personal and social exploration of the world was investigated among 198 youth making the transition to young adulthood. Youth who were in the foreclosure identity status category (see Chapter 6) were not open to new experiences (Clancy & Dollinger, 1993). Such youth might be missing, therefore, the opportunity to explore their world and find a means to identify a track, or to get back on one, that might afford a healthy adult life. In turn, youth who were in the moratorium identity status category spent more of their time experimenting with negative identities than exploring positive identities (Clancy & Dollinger, 1993). Here too a less than ideal use of the transition to adulthood period may have been occurring as young people explored problematic tracks rather than healthy ones.

One problematic path is having babies out of wedlock. Not only are poor women more likely to have such births, but out-of-wedlock childbearing during late adolescence is also associated with poverty after the transition to parenthood (Sullivan, 1993).

But the presence of developmental problems, even chronic ones, need not preclude achieving a successful transition to young adulthood. A study

MEET THE RESEARCHER BOX 15.1

LONNIE R. SHERROD
THE DEVELOPMENT OF CITIZENSHIP

Citizenship is as important an area of adult responsibility as work and the family; yet it has been the subject of far less research. It has been proposed that as a nation, we are confronting a crisis in civic engagement, particularly in youth. It is clear that we are not attending adequately to the political socialization of young people.

My research program is designed to understand how young people develop knowledge about, interest in, and become involved in the political system. Examples range from voting, campaigning, or other instances of active citizenship to helping out in one's community or doing service learning at school.

Quite interesting race and social class differences have been demonstrated in political engagement. My current research is based in three schools in a large urban city: a typical urban, disadvantaged high school; an academically, rigorous, highly selective urban high school (serving a similar population of youth); and a private parochial school serving a more middle-class, majority group of young people. The goal is to understand the developmental origins of individual differences in political engagement. These contrasting populations allow a particular focus on race and class differences.

Other researchers have demonstrated the importance of school climate and teachers' behavior to youth's political beliefs and attitudes. Individual factors, such as a general

Lonnie R. Sherrod is professor of psychology in Fordham University's applied developmental psychology program. He has been executive vice president of the William T. Grant Foundation, and has served on the staff of the Social Science Research Council. He edits *The Social Policy Reports*, and was chair of the Committee on Child Development, Public Policy, and Public Information of the Society for Research in Child Development.

prosocial orientation, academic involvement, and so forth, may also be important. Finally, commitment to family may influence, positively or negatively, the extent to which a young person feels a commitment to his or her nation. I hope to examine the potential interaction of these different factors in youth's civic engagement. The overall goal is to ask how we may promote more of a sense of social responsibility in youth.

I am directing a consortium of researchers from several disciplines in order to plan a general research agenda in this area. The consortium funded by the Grant Foundation represents an aspect of its program development and is intended to promote research on the topic from several social behavioral science disciplines.

Additionally, I am particularly interested in program evaluations and in the use of community-based programs serving youth as contexts for studying development—programs that aim to promote positive youth development, such as youth philanthropy, are of special concern. Finally, I have a particular interest in social policy and in using research to guide the development of policies as well as evaluating policies that are put in place—the latter two interests are reflected in my teaching and my work with SRCD's social policy committee. Dissemination of research is a critical ingredient of attention to policy, which is why I edit *SPR*.

using a nationally representative sample of 10,485 individuals who participated in the National Longitudinal Study of Youth (NLSY) provides a dramatic illustration of this point (Gortmaker et al., 1993). Of these youth, 1.9% were identified as having a chronic physical health condition between the ages of 14 and 21 years. These conditions involved such disorders as asthma, anomalies of the spine, diabetes mellitus, rheumatoid arthritis, epilepsy, cerebral palsy, scoliosis, congenital heart anomalies, eye, lower limb or foot anomalies, muscular dystrophy, and sickle cell anemia. Although youth who had very severe chronic health conditions had substantial limitations in their transitions to adulthood, such severely debilitating conditions were rare (Gortmaker et al., 1993). The great majority of chronically physically challenged youth made successful transitions to adulthood (Gortmaker et al., 1993).

Developmental Antecedents and Consequences of Behavior During the Transition to Young Adulthood

Issues to Consider

- What features of childhood and adolescent development may influence young adult development?
- How may young adult development influence later life?

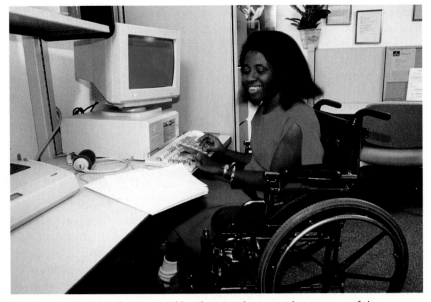

Youth with diverse abilities and backgrounds can make a successful transition to the world of work and young adulthood.

Getting back on track during the transition to young adulthood may be influenced by events in earlier developmental periods, that is, by *antecedents* of the transition. In turn, the degree to which the person functions well during the transition to young adulthood has consequences for behavior and development in later life.

In regard to the antecedents of behavior during the transition to young adulthood, in a 20-year follow-up of the children of about 250 African American teenage mothers, the bases of success in completing high school and in pursuing education beyond high school were explored (Brooks-Gunn, Gus, & Furstenberg, 1993). Among the participants in the study, 37% had dropped out of high school, 46% had completed high school, and 17% had gone on to postsecondary education (Brooks-Gunn et al., 1993). Completion of high school was associated with the number of years the father was present in the life of the girl, high maternal educational aspirations in the child's first year of life, being prepared for school, and not repeating a grade in elementary school (Brooks-Gunn et al., 1993). In turn, continuing education beyond high school was related to fewer years on welfare, high cognitive ability in preschool, attending a preschool, and no grade failures in elementary school (Brooks-Gunn et al., 1993).

In turn, in regard to the consequences of behavior during the transition of young adulthood on functioning in later life, in a study of about 4,700

men and women from their adolescence through their young adulthood, failure to complete high school was associated with psychological dysfunction in young adulthood (Kaplan, Damphousse, & Kaplan, 1996). Similarly, in a longitudinal study of about 2,000 young adults in Norway (Hammer, 1996), unemployment during the transition to adulthood was related to a greater tendency to pursue gender-typical adult roles (see Chapter 7). For instance, young women who were unemployed during the transition had a higher probability than other women of staying at home with children (Hammer, 1996).

In addition to behaviors associated with high school completion and employment during the transition, behaviors associated with interpersonal relationships during this period can have later-life influences. For example, cohabitation during the transition to young adulthood may be linked to some later-life problems. In a longitudinal study of unmarried young adults assessed when they were 18, 21, or 24 years of age and then retested 7 years later, when they were 25, 28, or 31 years old, respectively, cohabitation during the first assessment period was not related to depression at the time of the second assessment (Horwitz & White, 1998). However, men who had cohabited during the first assessment reported more alcohol problems than men who were single or married at the time; similarly, women who had cohabited reported more alcohol problems than women who were married during the first assessment (Horwitz & White, 1998).

In turn, and on a more positive note, having children or being married during the transition to adulthood is associated with having family-related goals (Salmela-Aro & Nurmi, 1997). The presence of these goals is related to both additional transitions in the family (e.g., having additional children) and feelings of well-being (Salmela-Aro & Nurmi, 1997).

Family Influences on the Success of the Transition to Young Adulthood

Issues to Consider

- How may the family promote positive development during young adulthood?
- How may the family have a detrimental influence?

As is true for other facets of youth development, the family appears to have a major influence on the nature of the transition to young adulthood and, as well, on behavior later in adult life. For example, in a longitudinal study of the bases of the pursuit of gender-atypical careers among 235 Finnish women, a nonagricultural vocational background of grandparents was related to a higher educational level among parents, which, in turn, was associated with both greater high school academic success and the attainment of gender-atypical careers (Nummenmaa & Nummenmaa, 1997).

Similarly, in a longitudinal study of about 80 two-parent families, educational attainment and healthy ego development in young adulthood were related to mothers and fathers behaving in ways that both promoted autonomy in their adolescents and maintained their relatedness to the family (Best, Hauser, & Allen, 1997). Moreover, youth who come from relatively small, intact, middle-class families, in which parents maintain the expectation for success of their children, attain more education and higher prestige jobs in young adulthood than do peers from other types of families (Bell et al., 1996). In addition, parents who encourage their children to pursue education beyond high school, and who encourage both the autonomy of their young adult children and their continuing relationship with them, are more likely to have youth who complete high school and who have better educa-

tional attainment and higher occupational prestige in young adulthood (Bell et al., 1996).

Other studies confirm that individuals who, as adolescents, had parents who granted autonomy to them are, as young adults, more psychologically healthy, for example, in regard to feelings of control and adjustment (Mayseless & Hai, 1998). Moreover, in such families, relationships between young adults and their parents tend to become more positive over time (Mayseless & Hai, 1998). Indeed, as young adults make transitions to marriage, to full-time employment, and even to cohabitation (but not to parenthood), relationships with parents become closer, more supportive, and less conflicted (Aquilino, 1997).

In turn, family conflict or poor parenting practices during the late adolescent period are often related to both problematic parent-child relations and to negative behavioral or emotional outcomes in young adulthood. For example, in a study of about 2,600 men and about 4,100 women from 39 countries on 6 continents, feelings of well-being among young adults were lower in families that had been characterized by marital conflict (Gohm et al., 1998).

Moreover, young adults do not generally receive help from parents involved in low-quality marriages (Amato, Rezac, & Booth, 1995); in addition, divorce lowers help between fathers and young adults but not between mothers and young adults. Similarly, low maternal communication and problem-solving ability, and high maternal depression, in adolescence are linked to delinquency during the transition to young adulthood (Klein et al., 1997). In turn, high levels of maternal problem-solving skill and the absence of maternal depression were linked to lower rates of delinquency during this transition (Klein et al., 1997).

Conclusions About the Challenges of the Young Adult Transition

The young adult transition challenges the young person to keep his or her train—the course of his development—on a healthy path or, if it is off course, the period represents an opportunity to find a healthy track. The person leaving the period of adolescence and entering young adulthood must, then, find a way to exit the world of adolescence—a world defined in large measure by the culture of high school (see Chapter 12)—and enter the realm of adults—a context defined in the main by commitment to work and career. In short, the transition to young adulthood is, in essence, a transition from school to work.

Accordingly, in trying to understand young adult life, and to take actions to enhance behavior and development during this period, it is crucial to focus attention on the nature of the connections between school and work. Applications Box 15.1 presents several programs that have been developed around the world to improve the chance that diverse youth will have positive and productive school-to-work connections across the young adult transitional period. In turn, in the next section of this chapter we discuss scholarship that has been central in helping researchers and practitioners conceptualize, study, and improve the school-to-work connection.

Understanding the School-to-Work Connection: The Theory and Research of Hamilton

Issues to Consider

- What is the nature of the transition from school to work in the United States?
- What does Hamilton envision as the motivation for youth to work hard in high school to forge a connection between school and work?
- How do the concepts of transparency and permeability enhance understanding of the transitions between school and work in different nations?

Almost all youth in the United States make a transition from school to work. The majority of these youth (about 75%; see Chapter 11) graduate from high school and then either try to enter the work force or, in turn, first pursue postsecondary education before beginning to look for full-time employment. In addition, about 95% of all men and women who become parents eventually earn a high

school degree (Hernandez, 1993), and most of these parents will seek employment outside of the home. Accordingly, for the vast majority of people in the United States, the connection between school and work is a very central part of their adult life.

How do people make this connection? How do they learn what they need to do to get a job in general or, more specifically, to obtain a particular type of job? How easy is it for them to enter the job of their choice? And what if they want to change jobs? How does one go about moving from one line of work to another? Are the answers to these questions the same for all young people? Or are there one set of answers for people who move directly from high school to work and another set for youth who first go to college before entering the world of work?

Clearly, the answers to these questions are critical for young people undergoing the transition to young adulthood. In addition, answers are central to society, given the importance of maximizing productivity and of citizens maintaining and perpetuating its institutions.

Stephen F. Hamilton (1994) has conducted the most important scholarship to date pertinent to understanding the connections between school to work that occur across the late adolescence to early adulthood transition. His scholarship provides theory and research that helps frame our understanding of the issues faced by youth trying to connect school and work. In addition, Hamilton offers ideas for policies

Vocational education facilitates youth in making a successful transition from school to work.

Enhancing the School-To-Work Connection Across the Transition of Young Adulthood

The Serowe Brigades
Serowe, Botswana

When the Serowe Brigades began in 1965, only 65% of Botswana's children attended primary school, with less than 10% receiving a secondary education. Now expanded throughout Botswana, the Brigades were created to provide the country's youth with practical education based on self-reliance. Although Botswana has experienced numerous political and economic changes since the 1960s, the Brigades continue to provide youth, ages 12 and older, with hands-on training as apprentices in more than 20 technical trades. As a result of their training, Brigade members attain marketable skills that are critical for acquiring jobs. The work of the Brigades benefits not only young people but the community as well, providing essential services such as construction and production of household goods. The Brigades are a highly effective and socially relevant alternative to formal education in Botswana. Indeed, participants are more likely to find work after graduation than graduates of formal schooling. As of 1999, 39 registered Brigades were training more than 3,000 youth annually.

Industrial Skills Training Program (ISTP)
Manila, Philippines

There are large numbers of idle out-of-school youth living in Tondo, Manila, Philippines. Lacking marketable skills, they often succumb to poverty and crime. Recognizing this crisis, in 1971 the Don Bosco Youth Center-Tondo established a vocational training center in Barrio Magsaysay, for unemployed dropouts, ages 17 to 23. The center offers an Industrial Skills Training Program (ISTP) that stresses positive work attitudes and exemplary industrial skills. Youth complete training in welding, technology, industrial electricity, automotive mechanics, and machine shop technology. The center's placement program then helps them find jobs. Unlike graduates of the country's traditional education system,

ISTP graduates are likely to find employment. Demand for vocational skills is high. In 1993, close to 94% of the program's machine shop graduates found full-time employment. Thus far, the Industrial Skills Training Program has trained 4,000 young people. Similar programs are offered in 13 Philippine provinces and in other countries where Don Bosco has a presence.

Industrial Technician Program (ITP)
Cebu City, Philippines

The Industrial Technician Program (ITP) uniquely integrates technical training and human development. It not only addresses the Philippines's need for unemployment reduction and more competent technicians, but it also provides future workers with a spiritual education that imbues them with professionalism and a social-oriented spirit. ITP was established by the Center for Industrial Technology and Enterprise for poor young men, ages 16 to 25, living in Cebu City. Although they have the ability to attain advanced education, these youth cannot afford it. Through a scholarship fund, they are able to complete a 3-year program that integrates technical training in electrical, electronic and mechanical technologies with values education. In addition to traditional classroom lectures, students participate in laboratory sessions, workshops, and an internship. Ultimately, the program produces middle level employees who are well trained and committed to their families, society, and exemplary work performance. In 1995, 83 of the first 97 participants graduated; all obtained jobs in well-established companies.

Programa Formación Professional (Professional Training Program)
Montevideo, Uruguay

All children in Uruguay have the advantage of a free elementary education, but one third of them drop out before completing the sixth grade. Also, the quality of education

and programs useful for enhancing the school-to-work connection for all youth and, in particular, for those adolescents who seek full-time employment immediately after completion of high school.

Hamilton's (1994; Hamilton & Hamilton, 1999; Hamilton & Lempert, 1996) scholarship has involved the study of adolescents and young adults from seven nations: the United States, Germany,

varies based on the economic strength of the community. Thus most young people find themselves ill equipped to enter the work world. The Programa Formación Professional (Professional Training Program) was founded to better train youth for the work force. Established in 1989, the program works with a wide range of related public and private institutions and serves about 500 youth annually, most of whom are school dropouts between the ages of 14 and 20. Participants attend classes and workshops to develop their skills in a chosen trade such as cooking, gardening, textile machinery, or electrical work. Complementing this training are sessions that strengthen students' personal development in areas such as drug prevention, sex education, and family relations. After they complete the program, students are assisted in their search for work and follow-up occurs for 6 months thereafter. Success, when measured by the number of youth employed, varies from year to year depending on the job market. In 1997, 40% of graduates found jobs. Additional studies show that youth have a better understanding of the society in which they live and a greater ability to face the challenges of daily life.

Jobs for America's Graduates (JAG)
Alexandria, Virginia

In the United States, 25% of all students are expected to drop out before completing high school; in some urban areas, this figure soars as high as 50%. Since its inception in 1980, Jobs for America's Graduates (JAG) has achieved extraordinary success in keeping at-risk and disadvantaged youth in school through graduation (or receipt of a GED) and assisting them with their transition into the workplace and/or to a postsecondary education. The program seeks to help young people secure work that will lead to a career with or without a postsecondary education. JAG uses a comprehensive approach combining dropout prevention and recovery activities with school-to-career transition activities. Trained job specialists work one on one with students, serving as mentors and helping youth overcome personal, academic, and economic barriers to success. JAG is the nation's largest, most consistently applied model of school-to-career transition for at-risk youth. It has graduated over 90% of program participants from high school and successfully placed over 80% in jobs, the military, postsecondary training, or a combination of all three. The program annually serves more than 65,000 young people in 1,100 high schools in 27 states. JAG's National Data Management System captures data regarding students served, services delivered, and outcomes achieved. JAG has also been replicated in the United Kingdom.

The Entrepreneurial Development Institute— TEDI
Washington, D.C.

In Washington, D.C., unemployment stands at crippling rates among young people. In communities such as this— where jobs are scarce—the solution to youth employment is not just job training, but job creation. The Entrepreneurial Development Institute (TEDI) was established in 1991 to serve as a catalyst for permanent social change, economic development, and community empowerment for youth and their families. TEDI is a national nonprofit dedicated to enabling disadvantaged youth, ages 7 to 21, to develop small businesses, avoid drugs and crime, sharpen their academic skills, and form positive attitudes about themselves and their communities. The program's strategy seeks to encourage entrepreneurship among disadvantaged youth. More than 3,300 participants annually have participated in the program, creating over 600 jobs in businesses serving local community needs. TEDI has established a consortium of youth serving agencies for replication of its model in 18 other U.S. cities. It has also launched five additional direct-service branch offices in Atlanta, New York, New Jersey, Los Angeles, and Cleveland.

Source: International Youth Foundation, 2001. <www.iyfnet.org>

Japan, Austria, Switzerland, Denmark, and Sweden. Hamilton (1994) observes that adolescents' expectations about the "payoff" in the labor market for achievement in secondary school motivates them to work hard in high school and forges a connection between the educational and work contexts of life. He points out that "Adolescents who believe their current efforts will bring them closer to a desirable future are far more likely to work hard in school and avoid self-destructive behavior than those who are either unable to think about the future or who believe their prospects are beyond their control" (Hamilton, 1994, pp. 267–268).

Hamilton (1994) explains that to attain the link they desire between their adolescent school context and their young adult work context, youth must consider two key facets of the worlds of education and work/career: transparency and permeability. Hamilton (1994) explains that **transparency** refers to the extent to which the young person can "see through" the intricacies of the stated and the unstated rules of the educational system and the labor market and, using this understanding, plan a course of action that will lead him or her from where they are in the present (e.g., a senior in high school) to a goal they have for the future (e.g., employment as an electrical engineer, as an accountant, or as a beautician). How easy is it to understand what one must do and what one must achieve to prepare in high school for a career as an engineer or as a beautician? To the extent that these pathways are clear and may be learned by any student interested in knowing them, the education-work/career system is transparent.

In turn, **permeability,** Hamilton notes, refers to the ease of movement from one part of the education-work/career market system to another. For example, permeability involves the amount of effort needed to move from, say, a plan involving becoming an electrical engineer to a plan involving becoming an orthodontist. A completely permeable system would be one where, after years of planning to be a beautician after high school, and working within the educational-work/career system to reach this goal, there would be no problems encountered, and it would be equally easy to now switch one's goal to electrical engineering, brain surgery, rocket science, or forestry.

Hamilton (1994) explains that formal credentials, or qualifications, are important in understanding both the transparency and the permeability of the education-work/career system. He finds an *inverse* relation between transparency and permeability (Hamilton, 1994). That is, the more there are particular and clearly specified qualifications for a given type of employment (e.g., 4 years of college, followed by 4 years of medical school, a 1-year internship, a 3-year residency in surgery, and a 3-year subspecialty residency in brain surgery for employment as a brain surgeon), the greater the transparency of the system. However, to the extent the qualifications are difficult to obtain, the system, although transparent, is not permeable (Hamilton, 1994).

Hamilton (1994) notes that in the United States the education-career/work system is, overall, not very transparent; it is, instead, opaque. For instance, what precise pathways can be specified for becoming a rock or a movie star, the CEO of a Fortune 500 company, the quarterback of a winning team, a successful lawyer and spouse/mother or father, or the proprietor of a successful e-commerce business? The education-work/career system in the Unites States is quite permeable, however (Hamilton, 1994). For example, Hamilton notes that it is possible to switch between the career of auto mechanic to the career of chef. Similarly, lawyers become entrepreneurs, teachers become store owners, and athletes become actors.

In turn, in other countries studied by Hamilton (1994) there are different connections between transparency and permeability. For example, in Germany the relation between credentials and employment are completely transparent. Youth are directed into particular educational paths that will lead either to a particular vocation (e.g., a machinist, a printer, or an electrician) or to university training and subsequent professional activity (e.g., as a physician, scientist, lawyer, or professor).

However, in all the countries Hamilton (1994) studied, professional life paths were quite similar. He noted that the connections between subsequent employment and preparation within universities for professional life were characterized in all countries by high transparency and low permeability. Becoming a surgeon, a contract lawyer, an aeronautical engineer, or a professor of human development requires, in all countries, attaining a quite formidable set of credentials. Although it is clear to anyone interested in these professional careers what these credentials are, the arduous tasks associated with meeting these qualifications makes their attainment quite difficult. This difficulty acts as a disincentive for moving out of the career and into another one, once one has finally obtained the requisite qualifications.

Transparency Extent to which young people can see through the intricacies of the rules of the education system and the world of work and then plan a course of action to lead them successfully from school to work.

Permeability Ease of movement from one part of the education-work/career system to another; permeability involves the amount of effort (e.g., additional education or training) needed to move from one occupation or career to another.

Implications of the School-to-Work System for Diverse Youth

Issue to Consider
- How did the School-to-Work Opportunities Act of 1994 facilitate school-to-work transitions in the United States?

Of course, not all youth, even in highly industrialized nations such as the United States, enter into professional career paths. For example, as we noted earlier, Sherrod, Haggerty, and Featherman (1993) pointed out that after high school half of the youth in America do not go on to college, and thus the nature of the transparency and permeability of professional career trajectories is, in effect, largely irrelevant to them. As we discussed, Sherrod et al. (1993) pointed to the need for public policies aimed at enhancing the success of the school-to-work transitions of this half of the American youth population.

Such a policy was introduced into the United States in 1994. As Hamilton and Lempert (1996) note,

> The School-to-Work Opportunities Act of 1994 responds to a serious gap in the United States' educational system: a gap between the completion of full-time schooling and entry into "adult" careers by young people who do not graduate from 4-year colleges and universities. (p. 427)

They also indicate that a core feature of the federal government's policy for economic development and educational reform is the provision of apprenticeships for American youth (Hamilton & Lempert, 1996).

Such apprenticeships have been common in some nations, most notably Germany. However, they have not been typical in the United States. Hamilton and Lempert believe that apprenticeships may be a key means to enhance the school-to-work connections for youth who do not attend 4-year colleges or universities.

A Vision for an American Apprenticeship System

Issue to Consider
- What are the key features of a useful apprenticeship system?

Based on what has been learned from the apprenticeship system in Germany, Hamilton and Lempert (1996) make several recommendations for building a developmental system in the United States to enhance the school-to-work transition of youth who seek adult employment after the completion of high school. As described by Hamilton and Lempert (1996), in the German system,

> Apprenticeships typically last for 3 years. Participants usually spend a day or a day-and-a-half each week attending a part-time vocational school (*Berufsschule*), where they receive instruction in German and social studies; in math, science, and other academic knowledge related to their occupation; and in the essential skills of their occupation, such as drafting or accounting. During their working time apprentices perform productive tasks and are paid, but they also receive instruction and the opportunity to gain proficiency in a range of new skills, which are specified for each occupation, as are the experiences and training they receive at work. Employers absorb the costs of training apprentices at work; state (*Land*) governments pay for schooling. Joint committees, with membership drawn from employers, workers, and government, design and monitor the system. The committees are convened by "chambers," nonvoluntary but self-governing associations of employers in related fields. Apprentices who pass the qualifying examination administered by the chamber at the completion of their training are certified as skilled workers and are thereby entitled to the compensation established for their occupation by collective bargaining agreements. They are privileged by law in applying for positions related to their career area; because they have received the training specified for their occupation, they have priority even if other applicants have more years of schooling. (pp. 430–431)

Accordingly, with the German system as a model for implementing the School-to-Work Opportunities Act of 1994, Hamilton and Lempert (1996) recommend the following:

1. The American apprenticeship system should be implemented with breadth being a key design principle. Youth should be trained in diverse and challenging tasks. "Occupations in which simple, highly repetitive tasks predominate should not be apprenticeable" (Hamilton & Lempert, 1996, p. 447).

2. Academic rigor must accompany occupational breadth. The courses taken by apprentices should focus on the theoretical components of

their occupations (e.g., the principles of electronics or of accounting). In addition, apprentices should take academic courses (for instance, in math or science) that are at the level of college preparatory courses (Hamilton & Lempert, 1996, p. 448).

3. Inclusion of diverse groups should be a hallmark of apprenticeship programs. Minority youth, women, and the poor must be afforded equal access to desirable occupations and to training with good firms or businesses (Hamilton & Lempert, 1996, p. 448).

4. Only high-quality firms or businesses should be allowed to participate in the apprenticeship system. "Apprenticeship training should be restricted to firms that are competent to teach 'all aspects of the industry,' to provide caring supervision, and to provide pedagogically sound training" (Hamilton & Lempert, 1996, p. 449).

Hamilton and Hamilton (1999) reviewed the successes of five different contexts within which the system they suggest has been implemented in the United States: single schools, school districts, regional collaborations among school districts, states, and corporate initiatives. They found that for school-to-work programs to function effectively, all these levels must work in harmony.

Indeed, Hamilton and Hamilton (1999) note that strong partnerships will be crucial to sustain the school-to-work system after the support provided by the 1994 federal legislation lapses. All levels of the system must make not only youth employment a priority but, as well, they must have youth participation in family and civic life as a central component of their efforts and an essential outcome of their programs. The ongoing research of Stephen F. Hamilton on education, employment, and the transition to young adulthood is presented in Meet the Researcher Box 15.2.

Conclusions: Integrating All Youth Into Civil Society

Issue to Consider

• How may the enhancement of the transition from school to work promote civil society?

As illustrated by the approach to research, policy, and programs pertinent to enhancing the school-to-work component of the transition to young adulthood, scholars and practitioners working with youth agree on a core set of ideas about promoting positive youth development. All components of the developmental system involved in adolescent life—including the active participation of young people themselves—need to be integrated to enhance the life chances of youth.

The developmental system of youth can—if engaged with a vision of civil society and with the values of social justice, and if coupled with the active application of the individual and ecological assets for healthy youth development—be a powerful basis for life success among the diverse youth of the nations of the world. It is my hope that you, as a reader of this book, can better appreciate this system. It is my hope as well that you, in your role as citizen, will actively and positively contribute to the developmental system in order to enhance the opportunities for positive lives for all young people and the chances that all of us will, together, live in a healthier, more just world.

MEET THE RESEARCHER BOX 15.2

STEPHEN F. HAMILTON
EDUCATION AND EMPLOYMENT
IN THE TRANSITION TO ADULTHOOD

Electronic technology and global competition have changed the work people do, increasing the demand for technical competence but also for personal and social competencies such as communication, teamwork, problem solving, and lifelong learning. A growing gap in earnings between those who have a college diploma and those without one demonstrates that employers are willing to pay a premium for these competencies, but also reveals a limitation in the American educational system. We have invested heavily in higher education but neglected other pathways to learning and to productive employment. When high school graduates, even dropouts, could get well-paid factory jobs, that neglect did not have such serious consequences as it has today when jobs that pay enough to support a family nearly all require academic and technical competence beyond the high school level.

Stephen F. Hamilton is professor of human development in the College of Human Ecology at Cornell University. As a Fulbright senior research fellow he studied the German apprenticeship system and wrote *Apprenticeship for Adulthood: Preparing Youth for the Future,* urging the adaptation of elements of that system in the United States.

German-style apprenticeship (variants are also found in Denmark, Austria, and Switzerland) combines part-time schooling with work experience that is carefully designed to teach competencies needed in specific occupations and more general competencies that can be used in other occupations and in other realms of adult life, especially civic activity. It bridges school and work, adolescence and adulthood. Many young people who do not learn well in school are diligent and adept learners in the workplace. In contrast to teenagers whose days are spent predominantly in the company of their peers, apprentices are surrounded by adults throughout the day, and some of those adults are charged with helping them succeed as workers. This gives apprentices access to adult mentors and role models who are neither their parents nor their classroom teachers, a decided advantage at the time in their life when they are faced with decisions about what kinds of adults they want to become.

The German system is embedded in German history, culture, law, and economic institutions; it cannot be transplanted intact to the United States. It serves rather as a point of comparison and source of ideas about how we might make the transition to adulthood smoother for those who do not graduate from college. Working with my wife, Mary Agnes Hamilton, I designed and directed a demonstration project to test how elements of German apprenticeship might be adapted in this country. We created apprenticeships for high school juniors and seniors in three broad occupational areas: manufacturing and engineering technology, health care, and administration and office technology. The occupational areas were defined much more broadly than in Germany because of the fluid nature of the American labor market and the need for people to be able to change occupations. Another critical adaptation was to tie youth apprenticeship closely to postsecondary education, assuring that enrollment in 2-year and 4-year colleges remained an option, avoiding career paths leading to dead ends.

Youth apprentices quickly learned to do work that is far more challenging than typical youth jobs. Many adults proved to be caring and competent mentors. Compared to their classmates in college-preparatory courses, apprentices were as likely to enroll in college, and when they did they were more likely to pursue a major related to their career interests. When they worked full time after high school graduation, apprentices earned more money, held higher level positions, and were more likely to be in jobs related to their career plans than their classmates. Without random assignment of youth to either apprenticeship or no apprenticeship, which was not feasible in this project, these differences cannot be attributed with certainty to participation in the program; but they are encouraging indicators.

Making apprenticeships like these available to large numbers of adolescents will require employers to invest in training youth and schools to work closely with employers to coordinate school-based with work-based learning. Even if we do not create a fully developed apprenticeship system, the example of the German system and its adaptation in the United States suggests smaller scale improvements, notably more work-based learning (e.g., cooperative education, internships) and more opportunities for adolescents to work with adults toward common goals (e.g., in joint community service projects).

Summary

- At the end of adolescence, people make a transition to young adulthood, a time of serious choices about life roles and relatively permanent commitments, for instance, involving marriage, children, occupation, and lifestyle.
- Erik Erikson believed that young adulthood is a period characterized by the crisis of intimacy versus isolation.
- Daniel Levinson proposed a model of young adult development for males involving four tasks: forming a dream, finding an occupation, establishing a relationship with a mentor, and establishing love relationships, marriage, and a family.
- Young adulthood is a period of choice and commitment, and a person does not have an indefinitely long period within the life span to achieve these tasks.
- Extending the time taken to meet these tasks well into the adult years means the person is "off time," a situation experienced by the person and regarded by society as a problem.
- In contemporary society there is an increasing separation in time between reaching physical maturity and assuming adult roles.
- Transitions to young adulthood may involve moving from high school to college or to the workplace. However, relatively few programs or policies exist in contemporary society to facilitate adolescents' transitions to young adulthood.
- Young adulthood may constitute a period in which youth have a safe haven for testing out possible adult roles. The period may afford an opportunity to get back on a positive developmental track if the young person has had personal or social problems in adolescence. However, some explorations of life paths and experiences in young adulthood may not be beneficial to youth (e.g., having a baby out of wedlock).
- Development in young adulthood can influence development in later adult life.
- The family is a major influence on the young person's development during and after the transition to young adulthood.
- In the United States there is a strong connection between school and work. Almost all youth make a transition from school to work.
- Stephen F. Hamilton has studied the transition from school to work in the United States as well as in six other nations (Germany, Japan, Austria, Switzerland, Denmark, and Sweden). He has found that adolescents' expectations about the "payoff" in the labor market for achievement in secondary school, and their beliefs that their future prospects are within their control, motivate them to work hard in high school and to avoid self-destructive behaviors.
- Hamilton indicates that for youth to attain a positive link between school and work they must consider two issues summarized by the concepts of transparency and permeability.
- Transparency refers to the extent to which the young person can see through the intricacies of the rules of the education system and the world of work and then plan a course of action to lead them successfully from school to work.
- Permeability refers to the ease of movement from one part of the education-work/career system to another.
- There is typically an inverse relation between transparency and permeability.
- Hamilton notes that in the United States the education-work/career system is not very transparent; it is opaque (e.g., it is not clear what qualifications are needed to be a rock or movie star). However, the system is very permeable.
- In the other countries that Hamilton studied, the relation between transparency and permeability varies, but the paths to professional careers (e.g., becoming a physician, lawyer, or physicist) were similar.
- Although there is a great need for more public policies to enhance the school-to-work transition for all youth in the United States, the 1994 School-to-Work Opportunities Act was a useful law in that it established an apprenticeship system for American youth.
- Enhancing the school-to-work transition for all youth within a nation is an essential ingredient in expanding and sustaining civil society across generations.

Discussion Topics

1. What important choices have you made since graduating from high school? Have they changed at all since you have been in college? Has college made it more or less difficult for you to make significant commitments to people and to careers?

2. In what ways do you feel the experiences you have had since high school have made you a different person? Do you believe most people change significantly when they become young adults? In what ways do they change? Are these changes for the better?

3. Do the tasks of young adulthood described by theorists such as Erikson and Levinson correspond to your own experience? Do you and other people of your age feel pressure to form an enduring intimate relationship, to form a vision for life, to find a mentor, and to make a commitment to a career?

4. Do you feel time is running out for you to make important life commitments? When might you think the right time to make decisions such as these has passed?

5. How has your family influenced your transition to young adulthood? Who has been the major influence on the choices and commitments you have made during your young adulthood? Would your friends have analogous answers to this question?

6. How easy has it been for you to develop a plan to use your education to move you successfully into a career or occupation? What would have enhanced your ability to develop a plan? How might society (educational institutions, businesses, government) improve the opportunity for all youth—whether or not they are college bound—to make a successful transition from school to work?

Key Terms

mentor (p. 361)

permeability (p. 370)

transparency (p. 370)

APPENDIX

STUDYING ADOLESCENT DEVELOPMENT:

METHODS AND DESIGNS

Will Gandalf loved teaching high school psychology. It was a great break from the required American history courses he usually taught. Students in psychology elected to be there and they were eager to hear what he had to say.

Yes, he loved teaching the class, except of course when he got a question like the one he just received from Tina Frodo, one of the more oppositional students in the class.

"Where," she had asked, "does all this information come from? Who says that kids and their parents behave that way?"

"Well, Tina," he began, "scientists, psychologists or sociologists for example, find these things out. They do research. Like the research I am sure you learned about in biology, chemistry, or other science courses."

"But people are not like chemicals," Tina protested. "You can't put them in test tubes or dissect them like we did to frogs in biology."

"Well, of course not, Tina. But psychologists and sociologists have scientific methods for studying people, just like biologists have their methods for studying frogs."

"But Mr. Gandalf, that's just the point I'm making. People are different than frogs. You don't need scientific methods to study them. You can just ask them what they think about things."

"Yes." Mr. Gandalf smiled. He sensed a teachable moment coming his way. "You're right, Tina. Scientists can ask people what they think. And in fact this is something they often do! This is one method for doing research."

"Well," Tina proclaimed triumphantly, "if you can just ask somebody, why in the world do you need to do research?"

LEARNING OBJECTIVES

1. To understand the approach to knowledge embodied in the scientific method.
2. To learn the basic characteristics of the scientific method and why all sciences rests on empiricism (observation).
3. To learn the characteristics, assets, and limitations of the four major types of observational methods used to study human development (naturalistic, controlled, experimental, and questionnaires, interviews, and surveys).
4. To understand how research designs provide a plan through which scientists make their observations.
5. To recognize that to study development a design must involve two or more times of observation.
6. To understand how variation associated with age, birth cohort, and time of measurement may influence developmental change.
7. To learn the characteristics of the three designs that have been used traditionally to study human development (longitudinal, cross-sectional, and time-lag) designs.
8. To understand the concept of confounded observations and to learn the assets and limitations associated with each of these designs.
9. To understand the characteristics of sequential designs, why they represent improvements over traditional designs but also have limitations.
10. To understand the need for and the characteristics of ethical standards for research in human development.

Many people do not understand what scientists do and why what they do is deemed "scientific." We accept the fact that physicists, chemists, and astronomers are scientists and do not raise questions about whether their work reflects the appropriate practice of science. But when it comes to the social and behavioral sciences—the subject matter of psychology, sociology, anthropology, or human development, for instance—skepticism is often expressed about whether the work of researchers in these areas actually reflects science.

Typically, we think of a scientist as a person in a white lab coat, toiling over test tubes and charts and experimenting. Certainly, some scientists do these things; and some of them study human development. Yet a scientist—and science—is not defined by a uniform or a workplace. Rather it is defined by whether the person adheres to the scientific method.

Characteristics of the Scientific Method

Scientific method Series of steps taken by a researcher to assure that what is observed is accurate and able to be verified by other researchers.

Empirical Capable of being observed.

Issues to Consider

- What is the approach to knowledge termed the *scientific method*?
- What are the key characteristics of the scientific method?

All scientists—whether they are physicists, chemists, biologist, sociologists, or psychologists—are scientists because they work in accordance with the scientific method. However, when scholars speak of the scientific method, they are not referring per se to a particular way of doing research (e.g., using test tubes in a laboratory to assess the combination of chemicals, studying the speed of particles in a nuclear accelerator, or observing infants as they interact with their mothers in the natural setting of the home). Rather, the **scientific method** refers to a series of steps taken by a scholar to assure that what he or she observes (no matter how it is observed) is accurate and able to be verified by other researchers. In other words, the scientist adheres to certain principles to be certain that what he or she learns from research—his or her knowledge—is information that anyone else, following the same procedures, would have observed.

Of course, science is not the only route to knowledge. For instance, one may know certain things because of one's faith or religion. However, to know something scientifically means that one follows a series of steps to obtain and verify knowledge. These steps are the components of the scientific method (Kaufmann, 1968).

First, all science rests on *observations*. This foundational basis of science is termed *empiricism*. When something is **empirical**, it is capable of observation. In science, anything that enters into the knowledge of a scientist must, in some way, be observable; it must, in some manner, be empirical.

Observation—empiricism—is the most basic characteristic of the scientific method.

In addition, scientists do not just observe anything. Rather there is a *purpose* to their observations. For example, they may want to see if observations about parent-child relations are consistent with the idea of storm and stress during adolescence (see Chapter 1), or the purpose of their observations may be to learn if certain types of parenting (e.g., authoritative ones) are associated with healthy development among youth, as predicted by scholarship in the field of adolescent development (see Chapter 8).

To fulfill the purposes of their observations, scientists do not observe behavior haphazardly. Rather, scientists arrange an order or sequence for their observations. They observe *systematically*.

If scientists' systematic and purposeful observations are accurate, then if other scientists follow their procedures, they should be able to make the same observations. In other words, scientific observations must be **replicable.** Moreover, scientists cannot keep their observations secret. If scientists do not *communicate* their observations to other scientists (for example, through publications in journals or books, or through presentations at scientific conferences), there cannot be any hope of independent and objective replication (and thus verification of the accuracy of the scientist's observations).

When a scientist's observations are communicated, the scientific community (other scientists working in the same area of research) can then work to verify and/or correct the work of the scientist. In other

words, through communication within the scientific community, science has the characteristic of *self-correction*. Finally, then, when an observation has been subjected to communication, replication, and correction it may enter the knowledge base of an area of science. In this way, science is a *cumulative* endeavor, a community process whereby knowledge is shared, verified, and integrated by the group of scholars working on a particular problem of concern to them.

In sum, the seven characteristics of the scientific method (Kaufmann, 1968) are observation (empiricism), purposefulness, systematicity, replicability, communication, self-correction (by the scientific community), and cumulativeness. All areas of science share these characteristics.

> **Replicable** Capable of being repeatedly observed.

However, the manner—the specific empirical procedures—through which a scientist makes observations depends on the subject matter of his or her investigation. How we observe the molecules of a particular gas under a specific temperature differs from the way we observe 15-year-old adolescents interacting at a shopping mall. Accordingly, it is important to discuss the ways in which scientists interested in the study of adolescent development make their observations.

Methods of Observation

Issue to Consider
- What are the methods of observation available to researchers interested in studying development?

The scientific procedures (the particular observational methods) a scientist uses, even when he or she is working within the confines of one area of science (e.g., psychology or sociology), may be quite diverse. Indeed, because of their varied interests, scholars of adolescent development study youth in many ways. Nevertheless, each method allows systematic, purposeful observations to be made in a useful manner.

Scholars use different methods of scientific observation to pursue their interests because there are many different ways in which development occurs and can be best studied. In fact, we may say that four major types of scientific method of observation are used in the study of development: naturalistic observation, controlled observation, experimental observation, and observation through the use of questionnaires and/or interviews. We consider the characteristics, advantages, and disadvantages of each of these methods next.

Naturalistic Observation

Issues to Consider
- What are the characteristics of naturalistic observation?
- What are its assets and limitations?
- What is ecological validity?

Ecological validity Observation of behavior as it exists in its true ("real-world") context.

In naturalistic observation, the researcher attempts to see

Naturalistic observation may be used to study people's behavior in the actual settings of life.

things as they exist naturally; that is, the researcher tries to observe things uninterrupted and as they are actually happening in a real-life setting. For example, suppose a scientist was interested in the aggressive behavior shown by 12-year-olds during a recess period in middle school. Such behavior might be defined as hitting, pushing, and throwing things at others. The researcher might want to know if such behavior is shown by 12-year-olds, and if so, how often and in what manner. Naturalistic observation might be chosen as a way of making the observations necessary to find out these things.

The researcher would find a group of 12-year-old children during recess. After the youth got used to the researcher's presence (or through the use of unobtrusive film or videotape techniques), he or she would simply observe and record the behavior of the children. The researcher would in no way interfere with the children's behavior. Rather, their behavior, as it naturally occurred in the real-play situation, would be observed and recorded.

Such naturalistic observation has real-world, or ecological validity because it is *actually* an observation of behavior as it exists in its true ecology. If we want to see how aggressive behavior exists among 12-year-olds when they are playing, a good way to find this out is to observe 12-year-olds at play!

But naturalistic observation also has its disadvantages. Although we see behavior as it actually occurs in the real world, all we can do is describe how the behavior looks and when we saw it appear. We cannot be certain *why* the behavior happened as it did.

Because the researcher neither controls the situation nor **manipulates** (i.e., attempts to influence) the behavior, it is not known what caused or affected it. There are many reasons for the inability to know causes. One is that many things may be happening at once. The scientist, even with the help of cameras, may be unable to observe everything. And even if many things are observed, the researcher does not know that what has been chosen for observation is really important or relevant to the reason for the behavior's occurrence. Thus incomplete or biased observations may be obtained.

It may also be difficult to see the behavior of interest. In other words, there is no way to *ensure* that the behavior of interest (e.g., aggression) will be seen often enough to assure systematic observations of it. The behavior of interest may be so infrequent that no systematic or repeatable observations can be communicated, and naturalistic observations of infrequent behaviors can produce misleading conclusions. Because of these disadvantages, other methods of observation are also used to study development.

Controlled Observation

Issues to Consider

- What are the characteristics of controlled observations?
- What are its uses and limitations?

Rather than studying behavior based on observations of its occurrence in the real world, the methods of controlled observation can be employed to increase the likelihood of observing the behavior of interest. This goal is sought by controlling the situation in which the behavior will take place. If a researcher believes that aggression in 12-year-olds does not occur very frequently and yet wants to study this behavior, he or she might see the advantage of controlled observation. Suppose that two

12-year-olds are placed in a room with a very attractive video game that can be used by only one youth at a time. After putting the adolescents in this situation for a very short time we might expect to see some aggression as we defined it.

Controlled observation allows the scientist to influence the observations because he or she controls and manipulates the situation. Situations are chosen on the basis of their likelihood of producing the behavior of interest. Yet this technique also has a disadvantage: By itself it allows the scientist directly to manipulate the situation alone, not the behavior of the people in the study. The researcher knows that a certain type of behavior may be expected to occur in this standard, controlled situation with some certain degree of regularity, but may not know what in the situation influenced the behavior to take the form it took.

A **norm** is behavior we may typically expect from certain people in specific situations. Controlled observation can provide *normative* information; that is, by having people respond in standard, controlled situations, we learn what behavior to expect in such situations. In fact, when scientists use a special type of controlled observation technique—known as a **psychological test**—important normative information about such aspects of functioning as intelligence and personality may be discovered.

The Controlled Experiment

Issues to Consider

- What are the characteristics of a controlled experiment?
- What are its limitations?
- What are independent and dependent variables?
- What are controls?

The controlled experiment is the observational technique that gives the researcher the best understanding of the basis of people's behavior *in a particular situation*. In a controlled experiment the scientist actually attempts to manipulate events that he or she believes will influence the person's behavior. That is,

Manipulation Attempts by a researcher to influence behavior and/or the situation within which behavior is studied.

Norm Behavior typical of certain people at certain points in development and/or in specific situations.

Psychological test Standardized, or controlled, device used to elicit behavior from or information about a person.

besides controlling a situation, the researcher also controls exactly what happens to the person in the situation. Such **controls** are used to see what will result when people are exposed to certain specific events. The goal is to establish a cause-effect relationship, and the researcher hopes to find evidence that "a change in X will cause (have the effect of) a change in Y." In an experiment the researcher tries to control the important influencing factors that act on the participants of the study; of course, what the participants do *depends* on them.

The behavior of adolescents may be assessed in standardized testing situations.

To illustrate, a researcher might conduct an experiment to determine whether high school students learn better when their environment is quiet versus when music is playing. The researcher might ask, How will different students learn if one half are stimulated with (or distracted by) contemporary music while trying to study, and the other half are not stimulated (or distracted) by sound at all? The researcher would then randomly assign students to the two groups and expose them to the different events—either the "music" or the "quiet" stimulation. The researcher would be interested in observing if differences in learning resulted between students exposed to one condition as opposed to the other. In an experiment, then, the researcher tries to see if the person's behavior can be affected, or changed, as a consequence of the different conditions the researcher manipulates.

Controls Variables that a researcher holds constant in a research study because of their presumed potential to influence the dependent variable.

Variable Anything that can change or vary.

Independent variable Condition that a researcher chooses to vary in a research study and present to research participants.

Dependent variable Behavior shown in response to the presentation of the independent variable.

The Independent Variable

Anything that can change or vary is a **variable.** Noise (or sound level), age, height, intelligence, amount of tenseness, and years in college are all variables. Anything that can change (or vary) in terms of how much of it exists is a variable. The condition that the researcher chooses to vary, that is, the various events with which the researcher stimulates the participants, is called the **independent variable.** An independent variable is something the researcher chooses to vary through intentional manipulation in an experimental study of development. This variable is independent of the participant's behavior. It is what the researcher chooses to manipulate.

The Dependent Variable

Although the independent variables, or the stimulus conditions, are chosen by the researcher for manipulation and are thus independent of the participants, their effects on the participants' behaviors are not independent of the participants. How the participants behave in response to the different stimulations they receive *depends* on them, and in an experiment the behavior shown in response to an independent variable's stimulation is termed the **dependent variable.**

In an experiment the scientist alters a specific stimulus—the independent variable—to see its effect on the dependent variable (i.e., the participants' *responses* to the various stimuli). As in our example, the researcher manipulates the background sound stimulus (sound or quiet) to see what effect this change will have on the students' learning. In this illustrative experiment, then, the level of background sound is the independent variable, and the resulting degree of participant learning constitutes the dependent variable.

Controls Controlling the independent variable to which participants are exposed is important, but the researcher also has to control many other variables. In fact, in an ideal experiment the only thing that can be different between the two groups of students is that one studies with music playing while the other studies in a quiet environment. Any other stimulus that, if varied, could have some effect on the students' responses (on the dependent variable) must not be allowed to vary. Only through control will the researcher be sure that any changes in the participants' learning are due *only* to the changes in the independent (stimulus) variable.

Thus the scientist would want to make sure such factors as age, intelligence, and educational background of the two groups were not different before the study was conducted. If the scientist found differences in how well students learned when stimulated with music versus quiet, he or she would want to be sure such differences were due to this different stimulation between the two groups and did not arise because one group was composed of, say, 12-year-olds while the other group was composed of, say, 20-year-olds, or because one group consisted of very bright students while the other group contained students of average intelligence. If such differences existed between the two groups, the researcher could not be sure the differences found in the dependent variable were, after all, really due only to the variations introduced by the independent variable.

Unless an experiment is properly controlled, the differences could just as easily have been due to age, intelligence, or educational differences. When an experiment is properly controlled, the researcher can make sound determinations of what caused the variations in the dependent variable.

Controlled experimental observations have an advantage not found with either naturalistic observation or controlled observation. When the scientist observes how changes in the independent variable affect the students' behaviors, he or she may state that the difference in the participants' behaviors was the result of the different conditions to which they were exposed. In other words, experimental observation allows the researcher to discover a basis of a particular behavior within the specific situation used for study.

Suppose the group that studied with a quiet environment learned better than the group that studied with music. Given all the proper controls, the researcher examining this difference could now say that the basis of the different levels of learning seen in the situation used in the experiment was the different sound stimulation given the two groups. Hence experimental observations allow the researcher to discover bases of studied behavior within a controlled experimental setting.

The controlled experiment also has disadvantages, however. The results of an experiment tell us only the effect of a specific stimulus on a certain behavior in one specific situation. We cannot necessarily apply these results to a different situation, where perhaps other stimuli may be used and/or other things may or may not be controlled. Thus we cannot easily apply results of one experiment to other experimental situations *unless* everything about the two situations is identical. Moreover, in the real world everything is not as controlled as it is in an experiment. Things vary naturally, and because many variables stimulate a person at the same time (instead of one at a time), each of these variables may affect behavior singularly or in combination. Experimental observations give us important information about a basis for behavior in a specific situation, but that situation is rarely identical to events in the real world. Hence we must apply or "generalize" the results of controlled experimental observations cautiously to the real world.

A disadvantage of experimental observation—that it may not have real-world validity—is an advantage of naturalistic observation. The disadvantage of naturalistic observation—that it cannot easily discover a basis of a behavior—is an advantage of the controlled experiment. Ideally, a researcher interested in discovering the most accurate information about behavior should try to move back and forth between these two methods of scientific observation, observing reality in the natural world but testing hypotheses carefully under controlled conditions. Actually, researchers tend to use one or the other of the foregoing types of observation; or, because of the disadvantages associated with each technique, they may choose yet another type of method of observation.

Questionnaires and Interviews

Issues to Consider
- What are the characteristics of questionnaires and interviews?
- What are their uses and limitations?

Rather than try to observe all the possible variables that may influence behavior in all possible naturalistic situations, and/or try to study each variable separately in one experiment after another, many researchers choose merely to ask people about themselves. That is, researchers often ask people they are interested in studying a series of questions about behavior. The questions may pertain to just about anything—for example, beliefs about politics, religion, sex, or drug use; typical reactions to events; what experiences the respondents recall from childhood; and many, many more. How the questions are both asked and answered can also take many forms. A printed series of questions may be given to participants, or the same questions may be asked in an oral interview. Participants may respond to such questions through writing, speaking, or both.

Interviews are a frequently used means to study adolescents' attitudes, values, or ideas.

Such techniques have obvious disadvantages. People may lie; they may try to answer in a way they think is favorable to them, and/or they may respond with answers they think the researcher wants to hear. For example, when asked whether they have ever "engaged in illegal drug use," people may respond "no" because they think this makes them look better rather than because "no" is the truth. Similarly, when asked if they think people of one religion are inferior to people of another religion, participants may also respond "no" because they think that is the "politically correct" response or because they think researchers want to discover a lack of prejudice in people.

Another potential disadvantage is that what people say about their behavior may differ from how they behave. We may not be intentionally lying when we say we behave in certain ways; yet we may be too involved with ourselves to describe our behavior accurately. Hence we may unintentionally be distorting the facts of our behavior, or we may be forgetting and/or not remembering certain things accurately. For instance, we may report that we *always* obey traffic laws, and yet, a bit later, we may speed home to dinner.

Finally, researchers may include questions that make certain answers more likely than others, or their behavior may bias the participants' answers to questions. For instance, a researcher who establishes a warm rapport with an adolescent may elicit answers that differ from those elicited by a cold and/or hostile interviewer.

Despite these disadvantages, questionnaires and interviews do have important advantages. They allow scientists to obtain considerable information about behavior quickly. If a questionnaire has both written questions and answers, for instance, one scientist may obtain information from several hundred people at the same time. Moreover, some aspects of behavior may not be ethical or easy to investigate except through questionnaires or interviews. For instance, whereas few people would allow their sexual behavior to be observed daily, more people might provide anonymous information on a questionnaire about their sexuality.

Scientists have long favored questionnaires and interviews and have sought to overcome the disadvantages of such techniques (Cattell, 1973). For instance, techniques have been developed to measure people's tendency to lie on questionnaires, and scientists have attempted to devise ways to screen the actual purpose of the questions from the participant, or at least make it hard to guess.

Conclusions About Methods of Observation

A scientist may observe behaviors associated with human development in several different ways. However, a special observational task is presented to a scientist concerned with studying development. As explained in Chapter 1, development involves change. Change—an alteration over time in some characteristic of the person—cannot be observed by studying a person only once. To observe change, at least two points in time must be involved.

Accordingly, in order to study human development, researchers must plan—or **design**—their observations to encompass two or more occasions. In other words, measures related to development must be taken on at least two occasions in order to determine if a change has in fact occurred.

Designs of Developmental Research

Issues to Consider

- What are the ways in which researchers interested in studying development may design their observations?
- Why is variation associated with age, cohort, and time of measurement important to assess?
- How may these variables be confounded in designs of developmental research?

Many people who attempt to understand the basis of an individual's development do so by specifying age-related changes. An example is attributing storm and stress to the adolescent "stage of life." Although such age-related changes may be one source of a person's development, they are not the only processes that provide a basis for change. For example, if a prominent event occurs, as for instance the assassination of an important political figure, behaviors of people might be affected despite what stage or age of development they are in. As such, it is possible that time of measurement, as well as age-related phenomena, can influence development.

In addition, not only may age and a particular historical event influence behavior, but people may change as a consequence of being exposed to a particular *series* of historical events. Imagine that attitudes toward government were being measured and the participants in the study were people born during the Great Depression in the United States (1929 through the late 1930s). During this historical era, many of the institutions designed to afford economic security to American citizens (banks, for example) failed, and existing governmental policies were not able to deal with this situation. Accordingly, it may be expected that people who are members of the 1920s birth **cohort** (or group), and thus experienced the effects of the Depression during childhood, might have developed differently than people born well before or well after this historical era. Indeed, research has found this to be true (Elder, 1974).

So we may see at least three components of developmental change: **birth cohort**–related events, time of measurement, and age-related phenomena. Recognizing that reference is always made to phenomena that change in relation to these components, we may label these components *cohort, time,* and *age,* for convenience. Thus when we see change in a person from one point in the life span to another, we must be able to determine how processes associated with each of these three components may influence change.

Until the 1960s (Baltes, 1968; Schaie, 1965), the three commonly used designs for developmental research—termed *longitudinal, cross sectional,* and *time lag*—did not allow for an adequate determination of the contributions of age, time, and cohort. Developmental research typically involves a **confounding** of two of the three components of change, and as a consequence, the design's utility is severely limited. When a variable is confounded, its influence on behavior cannot be separated from that of another variable which could be simultaneously influencing behavior.

For instance, if we wanted to know whether males or females could score higher on a test of reading comprehension, we would not want all the males to be college educated and all the females grade school educated. If we did not equate the two sex groups on education level (if we did not "control" for the contributions of education), then we would not know if differences between the groups were influenced by their sex or by their

Design Plan for the observation of behavior.

Cohort Group of people experiencing an event in common.

Birth cohort Group of people who share a common birth year.

Confounding Situation in research in which the influence of one variable on behavior cannot be separated from the influence of another variable on behavior.

Adolescents' preferred styles of dress and grooming have changed across history.

educational disparities (or some combination of the two). Thus sex would be confounded with education. In other words, we could not separate the effects of the two variables. When the separate influence of two variables cannot be determined, these variables may be confounded, and any study that involves such a confounding has a potential methodological flaw.

Table A.1 presents the particular confounding factors in each of the three commonly used developmental designs. Refer to this table as our discussion turns to an examination of the characteristics of each of these designs and an explanation of why they confound what they do.

The Longitudinal Design

Issues to Consider

Longitudinal design Design in which the same group of people is studied repeatedly.

Panel design Another term used to label a longitudinal design.

- What are the characteristics of a longitudinal design?
- What are its assets and its limitations?

The **longitudinal design** (also known as a **panel design**) in-

volves observing the same group of people at more than one point in time. The main asset of this approach is that because the same people are studied over time, the similarities or changes in behavior across their development can be directly ascertained. If we did not repeatedly observe the same people, through use of longitudinal observations, we would not be able to know if and how a given behavior seen in a person early in life may be expressed by that same person later in life. Without longitudinal measurement, we would not know whether behavior stays the same or changes in a person. However, this asset of the longitudinal method leads directly to some limitations.

Table A-1	Some Characteristics of Longitudinal, Cross-Sectional, and Time-Lag Designs of Developmental Research	
Design	**Study Involves:**	**Confounded Components of Developmental Change**
Longitudinal	One birth cohort	Age with time
Cross sectional	One time of measurement	Age with birth cohort
Time lag	One age	Time with birth cohort

It obviously takes a relatively long time to do some longitudinal studies. If researchers wanted, for instance, to do a longitudinal study of personality development from birth through late adolescence, they would have to devote about 20 years of their own lives to such an endeavor. Such a commitment would be expensive, as well as time consuming, and thus relatively few long-term longitudinal studies have been done (e.g., see Jones, 1958; Kagan & Moss, 1962; Livson & Peskin, 1980; Thomas & Chess, 1977).

Other limitations of longitudinal studies pertain to the nature of the people studied and to problems with the measurements that may be used. Not everyone would be willing to be a participant in a study that required their continual observation over the course of many months or years of their lives. Hence samples tend to be small in such studies. Those people who are willing to take part may not be representative of most people. Thus longitudinal studies often involve unrepresentative, or "biased," samples of people. Results of such studies may not be easily applied, or "generalized," to a broader population; that is, such studies may not be externally valid. In addition, longitudinal samples typically become increasingly biased as the study continues. Some people drop out of the group, and we cannot assume the remaining people are identical to the former group. After all, the people who stay may be different just by virtue of the fact that they continue to participate.

Another problem with longitudinal studies is that after some time people may become accustomed to the tests of their behavior. They may learn "how to respond," or they may respond differently than they would if they had never been exposed to the test. Hence the meaning of a particular test to the participants may be altered over time through the repeated use of the instrument with the same sample. Such an occurrence would make it difficult to say the same variable was actually being measured at different times in the participants' lives.

Often the purpose of using a longitudinal design is to ascertain the developmental time course for a particular type of behavior or psychological function. Researchers also want information that they may apply to understanding development about future generations of people. Yet a longitudinal study is only studying people who are born in one historical era and who are measured at certain points in time. It is unclear whether findings about this one cohort can be generalized to people in other cohorts.

Thus a confounding of age and time occurs during such a study. Because a longitudinal design involves assessing one particular cohort of people (for example, a group of males and females born in 1975), such people can be age 15 at only one time of measurement (1990 in this case). Thus their behavior at age 15 may be due to age-related phenomena or to phenomena present at the time of measurement (or to both). Similarly, members of one birth cohort can only be age 20 at one time of measurement. Thus, as noted in Table A.1, age and time are confounded in a longitudinal study. One does not know if results of a longitudinal study can be applied to other 15- or 20-year-olds who are measured at other times.

Hence the findings about development gained from a longitudinal study reflect age-related changes, *or*, alternatively, they may reflect only characteristics of people born and studied at particular points in time. One does not know in a longitudinal study whether the findings are due to universal rules, or "laws," of development (i.e., rules that describe a person's development no matter when it occurs), *or* to particular times the participants are measured, *or* to some combination of all these influences. Because of such problems, alternatives to the longitudinal method are often used.

The Cross-Sectional Design

Issues to Consider
- What are the characteristics of a cross-section design?
- What are its assets and its limitations?

The most widely used developmental research design is the **cross-sectional design.** Here different groups of people are studied at one point in time, and hence all observations can be completed relatively quickly. The design is less expensive than longitudinal research and requires less time. Because of these characteristics, some have argued that the method allows for a more efficiently derived description of development. However, cross-sectional research has important limitations.

If we wanted to study the development of aggression in individuals who range in age from 2 to 20 years, we could use the cross-sectional method. Instead of observing one group of people every year, for example, for 18 years, we could observe groups of individuals at each age between 2 and 20 at one point in time. The first group of people would be 2-year-olds, a second group would be 3-year-olds, and so on, through the last group, which would be 20-year-olds.

However, it is difficult to fully and adequately control for all variables that may affect behavior differences. We may not be certain whether differences between the various age groups are reflections of real age changes or merely reflections of the groups not being really identical to begin with.

Sometimes the researcher attempts to match the individuals on a number of important variables other than age (e.g., race, father's or mother's educational background, income level, or type of housing) to ensure some degree of comparability. However, such comparability is difficult to achieve. Moreover, although it is possible to get less biased, more representative samples for cross-sectional research than for longitudinal studies (people cooperate more readily because they are only committed to be observed or interviewed once), such better sampling may still not lead to a useful description of the components of developmental change. This failure occurs because of a flaw in the rationale for the use of a cross-sectional method instead of a longitudinal one.

Cross-sectional design Design in which people of different ages are studied at one time of measurement.

The expectation in some cross-sectional studies is that they yield results comparable to those obtained from studying the same group of people over time, and do so more efficiently, as long as the only differences among cross-sectional groups are their ages. However, despite how adequately participants are matched, it is rarely the case that the results of cross-sectional and longitudinal studies are consistent (Schaie & Strother, 1968).

For example, when studying intellectual development with a cross-sectional design, most researchers report that highest performance occurs in the early 20s or 30s and considerable decreases in performance levels occur after this period (e.g., Horn & Cattell, 1966). With longitudinal studies of these same variables, however, often no decrease in performance is seen at all. In fact, some studies (e.g., Bayley & Olden, 1955) have found some increase in performance levels into the 50s. As has been pointed out, the characteristics of the participants typically used in the longitudinal design may be considerably different from those of the participants used in the cross-sectional study.

Longitudinal studies, as we have noted, may be composed of a select sample to begin with, and as the study proceeds, some people will drop out of the research. Such attrition may not be random. Rather, it may be due to the fact that the participants of lower intellectual ability leave the study. Hence, in the example of research on intellectual development, this bias could account for lack of decreases in level of performance. In addition, as Schaie and Strother (1968) point out, these longitudinal studies have not assessed intellectual development in the 60s and 70s, the age periods during which the greatest performance decreases have been seen in the cross-sectional studies (e.g., Jones, 1959). Thus comparisons of the age-associated changes found with the two methods are not appropriate.

Cross-sectional samples have not escaped criticism, however. Schaie (1959) has argued that such samples do not give the researcher a good indication of age-associated changes because it is difficult to control for extraneous variables in the samples used to represent people of widely different age ranges.

Although these arguments may be appropriately used to reconcile the discrepancies (or perhaps to explain them away), Schaie (1965) suggests that these arguments miss an essential point: They do not show a recognition of an essential *methodological* problem involved in the consideration of longitudinal and cross-sectional designs. Just as longitudinal studies are confounded (between age and time), cross-sectional studies also are confounded. As seen in Table A.1, the confounding is between age and cohort. Because the two types of studies involve different confounding, it is unlikely they will reveal the same results.

The confounding of age and cohort that exists in cross-sectional studies occurs because at any one time of measurement (e.g., 1990) people who are of different ages can only be so because they were born in different years. To be 20 in 1990, one has to have been born in 1970; to be 25 at this time of measurement, one has to be a member of the 1965 birth cohort. Consequently, because cross-sectional studies focus only on one time of measurement, there is no way of telling whether differences between age groups are due to age-related changes or to differences associated with being born in historically different eras.

The Time-Lag Design

Issues to Consider
- What are the characteristics of a time-lag design?
- What are its assets and its limitations?

Although not as frequently used in research as the cross-sectional or longitudinal designs, the **time-lag design** allows a researcher to see differences in behavior associated with particular ages at various times in history. Ir contrast to focusing on one cohort or one time of measurement, the time-lag design considers only one age level and looks at characteristics associated with being a particular age at different times in history. For example, when the focus of research is to discern the characteristics associated with being a particular age (e.g., 15 years old) at different times of measurement (e.g., 1960, 1970, 1980, and 1990), a time-lag design is implied.

Of course, such a design involves cross sections of people and has all the problems of control, matching, and sampling associated with such designs. But there are also additional problems. As indicated in Table A.1, because only one age is studied at different times, the different groups are members of different birth cohorts. Thus, in a time-lag

design, time and birth cohort are confounded, and we do not know, for example, whether the behaviors of 12-year-olds studied at two points in time are associated with events acting on all people—no matter what their age—at a particular test time *or* are due to historical events associated with membership in a specific cohort.

In sum, the three types of conventional designs of developmental research do not allow for the unconfounded assessment of the contributions of the three components of developmental change. Because of these shortcomings, it is difficult to decide which method gives a more useful depiction of developmental changes. Each method may potentially introduce serious, but different, distortions into measures of developmental changes. This is perhaps the major reason why information about developmental changes derived from the three techniques often is not consistent (Schaie & Strother, 1968). Although each design has some advantages, the problem of each places limitations on the ability of developmental researchers to describe adequately how individual, sociocultural, or historical influences can influence change.

This point might lead some to conclude that a bleak picture exists for the study of human development because the three conventional designs of developmental research have some methodological problems. But, of course, *no research method is without its limitation.* As such, our view is that *all* the conventional methods of developmental research may be used to enhance understanding *if* they are employed with a recognition of their limitations. These limitations, however, can be transcended, as we describe in the following section. Although these other methods also have their limitations (e.g., they typically require large samples of people and are quite expensive to implement), they offer a useful alternative to traditional approaches.

Sequential Strategies of Design

Issues to Consider
- What are the sequential designs?
- What are their strengths?
- What limits the use of these designs?

Due to the influence of K. Warner Schaie (1965), Paul B.

Time-lag design Design in which people of the same age are studied at different times in history.

MEET THE RESEARCHER BOX A.1

JOHN R. NESSELROADE
MODELING DEVELOPMENTAL PROCESS AND CHANGE

As developmental researchers have become more and more sophisticated in the way they ask their questions regarding change at both the individual and the context levels, the methods by which the answers are sought have also undergone remarkable transformation. Mathematical and statistical modeling are general mainstays of quantitative, rational science. In each disciplinary context, however, specialized applications of quantitative methods that usefully reflect the current levels of theory, concept definition, measurement, and so on, need to be evaluated and disseminated. In the past 30 years or so, for instance, we have witnessed a striking rise in the application of multivariate "thinking" and methods to the study of development. Much of my own career has been devoted to the creation and elaboration of rigorous methods of multivariate analysis by which the study of development could be better carried out.

Nearly three decades ago, my colleagues and I (Baltes, Reese, & Nesselroade, 1977) opined that the business of developmental psychology was to study intra-individual change patterns and inter-individual differences (and similarities) in those patterns of intra-individual change. In part, our arguments reflected the fact that not all of the interesting developmental questions could be answered by the methods of experimental psychology in which

John R. Nesselroade is Hugh Scott Hamilton Professor of Psychology at the University of Virginia. Previously, he was a faculty member at West Virginia University (Department of Psychology) and The Pennsylvania State University (Individual and Family Studies).

some important variables can be manipulated and others controlled by the researcher. The void created by the need to answer developmental questions that do not lend themselves to experimental manipulation has been increasingly filled by multivariate methodologies (e.g., structural equation modeling, latent growth curve modeling). These classes of models feature testing the goodness of fit between empirical data and theory-derived propositions regarding relationships among concepts and variables.

Even as the relatively sophisticated multivariate methods have settled into place among seasoned researchers and are being taught to new generations of graduate students, the attentive methodologist is hearing a new summons from several quarters. It is the call for rigorous methods of representing *dynamic* relationships in the patterning of changes in individual and in context. A major focus of my current work, which involves collaborations with Steve Boker (University of Notre Dame), Michael Browne (Ohio State University), Jack McArdle (University of Virginia), and Peter Molenaar (University of Amsterdam), is the development and testing of multivariate models that explicitly recognize the dynamic character of change and process. This is the future of developmental research methodology, but, more importantly, it is the future of developmental science in general.

Baltes (1968), and John R. Nesselroade (Nesselroade & Baltes, 1974), the problems of confounding involved in cross-sectional, longitudinal, and time-lag designs may be resolved. Some of John Nesselroade's recent work in regard to the methods used to study development is presented in Meet the Researcher Box A.1.

Schaie (1965) demonstrated how the conventional methods were part of a more **general developmental model.** Presentation of this model allowed him to offer a new type of approach to designing developmental research: sequential methods.

> **General developmental model** Conception guiding the design of developmental research which involves the idea that designs must unconfound variation associated with age, time of measurement, and cohort.
>
> **Multivariate** Many variables.

Sequential methods combine features of longitudinal and cross-sectional designs and allow the researcher to assess the relative contributions of age, cohort, and time in one study, and to know what differences (or portion of the differences) between groups are due to age differences, to cohort (historical) differences, or to time of testing differences. In addition, a sequential design allows these sources of differences to be ascertained in a relatively short period of time.

Research based on sequential designs is complex, due in part to the usual involvement of **multivariate** (many variable) statistical analyses and the numerous measurements that have to be taken of different groups. But a simplified example of such a design may be offered. It will suggest how use of such a design allows the developmental researcher to avoid the potential confounding involved with traditional cross-sectional and longitudinal approaches.

Basically, a **sequential design** involves the remeasurement of a cross-sectional sample of people after a given, fixed interval of time has passed. A researcher selects a cross-sectional sample composed of various cohorts and measures each cohort longitudinally (with the provision that each set of measurements occurs at about the same point in time for each cohort). In other words, this design calls for obtaining repeated measures from each of the different cohort groups included in a given cross-sectional sample and, as well, for obtaining data from "retest" control groups to assess effects of retesting. For example, if three times of testing are included as the longitudinal component of the design, then control cohort groups (for instance, assessed only at the third testing time) may be used to control for any retesting effects. The researcher is thus in a position to make statements about the relative influences of age, cohort, and times of measurement on any observed developmental changes in the results.

Cross-sectional and longitudinal sequences consist of sequences of either simple cross-sectional or longitudinal designs. The successive application of these strategies permits us to describe the extent to which behavior change is associated with age-related or history-related influences. Figure A.1 provides a contrast between the simple and sequential strategies. The top portion of the figure shows the simple cross-sectional and longitudinal designs described earlier; the bottom portion of the figure shows the two sequential strategies. Cross-sectional sequences involve successions of two or more cross-sectional studies completed at different times of measurement. Longitudinal sequences involve successions of longitudinal studies begun at different times of measurement. The strategies differ in that cross-sectional sequences involve independent measures on different individuals, and longitudinal sequences involve repeated measures of the same individuals. In practice, one can apply both strategies simultaneously. In any event, the application of sequential strategies permits the discrimination of within- and between-cohort sources of change.

To see how this works, consider a sample design of such a sequential study (presented in Table A.2 and recast in the form of a matrix in Figure A.2). Different

Student protests were ubiquitous during the Vietnam War.

cohort levels are composed of different groups of people born at different historical periods (1954, 1955, 1956, or 1957). Thus, at the time of the first testing (1970 for this design), the study has the attributes of a cross-sectional study. Indeed, there are three such cross-sectional studies in this particular design, one for each time of measurement (see Figure A.2). However, the sequential feature is introduced when these same participants are again measured in 1971 and 1972. Thus for each cohort there is now a longitudinal study. As seen in Figure A.2, each cohort in a sequential design of this sort is involved in its own short-term longitudinal study (there are four of these in the design shown in Figure A.2). Additionally, note that the diagonals of the design matrix of Figure A.2 represent time-lag studies; people of the same age are studied at different times. Thus a sequential study involves all combinations of observations of other designs in one integrated matrix of observations.

With such a matrix, the researcher can answer a number of questions involving the potentially interrelated influences of cohort, age, and time. Referring to Table A.2

Sequential designs Designs in which cross-sectional samples are studied longitudinally.

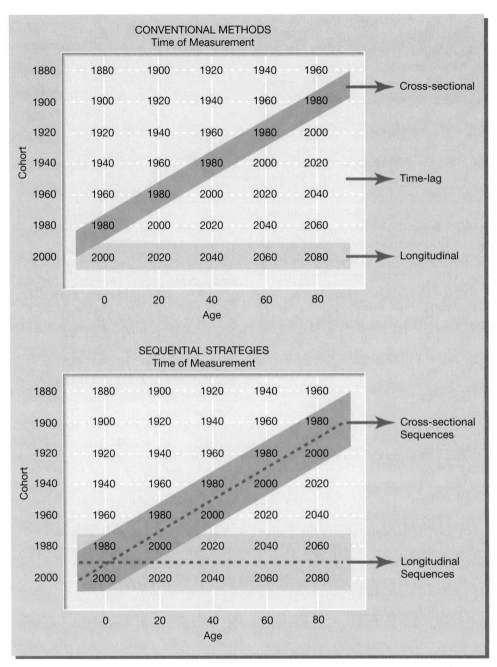

Figure A.1
Illustration of simple cross-sectional, longitudinal, and time-lag designs (top) and cross-sectional and longitudinal sequences (bottom). (*Source*: Baltes, Reese, & Nesselroade, 1977.)

and Figure A.2, if, for example, the cohort composed of people born in 1955 underwent changes between times of measurement 1 and 2 and were found to be different at age 16 from the people in the 1954 cohort group when they were 16, then there must be some historical difference between these two cohort levels. In other words, if differences were due simply to age-related changes, one should see the same performance for every cohort group, no matter when measured. If only age-related

| Table A-2 | The Design of a Sequential Study | | | | | | |

Birth Cohort	Time of Measurement 1	Age at Time 1	Time of Measurement 2	Age at Time 2	Time of Measurement 3	Age at Time 3	Time of Measurement of Retest Control Group	Age of Control Group
1957	1970	13	1971	14	1972	15	1972	15
1956	1970	14	1971	15	1972	16	1972	16
1955	1970	15	1971	16	1972	17	1972	17
1954	1970	16	1971	17	1972	18	1972	18

changes matter, then people of the same age should perform the same no matter what cohort they are from or when they are measured. A younger cohort group should perform similarly to that of an older cohort group as members of each group age *if* there were no historical differences between cohorts and if time of testing did not matter. Again from Table A.2 and Figure A.2, the 1957 cohort should show a level of performance on its second measurement comparable to that of the first measurement for the 1956 cohort *if* there were no historical differences between the generations.

In turn, if time of testing were a source of change, then people should respond the same despite their age or cohort. If events in 1972 were

the strongest influence on behavior, then one should see that people of all cohorts represented in Table A.2 and Figure A.2 respond the same way.

Finally, of course, if birth cohort was of most importance, then people of a particular cohort should respond in a given way no matter what age they are and no matter at what time they are measured. As illustrated by the example of children born in the Great Depression (Elder, 1974), membership in a particular cohort would override influences due to age or time of measurement.

Additionally, note that by including groups of participants to be tested for the first time at the end of the study (see Table A.2), sequential research provides a basis of assessing the issue of repeated

Figure A.2
The design of a sequential study put into the form of a matrix.

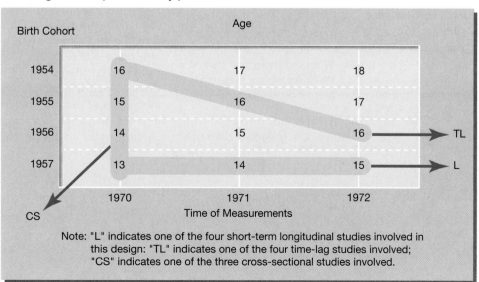

Note: "L" indicates one of the four short-term longitudinal studies involved in this design; "TL" indicates one of the four time-lag studies involved; "CS" indicates one of the three cross-sectional studies involved.

use of the measuring instruments, noted earlier. If participants in the core sample did not respond differently as a consequence of their having been repeatedly measured (for example, by the same tests of personality or IQ), then their behavior at the end of the study should be comparable to a group of participants matched in every way with them except for the fact that no repeated testing was given. If there are differences, however, between the core sample and these "retest" controls, then statistical techniques are available to researchers to measure the effects of retesting (Nesselroade & Baltes, 1974).

Despite the complexity of data analysis, and the more complex research design and reasoning process associated with it, sequential methodology has desirable attributes not associated with other techniques. It allows for the unconfounding of the components of developmental change functions in one research effort. As such, it allows the contributions of variables associated with multiple levels of influence to be evaluated adequately.

In fact, although sequential research studies are relatively few in number, the design illustrated in Table A.2 and Figure A.2 was used because it corresponds to the one employed by Nesselroade and Baltes (1974) in their classic sequential study of adolescent personality development (see Applications Box A.1).

Conclusions

Issues to Consider
- Why must all research about development be ethical and humane?

  - What are important standards for ethical research in human development?

Ethical standards Principles for the humane, caring, and responsible treatment of participants in research.

Scientists interested in the study of adolescent develop-ment have available to them a wide array of procedures for making systematic and purposeful observations. Moreover, there are several different designs of developmental research, and these observational plans afford the scientist several choices about how to make his or her observations of adolescent behavior and/or development systematic.

However, across all procedures used by developmental scientists, care must be taken to treat the participants of their research—youth, their parents and other family members, and all people involved in the lives of adolescents—in a humane, caring, and responsible manner. In other words, researchers must follow ethical principles when they work with youth and the other people in their social world (Fisher, 1993, 1994, 1997; Fisher & Brennan, 1992; Fisher & Fyrberg, 1994; Fisher et al., 1996a, 1996b; Fisher, Hoagwood, & Jensen, 1996; Fisher & Tryon, 1990). Applications Box A.2 (see page 396) presents the **ethical standards** for research with children followed by the Society for Research in Child Development (1999).

In summary, across this textbook I have discussed how adolescents living in today's complex society experience a world where opportunities are more abundant than ever before in history and yet, at the same time, where risks are rampant, poverty pervasive, and routes to positive life outcomes not equally available to all youth. To understand and enhance the life chances of all youth requires that scientists use their research (methodological) abilities to devise means to apply developmental science in the service of promoting civil society (Fisher et al. 1993; Fisher & Lerner, 1994; Lerner, Sparks, & McCubbin, 1999).

With such an applied developmental science, scholarship in adolescence may do more than support the wise observation made by the famous psychologist Kurt Lewin (1943), more than a half century ago, that nothing is as practical as a good theory. Such scholarship may also demonstrate that nothing is of greater value to society than a science devoted to using its expertise to improve the life chances of all young people.

applications box A.1

The Nesselroade and Baltes (1974) Sequential Study of Adolescent Personality Development

Noting that most conceptions of adolescent personality development suggest that age-related progressions are influential in this period of life, Nesselroade and Baltes (1974) argued that historical (cohort) and specific sociocultural (time) influences may also be involved. As such, they applied a sequential design to see how these three components contributed to changes in personality in the period from 1970 to 1972.

About 1,800 West Virginian male and female adolescents were measured in 1970, 1971, and 1972. These adolescents were from birth cohorts 1954 to 1957, and thus, as in Table A.2 and Figure A.2, ranged in age at the time of first measurement from 13 to 16. Personality questionnaires and measures of intelligence were administered to these participants.

Contrary to what is stressed by those theorists who focus on organismic components of adolescent development (e.g., Erik Erikson, 1968, and Anna Freud, 1969; see Chapter 2), Nesselroade and Baltes (1974) found that change at this time of life was quite responsive to sociocultural-historical influences. In fact, age per se was not found to be a very influential contributor to change. Rather, for these groups of adolescents developmental change was influenced more by 2-year historical period than by age-related sequences.

For instance, adolescents as a whole, *despite their age or birth cohort*, decreased in "superego strength," "socio-emotional anxiety," and achievement during the 1970 to 1972 period. Moreover, most adolescents, regardless of age or cohort, increased in independence during this period.

Accordingly, the Nesselroade and Baltes (1974) data show that it was the time at which all these differently aged adolescents were measured that was most influential in their changes. Perhaps due to the events in the society of that time (e.g., those associated with the Vietnam War), all adolescents performed similarly in regard to these personality domains. Despite where they were (in regard to age) on "entering" the 1970–1972 historical era, members of different cohorts changed in similar directions due to events surrounding them at the times they were tested.

Without sequential methodology, the role of the specific sociocultural setting on adolescents at that time could not have been suggested. This suggestion is supported by data derived from other sequential studies that have shown the influence of birth cohort on intellectual developments in children (Baltes, Baltes, & Reinert, 1970) and adults (Schaie, Labouvie, & Buech, 1973). These data imply that to understand developmental change, we should consider the dynamic interactions between individual and sociocultural-historical processes, a point emphasized in the developmental contextual view of human development. Indeed, sequential designs are of particular value in obtaining information pertinent to this view of development.

applications box A.2

Ethical Standards for Research with Children

The principles listed below were published in the 1990–91 Membership Directory of the Society for Research in Child Development, except for Principles 15 and 16 first published in the Fall 1991 editon of its *Newsletter.*

Principle 1. Non-harmful procedures: The investigator should use no research operation that may harm the child either physically or psychologically. The investigator is also obligated at all times to use the least stressful research operation whenever possible. Psychological harm in particular instances may be difficult to define; nevertheless its definition and means for reducing or eliminating it remain the responsibility of the investigator. When the investigator is in doubt about the possible harmful effects of the research operations, consultation should be sought from others. When harm seems inevitable, the investigator is obligated to find other means of obtaining the information or to abandon the research. Instances may, nevertheless, rise in which exposing the child to stressful conditions may be necessary if diagnostic or therapeutic benefits to the child are associated with the research. In such instances careful deliberation by an Institutional Review Board should be sought.

Principle 2. Informed consent: Before seeking consent or assent from the child, the investigator should inform the child of all features of the research that may affect his or her willingness to participate and should answer the child's questions in terms appropriate to the child's comprehension. The investigator should respect the child's freedom to choose to participate in the research or not by giving the child the opportunity to give or not give assent to participation as well as to choose to discontinue participation at any time. Assent means that the child shows some form of agreement to participate without necessarily comprehending the full significance of the research necessary to give informed consent. Investigators working with infants should take special effort to explain the research procedures to the parents and be especially sensitive to any indicators of discomfort in the infant. In spite of the paramount importance of obtaining consent, instances can arise in which consent or any kind of contact with the participant would make the research impossible to carry out. Non-intrusive field research is a common example. Conceivably, such research can be car-

ried out ethically if it is conducted in public places, participants' anonymity is totally protected, and there are no foreseeable negative consequences to the participant. However, judgments on whether such research is ethical in particular circumstances should be made in consultation with an Institutional Review Board.

Principle 3. Parental consent: The informed consent of parents, legal guardians or those who act *in loco parentis* (e.g., teachers, superintendents of institutions) similarly should be obtained, preferably in writing. Informed consent requires that parents or other responsible adults be informed of all the features of the research that may affect their willingness to allow the child to participate. This information should include the profession and institution affiliation of the investigator. Not only should the right of the responsible adults to refuse consent be respected, but they should be informed that they may refuse to participate without incurring any penalty to them or to the child.

Principle 4. Additional consent: The informed consent of any persons, such as school teachers for example, whose interaction with the child is the subject of the study should also be obtained. As with the child and parents or guardians, informed consent requires that the persons interacting with the child during the study be informed of all features of the research which may affect their willingness to participate. All questions posed by such persons should be answered and the persons should be free to choose to participate or not, and to discontinue participation at any time.

Principle 5. Incentives: Incentives to participate in a research project must be fair and must not unduly exceed the range of incentives that the child normally experiences. Whatever incentives are used, the investigator should always keep in mind that the greater the possible effects of the investigation on the child, the greater is the obligation to protect the child's welfare and freedom.

Principle 6. Deception: Although full disclosure of information during the procedure of obtaining consent is the ethical ideal, a particular study may necessitate withholding certain information or deception. Whenever withholding information or deception is judged to be essential to the conduct of the study, the investigator should satisfy research colleagues that such judgment is correct. If withholding information or deception is practiced, and there is reason to believe that the research participants will be negatively affected by it, adequate measures should be taken after the study to ensure the participant's understanding of the reasons for the deception. Investigators whose research is dependent upon deception should make an effort to employ deception methods that have no known negative effects on the child or the child's family.

Principle 7. Anonymity: To gain access to institutional records, the investigator should obtain permission from responsible authorities in charge of records. Anonymity of the information should be preserved and no information used other than that for which permission was obtained. It is the investigator's responsibility to ensure that responsible authorities do, in fact, have the confidence of the participant and that they bear some degree of responsibility in giving such permission.

Principle 8. Mutual responsibilities: From the beginning of each research investigation, there should be clear agreement between the investigator and the parents, guardians or those who act *in loco parentis,* and the child, when appropriate, that defines the responsibilities of each. The investigator has the obligation to honor all promises and commitments of the agreement.

Principle 9. Jeopardy: When, in the course of research, information comes to the investigator's attention that may jeopardize the child's well-being, the investigator has a responsibility to discuss the information with the parents or guardians and with those expert in the field in order that they may arrange the necessary assistance for the child.

Principle 10. Unforeseen consequences: When research procedures result in undesirable consequences for the participant that were previously unforeseen, the investigator should immediately employ appropriate measures to correct these consequences, and should redesign the procedures if they are to be included in subsequent studies.

Principle 11. Confidentiality: The investigator should keep in confidence all information obtained about research participants. The participants' identity should be concealed in written and verbal reports of the results, as well as in informal discussion with students and colleagues. When a possibility exists that others may gain access to such information, this possibility, together with the plans for protecting confidentiality, should be explained to the participants as part of the procedure of obtaining informed consent.

Principle 12. Informing participants: Immediately after the data are collected, the investigator should clarify for the research participant any misconceptions that may have arisen. The investigator also recognizes a duty to report general findings to participants in terms appropriate to their understanding. Where scientific or humane values justify withholding information, every effort should be made so that withholding the information has no damaging consequences for the participant.

Principle 13. Reporting results: Because the investigator's words may carry unintended weight with parents and children, caution should be exercised in reporting results, making evaluative statements, or giving advice.

Principle 14. Implications of findings: Investigators should be mindful of the social, political and human implications of their research and should be especially careful in the presentation of findings from the research. This principle, however, in no way denies investigators the right to pursue any area of research or the right to observe proper standards of scientific reporting.

Principle 15. Scientific misconduct: Misconduct is defined as the fabrication or falsification of data, plagiarism, misrepresentation, or other practices that seriously deviate from those that are commonly accepted within the scientific community for proposing, conducting, analyzing, or reporting research. It does not include unintentional errors or honest differences in interpretation of data.

The Society shall provide vigorous leadership in the pursuit of scientific investigation which is based on the integrity of the investigator and the honesty of research and will not tolerate the presence of scientific misconduct among its members. It shall be the responsibility of the voting members of Governing Council to reach a decision about the possible expulsion of members found guilty of scientific misconduct.

Principle 16. Personal misconduct: Personal misconduct that results in a criminal conviction of a felony may be sufficient grounds for a member's expulsion from the Society. The relevance of the crime to the purposes of the Society should be considered by the Governing Council in reaching a decision about the matter. It shall be the responsibility of the voting members of Governing Council to reach a decision about the possible expulsion of members found guilty of personal misconduct.

Source: Society for Research in Child Development, 1999.

Summary

- The scientific method refers to procedures used by researchers to assure that their observations are accurate and able to be verified by other researchers.

- Science is only one route to knowledge. However, scientific knowledge involves the use of the scientific method to obtain and verify knowledge.

- The most basic characteristic of the scientific method is empiricism. All science rests on making observations about the topic (the subject matter) one wants to know about (e.g., chemicals, planets, or adolescent behavior).

- Other characteristics of the scientific method are having a purpose for one's observations and making observations systematically (according to a specific plan).

- If scientists' systematic and purposeful observations are accurate, then other scientists should be able to replicate their observations.

- To enable replication scientists must communicate their observations, which enables science to be a self-correcting means of obtaining knowledge.

- After information is communicated and replicated or corrected, it can be added to the body of knowledge in an area of science. Such addition means science is a cumulative endeavor.

- Four major types of observational methods are used to study human development: naturalistic observation, controlled observation, experimental observation, and observation through the use of questionnaires, interviews, and surveys.

- When using naturalistic observation a researcher attempts to view behavior as it exists in its actual real-life setting. Such observations are therefore ecologically valid.

- Controlled observations can be used to increase the likelihood of viewing the behavior of interest. In controlled observation, the researcher controls and manipulates the situation within which the person is observed. However, the people in the situation are not directly influenced or manipulated.

- In a controlled experiment the researcher selects the observational setting and the quantity or quality of the events presented to research participants.

- The condition that the researcher selects to vary in an experiment is termed the *independent variable*. The behavior that is studied in the experiment is termed the *dependent variable*.

- Although enabling statements to be made about the influence of particular variables on particular behaviors among specific people studied in a specific situation, the results of controlled experiments may not necessarily be applied to other situations. They do not have ecological validity.

- Questionnaires and interviews use written and /or oral reports about behavior; these techniques do not directly observe the behavior of interest.

- Advantages of such techniques include the ability to collect a lot of information about one or several behaviors, from one or from large groups of people, in relatively efficient ways. Another advantage is the opportunity to collect information about behaviors (e.g., ones regarding sexual intimacy or voting behavior) that may not be easily or ethically available to a researcher.

- Disadvantages of such techniques include a possible lack of correspondence between reports about behavior and actual behavior and tendencies by participants to give researchers the answers they believe are being sought in the study.

- Techniques exist to assess if people are lying on questionnaires or in interviews.

- Because change can only be assessed across time, to study developmental researchers must develop a plan, or a design, for their observations that involves two or more times of observation.

- Developmental changes may be associated with variation in the age or stage of life of a person. These sort of changes may be labeled *age variation*.

- Variation may be associated also with the period in history when the person was born: People born at different historical times are in different birth cohorts, and there may be variation in the experiences of such groups. These sort of changes may be labeled *cohort variation*.

- Events occurring in the lives of people at the time that they are observed may also affect changes in their development. These sort of changes may be labeled *time* (of measurement) *variation*.

- Three designs of observation have been used traditionally to study human development: longitudinal, cross-sectional, and time-lag designs. A fourth time of design, described by K. Warner Schaie, is sequential designs.

- A confound in a research design occurs when the influence of one variable cannot be separated from the influence of another variable. Each of the three traditional designs of developmental research involves a confounding among two of the three sources of variation (age, cohort, and time) in development.

- A longitudinal (or panel) design involves repeatedly observing the same group of people. This design allows changes within people (intraindividual change) to be studied.

- In a cross-sectional design people of different ages are studied at the same point in time.

- In a time-lag design, people of the same age are observed at different times of measurement. As in cross-sectional designs, only differences between groups can be measured.
- Sequential designs combine features of longitudinal, cross-sectional, and time-lag designs. Cross-sectional groups of people are studied longitudinally. A longitudinal sequential design involves observing the same group of people from each cross-sectional group and therefore enables intraindividual change to be measured. Cross-sectional sequential designs involve observing different samples of people from the same birth cohort at each measurement time, and therefore enable only interindividual differences to be measured. In addition, such designs often include control groups to ascertain the effects of repeated testing.
- In all research, developmental scientists must be certain that they treat participants ethically and humanely. The Society for Research in Child Development offers a set of ethical standards for research with children that all people conducting human development research should follow.

Discussion Topics

1. Reflect on what you know and believe to be true. How much of your knowledge and beliefs rests on empirical observation? How much of what you believe do you accept on faith?

2. Does information from a research study have to correspond to what can be seen in the real world to be true? Would you believe the results of a study of adolescent development if the findings could only be demonstrated in a controlled experimental situation?

3. Would you volunteer to participate in a controlled observational study? What about an experiment or study using a questionnaire, interview, or survey? Do you think people from all walks of life would be willing to participate as much, less, or more than you? How might such willingness to participate in developmental research affect what we know about adolescence?

4. Why might cross-sectional, time-lag, and longitudinal studies attract different sorts of people as volunteers? What sorts of motivation might be required to remain in a longitudinal study for 20 or 30 years? Would all people who participate in a cross-sectional study be likely to have this motivation? Does it make a difference if they do not?

5. Much developmental research is supported by governmental grants, that is, from taxpayers' money. Are the results of longitudinal or sequential research worth their greater cost (as compared to cross-sectional research)?

6. Have you participated in a research study? Do you believe you were treated ethically and humanely? How do your experiences correspond to the experiences of others you know? What might be done to improve the ethical treatment of research participants? Does the age of the participant affect your answer? How so? Why?

Key Terms

birth cohort (p. 385)
cohort (p. 385)
confounding (p. 385)
controls (p. 382)
cross-sectional design (p. 388)
dependent variable (p. 382)
design (p. 385)
ecological validity (p. 380)

empirical (p. 378)
ethical standards (p. 394)
general developmental model (p. 390)
independent variable (p. 382)
longitudinal design (p. 386)
manipulation (p. 381)
multivariate (p. 390)

norm (p. 381)
panel design (p. 386)
psychological test (p. 381)
replicable (p. 379)
scientific method (p. 378)
sequential designs (p. 391)
time-lag design (p. 389)
variable (p. 382)

GLOSSARY

Ability grouping Placing students in a classroom based on their academic ability. [p. 269]

Accommodation Piagetian term used to define process of changing already existing knowledge to fit external stimulation. With assimilation, part of the equilibration process. [pp. 48, 91]

Acculturation Process of cultural change during which a member/group of one culture gives up his or her/their own values and customs and adopts those from a different culture. [p. 197]

Active leisure activities Free time events that require a large expenditure of energy by the participant. [p. 282]

Adaptive functioning Development that responds to biological, psychological, and social influences in ways that are healthy, positive, and successful. [p. 12]

Adolescence Period of transition spanning the second decade of life during which a person's biological, psychological, and social characteristics undergo change in an interrelated manner and the person goes from being childlike to adultlike. [p. 4]

Adolescent egocentrism Term introduced by Elkind in 1967 to label problems in adolescents' thoughts; the belief that others are preoccupied with them and that they are unique individuals. [p. 96]

Adulthood Stage 7 of Erikson's psychosocial theory. Involves a crisis between developing a sense of generativity versus stagnation. [p. 46]

Advantage index Index formed by scoring children on the basis of the absence of risk factors (such as factors pertinent to poverty) and the presence of more favorable circumstances in the children's lives. [p. 125]

AIDS (Acquired Immune Deficiency Syndrome) Condition of acquired deficiency of the immune system caused by the presence of a retrovirus. [p. 237]

Amenorrhea Failure to menstruate. [p. 76]

Anal musculature stage Stage 2 of Erikson's psychosocial theory. Involves a crisis between developing toward a sense of autonomy versus a sense of shame and doubt. [p. 45]

Anal stage Second psychosexual stage as defined by Freud. Occurs during second and third years of life, when the libido centers in the anal area. Gratification is obtained through exercising anal muscles, expelling or holding bowel movements. [p. 42]

Androgens Male sex hormones associated with the development of secondary sexual characteristics in boys. [p. 62]

Anorexia nervosa Eating disorder characterized by low body weight due to a person's misperception of his or her body image and by the mistaken belief that he or she is overweight. [p. 77]

Anxiety Unpleasant feeling state associated with such reactions as dread, fear, general uneasiness, or panic. [p. 299]

Applied developmental science Approach that uses research about human development to promote positive changes in individuals, families, and communities. [pp. 24, 33]

Assets (Developmental assets) Resources of a person (e.g., commitment to learning), a family (e.g., caring attitudes toward children), and a community (e.g., social support) that are needed for positive youth development. [p. 121]

Assimilation Piagetian term to define process of changing external stimulation to fit already existing knowledge. With accommodation, part of the equilibration process. [pp. 48, 91]

Attitudes Mental structures that have both an emotional and a cognitive component. [p. 244]

Authoritarian parenting Parenting marked by lack of warmth and rigid adherence to the rules set by parents. Authoritarian parents emphasize their power in the family and tend to use physical punishment. [p. 195]

400

Authoritative parenting Parenting marked by parental warmth and the use of rules and reasoning to promote obedience and keep discipline. Authoritative parents use nonphysical punishment and maintain consistency between their statements and actions across time. [p. 195]

Average reputation Peer reputation characterized by not showing extreme numbers of either positive or negative nominations. [p. 212]

Best practice Set of procedures or program attributes believed to be most effective in constituting a good program. [p. 340]

Birth cohort Group of people who share a common birth year. [p. 385]

Bulimia Eating disorder characterized by self-induced binge eating and purging behavior. [p. 77]

Burnouts Students who reject the school as a center for their social life. [p. 284]

Castration anxiety Boy's fear that father will punish him for his affections for his mother by performing castration. Fear leads boy to alter affection and turn to identify with father. [p. 43]

CDC (Centers for Disease Control) U.S. agency that works on promoting public health by looking at trends and researching the prevention and control of diseases, injuries, and disabilities. [p. 240]

Centration In Piaget's theory, a focus on one's own point of view, which involves therefore a lack of balance between assimilation and accommodation. [p. 96]

Civil society Society in which cultural and political values, as well as all nongovernmental and governmental institutions, both provide rights to people and require responsibilities of individuals. [p. 109]

Clique Subdivision of a crowd in which a set of three or more people with a key common identity or interest form a tightly knit and often exclusive group. [p. 213]

Cognitive reorganization Changes in the way a person thinks or reasons. [p. 17]

Cohort Group of people experiencing an event in common. [p. 385]

Comorbidity Simultaneous occurrence of two or more problem or risk behaviors or symptoms (e.g., violence and substance abuse often occur together). [p. 298]

Compensation Investing additional resources or substituting or applying additional means, geared toward the maintenance of functioning when the pathways youth follow to reach their goals fail. [p. 30]

Compulsory education System mandating that children and adolescents attend school up to a certain age. [p. 257]

Concrete operational stage Third stage of cognitive development as defined by Piaget. The child is capable of internalized, reversible actions. [p. 48]

Conditional reasoning Type of deductive reasoning, characterized by "if p, then q" statements. [p. 93]

Confounding Situation in research in which the influence of one variable on behavior cannot be separated from the influence of another variable on behavior. [p. 385]

Conscience Component of the superego that represents the internalization of society's standards, ethics, and morals. [p. 43]

Conspecifics Organisms that are members of the same species. [p. 195]

Context Environments in which an individual exists such as family, school, work, and culture. [p. 6]

"Continuous growth" Developmental path through adolescence characterized by smooth, nonabrupt change. [p. 19]

Controls Variables that a researcher holds constant in a research study because of their presumed potential to influence the dependent variable. [p. 382]

Controversial reputation Peer reputation characterized by receiving a lot of positive nominations and a lot of negative nominations. [p. 212]

Conventional morality Second level of moral development as defined by Kohlberg. The individual is bound by issues of the good-person orientation and is concerned with upholding social order and the institutional maintenance of morality. [p. 49]

Cooperative Extension System (CES) offices Offices, usually located in each county in a state, that coordinate the community-based programs of the land-grant university in that state; these programs pertain to youth, families, community and economic development, and agricultural issues. [p. 348]

Correlative transformation Process of thinking of all aspects of a problem by relating them to other problems. [p. 92]

Critical period Time in life when particular developments must occur if development is to proceed normally. [p. 45]

Cross-cultural variation Differences in values, beliefs, attitudes, and actions that occur between societies. [p. 19]

Cross-sectional design Design in which people of different ages are studied at one time of measurement. [p. 388]

Cross-sectional study Study that assesses a particular variable (e.g., youth-parent relations) at one point in time (e.g., during the year 2000). Often, different age groups are studied at this point in time. [p. 182]

Crowd (liaison) Collective group of similarly stereotyped individuals who may or may not spend time together. [p. 213]

Culturally conditioned Ideas, views, beliefs, attitudes, or values engendered by the social, cultural, and historical environment in which we live. [p. 16]

Deductive reasoning Type of reasoning that begins with a set of statements (premises) used to infer if another statement (conclusion) is valid. [p. 94]

Defense mechanisms Developed by the ego to take the pressures imposed by the id and place them into the unconscious part of the mind. [p. 46]

Delayed puberty Being behind schedule, for a given age group, in reaching puberty. [p. 76]

Dependent variable Behavior shown in response to the presentation of the independent variable. [p. 382]

Depression Emotional problem characterized by listlessness, lethargy, a blunting of affect, and disengagement from social activity. [p. 299]

Design Plan for the observation of behavior. [p. 385]

Developmental systems theories Theories which stress that development occurs as a consequence of organized and mutually influential relations among different levels of organization (e.g., biology, society, culture, history). [p. 32]

Developmental tasks Behavior that must be achieved at a particular age or stage in order for adaptive development to occur. [pp. 10, 134]

Developmental trajectories Individual's path through life as influenced by combinations of biology, psychology, and context unique to each person. [p. 6]

Disequilibration Cognitive process that occurs when our cognitive schemas (structures) are not in an agreement with one another, when there is an imbalance between assimilation and accommodation. [p. 91]

Display behaviors Actions designed to enhance one's attractiveness to others. [p. 217]

Diversity In development, systematic differences among individuals, groups, or institutions of society. [p. 33]

Down syndrome Genetic anomaly characterized by extra chromosome in the 21st pair of chromosomes. [p. 38]

Drive state Energizer of behavior that exists within the individual. [p. 41]

Dynamic interaction Interaction characterized by two different variables simultaneously influencing one another. For example, biological variables influence and are influenced by contextual variables. [p. 36]

Dysmenorrhea Difficult or painful menstruation. [p. 76]

Early maturers Adolescents who attain the physical maturation characteristics of puberty earlier than the rest of their same-age peers. [p. 65]

Ecological milieu Particular environmental settings of a species/individual. [p. 41]

Ecological validity Observation of behavior as it exists in its true ("real-world") context. [pp. 39, 380]

Ecology Levels of a person's social context that influences individual development. [pp. 7, 50]

"Efficacy research" Model of research conducted under optimal, university-based research conditions. [p. 335]

Ego One of three structures of the mind in psychoanalytic theory. Enables person to adapt to reality. [p. 46]

Ego ideal Component of the superego that represents the perfect, or ideal, person. [p. 43]

Egocentrism Cognitive focus on the self. Egocentrism changes as the child moves throughout Piagetian stages. [pp. 48, 91]

Electra complex For girls, the purported emotional crisis that occurs within the phallic stage of development in Freud's theory. [p. 43]

Empirical Capable of being observed. [p. 378]

Empowerment evaluation Procedures used to increase the ability of community members to prove the effectiveness of the program and to improve it. [p. 333]

Endocrine glands Ductless glands, such as the pituitary gland, that secrete their content into the bloodstream. [p. 61]

Equilibration Individual's attempt to maintain cognitive balance between existing cognitive structures and what is encountered in the environment. Maintained through continuous process of assimilation and accommodation. [pp. 48, 91]

Equivalency degrees Degrees equivalent to a high school diploma. [p. 266]

Estrogens Female sex hormones associated with the development of secondary sexual characteristics in girls. [p. 62]

Ethical standards Principles for the humane, caring, and responsible treatment of participants in research. [p. 394]

Evaluations Procedures used to ascertain if changes in program participants are due to the program. [p. 333]

Exocrine glands Glands with an opening (duct), such as salivary and mammary glands, that secrete their content directly into the environment. [p. 61]

Exosystem As defined by Bronfenbrenner, the third of several interrelated systems whose composition defines the ecology of human development. The formal and informal social structures that do not themselves contain the developing person but impinge on the setting within which the person exists. [p. 51]

Externalizing problems Behavior problems expressed through actions toward one's environment and, thereby, easily visible to others (e.g., aggression). [pp. 191, 299]

Extracurricular activities Events and activities that take place outside the academic realm of school. [p. 262]

Falsification strategies Proving one's ideas by trying to identify information that would disconfirm these ideas. [p. 95]

Fidelity Emotional orientation toward showing commitment to a role and ideology. [p. 138]

Five C's Five attributes (Competence, Connection, Character, Confidence, and Caring) representing positive developmental outcomes in youth. [p. 129]

Fixation Freudian term to describe an arrest of the development of the libido; the person attempts to obtain missed gratification of a previous stage. [p. 42]

Foreclosure Adopting a socially approved, easily available role and thereby avoiding the identity crisis. [p. 136]

Formal operational stage Fourth stage of cognitive development as defined by Piaget. Most representative of adolescents and adults in modern Western society. The person is capable of thinking counterfactually and hypothetically. Can think of all possible combinations of elements of a problem to find a solution. [pp. 48, 92]

Formal operational thought Fourth stage of Piaget's theory of cognitive development, when a person attains the ability to see that reality and his or her thoughts about reality are different, and when the person can generate and recognize hypotheses about reality. [p. 92]

Formative evaluation Procedures that seek to improve programs. [p. 333]

Friendship Voluntary and reciprocal relationship between individuals acknowledged by the people in it, with reciprocal affection and existing within a network of other relationships. [p. 212]

Full-service schools Schools that are part of a communitywide, multiagency, collaborative effort to prevent adolescent educational failure coupled with other risk behaviors. [p. 270]

"g" General intelligence/intellectual factor. [p. 85]

Gender intensification hypothesis Adolescents' socialization by institutions of society, such as the family, aimed at making the youth more gender stereotyped in their personal behavior. The hypothesis rests on the idea that adolescents experience quite different socialization by virtue of being either male or female. [p. 171]

Gender role behavior Behavioral functioning in accordance with the prescriptions set by the society one lives in. [p. 168]

Gender roles Socially and culturally defined set of behaviors linked to being a male or a female in a given society. [p. 162]

Gender role stereotypes Generalized beliefs that particular behaviors are more characteristic of one sex group than the other. [p. 168]

General developmental model Conception guiding the design of developmental research which involves the idea that designs must unconfound variation associated with age, time of measurement, and cohort. [p. 390]

Genital locomotor stage Stage 3 of Erikson's psychosocial theory. Involves a crisis between developing toward a sense of initiative versus guilt. [p. 45]

Genital stage Fifth psychosexual stage as defined by Freud. Occurs during puberty as the libido reemerges in the genital area, in an adult form. [p. 43]

Genotype Complement of genes transmitted to people at conception by the union of the sperm and ovum. [p. 36]

Goodness of fit Degree to which two individuals and/or groups match in goals or styles. [p. 268]

Group Collection of interacting individuals who have influence over one another and who have relationships based on common interests or circumstances. [p. 210]

Heteronomous morality Form of moral reasoning in which the person does not consider the interests of others or recognize that the interests of others differ from his or her own. [p. 111]

Heterosexism Sexual orientation to people of the opposite gender as oneself. [p. 236]

HIV Type of retrovirus (human immunodeficiency virus) responsible for AIDS. [p. 237]

Homonegativity Expressing negative attitudes toward homosexuals. [p. 236]

Homosexuality Sexual orientation to people of the same gender as oneself. [p. 236]

Hormones Chemicals released into the bloodstream that have specific regulatory effects on the activity of certain organs. [p. 61]

Id One of three structures of the mind in psychoanalytic theory. The initial source of the libido. [p. 46]

Identity Set of thoughts, feeling, values, attitudes, and behaviors that defines a person's self. [p. 135]

Identity conflict Crisis in which the person is uncertain of how to define self and is not sure about the role he or she wants to play in society. [p. 146]

Identity crisis Crisis between identity and role confusion elicited by the emotional upheaval provoked by the personal and social mandate to adopt a role in adolescence. [p. 135]

Identity deficit Identity crisis in which the person fails to resolve the identity crisis because of an inability to make decisions. [p. 146]

Identity diffusion Feeling an adolescent gets if he or she cannot resolve the identity crisis. The defining characteristic is a lack of commitment, about which the adolescent is not concerned. [p. 136]

Identity transformation Process of approaching a problem by recognizing the problem in terms of its singular attributes. [p. 92]

Ideology Set of attitudes, beliefs, and values that serves to define a role. [p. 136]

Imaginary audience Adolescents' belief that others are as preoccupied with the object of their own thoughts as they are. [pp. 48, 96]

In-between existence Balance between investing time in the social world of the school and the life in the community. [p. 284]

Independent variable Condition that a researcher chooses to vary in a research study and present to research participants. [p. 382]

Inductive reasoning When reasoning inductively we use our observations and experiences to draw conclusions about the general truth of a particular statement. [p. 94]

Indulgent parenting Parenting marked by overly permissive and condoning behavior toward one's child (e.g., "If my child wants something, I give it to him"). [p. 196]

INRC grouping Cognitive structure that characterizes formal operations and implies that all solutions to a problem may be obtained through the application of four components: identity, negation, reciprocity, and correlation. [p. 92]

Intellectualization Ego defense mechanism of highly abstract, intellectual reasoning used to justify behavior. [p. 47]

Inter-individual differences Variability between people that leads to different developmental outcomes. [p. 14]

Interaction Integration of the behaviors of two individuals into a social exchange of some duration. [p. 210]

Internalizing problems Behavior problems not expressed toward one's environment but rather directed to one's mental or emoting functioning (e.g., depression or anxiety). [pp. 191, 299]

Intervention program Program conducted by professionals or through community-based organizations that attempts to change a person's life for the better. [p. 330]

Interventions Actions planned to reduce or to prevent problems or to promote positive development. [p. 33]

Intervention studies Research designed to understand how changing aspects of the social world or an individual's behavior can lead to improvements in a person's life. [p. 9]

Intra-individual changes Alterations within a person that occur with development. [p. 14]

IQ The intelligence quotient. A numerical scale measuring level of intelligence. For example, to compute an IQ score, mental age (i.e., how much you know) is divided by chronological age (i.e., how much is known on average by others of your age) and multiplied by 100 (to eliminate fractions). [p. 85]

Jocks Students who use the school's extracurricular arena as a center for their social life. [p. 284]

Juvenile delinquency Violation of a law committed by a person prior to his or her 18th birthday, a violation that would have been a crime if committed by an adult. [p. 304]

Late maturers Adolescents who attain the physical maturation characteristics of puberty later than most of their same-age peers. [p. 65]

Latency Stage 4 of Erikson's psychosocial theory. Involves a crisis between developing toward a sense of industry versus inferiority. [p. 45]

Latency period Incubation period of a disease (period between the time an infection takes place and the time first symptoms of the infection appear). [p. 240]

Latency stage Fourth psychosexual stage as defined by Freud. Occurs around the fifth year of life until puberty. The libido is said to be latent in this stage. [p. 43]

Libido Freudian term that defines the finite amount of energy that each human is born with which governs human mental life. Localization of the libido within the body changes over the course of development. Placement of the libido within the body determines what stimulation is appropriate and what stimulation is inappropriate to the developing individual. [p. 42]

Life-span perspective Approach that characterizes individual development as occurring across a lifetime through the combination of internal and external influences; the approach stresses differences within and between people and attempts to optimize lifetime development. [p. 10]

Lifestyle Preferences and behaviors of adolescents regarding what they want to do, how and where they will spend their time, and with whom they want to interact. [p. 288]

Longitudinal design Design in which the same group of people is studied repeatedly. [p. 386]

Longitudinal research/studies Research composed of repeated observations. [p. 32]

Longitudinal study Study that assesses a particular variable (e.g., sibling relationships) repeatedly over time. [p. 182]

Loss-based selection When compensatory efforts fail or their costs outweigh their gains, individuals restructure their goal hierarchy, lower their standards, or look for new goals. [p. 53]

Macrosystem As defined by Bronfenbrenner, the fourth of several interrelated systems whose composition defines the ecology of human development. Composed of cultural values and beliefs and historical events that affect the other ecological systems. [p. 51]

Maintenance-actualization Function of schools in which students are both made happy about their current status and yet challenged to do better. [p. 257]

Manipulation Attempts by a researcher to influence behavior and/or the situation within which behavior is studied. [p. 381]

Maturity Stage 8 of Erikson's psychosocial theory. Involves a crisis between developing toward a sense of ego integrity versus despair. [p. 46]

Media Means through which information or entertainment is passed such as television, radio, movies, magazines, computers, pagers, cell phones, and video games. [p. 280]

Meiosis Process of division resulting in formation of sex cells, sperm, and ova. [p. 36]

Menarche Beginning of the first menstrual cycle. [p. 65]

Mentor Teacher, guide, or counselor to another person. The mentor is usually several years older than the person he or she mentors. [p. 361]

Mentoring One-on-one relationship that is structured and focuses on the needs of the person being mentored. [p. 352]

Mesosystem As defined by Bronfenbrenner, the second of several interrelated systems whose composition defines the ecology of human development. Composed of interrelations among the major settings containing the individual, the developing person at a particular point in his or her life. [p. 50]

Microsystem As defined by Bronfenbrenner, the first of several interrelated systems whose composition defines the ecology of human development. Composed of relations between the developing person and the environment in the immediate setting within which the person exists. [p. 50]

Moderate interaction theory Places equal stress on the influence of both nature and nurture but sees the two sources as independent of each other. [p. 42]

Monozygotic (MZ) twins Twins developed from one fertilized egg that splits after conception. In contrast, dizygotic (DZ) twins develop from separate fertilized eggs. [p. 36]

Moratorium Period in which an adolescent avoids commitment. [p. 136]

Multidisciplinary Research and knowledge from diverse fields. [p. 10]

Multilevel research/studies Research focusing on biological, psychological, and social facets of a phenomenon. [p. 32]

Multiple levels of organization Idea that development occurs as a consequence of relations among biology, person, social groups, culture, history, and other levels in the ecology of human development. [p. 31]

Multivariate Many variables. [p. 390]

Multivariate research/studies Research involving several variables. [p. 32]

Nature-nurture controversy Debate about whether or how biology and/or environment provide the basis of human behavior and development. [p. 31]

Negation operation Process of approaching a problem by canceling the existence of the problem. [p. 92]

Negative identity formation Resolving the identity crisis by adopting an available but socially disapproved role or ideology. [p. 136]

Neglected reputation Peer reputation characterized by receiving very few nominations, either positive or negative. [p. 212]

Neglectful parenting Parenting marked by inattentive, careless behavior toward one's child (e.g., "I really don't know what my child is up to. I don't really keep close tabs on her"). [p. 196]

Norm Behavior typical of certain people at certain points in development and/or in specific situations. [p. 381]

Nuclear family Intact family, characterized by the presence of both biological parents and one or more children. [p. 181]

Obesity Condition characterized by an excessive accumulation of fat in the body. [p. 76]

Oedipus complex Boy's emotional reaction to his mother at the time when the libido has moved to the boy's genital area and when he obtains gratification through stimu-

lation of the genitals. When the boy realizes his father is his rival for his mother's affection, the boy comes to fear his father will punish him by performing castration. The boy is so moved by his anxiety that he gives up desires for his mother and identifies with his father. [p. 43]

On-time maturers Adolescents who attain the physical maturation characteristics of puberty at the same time as most of their same-age peers. [p. 65]

Ontogeny Development, or life course, of an individual organism. [p. 40]

Operation Piagetian term referring to the internalized actions that are mentally reversible. [p. 48]

Optimization How youth acquire and refine the means to reach their goals. Describes process geared toward achieving higher levels of functioning. [p. 30]

Oral sensory stage Stage 1 of Erikson's psychosocial theory. Involves a crisis between developing a sense of basic trust versus mistrust toward one's world. [p. 45]

Oral stage First psychosexual stage defined by Freud. Occurs during the first year of life when the libido is said to be located in the region of the mouth. Gratification is obtained through stimulation of this region through sucking and biting. [p. 42]

Outcome or summative evaluation Procedures used to determine if a program is effective. [p. 333]

Outreach research Model of research conducted in real-world, community-based settings. [p. 335]

Panel design Another term used to label a longitudinal design. [p. 386]

Passive leisure activities Free time events that require little expenditure of energy on the part of the participant. [p. 282]

Penis envy Girl realizes she does not have a penis but, rather, an inferior (to Freud) organ, the clitoris. The girl experiences envy of the penis and this envy impels her to relinquish her incestuous love for her father and identify with her mother. [p. 43]

Permeability Ease of movement from one part of the education-work/career system to another; permeability involves the amount of effort (e.g., additional education or training) needed to move from one occupation or career to another. [p. 370]

Permissive parenting Parenting marked by lack of consistency in parents' use of rules. Permissive parents tend to have a laissez-faire attitude toward their child(ren)'s behaviors. The parents often overindulge their child(ren)'s requests and act more as a peer than as an independent observer. [p. 195]

Personal fable Belief that one is a unique, one-of-a-kind individual; the idea that one is a singular person having singular feelings and thoughts. [pp. 48, 97]

Phallic stage Third psychosexual stage as defined by Freud. Spans the period from about the third through fifth years when the libido moves to the genital area. Males and females experience this stage differently because their genitalia differ. See Oedipal complex and Electra complex. [p. 43]

Phenylketonuria (PKU) Illness characterized by body's inability to metabolize fatty substances due to lack of a particular digestive enzyme. [p. 39]

Phylogeny Evolutionary history of a species. [p. 41]

Plasticity Potential for systematic change across life. [p. 36]

Policies Actions (e.g., the enactment of laws) taken by social institutions, such as governments, to ensure or increase desired behaviors (e.g., better school performance) or to decrease unwanted behaviors (e.g., drunk driving). [p. 9]

Popular reputation Peer reputation characterized by receiving many positive nominations and few negative ones. [p. 212]

Postconventional morality Third level of moral development as defined by Kohlberg. The individual is concerned with legalistic reasoning oriented around principles and conscience. [p. 49]

Postpubescent phase Stage in pubertal maturation during which the bodily changes associated with adolescence are completed. [p. 61]

Post-traumatic stress disorder (PTSD) Psychological disorder experienced by individuals who have gone through some major traumatic experiences, such as a serious accident or war. [pp. 116, 312]

Precocious puberty Early or premature puberty. [p. 76]

Preconventional morality First level of moral development as defined by Kohlberg. The individual is bound by issues of punishment and obedience and naïve and egoistic reasoning. [p. 49]

Preoperational stage Second stage of cognitive development as defined by Piaget. The child can represent mentally absent objects and can use symbols to represent objects. [p. 48]

Prepubescent phase Stage in pubertal maturation during which some of the bodily changes associated with adolescence (e.g., changes in height, weight, fat and muscle distribution, glandular secretions, or sexual characteristics) have begun. [p. 61]

Primary sexual characteristics Physical attributes present at birth that involve internal and external genitalia (e.g., the penis in males and the vagina in females). [p. 62]

Process evaluation Procedures that seek to improve programs though enhancing the process through which the program provides its services. [p. 333]

Program effectiveness Concept indicating whether a program is accomplishing its goals by achieving what it attended to achieve. [p. 332]

Programs Standardized procedures followed to enable a person or group to increase desired behaviors (e.g., the enhancement of literacy through instruction in reading) or to decrease unwanted ones (e.g., school dropout). [p. 14]

Program scale Concept indicating whether a program is reaching the appropriate number of people for whom it could have positive benefits. [p. 334]

Program sustainability Concept indicating whether a program is maintained over time. [p. 334]

Projection Process of attributing one's own feelings to other objects or people. [p. 46]

Prosocial behavior Behavior that allows society to create a just and equitable system; individuals act in a way that contributes to a just social order. [p. 109]

Protective factors Strengths and assets of young people that keep them on a positive developmental path. [p. 339]

Psychological test Standardized, or controlled, device used to elicit behavior from or information about a person. [p. 381]

Psychopathology Serious problems of mental health that require professional treatment, for example, sustained and pervasive feelings of depression, anxiety, or the occurrence of a psychotic disorder. [p. 318]

Psychosis Severe mental disorder, characterized by problematic behaviors and thoughts that reflect a disengagement from reality. [p. 318]

Psychosocial development Emphasizes the role of the ego and, specifically, the role of society in determining what the ego must do to fulfill its function of adapting to the demands of reality. [p. 45]

Pubertal maturation Process through which the primary sexual characteristics develop into adult form and the secondary sexual characteristics associated with puberty emerge and develop. [p. 60]

Puberty period during which the primary sexual characteristics develop into adult form and the secondary sexual characteristics are emerging and developing and the capability to reproduce is attained. [p. 61]

Puberty and adolescence Stage 5 of Erikson's psychosocial theory. Involves a crisis between developing toward a sense of identity versus role confusion. [p. 45]

Pubescent phase Stage in pubertal maturation during which most of the bodily changes associated with adolescence have been initiated. [p. 61]

Public policy Standards or values for the conduct of individuals, organizations, and institutions that structure actions and indicate appropriate investment of resources. [pp. 129, 341]

Qualitative differences (in cognition) Differences in "kind" or "type" of thought shown by a person. [p. 90]

Rationalization Ego defense mechanism of applying plausible but untrue reasoning for behavior. [p. 46]

Reality principle Ego develops only to deal with reality, to allow the person to adjust to demands of real world and hence survive. [p. 44]

Recapitulation Developmental changes within the human life cycle that are the hypothetical repetition of the sequence of changes the species followed during evolution. [p. 40]

Reciprocal transformation Process of approaching a problem by considering and taking its opposite. [p. 92]

Rejected reputation Peer reputation characterized by receiving few positive nominations and many negative nominations. [p. 212]

Relationship Succession of interactions between two individuals known and committed to each other, which is influenced by the past interactions between the two individuals and by their expectations for the future. [p. 210]

Replicable Capable of being repeatedly observed. [p. 379]

Repression Ego defense mechanism by which unwanted desires and/or pressures are placed in the unconscious. [p. 46]

Reproductive assimilation When a person initially tries to deal with new information by treating it as something he or she already knows. [p. 91]

Resiliency Presence of considerable physical and physiological ability to overcome adversities. [p. 74]

Retrospection Constructing the past through memories. A technique used by Freud. [p. 44]

Reversibility Ability to know that by reversing one's actions on an object one can return the object to its original state. [p. 48]

Role Socially prescribed set of behaviors to which the person can show commitment. [pp. 136, 162]

Role confusion Feeling an adolescent gets if he or she cannot find a role that fits his or her biological, psychological, and social characteristics. [p. 136]

Role strain Often associated with maternal employment, the difficulty of balancing the demands of one's role as a worker and the demands of being a parent. [p. 193]

"Rotten outcomes" Problems of youth development associated with poverty. [p. 302]

School reform Altering the functions of a school. [p. 269]

School restructuring Altering the organization of a school. [p. 269]

Scientific method Series of steps taken by a researcher to assure that what is observed is accurate and able to be verified by other researchers. [p. 378]

Secondary process Functions (e.g., perception, reasoning) that enable ego to adjust to and deal with reality. [p. 44]

Secondary sexual characteristics Physical attributes that develop during puberty (e.g., breast devel-

opment in females and pigmented facial hair in males). [p. 62]

Secular trend Variation of adolescent bodily changes across history. [p. 67]

Selection How youth develop, structure, and commit to their goals. Gives direction to development by directing and focusing resources on certain domains of functioning and preventing diffusion of resources. [p. 30]

Self-definition Understanding of who you are as a person based on how you view yourself physically, psychologically, and socially. [p. 12]

Self-esteem Degree of positive or negative feelings one holds about the self. [p. 139]

Self-handicapping behaviors Actions of procrastination and not studying that lead to low achievement. [p. 260]

Self-regulation Feature of adolescent psychological and social functioning that allows the individual to select goals, find the means to attain those goals, and cope with failures or losses to reach the goals. [p. 140]

Sensorimotor stage First stage of cognitive development as defined by Piaget. The child develops the knowledge that external stimulation continues to exist even when not sensed by the person. [p. 48]

Sequential designs Designs in which cross-sectional samples are studied longitudinally. [p. 391]

Service learning Integration of classroom learning with the opportunity to perform community service. [p. 351]

Social careers Life built exclusively around participating in a particular social role. [p. 284]

Social cognition Thinking about interpersonal relationships and the social world. [p. 99]

Socialization Process by which one generation (the parental one) influences another (the adolescent one) to adopt the values, beliefs, and desired behaviors of society. [p. 181]

"Socially toxic" environment Environment in which one is exposed to multiple high-risk factors. [p. 312]

Social networks Distinct groups of relationships such as best friends, close friends, cliques, crowds, and romantic relationships. [p. 211]

Social role Socially prescribed set of behaviors that society believes is important for its maintenance and perpetuation. [p. 7]

Status offense Violation of the law involving a behavior that would not be illegal if engaged in by an adult. [p. 304]

STD (sexually transmitted diseases) Disease, such as HIV or gonorrhea, that is transmitted by sexual contact. [p. 240]

Stereotype Exceptionless generalization or commonly held belief about a group (e.g., adolescents) or social institution (e.g., fraternities or sororities). [pp. 15, 213]

Steroids Sex hormones (androgens in males and estrogens in females) that control development of physical and physiological changes associated with pubertal maturation. [p. 61]

Storm and stress Phrase often used to stereotype general and universal turmoil throughout the adolescent years. [p. 4]

Strong interaction theory Sees nature and nurture as reciprocally related and inextricably fused in all development. [p. 42]

Substitution Process of replacing one goal for another. [p. 46]

Superego Freudian personality structure made up of two components: the ego ideal and the conscience. Formed as a result of the resolution of the Oedipal complex. [pp. 43, 46]

"Surgent Growth" Developmental path through adolescence characterized by abrupt spurts or changes in behavior, but not necessarily with turmoil, storm, or stress. [p. 19]

Systems approach Approach to programs that deals with multiple problems simultaneously and engages all levels of the context to prevent problems and to promote the positive development of youth. [p. 266]

Thriving Concept defined and measured by Scales et al. Thriving is defined as involving the following seven attributes: school success, leadership, valuing diversity, physical health, helping others, delay of gratification, and overcoming adversity. [p. 125]

Time-lag design Design in which people of the same age are studied at different times in history. [p. 389]

Transparency Extent to which young people can see through the intricacies of the rules of the education system and the world of work and then plan a course of action to lead them successfully from school to work. [p. 370]

"Tumultuous growth" Developmental path through adolescence experienced by a minority of adolescents, characterized by turmoil, storm, and stress. [p. 19]

Variable Anything that can change or vary. [p. 382]

Weak interaction theory Places primary stress on one source (usually nature) as the determinant of the sequence and character of development. [p. 42]

Young adulthood Stage 6 of Erikson's psychosocial theory. Involves a crisis between developing toward a sense of intimacy versus isolation. [p. 45]

Youth charters Community-organized groups that enable adolescents and adults to promote positive youth developmental outcomes systematically and create a system by which civil society can be maintained and perpetuated. [p. 120]

Youth gangs Groups of youth potentially involved in criminal activity. [p. 303]

Youth policy Set of social policies that will enable the values of positive youth development to be translated into effective actions. [p. 341]

Zygote Fertilized egg. [p. 36]

REFERENCES

A

Abernathy, T. J., Massad, L., & Romano-Dwyer, L. (1995). The relationship between smoking and self-esteem. *Adolescence, 30*(120), 899–907.

Adam, K. S., Sheldon-Keller, A. E., & West, M. (1996). Attachment organization and history of suicidal behavior in clinical adolescents. *Journal of Consulting and Clinical Psychology, 64*(2), 264–272.

Adams, G. R. (1977). Physical attractiveness research: Toward a developmental social psychology of beauty. *Human Development, 20*, 217–239.

Adams, G. R. (1991). Runaways, negative consequences for. In R. M. Lerner, A. C. Petersen, & J. Brooks-Gunn (Eds.), *Encyclopedia of adolescence* (Vol. 2, pp. 947–950). New York: Garland.

Adams, G. R. (1997). Identity: A brief critique of a cybernetic model. *Journal of Adolescent Research, 12*(3), 358–362.

Adams, G. R., & Jones, R. M. (1983). Female adolescents' identity development: Age comparisons and perceived child-rearing experiences. *Developmental Psychology, 19*, 249–256.

Adams, G. R., & Marshall, S. K. (1996). A developmental social psychology of identity: Understanding the person-in-context. *Journal of Adolescence, 19*, 429–442.

Adelson, J. (1970, January 18). What generation gap? *New York Times Magazine* (Sec. 6), pp. 10–45.

Ahlburg, D. A., & De Vita, C. J. (1992). New realities of the American families. *Population Bulletin, 47*(2), 1–44.

Alan Guttmacher Institute. (1994). *Sex and America's teenagers*. New York: Author.

Allen, J. P., Hauser, S. T., Bell, K. L., & O'Connor, T. G. (1994). Longitudinal assessment of autonomy and relatedness in adolescent family interactions as predictors of adolescent ego development and self-esteem. *Child Development, 65*, 179–194.

Allen, J. P., Hauser, S. T., & Borman-Spurrell, E. (1996). Attachment theory as a framework for understanding sequelae of severe adolescent psychopathology: An 11-year follow-up study. *Journal of Consulting and Clinical Psychology, 64*(2), 254–263.

Allen, J. P., Hauser, S., Eickholt, C., Bell, K., & O'Connor, T. (1994). Autonomy and relatedness in family interactions as predictors of expressions of negative adolescent affect. *Journal of Research on Adolescence, 4*(4), 535–552.

Allen, J. P., Moore, C., Kuperminc, G., & Bell, K. (1998). Attachment and adolescent psychosocial functioning. *Child Development, 69*(5), 1406–1419.

Allen, J. P., Philliber, S., Herrling, S., & Kuperminc, G. P. (1997). Preventing teen pregnancy and academic failure: Experimental evaluation of a developmentally based approach. *Child Development, 64*(4), 729–742.

Allison, K. W. (1993). Adolescents living in "non-family" and alternative settings. In R. M. Lerner (Ed.), *Early adolescence: Perspectives on research, policy, and intervention* (pp. 37–50). Hilllsdale, NJ: Erlbaum.

Allport, G. W. (1954). *The nature of prejudice*. Reading, MA: Addison-Wesley.

Almeida, D. M., & Galambos, N. L. (1991). Examining father involvement and the quality of father-adolescent relations. *Journal of Research on Adolescence, 1*(2), 155–172.

Alnajjar, A. A. (1996). Adolescents' perceptions of family functioning in the United Arab Emirates. *Adolescence, 31*(122), 433–442.

Alsaker, F. D. (1992). Pubertal timing, overweight, and psychological adjustment. *Journal of Early Adolescence, 12*, 396–419.

Alsaker, F. D. (1995). Is puberty a critical period for socialization? *Journal of Adolescence, 18*, 427–444.

Alsaker, F., & Olweus, D. (1986). Assessment of global self-evaluations and perceived stability of self in Norwegian preadolescents and adolescents. *Journal of Early Adolescence, 6*, 269–278.

Alsaker, F., & Olweus, D. (1992). Is this right? Stability of global self-evaluations in early adolescence: A cohort longitudinal study. *Journal of Research on Adolescence, 2*, 123–145.

Alva, S., & Jones, M. (1994). Psychosocial adjustment and self-reported patterns of alcohol use among Hispanic adolescents. *Journal of Early Adolescence, 14*, 432–448.

Alvarez, R. (1992). *Assessing youth programs: An international perspective*. Unpublished manuscript. Battle Creek, MI: International Youth Foundation.

Amato, P. R., Rezac, S. J., & Booth, A. (1995). Helping between parents and young adult offspring: The role of parental marital quality, divorce, and remarriage. *Journal of Marriage and the Family, 57*, 363–374.

Ames, C., & Ames, R. (Eds.). (1989). *Research in motivation in educations: Vol. 3. Goals and cognitions*. New York: Academic Press.

Anastasi, A. (1958). Heredity, environment, and the question "how?" *Psychological Review, 65*, 197–208.

Anderman, E. M., Griesinger, T., & Westerfield, G. (1998). Motivation and cheating during early adolescence. *Journal of Educational Psychology, 90*(1), 84–93.

Anderson, T., & Dixon, W. E., Jr. (1995). Confirmatory factor analysis of the Wechsler Intelligence Scale for children—revised with normal and psychiatric adolescents. *Journal of Research on Adolescence, 5*(3), 319–332.

Andrews, J. A., Hops, H., Ary, D. V., & Tildesley, E. (1993). Parental influence on early adolescent substance use: Specific and nonspecific effects. *Journal of Early Adolescence, 13*(3), 285–310.

Annie E. Casey Foundation. (1996). *Kids Count Data Book 1996: State profiles of child well-being.* Baltimore: Author.

Annie E. Casey Foundation. (1997). *Kids Count Data Book 1997: State profiles of child well-being.* Baltimore: Author.

Annie E. Casey Foundation. (1998). *Kids Count Data Book 1998: State profiles of child well-being.* Baltimore: Author.

Annie E. Casey Foundation. (1999). *Kids Count Data Book 1999: State profiles of child well-being.* Baltimore: Author.

Annie E. Casey Foundation. (2000). *Kids Count Data Book: State profiles of child well-being.* Baltimore: Author.

Ansari, A. A., Gouthro, S., Ahmad, K., & Steele, C. (1996). Hospital-based behavior modification program for adolescents: Evaluation and predictors of outcome. *Adolescence, 31*(122), 469–476.

Ansuini, C. G., Fiddler-Woite, J., & Woite, R. S. (1996). The source, accuracy, and impact of initial sexuality information on lifetime wellness. *Adolescence, 31*(122), 283–289.

Anthony, J. (1969). The reaction of adults to adolescents and their behavior. In G. Caplan & S. Lebovici (Eds.), *Adolescence* (pp. 54–78). New York: Basic.

Aquilino, W. S. (1997). From adolescent to young adult: A prospective study of parent-child relations during the transition to adulthood. *Journal of Marriage and the Family, 59*, 670–686.

Araoye, M. O., & Adegoke, A. (1996). AIDS-related knowledge, attitude and behaviour among selected adolescents in Nigeria. *Journal of Adolescence, 19*, 179–181.

Archer, S. L. (1984, March). Rudiments of identity formation among early and mid-adolescents: An examination of process and content. In C. Cooper (Chair), *An assessment of adolescent identity research: An update with commentary on implications for future research.* Symposium conducted at the meetings of the Second Biennial Conference on Adolescent Research, Tucson, AZ.

Archer, S. L. (1985). Identity and the choice of social rules. *New Directions for Child Development, 30*, 79–99.

Archer, S. L. (1989). Adolescent identity: An appraisal of health and intervention. *Journal of Adolescence, 12*, 341–343.

Archer, S. L. (1991). Identity development, gender differences in. In R. M. Lerner, A. C. Petersen, & J. Brooks-Gunn (Eds.), *Encyclopedia of adolescence* (pp. 522–524). New York: Garland.

Archer, S. L. (1992). A feminist's approach to identity research. In G. R. Adams, T. P. Gullotta, & R. Montemayor (Eds.), *Adolescent identity formation* (pp. 25–49). Newbury Park, CA: Sage.

Archer, S. L., & Waterman, A. S. (1991). Ego development. In R. M. Lerner, A. C. Petersen, & J. Brooks-Gunn (Eds.), *Encyclopedia of adolescence* (Vol. 1, pp. 295–300). New York: Garland.

Armistead, L., Wierson, M., & Forehand, R. (1990). Adolescents and maternal employment: Is it harmful for a young adolescent to have an employed mother? Parent work and early adolescent development. [Special issue]. *Journal of Early Adolescence, 10*(3), 260–278.

Aseltine, R. H., & Gore, S. (1993). Mental health and social adaptation following the transition from high school. *Journal of Research on Adolescence, 3*, 247–270.

Ausubel, D. P., Montemayor, R., & Svajian, P. (1977). *Theory and problems of adolescent development* (2nd ed.). New York: Grune & Stratton.

B

Bäckman, L., & Dixon, R. A. (1992). Psychological compensation: A theoretical framework. *Psychological Bulletin, 112*, 259–283.

Bagley, C., Bolitho, F., & Bertrand, L. (1997). Sexual assault in school, mental health and suicidal behaviors in adolescent women in Canada. *Adolescence, 32*(126), 341–366.

Bagwell, C. L., Newcomb, A. F., & Bukowski, W. M. (1998). Preadolescent friendship and peer rejection as predictors of adult adjustment. *Child Development, 69*(1), 140–153.

Bahr, S. J., Maughan, S. L., Marcos, A. C., & Li, B. (1998). Family, religiosity, and the risk of adolescent drug use. *Journal of Marriage and the Family, 60*, 979–992.

Bakan, D. (1966). *The duality of human existence.* Chicago: Rand McNally.

Baltes, M. M., & Carstensen, L. L. (1996). The process of successful aging. *Aging and Society, 16*, 397–422.

Baltes, M. M., & Carstensen, L. L. (1998). Social-psychological theories and their applications to aging: From individual to collective. In V. L. Bengtson & K. W. Schaie (Eds.), *Handbook of theories of aging* (pp. 209–226). New York: Springer.

Baltes, P. B. (1968). Longitudinal and cross-sectional sequences in the study of age and generation effects. *Human Development, 11*, 145–171.

Baltes, P. B. (1987). Theoretical propositions of life-span developmental psychology: On the dynamics between growth and decline. *Developmental Psychology, 23*, 611–626.

Baltes, P. B. (1997). On the incomplete architecture of human ontology: Selection, optimization, and compensation as foundation of developmental theory. *American Psychologist, 52*, 366–380.

Baltes, P. B., & Baltes, M. M. (1990). Psychological perspectives on successful aging: The model of selective optimization with compensation. In P. B. Baltes & M. M. Baltes (Eds.), *Successful aging: Perspectives from the behavioral sciences* (pp. 1–34). New York: Cambridge University Press.

Baltes, P. B., Baltes, M. M., and Reinert, G. (1970). The relationship between time of measurement and age in cognitive development of children: An applicant of cross-sectional sequences. *Human Development, 13*, 258–268.

Baltes, P. B., Lindenberger, U., & Staudinger, U. M. (1998). Life-span theory in developmental psychology. In W. Damon (Series Ed.) & R. M. Lerner (Vol. Ed.), *Handbook of child psychology: Vol. 1. Theoretical models of human development* (5th ed., pp. 1029–1144). New York: Wiley.

Baltes, P. B., Reese, H. W., & Nesselroade, J. R. (1977). *Life-span developmental psychology: Introduction to research methods.* Monterey, CA: Brooks/Cole.

Baltes, P. B., Reese, H. W., & Nesselroade, J. R. (1988). *Life-span developmental psychology: An introduction to research methods.* Hillsdale, NJ: Erlbaum.

Baltes, P. B., Staudinger, U. M., & Lindenberger, U. (1999). Lifespan psychology: Theory and application to intellectual functioning. In J. T. Spence, J. M. Darley, & D. J. Foss (Eds.), *Annual review of psychology* (Vol. 50, 471–507). Palo Alto, CA: Annual Reviews.

Bandura, A. (1964). The stormy decade: Fact or fiction? *Psychology in the School, 1,* 224–231.

Barber, B. K. (1994). Cultural, family, and person contexts of parent-adolescent conflict. *Journal of Marriage and the Family, 56,* 375–386.

Barber, B. K., & Olsen, J. A. (1997). Socialization in context: Connection, regulation, and autonomy in the family, school, and neighborhood, and with peers. *Journal of Adolescent Research, 12*(2), 287–315.

Barnes, G. M. (1984). Adolescent alcohol abuse and other problem behaviors: Their relationships and common parental influences. *Journal of Youth & Adolescence, 13,* 329–348.

Barnes, G. M., & Farrell, M. P. (1992). Parental support and control as predictors of adolescent drinking, delinquency, and related problem behaviors. *Journal of Marriage and the Family, 54,* 763–776.

Barnes, G. M., Farrell, M. P., & Banerjee, S. (1994). Family influences on alcohol abuse and other problem behaviors among black and white adolescents in a general population sample. *Journal of Research on Adolescence, 4,* 183–202.

Barnes, H. L., & Olson, D. H. (1985). Parent-adolescent communication and the Circumplex model. *Child Development, 56*(2), 438–447.

Barrera, M., Li, S. A., & Chassin, L. (1995). Effects of parental alcoholism and life stress on Hispanic and non-Hispanic Caucasian adolescents: A prospective study. *American Journal of Psychology, 23*(4), 479–507.

Barrouillet, P., Fayol, M., & Lathulière, E. (1997). Selecting between competitors in multiplication tasks: An explanation of the errors produced by adolescents with learning disabilities. *International Journal of Behavioral Development, 21*(2), 253–275.

Barwick, M. A., & Siegel, L. S. (1996). Learning difficulties in adolescent clients of a shelter for runaway and homeless street youths. *Journal of Research on Adolescence, 6*(4), 649–670.

Basen-Enquist, K., Edmundson, E. W., & Parcel, G. S. (1996). Structure of health risk behavior among high school students. *Journal of Consulting and Clinical Psychology, 64*(4), 764–775.

Basinger, K. S., Gibbs, J. C., & Fuller, D. (1995). Context and the measurement of moral judgement. *International Journal of Behavioral Development, 18*(3), 537–556.

Battistich, V., Schaps, E., Watson, M., & Solomon, D. (1996). Prevention effects of the Child Development Project: Early findings from an ongoing multisite demonstration trial. *Journal of Adolescent Research, 11*(1), 12–35.

Baumeister, R. F. (1986). *Identity: Cultural change and the struggle for self.* New York: Oxford University Press.

Baumeister, R. F. (1991). Identity crisis. In R. M. Lerner, A. C. Petersen, & J. Brooks-Gunn (Eds.), *Encyclopedia of adolescence* (Vol. 1, pp. 518–521). New York: Garland.

Baumeister, R. F., & Muraven, M. (1996). Identity as adaptation to social, cultural, and historical context. *Journal of Adolescence, 19,* 405–416.

Baumeister, R. F., Shapiro, J. P., & Tice, D. M. (1985). Two kinds of identity crisis. *Journal of Personality, 53*(3), 407–424.

Baumrind, D. (1967). Child care practices anteceding three patterns of the preschool behavior. *Genetic Psychology Monographs, 75,* 43–88.

Baumrind, D. (1971). Current patterns of parental authority. *Developmental Psychology Monographs, 4*(1, Pt. 2).

Baumrind, D. (1991). The influence of parenting style on adolescent competence and substance use. *Journal of Early Adolescence, 11*(1), 56–95.

Baydar, N., Brooks-Gunn, J., & Furstenberg, F. F. (1993). Early warning signs of functional illiteracy: Predictors in childhood and adolescence. *Child Development, 64,* 815–829.

Bayley, N., & Olden, M. H. (1955). The maintenance of intellectual ability in gifted adults. *Journal of Gerontology, 10,* 91–107.

Bear, G., & Stewart, M. (1990). Early adolescents' acceptability of interventions: Influence of problem severity, gender, and moral development. *Journal of Early Adolescence, 10,* 191–208.

Beaty, L. A. (1995). Effects of paternal absence on male adolescents' peer relations and self-image. *Adolescence, 30,* 873–900.

Beaumont, S. L. (1996). Adolescent girls' perceptions of conversations with mothers and friends. *Journal of Adolescent Research, 11*(3), 325–346.

Bell, K. L., Allen, J. P., Hauser, S. T., & O'Connor, T. G. (1996). Family factors and young adult transitions: Educational attainment and occupational prestige. In J. A. Graber & J. Brooks-Gunn (Eds.), *Transitions through adolescence: Interpersonal domains and context* (pp. 345–366). Mahwah, NJ: Erlbaum.

Belsky, J., Lerner, R. M., & Spanier, G. B. (1984). *The child in the family.* Reading, MA: Addison-Wesley.

Bengtson, V. L., & Troll, L. (1978). Youth and their parents: Feedback and intergenerational influence in socialization. In R. M. Lerner & G. B. Spanier (Eds.), *Child influences on marital and family interaction: A life-span perspective.* New York: Academic Press.

Benson, M. J., Harris, P. B., & Rogers, C. S. (1992). Identity consequences of attachment to mothers and fathers among late adolescents. *Journal of Research on Adolescence, 2*(3), 187–204.

Benson, P. (1997). *All kids are our kids: What communities must do to raise caring and responsible children and adolescents.* San Francisco: Jossey-Bass.

Benson, P. L., Leffert, N., Scales, P. C., & Blyth, D. A. (1998). Beyond the "village" rhetoric: Creating healthy communities for children and adolescents. *Applied Developmental Science, 2*(3), 138–159.

Berndt, T. J., & Keefe, K. (1995). Friends' influence on adolescents' adjustment to school. *Child Development, 66,* 1312–1329.

Berndt, T. J., & Mekos, D. (1995). Adolescents' perceptions of the stressful and desirable aspects of the transition to junior high school. *Journal of Research on Adolescence, 5*(1), 123–142.

Berndt, T. J., Miller, K. E., & Park, K. (1989). Adolescents' perceptions of friends' and parents' influence on aspects of their school adjustment. *Journal of Early Adolescence, 9*(4), 419–435.

Berzonsky, M. D. (1993). A constructivist view of identity development: People as postpositivist self-theorists. In J. Kroger (Ed.), *Discussions on ego identity* (pp. 169–203). Hillsdale, NJ: Erlbaum.

Berzonsky, M. D. (1997). Identity development, control theory, and self-regulation: An individual differences perspective. *Journal of Adolescent Research, 12*(3), 347–353.

Berzonsky, M. D., & Neimeyer, G. J. (1994). Ego identity status and identity processing orientation: The moderating role of commitment. *Journal of Research in Personality, 28*(4), 425–435.

Best, K. M., Hauser, S. T., & Allen, J. P. (1997). Predicting young adult competencies: Adolescent era parent and individual influences. *Journal of Adolescent Research, 12*(1), 90–112.

Bills, D. B., Helms, L. B., & Ozcan, M. (1995). The impact of student employment on teachers' attitudes and behaviors toward working students. *Youth & Society, 27*(2), 169–193.

Bingham, C. R., & Crockett, L. J. (1996). Longitudinal adjustment patterns of boys and girls experiencing early, middle, and late sexual intercourse. *Developmental Psychology, 32*(4), 647–658.

Bishop, J. A., & Inderbitzen, H. M. (1995). Peer acceptance and friendship: An investigation of their relations to self-esteem. *Journal of Early Adolescence, 15*(4), 476–489.

Black, M. M., Ricardo, I. B., & Stanton, B. (1997). Social and psychological factors associated with AIDS risk behaviors among low-income, urban, African American adolescents. *Journal of Research on Adolescence, 7*(2), 173–195.

Blaske, D. M., Borduin, C. M., Henggeler, S. W., & Barton, M. J. (1989). Individual, family, and peer characteristics of adolescent sex offenders and assaultive offenders. *Developmental Psychology, 25,* 846–855.

Block, J. H. (1971). *Living through time.* Berkeley: Bancroft.

Block, J. H. (1973). Conceptions of sex roles: Some cross-cultural and longitudinal perspectives. *American Psychologist, 28,* 283–308.

Block, J. H., & Robins, R. W. (1993). A longitudinal study of consistency and change in self-esteem from early adolescence to early adulthood. *Child Development, 64,* 909–923.

Bloom, B. S. (1964). *Stability and change in human characteristics.* New York: Wiley.

Blyth, D. A., Hill, J., & Thiel, K. (1982). Early adolescents' significant others: Grade and gender differences in perceived relationships with familial and nonfamilial adults and young people. *Journal of Youth and Adolescence, 11,* 425–450.

Blyth, D. A., & Leffert, N. (1995). Communities as contexts for adolescent development: An empirical analysis. *Journal of Adolescent Research, 10*(1), 64–87.

Bogenschneider, K. (1997). Parental involvement in adolescent schooling: A proximal process with transcontextual validity. *Journal of Marriage and the Family, 59,* 718–733.

Bogenschneider, K., Small, S. A., & Tsay, J. C. (1997). Child, parent, and contextual influences on perceived parenting competence among parents of adolescents. *Journal of Marriage and the Family, 59,* 345–362.

Bogenschneider, K., Wu, M., Raffaelli, M., & Tsay, J. C. (1998a). Parent influences on adolescent peer orientation and substance use: The interface of parenting practicing and values. *Child Development, 69,* 1672–1688.

Bogenschneider, K., Wu, M.-Y., Raffaelli, M., & Tsay, J. C. (1998b). "Other teens drink, but not my kid": Does parental awareness of adolescent alcohol use protect adolescents from risky consequences? *Journal of Marriage and the Family, 60,* 356–373.

Bolognini, M., Plancherel, B., Bettschart, W., & Halfon, O. (1996). Self-esteem and mental health in early adolescence: Development and gender differences. *Journal of Adolescence, 19,* 233–245.

Boney-McCoy, S., & Finkelhor, D. (1995a). Prior victimization: A risk factor for child sexual abuse and for PTSD-related symptomatology among sexually abused youth. *Child Abuse and Neglect, 19,* 1401–1421.

Boney-McCoy, S., & Finkelhor, D. (1995b). Special populations: Psychosocial sequelae of violent victimization in a national youth sample. *Journal of Consulting and Clinical Psychology, 63*(5), 726–736.

Bornstein, M. H. (Ed.). (1995). *Handbook of parenting: Vol. 3. Status and social conditions of parenting.* Mahwah, NJ: Erlbaum.

Borus, M., Rosario, M., Van Rossem, R., & Reid, H. (1995). Prevalence, course, and predictors of multiple problem behaviors among gay and bisexual male adolescents. *Developmental Psychology, 1,* 75–85.

Bowman, H. A., & Spanier, G. B. (1978). *Modern marriage* (8th ed.). New York: McGraw-Hill.

Boyd, G. M., Howard, J., & Zucker, R. A. (1994). Preventing alcohol abuse among adolescents: Preintervention and intervention research. *Journal of Research on Adolescence, 4,* 175–181.

Boyer, C. B., & Hein, K. (1991). AIDS and the HIV infection in adolescents: The role of education and antibody testing. In R. M. Lerner, A. C. Petersen, & J. Brooks-Gunn (Eds.), *Encyclopedia of Adolescence* (Vol. 2, pp. 1028–1041). New York: Garland.

Boyer, C. B., Shafer, M., & Tschann, J. M. (1997). Evaluation of a knowledge- and cognitive-behavioral skills-building intervention to prevent STDs and HIV infection in high school students. *Adolescence, 32*(125), 25–42.

Brabeck, M. (1983). Moral judgment: Theory and research on differences between males and females. *Developmental Review, 3,* 274–291.

Brack, C., Brack, G., & Orr, D. P. (1996). Adolescent health promotion: Testing a model using multidimensional scaling. *Journal of Research on Adolescence, 6*(2), 139–149.

Brandtstädter, J. (1998). Action perspectives on human development. In W. Damon (Series Ed.) & R. M. Lerner (Vol. Ed.), *Handbook of child psychology: Vol. 1. Theoretical models of human development* (5th ed., pp. 807–863). New York: Wiley.

Brandtstädter, J. (1999). The self in action and development: Cultural, biosocial, and ontogenetic bases of intentional self-development. In J. Brandtstädter & R. M. Lerner (Eds.), *Action and self-development: Theory and research through the life span.* Thousand Oaks, CA: Sage.

Brandtstädter, J., & Wentura, D. (1995). Adjustment to shifting possibility frontiers in later life: Complementary adaptive modes. In R. A. Dixon & L. Bäckman (Eds.), *Psychological compensation: Managing losses and promoting gains* (pp. 83–106). Hillsdale, NJ: Erlbaum.

Bray, N., Hersh, R. E., & Turner, L. A. (1985). Selective remembering during adolescence. *Developmental Psychology, 21*(2), 290–294.

Breen, D. T., & Crosbie-Burnette, M. (1993). Moral dilemmas of early adolescents of divorced and intact families: A qualitative and quantitative analysis. *Journal of Early Adolescence, 13,* 168–182.

Brewster, K. L., Cooksey, E. C., Guilkey, D. K., & Rindfuss, R. R. (1998). The changing impact of religion on the sexual and contraceptive behavior of adolescent women in the United States. *Journal of Marriage and the Family, 60,* 493–504.

Brittain, C. V. (1963). Adolescent choices and parent-peer cross pressures. *American Sociological Review, 28,* 385–391.

Brody, F., & Forehand, R. (1990). Interparental conflict, relationship with the noncustodial father, and adolescent postdivorce adjustment. *Journal of Applied Developmental Psychology, 32*(4), 696–706.

Brody, G. H., Stoneman, Z., & Flor, D. (1995). Linking family processes and academic competence among rural African American youths. *Journal of Marriage and the Family, 57,* 567–579.

Brody, G. H., Stoneman, Z., & Flor, D. (1996). Parental religiosity, family processes, and youth competence in rural, two-parent African American families. *Developmental Psychology, 32*(4), 696–706.

Broman, S. (1979). Seven-year outcome of 4,000 children born to teenagers in the U.S. In K. G. Scott, T. Field, & E. Robertson (Eds.), *Teenage parents and their offspring* (pp. 195–226). New York: Grune & Stratton.

Bronfenbrenner, U. (1960). Freudian theories of identification and their derivatives. *Child Development, 31,* 15–40.

Bronfenbrenner, U. (1977). Toward an experimental ecology of human development. *American Psychologist, 32,* 513–531.

Bronfenbrenner, U. (1979). *The ecology of human development: Experiments by nature and design.* Cambridge: Harvard University Press.

Bronfenbrenner, U., & Morris, P. A. (1998). The ecology of developmental process. In W. Damon (Series Ed.) & R. M. Lerner (Vol. Ed.), *Handbook of child psychology: Vol. 1. Theoretical models of human development* (5th ed., pp. 993–1028). New York: Wiley.

Bronstein, P., Fitzgerald, M., Briones, M., & Pieniadz, J. (1993). Family emotional expressiveness as a predictor of early adolescent social and psychological adjustment. *Journal of Early Adolescence, 13,* 448–471.

Brook, J. S., Whiteman, M., Gordon, A. S., & Cohen, P. (1986). Some models and mechanisms for explaining the impact of maternal and adolescent characteristics on adolescent stages of drug use. *Developmental Psychology, 22,* 460–467.

Brookins, G. K. (1991). Socialization of African American adolescents. In R. M. Lerner, A. C. Petersen, & J. Brooks-Gunn (Eds.), *Encyclopedia of adolescence* (Vol. 2, pp. 1072–1076). New York: Garland.

Brooks-Gunn, J. (1987). Pubertal processes in girls' psychological adaptation. In R. M. Lerner & T. T. Foch (Eds.), *Biological-psychosocial interactions in early adolescence: A life-span perspective* (pp. 123–153). Hillsdale, NJ: Erlbaum.

Brooks-Gunn, J. (1989). Pubertal processes and the early adolescent transition. In W. Damon (Ed.), *Child development today and tomorrow. The Jossey-Bass social and behavioral science series* (pp. 155–176). San Francisco: Jossey-Bass.

Brooks-Gunn, J., & Chase-Lansdale, P. L. (1995). Adolescent parenthood. In M. H. Bornstein (Ed.), *Handbook of parenting: Vol. 3. Status and social conditions of parenting* (pp. 113–149). Mahwah, NJ: Erlbaum.

Brooks-Gunn, J., & Furstenberg, F. F. (1986). The children of adolescent mothers: Physical, academic, and psychological outcomes. *Developmental Review, 6*(3), 224–251.

Brooks-Gunn, J., & Furstenberg, F. F., Jr. (1987). Continuity and change in the context of poverty: Adolescent mothers and their children. In J. J. Gallagher & C. T. Ramey (Eds.), *The malleability of children* (pp. 171–188). Baltimore: Brooks.

Brooks-Gunn, J., Gus, G., & Furstenberg, F. F. (1993). Who drops out of and continues beyond high school? A 20-year follow-up of black urban youth. *Journal of Research on Adolescence, 3*(3), 271–294.

Brooks-Gunn, J., & Petersen, A. C. (1983). *Girls at puberty: Biological and psychosocial perspectives.* New York: Plenum.

Brooks-Gunn, J., Petersen, A. C., & Eichorn, D. (1985). The study of maturational timing effects in adolescence. *Journal of Youth & Adolescence, 14*(3), 149–161.

Broverman, I. K., Vogel, S. R., Broverman, D. M., Clarkson, F. E., & Rosenkrantz, P. S. (1972). Sex-role stereotypes: A current appraisal. *Journal of Social Issues, 28,* 59–78.

Brown, B. B. (1990). Peer groups and peer cultures. In S. S. Feldman & G. R. Elliott (Eds.), *At the threshold: The developing adolescent* (pp. 171–196). Cambridge: Harvard University Press.

Brown, B. B. (1996). Visibility, vulnerability, development, and context: Ingredients for a fuller understanding of peer rejection in adolescence. *Journal of Early Adolescence, 16*(1), 27–36.

Brown, B. B., Clasen, D. R., & Neiss, J. D. (1987, April). *Smoke in the looking glass: Adolescents' perceptions of peer group status.* Paper presented at the biennial meetings of the Society for Research in Child Development, Baltimore.

Brown, B. B., Mory, M. S., & Kinney, D. (1994). Casting adolescent crowds in a relational perspective: Caricature, channel, and context. In R. Montemayor, G. R. Adams, & T. P. Gullotta (Eds.), *Personal relationships during adolescence. Advances in adolescent development: An annual book series* (Vol. 6, pp. 123–167). Thousand Oaks, CA: Sage.

Brown, B. B., Mounts, N., Lamborn, S. D., & Steinberg, L. (1993). Parenting practices and peer group affiliation in adolescence. *Child Development, 62,* 1008–1029.

Browne, C. S., & Rife, J. C. (1991). Social, personality, and gender differences in at-risk and not-at-risk sixth-grade students. *Journal of Early Adolescence, 11,* 482–495.

Bubolz, M. M., & Sontag, M. S. (1993). Human ecology theory. In P. G. Boss, W. J. Doherty, R. LaRossa, W. R. Schumm, & S. K. Steinmetz (Eds.), *Sourcebook of family theories and methods: A contextual approach* (pp. 419–448). New York: Plenum.

Buchanan, C. M. (1991). Assessment of pubertal development. In R. M. Lerner, A. C. Petersen, and J. Brooks-Gunn (Eds.), *Encyclopedia of adolescence* (Vol. 2, pp. 875–883). New York: Garland.

Buchanan, C. M., Maccoby, E., & Dornbusch, S. M. (1991). Caught between parents: Adolescents' experience in divorced homes. *Child Development, 62,* 1008–1029.

Buchanan, C. M., Maccoby, E. E., & Dornbusch, S. M. (1992). Adolescents and their families after divorce: Three residential arrangements compared. *Journal of Research on Adolescence, 2*(3), 261–291.

Buehler, C., Krishnakumar, A., Stone, G., Anthony, C., Pemberton, S., Gerard, J., & Barber, B. K. (1998). Interparental conflict styles and youth problem behaviors: A two-sample replication study. *Journal of Marriage and the Family, 60,* 119–132.

Buhrmester, D. (1988, March). *Interpersonal competence and friuendship in early adolescence.* Paper presented at the Second Biennial Meeting of the Society for Research on Adolescence, Alexandria, VA.

Bukowski, W. M., Hoza, B., & Boivin, M. (1993). Popularity, friendship, and emotional adjustment during early adolescence. *New Directions for Child Development, 60,* 23–37.

Bukowski, W. M., & Kramer, T. L. (1986). Judgments of the features of friendship among early adolescent boys and girls. *Journal of Early Adolescence, 6*(4), 331–338.

Bukowski, W. M., & Newcomb, A. F. (1987, April). *Friendship quality and the "self" during early adolescence.* Paper presented at the Biennial Meeting of the Society for Research in Child Development, Baltimore.

Bulcroft, R. A., Carmody, D. C., & Bulcroft, K. A. (1996). Patterns of parental independence giving to adolescents: Variations by race, age, and gender of child. *Journal of Marriage and the Family, 58,* 866–883.

Bumpass, L., & Sweet, J. (1989). National estimates of cohabitation. *Demography, 26*(4), 615–625.

Buzwell, S., & Rosenthal, D. (1996). Constructing a sexual self: Adolescents' sexual self-perceptions and sexual risk-taking. *Journal of Research on Adolescence, 6*(4), 489–513.

Byrnes, J. P., & Takahira, S. (1993). Explaining gender differences in SAT-math items. *Developmental Psychology, 29,* 805–810.

C

Cairns, R. B., & Cairns, B. D. (1994). *Lifelines and risks: Pathways of youth in our time.* New York: Cambridge University Press.

Cairns, E., & Dawes, A. (1996). Children: Ethnic and political violence—a commentary. *Child Development, 67,* 129–139.

Cairns, R. B., Leung, M., Buchanan, L., & Cairns, B. D. (1995). Friendships and social networks in childhood and adolescence: Fluidity, reliability, and interrelations. *Child Development, 66,* 1330–1345.

Call, K. T., Mortimer, J. T., & Shanahan, M. J. (1995). Helpfulness and the development of competence in adolescence. *Child Development, 66,* 129–138.

Camarena, P. M., Stemmler, M., & Petersen, A. C. (1994). The gender-differential significance of work and family: An exploration of adolescent experience and expectation. In R. K. Silbereisen & E. Todt (Eds.), *Adolescence in context: The interplay of family, school, peers, and work in adjustment* (pp. 201–221). New York: Springer-Verlag.

Camino, L. A. (1995). Understanding intolerance and multiculturalism: A challenge for practitioners, but also for researchers. *Journal of Adolescent Research, 10*(1), 155–172.

Canals, J., Carbajo, G., Fernandez, J., Marti-Henneberg, C., & Domenech, E. (1996). Biopsychopathologic risk profile of adolescents with eating disorder symptoms. *Adolescence, 31*(122), 443–450.

Cannetti, L., Bachar, E., Galili-Weisstub, E., De-Nour, A. K., & Shalev, Arieh Y. (1997). Parental bonding and mental health in adolescence. *Adolescence, 32*(126), 381–394.

Capaldi, D. M. (1996). The reliability of retrospective report timing first sexual intercourse for adolescent males. *Journal of Adolescent Research, 11*(3), 375–387.

Capaldi, D. M., Crosby, L., & Stoolmiller, M. (1996). Predicting the timing of first sexual intercourse for at-risk adolescent males. *Child Development, 67,* 344–359.

Carlo, G., Eisenberg, N., & Knight, G. (1992). An objective measure of adolescents' prosocial moral reasoning. *Journal of Research on Adolescence, 2*(4), 331–349.

Carnegie Corporation of New York. (1992). *A matter of time: Risk and opportunity in the nonschool hours.* New York: Author.

Carnegie Corporation of New York. (1994). *Starting points: Meeting the needs of our youngest children.* New York: Author.

Carnegie Corporation of New York. (1995). *Great transitions: Preparing adolescents for a new century.* New York: Author.

Carnegie Council on Adolescent Development. (1989). *Turning points: Preparing American youth for the twenty-first century.* Washington, DC: Author.

Carroll, A., Durkin, K., Hattie, J., & Houghton, S. (1997). Goal setting among adolescents: A comparison of delinquent, at risk, and not-at-risk youth. *Journal of Educational Psychology, 89*(3), 441–450.

Carson, A., Madison, T., & Santrock, J. (1987). Relationships between possible selves and self-reported problems of divorced and intact family adolescents. *Journal of Early Adolescence, 7*(20), 191–204.

Carstensen, L. L., Hanson, K. A., & Freund, A. (1995). Selection and compensation in adulthood. In R. A. Dixon & L. Bäckman (Eds.), *Compensating for psychological deficits and declines: Managing losses and promoting gains* (pp. 107–126). Hillsdale, NJ: Erlbaum.

Casey, M. B., Nuttall, R., Pezaris, E., & Benbow, C. P. (1995). The influence of spatial ability on gender differences in mathematics college entrance test scores across diverse samples. *Developmental Psychology, 31*(4), 697–705.

Caspi, A., Henry, B., McGee, R. O., Moffitt, T. E., & Silva, P. A. (1995). Temperamental origins of child and adolescent behavior problems: From age three to age fifteen. *Child Development, 66,* 55–68.

Caspi, A., Lynam, D., Moffitt, T. E., & Silva, P. A. (1993). Unraveling girls' delinquency: Biological, dispositional, and contextual contributions to adolescent misbehavior. *Developmental Psychology, 29,* 19–30.

Caspi, A., & Silva, P. A. (1995). Temperamental qualities at age three predict personality traits in young adulthood: Longitudinal evidence from a birth cohort. *Child Development, 66,* 486–498.

Cassidy, L., & Hurrell, R. M. (1995). The influence of the victim's attire on adolescents' judgements of date rape. *Adolescence, 30*(118), 319–323.

Castellino, D. R., & Lerner, R. M. (1999, May). *Youth and vocational development: A developmental contextual perspective.* Paper presented at the Fourth National Conference of the Society for Vocational Psychology, a section of the Counseling Psychology Division of the American Psychological Association, on "Examining the interaction of person in environment: Role of context factors in vocational development," Milwaukee, WI.

Catell, R. B. (1963). Theory of fluid and crystallized intelligence: A critical experiment. *Journal of Educational Psychology, 54,* 1–22.

Cattell, R. B. (1973). *Personality and mood by questionnaire.* San Francisco: Jossey-Bass.

Cauffman, E., & Steinberg, L. (1996). Interactive effects of menarcheal status and dating on dieting and disordered eating among adolescent girls. *Developmental Psychology, 32*(4), 631–635.

Ceci, S. J., & Bronfenbrenner, U. (1985). "Don't forget to take the cupcakes out of the oven": Prospective memory, strategic time-monitoring, and context. *Child Development, 56*(1), 152–164.

Center for the Study of Social Policy. (1992). *1992 Kids Count Data Book: State profiles of child well-being.* Washington, DC: Author.

Center for the Study of Social Policy. (1993). *1993 Kids Count Data Book.* Washington, DC: Author.

Center for the Study of Social Policy. (1995). *Kids count data book.* Washington, DC: Author.

Centers for Disease Control and Prevention. (1998). Youth risk behavior surveillance—United States, 1997. *Morbidity and Mortality Weekly Report, 47,* (33-3).

Chamberlain, P., & Reid, J. B. (1998). Comparison of two community alternatives to incarceration for chronic juvenile offenders. *Journal of Consulting and Clinical Psychology, 66*(4), 624–633.

Chase-Lansdale, P. L., Cherlin, A. J., & Kiernan, K. E. (1995). The long-term effects of parental divorce on the mental health of young adults: A developmental perspective. *Child Development, 66,* 1614–1634.

Chase-Lansdale, P. L., Wakschlag, L. S., & Brooks-Gunn, J. (1995). A psychological perspective on the development of caring in children and youth: The role of the family. *Journal of Adolescence, 18,* 515–556.

Chassin, L. A., Presson, C. C., Sherman, S. J., Montello, D., & McGrew, J. (1986). Changes in peer and parent influence during adolescence: Longitudinal versus cross-sectional perspectives on smoking initiation. *Developmental Psychology, 22*(3), 327–334.

Chen, C., Lee, S.-Y., & Stevenson, H. W. (1996). Long-term prediction of academic achievement of American, Chinese, and Japanese adolescents. *Journal of Educational Psychology, 18*(4), 750–759.

Chen, C., & Stevenson, H. W. (1995). Motivation and mathematics achievement: A comparative study of Asian-American, Caucasian-American, and East Asian high school students. *Child Development, 66,* 1215–1234.

Chess, S., & Thomas, A. (1984). *The origins and evolution of behavior disorders: Infancy to early adult life.* New York: Brunner/Mazel.

Chibucos, T., & Lerner, R. M. (1999). *Serving children and families through community-university partnerships: Success stories.* Norwell, MA: Kluwer.

Children's Defense Fund. (1992). *Child poverty data from 1990 census.* Washington, DC: Author.

Children's Defense Fund. (1995). *The state of America's children yearbook.* Washington, DC: Author.

Children's Defense Fund. (2001). *The state of America's children yearbook.* Washington, DC: Author.

Chiu, M. L., Feldman, S. S., & Rosenthal, D. A. (1992). The influence of immigration on parental behavior and adolescent distress in Chinese families residing in two Western nations. *Journal of Research on Adolescence, 2,* 205–239.

Chubb, N. H., Fertman, C. I., & Ross, J. L. (1997). Adolescent self-esteem and locus of control: A longitudinal study of gender and age differences. *Adolescence, 32*(125), 113–129.

Clancy, S. M., & Dollinger, S. J. (1993). Identity, self, and personality: I. Identity status and the five-factor model of personality. *Journal of Research on Adolescence, 3*(3), 227–245.

Clark, J., & Barber, B. L. (1994). Adolescents in postdivorce and always-married families: Self-esteem and perceptions of fathers' interest. *Journal of Marriage and the Family, 56,* 608–614.

Clark-Lempers, D., Lempers, J., & Netusil, A. (1990). Family financial stress, parental support, and young adolescents' academic achievement and depressive symptoms. *Journal of Early Adolescence, 10*(1), 21–36.

Clausen, J. A. (1975). The social meaning of differential physical and sexual maturation. In S. E. Dragastin & G. H. Elder, Jr. (Eds.), *Adolescence in the life cycle* (pp. 25–97). New York: Wiley.

Clingempeel, W. G., Colyar, J. J., Brand, E., & Hetherington, E. M. (1992). Children's relationships with maternal grandparents: A longitudinal study of family structure and pubertal status effects. *Child Development, 63*(6), 1404–1422.

Coates, D. L. (1991). Social networks in adolescence. In R. M. Lerner, A. C. Petersen, & J. Brooks-Gunn (Eds.), *Encyclopedia of adolescence* (Vol. 2, pp. 1077–1085). New York: Garland.

Coates, D. L., & Van Widenfelt, B. (1991). Pregnancy in adolescence. In R. M. Lerner, A. C. Petersen, & J. Brooks-Gunn (Eds.), *Encyclopedia of adolescence* (Vol. 1, pp. 794–802). New York: Garland.

Cohler, B. J., & Musick, J. S. (1996). Adolescent parenthood and the transition to adulthood. In J. Graber, J. Brooks-Gunn, & A. C. Petersen (Eds.), *Transitions through adolescence: Interpersonal domains and context* (pp. 201–231). Mahwah, NJ: Erlbaum.

Colby, A. (1978). Evolution of a moral-development theory. *New Directions for Child Development, 2,* 89–104.

Colby, A., & Damon, W. (1992). *Some do care: Contemporary lives of moral commitment.* New York: Free Press.

Colby, A., Kohlberg, L., Gibbs, J., & Lieberman, M. (1983). A longitudinal study of moral judgment. *Monographs of the Society for Research in Child Development, 48* (200).

Cole, D. A., Peeke, L. G., Martin, J. M., Truglio, R., & Seroczynski, A. D. (1998). A longitudinal look at the relation between depression and anxiety in children and adolescents. *Journal of Consulting and Clinical Psychology, 66*(3), 451–460.

Collins, W. A. (1997). Relationships and development during adolescence: Interpersonal adaptation to individual change. *Personal Relationships, 4,* 1–14.

Collins, W. A., Laursen, B., Mortensen, N., Luebker, C., & Ferreira, M. (1997). Conflict processes and transitions in parent and peer relationships: Implications for autonomy and regulation. *Journal of Adolescent Research, 12,* 178–198.

Comer, J. (1989). Educating poor minority children. *Scientific American, 259*(5), 42–48.

Comite, F., Pescovitz, O., Sonis, W., Hench, K., McNemar, A., Klein, R. P., Loriaux, D., & Cutler, G. (1987). Premature adolescence: Neuroendocrine and psychosocial studies. In R. M. Lerner & T. T. Foch (Eds.), *Biological-psychosocial interactions in early adolescence* (pp. 155–171). Hillsdale, NJ: Erlbaum.

Compas, B. E., Howell, D. C., Phares, V., Williams, R. A., & Giunta, C. (1989). Risk factors for emotional/behavioral problems in young adolescents: A prospective analysis of adolescent and parental stress and symptoms. *Journal of Consulting & Clinical Psychology, 57*, 732–740.

Compas, B. E., Oppedisano, G., Connor, J. K., Gerhardt, C. A., Hinden, B. R., Achenbach, T. M., & Hammen, C. (1997). Gender differences in depressive symptoms in adolescence: Comparison of national samples of clinically referred and nonreferred youths. *Journal of Consulting and Clinical Psychology, 65*(4), 617–626.

Conger, K. J., Conger, R. D., & Scaramella, L. V. (1997). Parents, siblings, psychological control, and adolescent adjustment. *Journal of Adolescent Research, 12*(1), 113–138.

Conger, R. D., Conger, K. J., Elder, G. H., Jr., Lorenz, F. O., Simons, R. L., & Whitbeck, L. B. (1992). A family process model of economic hardship and adjustment of early adolescent boys. *Child Development, 63*, 526–541.

Conger, R. D., & Elder, G. H., Jr. (1994). *Families in troubled times: Adapting to change in rural America. Social institutions and social change.* New York: Aldine de Gruyter.

Conger, R. D., Lorenz, F. O., Elder, G. H., Jr., Melby, J. N., Simons, R. L., & Conger, K. J. (1991). A process model of family economic pressure and early adolescent alcohol use. *Journal of Early Adolescence, 11*, 430–499.

Conger, R. D., Patterson, G. R., & Ge, X. (1995). It takes two to replicate: A mediational model for the impact of parents' stress on adolescent adjustment. *Child Development, 66*, 80–97.

Connell, A., & Farrington, D. P. (1996). Bullying among incarcerated young offenders: Developing an interview schedule and some preliminary results. *Journal of Adolescence, 19*, 75–93.

Connell, J. P., Halpern-Felsher, B. L., Clifford, E., Crichlow, W., & Usinger, P. (1995). Hanging in there: Behavioral, psychological, and contextual factors affecting whether African American adolescents stay in high school. *Journal of Adolescence Research, 10*(1), 41–63.

Connell, J. P., Kubisch, A. C., Schorr, L. B., & Weiss, C. H. (1995). *New approaches to evaluating community initiatives: Concepts, methods, and contexts.* Washington, DC: The Aspen Institute.

Constantinople, A. (1969). An Eriksonian measure of personality development in college students. *Developmental Psychology, 1*, 357–372.

Cooper, C. R. (1994a). Cultural perspectives on continuity and change in adolescents' relationships. In R. Montemayor, G. R. Adams, & T. P. Gulotta (Eds.), *Advances in adolescent development: Vol. 6. Personal relationships during adolescence* (pp. 78–100). Thousand Oaks, CA: Sage.

Cooper, C. R. (1994b). Cultural perspectives on individuality and connectedness in adolescent development. In C. Nelson & A. Masten (Eds.), *Minnesota symposium on child psychology: Cultural processes in child development.* Hillsdale, NJ: Erlbaum.

Cooper, C. R., Grotevant, H. D., & Condon, S. M. (1983). Individuality and connectedness in the family as a context for adolescent identity formation and role-taking skill. *New Directions for Child Development, 22*, 43–59.

Cooper, C. R., Jackson, J. F., Azmitia, M., & Lopez, E. M. (1998). Multiple selves, multiple worlds: Ethnically sensitive research on identity, relationships, and opportunity structures in adolescence. In V. McLoyd & L. Steinberg (Eds.), *Conceptual and methodological issues in the study of minority adolescents and their families.* Hillsdale, NJ: Erlbaum.

Corbett, T. (1995). Changing the culture of welfare. *Focus, 16*, 12–22.

Cornell, D. G., Peterson, C. S., & Richards, H. (1999). Anger as a predictor of aggression among incarcerated adolescents. *Journal of Consulting and Clinical Psychology, 67*(1), 108–115.

Cornwell, G. T., Eggebeen, D. J., & Meschke, L. L. (1996). The changing family context of early adolescence. *Journal of Early Adolescence, 16*(2), 141–156.

Corvo, K. N. (1997). Community-based youth violence prevention: A framework for planners and funders. *Youth & Society, 28*(3), 291–316.

Costa, F. M., Jessor, R., Donovan, J. E., & Fortenberry, J. D. (1995). Early initiation of sexual intercourse: The influence of psychosocial unconventionality. *Journal of Research on Adolescence, 5*(1), 93–121.

Côté, J. E. (1996). Sociological perspectives on identity formation: The culture-identity link and identity capital. *Journal of Adolescence, 19*, 417–428.

Cotgrove, A., Zirinsky, L., Black, D., & Weston, D. (1995). Secondary prevention of attempted suicide in adolescence. *Journal of Adolescence, 18*, 569–577.

Cotterell, J. L. (1992). School size as a factor in adolescents' adjustment to the transition to secondary school. *Journal of Early Adolescence, 12*(1), 28–45.

Covell, K. (1996). National and gender differences in adolescents' war attitudes. *International Journal of Behavioral Development, 19*(4), 871–883.

Crockett, L., Losoff, M., & Petersen, A. C. (1984). Perceptions of the peer group and friendship in early adolescence. *Journal of Early Adolescence, 4*(2), 155–181.

Crockett, L., & Petersen, A. (1987). Pubertal status and psychosocial development: Findings from the Early Adolescence Study. In R. M. Lerner & T. Foch (Eds.), *Biological-psychosocial interactions in early adolescence* (pp. 173–188). Hillsdale, NJ: Erlbaum.

Crouter, A. C., Manke, B. A., & McHale, S. M. (1995). The family context of gender intensification in early adolescence. *Child Development, 66*, 317–329.

Crystal, D. S., & Stevenson, H. W. (1995). What is a bad kid? Answers of adolescents and their mothers in three cultures. *Journal of Research on Adolescence, 5*(1), 71–91.

Csapó, B. (1997). The development of inductive reasoning: Cross-sectional assessments in an educational context. *International Journal of Behavioral Development, 20*(4), 609–626.

Csikszentmihalyi, M., & Larson, R. (1987). Validity and reliability of the experience-sampling method. *Journal of Nervous & Mental Disease, 175*(9), 526–536.

Culp, A. M., Clyman, M. M., & Culp, R. E. (1995). Adolescent depressed mood, reports of suicide attempts, and asking for help. *Adolescence, 30*(120), 827–837.

Cutler, G. B. (1991). Adrenarche. In R. M. Lerner, A. C. Petersen, & J. Brooks-Gunn (Eds.), *Encyclopedia of adolescence.* (Vol. 1). New York: Garland.

Cunningham, M., & Spencer, M. B. (1996). The black male experiences measure. In R. L. Jones (Ed.), *Handbook of tests and measurements for black populations* (pp. 301–307). Hampton, VA: Cobb & Henry.

Curran, P. J., Stice, E., & Chassin, L. (1997). The relation between adolescent alcohol use and peer alcohol use: A longitudinal random coefficients model. *Journal of Consulting and Clinical Psychology, 65*(1), 130–140.

D

Damon, W. (1991). Problems of direction in socially shared cognition. In L. B. Resnick, J. M. Levine, & S. D. Teasley (Eds.), *Perspectives on socially shared cognition* (pp. 384–397). Washington, DC: American Psychological Association.

Damon, W. (1997). *The youth charter: How communities can work together to raise standards for all our children.* New York: Free Press.

Damon, W., & Gregory, A. (1997). The youth charter: Towards the formation of adolescent moral identity. *Journal of Moral Education, 26,* 117–131.

Damon, W., & Hart, D. (1988). *Self-understanding in childhood and adolescence.* New York: Cambridge University Press.

D'Angelo, L. L., Weinberger, D. A., & Feldman, S. S. (1995). Like father, like son? Predicting male adolescents' adjustment from parents' distress and self-restraint. *Developmental Psychology, 31*(6), 883–896.

D'Augelli, A. R., & Patterson, C. J. (Eds.). (1995). *Lesbian, gay, and bisexual identities over the lifespan: Psychological perspectives.* New York: Oxford University Press.

Davis, A. A., Rhodes, J. E., & Hamilton-Leaks, J. (1997). When both parents may be a source of support and problems: An analysis of pregnant and parenting female African-American adolescents' relationships with their mothers and fathers. *Journal of Research on Adolescence, 7*(3), 331–348.

Dawkins, M. P. (1997). Drug use and violent crime among adolescents. *Adolescence, 32*(126), 395–405.

De Gaston, J. F., Weed, S., & Jensen, L. (1996). Understanding gender differences in adolescent sexuality. *Adolescence, 31*(121), 217–231.

DeBaryshe, B. D., Patterson, G. R., & Capaldi, D. M. (1993). A performance model for academic achievement in early adolescent boys. *Developmental Psychology, 29,* 795–804.

Degirmencioglu, S. M., Urberg, K. A., Tolson, J. M., & Richard, P. (1998). Adolescent friendship networks: Continuity and change over the school year. *Merrill-Palmer Quarterly, 44*(3), 313–337.

Delaney, M. E. (1996). Across the transition to adolescence: Qualities of parent/adolescent relationships and adjustment. *Journal of Early Adolescence, 16*(3), 274–300.

Demetriou, A., Pachaury, A., Metallidou, Y., & Kazi, S. (1996). Universals and specificities in the structure and development of quantitative-relational thought: A cross-cultural study in Greece and India. *International Journal of Behavioral Development, 19*(2), 255–290.

Demo, D. H., & Acock, A. C. (1988). The impact of divorce on children. *Journal of Marriage and the Family, 50,* 619–648.

Demo, D. H., & Acock, A. C. (1996). Family structure, family process, and adolescent well-being. *Journal of Research on Adolescence, 6*(4), 457–488.

Demos, D. H., Allen, K., & Fine, M. (2000). *Handbook of family diversity.* New York: Oxford University Press.

Demos, V. (1986). Crying in early infancy: An illustration of the motivational function of affect. In T. B. Brazelton & M. W. Yogman (Eds.), *Affective development in infancy* (pp. 39–73). Norwood, NJ: Ablex.

Dietz, W. H., Jr., & Gortmaker, S. L. (1985). Do we fatten our children at the television set? Obesity and television viewing in children and adolescents. *Pediatrics, 75,* 807–812.

Dimant, R. J., & Bearison, D. J. (1991). Development of formal reasoning during successive peer interactions. *Developmental Psychology, 27,* 277–284.

di Mauro, D. (1995). *Sexuality research in the United States: An assessment of social and behavioral sciences.* New York: Social Science Research Council.

Dishion, T. J., Andrews, D. W., & Crosby, L. (1995). Antisocial boys and their friends in early adolescence: Relationship characteristics, quality, and interactional process. *Child Development, 66*(1), 139–151.

Dishion, T. J., Patterson, G. R., Stoolmiller, M., & Skinner, M. L. (1991). Family, school, and behavioral antecedents to early adolescent involvement with antisocial peers. *Developmental Psychology, 27*(1), 172–180.

Dixon, R. A., & Lerner, R. M. (1999). History and systems in developmental psychology. In M. Bornstein & M. Lamb (Eds.), *Developmental psychology: An advanced textbook* (4th ed., pp. 3–45). Mahwah, NJ: Erlbaum.

Dobkin, P. L., Tremblay, R. E., Masse, L. C., & Vitaro, F. (1995). Individual and peer characteristics in predicting boys' early onset of substance abuse: A seven-year longitudinal study. *Child Development, 66,* 1198–1214.

Doherty, W. J., & Needle, R. H. (1991). Psychological adjustment and substance use among adolescents before and after a parental divorce. *Child Development, 62,* 328–337.

Dolan, B. (1995). A Teen hot line. *Adolescence, 30*(117), 195–200.

Dolcini, M. M., Cohn, L. D., Adler, N. E., Millstein, S. G., Irwin, C. E., Kegeles, S. M., & Stone, G. C. (1989). Adolescent egocentrism and feelings of invulnerability: Are they related? *Journal of Early Adolescence, 9,* 409–418.

Donnelly, M. (1995). Depressions among adolescents in Northern Ireland. *Adolescence, 30*(118), 339–350.

Dornbusch, S. M., Carlsmith, J. M., Bushwall, S. J., Ritter, P. L., Leiderman, H., Hastorf, A. H., & Gross, R. T. (1985). Single parents extended households and the control of adolescents. *Child Development, 56,* 326–341.

Dornbusch, S. M., Carlsmith, J. M., Gross, R. T., Martin, J. A., Jennings, D., Rosenberg, A., & Duke, P. (1981). Sexual development, age, and dating: A comparison of biological and social influences upon one set of behaviors. *Child Development, 52,* 179–185.

Douglas, J. D., & Wong, A. C. (1977). Formal operations: Age and sex differences in Chinese and American children. *Child Development, 48,* 689–692.

Douvan, J. D., & Adelson, J. (1966). *The adolescent experience.* New York: Wiley.

Drumm, P., & Jackson, D. W. (1996). Developmental changes in questioning strategies during adolescence. *Journal of Adolescent Research, 11*(3), 285–305.

Dryfoos, J. G. (1990). *Adolescents at risk: Prevalence and prevention.* New York: Oxford University Press.

Dryfoos, J. G. (1994). *Full service schools: A revolution in health and social services for children, youth, and families.* San Francisco: Jossey-Bass.

Dryfoos, J. G. (1995). Full service schools: A revolution or fad? *Journal of Research on Adolescence, 5,* 149–150.

Dryfoos, J. G. (1998). *Safe passage: Making it through adolescence in a risky society.* New York: Oxford University Press.

Dubois, D. L., Eitel, S. K., & Felner, R. D. (1994). Effects of family environment and parent-child relationships on school adjustment during the transition to early adolescence. *Journal of Marriage and the Family, 56,* 405–414.

DuBois, D. L., Felner, R. D., Brand, S., Phillips, R. S. C., & Lease, A. M. (1996). Early adolescent self-esteem: A developmental-ecological framework and assessment strategy. *Journal of Research on Adolescence, 6*(4), 543–579.

Dubois, D. L., & Hirsch, B. J. (1993). School/nonschool friendship patterns in early adolescence. *Journal of Early Adolescence, 13*(1), 102–122.

Duncan, G. J. (1991). The economic environment of childhood. In A. C. Huston (Ed.), *Children in poverty: Child development and public policy* (pp. 23–50). Cambridge: Cambridge University Press.

Dunlop, R., & Burns, A. (1995). The sleeper effect—myth or reality? *Journal of Marriage and the Family, 57,* 375–386.

Dunn, M. E., & Goldman, M. S. (1998). Age and drinking-related differences in the memory organization of alcohol expectancies in 3rd-, 6th-, 9th-, and 12th-grade children. *Journal of Consulting and Clinical Psychology, 66*(3), 579–585.

DuRant, R. H., Getts, A. G., Cadenhead, C., & Woods, E. R. (1995). The association between weapon-carrying and the use of violence among adolescents living in or around public housing. *Journal of Adolescence, 18*(5), 579–592.

Durbin, D. L., Darling, N., Steinberg, L., & Brown, B. B. (1993). Parenting style and peer group membership among European-American adolescents. *Journal of Research on Adolescence, 3*(1), 87–100.

Dyl, J., & Wapner, S. (1996). Age and gender differences in the nature, meaning, and function of cherished possessions for children and adolescents. *Journal of Experimental Child Psychology, 62,* 340–377.

Dylan, B. (1964). My back pages. *Another side of Bob Dylan.* New York: Columbia Records.

E

East, P. L. (1989). Early adolescents' perceived interpersonal risks and benefits: Relations to social support and psychological functioning. *Journal of Early Adolescence, 2*(4), 374–395.

East, P. L. (1991). The parent-child relationships of withdrawn, aggressive, and sociable children: Child and parent perspectives. *Merrill-Palmer Quarterly, 37*(3), 425–443.

East, P. L. (1996). The younger sisters of childbearing adolescents: Their attitude, expectations, and behaviors. *Child Development, 67,* 267–282.

East, P. L., & Felice, M. E. (1996). *Adolescent pregnancy and parenting: Findings from a racially diverse sample.* Mahwah, NJ: Erlbaum.

East, P. L., Felice, M. E., & Morgan, M. C. (1993). Sisters' and girlfriends' sexual and childbearing behavior: Effects on early adolescent girls' sexual outcomes. *Journal of Marriage and the Family, 55,* 953–963.

East, P. L., Hess, L. E., & Lerner, R. M. (1987). Peer social support and adjustment of early adolescent peer groups. *Journal of Early Adolescence, 7*(2), 153–163.

East, P., Lerner, R. M., Lerner, J. V., Soni, R. T., Ohannessian, C. M., & Jacobson, L. P. (1992). Early adolescent-peer group fit, peer relations, and psychosocial competence: A short-term longitudinal study. *Journal of Early Adolescence, 12*(2), 132–152.

Ebata, A. T. (1996). Making university-community collaborations work: Challenges for institutions and individuals. *Journal of Research on Adolescence, 6*(1), 71–79.

Eccles, J. S. (1991). Academic achievement. In R. M. Lerner, A. C. Petersen, & J. Brooks-Gunn (Eds.), *Encyclopedia of adolescence* (Vol. 1, pp. 1–9). New York: Garland.

Eccles, J. S. (1996). The power and difficulty of university-community collaboration. *Journal of Research on Adolescence, 6*(1), 81–86.

Eccles, J. S., Early, D., Frasier, K., Belansky, E., & McCarthy, K. (1997). The relation of connection, regulation, and support for autonomy to adolescents' functioning. *Journal of Adolescent Research, 12*(2), 263–286.

Eccles, J. S., & Midgley, C. (1989). Stage-environment fit: Developmentally appropriate classrooms for young adolescents. In C. Ames & R. Ames (Eds.), *Research on motivation in education. Goals and cognitions* (Vol. 3, pp. 139–186). New York: Academic Press.

Eckert, P. (1995). Trajectory and forms of institutional participation. In L. J. Crockertt & A. C. Crouter (Eds.), *Pathways though adolescence: Individual development in relation to social contexts* (pp. 175–195). Mahway, NJ: Erlbaum.

Eder, D., & Kinney, D. A. (1995). The effect of middle school extracurricular activities on adolescents' popularity and peer status. *Youth & Society, 26*(3), 298–324.

Edwards, W. J. (1996). A sociological analysis of an invisible minority group. *Youth & Society, 27*(3), 334–355.

Eisenberg, N. (1986). *Altruistic emotion, cognition, and behavior.* Hillsdale, NJ: Erlbaum.

Eisenberg, N. (1991). Values, sympathy, and individual differences: Toward a pluralism of factors influencing altruism and empathy. *Psychological Inquiry, 2*(2), 128–131.

Eisenberg, N., Carlo, G., Murphy, B., & Van Court, P. (1995). Prosocial development in late adolescence: A longitudinal study. *Child Development, 66,* 1179–1197.

Eisenberg, N., & Fabes, R. A. (1998). Prosocial development. In N. Eisenberg (Ed.) & W. Damon (Ed. in chief), *Handbook of child psychology: Vol. 3. Social, emotional, and personality development* (5th ed., pp. 1097–1149). New York: Wiley.

Eisenberg, N., & McNally, S. (1993). Socialization and mothers' and adolescents' empathy-related characteristics. *Journal of Research on Adolescence, 3*(2), 171–191.

Eisenberg, N., & Mussen, P. (1989). *The roots of prosocial behavior in children.* Cambridge, England: Cambridge University Press.

Eisenberg-Berg, N. (1979). The development of children's prosocial moral judgment. *Developmental Psychology, 15,* 128–137.

Eisenberg-Berg, N., & Geisheker, E. (1979). Content of preachings and power of the model-preacher: Effect on children's generosity. *Developmental Psychology, 15*(2), 168–175.

Eiser, C., Havermans, T., & Eiser, J. R. (1995). The emergence during adolescence of gender differences in symptom reporting. *Journal of Adolescence, 18,* 307–316.

Elder, G. H., Jr. (1974). *Children of the Great Depression: Social change in life experiences.* Chicago: University of Chicago Press.

Elder, G. H., Jr. (1980). Adolescence in historical perspective. In J. Adelson (Ed.), *Handbook of adolescent psychology* (pp. 3–46). New York: Wiley.

Elder, G. H., Jr. (1998). The life course and human development. In W. Damon (Series Ed.) & R. M. Lerner (Vol. Ed.), *Handbook of child psychology: Vol. 1. Theoretical models of human development* (5th ed., pp. 939–991). New York: Wiley.

Elder, G. H., Jr. (1999). *Children of the Great Depression: Social change in life experience* (25th anniversary ed.). Boulder, CO: Westview Press.

Elder, G. H., Jr., & Conger, R. D. (2000). *Children of the land: Adversity and success in rural America.* Chicago: University of Chicago Press.

Elder, G. H., Jr., Modell, J., & Parke, R. D. (Eds.). (1993). Children in time and place: Developmental and historical insights. New York: Cambridge University Press.

Elkind, D. (1967). Egocentrism in adolescents. *Child Development, 38,* 1025–1034.

Elkind, D. (1968). Combinatorial thinking in adolescents from graded to ungraded classrooms. *Perceptual and Motor Skills, 27,* 1015–1018.

Elkind, D. (1980). The role of play in religious education. *Religious Education, 75,* 282–293.

Elkind, D., & Bowen, R. (1979). Imaginary audience behavior in children and adolescents. *Developmental Psychology, 15*(1), 38–44.

Elster, J. (1991). Local justice and interpersonal comparisons. In J. Elster & J. E. Roemer (Eds.), *Interpersonal comparisons of well-being. Studies in rationality and social change* (pp. 98–126). Cambridge: Cambridge University Press.

Emmons, L. (1996). The relationship of dieting to weight in adolescents. *Adolescence, 31*(121), 167–178.

Emshoff, J., Avery, E., Raduka, G., Anderson, D. J., & Calvert, C. (1996). Findings from SUPER STARS: A health promotion program for families to enhance multiple protective factors. *Journal of Adolescent Research, 11*(1), 68–96.

Enarson, H. L. (1989). *Revitalizing the landgrant mission.* Blacksburg: Virginia Polytechnic Institute and State University.

England, E. M., & Petro, K. D. (1998). Middle school students' perceptions of peer groups: Relative judgments about group characteristics. *Journal of Early Adolescence, 18*(4), 349–373.

Ennett, S. T., & Bauman, K. E. (1993). Peer group structure and adolescent cigarette smoking: A social network analysis. *Journal of Health & Social Behavior, 34*(3), 226–236.

Ennett, S. T., & Bauman, K. E. (1996). Adolescent social networks: School, demographic, and longitudinal considerations. *Journal of Adolescent Research, 11*(2), 194–215.

Enright, R. D., Lapsley, D. K., & Shukla, D. G. (1979). Adolescent egocentrism in early and late adolescence. *Adolescence, 14*(56), 687–695.

Enright, R. D., Shukla, D. G., & Lapsley, D. K. (1980). Adolescent egocentrism-sociocentrism and self-consciousness. *Journal of Youth and Adolescence, 9*(2), 101–116.

Ensminger, M. E., Lamkin, R. P., & Jacobson, N. (1996). School leaving: A longitudinal perspective including neighborhood effects. *Child Development, 67,* 2400–2416.

Epstein, J. L. (1983). Selection of friends in differently organized schools and classrooms. In J. L. Epstein & N. Karweit (Eds.), *Friends in school: Patterns of selection and influence in secondary schools* (pp. 73–92). New York: Wiley.

Epstein, J. L., & Dauber, S. L. (1995). Effects on students of an interdisciplinary program linking social studies, arts, and family volunteers in the middle grades. *Journal of Early Adolescence, 15*(1), 114–144.

Erikson, E. H. (1950). *Childhood and society.* New York: Norton.

Erikson, E. H. (1959). Identity and the lifecycle. *Psychological Issues, 1,* 18–164.

Erikson, E. (1963). *Childhood and society* (2nd ed.). New York: Norton.

Erikson, E. (1964). Inner and outer space: Reflections on womanhood. In R. J. Lifton (Ed.), *The woman in America* (pp. 1–26). Boston: Beacon Press.

Erikson, E. H. (1968). *Identity, youth and crisis.* New York: Norton.

Estrada, P. (1995). Adolescents' self-reports of prosocial responses to friends and acquaintances: The role of sympathy-related cognitive, affective, and motivational processes. *Journal of Research on Adolescence, 5*(2), 173–200.

Etaugh, C., & Liss, M. B. (1992). Home, school, and playroom: Training grounds for adult gender roles. *Sex Roles, 26* (3–4), 129–147.

F

Fabes, R. A., & Eisenberg, N. (1996). [An examination of age and sex differences in prosocial behavior and empathy.] Unpublished data. Arizona State University.

Falkner, F. (1972). Physical growth. In H. L. Bennett & A. H. Einhorn (Eds.), *Pediatrics.* New York: Appleton-Century-Crofts.

Farran, D. C., & Margolis, L. H. (1987). The family economic environment as a context for children's development. *New Directions for Child Development, 35,* 69–87.

Farrell, A. D., & White, K. S. (1998). Peer influence and drug use among urban adolescents: Family structure and parent–adolescent relationship as protective factors. *Journal of Consulting and Clinical Psychology, 66*(2), 248–258.

Faubert, M., Locke, D. C., Sprinthall, N. A., & Howland, W. H. (1996). Promoting cognitive and ego development of African-American rural youth: A program of deliberate psychological education. *Journal of Adolescence, 19,* 533–543.

Featherman, D. L., & Lerner, R. M. (1985). Ontogenesis and sociogenesis: Problematic for theory about development across the lifespan. *American Sociological Review, 50,* 659–676.

Featherman, D. L., Spenner, K. I., & Tsunematsu, N. (1988). Class and the socialization of children: Constancy, change, or irrelevance? In R. M. Lerner, E. M. Hetherington, & M. Perlmutter (Eds.), *Child development in life-span perspective* (pp. 67–90). Hillsdale, NJ: Erlbaum.

Feiring, C. (1996). Concepts of romance in 15-year-old adolescents. *Journal of Research on Adolescence, 6*(2), 181–200.

Feldman, B. (1995). The search for identity in late adolescence. In M. Sidoli & G. Bovensiepen (Eds.), *Incest fantasies and self-destructive acts: Jungian and post-Jungian psychotherapy in adolescence* (pp. 153–166). New Brunswick, NJ: Transaction.

Feldman, D. H. (2000). *Piaget's stages: The unfinished symphony.* Unpublished manuscript, Eliot-Pearson Department of Child Development, Tufts University.

Feldman, S. S., & Elliott, G. E. (1990). *At the threshold: The developing adolescent.* Cambridge: Harvard University Press.

Feldman, S. S., Fisher, L., Ransom, D. C., & Dimiceli, S. (1995). "Is what is good for the goose good for the gander?" Sex differences in relations between adolescent coping and adult adaptation. *Journal of Research on Adolescence, 5*(3), 333–359.

Feldman, S. S., Fisher, L., & Seitel, L. (1997). The effect of parents' marital satisfaction on young adults' adaptation: A longitudinal study. *Journal of Research on Adolescence, 7,* 55–80.

Feldman, S. S., Mont-Reynaud, R., & Rosenthal, D. A. (1992). When East moves West: The acculturations of values of Chinese adolescents in the U.S. and Australia. *Journal of Research on Adolescence, 2*(2), 147–173.

Feldman, S. S., Rosenthal, D. R., Brown, N. L., & Canning, R. D. (1995). Predicting sexual experience in adolescent boys from peer rejection and acceptance during childhood. *Journal of Research on Adolescence, 5*(4), 387–411.

Feldman, S. S., & Weinberger, D. A. (1994). Self-restraint as a mediator of family influences on boys' delinquent behavior: A longitudinal study. *Child Development, 65,* 195–211.

Feldman, S. S., & Wentzel, K. R. (1995). Relations of marital satisfaction to peer outcomes in adolescent boys: A longitudinal study. *Journal of Early Adolescence, 15*(2), 220–237.

Feldman, S. S., & Wood, D. N. (1994). Parents' expectations for preadolescent sons' behavioral autonomy: A longitudinal study of correlates and outcomes. *Journal of Research on Adolescence, 4*(1), 45–70.

Felner, R. D., Brand, S., DuBois, D. L., & Adan, A. (1995). Socioeconomic disadvantage, proximal environmental experiences, and socioemotional and academic adjustment in early adolescence: Investigation of a mediated effects model. *Child Development, 66,* 774–792.

Felner, R. D., Brand, S., DuBois, D. L., Adan, A. M., Mulhall, P. F., & Evans, E. G. (1995). Socioeconomic disadvantage, proximal environmental experiences, and socioemotional and academic adjustment in early adolescence: Investigation of a mediated effects model. *Child Development, 66,* 774–792.

Fenzel, L. M. (1992). The effect of relative age on self-esteem, role strain, GPA, and anxiety. *Journal of Early Adolescence, 12,* 253–266.

Fetterman, D. M., Kaftarian, S. J., & Wandersman, A. (Eds.). (1996). *Empowerment evaluation: Knowledge and tools for self-assessment and accountability.* Thousand Oaks, CA: Sage.

Fick, A. C., & Thomas, S. M. (1995). Growing up in a violent environment: Relationship to health-related beliefs and behaviors. *Youth & Society, 27*(2), 136–147.

Field, T. (1991). Mothers, adolescent and their young children. In R. M. Lerner, A. C. Petersen, & J. Brooks-Gunn (Eds.), *Encyclopedia of adolescence* (Vol. 2, pp. 669–674). New York: Garland.

Field, T., Grizzle, N., Scafidi, F., & Schanberg, S. (1996). Massage and relaxation therapies' effects on depressed adolescent mothers. *Adolescence, 31*(124), 903–911.

Field, T., Lang, C., Yando, R., & Bendell, D. (1995). Adolescents' intimacy with parents and friends. *Adolescence, 30*(117), 133–140.

Fine, M. A., & Kurdek, L. A. (1992). The adjustment of adolescents in stepfather and stepmother families. *Journal of Marriage and the Family, 54,* 725–736.

Finkelhor, D. (1994). Current information on the scope and nature of child sexual abuse. *Future of Children, 4*(2), 31–53.

Finkelstein, J. W. (1993). Familial influences on adolescent health. In R. M. Lerner (Ed.), *Early adolescence: Perspectives on research, policy, and intervention* (pp. 111–126). Hillsdale, NJ: Erlbaum.

Finken, L. L., & Jacobs, J. E. (1996). Consultant choice across decision contexts: Are abortion decisions different? *Journal of Early Adolescence, 11*(2), 235–260.

Fisher, C. B. (1993). Integrating science and ethics in research with high risk children and youth. *SRCD Social Policy Report, 7,* 1–27.

Fisher, C. B. (1994). Reporting and referring research participants: Ethical challenges for investigators studying children and youth. *Ethics and Behavior, 4,* 87–95.

Fisher, C. B. (1997). A relational perspective on ethics-in-science decision making for research with vulnerable populations. *IRB: A Review of Human Subjects Research, 19,* 1–4.

Fisher, C. B., & Brennan, M. (1992). Application and ethics in developmental psychology. In D. L. Featherman, R. M. Lerner, & M. Perlmutter (Eds.), *Lifespan development and behavior* (Vol. 11, pp. 189–219). Hillsdale, NJ: Erlbaum.

Fisher, C. B., & Fyrberg, D. (1994). Participant partners: College students weigh the costs and benefits of deceptive research. *American Psychologist, 49*(5), 417–427.

Fisher, C. B., Higgins, A., Rau, J. M., Kuther, T. L., & Belanger, S. (1996). Reporting and referring research participants at risk: Views from urban adolescents. *Child Development, 67,* 2086–2100.

Fisher, C. B., Higgins-D'Alessandro, A., Rau, J. B., Kuther, T. L., & Belanger, S. (1996). Referring and reporting research participants at risk: Views from urban adolescents. *Child Development, 67,* 2086–2100.

Fisher, C. B., Hoagwood, K., & Jensen, P. S. (1996). Casebook on ethical issues in research with children and adolescents with mental disorders. In K. Hoagwood & P. S. Jensen (Eds.), *Ethical issues in mental health research with children and adolescents* (pp. 135–266). Mahwah, NJ: Erlbaum.

Fisher, C. B., & Johnson, B. L. (1990). Getting mad at mom and dad: Children's changing views of family conflict. *International Journal of Behavioral Development, 13,* 31–48.

Fisher, C. B., & Lerner, R. M. (Eds.). (1994a). *Applied developmental psychology.* New York: McGraw-Hill.

Fisher, C. B., & Lerner, R. M. (1994b). Foundations of applied developmental psychology. In C. B. Fisher & R. M. Lerner (Eds.), *Applied developmental psychology* (pp. 3–20). New York: McGraw-Hill.

Fisher, C. B., Murray, J. P., Dill, J. R., Hagen, J. W., Hogan, M. J., Lerner, R. M., Rebok, G. W., Sigel, I., Sostek, A. M., Smyer, M. A., Spencer, M. B., & Wilcox, B. (1993). The national conference on graduate education in the applications of developmental science across the life span. *Journal of Applied Developmental Psychology, 14,* 1–10.

Fisher, C. B., & Tryon, W. W. (1990). Emerging ethical issues in an emerging field. In C. B. Fisher & W. W. Tryon (Eds.), *Ethics in applied developmental psychology: Emerging issues in an emerging field* (pp. 1–15). Norwood, NJ: Ablex.

Fisher, S. (1995). The amusement arcade as a social space for adolescents: An empirical study. *Journal of Adolescence, 18,* 71–86.

Fitzgerald, H. E., Abrams, A., Church, R. L., Votruba, J. C., & Imig, G. L. (1996). Applied developmental science at Michigan State University: Connecting university and community via programs for children, youth, and families. *Journal of Research on Adolescence,* 6(1), 55–69.

Fitzgerald, J. M., Nesselroade, J. R., & Baltes, P. B. (1973). Emergence of adult intellectual structure. *Developmental Psychology,* 9, 114–119.

Flanagan, C. A., & Eccles, J. S. (1993). Changes in parents' work status and adolescents' adjustment at school. *Child Development,* 64, 246–257.

Flannery, D. J., Vazsonyi, A. T., & Rowe, D. C. (1996). Caucasian and Hispanic early adolescent substance use: Parenting, personality, and school adjustment. *Journal of Early Adolescence,* 16(1), 71–89.

Fletcher, A. C., Darling, N. E., Steinberg, L., & Dornbusch, S. (1995). The company they keep: Relation of adolescents' adjustment and behavior to their friends' perceptions of authoritative parenting in the social network. *Developmental Psychology,* 31(2), 300–310.

Flisher, A. J., & Chalton, D. O. (1995). High-school dropouts in a working-class South African community: Selected characteristics and risk-taking behavior. *Journal of Adolescence,* 18, 105–121.

Foltz, C., Overton, W. F., & Ricco, R. B. (1995). Proof construction: Adolescent development from inductive to deductive problem-solving strategies. *Journal of Experimental Child Psychology,* 59, 179–195.

Ford, D. L., & Lerner, R. M. (1992). *Developmental systems theory: An integrative approach.* Newbury Park, CA: Sage.

Forehand, R., Miller, K. S., Dutra, R., & Chance, M. W. (1997). Role of parenting in adolescent deviant behavior: Replication across and within two ethnic groups. *Journal of Consulting and Clinical Psychology,* 65(6), 1036–1041.

Fortenberry, J. D., Costa, F. M., Jessor, R., & Donovan, J. E. (1997). Contraceptive behavior and adolescent lifestyles: A structural modeling approach. *Journal of Research on Adolescence,* 7(3), 307–329.

Foshee, V. A., & Hollinger, B. R. (1996). Maternal religiosity, adolescent social bonding, and adolescent alcohol use. *Journal of Early Adolescence,* 16(4), 451–468.

Foster-Clark, F. S., & Blyth, D. A. (1991). Peer relations and influences. In R. M. Lerner, A. C. Petersen, & J. Brooks-Gunn (Eds.), *Encyclopedia of adolescence* (Vol. 2, pp. 767–771). New York: Garland.

Foxcroft, D. R., & Lowe, G. (1995). Adolescent drinking, smoking and other substance use involvement: Links with perceived family life. *Journal of Adolescence,* 18, 159–177.

Freedland, J., & Dwyer, J. (1991). Nutrition in adolescent girls. In R. M. Lerner, A. C. Petersen, & J. Brooks-Gunn (Eds.), *Encyclopedia of Adolescence* (Vol. 2, pp. 714–723). New York: Garland.

Freedman-Doan, C. R., Arbreton, A. J., Harold, R. D., & Eccles, J. S. (1993). Looking forward to adolescence: Mothers' and fathers' expectations for affective and behavioral change. *Journal of Early Adolescence,* 13(4), 472–502.

Freud, A. (1969). Adolescence as a developmental disturbance. In G. Caplan & S. Lebovier (Eds.), *Adolescence* (pp. 5–10). New York: Basic.

Freund, A. M., & Baltes, P. B. (1998). Selection, optimization, and compensation as strategies of life-management: Correlation with subjective indicators of successful aging. *Psychology and Aging,* 13, 513–543.

Freund, A. M., & Baltes, P. B. (2000). The orchestration of selection, opitimization, and compensation: An action-theoretical conceptualization of a theory of developmental regulation. In W. J. Perrig & A. Grob (Eds.), *Control of human behavior, mental processes, and consciousness: Essays in honor of the 60th birthday of August Flammer* (pp. 35–58). New York: Erlbaum.

Freund, A. M., Li, K. Z. H., & Baltes, P. B. (1999). The role of selection, opitimization, and compensation in successful aging. In J. Brandtstädter & R. M. Lerner (Eds.), *Action and self-development: Theory and research through the life-span* (pp. 401–434). Thousand Oaks, CA: Sage.

Fuhrman, T., & Holmbeck, G. N. (1995). A contextual-moderator analysis of emotional autonomy and adjustment in adolescence. *Child Development,* 66, 793–811.

Fuligni, A. J. (1997). The academic achievement of adolescents from immigrant families: The roles of family background, attitudes, and behavior. *Child Development,* 68(2), 351–363.

Fuligni, A. J., & Eccles, J. S. (1993). Perceived parent-child relationships and early adolescents' orientation toward peers. *Developmental Psychology,* 29(4), 622–632.

Fuligni, A. J., Eccles, J. S., & Barber, B. L. (1995). The long-term effects of seventh-grade ability grouping in mathematics. *Journal of Early Adolescence,* 15(1), 58–89.

Fuligni, A. J., & Stevenson, H. W. (1995). Time use and mathematics achievement among American, Chinese, and Japanese high school students. *Child Development,* 66, 830–842.

Furman, D., & Buhrmester, D. (1992). Age and sex differences in perceptions of networks of person relationships. *Child Development,* 63, 103–115.

Furman, W. (1993). Theory is not a four letter word: Needed directions in the study of adolescent friendships. *New Directions for Child Development,* 60, 89–103.

Furman, W., & Brown, B. B. (Eds.). (1999). *The development of romantic relationships in adolescence. Cambridge studies in social and emotional development.* New York: Cambridge University Press.

Furstenberg, F. F., & Cherlin, A. J. (1991). *Divided families: What happens to children when parents part.* Cambridge: Harvard University Press.

Furstenberg, F. F., Jr., & Hughes, M. E. (1995). Social capital and successful development among at-risk youth. *Journal of Marriage and the Family,* 57, 580–592.

G

Galambos, N. L., & Almeida, D. M. (1992). Does parent-adolescent conflict increase in early adolescence? *Journal of Marriage and the Family,* 54, 737–747.

Galambos, N. L., Almeida, D. M., & Petersen, A. C. (1990). Masculinity, femininity, and sex role attitudes in early adolescence: Exploring gender intensification. *Child Development,* 61, 1905–1914.

Galambos, N. L., & Ehrenberg, M. F. (1997). The family as health risk and opportunity: A focus on divorce and working families. In J. Schulenberg, J. L. Maggs, & K. Hurrelmann (Eds.), *Health risks and developmental transitions during adolescence* (pp. 139–160). Cambridge: Cambridge University Press.

Galambos, N. L., & Maggs, J. L. (1990). Putting mothers' work-related stress in perspective: Mothers and adolescents in dual-earner families. *Journal of Early Adolescence, 10*(3), 313–328.

Galambos, N. L., & Maggs, J. L. (1991). Out-of-school care of young adolescents and self-reported behavior. *Developmental Psychology, 27*(4), 644–655.

Galambos, N. L., Sears, H. A., Almeida, D. M., & Kolaric, G. C. (1995). *Journal of Research on Adolescence, 5*(2), 201–223.

Gallatin, J. E. (1975). *Adolescence and individuality*. New York: Harper & Row.

Gallimore, M., & Kurdek, L. A. (1992). Parent depression and parent authoritative discipline as correlates of young adolescents' depression. *Journal of Early Adolescence, 12*(2), 187–196.

Gamoran, A., & Nystrand, M. (1991). Background and instructional effects on achievement in eighth-grade English and social studies. *Journal of Research on Adolescence, 1*(3), 277–300.

Garbarino, J. (1995). Growing up in a socially toxic environment: Life for children and families in the 1990s. In G. B. Melton (Ed.), The individual, the family, and social good: Personal fulfillment in times of change. *Nebraska Symposium on Motivation* (Vol. 42, pp. 1–20). Lincoln: University of Nebraska Press.

Garbarino, J. (1999). The effects of community violence on children. In L. Balter, C. S. Tamis-LeMonda (Eds.), *Child psychology: A handbook of contemporary issues* (pp. 412–425). Philadelphia: Psychology Press/Taylor & Francis.

Garbarino, J., & Kostelny, K. (1996). The effects of political violence on Palestinian children's behavior problems: A risk accumulation model. *Child Development, 67*, 33–45.

Garber, J., Robinson, N. S., & Valentiner, D. (1997). The relation between parenting and adolescent depression: Self-worth as a mediator. *Journal of Adolescent Research, 12*(1), 12–33.

Garn, S. M. (1980). Continuities and change in maturational timing. In O. G. Brim, Jr., & J. Kagan (Eds.), *Constancy and change in human development* (pp. 113–162). Cambridge: Harvard University Press.

Garnefski, N., & Okma, S. (1996). Addiction-risk and aggressive/criminal behaviour in adolescence: Influence of family, school and peers. *Journal of Early Adolescence, 19*, 503–512.

Garton, A. F., & Pratt, C. (1995). Stress and self-concept in 10- to 15-year-old school students. *Journal of Adolescence, 18*, 625–640.

Gauze, C., Bukowski, W. M., Aquan-Assee, J., & Sippola, L. K. (1996). Interactions between family environment and friendship and associations with self-perceived well-being during early adolescence. *Child Development, 67*, 2201–2216.

Gavazzi, S. M. (1995). The Growing Up FAST: Families and adolescents Surviving and Thriving program. *Journal of Adolescence, 18*, 31–47.

Gavin, L. A., & Furman, W. (1989). Age differences in adolescents' perceptions of their peer groups. *Developmental Psychology, 25*(5), 827–834.

Gavin, L. A., & Furman, W. (1996). Adolescent girls' relationships with mothers and best friends. *Child Development, 67*, 375–386.

Ge, X., Best, K. M., Conger, R. D., & Simons, R. L. (1996). Parenting behaviors and the occurence and co-occurence of adolescent depressive symptoms and conduct problems. *Developmental Psychology, 32*(4), 717–731.

Ge, X., Conger, R. D., & Elder, G. H., Jr. (1996). Coming of age too early: Pubertal influences on girls' vulnerability to psychological distress. *Child Development, 67*, 3386–3400.

Ge, X., Conger, R. D., Lorenz, F. O., Elder, G. H., Jr., Montague, R. B., & Simons, R. L. (1992). Linking family economic hardship to adolescent distress. *Journal of Research on Adolescence, 2*, 351–378.

Gilligan, C. (1982). New maps of development: New visions of maturity. *American Journal of Orthopsychiatry, 52*(2), 199–212.

Gillmore, M. A., Hawkins, J. D., Day, L. E., & Catalano, R. F. (1992). Friendship and deviance: New evidence on an old controversy. *Journal of Early Adolescence, 12*(1), 80–95.

Gillmore, M. R., Lewis, S. M., Lohr, M. J., Spencer, M. S., & White, R. D. (1997). Repeat pregnancies among adolescent mothers. *Journal of Marriage and the Family, 59*, 536–550.

Gjerde, P. F. (1986). The interpersonal structure of family interaction settings: Parent-adolescent relations in dyads and triads. *Developmental Psychology, 22*(3), 297–304.

Gjerde, P. F. (1995). Alternative pathways to chronic depressive symptoms in young adults: Gender differences in developmental trajectories. *Child Development, 66*, 1277–1300.

Gjerde, P. F., & Shimizu, H. (1995). Family relationships and adolescent development in Japan: A family-systems perspective on the Japanese family. *Journal of Research on Adolescence, 5*(3), 281–318.

Glasgow, K. L., Dornbusch, S. M., Troyer, L., Steinberg, L., & Ritter, P. L. (1997). Parenting styles, adolescents' attributions, and educational outcomes in nine heterogeneous high schools. *Child Development, 68*(3), 507–529.

Gohm, C. L., Oishi, S., Darlington, J., & Diener, E. (1998). Culture, parental conflict, parental marital status, and the subjective well-being of young adults. *Journal of Marriage and the Family, 60*, 319–334.

Goodenow, C. (1993). Classroom belonging among early adolescent students: Relationships to motivation and achievement. *Journal of Early Adolescence, 13*(1), 21–43.

Goodnow, J. J. (1962). A test of milieu differences with some of Piaget's tasks. *Psychological Monographs, 76*(36), 555.

Goodnow, J. J., & Bethon, G. (1996). Piaget's tasks: The effects of schooling and intelligence. *Child Development, 57*, 573–582.

Goossens, L., & Phinney, J. S. (1996). Commentary: Identity, context, and development. *Journal of Adolescence, 19*, 491–496.

Gordon, W. R., & Caltabiano, M. L. (1996). Urban-rural differences in adolescent self-esteem, leisure boredom, and sensation-seeking as predictors of leisure-time usage and satisfaction. *Adolescence, 31*(124), 883–901.

Gore, S., Aseltine, R. H., & Colten, M. E. (1993). Gender, social-relational involvement, and depression. *Journal of Research on Adolescence, 3*(2), 101–125.

Gortmaker, S. L., Perrin, J. M., Weitzman, M., Homer, C. J., & Sobol, A. M. (1993). An unexpected success story: Transition to adulthood in youth with chronic physical health conditions. *Journal of Research on Adolescence, 3*, 317–336.

Gottfredson, D. C., Gottfredson, G. D., & Skroban, S. (1996). A multimodel school-based prevention demonstration. *Journal of Adolescent Research, 11*(1), 97–115.

Gottlieb, G. (1991). The experiential canalization of behavioral development: Theory. *Developmental Psychology, 27,* 4–13.

Gottlieb, G. (1992). *Individual development and evolution: The genesis of novel behavior.* New York: Oxford University Press.

Gottlieb, G. (1997). *Synthesizing nature-nurture: Prenatal roots of instinctive behavior.* Mahwah, NJ: Erlbaum.

Gottlieb, G., Wahlsten, D., & Lickliter, R. (1998). The significance of biology for human development: A developmental psychobiological systems view. In W. Damon (Series Ed.) & R. M. Lerner (Vol. Ed.), *Handbook of child psychology: Vol. 1. Theoretical models of human development* (5th ed., pp. 233–273). New York: Wiley.

Gould, S. J. (1981). *The mismeasure of man.* New York: Norton.

Graafsma, T. L., Bosma, H. A., Grotevant, H. D., & de Levita, D. J. (1994). Identity and development: An interdisciplinary approach. In H. A. Bosma, T. L. G. Graafsma, H. D. Grotevant, & D. J. deLevita (Eds.), *Identity and development: An interdisciplinary approach.* Thousand Oaks, CA: Sage.

Graber, J. A., Brooks-Gunn, J., & Warren, M. P. (1995). The antecedents of menarcheal age: Heredity, family environment, and stressful life events. *Child Development, 66,* 346–359.

Graber, J. A., & Petersen, A. C. (1991). Cognitive changes at adolescence: Biological perspectives. In K. R. Gibson & A. C. Petersen (Eds.), *Brain maturation and cognitive development: Comparative and cross-cultural perspectives* (pp. 253–279). New York: Aldine de Gruyter.

Graham, S. (1992). "Most of the subjects were white and middle class": Trends in published research on African Americans in selected APA journals, 1970–1989. *American Psychologist, 47,* 629–639.

Graham, S., & Hudley, C. (1994). Attributions of aggressive and nonaggressive African American male early adolescents: A study of construct accessibility. *Developmental Psychology, 30*(3), 365–373.

Graham, S., Hudley, C., & Williams, E. (1992). Attributional and emotional determinants of aggression among African-American and Latino young adolescents. *Developmental Psychology, 28*(4), 731–740.

Graham, S., Taylor, A. Z., & Hudley, C. (1998). Exploring achievement values among ethnic minority early adolescents. *Journal of Educational Psychology, 90*(4), 606–620.

Gray, M. R., & Steinberg, L. (1999). Adolescent romance and the parent-child relationship: A contextual perspective. In W. Furman & B. B. Brown (Eds.), *The development of romantic relationships in adolescence. Cambridge studies in social and emotional development* (pp. 235–262). New York: Cambridge University Press.

Gray-Little, B., & Carels, R. A. (1997). The effect of racial dissonance on academic self-esteem and achievement in elementary, junior high, and high school students. *Journal of Research on Adolescence, 7*(2), 109–131.

Greenberger, E. (1984). Defining psychosocial maturity in adolescence. *Advances in Child Behavioral Analysis & Therapy, 3,* 1–37.

Greenberger, E., & Chen, C. (1996). Perceived family relationships and depressed mood in early and late adolescence: A comparison of European and Asian Americans. *Developmental Psychology, 32*(4), 707–716.

Greenberger, E., & Steinberg, L. D. (1986). *When teenagers work: The psychological and social costs of adolescent employment.* New York: Basic.

Greenfield, P. M. (1994). Video games as cultural artifacts. *Journal of Applied Developmental Psychology, 15,* 2–11.

Grob, A., Flammer, A., & Wearing, A. J. (1995). Adolescents' perceived control: Domain specificity, expectations, and appraisal. *Journal of Adolescence, 18,* 403–425.

Grossman, J. B., & Rhodes, J. E. (1999). The test of time: Predictors and effects of duration in youth mentoring relationships. Philadelphia: Public/Private Ventures.

Grotevant, H. D. (1987). Toward a process model of identity formation. *Journal of Adolescent Research, 2*(3), 203–222.

Grotevant, H. D. (1994). Assessment of parent-adolescent relationships. In C. B. Fisher & R. M. Lerner (Eds.), *Applied developmental psychology* (pp. 315–338). New York: McGraw-Hill.

Grotevant, H. D. (1997a). Family processes, identity development, and behavioral outcomes for adopted adolescents. *Journal of Adolescent Research, 12*(1), 139–161.

Grotevant, H. D. (1997b). Identity processes: Integrating social psychological and developmental approaches. *Journal of Adolescent Research, 12*(3), 354–357.

Grotevant, H. (1998). Adolescent development in family contexts. In W. Damon & N. Eisenberg (Eds.). *Handbook of child psychology: Vol. 3. Social, emotional, and personality development* (pp. 1097–1149). New York: Wiley.

Grotevant, H. D., & Bosma, H. A. (1994). History and literature. In H. A. Bosma, T. L. G. Graafsma, H. D. Grotevant, & D. J. deLevita (Eds.), *Identity and development: An interdisciplinary approach* (pp. 119–122). Thousand Oaks, CA: Sage.

Grotevant, H., & Cooper, C. R. (1983). *Adolescent development in the family.* San Francisco: Jossey-Bass.

Grotevant, H. D., & Cooper, C. R. (1985). Patterns of interaction in family relationships and the development of identity exploration in adolescence. *Child Development, 56*(2), 415–428.

Grotevant, H. D., & Cooper, C. R. (1986). Individuation in family relationships and the development of identity exploration. *Child Development, 56,* 415–428.

Grotevant, H. D., & Cooper, C. R. (1998). Individuality and connectedness in adolescent development: Review and prospects for research on identity, relationships, and context. In E. E. A. Skoe & A. L. von der Lippe (Eds.), *Adolescence and society* (pp. 3–37). New York: Routledge.

Grotpeter, J. K., & Crick, N. R. (1996). Relational aggression, overt aggression, and friendship. *Child Development, 67,* 2328–2338.

Grunseit, A., Kippax, S., Aggleton, P., Baldo, M., & Slutkin, G. (1997). Sexuality education and young people's sexual behavior: A review of studies. *Journal of Adolescent Research, 12*(4), 421–453.

Guerin, D. W., Gottfried, A. W., Oliver, P. H., & Thomas, C. W. (1994). Temperament and school functioning during early adolescence. *Journal of Early Adolescence, 14*(2), 200–225.

Guerney, L., & Arthur, J. (1984). Adolescent social relationships. In R. M. Lerner & N. L. Galambos (Eds.), *Experiencing adolescence: A sourcebook for parents, teachers, and teens* (pp. 87–118). New York: Garland.

Guerra, N. G., & Slaby, R. G. (1990). Cognitive mediators of aggression in adolescent offenders: Intervention. *Developmental Psychology, 26*(2), 269–277.

Guilford, J. P. (1967). *The nature of human intelligence.* New York: McGraw-Hill.

Gullotta, T. P., & Noyes, L. (1995). The changing of community health: The role of school-based health centers. *Adolescence, 30,* 107–115.

H

Hagell, A., & Newburn, T. (1996). Family and social contexts of adolescent re-offenders. *Journal of Adolescence, 19,* 5–18.

Hagen, J. W., Paul, B., Gibb, S., & Wolters, C. (1990). *Trends in research as reflected by publications in child development: 1930–1989.* Paper presented at the Biennial Meeting of the Society for Research on Adolescence, Atlanta, GA.

Hagestad, G. O., & Neugarten, B. L. (1985). Age and the life course. In R. H. Binstock & E. Shanas (Eds.), *Handbook of aging and the social sciences* (pp. 35–61). New York: Van Nostrand Reinhold.

Hagstrom, T., & Gamberale, F. (1995). Young people's work motivation and value orientation. *Journal of Adolescence, 18,* 475–490.

Hahn, A. B. (1994). Toward a national youth development policy for young African-American males: The choices policy makers face. In R. B. Mincy (Ed.), *Nurturing young black males* (pp. 165–186). Washington, DC: The Urban Institute Press.

Hall, G. S. (1904). *Adolescence* (Vols. 1 & 2). New York: Appleton.

Hall, G. S. (1922). *Senescence: The last half of life.* New York: Appleton.

Hamburg, D. A. (1992). *Today's children: Creating a future for a generation in crisis.* New York: Time.

Hamilton, S. F. (1994). Employment prospected as motivation for school achievement: Links and gaps between school and work in seven countries. In R. K. Silbereisen & E. Todt (Eds.), *Adolescence in context: The interplay of family, school, peers, and work in adjustment* (pp. 267–303). New York: Springer.

Hamilton, S. F. (1999). *A three-part definition of positive youth development.* Unpublished manuscript, College of Human Ecology, Cornell University.

Hamilton, S. F., & Hamilton, M. (1999). Creating new pathways to adulthood by adapting German apprenticeship in the United States. In W. R. Heinz (Ed.), *From education to work: Cross-national perspectives* (pp. 194–213). New York: Cambridge University Press.

Hamilton, S. F., & Lempert, W. (1996). The impact of apprenticeship on youth: A prospective analysis. *Journal of Research on Adolescence, 6*(4), 427–455.

Hammer, T. (1996). Consequences of unemployment in the transition from youth to adulthood in a life course perspective. *Youth & Society, 27*(4), 450–468.

Hanna, N. A., & Berndt, T. J. (1995). Relations between friendship, group acceptance, and evaluations of summer camp. *Journal of Early Adolescence, 15*(4), 456–475.

Hardesty, C., Wenk, D., & Morgan, C. S. (1995). Paternal involvement and the development of gender expectations in sons and daughters. *Youth & Society, 26*(3), 283–297.

Hardwick, P. J., & Rowton-Lee, M. A. (1996). Adolescent homicide: Towards assessment of risk. *Journal of Adolescence, 19,* 263–276.

Harold, G. T., & Conger, R. D. (1997). Marital conflict and adolescent distress: The role of adolescent awareness. *Child Development, 68*(2), 333–350.

Harrison, A. O., Stewart, R., Myambo, K., & Clarkston, T. (1997). Social networks among early adolescent Zimbabweans in extended families. *Journal of Research on Adolescence, 7*(2), 153–172.

Hart, B. I., & Thompson, J. M. (1996). Gender role characteristics and depressive symptomatology among adolescents. *Journal of Early Adolescence, 16*(4), 407–426.

Hart, D., & Fegley, S. (1995). Prosocial behavior and caring in adolescence: Relations to self-understanding and social judgement. *Child Development, 66,* 1346–1359.

Hart, L. R. (1995). MAPI personality correlates of comorbid substance abuse among adolescent psychiatric inpatients. *Journal of Adolescence, 18,* 657–667.

Harter, S. (1986). Processes underlying the construction, maintenance, and enhancement of the self-concept in children. In J. Suls & A. Greenwald (Eds.), *Psychological perspectives on the self* (pp. 136–181). Hillsdale, NJ: Erlbaum.

Harter, S. (1988). Cause, correlates, and the functional role of global self-worth: A life-span perspective. In J. Kolligan & R. J. Sternberg (Eds.), *Perceptions of competence and incompetence across the life-span.* New Haven, CT: Yale University Press.

Harter, S. (1998). The development of self-representations. In W. Damon (editor-in-chief) & N. Eisenberg (Ed.), *Handbook of child psychology: Vol. 3. Social, emotional, and personality development* (5th ed., pp. 1097–1149). New York: Wiley.

Harter, S., & Jackson, B. K. (1993). Young adolescents' perceptions of the link between low self-worth and depressed affect. *Journal of Early Adolescence, 13,* 383–407.

Harter, S., Stocker, C., & Robinson, N. S. (1996). The perceived directionality of the link between approval and self-worth: The liabilities of a looking glass self-orientation among young adolescents. *Journal of Research on Adolescence, 6*(3), 285–308.

Harter, S., Waters, P., & Whitesell, N. R. (1998). Relational self-worth: Differences in perceived worth as a person across interpersonal contexts among adolescents. *Child Development, 69*(3), 756–766.

Harton, H. C., & Latané, B. (1997). Social influence and adolescent lifestyle attitudes. *Journal of Research on Adolescence, 7*(2), 197–220.

Hartup, W. W. (1983). Peer relations. In P. H. Mussen (Ed.), *Handbook of child psychology* (Vol. 4, pp. 103–196). New York: Wiley.

Hartup, W. W. (1993). Adolescents and their friends. *New Directions for Child Development, 60,* 3–22.

Hartup, W. W. (1996). The company they keep: Friendships and their developmental significance. *Child Development, 67,* 1–13.

Hartup, W. W., & Overhauser, S. M. (1991). Friendships. In R. M. Lerner, A. C. Petersen, & J. Brooks-Gunn (Eds.), *Encyclopedia of adolescence* (Vol. 1, pp. 378–384). New York: Garland.

Harvey, S. M., & Spigner, C. (1995). Factors associated with sexual behavior among adolescents: A multivariate analysis. *Adolescence, 30*(118), 253–264.

Hatzichristou, C., & Hopf, D. (1996). A multiperspective comparison of peer sociometric status groups in childhood and adolescence. *Child Development, 67,* 1085–1102.

Hauser, S., Houlihan, J., Powers, S., Jacobson, A., Noam, G., Weiss-Perry, B., Follansbee, D., & Book, B. (1991). Adolescent ego development within the family: Family styles and family sequences. *International Journal of Behavioral Development, 14*(2), 165–193.

Hauser, S. T., Powers, S. I., & Noam, G. G. (1991). *Adolescents and their families: Paths of ego development.* New York: Free Press.

Hauser, S. T., Powers, S. I., Noam, G. G., Jacobson, A. M., Weiss, B., & Fallansbee, D. J. (1984). Familial contexts of adolescent ego development. *Child Development, 55,* 195–213.

Hauser, S. T., & Safyer, A. W. (1994). Ego development and adolescent emotions. *Journal of Research on Adolescence, 4*(4), 487–502.

Helwig, C. C. (1995). Adolescents' and young adults' conceptions of civil liberties: Freedom of speech and religion. *Child Development, 66,* 152–166.

Helwig, C. C. (1998). Children's conceptions of fair government and freedom of speech. *Child Development, 69*(2), 518–531.

Hendry, L. B., Glendinning, A., Shucksmith, J., Love, J., & Scott, J. (1994). The developmental context of adolescent life-styles. In R. K. Silbereisen & E. Todt (Eds.), *Adolescence in context: The interplay of family, school, peers, and work in adjustment* (pp. 66–81). New York: Springer.

Henggeler, S. W., Brondino, M. J., Melton, G. B., Scherer, D. G., & Hanley, J. H. (1997). Multisystemic therapy with violent and chronic juvenile offenders and their families: The role of treatment fidelity in successful dissemination. *Journal of Consulting and Clinical Psychology, 65*(5), 821–833.

Henggeler, S. W., Cunningham, P. B., Pickrel, S. G., Schoenwald, S. K., & Brondino, M. J. (1996). Multisystemic therapy: An effective violence prevention approach for serious juvenile offenders. *Journal of Adolescence, 19,* 47–61.

Henrich, C. C., Kuperminc, G. P., Sack, A., Blatt, S. J., & Leadbeater, B. J. (2000). Characteristics and homogeneity of early adolescent friendship groups: A comparison of male and female clique and nonclique members. *Applied Developmental Science, 4*(1), 15–26.

Henry, B., Caspi, A., Moffitt, T. E., & Silva, P. A. (1996). Temperamental and familial predictors of violent and nonviolent criminal convictions: Age 3 to age 18. *Developmental Psychology, 32,* 614–623.

Herdt, G. (Ed.). (1989). *Gay and lesbian youth.* New York: Haworth Press.

Herman, M. R., Dornbusch, S. M., Herron, M. C., & Herting, J. R. (1997). The influence of family regulation, connection and psychological autonomy on six measures of adolescent functioning. *Journal of Adolescent Research, 12*(1), 34–67.

Hernandez, D. J. (1993). *America's children: Resources for family, government, and the economy.* New York: Russell Sage Foundation.

Hernandez-Guzman, L., & Sanchez-Sosa, J. J. (1996). Parent-child interactions predict anxiety in Mexican adolescents. *Adolescence, 31*(124), 955–963.

Hershberger, S. L., Pilkington, N. W., & D'Augelli, A. R. (1997). Predictors of suicide attempts among gay, lesbian, and bisexual youth. *Journal of Adolescent Research, 12*(4), 477–497.

Herzberger, S. D., & Hall, J. A. (1993). Children's evaluations of retaliatory aggression against siblings and friends. *Journal of Interpersonal Violence, 8*(1), 77–89.

Hetherington, E. M. (1989). Coping with family transitions: Winners, losers, and survivors. *Child Development, 60,* 1–14.

Hetherington, E. M. (1991). Presidential address: Families, lies, and videotapes. *Journal of Research on Adolescence, 1*(4), 323–348.

Hetherington, E. M., Anderson, E. R., & Hagan, M. S. (1991). Divorce: Effects on adolescents. In R. M. Lerner, A. C. Petersen, & J. Brooks-Gunn (Eds.), *Encyclopedia of adolescence* (Vol. 1, pp. 237–243). New York: Garland.

Hetherington, E. M., & Clingempeel, W. G. (1988, March). *Coping with remarriage: The first two years.* Symposium presented at the Conference on Human Development, Charleston, SC.

Hetherington, E. M., Cox, M., & Cox, R. (1985). Long-term effects of divorce and remarriage on the adjustment of children. *Journal of the American Academy of Child Psychiatry, 24*(5), 518–530.

Hill, J. P., & Holmbeck, G. (1987). Familial adaptation to biological change during adolescence. In R. M. Lerner & T. Foch (Eds.), *Biological-psychosocial interactions in early adolescence* (pp. 207–223). Hillsdale, NJ: Erlbaum.

Hill, J. P., Holmbeck, G. N., Marlow, L., Green, T. M., & Lynch, M. E. (1985a). Menarcheal status and parent-child relations in families of seventh-grade girls. *Journal of Youth and Adolescence, 14,* 301–316.

Hill, J. P., Holmbeck, G. N., Marlow, L., Green, T. M., & Lynch, M. E. (1985b). Pubertal status and parent-child relations in families of seventh-grade boys. *Journal of Early Adolescence, 5,* 31–44.

Hill, J. P., & Lynch, M. E. (1983). The intensification of gender-related role expectations during early adolescence. In J. Brooks-Gunn & A. C. Petersen (Eds.), *Girls at puberty* (pp. 201–228). New York: Plenum.

Hinden, B. R., Compas, B. E., Howell, D. C., & Achenbach, T. M. (1997). Covariation of the anxious–depressed syndrome during adolescence: Separating fact from artifact. *Journal of Consulting and Clinical Psychology, 65*(1), 6–14.

Hines, A. M. (1997). Divorce-related transitions, adolescent development, and the role of the parent-child relationship: A review of the literature. *Journal of Marriage and the Family, 59,* 375–388.

Hockenberry-Eaton, M., Richman, M. J., DiIorio, C., Rivero, T., & Maibach, E. (1996). Mother and adolescent knowledge of sexual development: The effects of gender, age, and sexual experience. *Adolescence, 31*(121), 35–47.

Hodos, W., & Campbell, C. B. G. (1969). Scala naturae: Why there is no theory in comparative psychology. *Psychological Review, 76,* 337–350.

Hoffmann, J. P., & Johnson, R. A. (1998). A national portrait of family structure and adolescent drug use. *Journal of Marriage and the Family, 60,* 633–645.

Hogue, A., & Steinberg, L. (1995). Homophily of internalized distress in adolescent peer groups. *Developmental Psychology, 31*(6), 897–906.

Hohman, M., & LeCroy, C. W. (1996). Predictors of adolescent A.A. affiliation. *Adolescence, 31*(122), 339–352.

Hoksbergen, R. A. C. (1997). Turmoil for adoptees during their adolescence? *International Journal of Behavioral Development, 20*(1), 33–46.

Holmbeck, G., & Hill, J. P. (1988). Storm and stress beliefs about adolescence: Prevalence, self-reported antecedents, and effects of an undergraduate course. *Journal of Youth & Adolescence, 17*(4), 285–306.

Holmbeck, G. N., & Hill, J. P. (1991). Conflictive engagement, positive affect, and menarche in families with seventh-grade girls. *Child Development, 62*, 1030–1048.

Horn, J. L., & Cattell, R. B. (1966). Age differences in primary mental ability factors. *Journal of Gerontology, 21*, 210–220.

Horwitz, A. V., & White, H. R. (1998). The relationship of cohabitation and mental health: A study of a young adult cohort. *Journal of Marriage and the Family, 60*, 505–514.

Hoyle, R. H., & Leff, S. S. (1997). The role of parental involvement in youth sport participation and performance. *Adolescence, 32*(125), 233–243.

Hudley, C. A. (1995). Assessing the impact of separate schooling for African American male adolescents. *Journal of Early Adolescence, 15*(1), 38–57.

Huerta-Franco, R., Diaz de Leon, J., & Malacara, J. M. (1996). Knowledge and attitudes toward sexuality in adolescents and their associations with the family and other factors. *Adolescence, 31*, 179–191.

Hultsch, D. F., & Hickey, T. (1978). External validity in the study of human development: Theoretical and methodological issues. *Human Development, 21*, 76–91.

Hunt, E., Streissguth, A. P., Kerr, B., & Olson, H. C. (1995). Mothers' alcohol consumption during pregnancy: Effects on spatial-visual reasoning in 14-year-old children. *Psychological Society, 6*, 339–342.

Hunt, N. (1967). *The world of Nigel Hunt: The diary of a Mongoloid youth.* New York: Garrett.

Hunter, S. M., Vizelberg, I. A., & Berenson, G. S. (1991). Identifying mechanisms of adoption of tobacco and alcohol use among youth: The Bogalusa heart study. *Social Networks, 13*, 91–104.

Huston, A. C. (Ed.). (1991). *Children in poverty: Child development and public policy.* Cambridge: Cambridge University Press.

Huston, A. C., McLoyd, V. C., & Garcia Coll, C. (1994). Children and poverty: Issues in contemporary research. *Child Development, 65*, 275–282.

Huston, A. C., & Wright, J. C. (1998). Mass media and children's development. In W. Damon (Ed. in chief) & I. E. Sigel & K. A. Renninger (Eds.), *Handbook of child psychology: Vol. 4. Child psychology in practice* (5th ed., pp. 999–1058). New York: Wiley.

I

Inhelder, B., & Piaget, J. (1958). *The growth of logical thinking from childhood to adolescence.* New York: Basic.

J

Jaccard, J., Dittus, P. J., & Gordon, V. V. (1998). Parent-adolescent congruency in reports of adolescent sexual behavior and in communications about sexual behavior. *Child Development, 69*, 247–261.

Jacobs, F. (1988). The five-tiered approach to evaluation: Context and implementation. In H. B. Weiss & F. Jacobs (Eds.), *Evaluating family programs* (pp. 37–68). Hawthorne, NY: Aldine de Gruyter.

Jacobs, F. H., & Kapuscik, J. L. (2000). *Making it count: Evaluating family preservation services.* Medford, MA: Eliot-Pearson Department of Child Development, Tufts University.

Jacobs, J., Bennett, M., & Flanagan, C. (1993). A longitudinal study of the relation between representations of attachment in childhood and cognitive functioning in childhood and adolescence. *Journal of Early Adolescence, 13*(3), 245–266.

Jacobsen, T., Edelstein, W., & Hofmann, V. (1994). A longitudinal study of the relation between representations of attachment in childhood and cognitive functioning in childhood and adolescence. *Developmental Psychology, 30*, 112–124.

Jacobvitz, D. B., & Bush, N. F. (1996). Reconstructions of family relationships: Parent-child alliances, personal distress, and self-esteem. *Developmental Psychology, 32*(4), 732–743.

Jadack, R. A., Hyde, J. S., Moore, C. F., & Keller, M. L. (1995). Moral reasoning about sexually transmitted diseases. *Child Development, 66*, 167–177.

Jagers, R. J. (1996). Culture and problem behaviors among inner-city African-American youth: Further explorations. *Journal of Adolescence, 19*, 371–381.

Jakobsen, R. (1997). Stages of progression in noncoital sexual interactions among young adolescents: An application of the Mokken Scale analysis. *International Journal of Behavioral Development, 21*(3), 537–553.

Jenkins, J. E. (1996). The influence of peer affiliation and student activities on adolescent drug involvement. *Adolescence, 31*(122), 297–306.

Jensen, L. (1988). Rural-urban differences in the utilization of ameliorative effects on welfare programs. *Policy Studies Review, 7*, 782–794.

Jensen, P., Hoagwood, K., & Trickett, E. (1999). Ivory towers or earthen trenches?: Community collaborations to foster "real world" research. *Applied Developmental Science, 3*(4), 206–212.

Jessor, R. (1987). Problem-behavior theory, psychosocial development, and adolescent problem drinking. *British Journal of Addiction, 82*, 331–342.

Jessor, R. (1992). Risk behavior in adolescence: A psychosocial framework for understanding and action. *Developmental Review, 12*, 374–390.

Jessor, R., Donovan, J. E., & Costa, F. M. (1991). *Beyond adolescence: Problem behavior and young adult development.* Cambridge, England: Cambridge University Press.

Jessor, R., & Jessor, S. L. (1977). *Problem behavior and psychosocial development: A longitudinal study of the young.* New York: Academic Press.

Jessor, R., Van Den Bos, J., Vanderryn, J., & Costa, F. M. (1995). Protective factors in adolescent problem behavior: Moderator effects and developmental change. *Developmental Psychology, 31*(6), 923–933.

Joebgen, A. M., & Richards, M. H. (1990). Maternal education and employment: Mediating maternal and adolescent emotional adjustment. *Journal of Early Adolescence, 10*(3), 329–343.

Johanson, D. C., & Edey, M. A. (1981). *Lucy: The beginnings of humankind.* New York: Simon & Schuster.

Johnson, K., Strader, T., Berbaum, M., Bryant, D., Bucholtz, G., Collins, D., & Noe, T. (1996). Reducing alcohol and other drug use by strengthening community, family, and youth resiliency: An evaluation of the Creating Lasting Connections program. *Journal of Adolescent Research, 11*(1), 36–67.

Johnston, L. D., & Bachman, J. G. (1976). Educational institutions. In J. F. Adams (Ed.), *Understanding adolescence* (3rd ed., pp. 299–315). Boston: Allyn & Bacon.

Johnston, L. D., Bachman, J. G., & O'Malley, P. M. (1991). *Monitoring the future: Questionnaire responses from the nation's high school seniors.* Ann Arbor: Survey Research Center.

Johnston, L. D., Bachman, J. G., & O'Malley, P. M. (1998). *Monitoring the future.* Ann Arbor: Survey Research Center.

Johnston, L. D., Bachman, J. G., & O'Malley, P. M. (1999). *Monitoring the Future.* Ann Arbor: Survey Research Center.

Jones, H. E. (1958). Problems of method in longitudinal research. *Vita Humana, 1,* 93–99.

Jones, H. E. (1959). Intelligence and problem solving. In J. E. Birren (Ed.), *Handbook of aging and the individual.* Chicago: University of Chicago Press.

Jordan, W. J., Lara, J., & McPartland, J. M. (1996). Exploring the causes of early dropout among race-ethnic and gender groups. *Youth & Society, 28*(1), 62–94.

Jory, B., Rainbolt, E., Karns, J. T., Freeborn, A., & Greer, C. V. (1996). Communication patterns and alliances between parents and adolescents during a structured problem-solving task. *Journal of Adolescence, 19,* 339–346.

Jovanovic, J., & Lerner, R. M. (1994). Individual-contextual relationships and mathematics performance: Comparing American and Serbian young adolescents. *Journal of Early Adolescence, 14*(4), 449–470.

Juon, H.-S., Shin, Y., & Nam, J. J. (1995). Cigarette smoking among Korean adolescents: Prevalence and correlates. *Adolescence, 30*(119), 631–642.

Jurich, A. P., & Collins, O. P. (1996). 4-H Night at the Movies: A program for adolescents and their families. *Adolescence, 31*(124), 863–874.

Juvonen, J. (1991). Deviance, perceived responsibility, and negative peer reactions. *Developmental Psychology, 27*(4), 672–681.

Juvonen, J., & Murdock, T. B. (1995). Grade-level differences in the social value of effort: Implications for self-presentation tactics of early adolescents. *Child Development, 66,* 1694–1705.

K

Kagan, J., & Moss, H. A. (1962). *Birth to maturity: A study in psychological development.* New York: Wiley.

Kahlbaugh, P., & Haviland, J. M. (1991). Formal operational thinking and identity. In R. M. Lerner, A. C. Petersen, & J. Brooks-Gunn (Eds.), *Encyclopedia of adolescence* (Vol. 1, pp. 369–372). New York: Garland.

Kalil, A., & Eccles, J. S. (1998). Does welfare affect family processes and adolescent adjustment? *Child Development, 69*(6), 1597–1613.

Kandel, D. B. (1974). Inter- and intragenerational influences on adolescent marijuana use. *Journal of Social Issues, 30,* 107–135.

Kandel, D. B. (1986). Processes of peer influences in adolescence. In R. K. Silbereisen, K. Eyferth, & G. Rudinger (Eds.), *Development as action in context: Problem behavior and normal youth development* (pp. 203–227). New York: Springer.

Kandel, D. B., & Andrews, K. (1987). Processes of adolescent socialization by parents and peers. *International Journal of the Addictions, 22*(4), 319–344.

Kandel, D. B., & Lesser, G. S. (1969). Paternal and peer influences on educational plans of adolescents. *American Sociological Review, 34,* 213–223.

Kandel, D. B., & Lesser, G. S. (1972). *Youth in two worlds.* San Francisco: Jossey-Bass.

Kandel, D. B., Rosenbaum, E., & Chen, K. (1994). Impact of maternal drug use and life experiences on preadolescent children born to teenage mothers. *Journal of Marriage and the Family, 56,* 325–340.

Kandel, D. B., & Wu, P. (1995). The contributions of mothers and fathers to the intergenerational transmission of cigarette smoking and adolescence. *Journal of Research on Adolescence, 5*(2), 225–252.

Kaplan, D. S., Damphousse, K. R., & Kaplan, H. B. (1996). Moderating effects of gender on the relationship between not graduating from high school and psychological dysfunction in young adulthood. *Journal of Educational Psychology, 88*(4), 760–774.

Katchadourian, H. (1977). *The biology of adolescence.* San Francisco: Freeman.

Katz, P. A., & Ksansnak, K. R. (1994). Developmental aspects of gender role flexibility and traditionality in middle childhood and adolescence. *Developmental Psychology, 30,* 272–282.

Kaufmann, H. (1968). *Introduction to the study of human behavior.* Philadelphia: Saunders.

Kavsek, M. J., & Seiffge-Krenke, I. (1996). The differentiation of coping traits in adolescence. *International Journal of Behavioral Development, 19*(3), 651–668.

Keating, D. P. (1991). Cognition, adolescent. In R. M. Lerner, A. C. Petersen, &

J. Brooks-Gunn (Eds.), *Encyclopedia of adolescence* (Vol. 1, pp. 119–129). New York: Garland.

Keefe, K., & Berndt, T. J. (1996). Relations of friendship quality to self-esteem in early adolescence. *Journal of Early Adolescence, 16*(1), 110–129.

Keith, J. G., Nelson, C. S., Schlabach, J. H., & Thompson, C. J. (1990). The relationship between parental employment and three measures of early adolescent responsibility: Family-related, personal, and social. *Journal of Early Adolescence, 10*(3), 399–415.

Kellner, M. H., & Tutin, J. (1995). A school-based anger management program for developmentally and emotionally disabled high school students. *Adolescence, 30*(120), 813–825.

Kellogg Commission on the Future of State and Land-Grant Colleges. (1999). *Returning to our roots: The engaged institution.* Washington, DC: National Association of State Universities and Land-Grant Colleges.

Kendall, P. C., & Southam-Gerow, M. A. (1996). Long-term follow-up of a cognitive-behavioral therapy for anxiety-disordered youth. *Journal of Consulting and Clinical Psychology, 64*(4), 724–730.

Keniston, K. (1970). Youth: A "new" stage of life. *American Scholar, 39,* 631–641.

Kennedy, R. E. (1991). Delinquency. In R. M. Lerner, A. C. Petersen, & J. Brooks-Gunn (Eds.), *Encyclopedia of adolescence* (Vol. 1, pp. 199–206). New York: Garland.

Kenny, M., & Gallagher, L. (2000). Service-learning as a vehicle in training psychologists for revised professional roles. In F. T. Sherman & W. R. Torbert (Eds.), *Transforming social inquiry, transforming social action: New paradigms for crossing the theory/practice divide in universities and communities* (pp. 189–205). Norwell, MA: Kluwer Academic.

Kenny, M., Simon, L. A. K., Brabeck, K., & Lerner, R. M. (Eds.). (in press). *Learning to serve: Promoting civil society through service learning.* Norwell, MA: Kluwer Academic.

Kenny, M. E., Moilanen, D. L., Lomax, R., & Brabeck, M. M. (1993). Contributions of parental attachments to view of self and depressive symptoms among early adolescents. *Journal of Early Adolescence, 13*(4), 408–430.

Kenrick, D. T., Gabrielidis, C., Keefe, R. C., & Cornelius, J. S. (1996). Adolescents' age preferences for dating partners: Support for an evolutionary model of life-history strategies. *Child Development, 67,* 1499–1511.

Kerfoot, M., Harrington, R., & Dyer, E. (1995). Brief home-based intervention with young suicide attempters and their families. *Journal of Adolescence, 18,* 557–568.

Kerpelman, J. L., Pittman, J. F., & Lamke, L. K. (1997). Toward a microprocess perspective on adolescent identity development: An identity control theory approach. *Journal of Adolescent Research, 12*(3), 325–346.

Kershner, K. (1996). Adolescent attitudes about rape. *Adolescence, 31*(121), 29–33.

Ketterlinus, R. D., & Lamb, M. E. (Eds.). (1994). *Adolescent problem behaviors: Issues and research.* Hillsdale, NJ: Erlbaum.

Kidwell, J. S., Dunham, R. M., Bacho, R. A., Pastorino, E., & Portes, P. R. (1995). Adolescent identity exploration: A test of Erikson's theory of transitional crisis. *Adolescence, 30*(120), 785–793.

King, C. A., Akiyama, M. M., & Elling, K. A. (1996). Self-perceived competencies and depression among middle school students in Japan and the United States. *Journal of Early Adolescence, 16*(2), 192–210.

King, C. A., Radpour, L., Naylor, M. W., Segal, H. G., & Jouriles, E. N. (1995). Parents' marital functioning and adolescent psychopathology. *Journal of Consulting and Clinical Psychology, 63*(5), 749–753.

King, V., & Elder, G. (1995). American children view their grandparents: Linked lives across three rural generations. *Journal of Marriage and the Family, 57,* 165–178.

Kinsey, A. C., Pomeroy, W. B., & Martin, C. E. (1948). *Sexual behavior in the human male.* Philadelphia: Saunders.

Kinsey, A. C., Pomeroy, W. B., Martin, C. E., & Gebhard, P. H. (1953). *Sexual behavior in the human female.* Philadelphia: Saunders.

Kipke, M. D., Palmer, R. F., LaFrance, S., O'Connor, S. (1997). Homeless youths' descriptions of their parents' child-rearing practices. *Youth & Society, 28*(4), 415–431.

Kitchener, K. S., & Wood, P. K. (1987). Development of concepts of justification in German university students. *International Journal of Behavioral Development, 10,* 171–185.

Klaczynski, P. A., & Gordon, D. H. (1996). Self-serving influences on adolescents' evaluations of belief-relevant evidence. *Journal of Experimental Child Psychology, 62,* 317–339.

Klaw, E. L., & Rhodes, J. E. (1995). Mentor relationships and the career development of pregnant and parenting African-American teenagers. *Psychology of Women Quarterly, 19*(4), 551–562.

Klebanov, P., & Brooks-Gunn, J. (1992). Impact of maternal attitudes, girls' adjustment, and cognitive skills upon academic performance in middle and high school. *Journal of Research on Adolescence, 2,* 81–102.

Klein, K., Forehand, R., Armistead, L., & Long, P. (1997). Delinquency during the transition to early adulthood: Family and parenting predictors from early adolescence. *Adolescence, 32*(125), 61–80.

Klerman, L. V. (1991). The health of poor children: Problems and programs. In A. C. Huston (Ed.), *Children in poverty: Child development and public policy* (pp. 1–22). Cambridge: Cambridge University Press.

Kloep, M. (1995). Concurrent and predictive correlates of girls' depression and antisocial behavior under conditions of economic crisis and value change: The case of Albania. *Journal of Adolescence, 18,* 445–458.

Knight, G. P., Virdin, L. M., & Roosa, M. (1994). Socialization and family correlates of mental health outcomes among Hispanic and Anglo American children: Consideration of cross-ethnic scalar equivalence. *Child Development, 65,* 212–224.

Koch, P. B., Maney, D. W., & Susman, E. J. (1993). Introduction: Health promotion for early adolescents. In R. M. Lerner (Ed.), *Early adolescence: Perspectives on research, policy, and intervention* (pp. 241–245). Hillsdale, NJ: Erlbaum.

Koff, E., & Rierdan, J. (1995). Preparing girls for menstruation: Recommendations from adolescent girls. *Adolescence, 30*(120), 795–811.

Koff, E., Rierdan, J., & Stubbs, M. L. (1990). Gender, body image, and self-concept in early adolescence. *Journal of Early Adolescence, 10,* 56–68.

Kohlberg, L. (1958). *The development of modes of moral thinking and choice in the years ten to sixteen.* Unpublished doctoral dissertation, University of Chicago.

Kohlberg, L. (1963a). The development of children's orientations toward a moral order: Sequence in the development of moral thought. *Vita Humana, 6,* 11–33.

Kohlberg, L. (1963b). Moral development and identification. In H. Stevenson (Ed.), *Child psychology. 62nd yearbook of the National Society for the Study of Education* (pp. 277–332). Chicago: University of Chicago Press.

Kohlberg, L. (1964). Development of moral character and moral ideology. In M. L. Hoffman & L. W. Hoffman (Eds.), *Review of child development research* (Vol. 1, pp. 283–432). New York: Sage.

Kohlberg, L. (1970). Education for justice: A modern statement of the platonic view. In N. F. Sizer & T. R. Sizer (Eds.), *Moral education: Five lectures* (pp. 56–83). Cambridge: Harvard University Press.

Kohlberg, L. (1971). From is to ought: How to commit the naturalistic fallacy and get away with it in the study of moral development. In T. Mischel (Ed.), *Cognitive development and epistemology* (pp. 151–235). New York: Academic Press.

Kohlberg, L. (1976). Moral stages and moralization: The cognitive developmental approach. In T. Luckona (Ed.), *Moral development and behavior: Theory, research, and social issues.* New York: Holt.

Kohlberg, L. (1978). Revisions in the theory and practice of moral development. *New Directions for Child Development, 2,* 83–88.

Koizumi, R. (1995). Feelings of optimism and pessimism in Japanese students' transition to junior high school. *Journal of Early Adolescence, 15*(4), 412–428.

Kolaric, G. C., & Galambos, N. L. (1995). Face-to-face interactions in unacquainted female-male adolescent dyads: How do girls and boys behave? *Journal of Early Adolescence, 15*(3), 363–382.

Kramer, L. R. (1991). The social construction of ability perceptions: An ethnographic study of gifted adolescent girls. *Journal of Early Adolescence, 11,* 340–362.

Krampen, G. (1989). Perceived childrearing practices and the development of locus of control in early adolescence. *International Journal of Behavioral Development, 12,* 177–193.

Kretzmann, J. P., & McKnight, J. L. (1993). *Building communities from the inside out:*

A path toward finding and mobilizing a community's assets. Chicago: ACTA.

Kroger, J. (1995). The differentiation of "firm" and "developmental" foreclosure identity statuses: A longitudinal study. *Journal of Adolescent Research, 10*(3), 317–337.

Kuhn, D. (1976). Short-term longitudinal evidence for the sequentiality of Kohlberg's early stages of moral development. *Developmental Psychology, 12*, 162–166.

Kuhn, D. (1991). *The skills of argument*. New York: Cambridge University Press.

Kuhn, D., Amsel, E., & O'Loughlin, M. (1988). *The development of scientific thinking skills*. San Diego: Academic Press.

Kuperminc, G. P., Allen, J. P., & Arthur, M. W. (1996). Autonomy, relatedness, and male adolescent delinquency: Toward a multidimensional view of social competence. *Journal of Adolescent Research, 11*(4), 397–420.

Kurdek, L. A., Fine, M. A., & Sinclair, R. J. (1995). School adjustment in sixth graders: Parenting transitions, family climate, and peer norm effects. *Child Development, 66*, 430–445.

Kurtines, W., & Greif, E. B. (1974). The development of moral thought: Review and evaluation of Kohlberg's approach. *Psychological Bulletin, 81*, 453–469.

Kvernmo, S., & Heyerdahl, S. (1996). Ethnic identity in aboriginal Sami adolescents: The impact of the family and the ethnic community context. *Journal of Adolescence, 19*, 453–463.

L

Labouvie-Vief, G. (1981). Proactive and reactive aspects of constructivism: Growth and aging in life-span perspective. In R. M. Lerner & N. A. Busch-Rossnagel (Eds.), *Individuals as producers of their development: A life-span perspective* (pp. 197–230). New York: Academic Press.

Lamborn, S. D., Dornbusch, S. M., & Steinberg, L. (1996). Ethnicity and community context as moderators of the relations between family decision making and adolescent adjustment. *Child Development, 67*, 283–301.

Lamborn, S. D., Mounts, N. S., Steinberg, L., & Dornbusch, S. M. (1991). Patterns of competence and adjustment among adolescents from authoritative, authoritarian, indulgent, and neglectful families. *Child Development, 62*, 1049–1065.

Langer, L. M., Zimmerman, R. S., & Katz, J. A. (1995). Virgins' expectations and nonvirgins' reports: How adolescents feel about themselves. *Journal of Adolescent Research, 10*(2), 291–306.

Langhout, R. D., Osborne, L. N., Grossman, J. B., & Rhodes, J. E. (1999). An exploratory study of volunteer mentoring: Toward a typology of relationships. Unpublished manuscript. Cambridge, MA: Harvard University Graduate School of Education.

Lapsley, D. K. (1991). Egocentrism theory and the "new look" at the imaginary audience and personal fable in adolescence. In R. M. Lerner, A. C. Petersen, & J. Brooks-Gunn (Eds.), *Encyclopedia of adolescence* (Vol. 1, pp. 281–286). New York: Garland.

Larson, R. W. (1994). Youth organization, hobbies, and sports as developmental contexts. In R. K. Silbereisen & E. Todt (Eds.), *Adolescence in context: The interplay of family, school, peers, and work in adjustment.* (pp. 46–65). New York: Springer.

Larson, R. W. (1997). The emergence of solitude as a constructive domain of experience in early adolescence. *Child Development, 68*(1), 80–93.

Larson, R. W. (2000). Toward a psychology of positive youth development. *American Psychologist, 55*(1), 170–183.

Larson, R. W., Clore, G. L., & Wood, G. A. (1999). The emotions of romantic relationships: Do they wreak havoc on adolescents? In W. Furman & B. B. Brown (Eds.), *The development of romantic relationships in adolescence. Cambridge studies in social and emotional development* (pp. 19–49). New York: Cambridge University Press.

Larson, R. W., Gillman, S. A., & Richards, M. H. (1997). Divergent experiences of family leisure: Fathers, mothers, and young adolescents. *Journal of Leisure Research, 29*(1), 78–97.

Larson, R., & Richards, M. H. (1991). Daily companionship in late childhood and early adolescence: Changing developmental contexts. *Child Development, 62*, 284–300.

Larson, R. W., & Richards, M. H. (1994). Family emotions: Do young adolescents and their parents experience the same states? *Journal of Research on Adolescence, 4*(4), 567–583.

Larson, R. W., Richards, M. H., Moneta, G., & Holmbeck, G. (1996). Changes in adolescents' daily interactions with their

families from ages 10 to 18: Disengagement and transformation. *Developmental Psychology, 32*(4), 744–754.

Lasko, D. S., Field, T. M., Gonzalez, K. P., Harding, J., Yando, R., & Bendell, D. (1996). Adolescent depressed mood and parental unhappiness. *Adolescence, 31*(121), 49–57.

Lau, S., & Lau, W. (1996). Outlook on life: How adolescents and children view the life-style of parents, adults and self. *Journal of Adolescence, 19*, 293–296.

Laursen, B. (1993). Conflict management among close peers. *New Directions for Child Development, 60*, 39–54.

Laursen, B. (1995a). Conflict and social interaction in adolescent relationships. *Journal of Research on Adolescence, 5*(1), 55–70.

Laursen, B. (1995b). Variations in adolescent conflict and social interaction associated with maternal employment and family structure. *International Journal of Behavioral Development, 18*(1), 151–164.

Laursen, B., Coy, K. C., & Collins, W. A. (1998). Reconsidering changes in parent-child conflict across adolescence: A meta-analysis. *Child Development, 69*(3), 817–832.

Leadbeater, B. J. (1991). Relativistic thinking in adolescence. In R. M. Lerner, A. C. Petersen, & J. Brooks-Gunn (Eds.), *Encyclopedia of adolescence* (Vol. 2, pp. 921–925). New York: Garland.

Leadbeater, B. J. (1996). School outcomes for minority-group adolescent mothers at 28 to 36 months postpartum: A longitudinal follow-up. *Journal of Research on Adolescence, 6*(4), 629–648.

Leadbeater, B. J., Blatt, S. J., & Quinlan, D. M. (1995). Gender-linked vulnerabilities to depressive symptoms, stress, and problem behaviors in adolescents. *Journal of Research on Adolescence, 5*(1), 1–29.

Leadbeater, B. J., & Dionne, J. (1981). The adolescent's use of formal operational thinking in solving problems related to identity resolution. *Adolescence, 16*, 111–121.

Lee, M., & Larson, R. (1996). Effectiveness of coping in adolescence: The case of Korean examination stress. *International Journal of Behavioral Development, 19*(4), 851–869.

Lee, V. E., Burkam, D. T., Zimiles, H., & Ladewski, B. (1994). Family structure and its effect on behavioral and emotional problems in young adolescents. *Journal of Research on Adolescence, 4*(3), 405–437.

Leenaars, A. A., & Lester, D. (1995). The changing suicide pattern in Canadian adolescents and youth, compared to their American counterparts. *Adolescence, 30*(119), 539–547.

Leffert, N., Benson, P., Scales, P., Sharma, A., Drake, D., & Blyth, D. (1998). Developmental assets: Measurement and prediction of risk behaviors among adolescents. *Applied Developmental Science, 2*, 209–230.

Lenerz, K., Kucher, J., East, P., Lerner, J. V., & Lerner, R. M. (1987). Early adolescents' physical organismic characteristics and psychosocial functioning: Findings from the Pennsylvania Early Adolescent Transitions Study (PEATS). In R. M. Lerner & T. Foch (Eds.), *Biological-psychosocial interactions in early adolescence. Child Psychology* (pp. 225–247). Hillsdale, NJ: Erlbaum.

Leon, G. R. (1991). Bulimia nervosa in adolescence. In R. M. Lerner, A. C. Petersen, & J. Brooks-Gunn (Eds.), *Encyclopedia of adolescence* (Vol. 1). New York: Garland.

Lerman, R. I. (1985). *Who are the young absent fathers?* Paper prepared for the Department of Health and Human Services, Assistant Secretary for Policy and Evaluation. Waltham, MA: Brandeis University, Heller Graduate School.

Lerner, J. S. (1995). Foreword. In R. M. Lerner (Ed.), *America's youth in crisis: Challenges and options for programs and policies* (pp. xi–xii). Thousand Oaks, CA: Sage.

Lerner, J. V. (1994). *Working women and their families*. Thousand Oaks, CA: Sage.

Lerner, J. V., & Galambos, N. L. (1985). Mother role satisfaction, mother-child interaction, and child temperament: A process model. *Developmental Psychology, 21*(6), 1157–1164.

Lerner, J. V., & Galambos, N. L. (1991). *Employed mothers and their children*. New York: Garland.

Lerner, R. M, Castellino, D. R., Terry, P. A., Villarruel, F. A., & McKinney, M. H. (1995). A developmental contextual perspective on parenting. In M. H. Bornstein (Ed.), *Handbook of parenting: Biology and ecology of parenting* (Vol. 2, pp. 285–309). Mahwah, NJ: Erlbaum.

Lerner, R. M. (1976). *Concepts and theories of human development*. Reading, MA: Addison-Wesley.

Lerner, R. M. (1982). Children and adolescents as producers of their own development. *Developmental Review, 2*, 342–370.

Lerner, R. M. (1984). *On the nature of human plasticity*. New York: Cambridge University Press.

Lerner, R. M. (1985). Individual and context in developmental psychology: Conceptual and theoretical issues. In J. R. Nesselroade & A. von Eye (Eds.), *Individual development and social change: Explanatory analysis* (pp. 155–187). New York: Academic Press.

Lerner, R. M. (1986). *Concepts and theories of human development* (2nd ed.). New York: Random House.

Lerner, R. M. (1987). A life-span perspective for early adolescence. In R. M. Lerner & T. T. Foch (Eds.), *Biological-psychosocial interactions in early adolescence* (pp. 9–34). Hillsdale, NJ: Erlbaum.

Lerner, R. M. (1988). Early adolescent transitions: The lore and the laws of adolescence. In M. D. Levine & E. R. McArarney (Eds.), *Early adolescent transitions* (pp. 1–40). Lexington, MA: D.C. Heath.

Lerner, R. M. (1991a). Changing organism-context relations as the basic process of development: A developmental contextual perspective. *Developmental Psychology, 27*, 27–32.

Lerner, R. M. (1991b). Editorial: Continuities and changes in the scientific study of adolescence. *Journal of Research on Adolescence, 1*, 1–5.

Lerner, R. M. (1992a). Dialectics, developmental contextualism, and the further enhancement of theory about puberty and psychosocial development. *Journal of Early Adolescence, 12*, 366–388.

Lerner, R. M. (1992b). *Final solutions: Biology, prejudice, and genocide*. University Park: Penn State Press.

Lerner, R. M. (1993a). Early adolescence: Toward an agenda for the integration of research, policy, and intervention. In R. M. Lerner (Ed.), *Early adolescence: Perspectives on research, policy, and intervention*, pp. 1–13.

Lerner, R. M. (1993b). Investment in youth: The role of home economics in enhancing the life chances of America's children. *AHEA Monograph Series, 1*, 5–34.

Lerner, R. M. (1994). Schools and adolescents. In P. C. McKenry & S. M. Gavazzi (Eds.), *Visions 2010: Families and adolescents, 2*(1), pp. 14–15, 42–43. Minneapolis: National Council on Family Relations.

Lerner, R. M. (1995). *America's youth in crisis: Challenges and options for programs and policies*. Thousand Oaks, CA: Sage.

Lerner, R. M. (Ed). (1998a). Theoretical models of human development. In W. Damon (Ed.), *Handbook of Child Psychology* (5th ed., Vol. 1). New York: Wiley.

Lerner, R. M. (1998b). Theories of human development: Contemporary perspectives. In W. Damon (Series Ed.) & R. M. Lerner (Vol. Ed.), *Handbook of child psychology: Vol. 1. Theoretical models of human development* (pp. 1–24). New York: Wiley.

Lerner, R. M. (in press). *Concepts and theories of human development* (3rd ed.). Mahwah, NJ: Erlbaum.

Lerner, R. M., & Castellino, D. R. (1999). Adolescents and their families: A view of the issues. In R. M. Lerner & D. R. Castellino (Eds.), *Adolescents and their families: Structure, function, and parent-youth relations* (pp. ix–xiii). New York: Garland.

Lerner, R. M., & Castellino, D. R. (in press). Contemporary developmental theory and adolescence: Developmental systems and applied developmental science. *Journal of Adolescent Health*.

Lerner, R. M., Castellino, D. R., Terry, P. A., Villarruel, F. A., & McKinney, M. H. (1995). A developmental contextual perspective on parenting. In M. H. Bornstein (Ed.), *Handbook of parenting: Biology and ecology of parenting* (Vol. 2, pp. 285–309). Hillsdale, NJ: Erlbaum.

Lerner, R. M., Delaney, M., Hess, L. E., Jovanovic, J., & von Eye, A. (1990). Early adolescent physical attractiveness and academic competence. *Journal of Early Adolescence, 10*, 4–20.

Lerner, R. M., & Fisher, C. B. (1994). From applied developmental psychology to applied developmental science: Community coalitions and collaborative careers. In C. B. Fisher & R. M. Lerner (Eds.), *Applied developmental psychology* (pp. 502–522). New York: McGraw-Hill.

Lerner, R. M., Fisher, C. B., & Weinberg, R. A. (1997). Editorial: Applied developmental science: Scholarship for our times. *Applied Developmental Science, 1*, 2–3.

Lerner, R. M., Fisher, C. B., & Weinberg, R. A. (2000a). Toward a science for and of the people: Promoting civil society through the application of developmental science. *Child Development, 71*, 11–20.

Lerner, R. M., Fisher, C. B., & Weinberg, R. A. (2000b). Applying developmental science in the twenty-first century: International scholarship for our times. *International Journal of Behavioral Development, 24,* 24–29.

Lerner, R. M., & Foch, T. T. (Eds.). (1987). *Biological-psychosocial interactions in early adolescence.* Hillsdale, NJ: Erlbaum.

Lerner, R. M., Freund, A. M., DeStefanis, I., & Habermas, T. (2001). Understanding developmental regulation in adolescence: The use of the selection, optimization, and compensation model. *Human Development, 44,* 29–50.

Lerner, R. M., & Galambos, N. L. (1998). Adolescent development: Challenges and opportunities for research, programs, and policies. In J. T. Spence (Ed.), *Annual Review of Psychology* (Vol. 49, pp. 413–446). Palo Alto, CA: Annual Reviews.

Lerner, R. M., & Hoopfer, L. C. (1993, October 12). The family answer book: Teens and tweens. *Family Circle,* p. 43.

Lerner, R. M., & Hultsch, D. F. (1983). *Human development: A life-span perspective.* New York: McGraw-Hill.

Lerner, R. M., Karson, M., Meisels, M., & Knapp, J. R. (1975). Actual and perceived attitudes of late adolescents and their parents: The phenomenon of the generation gaps. *Journal of Genetic Psychology, 126,* 195–207.

Lerner, R. M., & Kauffman, M. B. (1985). The concept of development in contextualism. *Developmental Review, 5,* 309–333.

Lerner, R. M., & Knapp, J. R. (1975). Actual and perceived intrafamilial attitudes of late adolescents and their parents. *Journal of Youth and Adolescence, 4,* 17–36.

Lerner, R. M., & Lerner, J. V. (1983). Temperament-intelligence reciprocities in early childhood: A contextual model. In M. Lewis (Ed.), *Origins of intelligence: Infancy and early childhood* (pp. 399–421). New York: Plenum.

Lerner, R. M., & Lerner, J. V. (1987). Children in their contexts: A goodness-of-fit model. In J. B. Lancaster & J. Altmann (Eds.), *Parenting across the life span: Biosocial dimensions* (pp. 377–404). Hawthorne, NY: Aldine.

Lerner, R. M., & Lerner, J. V. (1989). Organismic and social contextual bases of development: The sample case of early adolescence. In W. Damon (Ed.), *Child development today and tomorrow* (pp. 69–85). San Francisco: Jossey-Bass.

Lerner, R. M., Lerner, J. V., Hess, L. E., Schwab, J., et al. (1991). Physical attractiveness and psychosocial functioning among early adolescents. *Journal of Early Adolescence, 11,* 300–320.

Lerner, R. M., & Miller, J. R. (1993). Integrating human development research and intervention for America's children: The Michigan State University Model. *Journal of Applied Developmental Psychology, 14,* 347–364.

Lerner, R. M., & Olson, C. K. (1994, February). The imaginary audience. *Parents,* pp. 133–134.

Lerner, R. M., & Olson, C. K. (1994, December). "Don't talk back!" *Parents,* pp. 97–98.

Lerner, R. M., & Olson, C. K. (1995, February). My body is so ugly! *Parents,* pp. 87–88.

Lerner, R. M., & Olson, C. K. (1995, September). Teen idols. *Parents,* pp. 91–92.

Lerner, R. M., & Olson, C. K. (1996, September). Keeping tabs . . . without being a nag. *Parents,* pp. 111–112.

Lerner, R. M., Ostrom, C. W., & Freel, M. A. (1995). Promoting positive youth and community development through outreach scholarship: Comments on Zeldin and Peterson. *Journal of Adolescent Research, 10,* 486–502.

Lerner, R. M., Ostrom, C. W., & Freel, M. A. (1997). Preventing health compromising behaviors among youth and promoting their positive development: A developmental contextual perspective. In J. Schulenberg, J. L. Maggs, & K. Hurrelmann (Eds.), *Health risks and developmental transitions during adolescence* (pp. 498–521). New York: Cambridge University Press.

Lerner, R. M., & Simon, L. A. K. (1998). The new American outreach university: Challenges and options. In R. M. Lerner & L. A. K. Simon (Eds.), *University-community collaborations for the twenty-first century: Outreach scholarship for youth and families* (pp. 3–23). New York: Garland.

Lerner, R. M., & Spanier, G. B. (Eds.). (1978a). *Child influences on marital and family interaction: A life span perspective.* New York: Academic Press.

Lerner, R. M., & Spanier, G. B. (1978b). A dynamic interactional view of child and family development. In R. M. Lerner & G. B. Spanier (Eds.), *Child influences on marital and family interaction: A life-span perspective* (pp. 1–22). New York: Academic Press.

Lerner, R. M., & Spanier, G. B. (1980). A dynamic interactional view of child and family development. In R. M. Lerner & G. B. Spanier (Eds.), *Child influences on marital and family interaction: A life-span perspective* (pp. 1–20). New York: Academic Press.

Lerner, R. M., Sparks, E., & McCubbin, L. (1999). *Family diversity and family policy: Strengthening families for America's children.* Norwell, MA: Kluwer.

Lerner, R. M., Sparks, E., & McCubbin, L. (2000). Family diversity and family policy. In D. Demo, K. R. Allen, & M. A. Fine (Eds.), *Handbook of family diversity* (pp. 380–401). New York: Oxford University Press.

Lerner, R. M., & Villarruel, F. A. (1994). Adolescence. In T. Husen & N. Postlethwaite (Eds.), *International encyclopedia of education* (2nd ed., Vol. 1, pp. 83–89). Oxford: Pergamon.

LeRoux, J. (1996). Street children in South Africa: Findings from interviews on the background of street children in Pretoria, South Africa. *Adolescence, 31*(122), 423–431.

Levinson, D. J. (1978). Mid-life transition period in adult psychosocial development. *Psychiatry, 129,* 173–174.

Levitt, M. J., Guacci-Franco, N., & Levitt, J. L. (1993). Convoys of social support in childhood and early adolescence: Structure and function. *Developmental Psychology, 29,* 811–818.

Levitt, M. J., Guacci-Franco, N., & Levitt, J. L. (1994). Social support and achievement in childhood and early adolescence: A multicultural study. *Journal of Applied Developmental Psychology, 15*(2), 207–222.

Levitt, M. Z., Selman, R. L., & Richmond, J. B. (1991). The psychosocial foundations of early adolescents' high-risk behavior: Implications for research and practice. *Journal of Research on Adolescence, 1*(4), 349–378.

Levy, G. D., Taylor, M. G., & Gelman, S. A. (1995). Traditional and evaluative aspects of flexibility in gender roles, social conventions, moral rules, and physical laws. *Child Development, 66,* 515–531.

Lewin, K. (1943). Psychology and the process of group living. *Journal of Social Psychology, 17,* 113–131.

Li, X., Sano, H., & Merwin, J. C. (1996). Perception and reasoning abilities among American, Japanese, and Chinese adolescents. *Journal of Adolescent Research, 11*(2), 173–193.

Linn, M. C. (1991). Scientific reasoning, adolescent. In R. M. Lerner, A. C. Petersen, & J. Brooks-Gunn (Eds.), *Encyclopedia of adolescence* (Vol. 2, pp. 981–986). New York: Garland.

Linn, M., & Petersen, A. (1985). Emergence and characterization of sex differences in spatial ability: A meta-analysis. *Child Development, 56*(6), 1479–1498.

Lintunen, T., Leskinen, E., Oinonen, M., Salinto, M., & Rahkila, P. (1995). Change, reliability, and stability in self-perceptions in early adolescence: A four-year follow-up study. *International Journal of Behavioral Development, 18*(2), 351–364.

Lipsitz, J. (1977). *Growing up forgotten.* Lexington, MA: Lexington.

Lipsitz, J. (1991). Public policy and young adolescents: A 1990s context for researchers. *Journal of Early Adolescence, 11,* 20–37.

Litchfield, A. W., Thomas, D. L., & Li, B. D. (1997). Dimensions of religiosity as mediators of the relations between parenting and adolescent deviant behavior. *Journal of Adolescent Research, 12*(2), 199–226.

Litt, I. F. (1991). Eating disorders, medical complications of. In R. M. Lerner, A. C. Petersen, & J. Brooks-Gunn (Eds.), *Encyclopedia of Adolescence* (Vol. 1, pp. 278–280). New York: Garland.

Little, R. R. (1993). *What's working for today's youth: The issues, the programs, and the learnings.* Paper presented at the ICYF Fellows Colloquium, Michigan State University.

Livson, N., & Peskin, H. (1980). Perspectives on adolescence from longitudinal research. In J. Adelson (Ed.), *Handbook of adolescent psychology* (pp. 47–98). New York: Wiley.

Lord, S. E., Eccles, J. S., & McCarthy, K. A. (1994). Surviving the junior high school transition: Family processes and self-perceptions as protective and risk factors. *Journal of Early Adolescence, 14,* 162–199.

LoSciuto, L., Rajala, A. K., Townsend, T. N., & Taylor, A. S. (1996). An outcome evaluation of Across Ages: An intergenerational mentoring approach to drug prevention. *Journal of Adolescent Research, 11*(1), 116–129.

Lourenço, O. M. (1990). From cost-perception to gain-construction: Toward a Piagetian explanation of the development of altruism in children. *International Journal of Behavioral Development, 13,* 119–132.

Luster, T., & McAdoo, H. P. (1994). Factors related to the achievement and adjustment of young African American children. *Child Development, 65,* 1080–1094.

Luster, T., & McAdoo, H. P. (1995). Factors related to self-esteem among African-American youths: A secondary analysis of the High/Scope Perry Preschool data. *Journal of Research on Adolescence, 5*(4), 451–467.

Luster, T., & McAdoo, H. (1996). Family and child influences on educational attainment: A secondary analysis of the High/Scope Perry Preschool data. *Developmental Psychology, 32*(1), 26–39.

Luster, T., & Small, S. A. (1997). Sexual abuse history and problems in adolescence: Exploring the effects of moderating variables. *Journal of Marriage and the Family, 59,* 131–142.

Luthar, S. S. (1995). Social competence in the school setting: Prospective cross-domain associations among inner-city teens. *Child Development, 66,* 416–429.

Luthar, S. S., & McMahon, T. J. (1996). Peer reputation among inner-city adolescents: Structure and correlates. *Journal of Research on Adolescence, 6*(4), 581–603.

Lynch, M. E. (1991). Gender intensification. In R. M. Lerner, A. C. Petersen, & J. Brooks-Gunn (Eds.), *Encyclopedia of adolescence* (Vol. 1, pp. 389–391). New York: Garland.

Lyon, M., Chatoor, I., Atkins, D., Silber, T., Mosimann, J., & Gray, J. (1997). Testing the hypothesis of the multidimensional model of anorexia nervosa in adolescents. *Adolescence, 32*(125), 101–111.

Lysne, M., & Levy, G. D. (1997). Differences in ethnic identity in Native American adolescents as a function of school context. *Journal of Adolescent Research, 12*(3), 372–388.

M

Maccoby, E., & Martin, J. (1983). Socialization in the context of the family: Parent-child interaction. In E. M. Hetherington (Ed.), *Handbook of child psychology: Socialization, personality, and social development* (Vol. 4, pp. 1–101). New York: Wiley.

Mac Iver, D. J., & Reuman, D. A. (1988, April). *Decision-making in the classroom and early adolescents' valuing of mathematics.* Paper presented at the annual meeting of the American Educational Research Association, New Orleans.

Macksoud, M. S., & Aber, J. L. (1996). The war experiences and psychosocial development of children in Lebanon. *Child Development, 67,* 70–88.

Maggs, J. L., Almeida, D. M., & Galambos, N. L. (1995). Risky business: The paradoxical meaning of problem behavior for young adolescents. *Journal of Early Adolescence, 15*(3), 344–362.

Maggs, J. L., & Galambos, N. L. (1993). Alternative structural models for understanding adolescent problem behavior in two-earner families. *Journal of Early Adolescence, 13*(1), 79–101.

Maggs, J. L., & Hurrelmann, K. (1998). Do substance use and delinquency have differential associations with adolescents' peer relations? *International Journal of Behavioral Development, 22*(2), 367–388.

Magnusson, D. (1988). Individual development from an interactional perspective. In D. Magnusson (Ed.), *Paths through life* (Vol. 1, pp. 3–31). Hillsdale, NJ: Erlbaum.

Magnusson, D., & Stattin, H. (1998). Person-context interaction theories. In W. Damon (Series Ed.) & R. M. Lerner (Vol. Ed.), *Handbook of child psychology: Vol. 1. Theoretical models of human development* (5th ed., pp. 685–759). New York: Wiley.

Magnusson, D., Stattin, H., & Allen, V. L. (1986). Differential maturation among girls and its relations to social adjustment: A longitudinal perspective. In P. B. Baltes, D. L. Featherman, & R. M. Lerner (Eds.), *Life-span development and behavior* (pp. 135–172). Hillsdale, NJ: Erlbaum.

Maguin, E., Zucker, R. A., & Fitzgerald, H. E. (1994). The path to alcohol problems through conduct problems: A family-based approach to very early intervention with risk. *Journal of Research on Adolescence, 4,* 249–269.

Mann-Feder, V. R. (1996). Adolescents in therapeutic communities. *Adolescence, 31*(121), 17–28.

Marcia, J. E. (1964). *Determination and construct validity of ego identity status.* Unpublished doctoral dissertation. Ohio State University.

Marcia, J. (1966). Development and validations of ego-identity status. *Journal of Personality and Social Psychology, 5,* 551–558.

Marcia, J. E. (1980). Identity in adolescence. In J. Adelson (Ed.), *Handbook of adolescent psychology* (pp. 159–187). New York: Wiley.

Marcia, J. (1991). Identity and self-development. In R. M. Lerner, A. C. Petersen, & J. Brooks-Gunn (Eds.), *Encyclopedia of adolescence* (Vol. 1, pp. 529–533). New York: Garland.

Marcia, J. E., Waterman, A. S., Matteson, D. R., Archer, S., & Orlofsky, J. (1992). *Ego identity: A handbook for psychosocial research*. British Columbia, Canada: Simon Fraser University. (Original work published 1985)

Marcus, R. F. (1996). The friendships of delinquents. *Adolescence, 31*(121), 145–158.

Marcus, R. F., & Betzer, P. D. S. (1996). Attachment and antisocial behavior in early adolescence. *Journal of Early Adolescence, 16*(2), 229–248.

Marini, Z., & Case, R. (1994). The development of abstract reasoning about the physical and social world. *Child Development, 65*, 147–159.

Markstrom-Adams, C., & Smith, M. (1996). Identity formation and religious orientation among high school students from the United States and Canada. *Journal of Adolescence, 19*, 247–261.

Marlatt, G. A., Baer, J. S., Kivlahan, D. R., Dimeff, L. A., Larimer, M. E., Quigley, L. A., Somers, J. M., & Williams, E. (1998). Screening and brief intervention for high-risk college student drinkers: Results from a 2-year follow-up assessment. *Journal of Consulting and Clinical Psychology, 66*(4), 604–615.

Marsh, H. W., & Roche, L. A. (1996). Structure of artistic self-concepts for performing arts and non-performing arts students in a performing arts high school: "Setting the stage" with multigroup confirmatory factor analysis. *Journal of Educational Psychology, 88*(3), 461–477.

Marshall, W. A., & Tanner, J. M. (1986). Puberty. In F. Falkner & J. M. Tanner (Eds.), *Human growth* (2nd ed., Vol. 2, pp. 171–209). New York: Plenum.

Marsiglio, W. (1987). Male teenage fertility: An analysis of fatherhood commitment and its association with educational outcomes and aspirations. *Dissertation Abstracts International, 48*(2-A), 358.

Marsiske, M., Lang, F. R., Baltes, P. B., & Baltes, M. M. (1995). Selective optimization with compensation: Life-span perspectives on successful human development. In R. A. Dixon & L. Bäckman (Eds.), *Compensating for psychological deficits and declines: Managing losses and promoting gains* (pp. 35–79). Mahwah, NJ: Erlbaum.

Mason, C. A., Cauce, A. M., Gonzales, N., & Hiraga, Y. (1996). Neither too sweet nor too sour: Problem peers, maternal control, and problem behavior in African American adolescents. *Child Development, 67*, 2115–2130.

Masten, A. S., Coatsworth, J. D., Neeman, J., Gest, S. D., Tellegen, A., & Garmezy, N. (1995). The structure and coherence of competence from childhood through adolescence. *Child Development, 66*, 1635–1659.

Matthews, D. J., & Keating, D. P. (1995). Domain specificity and habits of mind: An investigation of patterns of high-level development. *Journal of Early Adolescence, 15*(3), 319–343.

Mayseless, O., & Hai, I. (1998). Leaving home transition in Israel: Changes in parent-adolescent relationships and adolescents' adaptation to military service. *International Journal of Behavioral Development, 22*(3), 589–609.

Mboya, M. M. (1995). Variations in parenting practices: Gender and age-related differences in African adolescents. *Adolescence, 30*(120), 955–962.

McAdoo, H. P. (1995). Stress levels, family help patterns, and religiosity in middle- and working-class African American single mothers. *Journal of Black Psychology, 21*, 424–449.

McAdoo, H. P. (1998). African American families: Strength and realities. In H. C. McCubbin, E. Thompson, & J. Futrell (Eds.), *Resiliency in ethnic minority families: African American families* (pp. 17–30). Thousand Oaks, CA: Sage.

McAdoo, H. P. (1999). Diverse children of color. In H. E. Fitzgerald, B. M. Lester, & B. S. Zuckerman (Eds.), *Children of color: Research, health, and policy issues* (pp. 205–218). New York: Garland.

McCandless, B. R. (1967). *Children.* New York: Holt, Rinehart and Winston.

McCandless, B. (1970). *Adolescents.* Hinsdale, IL: Dryden Press.

McClearn, G. E. (1981). Evolution and genetic variability. In E. S. Gollin (Ed.), *Developmental plasticity: Behavioral and biological aspects of variations in development* (pp. 3–31). New York: Academic Press.

McCreary, M. L., Slavin, L. A., & Berry, E. J. (1996). Predicting problem behav-
ior and self-esteem among African American adolescents. *Journal of Adolescent Research, 11*(2), 216–234.

McCullum, C., & Achterberg, C. L. (1997). Food shopping and label use behavior among high school-aged adolescents. *Adolescence, 32*(125), 181–197.

McDermott, P. A., & Spencer, M. B. (1997). Racial and social class prevalence of psychopathology among school-age youth in the United States. *Youth & Society, 28*(4), 387–414.

McHale, S. M., Crouter, A. C., Fennelly, K., Tomascik, C. A., Updegraff, K. A., Graham, J. E., Baker, A. E., Dreisbach, L., Ferry, N., Manlove, E. E., McGroder, S. M., Mulkeen, P., & Obeidallah, D. A. (1996). Community-based interventions for young adolescents: The Penn State PRIDE Project. *Journal of Research on Adolescence, 6*(1), 23–36.

McHale, S. M., & Lerner, R. M. (1996). University-community collaborations on behalf of youth. *Journal of Research on Adolescence, 6*(1), 1–7.

McKechnie, J., Lindsay, S., Hobbs, S., & Lavalette, M. (1996). Adolescents' perceptions of the role of part-time work. *Adolescence, 31*(121), 193–204.

McKeown, R. E., Garrison, C. Z., Jackson, K. L., Cuffe, S. P., Addy, C. L., & Waller, J. L. (1997). Family structure and cohesion, and depressive symptoms in adolescents. *Journal of Research on Adolescence, 7*, 267–281.

McKinney, M., Abrams, L. A., Terry, P. A., & Lerner, R. M. (1994). Child development research and the poor children of America: A call for a developmental contextual approach to research and outreach. *Family and Consumer Sciences Research Journal, 23*, 26–42.

McLaughlin, C. S., Chen, C., Greenberger, E., & Biermeier, C. (1997). Family, peer, and individual correlates of sexual experience among Caucasian and Asian American late adolescents. *Journal of Research on Adolescence, 7*(1), 33–53.

McLaughlin, J.-A., Miller, P., & Warwick, H. (1996). Deliberate self-harm in adolescents: Hopelessness, depression, problems and problem-solving. *Journal of Adolescence, 19*, 523–532.

McLean, P. E. (1995). Sexual behaviors and attitudes of high school students in the kingdom of Swaziland. *Journal of Adolescent Research, 10*(3), 400–420.

McLernon, F., Ferguson, N., & Cairns, E.

(1997). Comparison of Northern Irish children's attitudes to war and peace before and after the paramilitary ceasefires. *International Journal of Behavioral Development, 20*(4), 715–730.

McLoyd, V. C. (1994). Research in the service of poor and ethnic/racial minority children: A moral imperative. *Family and Consumer Sciences Research Journal, 23*, 56–66.

McLoyd, V. C., & Wilson, L. (1991). The strain of living poor: Parenting, social support, and child mental health. In A. C. Huston (Ed.), *Children in poverty: Child development and public policy.* Cambridge: Cambridge University Press.

McLoyd, V. C., & Wilson, L. (1992). Telling them like it is: The role of economic and environmental factors in single mothers' discussions with their children. *American Journal of Community Psychology, 20*(4), 419–444.

McMaster, L. E., & Wintre, M. G. (1996). The relations between perceived parental reciprocity, perceived parental approval, and adolescent substance use. *Journal of Adolescent Research, 11*(4), 440–460.

Mead, M. (1928). *Coming of age in Samoa: A psychological study of primitive youth for Western civilization.* New York: Morrow.

Mead, M. (1930). *Growing up in New Guinea.* New York: Morrow.

Mead, M. (1935). *Sex and temperament in three primitive societies.* New York: Morrow.

Meeus, W., & Dekovic, M. (1995). Identity development, parental and peer support in adolescence: Results of a national Dutch survey. *Adolescence, 30*(120), 931–944.

Melby, J. N., & Conger, R. D. (1996). Parental behaviors and adolescent academic performance: A longitudinal analysis. *Journal of Research on Adolescence, 6*(1), 113–137.

Merten, D. E. (1996). Visibility and vulnerability: Responses to rejection by nonaggressive junior high school boys. *Journal of Early Adolescence, 16*(1), 5–26.

Meyer, J. W. (1988). The social construction of the psychology of childhood: Some contemporary processes. In E. M. Hetherington, R. M. Lerner, & M. Perlmutter (Eds.), *Child development in life-span perspective* (pp. 47–65). Hillsdale, NJ: Erlbaum.

Midgley, C., Anderman, E., & Hicks, L. (1995). Differences between elementary and middle school teachers and students:

A goal theory approach. *Journal of Early Adolescence, 15*(1), 90–113.

Midgley, C., Arunkumar, R., & Urdan, T. C. (1996). "If I don't do well tomorrow, there's a reason": Predictors of adolescents' use of academic self-handicapping strategies. *Journal of Educational Psychology, 88*(3), 423–434.

Midgley, C., & Feldlaufer, H. (1987). Students' and teachers' decision-making fit before and after the transition to junior high school. *Journal of Early Adolescence, 7*(2), 225–241.

Midgley, C., Feldlaufer, H., & Eccles, J. S. (1989a). Changes in teacher efficacy and student self- and task-related beliefs in mathematics during the transition to junior high school. *Journal of Educational Psychology, 81*, 247–258.

Midgley, C., Feldlaufer, H., & Eccles, J. S. (1989b). Student/teacher relations and attitudes toward mathematics before and after the transition to junior high school. *Child Development, 60*, 981–992.

Midgley, C., & Urdan, T. (1995). Predictors of middle school students' use of self-handicapping strategies. *Journal of Early Adolescence, 15*(4), 389–411.

Mihalic, S. W., & Elliot, D. (1997). Short- and long-term consequences of doing work. *Youth & Society, 28*(4), 464–498.

Miller, K. E. (1996). The effects of state terrorism and exile on indigenous Guatemalan refugee children: A mental health assessment and an analysis of children's narratives. *Child Development, 67*, 89–106.

Millett, R. A. (1996). Empowerment evaluation and the W. K. Kellogg Foundation. In D. M. Fetterman, S. J. Kaftarian, & A. Wandersman (Eds.), *Empowerment evaluation: Knowledge and tools for self-assessment & accountability* (pp. 65–76). Thousand Oaks, CA: Sage.

Mills, R., & Mills, R. (1996). Adolescents' attitudes toward female gender roles: Implications for education. *Adolescence, 31*(123), 741–745.

Millstein, S. G. (1989). Adolescent health: Challenges for behavioral scientists. *American Psychologist, 44*(5), 837–842.

Mincy, R. B. (1994). *Nurturing young black males: Challenges to agencies, programs, and social policy.* Washington, DC: Urban Institute Press.

Miron, L. F., & Lauria, M. (1995). Identity politics and student resistance to inner-city public schooling. *Youth & Society, 27*(1), 29–54.

Misiak, H., & Sexton, V. S. (1966). *Histo-*

ry of psychology in overview. New York: Grune & Stratton.

Mitchell, C. M., O'Nell, T. D., Beals, J., Dick, R. W., Keane, E., & Manson, S. M. (1996). Dimensionality of alcohol use among American Indian adolescents: Latent structure, construct validity, and implications for developmental research. *Journal of Research on Adolescence, 6*(2), 151–180.

Modell, J. (1985). *A social history of American adolescents 1945–1985.* Unpublished manuscript. Pittsburgh: Department of History, Carnegie-Mellon University.

Molina, B. S. G., & Chassin, L. (1996). The parent-adolescent relationship at puberty: Hispanic ethnicity and parent alcoholism as moderators. *Developmental Psychology, 32*, 675–686.

Montemayor, R. (1986). Family variation in parent-adolescent storm and stress. *Journal of Adolescent Research, 1*, 15–31.

Montemayor, R., Eberly, M., & Flannery, D. (1993). Effects of pubertal status and conversation topic on parent and adolescent affective expression. *Journal of Early Adolescence, 13*(4), 431–447.

Montemayor, R., & Flannery, D. J. (1991). Parent-adolescent relations in middle and late adolescence. In R. M. Lerner, A. C. Petersen, & J. Brooks-Gunn (Eds.), *Encyclopedia of adolescence* (Vol. 2, pp. 729–738). New York: Garland.

Moore, K. A., & Glei, D. (1995). Taking the plunge: An examination of positive youth development. *Journal of Adolescent Research, 10*(1), 15–40.

Moore, S. M. (1995). Girls' understanding and social constructions of menarche. *Journal of Adolescence, 18*, 87–104.

Moore, S. M., Laflin, M. T., & Weis, D. L. (1996). The role of cultural norms in the self-esteem and drug use relationship. *Adolescence, 31*(123), 523–542.

Morelli, G. A., & Verhoef, H. (1999). Who should help me raise my child? A Cultural approach to understanding non-maternal child care decisions. In C. Le Monda & L. Balter (Eds.), *Child psychology: A handbook of contemporary issues* (pp. 491–509). Philadelphia: Psychology Press/Taylor & Francis.

Moreno, A. B., & Thelen, M. H. (1995). Eating behavior in junior high school females. *Adolescence, 30*(117), 171–174.

Morison, P., & Masten, A. S. (1991). Peer reputation in middle childhood as a predictor of adaptation in adolescence: A seven-year follow-up. *Child Development, 62*, 991–1007.

Morrison, T. G., McLeod, L. D., Morrison, M. A., Anderson, D., & O'Connor, W. E. (1997). Gender stereotyping, homonegativity, and misconceptions about sexually coercive behavior among adolescents. *Youth & Society, 28*(3), 351–382.

Mortimer, J. T. (1991). Employment. In R. M. Lerner, A. C. Petersen, & J. Brooks-Gunn (Eds.), *Encyclopedia of adolescence* (Vol. 1, pp. 311–318). New York: Garland.

Mortimer, J. T., Finch, M. D., Ryu, S., Shanahan, M. J., & Call, K. T. (1996). The effects of work intensity on adolescent mental health, achievement, and behavioral adjustment: New evidence from a prospective study. *Child Development, 67*, 1243–1261.

Mortimer, J. T., Shanahan, M., & Ryu, S. (1994). The effects of adolescent employment on school-related orientation and behavior. In R. K. Silbereisen & E. Todt (Eds.), *Adolescence in context: The interplay of family, school, peers, and work in adjustment* (pp. 304–326). New York: Springer-Verlag.

Moshman, D., & Franks, B. A. (1986). Development of the concept of inferential validity. *Child Development, 57*(1), 153–165.

Mounts, N. S., & Steinberg, L. (1995). An ecological analysis of peer influence on adolescent grade point average and drug use. *Developmental Psychology, 31*(6), 915–922.

Mukai, T. (1996). Mothers, peers, and perceived pressure to diet among Japanese adolescent girls. *Journal of Research on Adolescence, 6*(3), 309–324.

Muller, C. (1995). Maternal employment, parent involvement, and mathematics achievement among adolescents. *Journal of Marriage and the Family, 57*, 85–100.

Munsch, J., & Kinchen, K. M. (1995). Adolescent sociometric status and social support. *Journal of Early Adolescence, 15*(2), 181–202.

Murray, V. M. (1996). An ecological analysis of coital timing among middle-class African American adolescent females. *Journal of Adolescent Research, 11*(2), 261–279.

Mussen, P. H., Harris, S., Rutherford, E., & Keasey, C. B. (1970). Honesty and altruism among preadolescents. *Developmental Psychology, 3*, 169–194.

Mutz, D. C., Roberts, D. F., & van Vuuren, D. P. (1993). Reconsidering the displacement hypothesis: Television's influence on children's time use. *Communication Research, 20*(1), 51–75.

Muuss, R. E. (1996). *Theories of adolescence* (6th ed.). New York: McGraw-Hill.

Myrtek, M., Scharff, C., Brugner, G., & Muller, W. (1996). Physiological, behavioral, and psychological effects associated with television viewing in schoolboys: An exploratory study. *Journal of Early Adolescence, 16*(3), 301–323.

N

National Research Council. (1993). *Losing generations: Adolescents in high-risk settings.* Washington, DC: National Academy Press.

Neimark, E. D. (1975). Intellectual development during adolescence. In F. D. Horowitz (Ed.), *Review of child development research* (Vol. 4, pp. 541–594). Chicago: University of Chicago Press.

Neimark, E. D. (1979). Current status of formal operations research. *Human Development, 22*, 60–67.

Nelson-Le Gall, S. (1990). Academic achievement and help-seeking behavior in early adolescent girls. *Journal of Early Adolescence, 10*, 176–190.

Nesselroade, J. R., & Baltes, P. B. (1974). Adolescent personality development and historical changes: 1970–1972. *Monographs of the Society for Research in Child Development, 39* (Whole No. 154).

Neugarten, B. L., & Moore, J. W. (1968). The changing age-status system. In B. L. Neugarten (Ed.), *Middle age and aging.* Chicago: University of Chicago Press.

Neville, B., & Parke, R. D. (1991). Fathers, adolescent. In R. M. Lerner, A. C. Petersen, & J. Brooks-Gunn (Eds.), *Encyclopedia of adolescence* (Vol. 1, pp. 354–359). New York: Garland.

Newcombe, N., & Dubas, J. S. (1992). A longitudinal study of predictors of spatial ability in adolescent females. *Child Development, 63*, 37–46.

Nottlemann, E. D., Susman, E. J., Blue, J. H., Inoff-Germain, G., Dorn, L. D., Loriaux, D. L., Cutler, G. B., Jr., & Chrousos, G. P. (1987). Gonadal and adrenal hormone correlates of adjustment in early adolescence. In R. M. Lerner & T. T. Foch (Eds.), *Biological-psychosocial interactions in early adolescence* (pp. 303–323). Hillsdale, NJ: Erlbaum.

Nucci, L., & Turiel, E. (1993). God's word, religious rules, and their relation to Christian and Jewish children's concepts of morality. *Child Development, 64*, 1475–1491.

Nummenmaa, A. R., & Nummenmaa, T. (1997). Intergenerational roots of Finnish women's sex-atypical careers. *International Journal of Behavioral Development, 21*(1), 1–14.

Nurmi, J.-E., Berzonsky, M. D., Tammi, K., & Kinney, A. (1997). Identity processing orientation, cognitive and behavioural strategies and well-being. *International Journal of Behavioral Development, 21*(3), 555–570.

Nurmi, J.-E., Poole, M. E., & Kalakoski, V. (1996). Age differences in adolescent identity exploration and commitment in urban and rural environments. *Journal of Adolescence, 19*, 443–452.

O

O'Connell, B. (1999). *Civil society: The underpinnings of American democracy.* Hanover, NH: University Press of New England.

Oden, S. (1995). Studying youth programs to assess influences on youth development: New roles for researchers. *Journal of Adolescent Research, 10*(1), 173–186.

Oettingen, G. (1999). Free fantasies about the future and the emergence of developmental goals. In J. Bandtstädter, & R. M. Lerner (Eds.), *Action and self-development: Theory and research through the life-span* (pp. 315–342). Thousand Oaks, CA: Sage.

Offer, D. (1969). *The psychological world of the teen-ager.* New York: Basic.

Ohannessian, C. M., Lerner, R. M., Lerner, J. V., & von Eye, A. (1995). Discrepancies in adolescents' and parents' perceptions of family functioning and adolescent emotional adjustment. *Journal of Early Adolescence, 15*(4), 490–516.

Okagaki, L., & Frensch, P. A. (1994). Effects of video game playing on measures of spatial performance: Gender effects in late adolescence. *Journal of Applied Developmental Psychology, 15*, 33–58.

O'Koon, J. (1997). Attachment to parents and peers in late adolescence and their relationship with self-image. *Adolescence, 32*(126), 471–482.

Oláh, A. (1995). Coping strategies among adolescents: A cross-cultural study. *Journal of Adolescence, 18*, 491–512.

Osofsky, J. D., & Eberhart-Wright, A. (1988). Affective exchanges between high risk mothers and infants. *International Journal of Psycho-Analysis, 69*(2), 221–231.

Ostrom, C. W., Lerner, R. M., & Freel, M. A. (1995). Building the capacity of youth and families through university-community collaborations: The development-in-context evaluation (DICE) model. *Journal of Adolescent Research, 10*(4) 427–448.

Oswald, M. A. (1994). Perceptions of autonomy, perfectionism, and social ineffectiveness in women with disordered eating patterns. *Dissertation Abstracts International Section A: Humanities & Social Sciences, 55*(3-A), 472.

Overton, W. F. (1990). *Reasoning, necessity, and logic: Developmental perspectives*. Hillsdale, NJ: Erlbaum.

Overton, W. F. (1991). The structure of developmental theory. In H. W. Reese & W. Hayne (Ed.), *Advances in child development and behavior* (Vol. 23, pp. 1–37). San Diego, CA: Academic Press.

Overton, W. (1998). Developmental psychology: Philosophy, concepts, and methodology. In W. Damon (Series Ed.) & R. M. Lerner (Ed.), *Handbook of child psychology: Vol. 1. Theoretical models of human development* (5th ed., pp. 107–187). New York: Wiley.

Overton, W. F., & Byrnes, J. P. (1991). Cognitive development. In R. M. Lerner, A. C. Petersen, & J. Brooks-Gunn (Eds.), *Encyclopedia of adolescence* (Vol. 1, pp. 151–156). New York: Garland.

Overton, W., Byrnes, J., & O'Brien, D. (1985). Developmental and individual differences in conditional reasoning: The role of contradiction training and cognitive style. *Developmental Psychology, 21*(4), 692–701.

Oyserman, D., Radin, N., & Benn, R. (1993). Dynamics in a three-generational family: Teens, grandparents, and babies. *Developmental Psychology, 29*(3), 564–572.

P

Pakiz, B., Reinherz, H. Z., & Frost, A. K. (1992). Antisocial behavior in adolescence: A community study. *Journal of Early Adolescence, 12*(3), 300–313.

Papini, D., & Datan, N. (1983, April). *Transition into adolescence: An interactionist perspective.* Paper presented at the Biennial Meetings of the Society for Research in Child Development, Detroit, MI.

Papini, D. R., & Roggman, L. A. (1992). Adolescent perceived attachment to parents in relation to competence, depression, and anxiety: A longitudinal study. *Journal of Early Adolescence, 12*(4), 420–440.

Papini, D. R., Roggman, L. A., & Anderson, J. (1991). Early-adolescent perceptions of attachment to mother and father: A test of the emotional-distancing and buffering hypotheses. *Journal of Early Adolescence, 11*(2), 258–275.

Park, E. K. (1995). Voices of Korean-American students. *Adolescence, 30*(120), 945–953.

Parke, R. D., Burks, V., Carson, J., Neville, B., & Boyum, L. (1994). Family-peer relationships: A tripartite model. In R. D. Parke & S. Kellam (Eds.), *Advances in family research: Vol. 4. Family relationships with other social systems* (pp. 115–145). Hillsdale, NJ: Erlbaum.

Parker, J. G., & Asher, S. R. (1987). Peer relations and later personal adjustment: Are low-accepted children at risk? *Psychological Bulletin, 102*(3), 357–389.

Paschall, M. J., & Hubbard, M. L. (1998). Effects of neighborhood and family stressors on African American male adolescents' self-worth and propensity for violent behavior. *Journal of Consulting and Clinical Psychology, 66*(5), 825–831.

Patrikakou, E. N. (1996). Investigating the academic achievement of adolescents with learning disabilities: A structural modeling approach. *Journal of Educational Psychology, 88*(3), 435–450.

Pattishall, E. (1984). Health issues in adolescence. In R. M. Lerner & N. L. Galambos (Eds.), *Experiencing adolescents: A sourcebook for parents, teachers, and teens. Guidance and counseling series* (pp. 191–230). New York: Teachers College Press.

Paulson, S. E. (1994). Relations of parenting style and parental involvement with ninth-grade students' achievement. *Journal of Early Adolescence, 14*, 250–267.

Paulson, S. E., Hill, J. P., & Holmbeck, G. N. (1991). Distinguishing between perceived closeness and parental warmth in families with seventh-grade boys and girls. *Journal of Early Adolescence, 11*, 276–293.

Peiser, N. C., & Heaven, P. C. L. (1996). Family influences on self-reported delinquency among high school students. *Journal of Adolescence, 19*, 557–568.

Peluffo, N. (1962). The notions of conserva-

tion and causality in children of different physical and sociocultural environments. *Archives de Psychologie, 38*, 275–291.

Peluffo, N. (1967). Culture and cognitive problems. *International Journal of Psychology, 2*, 187–198.

Pendley, J. S., & Bates, J. E. (1996). Mother/daughter agreement on the eating attitudes test and the eating disorder inventory. *Journal of Early Adolescence, 16*(2), 179–191.

Perkins, D. F., & Lerner, R. M. (1995). Single and multiple indicators of physical attractiveness and psychosocial behaviors among young adolescents. *Journal of Early Adolescence, 15*(3), 269–298.

Perkins, D. F., Luster, T., Villarruel, F. A., & Small, S. (1998). An ecological, risk-factor examination of adolescents' sexual activity in three ethnic groups. *Journal of Marriage and the Family, 60*, 660–673.

Perry, C. M., & McIntire, W. G. (1995). Modes of moral judgement among early adolescents. *Adolescence, 30*(119), 707–715.

Petersen, A. C. (1985). Pubertal development as a cause of disturbance: Myths, realities, and unanswered questions. *Genetic, Social, & General Psychology Monographs, 111*(2), 205–232.

Petersen, A. C. (1987). The nature of biological psychosocial interactions: The sample case of early adolescence. In R. M. Lerner & T. T. Fochs (Eds.), *Biological-psychosocial interactions in early adolescence: A life-span perspective* (pp. 35–61). Hillsdale, NJ: Erlbaum.

Petersen, A. C. (1988). Adolescent development. In M. R. Rosenzweig (Ed.), *Annual review of psychology* (Vol. 39, pp. 583–607). Palo Alto, CA: Annual Reviews.

Petersen, A. C., & Taylor, B. (1980). The biological approach to adolescence: Biological change and psychological adaptation. In J. Adelson (Ed.), *Handbook of adolescent psychology* (pp. 117–155). New York: Wiley.

Peterson, G. W. (1995). The need for common principles in prevention programs for children, adolescents, and families. *Journal of Adolescent Research, 10*(4), 470–485.

Peterson, P. L., Hawkins, J. D., Abbott, R. D., & Catalano, R. F. (1994). Disentangling the effects of parental drinking, family management, and parental alcohol norms on current drinking by black and white adolescents. *Journal of Research on Adolescence, 4*(2), 203–277.

Phares, V., & Renk, K. (1998). Perceptions of parents: A measure of adolescents' feelings about their parents. *Journal of Marriage and Family, 60,* 646–659.

Phillips, C. A., Rolls, S., Rouse, A., & Griffiths, M. D. (1995). Home video game playing in schoolchildren: A study of incidence and patterns of play. *Journal of Adolescence, 18,* 687–691.

Phinney, J. S., & Chavira, V. (1995). Parental ethnic socialization and adolescent coping with problems related to ethnicity. *Journal of Research on Adolescence, 5,* 31–53.

Phinney, J. S., & Cobb, N. J. (1996). Reasoning among intergroup relations among Hispanic and Euro-American adolescents. *Journal of Adolescent Research, 11,* 306–324.

Phinney, J. S., & Devich-Navarro, M. (1997). Variations in bicultural identification among African American and Mexican American adolescents. *Journal of Research on Adolescence, 7*(1), 3–32.

Phinney, J. S., Ferguson, D. L., & Tate, J. D. (1997). Intergroup attitudes among ethnic minority adolescents: A causal model. *Child Development, 68*(5), 955–969.

Piaget, J. (1950). *The psychology of intelligence.* New York: Harcourt Brace.

Piaget, J. (1965). *The moral judgment of the child.* New York: Free Press. (Original work published 1932)

Piaget, J. (1969). The intellectual development of the adolescent. In G. Caplan & S. Lebovici (Eds.), *Adolescence: Psychosocial perspective* (pp. 22–26). New York: Basic.

Piaget, J. (1970). Piaget's theory. In P. H. Mussen (Ed.), *Carmichael's manual of child psychology* (3rd ed., Vol. 1, pp. 703–723). New York: Wiley.

Piaget, J. (1972). Intellectual evolution from adolescence to adulthood. *Human Development, 15,* 1–12.

Piaget, J., & Inhelder, B. (1969). *The psychology of the child.* New York: Basic.

Pick, S., & Palos, P. A. (1995). Impact of the family on the sex lives of adolescents. *Adolescence, 30*(119), 667–675.

Pike, A., McGuire, S., Hetherington, E. M., Reiss, D., & Plomin, R. (1996). Family environment and adolescent depressive symptoms and antisocial behavior: A

multivariate genetic analysis. *Developmental Psychology, 32*(4), 574–589.

Pintrich, P. R., Roeser, R. W., & DeGroot, E. (1994). Classroom and individual differences in early adolescents' motivation and self-regulated learning. *Journal of Early Adolescence, 14*(2), 139–161.

Pirog-Good, M. A. (1995). The family background and attitudes of teen fathers. *Youth & Society, 26*(3), 351–376.

Pirog-Good, M. A. (1996). The education and labor market outcomes of adolescent fathers. *Youth & Society, 28*(2), 236–262.

Pittman, K. J. (1996, Winter). Community, youth, development: Three goals in search of connection. *New Designs for Youth Development,* pp. 4–8.

Pittman, K. J., & Irby, M. (1995, January 22–25). *Promoting investment in life skills for youth: Beyond indicators for survival and problem prevention.* Paper presented at the Monitoring and Measuring the State of Children: Beyond Survival, an interactional workshop, Jerusalem, Israel.

Pittman, K. J., Irby, M., & Cahill, M. (1995). *Mixing it up: Participatory evaluation as a tool for generating parent and community empowerment.* Unpublished manuscript. Cambridge, MA: Harvard Family Research Project, Harvard University.

Pittman, K. J., & Zeldin, S. (1994). From deterrence to development: Shifting the focus of youth programs for African-American males. In R. B. Mincy (Ed.), *Nurturing young black males* (pp. 45–55). Washington, DC: Urban Institute Press.

Pong, S.-L. (1997). Family structure, school context, and eighth-grade math and reading achievement. *Journal of Marriage and the Family, 59,* 734–746.

Powers, S. I., Hauser, S. T., Schwartz, J., Noam, G. G., & Jacobson, A. M. (1983). Adolescent ego development and family interactions: A structural-developmental perspective. In H. D. Grotevant & C. R. Cooper (Eds.), *Adolescent development in the family. New Directions for Child Development,* No. 22. San Francisco: Jossey-Bass.

Prince, F. (1995). The relative effectiveness of a peer-led and adult-led smoking intervention program. *Adolescence, 30*(117), 187–194.

Pulos, S. (1997). Adolescents' implicit theories of physical phenomena: A matter

of gravity. *International Journal of Behavioral Development, 20*(3), 493–507.

Punamäki, R.-L. (1996). Can ideological commitment protect children's psychosocial well-being in situations of political violence? *Child Development, 67,* 55–69.

Pungello, E. P., Kupersmidt, J. B., Burchinal, M. R., & Patterson, C. J. (1996). Environmental risk factors and children's achievement from middle childhood to early adolescence. *Developmental Psychology, 32*(4), 755–767.

R

Raffaelli, M., & Larson, R. (1987, April). *Sibling interaction in late childhood and early adolescence.* Paper presented at the Biennial Meeting of the Society for Research in Child Development, Baltimore, MD.

Ralston, P., Lerner, R. M., Mullis, A., Simerly, C., & Murray, J. (Eds.) (1999). Social change, public policy and community collaboration: Training human development professionals for the twenty-first century. Norwell, MA: Kluwer Academic Publishers.

Rathunde, K. (1996). Family context and talented adolescents' optimal experience in school-related activities. *Journal of Research on Adolescence, 6*(4), 605–628.

Ratti, L. A., Humphrey, L. L., & Lyons, J. S. (1996). Structural analysis of families with a polydrug-dependent, bulimic, or normal adolescent daughter. *Journal of Consulting and Clinical Psychology, 64*(6),1255–1262.

Ravert, A. A., & Martin, J. (1997). Family stress, perception of pregnancy, and age of first menarche among pregnant adolescents. *Adolescence, 32*(126), 261–270.

Reed, J. S., & Dubow, E. F. (1997). Cognitive and behavioral predictors of communication in clinic-referred and nonclinical mother-adolescent dyads. *Journal of Marriage and Family, 59,* 91–102.

Reid, P. T. (1991). Black female adolescents, socialization of. In R. M. Lerner, A. C. Petersen, & J. Brooks-Gunn (Eds.), *Encyclopedia of adolescence* (Vol. 1, pp. 85–87). New York: Garland.

Reimer, M. S., Overton, W. F., Steidl, J. H., Rosenstein, D. S., & Horowitz, H. (1996). Familial responsiveness and behavioral control: Influences on adolescent psychopathology, attachment, and cognition. *Journal of Research on Adolescence, 6*(1), 87–112.

Remafedi, G. J. (1985). Adolescent homosexuality: Issues for pediatricians. *Clinical Pediatrics, 24*(9), 481–485.

Remafedi, G. J. (1988). Preventing the sexual transmission of AIDS during adolescence. *Journal of Adolescent Health Care, 9*(2), 139–143.

Remafedi, G. (1991). Homosexuality, adolescent. In R. M. Lerner, A. C. Petersen, & J. Brooks-Gunn (Eds.), *Encyclopedia of adolescence* (Vol. 1, pp. 504–507). New York: Garland.

Reynolds, A. J., & Temple, J. A. (1998). Extended early childhood intervention and school achievement: Age thirteen findings from the Chicago longitudinal study. *Child Development, 69*(1), 231–246.

Rhodes, J. E., Contreras, J. M., & Mangelsdorf, S. C. (1994). Natural mentor relationships among Latina adolescent mothers: Psychological adjustment, moderating processes, and the role of early parental acceptance. *American Journal of Community Psychology, 22*(2), 211–227.

Rhodes, J. E., Ebert, L., & Fischer, K. (1992). Natural mentors: An overlooked resource in the social networks of young, African American mothers. *American Journal of Community Psychology, 20,* 445–461.

Rhodes, J. E., & Davis, A. B. (1996). Supportive ties between nonparent adults and urban adolescent girls. In B. J. Leadbeater & N. Way (Eds.), *Urban girls: Resisting stereotypes, creating identities* (pp. 213–225). New York: New York University Press.

Rhodes, J. E., Grossman, J. B., & Resch, N. L. (2000). Agents of change: Pathways through which mentoring relationships influence adolescents' academic adjustment. *Child Development, 71*(6), 1662–1671.

Rhodes, J. E., Haight, W. L., & Briggs, E. C. (1999). The influence of mentoring on the peer relationships of foster youth in relative and nonrelative care. *Journal of Research on Adolescence, 9*(2), 185–201.

Rice, K. G., & Mulkeen, P. (1995). Relationships with parents and peers: A longitudinal study of adolescent intimacy. *Journal of Adolescent Research, 10*(3), 338–357.

Richard, H. H., & Larson, R. W. (1993). Pubertal development and the daily subjective states of young adolescents. *Journal of Research on Adolescence, 3,* 145–169.

Richards, I., & Sullivan, A. (1996). Psychotherapy for delinquents? *Journal of Adolescence, 19,* 63–73.

Richards, M. H., Crowe, P. A., Larson, R., & Swarr, A. (1998). Developmental patterns and gender differences in the experience of peer companionship during adolescence. *Child Development, 69*(1), 154–163.

Richards, M. H., & Duckett, E. (1994). The relationship of maternal employment to early adolescent daily experience with and without parents. *Child Development, 65,* 225–236.

Richards-Colocino, N., McKenzie, P., & Newton, R. R. (1996). Project success: Comprehensive intervention services for middle school high-risk youth. *Journal of Adolescent Research, 11*(1), 130–163.

Richardson, R. A., Barbour, N. E., & Bubenzer, D. L. (1995). Peer relationships as a source of support for adolescent mothers. *Journal of Adolescent Research, 10*(2), 278–290.

Richardson, W. C. (1996). *A new calling for higher education.* Paper presented at the John W. Olswald Lecture, The Pennsylvania State University, University Park.

Riegel, K. F. (1976). From traits and equilibrium toward developmental dialectics. In W. J. Arnold & J. K. Cole (Eds.), *Nebraska symposium on motivation* (pp. 348–408). Lincoln: University of Nebraska Press.

Roberts, L. R., & Petersen, A. C. (1992). The relationship between academic achievement and social self-image during early adolescence. *Journal of Early Adolescence, 12*(2), 197–219.

Roberts, L. R., Sarigiani, P. A., Petersen, A. C., & Newman, J. L. (1990). Gender differences in the relationship between achievement and self-image during early adolescence. *Journal of Early Adolescence, 10*(2), 159–175.

Roberts, W., & Strayer, J. (1996). Empathy, emotional expressiveness, and prosocial behavior. *Child Development, 67,* 449–470.

Robinson, N. S. (1995). Evaluating the nature of perceived support and its relation to perceived self-worth in adolescents. *Journal of Research on Adolescence, 5*(2), 253–280.

Roeser, R. W., Midgley, C., & Urdan, T. C. (1996). Perceptions of the school psychological environment and early adolescents' psychological and behavioral functioning in school: The mediating role of goals and belonging. *Journal of Educational Psychology, 88*(3), 408–422.

Rohner, R., & Pettengill, S. (1985). Perceived parental acceptance-rejection and parental control among Korean adolescents. *Child Development, 56,* 524–528.

Rohr, M. E. (1996). Identifying adolescent runaways: The predictive utility of the personality inventory for children. *Adolescence, 31*(123), 605–623.

Rohrbach, L. A., Hodgson, C. S., Broder, B. I., Montgomery, S. B., Flay, B. R., Hansen, W. B., & Pentz, M. A. (1994). Parental participation in drug abuse prevention: Results for the midwestern prevention project. *Journal of Research on Adolescence, 4*(2), 295–318.

Roosa, M. W., & Tein, J. (1997). The relationship of childhood sexual abuse to teenage pregnancy. *Journal of Marriage and the Family, 59,* 119–130.

Rosario, M., Hunter, J., & Gwadz, M. (1997). Exploration of substance use among lesbian, gay, and bisexual youth: Prevalence and correlates. *Journal of Adolescent Research, 12*(4), 454–476.

Rosenstein, D. S., & Horowitz, H. A. (1996). Adolescent attachment and psychopathology. *Journal of Consulting and Clinical Psychology, 64*(2), 244–253.

Rosenthal, D. A., & Feldman, S. S. (1991). The influence of perceived family and personal factors on self-reported school performance of Chinese and Western high school students. *Journal of Research on Adolescence, 1*(2), 135–154.

Rosenthal, D. A., & Peart, R. (1996). The rules of the game: Teenagers communicating about sex. *Journal of Adolescence, 19,* 321–332.

Rosenthal, S. L., Lewis, L. M., & Cohen, S. S. (1996). Issues related to the sexual decision-making of inner-city adolescent girls. *Adolescence, 31*(123), 731–739.

Roth, J., Brooks-Gunn, J., Galen, B., Murray, L., Silverman, P., Liu, H., Man, D., & Foster, W. (1997). *Promoting healthy adolescence: Youth development frameworks and programs.* New York: Teachers College, Columbia University.

Rotherman-Borus, M. J., & Koopman, C. (1991). AIDS and adolescents. In R. M. Lerner, A. C. Petersen, & J. Brooks-Gunn (Eds.), *Encyclopedia of adolescence* (Vol. 1, pp. 29–36). New York: Garland.

Rubenstein, J. L., & Feldman, S. S. (1993). Conflict-resolution behavior in adolescent boys: Antecedents and adaptational correlates. *Journal of Research on Adolescence, 3*(1), 41–66.

Rubin, K. H., Bukowski, W., & Parker, J. G. (1998). Peer interactions, relationships, and groups. In W. Damon & N. Eisenberg (Eds.), *Handbook of child psychology: Vol. 3. Social, emotional, and personality development* (pp. 619–700). New York: Wiley.

Ruble, D. N., & Martin, C. L. (1998). Gender development. In N. Eisenberg (Ed.), *Handbook of child psychology: Vol. 1. Theoretical models of human development* (5th ed., pp. 933–1016). New York: Wiley.

Ruck, M. D., Abramovitch, R., & Keating, D. P. (1998). Children's and adolescents' understanding of rights: Balancing nurturance and self-determination. *Child Development, 64*(2), 404–417.

Rueter, M. A., & Conger, R. D. (1995a). Antecedents of parent-adolescent disagreements. *Journal of Marriage and Family, 57,* 435–448.

Rueter, M. A., & Conger, R. D. (1995b). Interaction style, problem-solving behavior, and family problem-solving effectiveness. *Child Development, 66,* 98–115.

S

Sack, W. H., Clarke, G. N., & Seeley, J. (1996). Multiple forms of stress in Cambodian adolescent refugees. *Child Development, 67,* 107–116.

Salmela-Aro, K., & Nurmi, J.-E. (1997). Goal contents, well-being, and life context during transition to university: A longitudinal study. *International Journal of Behavioral Development, 20*(3), 471–491.

Sam, D. L. (1995). Acculturation attitudes among young immigrants as a function of perceived parental attitudes toward cultural change. *Journal of Early Adolescence, 15*(2), 238–258.

Sameroff, A. (1975). Transactional models in early social relations. *Human Development, 18,* 65–79.

Sameroff, A. J. (1983). Developmental systems: Contexts and evolution. In W. Kessen (Ed.), *Handbook of child psychology: Vol. 1. History, theory, and methods* (pp. 237–294). New York: Wiley.

Sameroff, A. J., Seifer, R., Baldwin, A., & Baldwin, C. (1993). Stability of intelligence from preschool to adolescence: The influence of social and family risk factors. *Child Development, 64,* 80–97.

Sampson, R. J. (1997). Collective regulation of adolescent misbehavior: Validation results from eighty Chicago neighborhoods. *Journal of Adolescent Research, 12*(2), 227–244.

Sarigiani, P. A., Wilson, J. L., Petersen, A. C., & Vicary, J. R. (1990). Self-image and educational plans of adolescents from two contrasting communities. *Journal of Early Adolescence, 10,* 37–55.

Sauer, R. J. (1998). Furthering community youth development. In R. M. Lerner & L. A. K. Simon (Eds.), *University-community collaborations for the twenty-first century: Outreach scholarship for youth and families* (pp. 389–396). New York: Garland.

Savin-Williams, R. C. (1990). *Gay and lesbian youth: Expressions of identity.* New York: Hemisphere.

Savin-Williams, R. C. (1991). Gay and lesbian youth. In R. M. Lerner, A. C. Petersen, & J. Brooks-Gunn (Eds.), *Encyclopedia of adolescence* (pp. 385–388). New York: Garland.

Savin-Williams, R. C. (1994). Dating those you can't love and loving those you can't date. In R. Montemayor, G. R. Adams, & T. P. Gullotta (Eds.), *Personal relationships during adolescence. Advances in adolescent development* (Vol. 6, pp. 196–215). Thousand Oaks, CA: Sage.

Savin-Williams, R. C. (1995). An exploratory study of pubertal maturation timing and self-esteem among gay and bisexual male youths. *Developmental Psychology, 31*(1), 56–64.

Savin-Williams, R. C. (1999). Matthew Shepard's death: A professional awakening. *Applied Developmental Science, 3,* 150–154.

Savin-Williams, R. C., & Small, S. A. (1986). The timing of puberty and its relationship to adolescent and parent perceptions of family interactions. *Developmental Psychology, 22,* 342–347.

Scales, P., Benson, P., Leffert, N., & Blyth, D. A. (2000). The contribution of developmental assets to the prediction of thriving among adolescents. *Applied Developmental Science, 4*(1), 27–46.

Scales, P., & Leffert, N. (1999). *Developmental assets: A synthesis of the scientific research on adolescent development.* Minneapolis: Search Institute.

Schaie, K. W. (1959). Cross-sectional methods in the study of psychological aspects of aging. *Journal of Gerontology, 14,* 208–215.

Schaie, K. W. (1965). A general model for the study of developmental problems. *Psychosocial Bulletin, 64,* 92–107.

Schaie, K. W., Labouvie, G. V., & Buech, B. V. (1973). Generational and cohort-specific differences in adult cognitive functioning: A fourteen-year study of independent samples. *Developmental Psychology, 9,* 151–166.

Schaie, K. W., & Strother, C. R. (1968). A cross-sequential study of age changes in cognitive behavior. *Psychological Bulletin, 70,* 671–680.

Schiedel, D. G., & Marcia, J. E. (1985). Ego identity, intimacy, sex role orientation, and gender. *Developmental Psychology, 21*(1), 149–160.

Schneider, B. H., & Younger, A. J. (1996). Adolescent-parent attachment and adolescents' relations with their peers: A closer look. *Youth & Society, 28*(1), 95–108.

Schondel, C., Boehm, K., Rose, J., & Marlowe, A. (1995). Adolescent volunteers: An untapped resource in the delivery of adolescent preventive health care. *Youth & Society, 27*(2), 123–135.

Schonert-Reichl, K. A. (1994). Gender differences in depressive symptomatology and egocentrism in adolescence. *Journal of Early Adolescence, 14,* 49–65.

Schonfeld, W. A. (1969). The body and the body image in adolescents. In G. Caplan & S. Lebovici (Eds.), *Adolescence: Psychosocial perspectives.* New York: Basic.

Schönpflug, U., & Jansen, X. (1995). Self-concept and coping with developmental demands in German and Polish adolescents. *International Journal of Behavioral Development, 18*(3), 385–405.

Schorr, L. B. (1988). *Within our reach: Breaking the cycle of disadvantage.* New York: Doubleday.

Schorr, L. B. (1991). Effective programs for children growing up in concentrated poverty. In A. C. Huston (Ed.), *Children in poverty: Child development and public policy* (pp. 260–281). Cambridge: Cambridge University.

Schorr, L. (1997). *Common purpose: Strengthening families and neighborhoods to rebuild America.* New York: Doubleday.

Schwartz, R. (1999, October). *Superpredator or the boy next door? Policy trends in juvenile justice.* Paper presented at the Loyola Forum on the Child: Reclaiming childhood: Shaping policy for the future. Chicago: Loyola University.

Scott-Jones, D., & White, A. B. (1990). Correlates of sexual activity in early adolescence. *Journal of Early Adolescence, 10*(2), 221–238.

Selman, R. L., & Schultz, L. H. (1990). *Making a friend in youth: Developmental theory and pair therapy.* Chicago: University of Chicago Press.

Seltzer, V. C., & Waterman, R. P. (1996). A cross-national study of adolescent peer concordance on issues of the future. *Journal of Adolescent Research, 11*(4), 461–482.

Sessa, F., & Steinberg, L. (1991). Family structure and the development of autonomy during adolescence. *Journal of Early Adolescence, 11*(1), 38–55.

Shagle, S. C., & Barber, B. K. (1993). Effects of family, marital, and parent-child conflict on adolescent self-derogation and suicidal ideation. *Journal of Marriage and the Family, 55,* 964–974.

Shanahan, J. (1995). Television viewing and adolescent authoritarianism. *Journal of Adolescence, 18,* 271–288.

Shanahan, M. J., Elder, G. H., Jr., Burchinal, M., & Conger, R. D. (1996). Adolescent paid labor and relationships with parents: Early work-family linkages. *Child Development, 67,* 2183–2200.

Sharma, A. R., McGue, M. K., & Benson, P. L. (1998). The psychological adjustment of United States adopted adolescents and their nonadopted siblings. *Child Development, 69*(3), 791–802.

Sherrod, L. R., Haggerty, R. J., & Featherman, D. L. (1993). Introduction: Late adolescence and the transition to adulthood. *Journal of Research on Adolescence, 3,* 217–226.

Shoda, Y., Mischel, W., & Peake, P. K. (1990). Predicting adolescent cognitive and self-regulatory competencies from preschool delay of gratification: Identifying diagnostic conditions. *Developmental Psychology, 26,* 978–986.

Shorter-Gooden, K., & Washington, N. C. (1996). Young, black, and female: The challenge of weaving an identity. *Journal of Adolescence, 19,* 465–475.

Shucksmith, J., Hendry, L. B., & Glendinning, A. (1995). Models of parenting: Implications for adolescent well-being within different types of family contexts. *Journal of Adolescence, 18,* 253–270.

Shulman, S., & Knafo, D. (1997). Balancing closeness and individuality in adolescent close relationships. *International Journal of Behavioral Development, 21,* 687–702.

Shweder, R. A., Goodnow, J., Hatano, G., Kessel, F., LeVine, R. A., Markus, H.,

Miller, P., & Worthman, C. (1998). The cultural psychology of development: One mind, many mentalities. In W. Damon & R. M. Lerner (Eds.), *Handbook of child psychology: Vol. 1. Theoretical models of human development.* (5th ed., pp. 867–937). New York: Wiley.

Siegel, J., & Shaughnessy, M. F. (1995). There's a first time for everything: Understanding adolescence. *Adolescence, 30*(117), 217–221.

Sigelman, C., Derenowski, E., Woods, T., Mukai, T., Alfred-Liro, C., Durazo, O., & Maddock, A. (1996). Mexican-American and Anglo-American children's responsiveness to a theory-centered AIDS education program. *Child Development, 67,* 253–266.

Sigurdsson, J. F., & Gudjonsson, G. H. (1996). Psychological characteristics of juvenile alcohol and drug users. *Journal of Adolescence, 19,* 41–46.

Silbereisen, R. (1995). How parenting styles and crowd contexts interact in actualizing potential for development: Commentary. In L. J. Crockett & A. C. Crouter (Eds.), *Pathways through adolescence: Individual development in relation to social contexts* (pp. 197–207). Mahwah, NJ: Erlbaum.

Silbereisen, R., Noack, P., & Schönpflug, U. (1994). Comparative analyses of beliefs, leisure contexts, and substance abuse in West Berlin and Warsaw. In R. Silbereisen & E. Todt (Eds.), *Adolescence in context: The interplay of family, school, peers, and work in adjustment* (pp. 176–198). New York: Springer.

Silverberg, S. B., Marczak, M. S., & Gondoli, D. M. (1996). Maternal depressive symptoms and achievement-related outcomes among adolescent daughters: Variations by family structure. *Journal of Early Adolescence, 16*(1), 90–109.

Simmons, R. G., & Blyth, D. A. (1987). *Moving into adolescence: The impact of pubertal change and school context.* Hawthorne, NJ: Aldine.

Simmons, R. G., Carlton-Ford, S. L., Blyth, D. A. (1987). Predicting how a child will cope with the transition to junior high school. In R. M. Lerner & T. T. Foch (Eds.), *Biological-psychosocial interactions in early adolescence. Child psychology* (pp. 325–375). Hillsdale, NJ: Erlbaum.

Simmons, R., Rosenberg, F., & Rosenberg, M. (1973). Disturbances in the self-image in adolescence. *American Sociological Review, 38,* 553–568.

Simons, J. M., Finlay, B., & Yang, A. (1991). *The adolescent and young adult fact book.* Washington, DC: Children's Defense Fund.

Simons, R. L., Johnson, C., & Conger, R. D. (1994). Harsh corporal punishment versus quality of parental involvement as an explanation of adolescent maladjustment. *Journal of Marriage and the Family, 56,* 591–607.

Simons, R. L., Whitbeck, L. B., Beaman, J., & Conger, R. D. (1994). The impact of mothers' parenting, involvement by nonresidential fathers, and parental conflict on the adjustment of adolescent children. *Journal of Marriage and the Family, 56,* 356–374.

Singh, K., & Hernandez-Gantes, V. M. (1996). The relation of English language proficiency to educational aspirations of Mexican-American eighth graders. *Journal of Early Adolescence, 16*(3), 253–273.

Skoe, E. E., & Gooden, A. (1993). Ethic of care and real-life moral dilemma content in male and female early adolescents. *Journal of Early Adolescence, 13,* 154–167.

Slavin, R., Karweit, N., & Wasik, B. (1994). *Preventing early school failure: Research on effective strategies.* Boston: Allyn & Bacon.

Slonim-Nevo, V., Auslander, W. F., Ozawa, M. N., & Jung, K. G. (1996). The long-term impact of AIDS-preventive interventions for delinquent and abused adolescents. *Adolescence, 31*(122), 409–421.

Small, S. A. (1996). Collaborative, community-based research on adolescents: Using research for community change. *Journal of Research on Adolescence, 6*(1), 9–22.

Small, S. A., & Kerns, D. (1993). Unwanted sexual activity among peers during early and middle adolescence: Incidence and risk factors. *Journal of Marriage and the Family, 55,* 941–952.

Small, S. A., & Luster, T. (1994). An ecological risk-factor approach to adolescent sexual activity. *Journal of Marriage and the Family, 56,* 181–192.

Smetana, J. G. (1988). Concepts of self and social convention: Adolescents' and parents' reasoning about hypothetical and actual family conflicts. In M. R. Gunnar & W. A. Collins (Eds.), *Development during the transition to adolescence. Minnesota symposium on child psychology* (Vol. 21, pp. 79–122). Hillsdale, NJ: Erlbaum.

Smetana, J. G. (1993). Conceptions of parental authority in divorced and married mothers and their adolescents. *Journal of Research on Adolescence, 3*(1), 19–39.

Smetana, J. G. (1995). Parenting styles and conceptions of parental authority during adolescence. *Child Development, 66,* 299–316.

Smetana, J. G., & Asquith, P. (1994). Adolescents' and parents' conceptions of parental authority and personal autonomy. *Child Development, 65*(4), 1147–1162.

Smetana, J. G., Yau, J., & Hanson, S. (1991). Conflict resolution in families with adolescents. *Journal of Research on Adolescence, 1*(2), 189–206.

Smith, A. M. A., & Rosenthal, D. A. (1995). Adolescents' perceptions of their risk environment. *Journal of Adolescence, 18,* 229–245.

Smith, D. E., & Muenchen, R. A. (1995). Gender and age variations in the self-image of Jamaican adolescents. *Adolescence, 30*(119), 643–654.

Smith, R. E., & Smoll, F. L. (1990). Self-esteem and children's reactions to youth support coaching behaviors: A field study of self-enhancement processes. *Developmental Psychology, 26,* 987–993.

Smith, T. E. (1997). Adolescent gender differences in time alone and time devoted to conversation. *Adolescence, 32*(126), 483–496.

Snider, B. A., & Miller, J. P. (1993). The land-grant system and 4-H: A mutually beneficial relationship of scholars and practitioners in youth development. In R. M. Lerner (Ed.), *Early adolescence: Perspectives on research, policy, and intervention* (pp. 481–499). Hillsdale, NJ: Erlbaum.

Society for Research in Child Development. (1999). Ethical standards for research with children. In *The SRCD directory of members, 1999–2000* (pp. 283–284). Ann Arbor, MI: Author.

Solomon, Y., & Farrand, J. (1996). "Why don't you do it properly?" Young women who self-injure. *Journal of Adolescence, 19,* 111–119.

Spanier, G. B. (1997). *Enhancing the quality of life for children, youth, and families.* Unpublished manuscript. University Park: Pennsylvania State University.

Spanier, G. B. (1999). Enhancing the quality of life: A model for the 21st century land-grant university. *Applied Developmental Science, 3*(4), 199–205.

Spearman, C. (1927). *The abilities of man.* New York: Macmillan.

Speicher, B. (1994). Family patterns of moral judgment during adolescence and early adulthood. *Developmental Psychology, 30,* 624–632.

Spencer, M. B. (1990). Development of minority children: An introduction. *Child Development, 61,* 267–269.

Spencer, M. B. (1991). Identity, minority development of. In R. M. Lerner, A. C. Petersen, & J. Brooks-Gunn (Eds.), *Encyclopedia of adolescence* (Vol. 1, pp. 111–130). New York: Garland.

Spencer, M. B. (1995). Old issues and new theorizing about African American youth: A phenomenological variant of ecological systems theory. In R. L. Taylor (Ed.), *Black youth: Perspectives on their status in the United States* (pp. 38–69). Westport, CT: Praeger.

Spencer, M. B. (1999). Social and cultural influences on school adjustment: The application of an identity-focused cultural ecological perspective. *Educational Psychologist, 34,* 43–57.

Spencer, M. B., & Dornbusch, S. (1990). Challenges in studying minority youth. In S. Feldman & G. Elliott (Eds.), *At the threshold: The developing adolescent* (pp. 123–146). Cambridge: Harvard University Press.

Spencer, M. B., Dupree, D., & Hartmann, T. (1997). A phenomenological variant of ecological systems theory (PVEST): A self-organization perspective in context. *Development and Psychopathology, 9,* 817–833.

Spencer, M. B., & Markstrom-Adams, C. (1990). Identity process among racial and ethnic minority children in America. *Child Development, 61,* 290–310.

Spieker, S., & Bensley, L. (1994). Roles of living arrangements and grandmother social support in adolescent mothering and infant attachment. *Developmental Psychology, 30*(1), 102–111.

Spivack, G., Marcus, J., & Swift, M. (1986). Early classroom behaviors and later misconduct. *Developmental Psychology, 22*(1), 124–131.

Stallmann, J. I., & Johnson T. G. (1996). Community factors in secondary educational achievement in Appalachia. *Youth & Society, 27*(4), 469–484.

Stattin, H., & Magnusson, D. (1990). *Pubertal maturation in female development.* Hillsdale, NJ: Erlbaum.

Staudinger, V. M., Marsiske, M., & Baltes, P. (1995). Resilience and reserve capacity in later adulthood: Potentials and limits of development across the life-span. In D. Cicchetti & D. Cohen (Eds.), *Developmental psychopathology: Vol. 2. Risk disorder and adaptation* (pp. 801–847). New York: Wiley.

Stefanich, G. P., Wills, F. A., & Buss, R. R. (1991). The use of interdisciplinary teaming and its influence on student self-concept in middle schools. *Journal of Early Adolescence, 11*(4), 404–419.

Stein, D., & Reichert, P. (1990). Extreme dieting behaviors in early adolescence. *Journal of Early Adolescence, 10*(2), 108–121.

Steinberg, L. (1977). *A longitudinal study of physical growth, intellectual growth, and family interaction in early adolescence.* Unpublished doctoral dissertation, Cornell University, Ithaca, NY.

Steinberg, L. (1981). Transformations in family relations at puberty. *Developmental Psychology, 17,* 833–840.

Steinberg, L. (1983). The varieties and effects of work during adolescence. In M. Lamb, A. Brown, & B. Rogoff (Eds.), *Advances in developmental psychology* (Vol. 3). Hillsdale, NJ: Erlbaum.

Steinberg, L. (1987). The impact of puberty on family relations: Effects of pubertal status and pubertal timing. *Developmental Psychology, 23,* 833–840.

Steinberg, L. (1988). Reciprocal relation between parent-child distance and pubertal maturation. *Developmental Psychology, 24,* 122–128.

Steinberg, L. (1991). Developmental considerations in youth advocacy. In J. C. Westman (Ed.), *Who speaks for the children? The handbook of individual and class child advocacy* (pp. 23–27). Sarasota: Professional Resource Exchange.

Steinberg, L., & Dornbusch, S. M. (1991). Negative correlates of part-time employment during adolescence: Replication and elaboration. *Developmental Psychology, 27*(2), 304–313.

Steinberg, L., & Hill, J. (1978). Patterns of family interaction as a function of age, the onset of puberty, and formal thinking. *Developmental Psychology, 14,* 683–684.

Steinberg, L., Mounts, N. S., Lamborn, S. D., & Dornbusch, S. M. (1991). Authoritative parenting and adolescent adjustment across varied ecological niches. *Journal of Research on Adolescence, 1*(1), 19–36.

442 · REFERENCES

Stephenson, A. L., Henry, C. S., & Robinson, L. C. (1996). Family characteristics and adolescent substance use. *Adolescence, 31*(121), 59–77.

Stewart, S. M., Bond, M. H., McBride-Chang, C., Fielding, R., Deeds, O., & Westrick, J. (1998). Parent and adolescent contributors to teenage misconduct in Western and Asian high school students in Hong Kong. *International Journal of Behavioral Development, 22*(4), 847–869.

Stice, E., & Barrera, J. (1995). A longitudinal examination of the reciprocal relations between perceived parenting and adolescents' substance use and externalizing behaviors. *Developmental Psychology, 31*(2), 322–334.

Stiffman, A. R., Church, H., & Earls, F. (1992). Predictive modeling of change in depressive disorder and counts of depressive symptoms in urban youth. *Journal of Research on Adolescence, 2*(4), 295–316.

Stinson, M. S., Whitmire, K., & Kluwin, T. N. (1996). Self-perceptions of social relationships in hearing-impaired adolescents. *Journal of Educational Psychology, 88*(1), 132–143.

St. Lawrence, J. S., Brasfield, T. L., Jefferson, K. W., Alleyne, E., O'Bannon, R. E., III, & Shirley, A. (1995a). Cognitive-behavioral intervention to reduce African-American adolescents' risk for HIV infection. *Journal of Consulting and Clinical Psychology, 63*(2), 221–237.

St. Lawrence, J. S., Jefferson, K. W., Alleyne, E., & Brasfield, T. L. (1995b). Comparison of education versus behavioral skills training interventions in lowering sexual HIV-risk behavior of substance-dependent adolescents. *Journal of Consulting and Clinical Psychology, 63*(1), 154–157.

Stocker, C., & Dunn, J. (1991). Sibling relationships in adolescence. In R. M. Lerner, A. C. Petersen, & J. Brooks-Gunn (Eds.), *Encyclopedia of adolescence* (Vol. 2, pp. 1046–1048). New York: Garland.

Straker, G., Mendelsohn, M., Moosa, F., & Tudin, P. (1996). Violent political contexts and the emotional concerns of township youth. *Child Development, 67*, 46–54.

Straus, M. A., & Yodanis, C. L. (1996). Corporal punishment in adolescence and physical assaults on spouses in later life: What accounts for the link? *Journal of Marriage and Family, 58*, 825–841.

Strouse, J. S., Buerkel-Rothfuss, & Long, E. C. J. (1995). Gender and family as moderators of the relationship between music video exposure and adolescent sexual permissiveness. *Adolescence, 30*(119), 505–521.

Subkoviak, M. J., Enright, R. D., Wu, C.-R., Gassin, E. A., Freedman, S., Olson, L. M., & Sarinopoulos, I. (1995). Measuring interpersonal forgiveness in late adolescence and middle adulthood. *Journal of Adolescence, 18*, 641–655.

Suitor, J. J., & Reavis, R. (1995). Football, fast cars, and cheerleading: Adolescent gender norms, 1978–1989. *Adolescence, 30*(118), 265–272.

Sullivan, M. L. (1993). Culture and class as determinants of out-of-wedlock childbearing and poverty during late adolescence. *Journal of Research on Adolescence, 3*(3), 295–316.

Summers, P., Forehand, R., Armistead, L., & Tannenbaum, L. (1998). Parental divorce during early adolescence in Caucasian families: The role of family process variables in predicting the long-term consequences for early adult psychological adjustment. *Journal of Consulting and Clinical Psychology, 66*(2), 327–336.

Susman, E. J. (1997). Modeling developmental complexity in adolescence: Hormones and behavior in context. *Journal of Research on Adolescence, 7*(3), 283–306.

Sussman, T., & Duffy, M. (1996). Are we forgetting about gay male adolescents in AIDS-related research and prevention? *Youth & Society, 27*(3), 379–393.

Swanson, D. P., Spencer, M. B., & Petersen, A. (1998). Identity formation in adolescence. In K. Borman & B. Schneider (Eds.), *The adolescent years: Social influences and educational challenges: Ninety-seventh yearbook of the National Society for the Study of Education, Part I* (pp. 18–41). Chicago: National Society for the Study of Education.

Swenson, C. C., & Kennedy, W. A. (1995). Perceived control and treatment outcome with chronic adolescent offenders. *Adolescence, 30*(119), 565–578.

Switzer, G. E., Simmons, R. G., Dew, M. A., & Regalski, J. M. (1995). The effect of a school based helper program on adolescent self-image, attitudes, and behavior. *Journal of Early Adolescence, 15*(4), 429–455.

T

Takahashi, K., & Majima, N. (1994). Transition from home to college dormitory: The role of preestablished affective relationships in adjustment to a new life. *Journal of Research on Adolescence, 4*(3), 367–384.

Takanishi, R., & Hamburg, D. A. (1996). Great transitions: Preparing American youth for the 21st century—the role of research. *Journal of Research on Adolescence, 6*, 379–396.

Tanner, J. M. (1962). *Growth at adolescence.* Springfield, IL: Thomas.

Tanner, J. M. (1970). Physical growth. In P. H. Mussen (Ed.), *Carmichael's manual of child psychology* (Vol. 1, pp. 77–155). New York: Wiley.

Tanner, J. M. (1973). Growing up. *Scientific American, 229*, 34–43.

Tanner, J. M. (1991). Menarche, secular trend in age of. In R. M. Lerner, A. C. Petersen, & J. Brooks-Gunn (Eds.), *Encyclopedia of adolescence* (Vol. 1, pp. 637–641). New York: Garland.

Taylor, C. S. (1990). *Dangerous society.* East Lansing: Michigan State University Press.

Taylor, C. S. (1993). *Girls, gangs, women, and drugs.* East Lansing: Michigan State University Press.

Taylor, C. S. (1996). *The unintended consequences of incarceration: Youth development, the juvenile corrections systems, and crime.* Paper presented at the Vera Institute Conference, Harriman, NY.

Taylor, R., Casten, R., Flickinger, S., Roberts, D., & Fulmore, C. D. (1994). Explaining the school performance of African-American adolescents. *Journal of Research on Adolescence, 4*, 21–44.

Taylor, R. D. (1996). Adolescents' perceptions of kinship support and family management practices: Association with adolescent adjustment in African American families. *Developmental Psychology, 32*(4), 687–695.

Taylor, R. D., & Roberts, D. (1995). Kinship support and maternal and adolescent well-being in economically disadvantaged African-American families. *Child Development, 66*, 1585–1597.

Taylor-Gibbs, J. (1991). Black adolescents at risk: Approaches to prevention. In R. M. Lerner, A. C. Petersen, & J. Brooks-Gunn (Eds.), *Encyclopedia of adolescence* (Vol. 1, pp. 73–84). New York: Garland.

Terrell, N. E. (1997). Street life: Aggravated and sexual assaults among homeless and runaway adolescents. *Youth & Society, 28*(3), 267–290.

Thelen, E., & Smith, L. B. (1998). Dynamic systems theories. In W. Damon (Series Ed.) & R. M. Lerner (Vol. Ed.), *Handbook of child psychology: Vol. 1. Theoretical models of human development* (5th ed., pp. 563–633). New York: Wiley.

Thomas, A., & Chess, S. (1977). *Temperament and development.* New York: Brunner/Mazel.

Thomas, G., Farrell, M. P., & Barnes, G. M. (1996). The effects of single-mother families and nonresident fathers on delinquency and substance abuse in black and white adolescents. *Journal of Marriage and the Family, 58,* 884–894.

Thompson, K. L., Bundy, K. A., & Broncheau, C. (1995). Social skills training for young adolescents: Symbolic and behavioral components. *Adolescence, 30*(119), 723–734.

Thornberry, T. P., Smith, C. A., & Howard, G. J. (1997). Risk factors for teenage fatherhood. *Journal of Marriage and the Family, 59,* 505–522.

Thorndike, E. L. (1904). The newest psychology. *Educational Review, 28,* 217–227.

Timko, C., Stovel, K. W., Baumgartner, M., & Moos, R. H. (1995). Acute and chronic stressors, social resources, and functioning among adolescents with juvenile rheumatic disease. *Journal of Research on Adolescence, 5*(3), 361–385.

Tisak, M. S., & Tisak, J. (1996). My sibling's but not my friend's keeper: Reasoning about responses to aggressive acts. *Journal of Early Adolescence, 16*(3), 324–339.

Tobach, E. (1971). Some evolutionary aspects of human gender. *Journal of Orthopsychiatry, 41,* 710–715.

Tobach, E. (1972). The meaning of cryptanthroparion. In L. Ehrman, G. Omenn, & E. Caspari (Eds.), *Genetics, environment, and behavior* (pp. 219–239). New York: Academic Press.

Tobach, E. (1981). Evolutionary aspects of the activity of the organism and its development. In R. M. Lerner & N. A. Busch-Rossnagel (Eds.), *Individuals as producers of their development: A lifespan perspective* (pp. 37–68). New York: Academic Press.

Tobach, E., & Schneirla, T. C. (1968). The biopsychology of social behavior of animals. In R. E. Cooke & S. Levin (Eds.), *Biologic basis of pediatric practice* (pp. 68–82). New York: McGraw-Hill.

Todt, E., Drewes, R., & Heils, S. (1994). The development of interests during adolescence: Social context, individual differences, and individual significance. In R. K. Silbereisen & E. Todt (Eds.), *Adolescence in context: The interplay of family, school, peers, and work in adjustment* (pp. 82–95). New York: Springer.

Torres, R., Fernandez, F., & Maceira, D. (1995). Self-esteem and value of health as correlates of adolescent health behavior. *Adolescence, 30*(118), 403–412.

Travers, R., & Schneider, M. (1996). Barriers to accessibility for lesbian and gay youth needing addictions services. *Youth & Society, 27*(3), 356–378.

Treboux, D., & Busch-Rossnagel, N. A. (1995). Age differences in parent and peer influences on female sexual behavior. *Journal of Research on Adolescence, 5*(4), 469–487.

Trickett, E. J., Barone, C., & Buchanan, R. M. (1996). Elaborating developmental contextualism in adolescent research and intervention: Paradigm contributions from community psychology. *Journal of Research on Adolescence, 6*(3), 245–269.

Tubman, J. G., Windle, M., & Windle, R. C. (1996). The onset and cross-temporal patterning of sexual intercourse in middle adolescence: Prospective relations with behavioral and emotional problems. *Child Development, 67,* 327–343.

Turiel, E. (1969). Developmental processes in the child's moral thinking. In P. H. Mussen, J. Langer, & M. Covington (Eds.), *Trends and issues in developmental psychology* (pp. 92–133). New York: Holt.

Turner, H. A., & Finkelhor, D. (1996). Corporal punishment as a stressor among youth. *Journal of Marriage and Family, 58,* 155–166.

Turner, R. A., Irwin, C. E., & Millstein, S. G. (1991). Family structure, family processes, and experimenting with substances during adolescence. *Journal of Research on Adolescence, 1*(1), 93–106.

Turner, S., & Scherman, A. (1996). Big Brothers: Impact on Little Brothers' self-concepts and behaviors. *Adolescence, 31*(124), 875–882.

U

Underwood, M. K., Kupersmidt, J. B., & Coie, J. D. (1996). Childhood peer sociometric status and aggression as predictors of adolescent childbearing. *Journal of Research on Adolescence, 6*(2), 201–223.

United States Department of Commerce. (1993). *Poverty in the United States: 1993* (Current Population Reports, Series P-60, No. 178). Washington, DC: U.S. Government Printing Office.

United States Department of Health and Human Services. (1996). *Trends in the well-being of America's children and youth: 1996.* Washington, DC: Author.

United States General Accounting Office. (1993). *School-linked human services: A comprehensive strategy for aiding students at risk of school failure* (GAO/HRD-94-21). Washington, DC.

Upchurch, D. M. (1993). Early schooling and childbearing experiences: Implications for postsecondary school attendance. *Journal of Research on Adolescence, 3*(4), 423–443.

Urberg, K. A., Degirmencioglu, S. M., & Pilgrim, C. (1997). Close friend and group influence on adolescent cigarette smoking and alcohol use. *Developmental Psychology, 33*(5), 834–844.

Urberg, K. A., Degirmencioglu, S. M., & Tolson, J. M. (1998). Adolescent friendship selection and termination: The role of similarity. *Journal of Social & Personal Relationships, 15*(5), 703–710.

Urberg, K. A., Degirmencioglu, S. M., Tolson, J. M., & Halliday-Scher, K. (1995). The structure of adolescent peer networks. *Developmental Psychology, 31*(4), 540–547.

Urberg, K. A., Degirmencioglu, S. M., Tolson, J. M., & Halliday-Scher, K. (2000). Adolescent social crowds: Measurement and relationship to friends. *Journal of Adolescent Research, 15*(4), 427–445.

Urdan, T., Midgley, C., & Wood, S. (1995). Special issues in reforming middle level schools. *Journal of Early Adolescence, 15*(1), 9–37.

Usdan, M. (1994, January). The relationship between school boards and general purpose government. *Phi Delta Kappan,* pp. 374–377.

Useem, E. L. (1991). Student selection into course sequences in mathematics: The impact of parental involvement and school policies. *Journal of Research on Adolescence, 1*(3), 231–250.

V

van der Velde, M. E. G., Feij, J. A., & van Emmerik, H. V. (1998). Change in work values and norms among Dutch young adults: Aging or societal trends? *Interna-*

tional Journal of Behavioral Development, 22(1), 55–76.

Van de Ven, P. (1995). Talking with juvenile offenders about gay males and lesbians: Implications for combating homophobia. *Adolescence, 30*(117), 19–42.

Vartanian, L. R., & Powlishta, K. K. (1996). A longitudinal examination of the social-cognitive foundations of adolescent egocentrism. *Journal of Early Adolescence, 16*(2), 157–178.

Vernberg, E. M., Ewell, K. K., Berry, S. H., & Abwender, D. A. (1994). Sophistication of adolescents' interpersonal negotiation strategies and friendship formation after relocation: A naturally occurring experiment. *Journal of Research on Adolescence, 4*(1), 5–19.

Vicary, J. R., Klingaman, L. R., & Harkness, W. L. (1995). Risk factors associated with date rape and sexual assault of adolescent girls. *Journal of Adolescence, 18*, 289–306.

Villarruel, F. A., & Lerner, R. M. (Eds.). (1994). *Promoting community-based programs for socialization and learning.* San Francisco: Jossey-Bass.

Vitaro, F., Ladouceur, R., & Bujold, A. (1996). Predictive and concurrent correlates of gambling in early adolescent boys. *Journal of Early Adolescence, 16*(2), 211–228.

Vitaro, F., Tremblay, R. E., Kerr, M., Pagani, L., & Bukowski, W. M. (1997). Disruptiveness, friends' characteristics, and delinquency in early adolescence: A test of two competing models of development. *Child Development, 68*(4), 676–689.

Vondracek, F. W. (1994). Vocational identity development in adolescence. In R. K. Silbereisen & E. Todt (Eds.), *Adolescence in context: The interplay of family, school, peers, and work in adjustment* (pp. 284–303). New York: Springer.

Vondracek, F. W. (1999, May). *Applications of systemic models in the study of vocational development.* Paper presented at the Fourth National Conference of the Society for Vocational Psychology, a section of the Counseling Psychology Division of the American Psychological Association, on Examining the interaction of person in environment: Role of context factors in vocational development, Milwaukee, WI.

Vondracek, F. W., Lerner, R. M., & Schulenberg, J. E. (1986). *Career development: A life-span developmental approach.* Hillsdale, NJ: Erlbaum.

Vondracek, F. W., Schulenberg, J., Skorikov, V., Gillespie, L. K., & Wahlheim, C. (1995). The relationship of identity status to career indecision during adolescence. *Journal of Adolescence, 18*, 17–29.

Vuchinich, S., Angelelli, J., & Gatherum, A. (1996). Context and development in family problem solving with preadolescent children. *Child Development, 67*, 1276–1288.

Vuchinich, S., Hetherington, E. M., Vuchinich, R. A., & Clingempeel, W. G. (1991). Parent-child interaction and gender differences in early adolescents' adaptation to stepfamilies. *Developmental Psychology, 27*, 618–626.

W

Wadsworth, B. J. (1971). *Piaget's theory of cognitive development.* New York: McKay.

Wagenaar, A. C., & Perry, C. L. (1994). Community strategies for the reduction of youth drinking: Theory and application. *Journal of Research on Adolescence, 4*(2), 319–347.

Wagner, B. M., Cohen, P., & Brook, J. S. (1996). Parent/adolescent relationships: Moderators of the effects of stressful life events. *Journal of Adolescent Research, 11*(3), 347–374.

Wagner, J. A. (1987). Formal operations and ego identity in adolescence. *Adolescence, 22*(85), 23–35.

Wainryb, C. (1995). Reasoning about social conflicts in different cultures: Druze and Jewish children in Israel. *Child Development, 66*, 390–401.

Wainryb, C., Shaw, L. A., & Maianu, C. (1998). Tolerance and intolerance: Children's and adolescents' judgements of dissenting beliefs, speech, persons, and conduct. *Child Development, 69*(6), 1541–1555.

Waldner-Haugrud, L. K., & Magruder, B. (1996). Homosexual identity expression among lesbian and gay adolescents: An analysis of perceived structural associations. *Youth & Society, 27*(3), 313–333.

Walker, L. J. (1984). Sex differences in the development of moral reasoning: A critical review. *Child Development, 55*, 677–691.

Walker, L., & Richards, B. (1976). The effects of a narrative model on children's moral judgments. *Canadian Journal of Behavioral Science, 8*, 169–177.

Walker, L. J., & Taylor, J. H. (1991). Family interactions and the development of moral reasoning. *Child Development, 62*, 264–283.

Warton, P. M., & Goodnow, J. J. (1991). The nature of responsibility: Children's understanding of "your job." *Child Development, 62*, 156–165.

Wassef, A., Collins, M. L., Ingham, D., & Mason, G. (1995a). In search of effective programs to address students' emotional distress and behavioral problems. II: Critique of school- and community-based programs. *Adolescence, 30*(120), 757–777.

Wassef, A., Ingham, D., Collins, M. L., & Mason, G. (1995b). In search of effective programs to address students' emotional distress and behavioral problems. I: Defining the problem. *Adolescence, 30*(119), 523–538.

Wassef, A., Mason, G., Collins, M. L., O'Boyle, M., & Ingham, D. (1996). In search of effective programs to address students' emotional distress and behavioral problems. III: Student assessment of school-based support groups. *Adolescence, 31*(121), 1–16.

Waterman, A. S. (1982). Identity development from adolescence to adulthood: An extension of theory and a review of research. *Developmental Psychology, 18*, 341–358.

Wehlage, G., Rutter, R., Smith, G., Lesko, N., & Fernandez, R. (1989). *Reducing the risk: Schools as communities of support.* New York: Falmer.

Weinbender, M. L. M., & Rossignol, A. M. (1996). Lifestyle and risk of premature sexual activity in a high school population of Seventh-Day Adventists: Valuegenesis 1989. *Adolescence, 31*(122), 265–281.

Weinberg, R. A., & Erickson, M. F. (1996). Minnesota's Children, Youth, and Family Consortium: A university-community collaboration. *Journal of Research on Adolescence, 6*(1), 37–53.

Weiss, H. B., & Greene, J. C. (1992). An empowerment partnership for family support and education programs and evaluations. *Family Science Review, 5*, 131–148.

Weiss, L. H., & Schwarz, J. C. (1996). The relationship between parenting types and older adolescents' personality, academic achievement, adjustment, and substance use. *Child Development, 67*, 2101–2114.

Weller, A., Florian, V., & Mikulincer, M. (1995). Adolescents' reports of a parental division of power in a multicultural society. *Journal of Research on Adolescence, 5*(4), 413–429.

Wentzel, K. R. (1991). Relations between social competence and academic achievement in early adolescence. *Child Development, 62*, 1066–1078.

Wentzel, K. R. (1993). Motivation and achievement in early adolescence: The role of multiple classroom goals. *Journal of Early Adolescence, 13*(1), 4–20.

Wentzel, K. R. (1996). Social and academic motivation in middle school: Concurrent and long-term relations to academic effort. *Journal of Early Adolescence, 16*(4), 390–406.

Wentzel, K. R. (1997). Student motivation in middle school: The role of perceived pedagogical caring. *Journal of Educational Psychology, 89*(3), 411–419.

Wentzel, K. R. (1998). Social relationships and motivation in middle school: The role of parents, teachers, and peers. *Journal of Educational Psychology, 90*(2), 202–209.

Wentzel, K. R., & Asher, S. R. (1995). The academic lives of neglected, rejected, popular, and controversial children. *Child Development, 66*, 754–763.

Wentzel, K. R., & Caldwell, K. (1997). Friendships, peer acceptance, and group membership: Relations to academic achievement in middle school. *Child Development, 68*(6), 1198–1209.

Wentzel, K. R., & Erdley, C. A. (1993). Strategies for making friends: Relations to social behavior and peer acceptance in early adolescence. *Developmental Psychology, 29*(5), 819–826.

Wentzel, K. R., & Feldman, S. S. (1996). Relations of cohesion and power in family dyads to social and emotional adjustment during early adolescence. *Journal of Research on Adolescence, 6*(2), 225–244.

Wentzel, K. R., Feldman, S. S., & Weinberger, D. A. (1991). Parental child rearing and academic achievement in boys: The mediational role of social-emotional adjustment. *Journal of Early Adolescence, 11*(3), 321–339.

Wentzel, K. R., Weinberger, D. A., Ford, M. E., & Feldman, S. S. (1990). Academic achievement in preadolescence: The role of multiple classroom goals. *Journal of Early Adolescence, 13*(1), 4–20.

Werner, E., & Smith, R. (1982). *Vulnerable but invincible.* New York: McGraw-Hill.

Werner, E. E., & Smith, R. S. (1992). *Overcoming the odds: High risk children from birth to adulthood.* Ithaca, NY: Cornell University Press.

Whalen, S. P., & Wynn, J. R. (1995). Enhancing primary services for youth through an infrastructure of social services. *Journal of Adolescent Research, 10*(1), 88–110.

Whitbeck, L. B. (1987). Modeling efficacy: The effect of perceived parental efficacy on the self-efficacy of early adolescents. *Journal of Early Adolescence, 7*(2), 165–177.

Whitbeck, L. B., Simons, R. L., Conger, R. D., & Lorenz, F. O. (1989). Value socialization and peer group affiliation among early adolescents. *Journal of Early Adolescence, 9*(4), 436–453.

Whitbeck, L. B., Simons, R. L., & Kao, M. (1994). The effects of divorced mothers' dating behaviors and sexual attitudes on the sexual attitudes and behaviors of their adolescent children. *Journal of Marriage and the Family, 56*, 615–621.

Whitbourne, S. K., & Tesch, S. A. (1985). A comparison of identity and intimacy statuses in college students and alumni. *Developmental Psychology, 21*(6), 1039–1044.

White, S. H. (1968). The learning-maturation controversy: Hall to Hull. *Merrill-Palmer Quarterly, 14*, 58–65.

White, S. H. (1970). The learning theory tradition and child psychology. In P. H. Mussen (Ed.), *Carmichael's manual of child psychology* (3rd ed., pp. 657–701). New York: Wiley.

Whiting, B. B., & Whiting, J. W. M. (1991). Preindustrial world, adolescence in. In R. M. Lerner, A. C. Petersen, & J. Brooks-Gunn (Eds.), *Encyclopedia of adolescence* (Vol. 2, pp. 814–849). New York: Garland.

Wickrama, K. A. S., Conger, R. D., & Lorenz, F. O., Elder, G. H., Jr. (1998). Parental education and adolescent self-reported physical health. *Journal of Marriage and the Family, 60*, 967–978.

Wigfield, A., & Eccles, J. S. (1994). Children's competence beliefs, achievement values, and general self-esteem: Change across elementary and middle school. *Journal of Early Adolescence, 14*(2), 107–138.

Wigfield, A., Eccles, J. S., MacIver, D., Reumann, D. A., & Midgley, C. (1991). Transitions during early adolescence: Changes in children's domain-specific self-perceptions and general self-esteem across the transition to junior high. *Developmental Psychology, 27*, 552–565.

Windle, M. (1994). A study of friendship characteristics and problem behaviors among middle adolescents. *Child Development, 65*, 1764–1777.

Windle, M., Miller-Tutzauer, C., Barnes, G. M., & Welte, J. (1991). Adolescent perceptions of help-seeking resources for substance abuse. *Child Development, 62*, 179–189.

Windle, M., Miller-Tutzauer, C., & Domenico, D. (1992). Alcohol use, suicidal behavior, and risky activities among adolescents. *Journal of Research on Adolescence, 2*(4), 317–330.

Witt, S. D. (1997). Parental influence on children's socialization to gender roles. *Adolescence, 32*(126), 253–259.

Wolfson, A. R., & Carskadon, M. A. (1998). Sleep schedules and daytime functioning in adolescents. *Child Development, 69*(4), 875–887.

Wong, C. T., Day, J. D., Maxwell, S. E., & Meara, N. M. (1995). A multitrait-multimethod study of academic and social intelligence in college students. *Journal of Educational Psychology, 87*(1), 117–133.

Wood, P. B., & Clay, W. C. (1996). Perceived structural barriers and academic performance among American Indian high school students. *Youth & Society, 28*(1), 40–61.

Worell, J. (1981). Life-span sex roles: Development, continuity, and change. In R. M. Lerner & N. A. Busch-Rossnagel (Eds.), *Individuals as producers of their development: A life-span perspective* (pp. 313–347). New York: Academic Press.

World Health Organization. (1993). *The health of young people: A challenge and a promise.* Geneva: Author.

Wright, D. W., Peterson, L., & Barnes, H. L. (1990). The relation of parental employment and contextual variables with sexual permissiveness and gender role attitudes of rural early adolescents. *Journal of Early Adolescence, 10*(3), 382–393.

Y

Yates, M., & Youniss, J. (1996). Community service and political-moral identity in adolescents. *Journal of Research on Adolescence, 6*(3), 271–284.

Yau, J., & Smetana, J. G. (1996). Adolescent-parent conflict among Chinese adolescents in Hong Kong. *Child Development, 67,* 1262–1275.

Yax, L. K. (1999). *Resident population estimates of the United States by age group and sex: April 1, 1990 to October 1, 1999.* Washington, DC: U. S. Census Bureau, Population Estimates Program, Population Division.

Yildirim, A. (1997). Gender role influences on Turkish adolescents' self-identity. *Adolescence, 32*(125), 216–231.

Young, M. H., Miller, B. C., Norton, M. C., & Hill, E. J. (1995). The effect of parental supportive behaviors on life satisfaction of adolescent offspring. *Journal of Marriage and Family, 57,* 813–822.

Youniss, J., & Dean, A. (1974). Judgment and imagery aspects of operations: A Piagetian study with Korean and Costa Rican children. *Child Development, 45,* 1020–1031.

Youniss, J., Yates, M., & Su, Y. (1997). Social integration: Community service and marijuana use in high school seniors. *Journal of Adolescent Research, 12*(2), 245–262.

Z

Zabin, L. S., Astone, N. M., & Emerson, M. R. (1993). Do adolescents want babies? The relationship between attitudes and behavior. *Journal of Research on Adolescence, 3,* 67–86.

Zani, B., DiPalma, A., & Vullo, C. (1995). Psychosocial aspects of chronic illness in adolescents with thalassaemia major. *Journal of Adolescence, 18,* 387–402.

Zarbatany, L., Ghesquiere, K., & Mohr, K. (1992). A context perspective on early adolescents' friendship expectations. *Journal of Early Adolescence, 12*(1), 111–126.

Zaslow, M. J. (1988). Sex differences in children's response to parental divorce: I. Research methodology and postdivorce family forms. *American Journal of Orthopsychiatry, 58*(3), 355–378.

Zaslow, M. J. (1989). Sex differences in children's response to parental divorce: II. Samples, variables, ages, and sources. *American Journal of Orthopsychiatry, 59*(1), 118–141.

Zaslow, M., Tout, K., Smith, S., & Moore, K. (1998). Implications of the 1996 welfare legislation for children: A research perspective. *SRCD Social Policy Report, 12* (3).

Zeldin, S. (1995). Community-university collaborations for youth development: From theory to practice. *Journal of Adolescent Research, 10*(4), 449–469.

Zeldin, S., & Price, L. A. (1995). Creating supportive communities for adolescent development: Challenges to scholars: An introduction. *Journal of Adolescent Research, 10*(1), 6–14.

Zhang, J., & Jin, S. (1996). Determinants of suicide ideation: A comparison of Chinese and American college students. *Adolescence, 31*(122), 451–467.

Zimet, G. D., Sobo, E. J., Zimmerman, T., Jackson, J., Mortimer, J., Yanda, C. P., & Lazebnik, R. (1995). Sexual behavior, drug use, and AIDS knowledge among Midwestern runaways. *Youth & Society, 26*(4), 450–462.

Zimiles, H., & Lee, V. (1991). Adolescent family structure and educational progress. *Developmental Psychology, 27*(2), 314–320.

Zimmerman, M. A., Salem, D. A., & Maton, K. I. (1995). Family structure and psychosocial correlates among urban African-American adolescent males. *Child Development, 66,* 1598–1613.

Zimmerman, R. S., Sprecher, S., Langer, L. M., & Holloway, C. D. (1995). Adolescents' perceived ability to say "no" to unwanted sex. *Journal of Adolescent Research, 10*(3), 383–399.

CREDITS

Photographs

CO photos Photos at the top of pages, Digital Vision/Children and Teenagers (168121B, 168060A,168129A); large photos, PhotoDisk/Teens.

Chapter 1 Page 5 Young-Wolff, PhotoEdit; p. 6 Jonathan Nourok, PhotoEdit; p. 8 Glen Elder; p. 11 Nancy Galambos; p. 12 Michael Newman, PhotoEdit; p. 13 Bob Daemmrich, The Image Works; p. 18 Michael Newman, PhotoEdit; p. 20 Monika Graff, The Image Works.

Chapter 2 Page 30 R. Sidney, The Image Works; p. 31 Myrleen Ferguson, PhotoEdit; p. 35 Celia Fisher; p. 37 (top) Richard Weinberg; p. 37 (bottom) Mary Kate Denny, PhotoEdit; p. 38 © Chemical Design Ltd./SPL/Science Source/ Photo Researchers, Inc,; p. 44 Topham, The Image Works; p. 52 Paul B. Bates.

Chapter 3 Page 60 Spencer Grant, Stock Boston; p. 67 Young-Wolff, PhotoEdit; p. 69 Elizabeth Susman; p. 71 Bob Daemmrich, The Image Works; p. 72 Paul Conklin, PhotoEdit; p. 75 David Magnusson.

Chapter 4 Page 86 D. Young-Wolff, PhotoEdit; p. 91 Peter Menzel, Stock Boston; p. 93 Bill Overton; p. 94 Dick Blume, The Image Works; p. 96 David R. Frazier, Photo Researchers, Inc.; p. 97 Rich Weinberg; p. 101 Felicia Martinez, PhotoEdit.

Chapter 5 Page 109 Mary Kate Denny, PhotoEdit; p. 113 Bob Daemmrich, Stock Boston; p. 118 Nancy Eisenberg; p. 121 Tony Freeman, PhotoEdit; p. 122 William Damon; p. 125 Mary Kate Denny, PhotoEdit; p. 126 Peter Benson.

Chapter 6 Page 134 David Young-Wolff, PhotoEdit; p. 139 Bob Daemmrich, Stock Boston; p. 141 Gerry Adams; p. 143 Sally Archer; p. 144 Alan Waterman; p. 145 David Young-Wolff, PhotoEdit; p. 149 Harold D. Grotevant; p. 150 Richard Hutchings,

PhotoEdit; p. 152 Mike Greenlar, The Image Works; p. 154 Margaret Beale Spencer.

Chapter 7 Page 162 Bob Daemmrich, The Image Works; p. 163 Michael Schwartz, The Image Works; p. 165 Bob Daemmrich, The Image Works; p. 167 Jeylan T. Mortimer; p. 168 Stock Boston; p. 170 Bill Aron, PhotoEdit; p. 173 Fred Vondracek.

Chapter 8 Page 181 Bob Daemmrich, Stock Boston; p. 184 Donald J. Hernandez; p. 185 (left) © Mary Evans Picture Library/Photo Researchers, Inc.; p. 185 (right) Bob Daemmrich, The Image Works; p. 188 Rafael Macia, Photo Researchers, Inc.; p. 189 Harriette P. McAdoo; p. 190 Ronald Taylor; p. 191 Bill Lai, The Image Works; p. 194 Photo Researchers, Inc.; p. 199 David Young-Wolff, PhotoEdit.

Chapter 9 Page 211 Mike Doyle, Unicorn Stock Photos; p. 213 Robert Brenner, PhotoEdit; p. 215 Michael Newman, PhotoEdit; p. 216 Mike Mazzaschi, Stock Boston; p. 217 Spencer Grant, Stock Boston; p. 222 Brett Laursen.

Chapter 10 Page 231 Michael Newman, PhotoEdit; p. 234 David Young-Wolff, PhotoEdit; p. 235 Ritch Savin-Williams; p. 237 Spencer Grant, PhotoEdit; p. 240 Mark Richards, PhotoEdit; p. 243 Michael Newman, PhotoEdit; p. 247 Patricia East.

Chapter 11 Page 257 Mark C. Burnett, Stock Boston; p. 259 Cynthia García Coll; p. 260 Tony Freeman, PhotoEdit; p. 261 Carol Midgley; p. 262 Elizabeth Crews Photography; p. 263 Kathryn Wentzel; p. 268 Bob Daemmrich, The Image Works; p. 270 Will Hart, PhotoEdit; p. 272 G & M David de Lossy, The Image Bank.

Chapter 12 Page 280 David Young-Wolff, PhotoEdit; p. 281 Tony Freeman, PhotoEdit; p. 282 Spencer Grant, Stock Boston; p. 283 Will Hart, PhotoEdit; p. 284 Tony Freeman,

PhotoEdit; p. 287 Dr. Reed Larson; p. 289 Mark Richards, PhotoEdit.

Chapter 13 Page 300 Lisa Crockett; p. 302 N.P. Alexander, Unicorn Stock Photos; p. 306 Steve Starr, Stock Boston; p. 307 Carl Taylor; p. 309 Matthew Neal McVay, Stock Boston; p. 313 Dr. P. Marazzi/Science Photo Library, Photo Researchers, Inc.; p. 314 James Garbarino; p. 315 Mary Lewis, Unicorn Stock Photos; p. 317 Michael Windle; p. 319 Nancy Richmond, The Image Works; p. 320 Jacksonville Journal Courier, The Image Works.

Chapter 14 Page 330 Jodie Roth; p. 332 Mary Kate Denny, PhotoEdit; p. 333 Mary Kate Denny, PhotoEdit; p. 340 Myrleen Ferguson Cate, PhotoEdit; p. 345 Aletha Huston; p. 347 Karen Pittman; p. 352 Skjold, PhotoEdit; p. 353 Jean Rhodes.

Chapter 15 Page 361 David Young-Wolff, PhotoEdit; p. 362 Eric R. Berndt, Unicorn Stock Photos; p. 364 Lonnie Sherrod; p. 365 Bob Daemmrich, Stock Boston; p. 367, Michael Newman, PhotoEdit; p. 373 Stephen Hamilton.

Appendix Page 379 (left) David Parker/Science Photo Laboratory, Photo Researchers, Inc.; p. 379 (top right) Elena Rooraid, PhotoEdit; p. 379 (bottom right) Ray Stott, The Image Works; p. 380 Bill Aron, PhotoEdit; p. 382 © Richard T. Nowitz/CORBIS; p. 384 Michael Newman, PhotoEdit; p. 386 (left) © Hulton-Deutsch/CORBIS; p. 386 (top right) © Vince Streano/CORBIS; p. 386 (bottom right) Andrew Lichtenstein, The Image Works; p. 390 John Nesselroade; p. 391 Don Carl Steffen, Photo Researchers, Inc.

Figures and Tables

Chapter 1 IFP Box 1.1 "Don't Talk Back" by R. M. Lerner and C. K. Olson, *Parents*, December 1994. Copyright © 1994 by Gruner & Jahr USA Publishing. Reprinted from PARENTS magazine by permission.

Chapter 2 Table 2-1 From CONCEPTS AND THEORIES OF HUMAN DEVELOPMENT 2nd edition by Richard M. Lerner, 1996, Random House. Reprinted by permission of the author.

Chapter 3 Figures 3.1, 3.2, 3.3, & 3.4 Figures redrawn from GROWTH AT ADOLESCENCE 2nd edition by J. M. Tanner. Copyright © 1962. Reprinted by permission of Blackwell Scientific Publications; Figure 3.5 Illustration courtesy of Nelson H. Prentiss. Graph by Ilil Arbel from "Growing Up" by J. M. Tanner in *Scientific American*, September 1973, v. 229. Copyright © 1973 by Scientific American, Inc.; Table 3-1 "Ethnic Differences in Growth and Development" by Jean Hiernaux, *Eugenics Quarterly*, 1968, 15, pp. 12–21. Reprinted by permission of Kenneth C. Land, Duke University, Editor of *Social Biology*; Figure 3.7 From "Pubertal Processes in Girls' Psychological Adaptations" in BIOLOGICAL-PSYCHOSOCIAL INTERACTIONS IN EARLY ADOLESCENCE: A Life-Span Perspective ed. by R. Lerner and T. T. Foch, Erlbaum, 1987. Reprinted by permission of Lawrence Erlbaum Associates, Inc.; Figures 3.8 & 3.9 From "Differential Maturation Among Girls and Its Relation to Social Adjustment: A Longitudinal Perspective" by Magnusson, et al., in LIFE-SPAN DEVELOPMENT AND BEHAVIOR ed. by P. B. Baltes, D. L. Fetherman, and R. M. Lerner, Erlbaum, 1986. Reprinted by permission of Lawrence Erlbaum Associates, Inc.; IFP Box 3.1 "Don't Talk Back!" by R. M. Lerner and C. K. Olson, *Parents*, February 1995. Copyright © 1995 by Gruner & Jahr USA Publishing. Reprinted from PARENTS magazine by permission.

Chapter 4 Applications Box 4.1 Reprinted by permission of International Youth Foundation, YouthNet International; Table 4-1 From CONCEPTS AND THEORIES OF HUMAN DEVELOPMENT 2nd edition by Richard M. Lerner, 1986, Random House. Reprinted by permission of the author; IFP Box 4.1 "The Imaginary Audience" by R. M. Lerner and C. K. Olson, *Parents*, February 1994. Copyright © 1994 by Gruner & Jahr USA Publishing. Reprinted from PARENTS magazine by permission.

Chapter 5 Table 5-1 Reprinted by permission of Thomas Lickona; Table 5-2 From "Beyond the 'Village' Rhetoric: Creating Healthy Communities for Children and Adolescents" by Benson, Leffert, Scales & Blyth, *Applied Developmental Science*, 2(3), 1998. Reprinted by permission of Lawrence Erlbaum Associates, Inc.; Figures 5.1, 5.2, & 5.3 From "Developmental Assets: Measurement and Prediction of Risk Behaviors Among Adolescents" by N. Leffert, P. Benson, P. Scales, A. Sharma, D. Drake, & D. Blyth, *Applied Developmental Science*, 2, 1998. Reprinted by permission of Lawrence Erlbaum Associates, Inc.; Figures 5.4, 5.5, & 5.6 From "The Contribution of Developmental Assets to the Prediction of Thriving Among Adolescents" by Scales, et al. from *Applied Developmental*

Science, 4(1), 2000. Reprinted by permission of Lawrence Erlbaum Associates, Inc.; Figure 5.7 From "Applying Developmental Science in the Twenty-First Century: International Scholarship for Our Times" by R. M. Lerner, C. B. Fisher, R. A. Weinberg, *International Journal of Behavioral Development*, vol. 24 (2000), pp. 24-29. Reprinted by permission of Taylor & Francis Ltd.

Chapter 6 Table 6-1 From CONCEPTS AND THEORIES OF HUMAN DEVELOPMENT 2nd edition by Richard M. Lerner, 1986, Random House. Reprinted by permission of the author; Applications Boxes 6.1 and 6.2 Reprinted by permission of International Youth Foundation, YouthNet International.

Chapter 7 Table 7.1 From "Sex-Role Stereotypes: A Current Appraisal" by I. K. Broverman, S. R. Vogel, D. M. Broverman, F. E. Clarkson, & P. S. Rosenkrantz in *Journal of Social Issues*, v. 28, 1972. Copyright © 1972. Reprinted by permission of Blackwell Publishers; Applications Box 7.1 Reprinted by permission of International Youth Foundation, YouthNet International.

Chapter 8 Table 8-1 From "A Developmental Contextual Perspective on Parenting" by Lerner, et al. in HANDBOOK OF PARENTING: Biology and Ecology of Parenting, Vol. 2, ed. by J. H. Bornstein, R. M. Lerner, D. R. Castellino, P. A. Terry, F. A. Villarruel, & M. H. McKinney, Erlbaum, 1995. Reprinted by permission of Lawrence ErlbaumAssociates, Inc.; Tables 8.2, 8.3, 8.4, & 8.5 From AMERICA'S CHILDREN by Donald Hernandez. Copyright © 1993 by Russell Sage Foundation, New York, NY. Reprinted by permission; IFP Box 8.1 "Teens and Tweens" by R. M. Lerner & L. C. Hoopfer, *Family Circle*, October 1993. Copyright © 1993 by Gruner & Jahr USA Publishing. Reprinted from FAMILY CIRCLE magazine by permission.

Chapter 9 Applications Box 9.1 Reprinted by permission of International Youth Foundation, YouthNet International.

Chapter 10 IFP Box 10.1 "Teen Idols" by R. M. Lerner & C. K. Olson, *Parents*, September 1995. Copyright © 1995 by Gruner & Jahr USA Publishing. Reprinted from PARENTS magazine by permission; Figure 10.1 Reproduced with the permission of The Alan Guttmacher Institute from the Alan Guttmacher Institute, SEX AND AMERICA'S TEENAGERS, New York; The Alan Guttmacher Institute, 1994; Applications Box 10.2 Reprinted by permission of International Youth Foundation, YouthNet International.

Chapter 11 Figure 11.1 From GREAT TRANSITIONS: Preparing Adolescents for a New Century. Copyright © 1995 by Carnegie Corporation of New York. Reprinted with permission; Applications Box 11.1 Reprinted by permission of International Youth Foundation, YouthNet International.

Chapter 12 Table 12-1 From "Trajectory and Forms of Institutional Participation" by Eckert in PATHWAYS THROUGH ADOLESCENTS: Individual Development in Relation to Social Contexts ed. by L. J. Crockett and A. C. Crouter, Erlbaum, 1995. Reprinted by permission of Lawrence Erlbaum Associates, Inc.; Application Box 12.1 Reprinted by permission of International Youth Foundation, YouthNet International.

Chapter 13 Table 13-1 Children's Defense Fund, *The State of America's Children Yearbook 2001*. Washington, D. C.: Children's Defense Fund, 2000. Used with permission of the Children's Defense Fund; Table 13-2 "Indicators of Child Well-Being" from KIDS COUNT DATA BOOK 2000: State Profiles of Child Well-Being by the Annie R. Casey Foundation. Copyright © 2000. Reprinted by permission. http://www.kidscount.org; Table 13-3 From "Theories of Human Development: Contemporary Perspectives" by Richard M. Lerner in HANDBOOK OF CHILD PSYCHOLOGY ed. by W. Damon. Volume 1 *Theoretical Models of Human Development* ed. by R. M. Lerner. Copyright © 1998. Reprinted by permission of John Wiley & Sons, Inc.; Applications Box 13.1 Reprinted by permission of International Youth Foundation, YouthNet International; Applications Box 13.2 Reprinted by permission of International Youth Foundation, YouthNet International; IFP Box 13.1 Adapted from "Keeping Tabs...Without Being a Nag" by R. M. Lerner & C. K. Olson, *Parents*, September 1996. Copyright © 1996 by Gruner & Jahr USA Publishing. Reprinted from PARENTS magazine by permission.

Chapter 14 Table 14-1 Table from *A Three-Part Definition of Positive Youth Development*, by S. F. Hamilton, unpublished manuscript, 1999. Reprinted by permission of Stephen F. Hamilton, Cornell University; Applications Box 14.1 Adapted from Jacobs, F. (1998). The Five-Tiered Approach to Evaluation: Context and Implementation. In H. Weiss and F. Jacobs (Eds.) (1998). Evaluating Family Programs. Hawthorne, NY: Aldine de Gruyter. Source: Jacobs, F. H. and Kapuscik, J. L. (2000). Making It Count: Evaluating Family Preservation Services. Medford, MA: Tufts University, Eliot-Pearson Department of Child Development. Reprinted by permission of F. H. Jacobs; Applications Box 14.2 From GREAT TRANSITIONS: Preparing Adolescents for a New Century. Copyright © 1995 by Carnegie Corporation of New York. Reprinted with permission.

Chapter 15 Applications Box 15.1 Reprinted by permission of International Youth Foundation, YouthNet International.

Appendix Figure A.1 From LIFE SPAN DEVELOPMENTAL PSYCHOLOGY: Introduction to Research Methods by Baltes, Reese, and Nesselroade, Brooks/Cole, 1977. Reprinted by permission of John R. Nesselroade; Applications Box A. 1 "Ethical Standards for Research with Children" by Society for Research in Child Development. Reprinted by permission.

NAME INDEX

SUBJECT INDEX